FileMaker Pro 5 Bible

FileMaker Pro 5 Bible

Steven A. Schwartz

IDG Books Worldwide, Inc.
An International Data Group Company

Foster City, CA ✦ Chicago, IL ✦ Indianapolis, IN ✦ New York, NY

FileMaker Pro 5 Bible

Published by
IDG Books Worldwide, Inc.
An International Data Group Company
919 E. Hillsdale Blvd., Suite 400
Foster City, CA 94404
www.idgbooks.com (IDG Books Worldwide
Web site)

ISBN: 0-7645-3406-8

Printed in the United States of America.

10 9 8 7 6 5 4 3

1B/QX/RS/ZZ/FC

Distributed in the United States by IDG Books Worldwide, Inc.

Distributed by CDG Books Canada Inc. for Canada; by Transworld Publishers Limited in the United Kingdom; by IDG Norge Books for Norway; by IDG Sweden Books for Sweden; by IDG Books Australia Publishing Corporation Pty. Ltd. for Australia and New Zealand; by TransQuest Publishers Pte Ltd. for Singapore, Malaysia, Thailand, Indonesia, and Hong Kong; by Gotop Information Inc. for Taiwan; by ICG Muse, Inc. for Japan; by Intersoft for South Africa; by Eyrolles for France; by International Thomson Publishing for Germany, Austria and Switzerland; by Distribuidora Cuspide for Argentina; by LR International for Brazil; by Galileo Libros for Chile; by Ediciones ZETA S.C.R. Ltda. for Peru; by WS Computer Publishing Corporation, Inc., for the Philippines; by Contemporanea de Ediciones for Venezuela; by Express Computer Distributors for the Caribbean and West Indies; by Micronesia Media Distributor, Inc. for Micronesia; by Chips Computadoras S.A. de C.V. for Mexico; by Editorial Norma de Panama S.A. for Panama; by American Bookshops for Finland.

For general information on IDG Books Worldwide's books in the U.S., please call our Consumer Customer Service department at 800-762-2974. For reseller information, including discounts and premium sales, please call our Reseller Customer Service department at 800-434-3422.

For information on where to purchase IDG Books Worldwide's books outside the U.S., please contact our International Sales department at 317-596-5530 or fax 317-596-5692.

For consumer information on foreign language translations, please contact our Customer Service department at 800-434-3422, fax 317-596-5692, or e-mail rights@idgbooks.com.

For information on licensing foreign or domestic rights, please phone +1-650-655-3109.

For sales inquiries and special prices for bulk quantities, please contact our Sales department at 650-655-3200 or write to the address above.

For information on using IDG Books Worldwide's books in the classroom or for ordering examination copies, please contact our Educational Sales department at 800-434-2086 or fax 317-596-5499.

For press review copies, author interviews, or other publicity information, please contact our Public Relations department at 650-655-3000 or fax 650-655-3299.

For authorization to photocopy items for corporate, personal, or educational use, please contact Copyright Clearance Center, 222 Rosewood Drive, Danvers, MA 01923, or fax 978-750-4470.

Library of Congress Cataloging-in-Publication Data
Schwartz, Steven A.
   FileMaker Pro 5 bible / Steven A. Schwartz.
     p. cm.
   ISBN 07645-3406-8 (alk. paper)
   1. FileMaker pro. 2. Database management. I. Title.
QA76.9.D3 S3364 1999
005.75'65–dc21   99-051489
                                     CIP

ABOUT IDG BOOKS WORLDWIDE

Welcome to the world of IDG Books Worldwide.

IDG Books Worldwide, Inc., is a subsidiary of International Data Group, the world's largest publisher of computer-related information and the leading global provider of information services on information technology. IDG was founded more than 30 years ago by Patrick J. McGovern and now employs more than 9,000 people worldwide. IDG publishes more than 290 computer publications in over 75 countries. More than 90 million people read one or more IDG publications each month.

Launched in 1990, IDG Books Worldwide is today the #1 publisher of best-selling computer books in the United States. We are proud to have received eight awards from the Computer Press Association in recognition of editorial excellence and three from Computer Currents' First Annual Readers' Choice Awards. Our best-selling *...For Dummies®* series has more than 50 million copies in print with translations in 31 languages. IDG Books Worldwide, through a joint venture with IDG's Hi-Tech Beijing, became the first U.S. publisher to publish a computer book in the People's Republic of China. In record time, IDG Books Worldwide has become the first choice for millions of readers around the world who want to learn how to better manage their businesses.

Our mission is simple: Every one of our books is designed to bring extra value and skill-building instructions to the reader. Our books are written by experts who understand and care about our readers. The knowledge base of our editorial staff comes from years of experience in publishing, education, and journalism — experience we use to produce books to carry us into the new millennium. In short, we care about books, so we attract the best people. We devote special attention to details such as audience, interior design, use of icons, and illustrations. And because we use an efficient process of authoring, editing, and desktop publishing our books electronically, we can spend more time ensuring superior content and less time on the technicalities of making books.

You can count on our commitment to deliver high-quality books at competitive prices on topics you want to read about. At IDG Books Worldwide, we continue in the IDG tradition of delivering quality for more than 30 years. You'll find no better book on a subject than one from IDG Books Worldwide.

John Kilcullen
Chairman and CEO
IDG Books Worldwide, Inc.

Steven Berkowitz
President and Publisher
IDG Books Worldwide, Inc.

*Eighth Annual
Computer Press
Awards ≥1992*

*Ninth Annual
Computer Press
Awards ≥1993*

*Tenth Annual
Computer Press
Awards ≥1994*

*Eleventh Annual
Computer Press
Awards ≥1995*

IDG is the world's leading IT media, research and exposition company. Founded in 1964, IDG had 1997 revenues of $2.05 billion and has more than 9,000 employees worldwide. IDG offers the widest range of media options that reach IT buyers in 75 countries representing 95% of worldwide IT spending. IDG's diverse product and services portfolio spans six key areas including print publishing, online publishing, expositions and conferences, market research, education and training, and global marketing services. More than 90 million people read one or more of IDG's 290 magazines and newspapers, including IDG's leading global brands — Computerworld, PC World, Network World, Macworld and the Channel World family of publications. IDG Books Worldwide is one of the fastest-growing computer book publishers in the world, with more than 700 titles in 36 languages. The "...For Dummies®" series alone has more than 50 million copies in print. IDG offers online users the largest network of technology-specific Web sites around the world through IDG.net (http://www.idg.net), which comprises more than 225 targeted Web sites in 55 countries worldwide. International Data Corporation (IDC) is the world's largest provider of information technology data, analysis and consulting, with research centers in over 41 countries and more than 400 research analysts worldwide. IDG World Expo is a leading producer of more than 168 globally branded conferences and expositions in 35 countries including E3 (Electronic Entertainment Expo), Macworld Expo, ComNet, Windows World Expo, ICE (Internet Commerce Expo), Agenda, DEMO, and Spotlight. IDG's training subsidiary, ExecuTrain, is the world's largest computer training company, with more than 230 locations worldwide and 785 training courses. IDG Marketing Services helps industry-leading IT companies build international brand recognition by developing global integrated marketing programs via IDG's print, online and exposition products worldwide. Further information about the company can be found at www.idg.com.   1/24/99

Credits

Acquisitions Editor
Ed Adams

Development Editors
Kathi Duggan
Colleen Dowling

Technical Editor
Dennis Cohen

Copy Editors
Timothy J. Borek
Marti Paul

CD-ROM
Media Development

Project Coordinators
Linda Marousek
Joe Shines

Graphics and Production Specialists
Mario Amador
Stephanie Hollier
Jude Levinson
Ramses Ramirez

Quality Control Specialist
Chris Weisbart

Cover Illustrators
Mary Jo Richards
Clint Lahnen
Brian Drumm
Karl Brandt
Kippy Thomsen

Proofreading and Indexing
York Production Services

About the Author

In 1978, **Dr. Steven Schwartz** bought his first microcomputer, a new Apple II+. Determined to find a way to make money with it, he began writing software reviews, BASIC programs, and user tips for *Nibble* magazine. Shortly thereafter, he was made a contributing editor.

During the past 20 years, Steven has written hundreds of articles for more than a dozen computer magazines. He currently writes for *Macworld* magazine. He was also a founding editor of *Software Digest*, as well as business editor for *MACazine*. From 1985 to 1990, he was the director of technical services for Funk Software.

Steven is the author of nearly 40 books, including *Macworld Guide to ClarisWorks 2, Macworld ClarisWorks 2.0/2.1 Companion, Macworld ClarisWorks 3.0 Bible, Macworld ClarisWorks 4.0 Bible, Macworld ClarisWorks Office Bible, Macworld FileMaker Pro 2.0/2.1 Bible, Macworld FileMaker Pro 3.0 Bible, FileMaker Pro 4 Bible,* and dozens of popular game strategy guides.

Steven has a Ph.D. in psychology and presently lives in the fictional town of Lizard Spit, Arizona, where he writes books and reviews, consults on game development issues, and complains about the heat. He can be contacted via e-mail at fmprobible@hotmail.com.

This is for all the business, education, and home users who have made this the #1 best-selling book on FileMaker Pro

Preface

Why FileMaker Pro?

FileMaker Pro is a mature database product. I'm not talking about some company's latest brainchild that is being foisted — bug-laden — onto an unsuspecting public. In its various incarnations and from its various publishers, this product has been known as FileMaker; FileMaker 2; FileMaker IV; FileMaker Pro; FileMaker Pro 2, 3, and 4; and now FileMaker Pro 5. FileMaker Pro has been around the block — and I've been in lock step with it.

Unlike many computer products that are periodically "redefined" by having drastic changes made to the program's focus (changing a simple text editor into a desktop publishing program, for example), FileMaker Pro's versions have all shown a steady progression forward. This means that if you've used any version of FileMaker Pro — even one that is several years old — the information and experience you've gained have not been a waste of time. Much of your knowledge can be applied directly to the current version of the program.

Although I've reviewed computer programs for more than 20 years for magazines such as *Macworld, PC World,* and *Multimedia World,* only a surprisingly few products have impressed me enough to stick with them over the years. FileMaker Pro is such a program. Apparently, much of the computer community agrees with my assessment, because FileMaker Pro currently owns about 70 percent of the Mac database market, and it's making steady inroads into the world of Windows, too. Because it's safe to assume that you own a copy of FileMaker Pro, you're in excellent company.

About This Book

The *FileMaker Pro 5 Bible* is a different kind of computer book. First, it's not a manual. Many people don't like computer manuals — perhaps because they feel obligated to read a manual from cover to cover, or perhaps because manuals are designed to explain how features work rather than how to make a program work for you. The *FileMaker Pro 5 Bible* is not a book you *have* to read. It's a book I hope you'll *want* to read — because it provides easy-to-find, easy-to-understand explanations of the common tasks for which you bought FileMaker Pro in the first place. When you want to know how to use a particular program feature, you can use the extensive table of contents or the index to identify the section of the book you need to read.

Second, like the *FileMaker Pro 4 Bible,* this is a cross-platform book. Whether you use a Macintosh, Windows 95, 98, or Windows NT, the material in this book is applicable to you. Windows- and Mac-specific material are clearly delineated, so you never have to guess whether a particular procedure or explanation is relevant to you.

Note   When commands, dialog box titles, or other elements are different between the two platforms, they are shown as *Macintosh item/Windows item* (such as ⌘+S/Ctrl+S).

Third, although I hope you'll find some of the material in this book entertaining, the primary mission of the *FileMaker Pro 5 Bible* is to inform. I want you to really understand how FileMaker Pro works and to be able to make it do exactly what you want it to do. No matter where you turn in this book, if you find yourself with a puzzled look on your face after reading a section, I haven't done my job.

Finally, the philosophy of this book—as well as the other books in the Bible series from IDG Books—is that you don't want or need a handful of books to learn all about a computer program; one book should suffice. The *FileMaker Pro 5 Bible* is an all-in-one book that gives you a well-rounded knowledge of FileMaker Pro. You don't just learn how to perform an action; you also learn *when* and *why* you would perform that action. You can find almost anything you want to know about FileMaker Pro in this book.

Whom This Book Is For

The *FileMaker Pro 5 Bible* is for anyone who uses Version 5 of FileMaker Pro:

+ If you're a beginning FileMaker Pro user, step-by-step instructions help you get up to speed quickly with explanations of how to perform common (and not so common) FileMaker Pro features and procedures.

+ If you're an intermediate or advanced FileMaker Pro user—someone who doesn't need much handholding—tips and insights in each chapter help you get the most from FileMaker Pro. You'll find the information provided in the sidebars to be handy tools for your FileMaker Pro toolbox.

How This Book Is Organized

Each chapter is self-contained. When you need to perform a particular FileMaker Pro task, scan the table of contents to locate the chapter that addresses your needs. You can also flip through the pages of the book to find the chapter you need quickly. *FileMaker Pro 5 Bible* is divided into six parts:

Part I: The Fundamentals

This part is a gentle introduction to database concepts, essential FileMaker Pro concepts and procedures, and what's new in FileMaker Pro 5.

Part II: Database Design Basics

This part instructs you in using the various design tools to construct databases and to design different types of layouts.

Part III: Working with Databases

Here you will learn about working with databases: entering and editing data, searching for particular records, sorting, designing reports, and printing.

Part IV: Putting FileMaker Pro to Work

This part covers material that helps you make more productive use of FileMaker Pro. It isn't essential to learn about these features immediately, but you will want to tackle them after you're comfortable with the FileMaker Pro basics.

Part V: Mastering FileMaker Pro

Material in this part will interest more experienced FileMaker Pro users and would-be developers, including information on using relations and lookups to link databases, publishing databases on the Internet, using FileMaker Pro Server, and using ODBC to link with non-FileMaker databases.

Part VI: Appendixes

The appendixes show how to install and use the templates, programs, and demos on the *FileMaker Pro 5 Bible* CD-ROM; present all keyboard shortcuts for the Macintosh and Windows versions of FileMaker Pro 5; list additional resources to which you can turn to learn more about FileMaker Pro; and explain common computer, system software, database, and FileMaker Pro terms that you may not know.

Conventions Used in This Book

The book contains the following icons:

The New Feature icon identifies new features found in FileMaker Pro 5. All other features are available to FileMaker Pro 4.0/4.1 users.

The Note icon highlights a special point of interest about the topic being discussed — information that is not necessarily vital to performing a task. Look here if you're interested in achieving a well-rounded knowledge of FileMaker Pro.

The Tip icon marks a timesaving shortcut or technique that will help you work smarter.

The Caution icon alerts you that the action or operation being described can cause problems if you are not careful.

The Mac-Only and Windows-Only icons make it easy to identify material that is specific to only one computer platform (Macintosh or Windows). All other material is equally relevant to *both* platforms.

How to Use This Book

I won't tell you how to read this book. Reading and learning styles are all very personal. When I get a new computer program, I frequently read the manual from cover to cover before even installing the software. Of course, I'll be flattered if you read the *FileMaker Pro 5 Bible* the same way — but I'll also be surprised.

This book is written as a reference to "all things FileMaker Pro." When you want to learn about defining fields, there's a specific chapter to which you can turn. If you just need to know how to use the spelling checker, you can flip to the table of contents or the index and find the pages where this feature is discussed. Most procedures are explained in step-by-step fashion, so you can quickly accomplish even the most complex tasks. Thus, you can read this book as you would a novel, read just the chapters that interest you, or use it as a quick reference for when you need to learn about a particular feature or procedure.

For those who prefer a little more direction than "whatever works for you," some general guidelines are suggested in the following paragraphs — arranged according to your level of computer expertise and previous FileMaker Pro experience.

However, I do have one general suggestion: *If at all possible, read this book with FileMaker Pro on-screen*. Sure, you can read about editing a user dictionary for the spelling checker while relaxing in the tub, but—unless you have exceptional recall—what you read will be more meaningful if you're sitting in front of the computer.

For the beginner

Like the manuals of most computer programs, this book assumes you have a general grasp of the procedures necessary to use your computer, such as using the mouse, choosing commands from menus, and printing documents. If FileMaker Pro is your first program and you have not yet taken the time to work through the manuals that came with your computer, stop reading now. It's time to drag out the manuals for your computer, printer, and system software. Once you fill in the gaps in your computer education, you'll feel more confident and comfortable tackling FileMaker Pro and any other programs you eventually purchase.

If you're relatively new to computers and FileMaker Pro, start by reading all of Part I. This part will acquaint you with database concepts and the FileMaker Pro basics. Next, work through the tutorial presented in Chapter 4. This chapter gently leads you through the process of creating your first database, a full-featured address book in which you can record your business and personal contacts. Finish up by reading the remaining chapters of Part II (Chapters 5 through 7) and at least the first three chapters of Part III (Chapters 8 through 10). This material will provide you with a sufficient grounding in FileMaker Pro concepts and features to enable you to tackle basic database projects. Then, as you find it necessary to explore additional program features, such as printing or creating calculations, you can simply jump to the appropriate chapter.

The more advanced stuff is saved for Parts IV and V. Although you'll eventually want to check out the material in those parts, too, I've purposely separated the advanced matters from the basics in order to keep new users from being overwhelmed.

For the more experienced computer user

If you're familiar with databases, you can safely skip Chapter 1. The material in this chapter is very basic and is probably second-hand to you. If FileMaker Pro is your first database program, however, you should at least skim through the material in Chapter 1.

Chapter 2 is a must-read for every FileMaker Pro user. Many FileMaker Pro tasks, such as using the tools, are discussed here.

Parts II and III are the real meat-and-potatoes chapters for new FileMaker Pro users. Many of the topics covered in these parts are at least touched upon in Chapter 4. After completing this tutorial chapter, you may feel sufficiently confident to tackle some of your own database projects. You can treat the remainder of the book as reference material and read it as needed.

For an owner of a previous version of FileMaker Pro

As mentioned earlier, FileMaker (in its various incarnations) has always worked basically the same. Through the years, however, new features and capabilities have been added. If you are familiar with an older version of FileMaker, you should pay particular attention to material in the following chapters:

+ Chapter 3 provides a brief description of all changes and new features introduced in FileMaker Pro 4.

+ Chapter 14 explains how to create calculations, and it summarizes all FileMaker Pro built-in functions. (For a complete reference to the functions, see Appendix E.)

+ Chapter 15 discusses ScriptMaker and explains how to create auto-entry data fields.

+ Chapter 16 explains the procedures for moving data between FileMaker Pro and other programs.

+ Chapter 18 discusses FileMaker Pro's relational and lookup capabilities, enabling you to use data from an external database in the current database.

+ Chapter 19 discusses FileMaker Pro Server, explains how FileMaker Pro works on a network (with or without Server), and shows how to create passwords and groups to restrict access privileges for different users.

+ Chapter 20 tells how to use the new Web Companion plug-in to host databases on the World Wide Web or a corporate Intranet.

+ Chapter 21 explains how to use the ODBC support of FileMaker Pro 4.1 and higher to exchange data with high-end/corporate databases.

The FileMaker Pro 5 Bible CD-ROM

Bound into this book is the *FileMaker Pro 5 Bible* CD-ROM, a massive collection of ready-to-run FileMaker Pro templates, example databases, demos, and utilities. Whether you just want to get up and running quickly, need some help with the more advanced topics covered in the book, or are looking for new ways to use FileMaker Pro, I strongly encourage you to check out the CD-ROM.

Note: The *FileMaker Pro 5 Bible* CD-ROM is neither a product of nor endorsed by FileMaker, Inc.

Acknowledgments

I am grateful to the many people who offered their encouragement and support while I was working on this update, including Kevin Mallon and Sue Hart (FileMaker, Inc.); Andy Cummings, Ed Adams, Kathi Duggan, Colleen Dowling, Tim Borek, and Marti Paul (IDG Books Worldwide, Inc.); and my agent and friend, Matt Wagner. I also wish to extend a special thank you to all the individuals who graciously contributed material to the *FileMaker Pro 5 Bible* CD-ROM and to Dennis Cohen for doing the technical editing for this new edition.

Contents at a Glance

Contents

● ●

Part II: Database Design Basics   65

Chapter 4: Creating Your First Database 67

Chapter 5: Defining Fields 123

Part III: Working With Databases   257

Part IV: Putting FileMaker Pro to Work　　　401

Chapter 14: Calculations and Computations 403

Chapter 15: Automating FileMaker Pro 419

Chapter 16: Exchanging Data Between Applications 495

Part V: Mastering FileMaker Pro   531

The Fundamentals

◆ ◆ ◆ ◆

◆ ◆ ◆ ◆

What Is a Database?

Before exploring FileMaker Pro 5.0, you need to understand what a database is. A *database* is an organized collection of information, usually with one central topic. In a computer database (as opposed to a paper database), the program you use to enter and manipulate the data is called a database program or a database management program.

The word *organized* is a key part of this definition. Otherwise, a shoebox stuffed with business receipts might be considered a database. In general, if you need to look at every scrap of data before finding the one for which you're searching, you don't have a database. You just have a shoebox full of stuff.

Even if you have never used a computer database, you're already familiar with many examples of paper databases:

✦ Address books and business card files

✦ Employee records

✦ Recipe card files

✦ Telephone books

✦ Holiday greeting card lists

Every database — whether on paper, in a hand-held elec-tronic organizer, or in a computer — is composed of records. A *record* contains all the information that has been collected on one individual or entity in the database. In the preceding examples, a record holds all the address data on one friend or business associate (address book or business card file); the employment information on one employee (employee records); the ingredients and cooking instructions for one recipe (recipe card file); the name, street address, and phone number for one person or business in the area (telephone book); and the name of one person or family whom you previously received a card from or intend to send a card to (holiday greeting card list).

Records are divided into fields. A *field* contains a single piece of information about the subject of the record. In an address database, for example, the fields may include first name, last name, address, city, state, zip code, and phone number. Figure 1-1 shows the relationship among the components of a database.

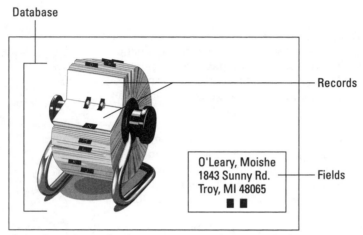

Figure 1-1: Every database is composed of records that contain fields.

What distinguishes a database from any old hodgepodge of information is that the data within each record is organized. Fields are responsible for this organization. The fields appear in the same place on every record and are reserved for a particular type of information. In the example in Figure 1-1, the field for the last name is always in the upper-left corner of the address card, and it always contains a person's last name. No matter which address card you pull, you will find a last name at that spot on the card.

Of course, in some paper databases, maintaining this level of organization can be difficult. When you are writing or typing an address card, for example, you may occasionally reverse the order of the last and first names or enter a company name in that location. Organization in informal paper databases comes exclusively from your own consistency—or lack of it.

When consistency is critical, such as when you are recording information on employees or filling out a customer invoice, records are often designed as forms. Spaces on the form have labels so you always know which piece of information belongs where. You can still type a phone number in the space labeled "Social Security number," but at least the labels make catching and correcting mistakes easier. Forms help organize the data in much the same way a computer-based database does. In fact, this type of paper database is frequently the basis for a computer database.

Paper Databases versus Computer Databases

So what's wrong with paper databases? Many homes and businesses rely heavily on them. The following sections discuss some of the shortcomings of paper databases and explain how computer databases can avoid these limitations.

Limitations of paper databases

First, consider some of the shortcomings of paper databases:

✦ *It's easy to make data-entry errors.* Even when you are using a typeset form, nothing prevents you from entering the wrong data in a field or forgetting to fill in a critical field, such as the hire date or medical history.

✦ *Maintenance can be difficult.* For records to be easy to locate, they must be in some rational order. Whenever you return or add a record to a folder or the filing cabinet, you have to be careful to place it in the correct spot. If you put the vendor file for Alpha Gamma Corp. in the Q folder, you may never find it again!

✦ *Updating records can be time-consuming.* Because of changes in information, such as addresses, phone numbers, and salaries, few databases are static. Updating a paper record may require several steps, including finding the record, erasing the old information, writing in the new information (or typing a whole new record), and returning the form to the filing cabinet. Making an across-the-board change — such as granting an incremental salary increase to all employees — can take a long time.

✦ *Sorting records, selecting subgroups of records, and creating reports are cumbersome tasks.* Suppose the boss walks into your office and says, "We're thinking about putting in a day-care center. How many of our 149 employees have kids under the age of five? Or you may be thinking of sending a direct-mail piece to your local customers. To determine printing and postage costs, you need to know how many customers are in the target zip code or are within a particular range of zip codes.

In either case, you'll probably have to examine every record in the paper database. Whenever a task requires sorting, organizing, or summarizing the data in a different way, you can look forward to a nightmare of paper shuffling. And when you're through, you'll have to restore all the records to their original order!

✦ *Sharing records is difficult.* When a supervisor borrows some employee records, for example, the office manager no longer has easy access to those records. (They're no longer in the file drawer.)

✦ *Information is hard to reuse.* If you want to use the information in a paper database for any purpose other than just reading it (addressing envelopes, for example), someone has to drag out the typewriter. Photocopying an address and then taping it onto a letter is considered bad form — unless you're creating a ransom note.

Advantages of computer databases

Computer databases, on the other hand, offer the following benefits:

✦ *Entering error-free information is easier.* Most database programs have features that speed data entry. Setting default values for some fields can save an incredible amount of typing time and ensure that information is entered consistently. (Using *CA* as the default entry for a State field, for example, ensures that you don't end up with records that variously contain CA, Calif., and California in the same field.) Other useful data-entry features include auto-incrementing fields (which automatically assign invoice or record numbers to new records), field types (which, for example, can prevent you from entering alphabetic information in a field that was designed to record salary data), range checking (which accepts only numbers within a particular range), and required fields (which warn you if you do not fill in a critical field).

✦ *You can easily add, delete, or change data.* Making a change to a record merely involves bringing the record up on-screen, editing it, and then closing the file. Because you make all changes on a computer, you don't need to search through file drawers or hunt for an eraser. And if you need additional copies of records, you can quickly print them. As you can see, the ease with which you can manage data is one of the key reasons for buying and using a database program such as FileMaker Pro.

✦ *Finding records is simple.* A Find feature enables you to jump directly to the record or records of interest.

✦ *You can specify criteria for sorting data.* Arranging records in a different order is as simple as issuing a Sort command. You can rearrange records in order of salary, record creation date, or any other field that is in the database. Most database programs also enable you to sort by multiple fields simultaneously. For example, you can sort a client database by city within each state.

✦ *You can work with discrete groups of records.* Using the database program's record selection tools, you can select a subgroup of records that is based on any criteria you want. You may, for example, want to see only recipes that have chicken as the main ingredient, or group employee records according to salary ranges or by department.

✦ *Database programs can perform calculations, frequently offering many of the same calculation capabilities that spreadsheet programs offer.* Instead of using a hand calculator to compute the sales tax and total for an invoice, you can have a database program automatically make the computations for you. In addition to performing computations within individual records, database programs can also generate summary statistics across all records or for selected groups of records. For example, you can easily summarize the efforts of different sales teams by calculating sales totals and averages by region.

✦ *Many people can simultaneously access the database.* If several people in a company need to view or modify the information in a database, you can use a database program on a network.

✦ *You can readily use information for multiple purposes.* For example, you can use the address information in records to print mailing labels, envelopes, a pocket-sized address book, or personalized form letters.

✦ *You can create custom reports.* Only you are in a position to decide which reports are essential to running your business, department, class, bowling league, or home. In most database programs, you can create your own reports and lay them out in any format that meets your information needs. Because you can save report formats on disk, you can reuse a format whenever you want to generate a current report.

✦ *You can use data from one program in another program.* Most database programs can import and export data.

Importing enables you to bring information into the database from other programs. For example, you may already have an address book program in which you've recorded the addresses of friends and business associates. Rather than retyping those addresses in your database program, you can export them from the original program (creating a file your database program can read) and then import them into a database.

Exporting, on the other hand, enables you to use fields and records in a database to create a file that other programs can read. For example, you can easily export numeric data so you can graph it with a spreadsheet program.

When should you use a database program?

Although there's a long list of reasons why computer databases are superior to paper databases, you also need to recognize that not every database is a good candidate for computerization. Specifically, when you are deciding between using a paper database and using a computer database, you need to ask yourself the following questions (the more Yes answers you give, the more reasons you have for using a database program):

✦ *Will the contents of individual records change frequently?* If the information for each record is not static and editing is often necessary, choose a computer database.

✦ *Is much of the information repetitive?* As mentioned previously, you can use a database program to create default entries for fields. If much of the information that you'll enter is repetitive, using a database program can help you avoid unnecessary typing.

✦ *Will the records need to be grouped or sorted in different ways?* Database programs can quickly sort and select records for even very large collections of data.

✦ *Will calculations be necessary?* The more complex the calculations, the more you need a database program.

✦ *Will printed output be required?* Unless photocopies are satisfactory, use a database program.

✦ *Will reports be necessary?* Summarizing information is a task at which database programs excel. If your reports go beyond simple record counts, a database program may be the best choice.

Flat-file and relational databases

You can roughly classify every database program as either flat file or relational, according to the program's relational capabilities — that is, its capability to simultaneously draw information from more than one database on the basis of shared fields.

That explanation is quite a mouthful, isn't it? A couple of definitions and an example may make it easier to swallow:

✦ A *flat-file database* always consists of a single file. All fields that are required have to be contained within that data file.

✦ A *relational database* consists of two or more interrelated data files that have one or more key fields in common.

Instead of designing a single customer database that contains all your customer information (as you would in a flat-file database program), you might create several smaller databases. For example, you could create one database called "Addresses" to contain just customer addresses, and another called "Orders" to hold information about the customers' previous orders. To link the records in the two databases, you could assign a unique identification number to each customer. By placing this I.D. field in both data files, you can relate the two sets of information. For example, you can generate a statement from the Orders database and instruct the program to pull the customer's mailing address from the Addresses database after finding the record that contains the matching I.D. number, as shown in Figure 1-2.

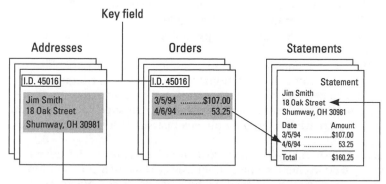

Figure 1-2: Relational database programs can create a report by extracting information from several files.

Both types of database programs have advantages. Conceptually, flat-file database programs are easier to understand and learn to use. All the important data is in a single file. If you need to record additional information, you just add more fields.

On the other hand, because of the multi-file approach that relational database programs use, the files tend to be smaller and, hence, faster to work with for common tasks such as sorting and searching. Because of their power and flexibility, relational database programs are frequently used for large record-keeping projects or projects that have complex requirements. Another significant advantage of relational databases is their ability to reuse (or re-purpose data). For example, a high school might maintain a series of databases for extracurricular activities, but draw all the name and address information from a single student registration database.

Learning to use a relational database program can be difficult because of the complexity of the relational concept and the fact that much of the program's power frequently comes from a programming language that you must use to create advanced databases. In addition, designing relational databases often requires substantial planning. You must usually decide on the relational (or key) fields ahead of time and determine what data will be collected in each file. Unlike a flat-file database, a relational database is not easy to toss together.

Introducing FileMaker Pro

Because this book is about FileMaker Pro, you may well be asking yourself where it fits into the "relational versus flat-file" classification scheme. Up through FileMaker Pro 2.1, FileMaker Pro was a flat-file database program with some relational capabilities. Specifically, you could use its Lookup feature to look up information in a secondary file and then copy that information into the current file.

Since version 3.0, however, FileMaker Pro has had full relational capabilities. In addition to lookups, you can define relationships between files that merely display the related data from a secondary file rather than copy it into the primary file. Depending on the nature and extent of your data, you can save substantial amounts of hard-disk space by creating related databases instead of relying on lookups.

If you run a business, you may already have an invoice database, for example. Instead of retyping a customer's name and address (or using a series of lookups to copy this information from another file) whenever he or she places another order, you can store the address information in a separate customer address database and then merely reference it in the invoice file. No matter how many invoices you create for a customer, the name and address information is only recorded once and is always current.

FileMaker concepts

Even before you sit down to try out FileMaker Pro, it's important that you understand a few key concepts and features. Although all database programs have much in common with each other (as explained earlier in this chapter), FileMaker Pro has distinct ways of doing things that clearly distinguish it from other programs. (These differences explain — at least partially — why FileMaker Pro has long been the database program of choice for Macintosh users and is making great strides in the Windows world.) The remainder of this chapter provides an introduction to these key concepts and an explanation of how you can use FileMaker Pro to tackle many database needs — both in the business and home arenas.

Understanding layouts

Much of FileMaker Pro's power comes from a feature called layouts. A *layout* is an arrangement of a set of database fields for a particular file. Every layout is a view or window into the contents of a database, and different layouts present different views (frequently using different groups of fields). You can create separate layouts for doing data entry, generating reports (on-screen or printed), and printing labels or envelopes. And you can have as many layouts for each file as you need.

Whenever you create a new database and define its fields, FileMaker Pro automatically generates a layout that is a standard arrangement of all the fields you have defined (see Figure 1-3). If a quick-and-dirty database is all you need, you can use this standard layout to start entering data immediately.

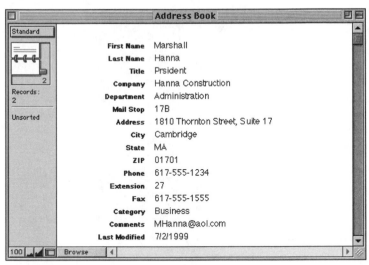

Figure 1-3: A standard database layout

On the other hand, you can customize a database layout by doing any of the following:

✦ Changing the placement of fields (to create a columnar report, for example)

✦ Eliminating fields from the layout that you do not want to display (while still being able to use them in other layouts where they *will* display)

✦ Removing some or all of the field labels or moving the labels to different positions (field labels are not attached to fields)

✦ Embellishing the layout by adding text and graphics and by modifying the font, style, color, pattern, or border for fields

✦ Eliminating layout parts (which are explained later in this chapter) that are not needed, or adding parts that display summary statistics or present information that repeats on every page

Figure 1-4 shows a custom layout for the same database as the one previously shown in Figure 1-3. The data-entry screen is more attractive because of the rearrangement of the fields, changes in font sizes and styles, and the addition of color and graphics. The capability to produce custom layouts is one of the many features that attracts users to FileMaker Pro.

New
Feature

Standard layouts, such as the one shown in Figure 1-3, no longer have to be plain. By choosing a FileMaker Pro 5 *theme* when creating the layout, you can add background colors and field borders.

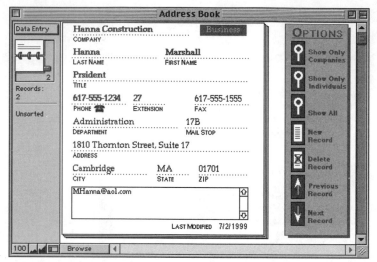

Figure 1-4: A custom layout

Every layout you create for a database is separate from every other layout, but it draws from the same set of fields. When you design a new layout, you select only the fields you need. In a customer database, for example, you can use one layout to display invoice information, such as the customer's name, address, items or services purchased, and a total. A second layout may contain only name and address information that is formatted as a mailing label. You can create a third layout to print or display a client phone book or monthly client purchase totals. Figure 1-5 shows two different layouts for the same database.

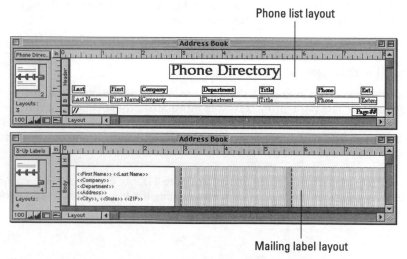

Figure 1-5: Layouts for a phone book and mailing labels

No practical restrictions limit the number of fields you can use in a layout. Data-entry screens, for example, frequently have many fields so you can easily enter all important information for a record in a single layout. At the other extreme, a help screen or menu layout may contain only static text and buttons — no fields at all.

As you design layouts for a database, you may need to create additional fields that are specific to a single layout. For example, a field that shows a total for each customer order is important in an invoice layout but unnecessary (or pointless) in an address label layout. Conversely, you do not have to include every field you define. You may want to create a field to use only as a test for a calculation (determining whether another field is blank, for example) and not place it on any layout.

Keep in mind that data you enter in one layout automatically appears in any other layouts that use those same fields. And although you can — and usually will — create an all-encompassing layout for data entry, you can use the other layouts for data entry, too.

Because you can make new layouts whenever you like — even after a database contains records — you can design additional reports, labels, and data-entry screens as the need arises. And if you didn't originally remember to create a field that is critical to a layout, you can just add fields as you need them.

Remember the following important points about layouts:

✦ Every database can have as many different layouts as you need.

✦ Every layout can use as many or as few of the defined fields as you like.

✦ A database can have fields that are not included in any layout.

✦ As with the process of defining new fields, you can create or modify layouts whenever the need presents itself.

Understanding layout parts

Layouts are divided into parts. Like a word-processing document, a layout can have, for example, a body, a header, and a footer. Each of these elements is a *part*. Every part can contain database fields, graphics, static text, and other embellishments. (As you will learn in Chapter 5, information in some parts is visible both on-screen and in reports, but you can see information in other parts only when you print a report or use the Preview command.)

The following layout parts are available to you in FileMaker Pro:

✦ *Title header and title footer*. This special header or footer appears only on the first page of a report and substitutes for any other header or footer part that has been defined for the layout.

✦ *Header and footer:* Headers and footers appear at the top or bottom, respectively, of every page of a report or other type of layout. (If you create a title header or footer, it takes precedence on the first page of the report.) Page numbers, logos, and the current date are popular items to place in a header or footer.

✦ *Body:* Unlike the other layout parts, information in the body appears in every record in the database. For this reason, you normally place most fields in the body.

✦ *Sub-summaries:* You use sub-summary parts to summarize groups of related records after you have sorted the database by the contents of a particular field. For example, after sorting an address database by city, you can use a sub-summary field to display a count of records in each city. Sub-summaries can appear above or below each group of records, and they are visible only in Preview mode and in printed output. (Preview and other FileMaker Pro modes are discussed in the next section.)

✦ *Grand summaries:* Statistics that appear in a grand summary apply to all records that are currently visible (that is, they are being browsed). A grand summary can appear at the beginning (leading grand summary) or end (trailing grand summary) of a report, and it is visible only in Preview mode and in printed output.

When you first create a layout, it starts with only a body, header, and footer. You can remove unnecessary parts and add other parts, as you like. Figures 1-6a and 1-6b show a layout that has several parts. The figures illustrate the relationship between the layout and an on-screen preview of the report.

Understanding modes

FileMaker Pro has four modes of operation: Browse, Layout, Find, and Preview. The mode you are in at any given moment governs the types of activities you can perform:

✦ *Browse mode:* You use this mode to create and delete records, as well as to enter and edit data. (You perform all data entry in Browse mode.)

✦ *Layout mode:* You design, edit, reorder, or delete database layouts in Layout mode.

✦ *Find mode:* In Find mode, you can search for or hide records that meet criteria you specify.

✦ *Preview mode:* Use Preview mode to preview a report or layout on-screen (usually prior to printing).

Thus, when you want to enter a new record, you must switch to Browse mode. To modify any portion of a layout (to add or resize a graphic, for example), you have to be in Layout mode. If you're not sure what mode you're in, check the Mode indicator at the bottom of the database window.

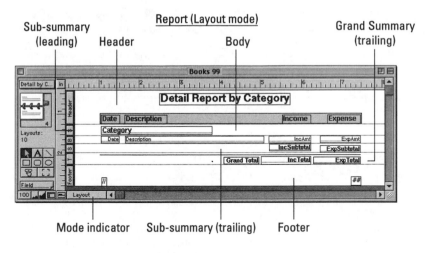

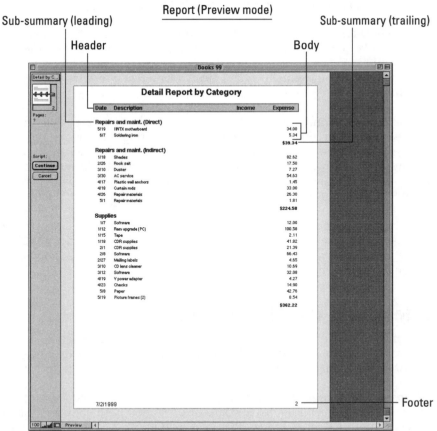

Figure 1-6: Layout parts (as displayed in Layout and Preview mode)

Preview your documents before printing

When examining a report or other type of layout in Preview mode, whatever is shown on the preview screen is precisely what will be sent to the printer. If your printout doesn't look like what you expected, use Preview mode to check your changes until the printout is correct. This saves time and paper when printing layouts, labels, and reports, for example.

Getting "The Big Picture"

Now that you understand what a database program is and does, and how to determine when it's the right tool for the job, you may be facing a problem common to anyone who buys a new type of program. You probably wonder what you can do with FileMaker Pro. (Yes, many of us often purchase software solutions before clearly defining the problems they were intended to solve.)

Although FileMaker Pro is a wonderful piece of technology, it's only as useful as you make it. And, like so many other things in life, understanding how something works is not the same as knowing *when* to use it. If you've ever taken an advanced math or statistics course, you understand what I mean. Memorizing formulas is not the same as knowing when they should be applied.

If you've already experimented with the sample files and templates that are included with FileMaker Pro 5.0, it should be obvious that they are not meant to serve all your database needs. (Neither are the templates included with this book, by the way.) Before long, you will be faced with the prospect of designing and using your own databases. And if you're new to databases, your biggest initial problem will not be learning how to use the program, but rather what to use it for.

To get you into the proper mind-set, this chapter concludes with a list of some uses to which FileMaker Pro can be put — some general and some very specific. Hopefully, these examples will give you ideas for databases that you may want to create, moving you from the thinking stage to the doing stage.

Business uses for FileMaker Pro

Because of the ease with which you can create functional, useful databases (regardless of your prior database experience), FileMaker Pro has long been a favorite program among business users. Here are a few of the things you can do:

✦ *Automate business forms.* Most businesses rely on forms, and many of these forms are perfect candidates for databases. A petty cash voucher system is one example. Rather than just fill out a slip of paper that gets tossed into a cash box or drawer, you can duplicate the voucher as a FileMaker Pro data-entry form. Features such as date-stamping and assigning serial numbers can be automatically applied to each new voucher. And by creating appropriate report layouts, you can break down disbursements by time periods, departments, or individuals.

✦ *Improve shipping records.* Rather than frantically searching for a shipping receipt or bill of lading whenever a shipment goes awry, FileMaker Pro can help you keep track of incoming and outgoing shipments. The program's search capabilities make it easy to locate any shipment documentation that normally might be tucked away in a file drawer. FileMaker Pro can also help you organize your receipts and create appropriate reports — grouping them and showing total shipments to each customer, for example.

✦ *Reuse existing customer data.* For many businesses, the customer list is its most valuable asset. Sadly, many businesses — both small and large — still attempt to maintain their customer records on paper only. Entering customer information into a database makes it possible to do mass mailings to announce sales, easily update and correct information (a change of address, for example), examine customer buying patterns, and determine when an additional sales call or purging from your list is necessary.

✦ *Track rental information.* Small businesses that do rentals are excellent candidates for FileMaker Pro. By creating appropriate formulas, scripts, and reports, you can instruct the program to find all rentals that are late, calculate late charges, and determine who your best customers are, for example.

✦ *Examine employee performance.* Although not the best choice for project tracking (there are many programs designed specifically for this task), you can certainly create a simple assignment-oriented database that records each assignment you hand out, including its due date, progress notes, and completion date. By adding fields for "quality of work," the database can help you perform (and document) the dreaded salary review.

✦ *Schedule company resources.* Conference rooms, audio-visual equipment, and other limited company resources are often in high demand. If you're the office manager, you may want to create a database of resource requests. You can then sort by resource, date, and time to quickly flag duplicate requests.

✦ *Share information between branches.* FileMaker Pro's ability to host multi-user databases on the Internet or a company intranet provides an ideal way for you to share data between distant branches of your company or among the users on your corporate LAN.

Home uses for FileMaker Pro

FileMaker Pro isn't just for business. In fact, home users make up a substantial portion of those who purchase and use FileMaker Pro for their data recording needs. Here are some ways you can use FileMaker Pro for your own recordkeeping:

✦ *Maintain a home inventory.* If you know anyone who has had a large casualty loss due to a burglary, fire, or natural disaster, you understand the pressing need for documenting everything you own. An inventory database can be used to conveniently list your possessions along with their serial numbers, purchase date, and cost. A similar database that lists insurance policies, credit cards, and other important documents (and their locations) can also be very useful.

✦ *Track a collection.* A database program is perfect for recording purchases and catalog values for any set of collectibles, such as stamps, coins, baseball cards, comic books, paintings, books, wines, Pez dispensers, or Beanie Babies. If you have a scanner or digital camera, you can also include graphic images of the items in the database.

✦ *Record credit card and checking account activity.* If you don't already have a home accounting program, you can use FileMaker Pro to create one. Every transaction (a check, deposit, charge, or payment) can be treated as a separate record.

✦ *Never a lender be.* Do you have neighbors, friends, and relatives who are great at borrowing but not so hot at returning items? Use a database to track what was lent, when, and to whom. By including a simple date calculation, you can automatically determine how long it has been since each item was lent, too. Even if you don't throw this information in the borrower's face ("Bill, you borrowed my hedge clippers 47 days ago!"), at least you'll always know where your stuff is.

✦ *Get a handle on your investments.* Say you just sold some stock and you don't remember what you paid for it. The IRS expects you to record this information in order to determine capital gains. FileMaker Pro can help you keep track of your buy and sell costs. And with all its calculation capabilities, you can also use FileMaker Pro to calculate gains and losses (in dollars and percentages), the number of days an investment was held, and so on.

Summary

✦ Every database is composed of records — one per person or entity in the database. Records are divided into fields, which are each designed to hold one particular piece of information.

✦ A database program, such as FileMaker Pro, enables you to store information for rapid retrieval and organize the data in ways that are extremely cumbersome and time-consuming if attempted with a paper database.

✦ Paper databases are most useful when the data collected is relatively static and your reporting requirements are minimal. A database program is a better choice when data frequently changes, when you need to use the information for multiple purposes, or when you want to be able to print the information. A database program is also a better choice when you want to perform calculations or you need summary information or reports.

✦ Layouts are arrangements of database fields. Different layouts enable you to view and present information in different ways. You can have as many layouts for a FileMaker Pro database as you like.

✦ Layouts are divided into sections called parts. Depending on the parts in which you place fields, text, and objects, they will be printed once for every record in the database (body), only at the top or bottom of each report page (header or footer), only at the top or bottom of the first report page (title header or title footer), once before or after each group of records sorted on the sort-by field (leading or trailing sub-summary), or once before or after all of the records being browsed (leading or trailing grand summary).

✦ You do all work in FileMaker Pro in one of four modes: Browse, Layout, Find, or Preview. For example, you can enter data only when the database is in Browse mode. If you're ever unsure of the current mode, check the Mode indicator at the bottom of the database window.

✦ ✦ ✦

FileMaker Pro Basic Operations

In Chapter 1, you learned that FileMaker Pro is a mode-oriented program. That is, the mode you're in (Browse, Layout, Find, or Preview) determines the types of operations you can perform. Now that you understand the fundamental FileMaker Pro concepts of modes and layouts, you're ready to explore the basic — yet essential — program procedures for performing common operations.

Starting Up

You can start up FileMaker Pro using one of two methods. The method you use depends on whether you also want to open one or several databases as you're starting up.

Note When books, magazines, or manuals discuss *starting up* a program, they sometimes use the terms *run* and *launch*. All three terms mean the same thing.

To launch FileMaker Pro without opening an existing database, follow these steps:

1. Locate the FileMaker Pro icon on your hard disk (see Figure 2-1).

   If the program is stored on a disk whose window is closed, double-click the disk icon to open its window. Similarly, if the program is stored in a folder that is not presently open, double-click the folder to display its contents. Continue opening folders as necessary until you see the FileMaker Pro icon.

If you have Windows 95 or 98, you can launch FileMaker Pro by choosing its name from the Start ➪ Programs menu and then go to step 3. As an alternative, you can create a shortcut for FileMaker Pro and drag it onto the Quick Launch bar (found to the right of the Start button).

If you have recently run FileMaker Pro on your Mac, you can also launch it by choosing its name from the Recent Applications folder in the Apple menu. You may also find it helpful to make an alias of FileMaker Pro (select its icon and press ⌘+M) and then drag the alias into the Apple Menu Items folder inside the System Folder. Doing so will enable you to launch FileMaker Pro by choosing its name from the Apple menu.

If you're running OS 8.5 or later, you can put the alias in your Favorites folder and then run FileMaker Pro by choosing Apple ⇨ Favorites. To create and store the alias, select the FileMaker Pro program icon and choose File ⇨ Add to Favorites.)

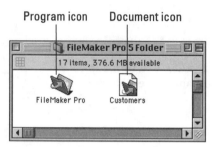

Figure 2-1: The FileMaker Pro program icon and a document icon

2. Double-click the FileMaker Pro program icon.

FileMaker Pro loads into memory and presents you with the New Database dialog box (see Figure 2-2).

Figure 2-2: This dialog box appears when the program starts.

3. Click the appropriate radio button in the New Database dialog box.

- To create a new database from one of the included templates, click the radio button labeled "Create a new file using a template," choose a category from the pop-up menu, and then choose a database template from the list that appears.

- To create a new database from scratch, click the radio button labeled "Create a new empty file."

- To open an existing database, click the radio button labeled "Open an existing file."

4. Complete your choice by clicking OK.

- If you chose "Create a new file using a template," FileMaker Pro automatically generates a new, empty copy of the chosen database template.

- If you chose "Create a new empty file," a file dialog box appears, like the one shown in Figure 2-3. Type a name for the new file, select a location on disk in which to store the database, and click Save. The Define Fields dialog box appears, enabling you to complete the initial database definition.

  Define the necessary fields and click Done. A standard layout is created for you, the first record of the database is displayed, and you are switched into Browse mode, where you can begin entering data for the first record. (The details of defining fields and designing layouts are covered in Chapters 5 and 6.)

- If you chose "Open an existing file," a file dialog box appears. Navigate to the drive and folder that contains your database, choose its name in the file list, and click Open.

Tip If you prefer, you can just dismiss the New Database dialog box by clicking the Cancel button. You can then use commands from the File menu to create new databases (New Database) or open existing databases (Open). Note that New Database and Open work the same whether you select them in the New Database dialog box or choose their commands from the File menu.

Dealing with the New Database dialog box can be a nuisance—and totally unnecessary if the database you want to work with already exists. You can simultaneously launch FileMaker Pro and open a database by double-clicking the database's file icon. FileMaker Pro launches, and the database is automatically opened.

Tip You can stop the New Database dialog box from appearing at startup by clicking the "No longer show this dialog" check box (refer to Figure 2-2).

Macintosh

Enter a new file name here   Click to create
a new document

Windows

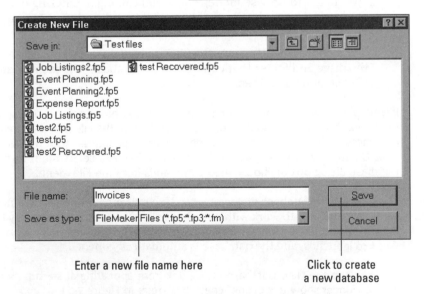

Enter a new file name here   Click to create
a new database

Figure 2-3: This file dialog box is presented when you create a new database (OS 8.5 and higher).

If you want, you can simultaneously launch FileMaker Pro and open several databases, as follows:

1. Locate the file icons of the databases you wish to open.

   To open more than one database simultaneously, you must have all the database files on the same disk and in the same folder (or in the root directory of the same disk). (Note that if you have OS 8.5.*x* and view the files in list view, they need only be on the same disk.)

2. Drag a selection rectangle around all the databases of interest.

   —or—

   Click one of the databases to select it and then, while holding down the Shift/Ctrl key, click the additional databases you want to open.

3. *Macintosh*: Choose File ➪ Open or press ⌘+O. FileMaker Pro launches, and all the selected databases are automatically opened.

   Windows: Right-click one of the selected files. A pop-up menu appears. Choose the Open command.

Tip   You can create aliases (Mac) or shortcuts (Windows) for frequently used databases, so you can easily find and open them.

FileMaker Pro and memory usage

When you launch FileMaker Pro and open a database, the entire database is not always loaded into memory. FileMaker Pro uses a disk-caching scheme, loading only the data it requires at the moment (based on your find requests, the layout in use, and so on). When the program needs to display additional records or a different layout, it reads the information from the disk, replacing the data that was previously in memory with the new data. This way, you can open a 12MB database with a machine that only has 8MB of RAM (*Random Access Memory*), for example. Disk caching is common to many programs that deal with large quantities of data.

An important consequence of this disk-caching scheme can be seen if you are using FileMaker Pro with a laptop computer. With large databases, you can expect more disk accesses than normal, which will quickly use up the battery charge. Unless you can plug your laptop into a wall outlet (rather than run it from its battery), you are well-advised to restrict your work to smaller databases or to use larger databases sparingly — closing them as soon as you've accomplished the task at hand.

FileMaker Pro and the power switch

Just as it's a bad idea to shut down your Mac or PC by simply cutting the power instead of using the Shut Down command, turning off the juice is also a poor substitute for using a program's Quit/Exit command. Although FileMaker Pro does indeed save your work automatically and even has a command that can be used to recover a damaged database file, you shouldn't take unnecessary risks with your data. Unless circumstances beyond your control prevent doing so (your system crashes, lightning strikes, or your puppy yanks out the computer's power cord), you should always use the Quit/Exit command to end a FileMaker Pro session.

Quitting

When you're ready to end a FileMaker Pro session, choose Quit/Exit from the File menu (or press ⌘+Q/Alt+F4). Any open data files are closed as part of the Quit/Exit process. Because FileMaker Pro automatically saves changes to files as you work with them, you don't need to issue any Save commands. (For more information on how FileMaker Pro saves data, see "Saving files," later in this chapter.)

File-Handling Procedures

While you are working in FileMaker Pro, you may want to open additional database files, create new files, close files, or make a backup copy of a database you are using. The information in this section explains how to perform these common procedures.

Opening, creating, and closing databases

You use the File menu or a keyboard shortcut to open an existing database, create a new database, or close a database. To open an existing database, follow these steps:

1. Choose File ➪ Open (or press ⌘+O/Ctrl+O).

A standard file dialog box appears, as shown in Figure 2-4.

Macintosh

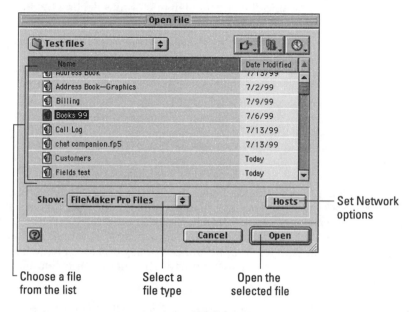

Choose a file   Select a   Open the
from the list   file type   selected file

Windows

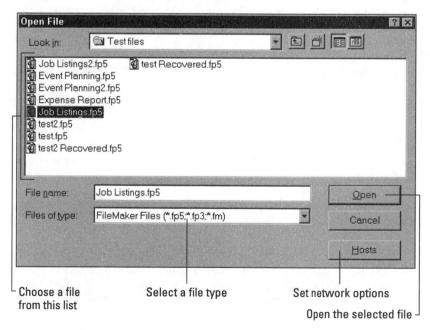

Choose a file   Select a file type   Set network options
from this list

Open the selected file

Figure 2-4: This file dialog box appears when you choose the Open command (OS 8.5.x).

2. Navigate to the drive and folder where the database file is stored.

3. Open the file by double-clicking its filename or by selecting the filename and then clicking the Open button.

As mentioned previously, you can have several FileMaker Pro databases open at the same time, if you like. To open additional databases, simply repeat these steps.

Tip   FileMaker Pro's Open dialog box has a Show:/Files of Type: pop-up menu that you can use to filter the file list to display only particular types of files. By default, FileMaker Files is selected. Select a different file format, such as Tab-Separated Text Files, only when you want to convert an existing file into a FileMaker Pro 5.0 database. The procedure for doing this is described in Chapter 16.

FileMaker Pro has a feature that makes it simple to open any recently used database. You can choose a database to open from the list that appears at the bottom of the File menu. To enable this feature, choose Edit ⇨ Preferences ⇨ Application. Then, click the check box for "Show recently opened files" in the General section of the Application Preferences dialog box (see Figure 2-5). The number you specify for this option determines the number of recent files that will be listed at the bottom of the File menu.

To create a new database file from scratch or from a FileMaker-provided template, choose File ⇨ New Database. A modified version of the New Database dialog box (previously shown in Figure 2-2) appears, with the "Open an existing file" option eliminated. Follow the instructions presented earlier in this chapter for working with the New Database dialog box.

Note   Windows determines which program is associated with a given file by the file's *extension* — a three-character suffix, such as .doc or .zip. When you create a FileMaker Pro 5 database in Windows, the filename automatically includes an .fp5 extension, such as Sales.fp5. Mac filenames, on the other hand, do not need to have extensions. But if you want a Mac database to be recognized by the Windows version of FileMaker Pro, add the .fp5 to the end of the filename. (Windows databases created with FileMaker Pro 3.0-4.1 had an .fp3 extension. FileMaker Pro 5 can convert and open these files.)

When you're through working with a database, you can close its file by performing any one of the following actions:

✦ Choose File ⇨ Close (or press ⌘+W/Ctrl+W).

✦ Click the file's close box. Mac users will find the close box in the upper-left corner of the document window. In Windows applications, the close box is the tiny *x* in the upper-right corner of the document window.

✦ Choose File ➪ Quit/Exit (or press ⌘+Q/Alt+F4). Quitting automatically closes any open database files and records any unsaved changes.

Note   When you are working in FileMaker Pro, remember that you do not have to close *any* files. You can have as many open files as will fit in your computer's available memory.

Macintosh

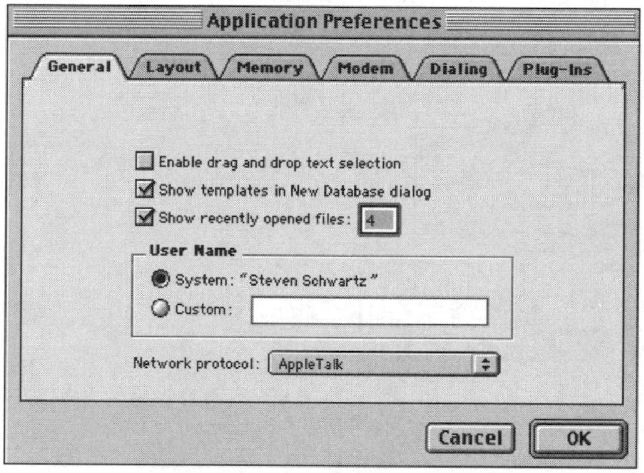

![Macintosh Application Preferences dialog]

Windows

![Windows Application Preferences dialog]

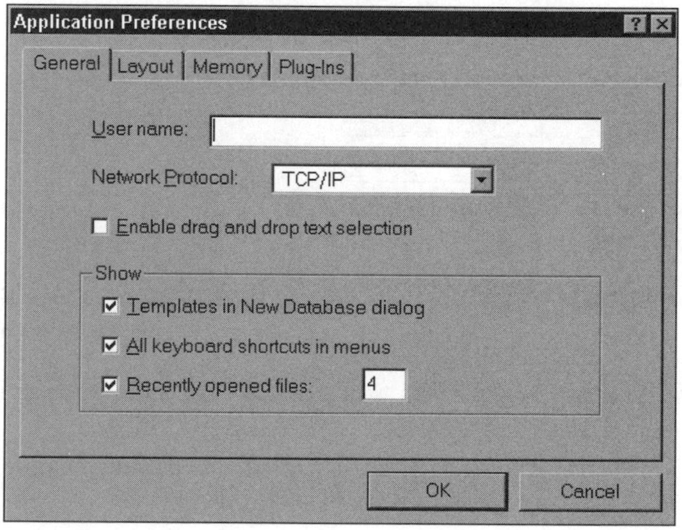

Figure 2-5: To make it easy to open recently used databases, enable the option to "Show recently opened files."

New Mac file-handling helpers

If you are running FileMaker Pro on a Macintosh with OS 8.5 or higher, you'll note that file dialog boxes offer several new options. There are now three buttons in the upper-right corner of the dialog box. When clicked, the buttons present drop-down menus that enable you to:

✦ Switch to any drive or network volume

✦ Open any FileMaker database that you've added to the Favorites list

✦ Open any recently opened database, folder, drive, or server

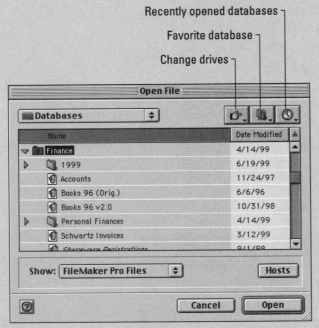

Click these buttons to switch drives, open favorite databases, or open a recently used database.

Another useful new feature of dialog boxes is that drive, folder, and file lists in dialog boxes now work the same as viewing them in the Finder using List view. That is, in addition to using the normal procedures to open a folder or drive (by double-clicking it, or by selecting it and clicking Open), you can also view the contents of any drive or folder by merely clicking the triangle in front of the drive or folder name.

To make it simple to find any frequently used database, you can add it to the drop-down Favorites list. Select the database in the file list, click the Favorites button, and choose Add to Favorites.

To remove an item from the Favorites menu, click the Favorites button and choose Remove from Favorites. The Remove Favorites dialog box appears. Highlight the database you want to remove, and click Remove.

Select the database you wish to remove from the Favorites list.

Saving files

In most programs, the procedure for saving a new file or for saving changes you've made to an older file is to choose the File ⇨ Save or File ⇨ Save As command. In FileMaker Pro, however, you do not use these methods. In fact, if you examine the File menu (see Figure 2-6), you'll note that it does not have Save or Save As commands. These commands are missing because FileMaker Pro automatically saves changes as you work with a file. And when you close a file or quit the program, you never see a dialog box asking whether you want to save your changes — the program has already saved them.

Tip   You can, however, exert some control over *when* FileMaker Pro saves files. Choose Edit ⇨ Preferences ⇨ Application. The Application Preferences dialog box appears. Click the Memory tab. You can instruct FileMaker to save only during idle time or every so many minutes. The latter option is most useful if you are using a notebook or laptop. By setting the minutes between saves to a relatively high number, you can conserve battery power by reducing the frequency of "hits" on the internal hard disk or floppy drive. Select a setting with which you're comfortable. For instance, if you set 15 minutes as the save period, you are risking up to 15 minutes worth of data in the event that your computer crashes before the data is saved. Don't worry if you quit before the time is up, though. FileMaker Pro automatically saves all data when you quit.

Macintosh   Windows

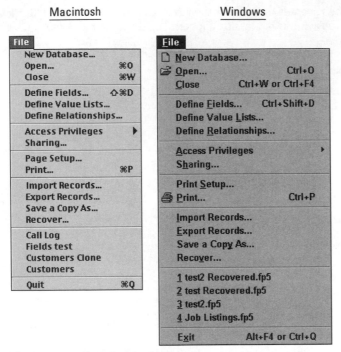

Figure 2-6: FileMaker Pro's File menu

Because the integrity of your data is paramount, FileMaker Pro's approach to saving goes a long way toward reducing the risk of data loss. The only negative side to auto-saving is that FileMaker Pro saves all changes — both good and bad — that you make to a database. For example, if you experiment with a layout, FileMaker Pro records the changes. Two options are available for recovering from inadvertent changes:

✦ Immediately choose the Edit ➪ Undo command (or press ⌘+Z/Ctrl+Z).

✦ Create a backup of the file before you make any major changes (as discussed in the next section, "Making a backup copy of a file").

The Undo command has two limitations. First, you can undo only the most recent modification made to the database. (The wording of the Undo command automatically changes to reflect the most recent action that you can undo.) For example, if you delete some text from a field and then type information into another field, you cannot undo the deletion. (However, as long as you have not switched to a different record, you can use the Records ➪ Revert Record command to undo *all* changes made to an individual record.)

Second, some commands simply cannot be undone. When you can't use the Undo command, it changes to Can't Undo. Actions that cannot be undone include using most of the Delete commands, such as Delete Record, Delete All Records, Delete Layout, and the Delete command in the Define Fields dialog box.

The moral is that relying on the Undo command to save you from major mistakes can be a major mistake itself. The only safe approach is to keep backups of important files, ensuring that you can recover from even the most horrendous mistake or computer calamity.

Making a backup copy of a file

Don't trust computers! Do I have your attention now? Although you may have spent thousands of dollars on your computer and programs, they're not infallible. Regardless of how many times they hear this, most new computer users appear to feign deafness. Then they wake up one morning to find that their hard disk has bit the dust, the kids threw out the folder that contained the family's financial records, or a thief has walked off with the computer. Without a backup of your important data, you're back at square one.

Because your data and layouts are important to you, FileMaker Pro provides several ways to make backup copies. In the event that something happens to the original file, you can use the backup copy to get the database up and running again. In addition to using the backup procedures provided by FileMaker Pro, you can make copies using the Finder (Macintosh), Windows desktop, or a commercial backup program, such as Retrospect from Dantz Development.

In particular, you may want to make a backup copy of a file for the following reasons:

✦ As a general precaution against data loss due to user error, hardware failure, or software problems (a crash, for example)

✦ When you are planning to make a major change to a database, such as deleting records or modifying a layout

✦ When you want to create a database template for someone else or for your own use

You can make an exact duplicate of a database file (containing all the data and layouts) from the Finder/Windows desktop, using a commercial backup program, or from within FileMaker Pro. However, you can make *templates* (databases without data) only from within FileMaker Pro.

To duplicate a FileMaker Pro database file from within FileMaker Pro, do the following:

1. In FileMaker Pro, open the database you want to copy.

2. Choose File ➪ Save a Copy As.

   A file dialog box appears, as shown in Figure 2-7.

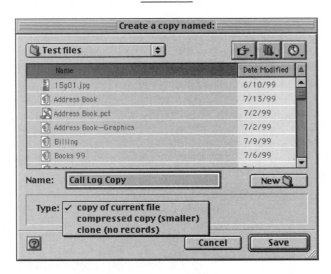

Figure 2-7: This dialog box enables you to save a copy of a FileMaker Pro database in any of three formats.

3. Click the Type:/Save a: pop-up menu, and select the type of file you want to create:

- *Copy of current file*: Use this choice when you want an exact duplicate of a database, including all the layouts and data it contains.

- *Compressed copy (smaller)*: This choice produces a usable copy of a database, but the copy is compressed to save disk space. This option is particularly useful when you are *archiving* a database (storing it for posterity or as a backup) or when a database is too large to fit on a floppy disk.

- *Clone (no records)*: Select this option when you want to create a template from the database. All formulas, field definitions, and layouts are retained in the new file, but it contains no records.

4. Enter a new filename for the copy or leave the displayed default name as is.

The default name that FileMaker Pro presents is one of the following, depending on the type of file you selected in step 3:

- *Current filename* Copy (if you chose "copy of current file" or "compressed copy")

- *Current filename* Clone (if you chose "clone")

If you are running FileMaker Pro 5 for Windows, the .fp5 extension is automatically added for you.

5. Using standard file dialog box procedures, navigate to the disk and folder in which you want to save the copy.

6. Click Save (or press Enter or Return).

The copy is saved in the format you selected.

Automatic backups

If you're worried about making inadvertent changes to a database or concerned that something catastrophic may happen to it, you can create a FileMaker Pro script that automatically creates a backup every time you open the database. (Yes, I know we're getting ahead of ourselves. Scripting is covered much later in this book. If you don't feel comfortable with scripting at this moment, return to this section when you do. You'll find it surprisingly easy.) You can add a copy of the Automatic Backup script to the Scripts menu so you can create backups during a session, too.

To create an automatic backup script, follow these steps:

1. Launch FileMaker Pro and open the database.

More about clones

A FileMaker Pro clone is the equivalent of a template or stationery file you create in most other programs. It's an empty database, ready for you to begin adding records. However, unlike icons for templates or stationery files that you might create in other programs, the icon for a clone looks exactly like the icon for any other FileMaker Pro database file — so recognizing that it's a clone is difficult. And because it's not a real template or stationery file, when you open a clone, you aren't opening a copy of it; you're opening the actual file. Any data you add to the clone is automatically saved as part of the file. If you want to preserve the clone, make a copy of it (or make a second clone), and make changes to the copy rather than to the original.

Clones are particularly useful when you have databases that you routinely need to start over from scratch (for example, a bookkeeping database that you clear monthly or annually), when you want to experiment with a layout or scripts, or when you want to provide a template for other users but don't want them to have your data.

When you open a clone for the first time, it will not contain any records. To begin using the file, choose Records ➪ New Record (⌘+N/Ctrl+N).

2. Choose ScriptMaker from the Scripts menu.

The Define Scripts dialog box appears (see Figure 2-8). The dialog box displays all scripts that have been defined for the database.

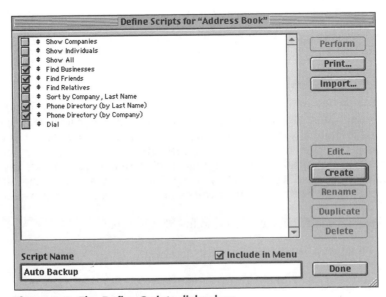

Figure 2-8: The Define Scripts dialog box

3. Type a name for the script in the Script Name box.

If the "Include in Menu" check box does not contain a check mark, click once in the box to add the check mark.

4. Click Create to define the script.

The Script Definition dialog box appears, as shown in Figure 2-9.

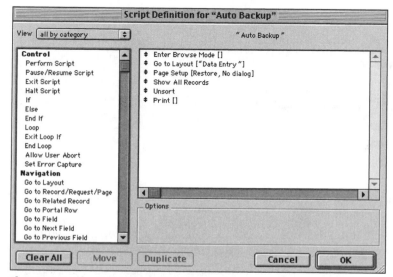

Figure 2-9: The Script Definition dialog box

5. Click Clear All to clear the script definition list on the right side of the dialog box.

6. Scroll down the steps list until the choice "Save a Copy as" appears.

7. Select "Save a Copy as" and then click the Move button.

The script step is copied to the script list on the right and is automatically highlighted.

8. Click the Specify File/File button.

A standard file dialog box appears, as shown in Figure 2-10.

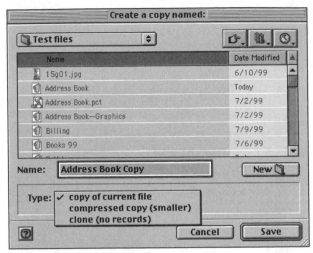

Figure 2-10: You specify the name, location, and type of backup file in this dialog box.

9. Navigate to the drive and folder where you intend to store the backup files made by the script.

   By default, FileMaker Pro offers to name the backup file *filename* Copy, but you can change the name of the file using normal editing techniques.

10. At the bottom of the dialog box, click the Type:/Save a: pop-up menu and choose either "copy of current file" or "compressed copy (smaller)."

   Either option will save a complete copy of the database, including all records, layouts, and field definitions. If disk space is at a premium, you may prefer to use the compressed copy option.

11. Click the Save button.

12. To complete the script, click OK and then click Done in the dialog boxes that appear.

   The script is added to the bottom of the Scripts menu.

13. To make the script execute automatically whenever you open the database file, choose Edit ➪ Preferences ➪ Document.

   The Document Preferences dialog box appears (as shown in Figure 2-11).

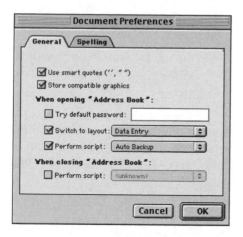

Figure 2-11: The Document Preferences dialog box

14. Click the General tab.

15. Click the "Perform script" check box in the "When opening" section of the dialog box.

16. Choose the automatic backup script from the pop-up list that appears ("Auto backup," in this case).

17. Click Done.

The changes are recorded, and the dialog box disappears.

Keep the following in mind when you are using this backup script:

✦ Each time a new backup is created, it writes over the previous backup file. If you need to keep multiple generations of backups, you should return to the desktop and manually rename the backup before or at the end of each FileMaker Pro session.

✦ Remember that the backup file is an exact copy of the original. Thus, it also contains the automatic backup script. If you ever need to use the backup file, be sure to rename it before opening it in FileMaker Pro. Otherwise, an error dialog box will appear, informing you that FileMaker was unable to create a backup (because the script is attempting to make a copy of the currently open database, using its own name).

Note

As you probably noted in step 15, there is also an option to make the backup script automatically run each time you *close* the database. Whether you run the script on opening or closing is entirely up to you.

Issuing Commands

Issuing commands in FileMaker Pro is no different from issuing them in any other program. For those of you who are new computer users, the following discussion will be helpful.

To issue a command in FileMaker Pro—to create a new record or add formatting to a field, for example—you can use the mouse to choose the command from a menu or, if the command has a keystroke equivalent, you can press a special combination of keys. Figure 2-12 shows an example of selecting a command from a menu.

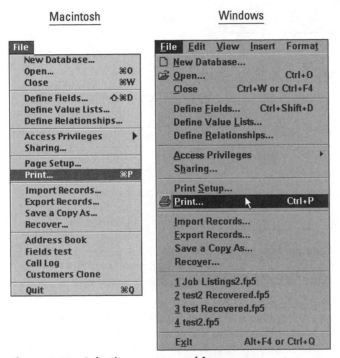

Figure 2-12: Selecting a command from a menu

Some menu commands may be gray. These grayed-out commands are not presently available, usually because they are not relevant to the operation you are attempting to perform. For example, when you're in Browse mode and a field is not currently selected, text-formatting commands in the Format menu are grayed-out (as is the entire Text Ruler toolbar, if enabled). This is because the formatting commands can only be executed when something is selected that you can format. Grayed-out commands become available only when they are relevant to the current state of the database and what you are doing at the moment.

To choose a menu command in Mac System 7.6 or earlier, do the following:

1. Click the menu title that contains the command you want to issue.

   The menu drops down, exposing the commands within it.

2. While continuing to hold down the mouse button, drag the pointer until the command you want to issue is highlighted (turns black).

3. Release the mouse button.

   The command executes.

To choose a menu command under Windows or Mac OS 8, do the following:

1. Click the menu title that contains the command you want to issue.

   The menu drops down, exposing the commands within it.

2. Click the command you want to execute.

   The command executes.

Under Windows, you can also select a menu command using the up- and down-arrow keys.

You can issue any menu command that is followed by a letter, number, or symbol without using the mouse or the menus. Such a command is said to have a keyboard shortcut, a keyboard equivalent, or a Command-key equivalent (all three terms mean the same thing).

On a Mac, a propeller-shaped symbol and a letter follow some menu commands. This symbol represents the Command key (shown on most keyboards as ⌘).

On a PC, the Ctrl and Alt keys are the keys used for keyboard shortcuts.

To issue a keyboard shortcut, follow these steps:

1. Press and hold the modifier key (or keys) that precedes the letter, number, or symbol in the menu.

   The modifier keys that FileMaker Pro uses for Mac menu shortcuts include the Shift, Option, and ⌘ keys. In the Windows version, these modifier keys are the Ctrl and Shift keys. They are called *modifier keys* because they have an effect only when you press them in combination with a letter, number, or symbol key. They modify the meaning of that key. Figure 2-13 shows the symbols used to represent these keys on the Mac.

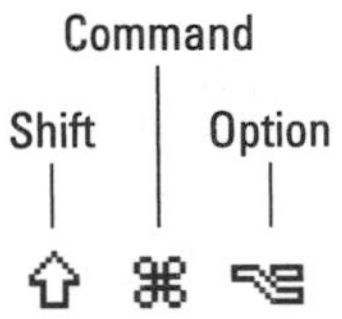

Figure 2-13: Modifier key symbols as displayed in Mac FileMaker Pro menus

2. While holding down the modifier key (or keys), press the letter, number, or symbol key that completes the keyboard shortcut.

   The command executes.

Note   A complete list of the keyboard shortcuts available in FileMaker Pro 5.0 can be found in Appendixes B and C.

You can also use keyboard shortcuts in some dialog boxes. For example, you can click the default button in dialog boxes by pressing Enter or Return, and you can choose the Cancel command by pressing Esc. If you are running Windows, any command or choice in a dialog box that contains an underlined letter can be executed or chosen by pressing Alt in combination with the underlined letter. For instance, in the Define Fields dialog box, all field types and buttons can be chosen or clicked in this manner.

Using Tools and Palettes

This section provides a brief introduction to the tools and palettes that are available in FileMaker Pro 5.0. Later chapters describe the tools and palettes in detail.

Figure 2-14 shows FileMaker Pro in Layout mode. This figure shows all tools except the few that are specific to Find mode.

The following list briefly describes the basic FileMaker tools and palettes:

✦ *Layout pop-up menu* (available in all modes): Click this icon to display a menu of the names of all layouts that have been created for the current database. Selecting a different layout from the menu switches to that layout.

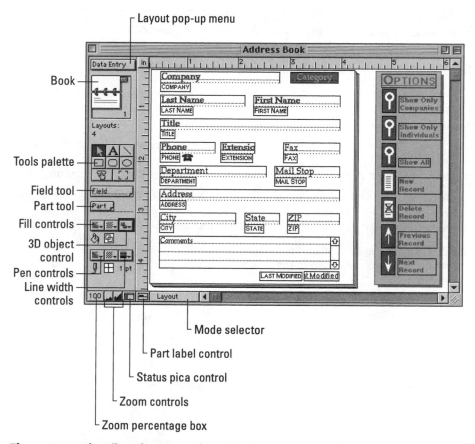

Figure 2-14: The FileMaker Pro tools and palettes

✦ *Book*: In Browse mode, you use the Book tool to switch to different records. In Layout mode, you use it to switch to different layouts. In Find mode, you use it to switch between multiple find requests. In Preview mode, you use it to switch between different pages of a report.

✦ *Tools palette* (Layout mode only): From the top left, these tools are used to select objects (the Pointer tool), add or edit text (the A tool), draw lines (the Line tool), draw rectangles and squares (the Rectangle tool), draw rounded rectangles and rounded squares (the Rounded Rectangle tool), draw ovals and circles (the Oval tool), create buttons, and create portals to display fields from a related database.

Commands with ellipses and triangles

If you browse through FileMaker Pro's menus, you'll notice that two unusual elements are tacked onto the end of some commands: ellipses and triangles.

An *ellipsis* is a series of three dots. It indicates that the command displays a dialog box to which you have to respond. In contrast, menu commands that do not have ellipses are executed immediately.

A triangle that follows a menu command indicates that the command is accompanied by a hierarchical menu (also called a submenu). When the mouse pointer slides over one of these menu commands, another menu pops out to the side of the original menu.

✦ *If you're using Mac System 7.6 or earlier*, you need to continue to hold down the mouse button while you move the pointer and highlight the appropriate command in the submenu. Then release the mouse button to choose the command.

✦ *For Windows or Mac OS 8*, click to open the menu and then slide the pointer until the appropriate command in the submenu is highlighted. Then click to choose the command.

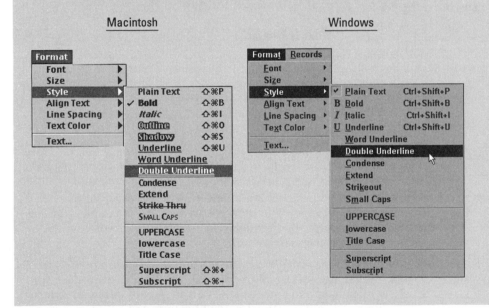

✦ *Field and part tools* (Layout mode only): These tools enable you to place additional fields and parts on a layout.

✦ *Fill and pen controls* (Layout mode only): You use the fill controls to set fill colors and patterns for objects. You use the pen controls to set line and border colors. Figure 2-15 shows the pop-up palettes that appear when you click the fill, pattern, or line width controls.

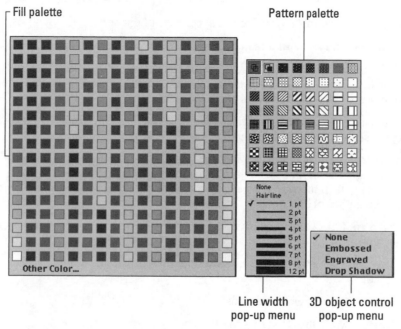

Figure 2-15: Select a color, pattern, or line width by clicking in these palettes.

✦ *3D object control* (Layout mode only): This control enables you to add 3D embossing, engraving, or a drop shadow to any selected object. (This is a new feature in FileMaker Pro 5.)

✦ *Line width control* (Layout mode only): This control enables you to set the thickness of any line (in points).

✦ *Zoom percentage box* (all modes): This box shows the current zoom level. (Zooming enlarges or shrinks your view of what's on-screen.) Click the box to switch between the current zoom level and 100 percent.

✦ *Zoom controls* (all modes): Click the left icon to reduce the view to a "bird's eye" perspective. Click the right icon to increase the document's zoom (magnification) level.

Overcoming keystroke conflicts

If using a keyboard shortcut produces an unusual effect (a dialog box appears that seems to have nothing to do with FileMaker Pro or a program launches, for example), you probably have a utility running in the background that is conflicting with FileMaker Pro. Many background programs are constantly scanning for the particular key combination that activates them. On my Mac, for example, attempting to execute the keyboard shortcut for Define Fields (Shift+⌘+D) results in the launching of DiskTop—a file-manipulation utility.

Several options are available for overcoming conflicts of this sort:

✦ Reconfigure the utility so it responds to a different key combination.

See the utility's manual for instructions. Assuming reconfiguration is possible, this is the best solution. To avoid additional conflicts, try to choose key combinations that are unlikely to conflict with your main programs.

✦ If you cannot reconfigure the utility, turn it off when you are using FileMaker Pro. (Again, see the manual for details.)

No matter how helpful utilities are, few of them are as critical as the work you do in a major application, such as a database, word processing program, or spreadsheet. If a utility gets in the way, temporarily shut it down. If you can't reconfigure it or shut it down, get rid of it.

✦ When a conflict occurs, restrict yourself to using FileMaker Pro's menus to select the command.

This solution is better than nothing, but not by much. It may remind you of this old joke:

Patient: "It hurts when I do this."

Doctor: "Well, then don't do that!"

✦ *Status area control* (all modes): Click this control to show or hide the entire status area, including all tools.

✦ *Part label control* (Layout mode only): Click this control to switch between displaying layout part labels horizontally and vertically.

✦ *Mode selector* (all modes): This displays the current mode. Click the mode selector to display a pop-up menu (see Figure 2-16) that enables you to switch between the four program modes: Browse, Layout, Find, and Preview.

Figure 2-16: The Mode pop-up menu

In addition to these tools, a few special tools are introduced in Find mode, as shown in Figure 2-17.

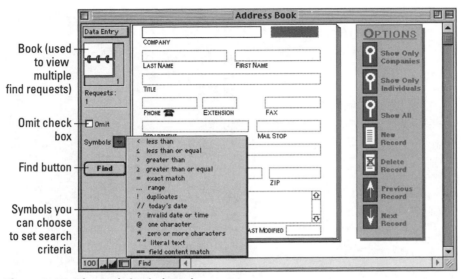

Figure 2-17: The tools in Find mode

You use these Find tools as follows:

✦ *Omit check box*: Check this box to exclude records from the found set that match the find criteria. For example, if the criterion is Sales > 100000, you can create a found set of records that includes everyone *except* salespeople with sales of more than $100,000.

✦ *Symbols pop-up menu*: Instead of typing conditional symbols and special characters when you are entering find criteria, you can select them from this pop-up menu.

✦ *Find button*: Click this button when you are ready to execute a find request (or multiple find requests).

Using Toolbars

In order to be certified as Office 98/2000-compliant, FileMaker Pro 5 now has toolbars similar to the ones in Microsoft Office (see Figure 2-18). The two toolbars are referred to as Standard and Text Formatting.

Standard toolbar

Text formatting toolbar

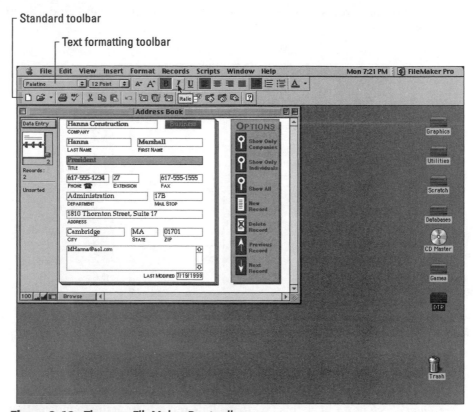

Figure 2-18: The new FileMaker Pro toolbars

You can click buttons in the Standard toolbar to issue common FileMaker Pro commands, such as opening a file, deleting the current record, or summoning help. The icons in the Standard toolbar change to reflect the mode you're in (Browse, Layout, Find, or Preview).

You can click the icons in the Text Formatting toolbar to format selected text or to set a paragraph alignment. You can change the font or size of currently selected text by choosing options from the drop-down menus.

If you're uncertain what an icon in a toolbar does, let your cursor rest over it for a moment. A tiny description automatically appears. To hide or show either toolbar, choose the toolbar's name from the View ➪ Toolbars submenu. When the name is shown with a check mark, it is visible.

Getting Help

Not all FileMaker topics are covered in the manual. To make it simple for you to find the help information that you need while running FileMaker Pro, the program provides an extensive Help system.

Help for Windows users

If you're using the Windows version of FileMaker Pro, you can obtain the following types of online help:

✦ *Toolbar help*: When FileMaker Pro 5 toolbars are displayed, rest the cursor over any toolbar button or menu for a few seconds. A pop-up label for the button will appear.

✦ *Context-sensitive help with FileMaker Pro windows*: Choose Help ➪ What's This? (or press Shift+F1). The cursor changes to a question mark (?). Click any element in a FileMaker Pro document window to view detailed help information related to the element you clicked on.

✦ *Context-sensitive help with dialog boxes*: You can summon context-sensitive help when working in a FileMaker dialog box by choosing Help ➪ FileMaker Pro Help, pressing the F1 key, or clicking the Help button (if one is available). You can summon help when working in the New Layout/Report wizard by pressing F1 or by clicking the Help button.

Many FileMaker Pro dialog boxes have a question mark (?) in the upper-right corner. Click it to change the cursor into a question mark, and then click any element in the dialog box for a brief explanation of the element (see Figure 2-19).

✦ *General help*: You can browse through the FileMaker help information by choosing Help ➪ FileMaker Pro Help, choosing Help ➪ Contents and Index, or pressing the F1 key. The Help Topics window appears, open to the Contents, Index, or Find tab. (By default, the window opens to the last tab you used.)

To browse Help by topic, click the Contents tab. Expand items until you find a topic of interest. Highlight the topic and click Display to view the help information for that topic.

Click the Index tab to view an alphabetical index of help topics. You can manually scroll to a topic of interest or type the first few letters of the topic. Highlight a topic and click Display to view the help information for that topic.

To search Help for a particular topic, click the Find tab. Enter your search string and criteria and then click Search. All topics that meet your search criteria are listed in the bottom part of the dialog box. Highlight a topic and click Display to view the help information for that topic.

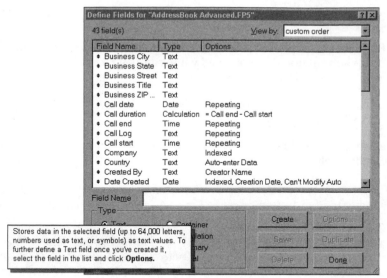

Figure 2-19: Click the question mark button for help with a dialog box.

Note   The first time you click the Find tab, the Help information is indexed for you.

✦ *Web help*: If you have an active Internet connection, you can visit the FileMaker Web site. Choose Help ➪ FileMaker on the Web. A standard Web page opens in your default browser (see Figure 2-20). Click the "Visit the FileMaker website" link to go to the support area of the FileMaker Web site.

The FileMaker Help system has additional capabilities that you may also want to use. You can bookmark particular topics, making them easier for you to find a second time. You can also add your own notes to topics. To learn more about these and other additional Help features, choose Help ➪ Contents and Index, click the Contents tab, and expand the following help topic: Reference ➪ Using FileMaker Pro Help (Windows).

Click here

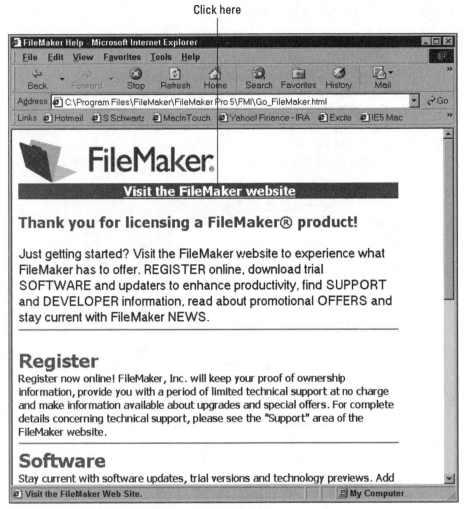

Figure 2-20: Click the text link to visit the FileMaker site.

Help for Macintosh users

If you're using the Macintosh version of FileMaker Pro, you can obtain the following types of online help:

✦ *Toolbar help*: When FileMaker Pro 5 toolbars are displayed, rest the cursor over any toolbar button or menu for a few seconds. A pop-up label for the button will appear.

✦ Balloon help: Choose Help Í Show Balloons. Whenever you move the cursor over a FileMaker Pro element for which help is available, a cartoon balloon appears that contains a brief description of the item (see Figure 2-21).

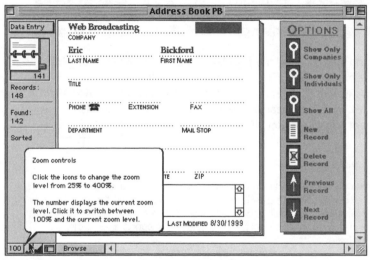

Figure 2-21: Enable Balloon help when you're not sure what a control or tool does.

Note that Balloon help is a part of the Macintosh system software. When enabled, Balloon help is simultaneously available for all applications that are running, as well as for the Finder and other system software components. To turn off Balloon help, choose Help ➪ Hide Balloons.

✦ *Help with dialog boxes*: You can summon context-sensitive help when working in a FileMaker dialog box by choosing Help ➪ FileMaker Pro Help, pressing ⌘+?, or pressing the Help key (if you have an Extended keyboard). You can summon help when working in the New Layout/Report wizard by performing the same actions or by clicking the Help icon.

✦ *General help*: You can browse through the FileMaker help information by choosing Help ➪ FileMaker Pro Help, choosing Help ➪ Contents and Index, pressing ⌘+?, or pressing the Help key (if you have an Extended keyboard). FileMaker Help Viewer launches and displays the Topics: FileMaker Pro Help window (see Figure 2-22) — open to the Contents, Index, or Find tab. (By default, Help Viewer opens to the last tab you used.)

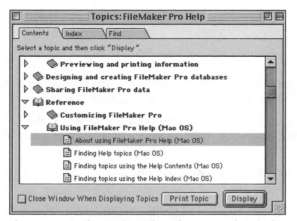

Figure 2-22: The Topics: FileMaker Pro Help window

To browse Help by topic, click the Contents tab. Expand items until you find a topic of interest. Highlight the topic and click Display to view the help information for that topic.

Click the Index tab to view an alphabetical index of help topics. You can manually scroll to a topic of interest or type the first few letters of the topic. Highlight a topic and click Display to view the help information for that topic.

To search Help for a particular topic, click the Find tab. Enter your search string and criteria and then click Search. All topics that meet your search criteria are listed in the bottom part of the dialog box. Highlight a topic and click Display to view the help information for that topic.

✦ *Web help*: If you have an active Internet connection, you can visit the FileMaker Web site. Choose Help ➪ FileMaker on the Web. A standard Web page opens in your default browser. Click the "Visit the FileMaker Website" link to go to the support area of the FileMaker Web site.

The FileMaker Help Viewer has additional capabilities that you may also want to use. You can bookmark particular topics, making them easier for you to find a second time. You can also add your own notes to topics. To learn more about these and other additional Help features, choose Help ➪ Contents and Index, click the Contents tab, and expand the following help topic: Reference ➪ Using FileMaker Pro Help (Mac OS).

Tip   The FileMaker Help Viewer is a separate program from FileMaker Pro. Help Viewer is responsible for displaying all general and context-sensitive FileMaker Pro help information. Although you will typically be running FileMaker when you access Help Viewer, you can also summon it by double-clicking the FileMaker Pro Help icon (found inside of the FileMaker Help folder). When you quit FileMaker Pro, FileMaker Help Viewer automatically quits, too. If you need to free up some additional memory, however, you can quit FileMaker Help Viewer by choosing File ➪ Quit (or by pressing ⌘+Q).

Summary

✦ Double-clicking a database icon on the desktop is the quickest way to launch FileMaker Pro and simultaneously open the database.

✦ Changes you make to a database are automatically saved for you. If you want to preserve a database, you can use the Save a Copy As command to make a backup copy.

✦ You can issue commands by choosing from menus and, in some cases, by pressing keyboard shortcuts.

✦ FileMaker Pro makes extensive use of tools and palettes, particularly for designing database layouts.

✦ FileMaker Pro 5 has two toolbars that enable you to execute common commands and format text.

✦ FileMaker Pro offers several different types of help information. You can summon help when working in most parts of the program by choosing a command from the Help menu, pressing a keyboard shortcut, or clicking a Help button.

✦   ✦   ✦

What's New in FileMaker Pro 5?

As it has in the past, FileMaker Pro 5 builds upon
the capabilities and features of previous versions
of the program. If you've used FileMaker Pro in any of its earlier
incarnations, this chapter will help smooth your transition to
FileMaker Pro 5 by pointing out the changes and additions you'll
have to learn about. The sections in this chapter briefly describe
the new features and how to use them in your own databases.

The FileMaker Pro 5 Product Family

In FileMaker Pro 5, FileMaker Inc. clearly delineates a line of
inter-related products, each designed to address a specific
database need:

> ✦ *FileMaker Pro 5*: Regardless of how the database will
> eventually be used (as a single-user database, shared
> on a network, or published on an intranet or the World
> Wide Web), it is designed and modified using FileMaker
> Pro 5. To work with any FileMaker Pro database (other
> than those published on the Web or those created as
> stand-alone or run-time solutions), each user must have
> his or her own copy of FileMaker Pro. Web published
> databases are viewed and modified using a browser,
> such as Internet Explorer or Netscape Communicator.
>
> Unlike previous versions, FileMaker Pro 5 is now usable
> only by small workgroups. If more than 10 users will
> need to simultaneously share a database on a network,
> they *must* host the database with FileMaker Pro Server.

✦ *FileMaker Pro Server 5*: FileMaker Server is used to host databases on a network where more than 10 users must simultaneously be able to access the database. Server supports up to 250 simultaneous guests. Each user must also have his or her own copy of FileMaker Pro.

✦ *FileMaker Pro5 Unlimited*: Unlimited is a similar product to FileMaker Server, but is for hosting high-traffic databases on the Web or an Intranet.

✦ *FileMaker Developer5*: Although developers can easily create databases for their company or for resale using a standard copy of FileMaker Pro 5, Developer 5 offers special developer tools, as well as the ability to create stand-alone databases that can be run by Mac or Windows users who do not have a copy of FileMaker Pro.

Global Changes

FileMaker Pro 5 introduces several global changes that are unrelated to a specific mode or program state.

Microsoft Office compliance and integration

This is the most sweeping change introduced in FileMaker Pro 5. Menus have been renamed and reorganized to make them Office 98/2000-compliant. And FileMaker Pro now has Office-style toolbars that make it simple to execute common commands by clicking icons and choosing from pop-up menus. The toolbars change to reflect the mode you're in. Moving data between FileMaker Pro and Microsoft Office components has also been simplified.

New file format

The file formats for databases created in FileMaker Pro 3.0, 4.0, and 4.1 were identical. Users of these versions could open a database created in any of the other versions. The Windows file extension (.fp3) remained the same for all three versions. As long as a database didn't rely on features that were available only in FileMaker Pro 4.0 or 4.1, there were no differences in the database's functionality when opened in FileMaker Pro 3.0.

FileMaker Pro 5, however, introduces a new file format and extension (.fp5). Earlier versions of FileMaker Pro cannot open FileMaker Pro 5 databases. When FileMaker Pro 5 is used to open a database created in any earlier version of FileMaker Pro, the database must be converted to FileMaker Pro 5 format.

Resizable dialog boxes

FileMaker Pro 5 has made it easier to view the contents of the Define Fields, Define Relationships, Define Value Lists, and Script Definition dialog boxes by enabling you to resize them. To resize one of these dialog boxes, you just drag its lower-right corner (see Figure 3-1).

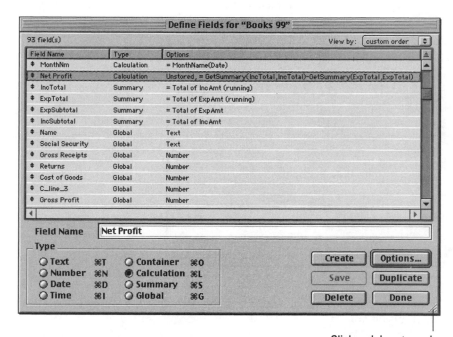

Click and drag to resize

Figure 3-1: You can resize the Define Fields dialog box to display long formulas.

FileMaker Pro 5 also enables you to simultaneously select multiple items in many of its dialog boxes. For instance, in the Define Fields dialog box, you can select several field names and delete them as a group.

Enhanced Open dialog box

If you are running Mac OS 8.5 or higher, the Open File dialog box has three new buttons (see Figure 3-2). From left to right, they enable you to quickly change drives or servers, add a database to your Favorites list (or open an existing favorite), or open a recently opened database. In addition, you can now open folders either by double clicking or expanding them.

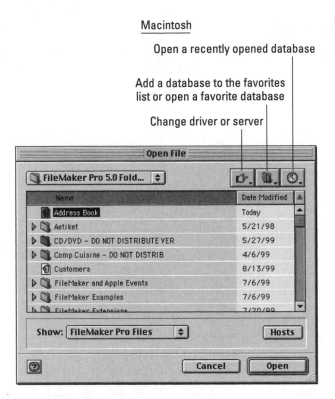

Macintosh

Open a recently opened database

Add a database to the favorites
list or open a favorite database

Change driver or server

Figure 3-2: The Open
File dialog box
(Macintosh)

Note   If you are using an earlier version of the Mac OS, you will see the standard
Open dialog box.

Hosting files as Multi-User (Hidden)

Shared databases can now be opened as Multi-User or Multi-User (Hidden). The
latter option keeps other users from being able to see the database. For instance,
you might want to open an essential related database as Hidden to prevent other
users from accessing it.

FileMaker Pro 5 can be controlled via ActiveX applications. Such applications can span
multiple programs and present a custom interface to the user.

Browsing Features

In browse mode, you can now view any database layout as a spreadsheet-like
table. FileMaker Pro 5 also includes enhanced QuickTime support and conditional
value lists.

Table View

In addition to being able to view any layout as a single-record form or as a record list, FileMaker Pro 5 introduces *table view*. Choose View ➪ View as Table to display all fields in the current layout in a spreadsheet-style grid.

To set the properties for a table view, switch to Layout mode, choose Layouts ➪ Layout Setup, click the Views tab in the Layout Setup dialog box, and click the Properties button (to the right of Table View). Options (see Figure 3-3) include the grid color and pattern; whether a header and/or footer are displayed; and whether you can resize, rearrange, and/or sort by column headers.

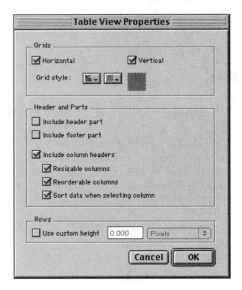

Figure 3-3: The Table View Properties dialog box

 Tip By default, the option to "Sort data when selecting column" is disabled. When it is enabled, you can click any column heading to sort the database by the contents of that column, and click the same column heading again to reverse the sort order. When all you want to do is sort records by a single field, this method is much faster than choosing the Records ➪ Sort command, so you probably want to turn this option on and keep it on.

Improved QuickTime support

In addition to QuickTime movies, you can now insert QuickTime VR (virtual reality) and QuickTime audio clips into Container fields. Movies in Container fields can also be played in databases that you publish on the Web or an Intranet. (These features require QuickTime 3.0 and QuickTime VR 3.0.)

Value Lists based on relationships

Value lists can now be created based on a relationship, allowing different values to be presented for each record, depending on the match field. For example, in a bookkeeping database, you could display a value list containing only income categories or only expense categories, depending on whether "Income" or "Expense" was selected for the record.

Layout Features

The new layout-related features include a software assistant that helps you design layouts, support for additional color palettes, and 3D effects for fields and other objects.

New Layout/Report assistant

As in earlier versions, the first layout created for a new database is a standard arrangement of all defined fields, one above the other. Additional layouts, on the other hand, are all designed in the New Layout/Report assistant (see Figure 3-4). To start this assistant, switch to Layout mode and choose Layouts ⇨ New Layout/Report. A series of dialog boxes walks you though the layout creation process. In addition to choosing a layout style, you can select a design *theme* (a color scheme for the layout parts and fields), choose break fields, specify sorting instructions, and create a default script that presents the layout in Preview mode.

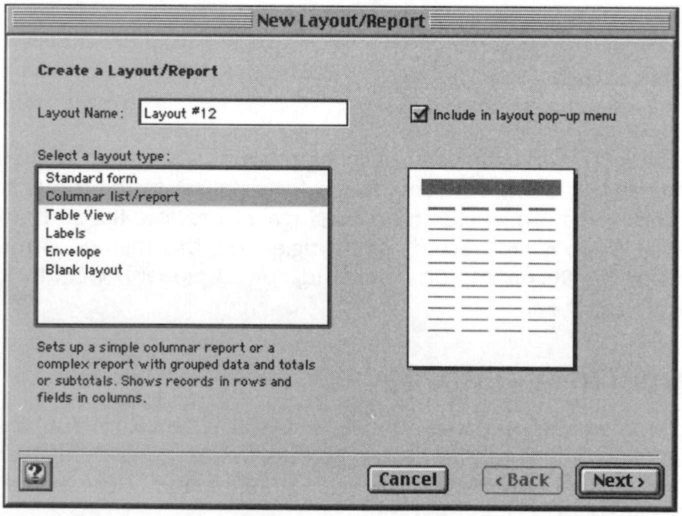

Figure 3-4: The New Layout/Report assistant

Note

Two of the former layout styles, columnar report and extended columnar, have been combined into a single style—columnar list/report). A new Table View style has been added for displaying fields in a spreadsheet-style grid.

Color palettes

Color choices in previous versions of FileMaker Pro were restricted to those available in an 88-color palette. By choosing Edit ➪ Preferences ➪ Application and then clicking the Layout tab (see Figure 3-5), you now can select from *three* color palettes:

✦ Standard system palette (256 colors)

✦ System subset (88 colors)

✦ Web palette (216 colors)

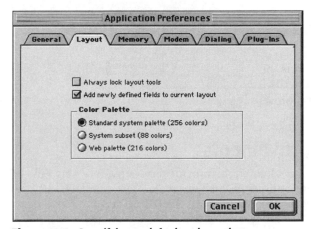

Figure 3-5: Specifying a default color palette

If you intend to publish a database on the Web or an intranet, the Web palette offers a set of browser-safe, platform-independent color choices.

3D effects

In Layout mode, a new item has been added to the Tools panel. To the right of the fill color and pattern palettes, you'll find the Effects pop-up menu. Choose Embossed, Engraved, or Drop Shadow to add 3D effects to fields and other layout objects.

ScriptMaker Features

The Define Scripts dialog box has two new buttons: Print and Import (see Figure 3-6).

New buttons

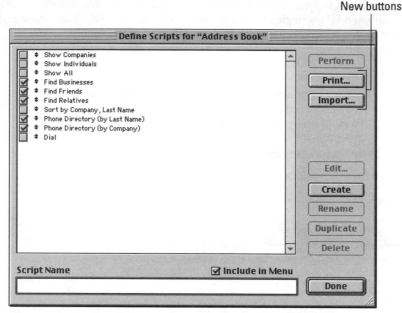

Figure 3-6: The new Define Scripts dialog box

Script printing improvements

FileMaker Pro users have always been able to print scripts by choosing File ➪ Print and selecting the appropriate options in the Print dialog box. In FileMaker Pro 5, you can print any script by selecting its name in the Define Scripts dialog box and clicking the Print button. There are no options to choose first, as there are if you print by choosing the File ➪ Print command.

Printed scripts are easier to read and understand. Script steps are printed in bold; data associated with a step is surrounded by brackets and follows the step; and field references are underlined.

Importing scripts from other databases

If you've created complex scripts in other databases that you'd like to reuse, there's no longer a reason to create them again from scratch—or by printing out the old scripts and then duplicating the steps. To add these scripts to the current database, choose Scripts ➪ ScriptMaker, click the Import button in the Define Scripts dialog box, choose a database, and then select the scripts to be imported. The imported scripts are named *script name* imported. Be sure to check the imported scripts to see that the steps refer to appropriate field names, layouts, and so on.

Importing and Exporting Features

FileMaker Pro 5 introduces several enhancements to data importing and exporting, as described in the following paragraphs.

Excel import

It's now simple to import Excel 98 (Macintosh) or Excel 2000 (Windows) spreadsheets into FileMaker Pro 5. You can either drag a worksheet onto the FileMaker Pro icon or open it directly in FileMaker Pro 5. The first row of the spreadsheet can be treated as column headings or data. If they are headings, they can be converted to FileMaker field names. Field types are automatically assigned, based on the spreadsheet contents.

When the converted file is opened in FileMaker Pro, two layouts are created for the spreadsheet data. Layout #1 is a standard layout in which each former spreadsheet row is a record. In Layout #2, the entire data set is displayed in table view.

Updating records on import

In previous versions of FileMaker Pro, imported records either replaced the existing records or they were appended to the database. In FileMaker Pro 5, you can elect to *update* the current records based on imported data. This feature makes it possible to keep two copies of a database in synch with each other. To update records, choose File ➪ Import Records, specify one or more "match fields" (to identify matching records), and click the "Update matching records in current found set" radio button. Non-matching records can either be ignored or added to the database.

New ODBC Capabilities

ODBC (Open Database Connectivity) support was introduced in FileMaker Pro 4.1, enabling you to query and import data from ODBC data sources into FileMaker Pro. In FileMaker Pro 5, the reverse is now also true — you can access FileMaker data from any ODBC-compliant program. In addition, you can create a front-end to a FileMaker Pro database using other applications, such as Microsoft Visual Basic.

FileMaker Pro 5 includes two new plug-ins in support of ODBC. The Local Data Access companion allows you to receive queries from an ODBC-compliant application on the same computer. The Remote Data Access Companion allows you to receive queries from an ODBC-compliant application over the Internet (via TCP/IP).

To enable the plug-ins, choose Edit ➪ Preferences ➪ Application and click the Plug-Ins tab at the top of the Application Preferences dialog box, as shown in Figure 3-7. Then choose File ➪ Sharing to enable Companion Sharing.

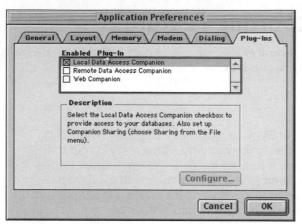

Figure 3-7: The Plug-Ins section of the Application Preferences dialog box

Web Publishing Features

Several enhancements have been made to Instant Web Publishing and the Web Companion plug-in. First, each published database can now have a layout *style* that improves its appearance and functionality. Second, support for *cascading style sheets* makes it possible for Web published databases to look more like they would if opened in FileMaker Pro.

New security features have also been added. You can specify a list of IP addresses (or prefixes) that can view a published database. In addition, you can also specify that several log files be kept, enabling you to track activity for the database.

✦   ✦   ✦

Database Design Basics

Creating Your First Database

When I first conceptualized this chapter, I imagined walking you through the steps of creating a simple FileMaker Pro database. But the more I thought about it, the more pointless that approach seemed. The purpose of this book is to give you a solid understanding of FileMaker Pro's features and capabilities, not just a quick glimpse of them. So the chapter took a dramatic turn.

Instead of helping you design a simple database, this chapter steps you through the creation of a full-featured database called Address Book, a database that has graphics, multiple layouts, buttons, scripts, and reports. Figure 4-1 shows the data entry layout for the completed database and points out some of its features.

Pop-up menu   Special field border   Pop-up menu   Button scripts

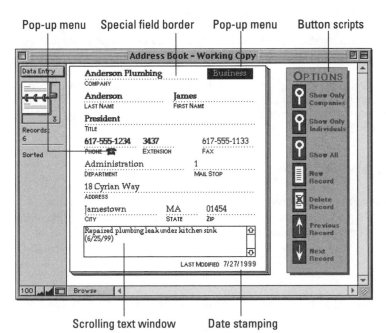

Scrolling text window   Date stamping

Figure 4-1: The data entry layout for Address Book

This extended exercise will help you become familiar with many of the important functions of FileMaker Pro while you create a database that you may actually want to use. After you finish making the database, you will have at least a passing familiarity with how FileMaker Pro works and its many capabilities. Later chapters provide in-depth instructions on using the program features that this chapter discusses.

The *FileMaker Pro 5 Bible CD* includes two templates for the database: Address Book and Address Book—Graphics. You'll find them in the FileMaker Pro Bible folder. Address Book is the finished database. Before launching into this tutorial, you may want to play with Address Book to see what you are going to accomplish. Address Book—Graphics contains the background graphics you use to make the database more attractive. If you haven't already done so, install the database templates onto your hard disk. (See Appendix A for instructions.)

Designing a database that does exactly what you want (collecting the proper data and presenting it in ways that meet your specific needs) is seldom a linear process. Unless you spend an inordinate amount of time planning a database before you begin the actual construction work in FileMaker Pro, you are likely to add more fields, delete some fields that—in retrospect—you didn't really need, design additional reports, and tweak the layout (trying out different fonts and alignments, for example). In the design process, you'll repeatedly bounce between Layout, Browse, and Preview modes, as well as in and out of ScriptMaker.

Like most tutorials, this tutorial is in a step-by-step, linear format. But don't be fooled. This relatively simple database took me a full day to construct, and the process was far from linear. So don't be surprised if the process you go through in designing your own databases doesn't match the Step 1 ➪ Step 2 ➪ Step 3 approach that you find in this chapter. (Of course, planning does help. The more time you spend deciding which fields, reports, and scripts you need, how to format fields, and what you want the layouts to look like, the faster the creation process will go.)

Even if you've gone through this tutorial in a previous edition of this book, I strongly recommend that you at least skim through this material. You'll find many useful tips for creating better databases, as well as many changes specific to FileMaker Pro 5.

Step 1: Create a New Database

If FileMaker Pro isn't already running, double-click the FileMaker Pro icon to launch the program. To begin the process of creating the database, choose "Create a new empty file" from the New Database dialog box, and click OK.

—or—

If FileMaker Pro is already running, choose the File ➪ New Database command. The New Database dialog box appears. Choose "Create a new empty file," and then click OK.

In either case, one of the file dialog boxes shown in Figure 4-2 appears, depending on whether you are using a Mac or Windows.

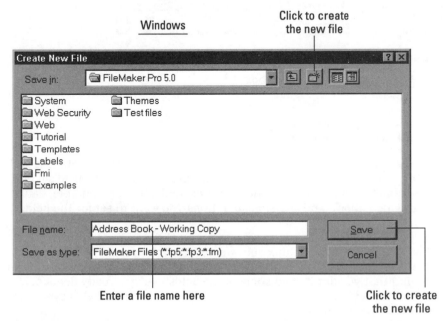

Figure 4-2: Creating a new database on a Mac with OS 8.5.x (top) and in Windows (bottom)

Select the disk drive and folder in which you want to store the new database, enter a name for it (Address Book — Working Copy, for example), and click Save. The Define Fields dialog box appears, as shown in Figure 4-3.

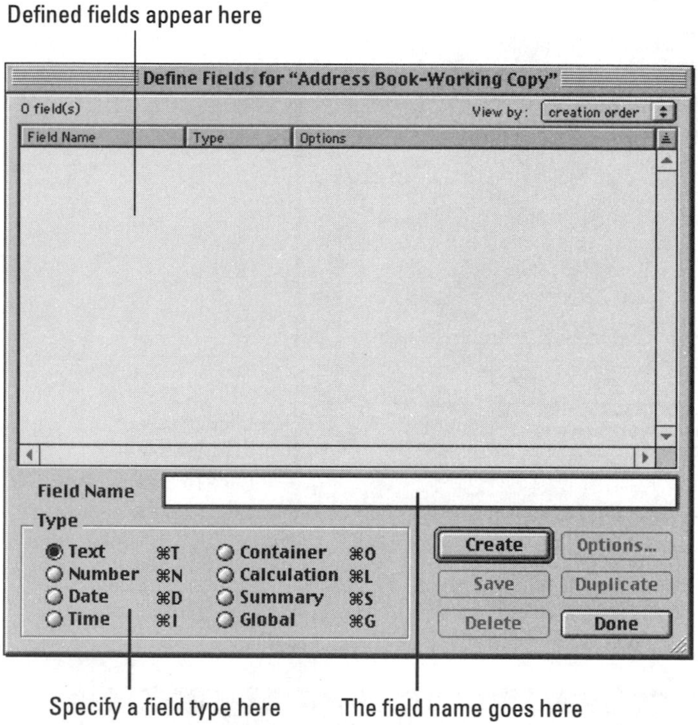

Defined fields appear here

```
┌──────────────────────────────────────────────────────────┐
│ ▦▦▦  Define Fields for "Address Book-Working Copy" ▦▦▦    │
│ 0 field(s)                          View by : [creation order ⇕]│
│ ┌──────────┬────────┬──────────────────────────────┐▲    │
│ │Field Name│  Type  │ Options                      │      │
│ │          │        │                              │      │
│ │          │        │                              │      │
│ │          │        │                              │      │
│ │          │        │                              │      │
│ │          │        │                              │      │
│ │          │        │                              │      │
│ │          │        │                              │▼     │
│ └◄─────────┴────────┴──────────────────────────►──┘      │
│                                                           │
│  Field Name  [                                    ]       │
│ ┌Type────────────────────────┐ ┌─────────┐ ┌─────────┐  │
│ │ ● Text      ⌘T  ○ Container ⌘O│ │ Create │ │Options..│  │
│ │ ○ Number    ⌘N  ○ Calculation⌘L│└─────────┘ └─────────┘  │
│ │ ○ Date      ⌘D  ○ Summary   ⌘S│ │  Save  │ │Duplicate│  │
│ │ ○ Time      ⌘I  ○ Global    ⌘G│ │ Delete │ │  Done  │  │
│ └──────────────────────────────┘ └────────┘ └─────────┘  │
└──────────────────────────────────────────────────────────┘
```

Specify a field type here   The field name goes here

Figure 4-3: The Define Fields dialog box

Step 2: Define Fields

As with any new database, the first task is to define the fields the database will use to store and present the data. A *field definition* consists of the field's name, the type of information the field will contain (for example, text or a number, date, time, picture, or calculation), and any special options you want to set for the field.

Defining fields for a database often requires several steps. You normally begin by defining all the fields you think you will need. In the process of designing the database, however, you'll often discover that you should have created additional fields or find that you don't need some of the fields you've already defined. Making a change in the fields is not a problem. You can add or remove fields even after you create records and enter data.

To keep things simple, there are only two field types used in the Address Book database: Text and Date. Table 4-1 lists the database fields that you need to define.

Table 4-1
Field Definitions for Address Book

Field Name	Type	Options	Field Contents
First Name	Text		First name of contact
Last Name	Text		Last name of contact
Title	Text		Person's title
Company	Text		Company affiliation
Department	Text		Department
Mail Stop	Text		Mail stop
Address	Text		Street address
City	Text		City
State	Text		State
Zip	Text		Zip code
Phone	Text		Area code and phone number
Extension	Text		Phone extension
Fax	Text		Area code and fax number
Category	Text	By ValueList, Strict, Required Value, Message	Classification for the record
Comments	Text		Notes
Last Modified	Date	Modification Date	Date the record was last altered

Text or number fields?

Although the Phone, Extension, Fax, and ZIP fields contain numbers, these fields are defined as Text fields rather than Number fields in Address Book. In FileMaker Pro, you should define a field as a Number field for the following reasons:

✦ You intend to use the contents of the field in a calculation.

✦ You want to restrict the contents of the field to numbers only.

Because you are not going to base a calculation on any of these four fields and because they can legitimately contain letters or special characters — such as (619) 443-5555, 1-800-SUCCESS, and N9B 3P7 (a Canadian Postal Code) — it makes better sense to treat them as text than to define them as numbers. In addition, some U.S. ZIP codes start with a 0, which would not show up in a numeric field. Furthermore, there are nine-digit ZIP codes with an embedded dash.

You need to set options for only two fields: Category and Last Modified. Although you can set field options when you are defining the field, for this example you define all the fields first and then set all necessary field options.

To define the first field, type **First Name** in the Field Name text box of the Define Fields dialog box. Because Text is already chosen as the field type and you are not assigning any options to the field, click the Create button. The field is added to the scrolling list at the top of the dialog box (see Figure 4-4).

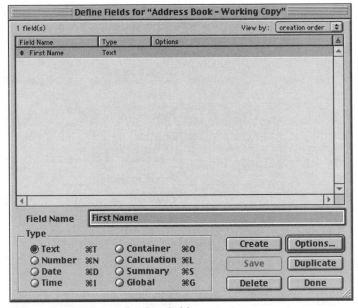

Figure 4-4: Defining the first field

To create the Last Name field, type **Last Name** in the Field Name text box and click Create again. Continue this process, defining every Text field in Table 4-1 (the First Name field through the Comments field).

Tip   You can make the field definition process go faster by pressing Return or Enter immediately after you type each field name. Whenever the Create button — or any other button in a dialog box — is surrounded by a thick line/drop shadow, you can choose it by pressing Return or Enter. Of course, you can still click the button with the mouse, if you prefer.

Finally, create the Last Modified field. Type **Last Modified**, choose Date as the field type, and click Create. The Last Modified field will automatically store the date that each record was last modified, giving you an idea of how current the information is.

The Define Fields dialog box can be resized by clicking and dragging its bottom-right corner. This comes in handy for examining fields that have multiple options, as well as for lengthy Calculation fields. Other resizable dialog boxes include Define Relationships, Define Value Lists, and Script Definition.

Step 3: Set Field Options

You can use various field options to help you automatically enter information (such as the current date or a serial number), verify that only appropriate data has been entered, or create repeating fields. To give you a sample of these capabilities, this section shows you how to define options for two fields: Last Modified and Category.

Select the Last Modified field in the Define Fields dialog box and click the Options button. The Options for Field "Last Modified" dialog box appears, as shown in Figure 4-5.

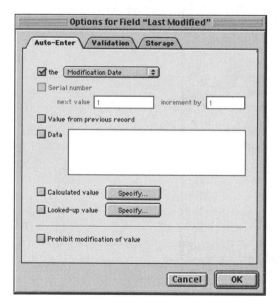

Figure 4-5: Setting an option for the Last Modified field

Regardless of the field for which you are setting options, the dialog box always looks the same. However, the name of the dialog box changes to reflect the name of the field for which you are setting options.

Click the Auto-Enter tab at the top of the dialog box (if it is not already displayed), and then choose Modification Date from the pop-up menu (refer to Figure 4-5). FileMaker Pro will automatically check the check box. Click OK to return to the Define Fields dialog box. You'll see that the Last Modified field now lists "Modification Date" in the Options column. (When you set options for any field, they are noted in the Options column.)

When the database is finished, you will use the Category field to assign a general classification to every record: Business, Friend, or Relative. (Even if you would prefer other classifications, please use these for the example. You can change them to something more appropriate later.)

You should make Category a required field — one that cannot be empty. This ensures that when you are entering data, FileMaker Pro displays a warning if you attempt to leave a record without first making a Category choice. To set this and other validation options for the Category field, follow these steps:

1. In the Define Fields dialog box, select the Category field and then click Options.

   The Options for Field "Category" dialog box appears.

2. Click the Validation tab at the top of the dialog box (see Figure 4-6). Click the check box labeled "Not empty."

Figure 4-6: The Validation section of the Options for Field dialog box

3. To make sure this requirement is enforced, click the check box labeled "Strict: Do not allow user to override data validation."

4. Click the check box labeled "Display custom message if validation fails," and type the following message in the text box: **You must choose a category for every record.**

   If you (or another user doing the data entry) fail to select a category for a new record, the custom message will be presented automatically.

5. Click the check box labeled "Member of value list," and choose Define Value Lists from the pop-up menu to the right.

The Define Value Lists dialog box appears, as shown in Figure 4-7. Value lists are created, edited, and deleted in this dialog box.

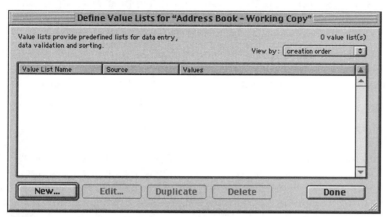

Figure 4-7: The Define Value Lists dialog box

6. Click the New button.

The Edit Value List dialog box appears (see Figure 4-8).

Defined fields appear here

Values are typed directly into this list box

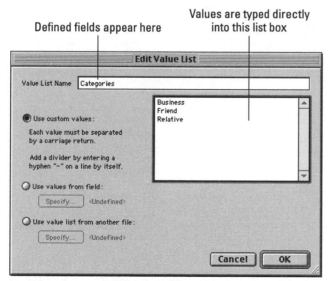

Figure 4-8: You define all value lists in the Edit Value List dialog box.

7. Type a name (such as **Categories**) for the new value list in the Value List Name text box.

   Any values you enter in this dialog box will appear as a pop-up menu or list when you click or tab into the Category field. The order in which you type the values is the order in which they will appear.

8. With the "Use custom values" radio button selected, type the three lines of text previously shown in the Edit Value Lists dialog box in Figure 4-8, pressing Return/Enter after typing the first and second values.

9. After you enter the values, click OK to accept them and click Done.

10. Click OK to return to the Define Fields dialog box.

After you've defined all the fields and set their options, click Done. A standard layout is automatically created for you, as shown in Figure 4-9. As you can see, a standard layout is a vertical arrangement of all the database fields. Each field includes a label that matches whatever you named the field in the Define Fields dialog box.

Note   Note that the Last Modified field is automatically filled in with today's date. This happens whenever you create a new record or modify an existing one.

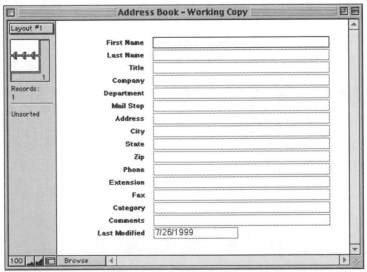

Figure 4-9: The initial database arranged in a standard layout

If you are interested in only a quick-and-dirty database, you can stop right here. Address Book—Working Copy is ready to receive data. However, in keeping with the goal of this chapter—to teach you how to create a full-featured database—the next step involves rearranging the fields, adding field formatting, and including some graphics to make this layout more visually appealing.

When you'd like to learn more about defining fields and setting field options, see Chapter 5.

Step 4: Design the Data Entry Layout

If you want to take a standard layout beyond the functional stage — all the way to attractive and pleasant to use — you may find that you spend more time on this task than on any other database development task. Frankly, however, not every database is worth the extra effort required to "pretty it up." Many databases, such as those intended only for your personal use, need never evolve beyond the functional stage. A database that you use daily or one that you intend to distribute to others, on the other hand, should look good and contain scripts that make it easy to perform common tasks. In this step, you do some of the work that's required to create an attractive layout.

Altering the layout parts

Normally, the standard layout that FileMaker Pro automatically creates is a good starting point for a custom layout such as the one you are going to create for Address Book. Because I know the height of the graphics that you are going to place in the background, however, I'll save you a little grief by having you change the size of the layout before you add the graphics and arrange the fields. Specifically, you'll remove the header and footer layout parts (because they serve no purpose in the Data Entry layout) and enlarge the body layout part (to make room for the graphics and fields).

Note

When FileMaker Pro creates a standard layout, it automatically generates three basic sections (called *parts*) for the layout: header, body, and footer. As your needs dictate, you can remove unnecessary parts and create additional parts, such as a title header (for the first page in a report layout) and subsummary parts (for numerically summarizing data across records in the database).

To delete the unnecessary layout parts, you'll need to switch to Layout mode. Choose View ➪ Layout Mode, press ⌘+L/Ctrl+L, or choose Layout from the mode pop-up menu at the bottom of the database windows. Then choose Layouts ➪ Part Setup. The Part Setup dialog box appears (see Figure 4-10). To remove the header part, select Header and click the Delete button. Then delete the footer part in the same manner. Finally, click Done to close the dialog box and return to the layout. Notice that it now contains only one part — the body.

The body needs to be about 5.5 inches high. If you don't see a ruler down the left side of the layout, choose the View ➪ Graphic Rulers command. To increase the height of the body, drag the body part indicator (labeled with the word "Body") down until you reach the 5.5-inch mark.

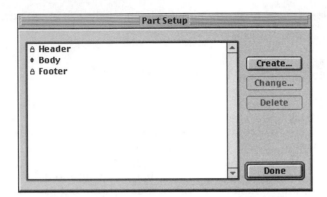

Figure 4-10: The Part Setup dialog box

Adding graphics

Next, add the background graphics. The graphics are stored in the file named Address Book—Graphics on the CD. Having the graphics in place enables you to arrange the fields so they fit correctly. (After you begin to create your own databases, you can design your own graphics in any graphics program, buy ready-made graphics called *clip art*, or—if you don't intend to resell or distribute the databases—copy graphics from files you obtain from user groups and online information services.)

Follow these steps to transfer graphics from Address Book—Graphics to Address Book—Working Copy (or whatever you named the database you are creating):

1. If your copy of the Address Book—Working Copy database isn't already open, choose File ➪ Open, choose the Address Book—Working Copy database, and click Open.

2. Switch to Layout mode by choosing View ➪ Layout Mode.

   All design work is done in Layout mode.

3. Open the database that contains the graphics by choosing File ➪ Open and then selecting the Address Book—Graphics file.

4. Switch to Layout mode by choosing View ➪ Layout Mode.

   Because the database opens in Browse mode, you can see the graphics when you open the file, but you can't select them. You have to be in Layout mode to copy or otherwise manipulate elements in a layout.

5. In Address Book—Graphics, click to select the graphics.

   Because the graphics have been grouped (so you can work with them as a single unit instead of as the mass of little images they really are), clicking anywhere within the graphics selects everything. (When an object is selected, a black dot called a *handle* appears at each of the object's four corners, as shown in Figure 4-11.) Later, you will use the Ungroup command so you can deal with the graphic elements individually.

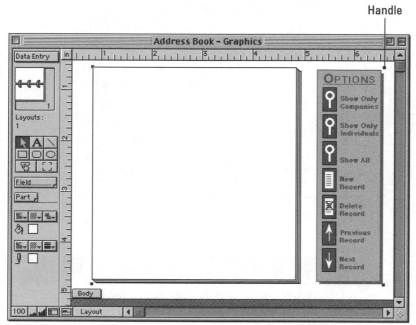

Figure 4-11: The Address Book—Graphics database with the graphics selected

6. If drag-and-drop is enabled on your computer, drag the graphics into the current layout in Address Book—Working Copy.

   A copy of the graphics is transferred. Now close Address Book—Graphics by choosing File ⇨ Close from the File menu, and go to step 9 in this procedure.

   — or —

   Choose Edit ⇨ Copy (or press ⌘+C/Ctrl+C).

   A copy of the graphics is stored in memory.

7. Choose File ⇨ Close (to close Address Book—Graphics).

8. Choose Edit ⇨ Paste (or press ⌘+V/Ctrl+V).

   The graphics are pasted onto the layout in Address Book—Working Copy.

9. Because you want the graphics to appear behind the data fields instead of obscuring them, choose Arrange ⇨ Send to Back.

10. Drag the graphics so they approximately match the placement shown in Figure 4-12.

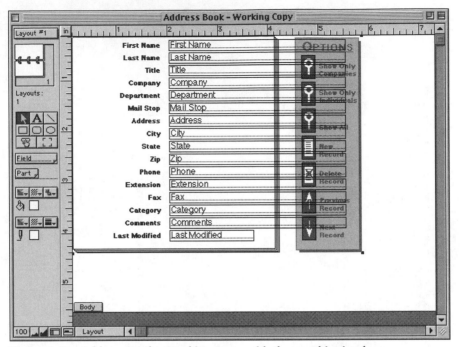

Figure 4-12: Address Book — Working Copy, with the graphics in place

Setting field attributes

Instead of immediately moving the fields and labels to their final resting place on the layout, you will use the initial stacked format to select the fields and assign text attributes (font, size, style, alignment, and color) and field borders to them, as described in the following sections.

Text attributes

All the field labels are displayed in the finished database with the same font and format, so start by selecting them. To select multiple objects, first select the Pointer tool by clicking its icon in the Tools palette. Then do either of the following:

✦ Drag a selection rectangle that completely surrounds the objects of interest.

✦ Hold down the Shift key and click every object that you want to include in the selection.

You can also combine the two approaches. In this case, however, because the field labels are all stacked in a nice, neat column, the first approach is simplest. The selected labels should look like the ones in Figure 4-13.

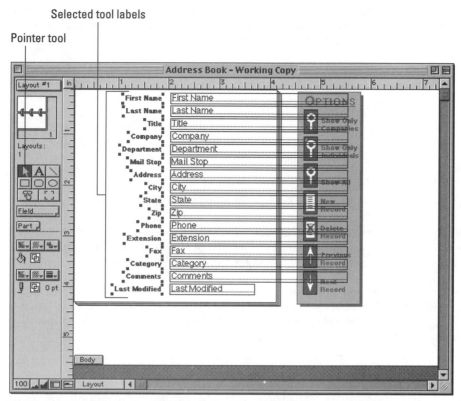

Figure 4-13: Selecting the field labels

Tip   Another way to select multiple items on a layout is to hold down the ⌘/Ctrl key as you drag the selection rectangle. Rather than having to surround the objects you're selecting, it's sufficient to merely touch them with the selection rectangle.

Preselecting text-formatting settings

Whenever you enter Layout mode and set a new font, style, color, and so on without first selecting a field or object to which the formatting will be applied, those formatting options become the new defaults. The next field, label, or object you create will automatically use those preselected settings. Thus, you can use this trick to preselect the text formatting for fields and save yourself the trouble of having to reformat each field manually after FileMaker Pro generates the layout. (Pressing ⌘/Ctrl and clicking a field or object also changes the default setting to that of the clicked field or object.)

The format for each of the field labels is left-aligned, 9-point Helvetica, with small caps. With the field labels still selected, choose the following commands from the appropriate submenus of the Format menu:

✦ Choose Format ➪ Font ➪ Helvetica (or Helvetica Regular). If Helvetica does not appear as a choice in the Font submenu, choose a similar font, such as Arial.

✦ Choose Format ➪ Size ➪ 9 Point.

✦ Choose Format ➪ Style ➪ Bold or Format ➪ Align Text ➪ Plain Text. (Either command will remove the boldface that was assigned by default to the field labels.)

✦ Choose Format ➪ Style ➪ Small Caps.

✦ Choose Format ➪ Align Text ➪ Left and Format ➪ Align Text ➪ Top.

Next, format the fields. In the layout, each field appears as a rectangle surrounding a field name. As you apply different formatting attributes to a field, the formatting of the field name automatically changes to reflect the new attributes.

Select individual fields or groups of fields, as described in Table 4-2, and apply the designated formats. Each column in the table corresponds to a text attribute command in the Format menu. Working with a single row of the table at a time is easiest.

Table 4-2 **Field Text Attributes**					
Field Name(s)	*Font*	*Size*	*Style*	*Align Text*	*Text Color*
First Name, Last Name, Title, Company, Phone, Extension	Palatino, Palatino Roman, Times, Times Roman, or Times New Roman	12	Bold	Left, Top	Dark blue
Department, Mail Stop, Address, City, State, Zip, Fax	Palatino, Palatino Roman, Times, Times Roman, or Times New Roman	12	Plain	Left, Top	Black
Category	Palatino, Palatino Roman, Times, Times Roman, or Times New Roman	12	Plain	Center, Top	Faint blue

Field Name(s)	Font	Size	Style	Align Text	Text Color
Comments Roman, Times, Times Roman, or Times New Roman	Palatino, Palatino	10	Plain	Left, Top	Black
Last Modified	Helvetica or Arial	10	Plain	Right, Top	Black

Simultaneously choosing several Text Format options

Try the following shortcut when making multiple Format menu selections: After you select each field or group of fields, choose Format ⇨ Text. In the Text Format dialog box that appears, you can simultaneously set all the text formats for the selected fields.

You can also set most text formatting options by choosing from the drop-down menus and clicking the icons in the new Text Formatting toolbar shown the following figure. If this toolbar isn't visible, choose View ⇨ Toolbars ⇨ Text Formatting.

Text Formatting toolbar

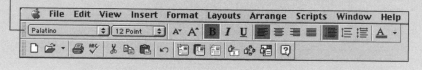

Field borders

If you take another peek at the finished version of Address Book previously shown in Figure 4-1, you'll note that many fields have a dotted line as a bottom border. Although FileMaker Pro does not have a specific feature for creating dotted lines, you can use the trick described in the following steps:

1. Select all fields except Category, Comments, and Last Modified. (Be sure to select only the fields — *not* the field labels.)

2. Choose Format ⇨ Field Borders.

   The "Field Borders for selected objects" dialog box appears, as shown in Figure 4-14.

3. Click the Bottom check box.

4. At the bottom of the dialog box, click the pattern pop-up menu (the second icon from the left) and choose the pattern indicated in Figure 4-14.

Note that as you are choosing the new pattern, the previous pattern (the solid fill on the left side of the pattern pop-up menu) is still selected. When you release the mouse button, a sample showing the dotted-line pattern appears in the Sample box—replacing the former pattern.

5. Click OK.

The new border settings are accepted, and the dialog box closes.

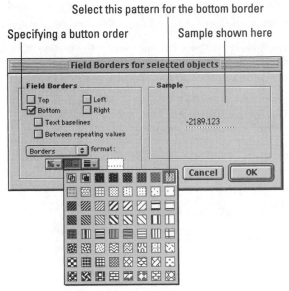

Figure 4-14: Selecting a pattern for a bottom border

To ensure that the Comments field is always visible, we'll surround it with a border. To create the border, switch to Layout mode and select the Comments field; choose Format ➪ Field Borders; place a check mark in the Top, Bottom, Left, and Right check boxes of the Field Borders dialog box; and click OK.

Field formats

The Format menu has a few commands that you haven't used in the Address Book database. The final option you are going to use is the Field Format command. You use it in this database to make the Comments field into a scrolling text window. This feature is particularly useful when you want to store a lot of text in a relatively small area on a layout.

Follow these steps to create a scrolling text window for the Comments field:

1. Select the field on the layout (in this case, the Comments field).

2. Choose Format ⇨ Field Format.

   The Field Format for "Comments" dialog box appears, as shown in Figure 4-15.

Add a scroll bar

Figure 4-15: The Field Format for "Comments" dialog box

3. Be sure the "Standard field" radio button at the top of the dialog box is selected and then click the check box labeled "Include vertical scroll bar."

4. Click OK.

   The dialog box closes, and a vertical scroll bar is added to the right side of the Comments field.

Setting field dimensions and placement

The last two major field-arrangement tasks are resizing the fields and placing them in their proper places on the layout. You can alter the size of fields, field labels, and graphic objects on a layout in two ways:

✦ *Manually*: By selecting an object and dragging one of its handles in the appropriate direction.

✦ *Precisely*: By entering one or more dimensions in the Size windoid.

Note A *windoid* is a tiny, special-purpose window provided by some programs to display options that you need to use frequently, such as color, pattern, and other palettes. Windoids float freely on-screen and can be moved (by dragging the title bar) or closed (by clicking the close box) whenever you wish. Windoids have a look that immediately distinguishes them from normal windows.

To see the tiny Size windoid (see Figure 4-16), choose the View ➪ Object Size command.

Distance from top edge

Distance from left edge

Distance from right edge

Distance from bottom edge

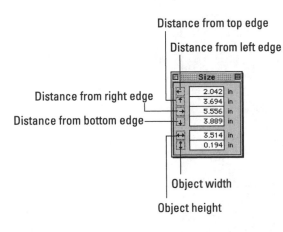

Object width

Object height

Figure 4-16: The Size windoid enables you to see and change the dimensions and location of any selected object.

Because your task in this tutorial is to duplicate the layout shown in Figure 4-1 — rather than make a rough approximation of it — you can use the Size windoid to avoid all the manual dragging and resizing. However, because most of the databases you'll design from scratch won't have a template that you're attempting to match, you also need to explore the manual method.

Manually sizing and placing objects on the layout

So that you'll have some fields with which to work, start by selecting the following fields and their field labels: First Name, Last Name, and Title. Choose the Edit ➪ Duplicate command. (Duplicate is a shortcut for the normal Copy and Paste procedure.) Duplicates of these fields and labels appear on the layout and are automatically selected. With the duplicate objects still selected, drag them to the right until they cross the vertical dashed line that marks the page break. Moving the objects to this area gives you plenty of room to experiment without fear of disturbing the "real" fields, labels, and graphics. (You may have to resize the database window in order to accomplish the move.)

Note When you finish trying out the manual sizing and placement procedures, be sure to select the duplicate fields and labels, and then remove them by pressing the Delete key.

Before modifying any of the duplicate objects, you may want to turn on some of the helpful tools in the View and Arrange menus. For example, the Arrange ➪ Object Grids command simplifies creating equal-sized fields and arranging them in a uniform manner by restricting field movements and adjustments to those that coincide with grid coordinates. The T-Squares tool (in the View menu) can help you make sure that fields are properly aligned with one another — in straight rows and columns. You may also want to choose View ➪ Show ➪ Text Boundaries. This command places a bounding box around every field label and text object on the layout, enabling you to visually determine whether these objects are correctly positioned and in alignment with other objects. Finally, the graphic rulers (choose View ➪ Graphic Rulers) are an enormous help when placing and aligning objects. As you drag any object, its exact position is shown on the horizontal and vertical rulers.

Now you can experiment with manually changing field sizes. Whether you're working with a field, a label, or another layout object, you always begin by selecting the object. (A selected object has a black dot called a *handle* at each of its corners.) To change a field's size or shape, drag any handle to a new location. Dragging options include the following:

✦ *Dragging*: The normal dragging procedure enables you to change the height, width, or both dimensions as you drag. (If the Object Grids feature is on and you're reasonably careful, it is fairly easy to make sure that only one dimension changes.)

✦ *Shift-dragging*: If you press the Shift key as you drag, you restrict size changes to one dimension — horizontal or vertical. When you want to keep all text fields the same height, for example, this technique is ideal for ensuring that only the field's width changes.

✦ *Option-dragging/Ctrl-dragging*: Depending on the shape of the object you're resizing, pressing the Option/Ctrl key as you drag forces the object's final shape to a square, a square with rounded corners, or a circle.

Manually placing an object is also a simple task. Click anywhere within the center of the object and drag it to a new spot on the layout. As you drag, FileMaker Pro displays an outline of the object so you can easily see the object's precise location before you release the mouse button.

 Tip   You can "nudge" any selected field, label, or other object slightly by pressing any arrow key. This technique works even when the Object Grids command is in effect.

After resizing and rearranging the fields and labels, you may also want to try out FileMaker Pro's alignment commands. To keep things nice and uniform, you can use Align and Set Alignment to align the edges of any group of fields or to align fields and their labels, for example. These commands are especially helpful when you have nudged several objects with the arrow keys or have been aligning objects by using the "eyeball method" — as in, "Hmm . . . looks like the First Name and Last Name fields are lined up now."

The following steps describe how to align selected objects:

1. Select the objects you want to align with each other by selecting the Pointer tool and then drawing a selection rectangle around the objects, Shift-clicking the objects, or using a combination of the two selection methods.

2. Choose Arrange ➪ Set Alignment.

   The Set Alignment dialog box appears, as shown in Figure 4-17.

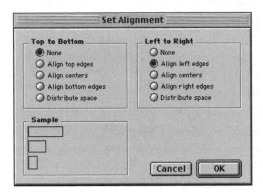

Figure 4-17: The Set Alignment dialog box

3. Select an option from the Top to Bottom area of the dialog box and an option from the Left to Right area of the dialog box. For example, to align the left-most fields and labels along their left edges, you would set Top to Bottom as "None" and Left to Right as "Align left edges."

   As you choose options, the Sample area of the dialog box shows what effect your choices will have on the selected objects.

4. Click OK.

   The dialog box closes, and FileMaker Pro executes the alignment options. If the result is not what you intended, you can restore the objects to their previous locations by immediately choosing Undo Align from the Edit menu (or by pressing ⌘+Z/Ctrl+Z).

Note

The options you choose in the Set Alignment dialog box remain in effect until you choose new options or until you quit the program. These options are also the ones that will be used whenever you choose the Arrange ➪ Align command (or press ⌘+K/Ctrl+K). Unlike the Set Alignment command, Align is immediately executed on the selected objects. No dialog box appears.

If you want to become more familiar with the process of manually sizing and placing fields, refer to Figure 4-1 (shown previously) and attempt to match the field widths and placements as best you can. When you're done, you can use the information in Tables 4-3 and 4-4 in the next section to see how well you have done and to correct any mistakes you have made.

Using the Size windoid to size and place objects

You can use the Size windoid (shown previously in Figure 4-16) to perform the following functions:

✦ Determine the exact location and dimensions of any object on a layout

✦ Move an object to a precise location

✦ Change the dimensions of an object

Instead of using the Align command to arrange several fields in a perfect column, for example, you can select each field and then enter the same distance from the left edge of the page in the first text box in the Size windoid. Also, by clicking several objects one by one, you can check to make sure they are all exactly the same distance from a particular edge or that they are all the same height or width.

In this tutorial, however, your use of the Size windoid will be a bit unorthodox. You'll combine the second and third uses of the Size windoid from the preceding list to size and precisely place every field and label on the layout — and do *both* at the same time. Using the Size windoid in this manner is very much like having a robot slave who happily and mindlessly pushes the fields around the page for you.

Although this exercise doesn't have a practical application — after you start designing your own databases, that is — it does serve two important purposes. First, it enables you to match the placement of fields and labels with those in the finished Address Book database. Second, it makes you an expert on using the Size windoid. When you have a real need for it, you won't have to flip through the manual or this book to see how the Size windoid works.

To resize and place the fields and labels, read the following instructions for using the Size windoid and then, using the information in Tables 4-3 and 4-4, enter the appropriate numbers in the windoid's text boxes to size and place the fields and field labels, respectively.

1. If the Size windoid isn't visible, choose View ➪ Object Size.

   The Size windoid appears (as previously shown in Figure 4-16). If you want to change the measurement units for the Size windoid, click one of the units to the right of any number entry in the windoid. Each mouse click chooses one of the three possible measurement units: inches, centimeters, or pixels. Note that visible text or graphics rulers will simultaneously change to reflect the chosen unit.

Tip When graphic rulers are displayed, the current measurement unit is also displayed in the intersection of the ruler bars.

2. Select the object whose placement or size you want to modify.

   Handles (black dots) appear at the object's corners to show that it is selected.

3. To change the position of the selected object, type numbers into any of the top four text boxes in the Size windoid. In order, these boxes represent the distance from:

- *Left*: The left edge of the object to the left edge of the layout
- *Top*: The top edge of the object to the top of the layout
- *Right*: The right edge of the object to the left edge of the layout
- *Bottom*: The bottom edge of the object to the top of the layout

Tip   You can precisely set the location of any object by specifying any pair of vertical and horizontal numbers, such as the distance from the left and distance from the top. As you make changes to the chosen pair of figures, the numbers in the other pair automatically change to reflect the object's new location.

4. To change the dimensions of the selected object, type numbers into the bottom two text boxes: width and height.

5. To execute the changes on a Mac, press Tab or Return to move to the next text box, press Enter to stay in the same text box, or use the mouse to click in a different text box. To execute the changes on a Windows PC, press Return or Enter, or press Tab to move to the next text box.

As an example of using the Size windoid, you can set the size and location of the First Name field and the other fields in the database by following these steps:

1. Using the Pointer tool, select the First Name field.

2. In the Size windoid, type the numbers shown in the First Name row of Table 4-3.

   Move from one text box to another by pressing Tab or clicking in the next box with the mouse.

3. Next, without closing the Size windoid, individually select each additional field and — one by one — enter the appropriate settings from Table 4-3.

Table 4-3 lists the size and placement for the fields in the Address Book database. Note that the height dimension remains constant for most of the fields. This consistency is natural, because most fields contain data that is formatted with the same font and size.

Table 4-3
Field Size and Placement (in Inches)

Field Name	Left Edge	Top Edge	Width	Height
First Name	2.472	.944	1.681	.222
Last Name	.639	.944	1.681	.222
Title	.639	1.403	3.514	.222

Field Name	Left Edge	Top Edge	Width	Height
Company	.639	.486	2.347	.222
Department	.639	2.319	2.097	.222
Mail Stop	2.889	2.319	1.264	.222
Address	.639	2.778	3.514	.222
City	.639	3.236	1.514	.222
State	2.319	3.236	.681	.222
Zip	3.139	3.236	1.014	.222
Phone	.639	1.861	1.097	.222
Extension	1.833	1.861	.681	.222
Fax	3.056	1.861	1.097	.222
Category	3.181	.486	.931	.222
Comments	.639	3.694	3.514	.639
Last Modified	3.472	4.375	.681	.194

Table 4-4 contains the data you need to position the field labels. It does not include width and height dimensions because every label is already the correct size. Because neither the Comments nor the Category field has a field label in the final layout, remove these two labels by selecting them and pressing Delete. Then, one by one, select each field label listed in Table 4-4 and enter its pair of placement figures in the Size windoid.

Table 4-4
Field Label Placement (in Inches)

Field Label	Left Edge	Top Edge
First Name	2.472	1.167
Last Name	.639	1.167
Title	.639	1.625
Company	.639	.708
Department	.639	2.542
Mail Stop	2.889	2.542
Address	.639	3.000

Continued

Table 4-4 *(continued)*		
Field Label	*Left Edge*	*Top Edge*
City	.639	3.458
State	2.319	3.458
Zip	3.139	3.458
Phone	.639	2.083
Extension	1.833	2.083
Fax	3.056	2.083
Last Modified	2.611	4.389

Finally, to move the background graphic into position, select the background graphic and enter the following numbers (in inches) for the distance from the left and top edges: **0.347** and **0.431**, respectively.

Adding the finishing touches

In designing the data entry layout, a few small tasks remain:

✦ Naming the layout

✦ Setting the final size of the layout

✦ Completing the formatting of the Category field

✦ Ungrouping the background graphics

✦ Inserting a phone icon (to be used as a dialing button)

Naming the layout

Layout #1 is the default name assigned by FileMaker Pro to the first layout created for a database. Because this database will have more than one layout, you should give each layout a more descriptive name. The following steps describe how to assign a name to a layout:

1. Choose View ➪ Layout Mode.

2. If the database has more than one layout, switch to the layout you want to rename by choosing its current name from the layout pop-up menu in the upper-left corner of the document window. (At this point, Address Book has only a single layout, so this step is unnecessary.)

3. Choose Layouts ➪ Layout Setup.

   The Layout Setup dialog box appears, open to the General tab (see Figure 4-18). The current name of the layout is shown in the Layout Name text box.

4. Type the new name for the layout and then click OK. In this example, type **Data Entry**.

You do not have to assign a name to a layout at any specific time. You can assign and change layout names whenever the mood strikes you. However, because some FileMaker Pro scripts refer to layouts by name, setting layout names early in the design process — and certainly before you begin to create any scripts — is the best method.

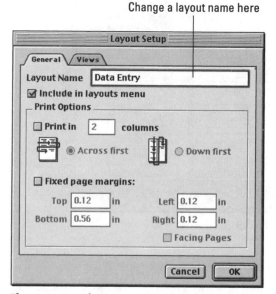

Change a layout name here

Figure 4-18: The Layout Setup dialog box

Setting the final size of the layout

Because you will use the Data Entry layout only for data entry and you will never use it to view more than one record at a time, the layout will look better if you eliminate all unnecessary white space that surrounds the graphics. To eliminate the unnecessary white space, follow these steps:

1. Change to Layout mode (choose View ➪ Layout Mode or press ⌘+L/Ctrl+L).

2. Choose Edit ➪ Select All (or press ⌘+A/Ctrl+A).

   This command selects all the objects on the layout (in this case, the fields, field labels, and the background graphic).

3. Drag the objects so their edges are closer to the top and left edges of the layout.

4. Click the Body part indicator and drag it up, removing the unnecessary space at the bottom of the layout.

5. If you like, you can drag the window's size box (in the bottom-right corner of the window) to match the size of the Data Entry layout.

Your version of the Data Entry layout should now look similar to the one shown in Figure 4-19.

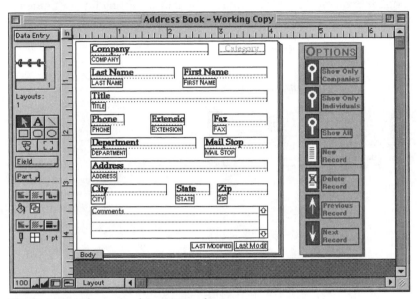

Figure 4-19: The resized Data Entry layout

Formatting the Category field

Because the text for the Category field is set in a light-colored font, adding a fill color to the field enables you to read the text easily and makes the field stand out. To add a fill color, follow these steps:

1. Switch to Layout mode (choose View ➪ Layout Mode menu or press ⌘+L/Ctrl+L).

2. Select the Category field.

3. In the fill color pop-up palette, select a dark blue (similar to the shade that you chose for the text in the Company, Last Name, First Name, Phone, and Extension fields).

Although you created and attached the Categories value list to this field, you have not yet specified a format for the list. FileMaker Pro can present any value list as a pop-up list, pop-up menu, check boxes, or radio buttons. For this example, you'll make it a pop-up list by following these steps:

1. In Layout mode with the Category field still selected, choose Format ➪ Field Format.

The Field Format for "Category" dialog box appears, as shown in Figure 4-20.

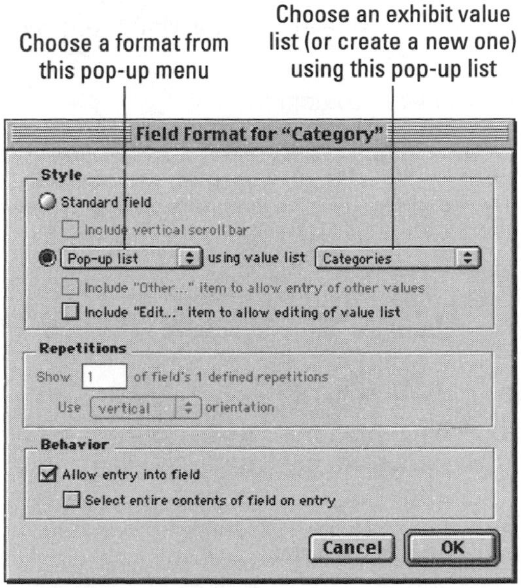

Figure 4-20: The Field Format for "Category" dialog box

2. Choose "Pop-up list" from the pop-up menu in the Style section of the dialog box, and choose the "Categories" value list from the pop-up menu to the right.

3. Click OK to dismiss the dialog box.

Now when you switch to Browse mode and tab into the Category field, the pop-up list is automatically presented.

Ungrouping the background graphics

To make manipulating the background graphics safer when you were in the design phase of creating the Data Entry layout, the graphics were initially grouped. (To group objects, you switch to Layout mode, select the graphic elements to be grouped, and then choose the Arrange ⇨ Group command.) Grouping enables you to treat two or more graphic elements as a single entity. As a result, you can move the graphics without fear of leaving some elements behind, and you can apply formatting commands that simultaneously affect all the graphic elements in the group. Grouping also enables you to maintain the relative alignment and positioning of the grouped objects.

After you ungroup the graphics, you can treat each graphic element, such as the buttons in the Control palette, individually. You can move, format, or assign a script to just one element, for example.

Follow these steps to ungroup previously grouped objects (in this case, the background graphics):

1. Change to Layout mode by choosing View ⇨ Layout Mode (or pressing ⌘+L/Ctrl+L).

2. Select the graphic element you want to ungroup.

   Because all the graphics form a single group, click anywhere in the background graphic (the Control palette on the right, for example). Handles appear at the corners of the graphic to show that it is selected.

3. Choose the Arrange ⇨ Ungroup command (or press Shift-⌘+G/Shift+Ctrl+G).

   Every element in the selected object that was previously grouped is now displayed with its own handles, showing that it is ungrouped.

Inserting an icon for a phone dialing button

FileMaker Pro 5 supports phone dialing through a modem or the computer's speaker. Rather than add an ordinary button that says "Dial" or "Phone," it's much cooler to use an icon.

To add the phone dialing icon, follow these steps:

1. Change to Layout mode by choosing View ⇨ Layout Mode menu (or pressing ⌘+L/Ctrl+L).

2. Choose Insert ⇨ Picture.

   A standard file dialog box appears.

3. Navigate to the drive and folder that contains the graphics file named Phone.jpg.

   You'll find Phone.jpg in the same folder as Address Book — Graphics (the file that contained the background graphics for this database).

4. Select Phone.jpg in the file list, and click Open.

   A copy of the phone icon appears in the layout.

5. Drag the phone icon just to the right of the Phone field label (which is under the Phone field name).

   If you prefer, you can place the phone icon using the Size windoid. Set the distance from the left to 0.917 inches and the distance from the top to 1.819 inches.

Although you will later assign scripts that interact with the Data Entry layout, the design work is now done. The layout you just created should look very much like the one shown in Figure 4-21.

Cross-Reference For more information on designing and modifying layouts, see Chapter 6.

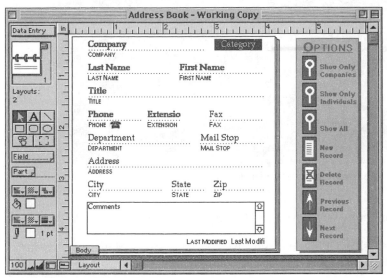

Figure 4-21: The finished Data Entry layout

Step 5: Design a Report Layout

Although the Data Entry layout is excellent for its intended purpose (entering address and contact information), most users wouldn't have much interest in using this layout to create reports.

Note If you're curious, open the finished Address Book database, make sure the Data Entry layout is selected, create a few records, and then choose View ⇨ Preview Mode. Preview mode shows what you would get if you printed the current layout. As you can see, only two records fit on a page, and the information in each record is arranged in exactly the same way it looks when you're in Browse mode — pretty, but hardly functional.

Unless you have designed an all-purpose layout for a database, you're usually better off creating one layout for data entry and other layouts for reports. As an example of the kinds of reports you can produce from the Address Book database, you will now create a layout for a phone directory. The Phone Directory layout is a columnar report layout. As with most such layouts, you can print reports that you generate from the layout or view them on the monitor. The finished layout looks like the one in Figure 4-22.

Address Book - Working Copy
Phone Directory
Last Name
First
Company
Department
Title
Phone
Ext.
Layout #3
Layouts:
3
Field
Part
1 pt
100
Layout

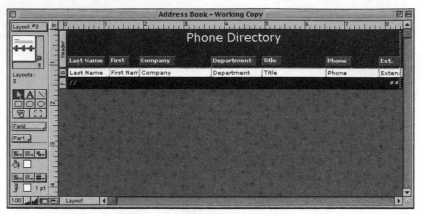

Figure 4-22: The completed Phone Directory layout

To create the Phone Directory layout, follow these steps:

1. Change to Layout mode by choosing View ➪ Layout Mode (or pressing ⌘+L/Ctrl+L).
2. Choose Layouts ➪ New Layout/Report (or press ⌘+N/Ctrl+N).

   The opening screen of the New Layout/Report assistant appears, as shown in Figure 4-23. (This is a new feature of FileMaker Pro 5.)

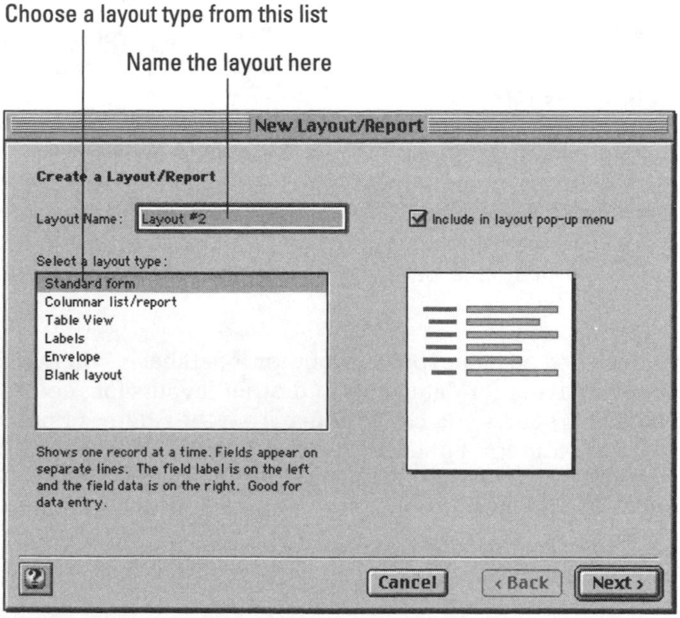

Choose a layout type from this list
Name the layout here
New Layout/Report
Create a Layout/Report
Layout Name:
Layout #2
Include in layout pop-up menu
Select a layout type:
Standard form
Columnar list/report
Table View
Labels
Envelope
Blank layout
Shows one record at a time. Fields appear on separate lines. The field label is on the left and the field data is on the right. Good for data entry.
Cancel
‹ Back
Next ›

Figure 4-23: The New Layout/Report assistant

3. Type a name for the layout in the Layout Name text box. (In this case, type **Phone Directory**.)

Note

Instead of accepting the default name for the layout (Layout #2, in this example) or naming it later in the process as you did with the Data Entry layout, you can name this layout when you create it. Only the first layout created for a database is automatically named Layout #*x*.

4. Choose "Columnar list/report" as the layout type, and click Next.

5. Click the "Columnar list/report" radio button, but leave the "Constrain to page width" check box unchecked.

Note

Leaving the "Constrain to page width" check box unchecked corresponds to the Extended Columnar layout in FileMaker Pro 4.1 and earlier. If we wanted to restrict the width of the report to a single page width, we would check the option to "Constrain to page width" (corresponding to the old Columnar report layout).

6. Click Next.

The Specify Fields screen appears, as shown in Figure 4-24.

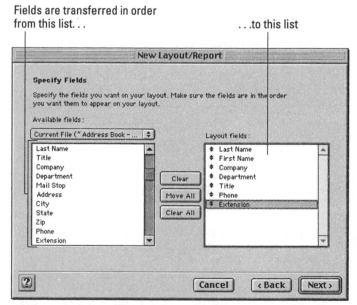

Fields are transferred in order from this list. . .

. . .to this list

Figure 4-24: The Specify Fields screen

7. Select fields in the left side of the dialog box, click Move to transfer them to the Layout fields list on the right, and — when you have finished — click Next. Alternatively, instead of clicking the field and then clicking Move, you can simply double-click the field you want to move.

The Specify Fields screen has two functions. You use it to select the initial set of fields you want to appear in the layout, as well as to set the order in which the fields appear. For the Phone Directory layout, select and move the following fields (in order): Last Name, First Name, Company, Department, Title, Phone, and Extension.

8. The Sort Records screen appears. Move the following fields (in order): Company, Last Name, and First Name. By default, each is sorted in ascending order. Click Next.

The Select a Theme screen appears (see Figure 4-25).

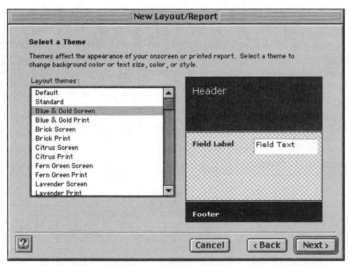

Figure 4-25: By selecting a Screen or Print theme, you can make short work of much of the design phase.

9. We're going to make this an on-screen report, so we'll add some features to make it more visually appealing. Choose "Blue & Gold Screen," and click Next.

The Header and Footer Information screen appears (see Figure 4-26).

10. In the Header section, click the Top center pop-up menu and choose "Large Custom Text." Type **Phone Directory** in the dialog box that appears, and click OK.

11. In the Footer section, choose Current Date from the Bottom left pop-up menu and Page Number from the Bottom right pop-up menu. Click Next.

The Create a Script for this Report screen appears.

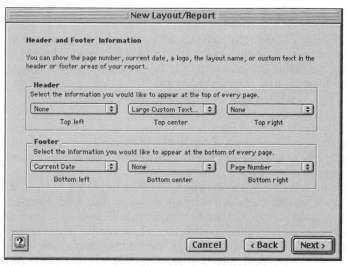

Figure 4-26: Specify header and footer information that you want to display on every page of the report.

12. We won't create a script now, but will do so later in this chapter. Select the "Do not create a script" radio button, and click Next.

    The final screen appears.

13. Because we will want to make some changes to the layout, choose "View the report in Layout mode" and then click Finish.

    The report layout is generated.

If you scroll the Phone Directory layout from side to side, you'll see that it extends beyond the current page width. Several possible solutions are available for handling this problem:

✦ Set the printing for landscape mode (sideways) using the Page Setup command.

✦ Remove some of the fields.

✦ Change the layout by reducing the size of some fields and sliding them to the left.

Although using either of the first two approaches is an easy way to resolve the width problem, assume that you have your heart set on producing a phone directory report that you can view in portrait mode and that you want it to include every one of the chosen fields. In this case, you will proceed with the third option — reducing field sizes and sliding them left so they fit within the width of a single page.

Resizing the fields

Try using the "eyeball" (best approximation) approach to resize and move the fields manually so they fit on the layout. You can refer back to Figure 4-22 and use it as a rough guideline for how wide the fields should be. (Unless you're feeling adventuresome, however, leave the column headings where they are. In the next section, you'll learn an easy way to move them.)

When you alter the width of each field, hold down the Shift key as you drag. Doing so ensures that only one dimension of the field will change—the width, in this case. Because the same font is used in every field, the height of each field is already correct.

When you're through manually resizing and shuffling the fields to the left, check your results against the Size windoid settings shown in Table 4-5. Please note that no settings are right or wrong. As long as you leave sufficient room for each field to display its intended contents, the layout is fine. However, if the data from any record doesn't fit within a field's new dimensions (a record may contain an extra-long company name, for example), the extra characters will be truncated (chopped off) when the report is printed. When setting field widths, err on the plus side if possible.

As before, to examine or alter the dimensions or placement of any field, select the field on the layout and then check its size and location in the Size windoid.

Table 4-5 Field Dimensions (in Inches)		
Field Name	**Distance from Left Edge**	**Field Width**
Last Name	0.125	1.000
First Name	1.139	0.819
Company	1.972	1.736
Department	3.722	1.236
Title	4.972	1.569
Phone	6.556	1.292
Extension	7.861	0.514

Formatting the header

In a columnar report, the field labels for the columns are normally placed in the header layout part rather than in the body layout part. That way, when you scroll the report on-screen or print it, you can be assured that the column headers (the field labels) are always visible. As you have seen, the New Layout/Report assistant automatically placed the labels in the header. Thus, all we need to do now is align each label with its matching field.

To align the Last Name label with the Last Name field, follow these steps:

1. Select the Last Name field and its matching label by Shift-clicking the two elements.

2. Choose Arrange ⇨ Set Alignment.

3. Set options in the Set Alignment dialog box, as shown in Figure 4-27. In the Top to Bottom area, choose None; in the Left to Right area, choose "Align left edges."

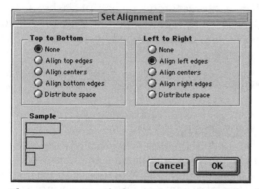

Figure 4-27: Match the settings in this dialog box.

4. Click OK.

   The dialog box closes, and the two fields are aligned.

After you set the proper alignment options, you can quickly align the remaining fields and labels by selecting each pair and pressing ⌘+K/Ctrl+K (the keyboard shortcut for the Align command).

The labels now have only one thing wrong with them — some of the labels are longer than their matching fields. Select the Text tool (the uppercase A) from the Tools palette. Change the wording of the First Name label to **First** and the Extension label to **Ext.** Then shorten their widths by clicking and dragging. Next, change the width of the Last Name label, so it isn't so close to the First Name label.

Finally, although the report already has a title (Phone Directory), it's too close to the field labels. To give it some breathing room, click the Body part and drag it down to a little below the 1-inch mark. Now select all the field labels and drag them down until they are just a hair above the Body part.

Formatting the footer

Like every other layout generated by FileMaker Pro, this one already has space reserved for a footer. Although the Data Entry layout doesn't need a footer, footers are often useful in report layouts, such as a Phone Directory. They can be used to present any information you want to see on every page, such as the page number, date, name of the database, or name of the user who created the report. While creating the layout, we specified that date-stamp and page number placeholders be included.

If you had decided to add these elements after closing the New Layout/Report assistant, all you'd have to do is choose Insert ➪ Date Symbol and Insert ➪ Page Number Symbol. The date symbol is represented by a pair of slashes (//), while the page number symbol is represented by a pair of pound signs (##). If you can't see these symbols in the current layout, make sure that View ➪ Show ➪ Sample Data is not checked.

Cross-Reference   For more information on working with layout parts, see Chapter 6.

Step 6: Create the Scripts

Strictly speaking, you could quit right here and still have an extremely functional database. But by adding scripts that automate many of the database operations, you can transform this functional database into an easy-to-use, time-conserving database. Carefully chosen scripts can eliminate an enormous amount of wasted effort. What's the point of constantly re-creating a particular find request or set of sort instructions, for example, when all you have to do is design a small script that performs these actions at the touch of a button?

Because the term *script* smacks of programming, many users shy away from the ScriptMaker feature. The simple but powerful scripts presented in this section show you what you have been missing and demonstrate just how easy ScriptMaker is to use. And no programming is required!

Address Book uses scripts in two ways: Some are assigned to buttons, and others are available only as commands in the Scripts menu. Furthermore, some of the scripts contain several steps, and some execute only a single command. By looking at the ways in which scripts are incorporated into this database, you can get a good idea of the kinds of things you can do with scripts in your own databases.

The script definition process

When creating a script, the first step is to use menu commands to perform all the actions that the script will eventually handle. Doing so "sets up" the database so all necessary command options are already selected. That is, while you are executing the steps you intend to include in the script, you set the correct Sort, Find, Page Setup, Print, Export, and Import options, for example. Setting these options is essential because you cannot specify sort fields, find logic, print options, or settings for other commands as you create the script. In fact, the following methods are the only ones you can use to set options for commands used in scripts:

✦ Instruct the script to present a dialog box that enables the user to verify the current settings or enter different ones.

✦ Instruct the script to use the command settings that were in effect at the moment the script was created.

If you are creating a generic sort, find, or export script, the first approach works well. Each time the script step is executed, the user can enter the appropriate settings in the dialog box that appears.

In many cases, however, you want scripts to perform steps that have preset options. For example, you could create a script that switches to a particular layout, finds only the records of employees who have arrived late more than three times in the last month, sorts the found records by salary, sets printing for landscape mode, and then prints the resulting report. Although you can instruct FileMaker Pro to present a dialog box for each of the last four actions (Find, Sort, Page Setup, and Print), doing so is a waste of time. Because you intend to use the same options every time you execute this script, incorporating the command options within the steps of the script is much simpler. Doing so adds consistency to the script's performance, and it ensures that no matter who runs the script (such as a temporary worker or an assistant who is sitting in for you), the result will always be the same.

After creating the necessary scripts in the following sections, you'll assign some of the scripts to the buttons in the background graphics. Other scripts will be available only as commands in the Scripts menu.

Revealing a script's Sort and Find instructions

You can easily reveal the sort and find instructions that are used in scripts in other people's databases. Perform the script and then immediately choose the Records ⇨ Sort (⌘+S/Ctrl+S) and Records ⇨ Modify Last Find (⌘+R/Ctrl+R) commands.

When you are examining the sort and find requests, performing the sort or find isn't necessary or even desirable. You simply use these commands to determine what options the creator of the database set for the scripts. You can exit the Sort dialog box by clicking Done and exit the find request by choosing View ⇨ Browse Mode (or by pressing ⌘+B/Ctrl+B).

The Address Book scripts

Address Book contains 10 scripts. Some are attached to buttons, others appear in the Scripts menu, and one is a special-purpose script that is used only as a step in another script. Each script is described in detail in the pages that follow. The first script, Show Companies, contains a complete walk-through of the script creation process. After creating the Show Companies script, you should have little difficulty creating the other scripts.

Before you start creating scripts, spend a few minutes entering some sample records for the database. You can more easily determine whether your scripts are working correctly if you have records in the database. (To create a new record, enter Browse mode and choose Records ➪ New Record.) Be sure that your records contain a sample of all three categories (Business, Friend, and Relative) and that some records include a company name and some do not. When you're ready to use your own data with the copy of Address Book that you have created, you can delete the dummy records.

The Show Companies script

This script limits visible records to those that have an entry in the Company field. The find request checks to see if the Company field has anything in it, and if it does, that record is included in the results of the search.

You are interested in looking at records sorted by company, so Company is selected as the first sort field. Because you may have several records for the same company, the records are further sorted by Last Name. Thus, all the personnel from a particular company will be listed in alphabetical order according to last name.

Follow these steps to create a script that sorts records by companies and last names:

1. If the Data Entry layout isn't currently displayed, choose Data Entry from the layout pop-up menu in the upper-left corner of the document window.

2. Choose View ➪ Find Mode (or press ⌘+F/Ctrl+F).

   A find request form appears, as shown in Figure 4-28.

3. Enter an asterisk (*) in the Company field.

   The asterisk stands for "anything." No characters follow the asterisk, so you are looking for records that contain anything in the Company field (that is, records in which this field is not blank). You can type the asterisk or choose it from the Symbols pop-up menu.

4. Click Find.

   The search executes.

Click to execute the find

Enter an * here

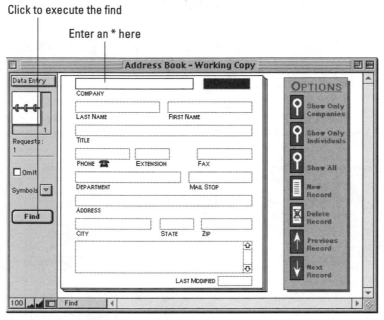

Figure 4-28: A find request form

5. Choose Records ➪ Sort (or press ⌘+S/Ctrl+S).

The Sort Records dialog box appears, as shown in Figure 4-29. The most recent sort specification is displayed, sorted by company, last name, and first name.

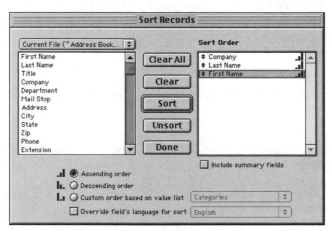

Figure 4-29: The Sort Records dialog box

6. In the Sort Order list, choose the First Name field and then click Clear.

7. Click Sort.

The database is sorted by the two fields (Company and Last Name).

You have completed the preparatory steps for creating the Show Companies script. Next, we'll build the actual script.

8. Choose Scripts ➪ ScriptMaker.

The Define Scripts dialog box appears, as shown in Figure 4-30.

Defined scripts are listed here   Click to creat the script

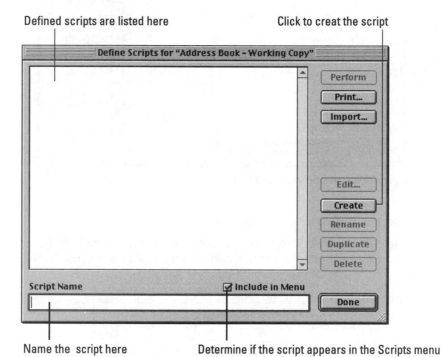

Name the script here   Determine if the script appears in the Scripts menu

Figure 4-30: To create a new script, enter a name for it in the Define Scripts dialog box and then click Create.

9. Type **Show Companies** in the Script Name text box, click the check box labeled "Include in Menu" to remove the check mark, and then click Create.

Note

Because this script will be attached to a button, there is no need to also list it in the Scripts menu.

The Script Definition dialog box appears (see Figure 4-31), listing FileMaker Pro's best guess at the steps that will be needed.

Script steps are chosen from this list   Current script steps

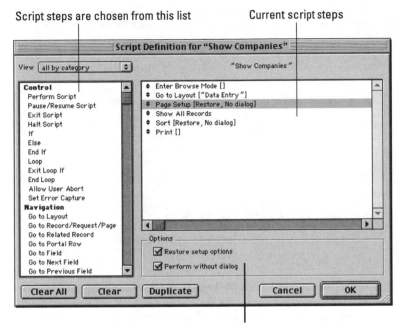

Options for selected script step are displayed here

Figure 4-31: The Script Definition dialog box

10. In the list of included script steps (on the right side of the dialog box), select the Page Setup/Print Setup step and then click the Clear button to remove this step.

11. Select the Print step from the list of included steps and click the Clear button to remove this step.

Note

Because this script has nothing to do with printing, you can eliminate both the Page Setup/Print Setup and Print steps. Although the Page Setup step can affect the on-screen and printed appearance of the layout, this database is always used with the standard, portrait-mode Page Setup options. Because you are not going to change the Page Setup/Print Setup, you do not need to restore these settings each time you execute the script. However, if you are ever going to print a layout with settings other than the default settings (such as landscape), you should keep the Page Setup/Print Setup step in the script.

12. Click OK to accept the script definition.

13. When the Define Scripts dialog box reappears, click Done to return to the database.

Table 4-6 shows all the steps in the Show Companies script. Details for some of the steps are listed in the second column (Special Instructions/Comments). You will create the remaining scripts for the database by following the instructions presented in the explanatory text and the tables.

Any text in brackets that is shown as part of a script step is an option you specify when you add or edit that script step, such as Perform Find [Restore]. Available options are always shown in the bottom-right corner of the Script Definition dialog box, either as check boxes, buttons, or pop-up menus. Quotation marks around text indicate a specific layout, file, field, or script name.

Table 4-6 **The Show Companies Script**	
Script Step	*Special Instructions/Comments*
Enter Browse Mode [ ]	
Go to Layout ["Data Entry"]	
Perform Find [Restore]	* in Company field
Sort [Restore, No dialog]	Sort by Company, Last Name

Script steps can be reordered, if necessary. To change the position of any step, move the mouse pointer into the list of currently selected steps. As the pointer passes over the double-arrow symbol at the beginning of any step, the pointer changes to a larger version of the double-arrow symbol. Click to select the step, and then drag it up or down in the steps list. When you release the mouse button, the step is fixed in its new position in the list.

The Show Individuals script

Table 4-7 shows the steps in the Show Individuals script. The find request in this script is straightforward. To find records of individuals (records that have no entry in the Company field), you search for Company fields that are empty (=).

Table 4-7 **The Show Individuals Script**	
Script Step	*Special Instructions/Comments*
Enter Browse Mode [ ]	
Go to Layout ["Data Entry"]	
Perform Find [Restore]	= in Company field
Sort [Restore, No dialog]	Sort by Last Name

The Show All script

Table 4-8 shows the steps in the Show All script. The purpose of this script is to make all records visible (the same as issuing a Show All Records command) and then sort them by Company and Last Name. Note that the Show All Records command does not use a Find layout to perform a search.

Table 4-8	
The Show All Script	
Script Step	*Special Instructions/Comments*
Enter Browse Mode [ ]	
Go to Layout ["Data Entry"]	
Show All Records	
Sort [Restore, No dialog]	Sort by Company, Last Name

The Find Businesses script

Table 4-9 shows the steps in the Find Businesses script. This script finds all records for which you have chosen Business in the Category field pop-up menu. Although the Find Businesses script serves a purpose similar to that of the Show Companies script, it finds all records that you have identified as being a business, rather than relying on the contents of the Company field. Many self-employed people, for example, operate businesses out of their homes but have no company names. Similarly, you may also have records that list home addresses of your business contacts. (Although the records may not contain a company name, you still consider them business contacts.) The Find Businesses script will locate all these records.

Table 4-9	
The Find Businesses Script	
Script Step	*Special Instructions/Comments*
Enter Browse Mode [ ]	
Go to Layout ["Data Entry"]	
Perform Find [Restore]	"Business" in Category field
Sort [Restore, No dialog]	Sort by Company, Last Name

The found records are sorted by the Company field and then by the Last Name field. Because your business contacts may or may not have a company name, also sorting them by company is important. Records without a company name (the Company field is blank) will appear first in the sorted found set.

You can later execute this script by selecting it from the Scripts menu. To do so, the script must have the "Include in Menu" option associated with it in the Define Scripts dialog box. (Make sure this option is set when defining the script.) Because this script is the first one added to the Scripts menu, FileMaker Pro assigns it a keyboard shortcut of ⌘+1/Ctrl+1.

The Find Friends script

Table 4-10 shows the steps for the Find Friends script. This script finds all records for which you have chosen Friend in the Category field pop-up menu. The found records are sorted by last name only. Although you can also sort by company name, you have identified the individuals in these records as being personal friends rather than business contacts, so you'll be able to locate them more easily if they're alphabetized by last name rather than by company.

Table 4-10 The Find Friends Script	
Script Step	*Special Instructions/Comments*
Enter Browse Mode [ ]	
Go to Layout ["Data Entry"]	
Perform Find [Restore]	"Friend" in Category field
Sort [Restore, No dialog]	Sort by Last Name

You can later execute this script by choosing it from the Scripts menu (place a check mark in the check box labeled "Include in Menu" in the Define scripts dialog box) or by pressing ⌘+2/Ctrl+2.

The Find Relatives script

Table 4-11 shows the steps for the Find Relatives script. This script works exactly like the Find Friends script described in the preceding section, but it finds only the records for which you have chosen Relative in the Category field pop-up menu. The found records are sorted by last name only.

Table 4-11 The Find Relatives Script	
Script Step	*Special Instructions/Comments*
Enter Browse Mode [ ]	
Go to Layout ["Data Entry"]	
Perform Find [Restore]	"Relative" in Category field
Sort [Restore, No dialog]	Sort by Last Name

You can later execute this script by choosing it from the Scripts menu (place a check mark in the check box labeled "Include in Menu" in the Define scripts dialog box) or by pressing ⌘+3/Ctrl+3.

The Sort by Company, Last Name script

This utility script performs just one action: sorting the database by company and last name. Its only purpose is to be part of the Phone Directory (by Last Name) script that is described in the next section. (A script that is executed by another script is known as a *sub-script*.) Thus, you will neither assign it to a button nor place it in the Scripts menu.

Follow these steps to create the script that will sort the database by the Company and Last Name fields:

1. Perform a sort, using Company and Last Name as the sort fields.

2. Choose Scripts ➪ ScriptMaker.

3. Type **Sort by Company, Last Name** in the Script Name text box, click to remove the check mark in the check box labeled "Include in Menu," and then click Create.

4. Click the Clear All button.

5. In the Available Steps list, double-click the Sort step.

6. Accept the default settings: Sort [Restore, No dialog].

7. Click OK, and then click Done.

The Phone Directory (by Last Name) script

Table 4-12 shows the steps for the Phone Directory (by Last Name) script. This script displays a phone directory that is alphabetized by last name only. As in the Show Individuals script, if your database will contain records for several individuals who share the same last name, you may want to modify the sort instructions by adding First Name as the second sort field.

Table 4-12
The Phone Directory (by Last Name) Script

Script Step	Special Instructions/Comments
Enter Browse Mode [ ]	
Go to Layout ["Phone Directory"]	Switch to the Phone Directory layout
Toggle Window [Maximize]	Open the window to the full screen dimensions
Show All Records	Use all records
Sort [Restore, No dialog]	Sort by Last Name
Pause/Resume Script [ ]	Wait for Continue button to be clicked
Go to Layout ["Data Entry"]	
Toggle Window [Unzoom]	Restore Data Entry window to its normal size
Perform Script [Sub-scripts, "Sort by Company, Last Name"]	Sort by Company, Last Name script

After you finish viewing the Phone Directory and click the Continue button, the script automatically returns to the Data Entry layout, and then performs the Sort by Company, Last Name script (sorting the records by company and last name).

You can later execute this script by choosing it from the Scripts menu (place a check mark in the check box labeled "Include in Menu" in the Define scripts dialog box) or by pressing ⌘+4/Ctrl+4.

Creating scripts based on other scripts

FileMaker provides a way for you to create scripts that are based on other scripts. For example, you could create the Phone Directory (by Company) script by duplicating the Phone Directory (by Last Name) script and then editing the duplicate, as follows:

1. Execute the new sort (using Company and Last Name as the sort fields).

2. Open ScriptMaker, select the Phone Directory (by Last Name) script, and click the Duplicate button.

3. Edit the name of the duplicate to read Phone Directory (by Company), and then click Rename.

4. With the renamed script selected, click the Edit button.

   The Script Definition dialog box appears.

5. Clear the Perform Script [Sub-scripts, "Sort by Company, Last Name"] step, and then click OK.

6. In the dialog box that appears, click Replace for the Sort Order (to tell it to use the most recent sort), click OK, and then click Done.

The Phone Directory (by Company) script

Table 4-13 shows the steps for the Phone Directory (by Company) script. This script and the Phone Directory (by Last Name) script are different in two small ways. First, this script sorts by the Company and Last Name fields rather than only by the Last Name field. Thus, the list is alphabetized by company and, within each company, employees are listed alphabetically according to their last names. Second, because the Sort command arranges the database in the same order that it needs to be in after the script is finished, you don't need to perform another sort as the final script step.

Table 4-13 The Phone Directory (by Company) Script	
Script Step	**Special Instructions/Comments**
Enter Browse Mode [ ]	
Go to Layout ["Phone Directory"]	Switch to the Phone Directory layout
Toggle Window [Maximize]	Open the window to the full screen dimensions
Show All Records	Use all records
Sort [Restore, No dialog]	Sort by Company, Last Name
Pause/Resume Script [ ]	Wait for Continue button to be clicked
Go to Layout ["Data Entry"]	
Toggle Window [Unzoom]	Restore Data Entry window to its normal size

You can later execute this script by choosing it from the Scripts menu (place a check mark in the check box labeled "Include in Menu" in the Define scripts dialog box) or by pressing ⌘+5/Ctrl+5.

The Dial script

Because you've gone to the trouble of importing a telephone icon into the Data Entry layout, you can change it into a button by creating a simple dialing script and then attaching it to the icon. The Dial script consists of only one script step: Dial Phone.

To set up the Dial script, follow these steps:

1. Choose Scripts ⇨ ScriptMaker, and enter **Dial** as the name of the script.

   Because you do not want to list this script in the Scripts menu, remove the check mark from the check box labeled "Include in Menu."

2. Click Create to define the script.

3. Click Clear All to eliminate the predefined steps.

4. Select the Dial Phone step, and click Move to add it to the script.

5. Click the check box labeled "Perform without dialog," and then click the Specify button.

   The Dial Phone dialog box appears, as shown in Figure 4-32.

Figure 4-32: The Dial Phone dialog box

6. Click the Field Value radio button in the Dial Phone dialog box. Select Phone as the field to be dialed.

   If you have set (or intend to set) dialing preferences, click the "Use Dialing Preferences" check box. (To set your dialing preferences, choose Edit ⇨ Preferences ⇨ Application and click the Dialing tab.)

7. To exit from ScriptMaker, click OK, click OK again, and then click Done.

In the next section, you will attach the script to the telephone icon.

For more help with designing and editing scripts, see Chapter 15.

Assigning scripts to buttons

After defining all the scripts, you can attach several of them to the graphic buttons in the Data Entry layout. (Any object on a layout can be made into a button by simply attaching a script or script step to the object.) Whenever a button is clicked, the attached script or script step is instantly performed. Many users find it more convenient to click a button than to pull down the Scripts menu and select a script. (Note, however, that there is nothing to prevent you from attaching the same script to a button *and* adding the script to the Scripts menu.)

Follow these steps to assign a script to a button:

1. Switch to Layout mode (choose View ➪ Layout Mode or press ⌘+L/Ctrl+L).
2. Using the Pointer tool, select the button or object to which you want to attach the script.
3. Choose the Format ➪ Button command.

    The Specify Button dialog box appears, as shown in Figure 4-33.

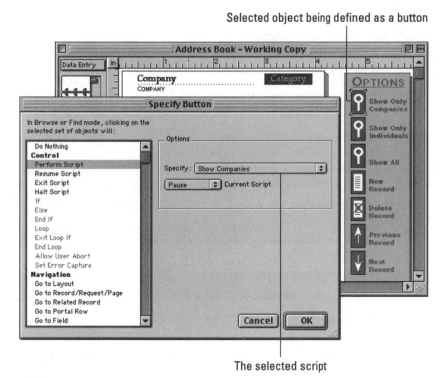

Figure 4-33: The Specify Button dialog box

4. Select Perform Script and choose the specific script in the Specify pop-up menu.
5. Click OK.

    FileMaker Pro assigns the script (or action) to the button you selected.

Use this procedure to attach scripts to the top three buttons in the Data Entry layout (see Figure 4-34). Finally, using the same procedure, select the phone icon on the layout, and assign the Dial script to it.

You have not yet created scripts for the other four button icons (New Record, Delete Record, Previous Record, and Next Record) because you can control each button by a single script step. Instead of using ScriptMaker to design a script for these buttons, you can simultaneously create and assign the scripts using only the Format ➪ Button command.

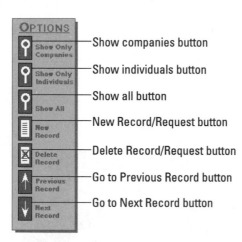
—Show companies button
—Show individuals button
—Show all button
—New Record/Request button
—Delete Record/Request button
—Go to Previous Record button
—Go to Next Record button

Figure 4-34: Attach the Show Companies, Show Individuals, and Show All scripts to the buttons shown.

The button definition process is similar to the one you used to assign scripts to the first three buttons. The only difference is that you select a specific FileMaker Pro script step in Step 4 instead of choosing an existing script to be performed.

To assign functions to the remaining four buttons, select each button and assign the following actions to them (in order):

✦ New Record/Request

✦ Delete Record/Request (leave "Perform without dialog" check box unchecked)

✦ Go to Record/Request/Page (and choose Previous from the Specify pop-up menu)

✦ Go to Record/Request/Page (and choose Next from the Specify pop-up menu)

When you later use the database and switch to Browse mode, clicking these four buttons will create a new record, delete the current record, switch to the previous record in the current sort order, and switch to the following record in the current sort order, respectively. Of course, you can also perform these actions by choosing menu commands (New Record or Delete Record), pressing keyboard shortcuts (⌘+N/Ctrl+N or ⌘+E/Ctrl+E), and clicking book pages in the status area. Because these functions are common, however, providing them as buttons is a thoughtful touch.

Note that the Delete Record/Request/Page script step has an option that enables you to delete records without having to respond to a dialog box that asks whether you are sure you want to delete the record. Unless you're a very careful computer user, you should not set this option. If, in a moment of carelessness, you click the Delete Record button when you meant to click the New Record or Previous Record button, the record will be deleted instantly. Unfortunately, you cannot use the Undo command to restore deleted records, but presenting the Delete dialog box (as is done in Address Book) can help you avoid deleting records by mistake.

 Cross-Reference For more information about attaching scripts to buttons, see Chapter 15.

The Button tool

FileMaker Pro 5 includes a feature specifically designed to create buttons: the Button tool. By switching to Layout mode, selecting the Button tool from the Tools palette, and then drawing, you can create attractive 3D buttons. Although this feature is not used in the Address Book database, you can learn about it in Chapter 6.

Step 7: Set Startup Actions

To complete the Address Book database, you can add one last option to make the database even easier to use. You can specify startup actions that will occur whenever you open the database. For example, you can make the Data Entry layout automatically appear, regardless of the layout you last used.

Follow these steps to set database startup actions:

1. Choose Edit ➪ Preferences ➪ Document.

   The Document Preferences dialog box appears (see Figure 4-35).

2. To set the general preferences for the current database, click the General tab at the top of the Document Preferences dialog box (if it is not already displayed).

3. Click the check box labeled "Switch to layout" in the "When opening" section of the dialog box, and choose Data Entry from the pop-up layout menu.
4. Click OK.

   The dialog box closes, and the changes are recorded.

Select this option to force the database
to always open a particular layout

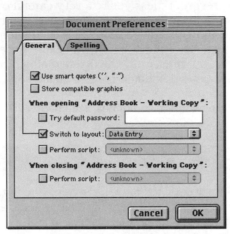

Figure 4-35: The Document Preferences dialog box

By choosing Data Entry from the "Switch to layout" pop-up menu, you ensure
that the database will automatically open to the Data Entry layout, regardless
of the layout you were in when you last closed the database. Because the primary
purpose of Address Book is entering, editing, and viewing address records, you can
save a little time and effort by making sure the Data Entry layout always appears
when you first open the database.

Cross-
Reference

For additional information on setting preferences, see Chapter 7.

Summary

✦ Creating a database can be as simple as defining fields and then using the
default layout that FileMaker Pro provides. However, taking the time to enhance
the database by creating custom layouts, adding graphics, and designing
scripts can greatly improve a database's functionality and ease of use.

✦ Each field in a database is a specific type. The field type determines the kind
of information the field can contain, such as text, numbers, dates, or pictures.

✦ You can resize and move fields as necessary. You can also apply different
formatting options to fields, such as fonts, styles, sizes, and colors.

✦ A database can have as many different layouts as are needed to collect
and display the data in the ways you want. For example, it is not unusual
to create one layout specifically for entering and editing data and other
layouts for generating reports and mailing labels. Every layout draws
on the same information contained in the database; FileMaker simply
arranges the data in a different way.

✦ Scripts enable you to automate common and not-so-common database procedures. ScriptMaker sets many script options for you by "watching" the actions you perform.

✦ You can use graphic or text objects on a layout as buttons, or you can use the Button tool to create 3D buttons. When you click a button, it executes the script or script step that has been attached to it.

✦ To make it easier to create new layouts, FileMaker Pro 5 introduces the New Layout/Report assistant. You can use the assistant to create layouts that conform to an overall style, as well as specify sorting instructions and create a basic script to print or preview the layout as a report.

✦　　✦　　✦

Defining Fields

As explained in Part I of this book, fields are the building blocks from which databases are constructed. In this chapter, you learn all about defining fields, selecting field types, and setting field options.

Setting Field Definitions

Until you define fields for a database, you cannot store data in the database. (Technically, it isn't even a database until fields have been defined.) After you select the drive and folder in which you want to store the new database and give the database a name, the next step is to define the fields. The process of defining a field includes the following:

+ Naming the field

+ Setting a type for the field (the type of information the field will store)

+ Setting options for the field (data validation procedures, auto-entry options, and so on)

The first two steps, naming the field and selecting a data type for the field, are required. Setting options is optional, naturally. You create all fields in the Define Fields dialog box, shown in Figure 5-1.

You can reach the Define Fields dialog box in one of two ways:

+ Create a new file. When you create a new database file (by choosing "Create a new empty file" from the New Database dialog box or by choosing File ➪ New Database), the Define Fields dialog box automatically appears after you name the new database.

+ Choose File ➪ Define Fields (or press Shift+⌘+D /Shift+Ctrl+D). When you want to create new fields or examine, edit, or delete existing field definitions, choose the Define Fields command.

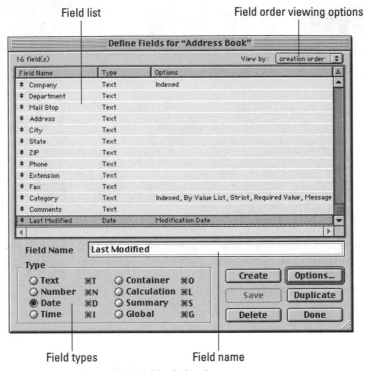

Figure 5-1: The Define Fields dialog box

Follow these steps to define a field:

1. To create a new database when launching FileMaker Pro, choose "Create a new empty file" from the New Database dialog box. Enter a filename for the database in the file dialog box that appears and click Save.

   — or —

   To create a new database when FileMaker Pro is already running, choose File ➪ New Database and then choose "Create a new empty file" from the New Database dialog box. Enter a filename for the database in the file dialog box that appears and click Save.

   — or —

   For an existing database, choose File ➪ Define Fields (or press Shift+⌘+D/ Shift+Ctrl+D).

   In all of these cases, the Define Fields dialog box then appears.

2. Type a name for the new field (up to 60 characters long) in the Field Name box.

   If you think that you may want to use the field in a calculation formula, be sure that the name does not contain a number, period, comma, quotation mark, math symbol, or a logical keyword (AND, OR, NOT). In addition, the name cannot be the same as any of the FileMaker Pro built-in functions. (Refer to Chapter 14 for the names of FileMaker Pro functions.) Such symbols and words will be improperly interpreted as being part of the formula. To prevent such occurrences, FileMaker Pro routinely warns you if you enter an improper name, as shown in Figure 5-2.

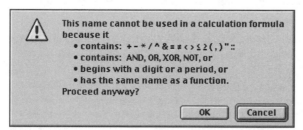

Figure 5-2: This warning appears if you enter an improper field name.

3. Click a radio button to select a data type for the field.

As Figure 5-1 showed, a field type can also be selected by pressing the keyboard equivalent, such as ⌘+D/Alt+D for a Date field. Field types are explained in "All about field types," later in this chapter.

4. Click Create.

If you select Calculation, Summary, or Global as the field type, another dialog box appears in which you specify additional required settings (such as a formula). For any other field type, the basic definition process ends when you click Create.

5. To define additional fields, repeat steps 2 through 4. Click Done when you are through defining fields.

Tip

If you intend to publish the database on the Web or use it in conjunction with ODBC, use underscore characters rather than spaces when creating field names (for example, **Sales_Total**, rather than **Sales Total**).

After you create a field, you can set options for it, as described in "Setting Field Options," later in this chapter.

When you create a database, you normally begin by defining all its fields. You should note, however, that you are not locked in to this set of fields. You can later add new fields, delete fields, set and change field options, or even change field types (from Number to Text, for example). You can change field definitions at any time by choosing File ↪ Define Fields (or pressing Shift+⌘+D/Shift+Ctrl+D). For additional information, see "Modifying Field Definitions, Names, and Options," later in this chapter.

Breaking up complex fields

When you are defining fields for a database, think seriously about dividing complex fields into their logical components. For example, instead of defining a single Name field, you may want to define Title, First Name, and Last Name fields. This approach makes sorting by last name simple. If you attempt to sort a single Name field, on the other hand, FileMaker Pro will list everyone alphabetically by their first name or — worse yet — by their title, such as Mr., Dr., or Ms.

Using different fields for Title, First Name, and Last Name also makes performing a mail merge easy. You can create the salutation by combining the Title and Last Name fields, as in

```
Dear <<Title> <<Last Name>:
```

rather than

```
Dear <<Name>:
```

Thus, instead of saying "Dear Dr. John Abrams:", the form letter would read "Dear Dr. Abrams:".

As you can see, combining several specific fields is much easier than attempting to dismantle and work with a single general field. Plan ahead.

All about field types

Every field in a FileMaker Pro database must have a field type. The *field type* determines the kind of data you can enter and store in a field. Number fields, for example, store numeric data. Because Number fields contain numbers, you can use them to perform calculations, such as SALE * .05 for a field that computes a commission.

FileMaker Pro 5 has eight field types from which you can choose: Text, Number, Date, Time, Container, Calculation, Summary, and Global. Each field must be defined as being one — and only one — type.

In order to improve the speed of executing find requests, FileMaker Pro can keep track of data that has been entered in any field and maintain an index for that field. Depending on the field type you assign to a field and the indexing option you select, FileMaker Pro indexes all data for that field, only part of the data, or no data at all, as Table 5-1 summarizes and the following sections describe.

Table 5-1		
Field Type Specifications		
Field Type	*Field Content and Restrictions*	*Indexed Information*
Text	Up to 64,000 characters of any type	First 20 alphanumeric characters of every word
Number	Up to 255 characters (must be on one line)	First 122 numeric characters (nonnumeric characters are ignored)
Date	One date between year 1 and 3000 (8 characters — month, day, and year — plus separators)	Entire date
Time	One time (8 characters — hours, minutes, and seconds separated by colons)	Entire time
Container	One picture, QuickTime movie or audio clip, sound, or OLE object	Not indexed
Calculation	One formula with a text, numeric, date, time, or container result	Calculation result (the amount of data indexed corresponds to the result type)
Summary	Result of one summary function	Not indexed
Global	A text string, number, date, time, or container item, depending on the data type chosen	Not indexed

In addition, field data used in any of the following manners is automatically indexed (unless you specifically turn off indexing for the affected fields):

✦ Finding duplicates

✦ Using a value list

✦ Validating fields that have the unique or existing value validation criterion set for them

✦ Matching fields in a lookup, related, or master file (based on a relationship)

Text fields

A Text field can store any type of information: text, numbers, and other characters. With a maximum of 64,000 characters, Text fields are ideal for handling large amounts of information, such as comments and notes. If indexing has been turned on for a given Text field, searching for any word in the field is easy because

FileMaker Pro automatically indexes every word—not just the first one. However, indexing (especially on large Text fields) can significantly increase the size of the database file. For this reason, you are better off disabling indexing on large Text fields that you do not intend to use in searches. Because you can enter any type of data in a Text field, a majority of database fields are defined as Text fields.

Number fields

Although its name implies otherwise, you can also enter anything in a Number field—text and symbols, in addition to numeric characters. Number fields, however, have greater restrictions than Text fields. They can contain a maximum of only 255 characters, and you must enter data as a single line. If you attempt to press Return/Enter when typing an entry in a Number field, FileMaker Pro beeps and ignores the Return. Because the numeric information in Number fields is readily accessible for use in formulas and computations, the contents of Number fields are frequently used as the basis for Calculation fields (discussed later in this chapter).

When indexing is turned on for a Number field, only the first 122 numeric characters (numbers, decimal points, and signs) are indexed. Text and other characters are ignored. If you enter both text and numbers in a Number field, individual numbers in the field are combined to form a single number. As an example, suppose you have entered the following address in a Number field:

```
23 East Elm Street, Apt. #7
```

For indexing purposes, FileMaker Pro treats this field as though it contains the number 237. (It appends the 7 to the end of the number 23.) This method of operating also affects searches (performed with the Find command). If you enter 23 or 7 as the search string, the search will fail. Similarly, because text in a Number field is not indexed, searching for Elm also fails. On the other hand, searching for 237—the concatenated numbers—successfully finds this record.

This discussion of concatenation leads to an important point: If you think you will need to enter both text and numeric information in a field, you may be happier if you define it as a Text field rather than as a Number field. If you're just interested in making sure that only legitimate numbers can be entered into a Number field, you have to set the "Numeric only" validation option for the field. See "Setting Field Options," later in this chapter, for instructions.

Date fields

Date fields are reserved for dates. Each date can contain up to eight characters plus separators (MM/DD/YYYY), and the entire date is indexed as a single string (when indexing is turned on for the field). When you type dates, you must use only numbers and the following separators: slash (/), hyphen (-), period (.), or a space. Thus, all the following dates are proper FileMaker Pro dates: 3/14/99, 3-14-99,

3.14.99, 3 14 99, and 3/14/1999. Leading zeros (as in 07/09/99) are optional. The year portion of the date must be between 1 and 3000.

When you enter the month or day part of a date, you can use one or two digits. As shown in Table 5-2, the allowable number of digits in the year portion of a date depends on which year it is.

Caution   Be sure to check out Table 5-2. In order to address Y2K issues, FileMaker Pro 5 handles the entering of years in a different manner from previous versions of the program. And when displaying the year portion of any date, four digits are *always* used — regardless of the formatting options set for the Date field.

Table 5-2 Entering Years in Dates	
For a year in the range . . .	**Enter this . . .**
1–9	Two or three zeros, followed by a single digit (004 or 0004, for example)
10–99	One or two zeros, followed by two digits (057 or 0057, for example)
100–999	Three or four digits (756 or 0756, for example)
1000–1909	Four digits — the actual year (1847, for example)
1910-1999	Two or four digits (94 or 1994, for example)
2000-2009	One, two, or four digits (2, 02, or 2002, for example)
2010–3000	Four digits (2017, for example)

Tip   While Table 5-2 suggests that entering dates is terribly confusing, here's a shortcut. Any year between 1910 and 2009 (the majority of years you'll probably use) can be entered with two digits. Any other year can be entered using four digits.

The manner in which the date is *displayed*, on the other hand, is determined by the format you've set for the field using the Format ⇨ Date command (see "Setting Field Formatting" in Chapter 6). Note that when you base a find request on the contents of a Date field, you must enter a date that is in keeping with the restrictions listed in Table 5-2.

Tip   Here's another way to avoid some typing. When you enter a date for the current year, you don't have to include the year at all. If you type **10/17**, for example, FileMaker Pro fills in the current year for you.

Time fields

Like Date fields, a Time field can hold one time (up to eight characters in length), and it is indexed as a single string (if indexing is turned on for the field). You can enter times as hours (5); hours and minutes (5:12); or hours, minutes, and seconds (5:12:43). When you enter data in a Time field, you have to separate the parts of the time with colons (see Figure 5-3). Leading zeros are optional (both 5:07 and 5:7 are acceptable, for example). You can also append AM or PM to the end of a time string. You can set a display format for a Time field by using the Format ➪ Time command (see "Setting Field Formatting" in Chapter 6).

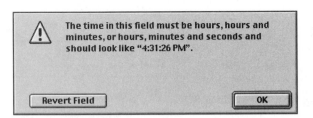

Figure 5-3: This message shows the correct way to enter a time. You can click Revert Field to restore the previous contents of the current Time field.

Container fields

A Container field can store one of three types of material: a picture, a QuickTime movie or audio clip, or a sound.

In the Windows version of FileMaker Pro 5, a Container field can also store OLE (Object Linking and Embedding) objects.

You can play movies and sounds from within a database by double-clicking the Container field in which the data is stored. You can also play QuickTime movies and audio by clicking the play button in the QuickTime control bar, as shown at the top of Figure 5-4. You can copy pictures and QuickTime movies and paste them into the field, or you can add them by choosing a command from the Insert menu. (See Chapter 16 for instructions.) You can copy and paste sound clips into a Container field, or you can record them directly into the field if you have the necessary hardware. The bottom image in Figure 5-4 shows a Container field that contains a sound.

Information in a Container field is not indexed, so you cannot perform a find operation based on the contents of the field. Of course, this limitation makes sense because the information in the field isn't labeled in any way — there's nothing for which to search. If you want to search for a particular picture, sound, or movie, create a separate Text field to store a title or set of keywords that describe the picture, sound, or movie, and then base your find request on the contents of the Text field.

QuickTime movie

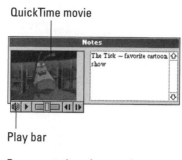

Figure 5-4: A QuickTime movie (top) and a sound (bottom) in a Container field

Play bar

Representation of a sound

Inserting OLE objects into Container fields

If you use Windows, you can insert an OLE object into a Container field in one of two ways. You can embed the object in the field, or you can link the object to the field. *Embedding* objects results in a "portable" database; that is, when you give a copy of the database to someone, the person gets all the actual objects. However, if the objects are large, the database file can become huge. *Linking* an object simply stores a "pointer" to where the object is stored on your hard drive or network. Linking saves space in the database file, but it makes it difficult to transfer the database to someone.

Another difference between linked and embedded objects is that linked objects can be set to update automatically whenever the original object is modified. (Browse the relevant record and choose Edit ⇨ Objects ⇨ Links to set update options.) Embedded objects, on the other hand, are static. Even if the original object changes, the embedded object remains the same.

You'll quickly discover that there are *many* types of OLE objects, such as Adobe Acrobat documents, ClarisWorks equations, Paint Shop Pro images, and WordPad documents. FileMaker Pro 5 enables you to insert OLE objects from a file or create them from scratch (as long as you have the program that is required to do so).

To insert an OLE object into a Container field, follow these steps:

1. In Browse mode, click to select a Container field.

2. Choose Insert ⇨ Object (or right-click the field and choose Insert Object from the pop-up menu that appears).

The Insert Object dialog box appears (refer to the top half of the figure shown below).

Continued

Continued

3. To create a new OLE object, click the Create New radio button, and select an object type. Type from the scrolling list. If you want to display an icon in the field rather than the actual object, click the Display As Icon check box. Click OK.

The creator program opens (assuming that you have the program). Design the object or document.

— or —

To insert an existing object into the field, click the Create from File radio button (refer to the bottom half of the figure shown below). To insert a link to the object's file rather than embed the object, click the Link button. Select the file to insert by typing its path or by clicking the Browse button. If you want to display an icon in the field rather than the actual object, click the Display As Icon check box. Click OK.

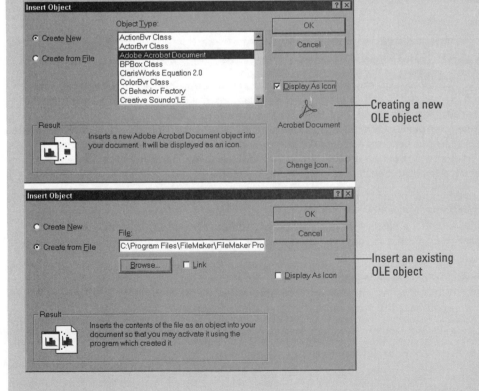

Creating a new OLE object

Insert an existing OLE object

You can view or modify the original OLE object by double-clicking the Container field that holds the object (or by right-clicking the field and choosing the Edit or Open command from the pop-up menu that appears). Windows launches the application in which the object was created (if it's available), enabling you to view or edit the object. When you are done, you can close the creator application and update the FileMaker Pro record.

Calculation fields

Calculation fields perform numeric, text, date, or time calculations within each record. A calculation can include constants, any of FileMaker Pro's built-in functions, and references to other fields, as well as any combination of these items. The capability to perform calculations elevates a database from a nicely arranged stack of note cards to a powerful information source. For example, you can use any word processing program to type an invoice. But an invoice database that has Calculation fields can automatically total the purchases, compute the sales tax, and show you the number of days a payment is overdue, for example.

You specify the formula for a Calculation field in the Specify Calculation dialog box, which appears automatically when you select Calculation as the field type. You need to specify the result type for each Calculation field. A result can be text, a number, a date, a time, or a container. Table 5-3 gives examples of the types of calculations you can perform.

Table 5-3
Examples of Calculations

Formula	Result Type	Explanation
SalesTotal * .08	Number	Multiply the value in the SalesTotal field by 0.08 to compute the salesperson's commission.
First & " " & Last	Text	Concatenate each person's first and last name to show the full name. (First and Last are separated by a space.)
EndTime - StartTime	Time	Compute the amount of time spent on a particular task.
DueDate - Today	Number	Subtract today's date (Today) from the due date to determine the number of days that remain.
If (State="CA", Picture 1, Picture 2)	Container	If the state is California, display the image stored in the Picture 1 field; otherwise, use the image stored in the Picture 2 field.

By default, the results of Calculation field formulas are automatically stored on disk as part of the database. For calculations that change frequently, you can turn off the storage setting for the field—thereby instructing FileMaker Pro to calculate the formulas only as needed. For example, if a project management database has a field that computes the number of days until each project is due, you may want to turn off automatic storage for the field (because the field will have to be recalculated whenever you open the database).

To avoid erroneous results, FileMaker Pro will not let you modify the contents of a Calculation field. To emphasize this fact, Calculation fields are automatically skipped when you tab from field to field. However, if you want to copy the contents of a Calculation field, you can click the field and then choose Edit ➪ Copy (or press ⌘+C/Ctrl+C).

You cannot edit the results in a Calculation field, but you can auto-enter a calculation in any Text, Number, Date, Time, or Container field. Unlike a result in a Calculation field, auto-entered calculations can be edited. Whenever you create a new record, the auto-enter calculation is used to create a default value for the field. You might, for example, want to use today's date plus one day as a default entry in a Homework Due Date field. See "Setting Field Options," later in this chapter, for details.

Chapter 14 presents the details of creating formulas for Calculation fields, as well as descriptions of FileMaker Pro's built-in functions. Additional instructions for defining a Calculation field can be found in the section "Defining Calculation, Summary, and Global fields," later in this chapter.

Tip   You might be wondering how a Container could be the result type for a Calculation. As an example, in an address database, you could display a small state map that corresponds to the state each person lives in. To do this, store the map images in 50 Global fields (one per state). Then use a Case function to specify the match between state abbreviations and the global field in which each image can be found, as in:

```
Case (State = "AZ", MapAZ, State = "AK", MapAK)
```

Global fields

A Global field is used to hold the same value for all records in a database (a state sales tax percentage, for example). It can also be used to store script results temporarily. Each Global field is stored only once for the entire database. If placed in a layout, a Global field shows the same value in every record.

After defining a field as Global, the Options for Global Field "*field name*" dialog box appears (as shown in Figure 5-5). At a minimum, you must select a data type for the field by choosing Text, Number, Date, Time, or Container from the "Data type" pop-up menu. You can also make it a repeating field by clicking the Repeating field check box and entering a number for the maximum repetitions that the field will require. Additional instructions for defining a Global field can be found in the section "Defining Calculation, Summary, and Global fields," later in this chapter.

Figure 5-5: Setting options for a Global field

Summary fields

Instead of performing calculations within each record as Calculation fields do, Summary fields perform calculations *across* records. For example, in a database that tracks customer purchases, you could define a Summary field named Grand Total to total all the purchases by all customers.

A Summary field is based on the contents of a single Number, Date, Time, or Calculation field, and it summarizes the records you are currently browsing. When all records are visible, the Grand Total field provides the total of all purchases by all customers. If, on the other hand, you issue a Find request to restrict the visible records to only customers from Boston, the Grand Total field shows total purchases by Boston customers rather than by the entire database.

You can place Summary fields in any layout part: header, body, footer, and so on. If you place a Summary field in a subsummary part and sort the database by a particular field, you can generate group statistics, such as computing the average rainfall for cities in country A, country B, and so on. (Chapter 6 discusses the subsummary and other layout parts.)

FileMaker Pro automatically recalculates Summary fields whenever necessary. When you change the contents of a field on which a summary is based or when the set of browsed records changes, the summary figure is recalculated.

Functions for Summary fields include Total, Average, Count, Minimum, Maximum, Standard deviation, and Fraction of total. Defining Summary fields is discussed in the next section.

As it does with Calculation fields, FileMaker Pro prevents you from tabbing into a Summary field. However, you can click a Summary field and copy its contents. Summary fields are not indexed, nor can you base a Find on the contents of a Summary field.

Defining Calculation, Summary, and Global fields

You normally define field types by simply naming them, selecting a field type, and clicking Create. The definition procedure is slightly different for Calculation, Summary, and Global fields, however, as described in the step-by-step instructions in this section.

Follow these steps to define a Calculation field:

1. In the Define Fields dialog box, type a name for the new field (up to 60 characters) in the Field Name box.

2. In the Type section of the dialog box, click the Calculation radio button (or press ⌘+L/Alt+C).

3. Click Create.

   The Specify Calculation dialog box appears, as shown in Figure 5-6.

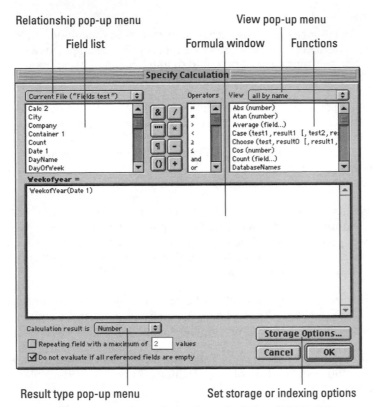

Figure 5-6: Create a formula for the Calculation field in this dialog box.

4. Enter the formula for the field in the scrolling text box in the center of the dialog box.

You can select field names, special symbols, operators, and functions by clicking the appropriate items in the upper part of the dialog box. You can also type directly into the Formula windows.

To make it easier to find the appropriate function in the list on the right side of the dialog box, you can set a different viewing preference by clicking the View pop-up menu, as shown in Figure 5-7.

By default, FileMaker lists the fields from the current file. If you've defined relationships for this file and want to base a calculation on a field in a related database, choose the name of the relationship from the pop-up menu in the upper-left corner of the dialog box. All fields from the related file are then displayed. (You can also create relationships by choosing Define Relationships from the same pop-up menu.)

Figure 5-7: The View pop-up menu

5. Choose a result type for the formula.

   You must choose a result type for every formula. Choose Text, Number, Date, Time, or Container from the "Calculation result is" pop-up menu.

6. By default, the check box labeled "Do not evaluate if all referenced fields are empty " is checked. If you want the calculation to always be performed — even if all of the referenced fields are blank — click the box to remove the check mark.

Note

The point of this option is to make sure that every displayed calculation shows a nonzero value. If you choose "Do not evaluate if all referenced fields are empty," FileMaker Pro will only perform the calculation if at least one referenced field contains an entry. However, this also means that if *some* of the referenced fields are empty, FileMaker Pro will still perform the calculation, resulting — in many cases — in a misleading and potentially incorrect computation. (It's too bad there isn't an option to keep the calculation from being performed if *any* of the referenced fields are blank.)

7. *Optional*: If you want the field to be a repeating field, click the check box labeled "Repeating field with a maximum of" and type a number for the maximum number of repeats you want the field to have.

   See "Repeating fields," later in this chapter, for more information.

8. *Optional*: To set indexing or storage options for the results of the calculation, click Storage Options.

9. Click OK.

   FileMaker Pro evaluates the formula and reports any errors it detects. When the formula is correct, it returns you to the Define Fields dialog box.

10. You can define additional fields by repeating steps 1–9, or you can click Done to dismiss the dialog box.

Cross-Reference

The process of creating Calculation fields is explained in greater detail in Chapter 14, where definitions and examples for each of the built-in functions are also provided.

Follow these steps to define a Summary field:

1. In the Define Fields dialog box, type a name for the new field (up to 60 characters) in the Field Name box.

2. In the Type section of the dialog box, click the Summary radio button (or press ⌘+S/Alt+S).

3. Click Create.

   The Options for Summary Field "*field name*" dialog box appears, as shown in Figure 5-8.

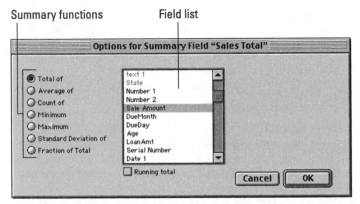

Figure 5-8: Select a summary function in this Options dialog box.

4. Choose a summary function by clicking a radio button.

   See the next section for a description of the summary functions and their options.

5. From the scrolling field list, select a field on which to base the summary.

6. *Optional*: At the bottom of the dialog box, many of the summary functions provide an option you can select by clicking the check box and, if required, choosing a field from the new list that appears (see Figure 5-9 and Table 5-4). The particular option displayed depends on the summary function chosen.

7. Click OK to accept the definition or Cancel to ignore the settings you have selected.

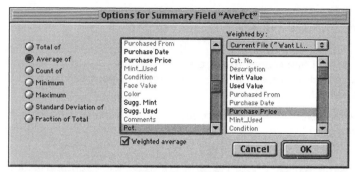

Figure 5-9: If you choose a weighted average summary function, for example, you must also choose a field that contains the weighting information.

Understanding summary functions

Table 5-4 lists the available summary functions and their options.

Table 5-4
Summary Functions and Options

Summary Function	Option
Total	Running total
Average	Weighted by field name
Count	Running count
Minimum	None
Maximum	None
Standard deviation	By population
Fraction of total	Subtotaled (when sorted by field x)

The following descriptions of the summary functions and their options can help you select the most appropriate function for any Summary field:

✦ *Total/Running total*: The Total function totals a selected field across all records that are being browsed.

Example: In a household expense database, you can create a Total Summary field that shows total expenses for the entire database. You can place the

Total Summary field in a subsummary part and then sort by Expense Category to calculate separate totals for each type of expense.

Select the "Running total" option if you prefer to see a cumulative total for the field as you flip from one record to another. To calculate subtotals for groups of records, place this Summary field in a subsummary part and then sort by the appropriate field.

✦ *Average/Weighted average*: The Average function calculates a simple numeric average of a selected field for the records being browsed. Place this Summary field in a subsummary part if you want to calculate group averages.

Example: If bowling scores of 112, 142, and 175 were being summarized, the average displayed would be 143—the sum of the scores (429) divided by the number of scores (3).

If you check the Weighted average option, the statistic is weighted by another field of your choice (instead of being calculated as a simple average).

Example: In my Want List database on the *FileMaker Pro 5 Bible* CD-ROM, one Calculation field displays the percentage of the catalog value at which each stamp was purchased. If you were to use the Average summary function to compute the average percentage, the result would have little meaning because—from a monetary standpoint—purchases for hundreds of dollars would be treated the same as purchases for pennies. Weighting the average by the purchase price, on the other hand, gives greater importance to the more expensive purchases.

✦ *Count/Running count*: Placed in any part other than a subsummary, the Count function shows the number of records that contain any value in the selected field across the records that are currently being browsed. This function is considerably more useful when placed in a subsummary part, however, where it shows how many qualifying records are in each group (after being sorted by the appropriate field).

Example: To determine how many records have an entry in an Address field, place a Count Summary field in any layout part other than a subsummary. The Count Summary field then shows the number of records from which you can create usable mailing labels. If you create a Count Summary field based on a field that is always filled in, place it in a subsummary part, and then sort by the appropriate field, you can get an accurate count of the number of members in each subgroup.

The Running count function is also more informative when placed in a subsummary part, where it shows the cumulative number of records in each group (after being sorted by the appropriate field). When you place a Running count Summary field in another layout part, it simply matches the record numbers—as in 1, 2, 3, 4, and so on.

✦ *Minimum*: When placed in any part other than a subsummary, the Minimum function shows the smallest value for the chosen field across all records being browsed. When you place it in a subsummary part, Minimum shows the smallest value for the chosen field for each group of records being browsed.

Example: In a software inventory database, a Minimum Summary field can show you the cheapest program in the lot. If you perform a Find based on a particular software category, the field displays the least expensive program of that type. Placed in a subsummary part and then sorted by software category, the Summary field shows the least expensive program for each type of software, on a category-by-category basis.

✦ *Maximum*: When placed in any part other than a subsummary, the Maximum function shows the largest value for the chosen field across all records being browsed. When placed in a subsummary part, Maximum shows the largest value for the chosen field for each group of records being browsed.

Example: In a software inventory database, a Maximum Summary field can show you the most expensive program in the lot. If you perform a Find based on a particular software category, the field displays the most expensive program of that type. Placed in a subsummary part and then sorted by software category, the Summary field shows the most expensive program for each type of software, on a category-by-category basis.

✦ *Standard deviation/by population*: This function computes a statistic called a standard deviation for the chosen field across all records being browsed. The "Standard deviation" function shows how widely the values summarized vary from one another.

If you check "by population," the formula used to compute the standard deviation is a population — rather than a sample — statistic.

Example: You can use a "Standard deviation" function in a student database to see how much the students' grades vary. Place the same field in a subsummary part and then sort by age, grade level, or teacher name, for example, to get the same information separately for each group.

✦ Fraction of total/Subtotaled: When placed in any part other than a subsummary, this function shows the portion of the total for a field that can be accounted for by each record. When placed in a subsummary part, the function shows the portion of the total for a field that can be accounted for by each group rather than by each record. If you check the Subtotaled option and sort the database by the selected field, the Fraction of total figures are fractions of each group rather than of all visible records; that is, the Fraction of total figures within each group will add up to 1.0 (or 100 percent).

Example: In a household expense database, place this field in any layout part other than a subsummary to determine the fraction of total expenses that each transaction accounted for. Place the same field in a subsummary part and then sort by Expense Category to see the fraction of the category that can be attributed to each expense item.

More help with Summary functions

If you're having trouble making sense of Summary fields, how the different functions work, and when you should use them, the quickest path to understanding is to create a test file and try out the various options. You can use Summary Field Tester, a sample file on the *FileMaker Pro 5 Bible CD-ROM* in the FileMaker Pro Bible folder.

Summary File Tester contains only six records and consists of the following four fields:

✦ City : A Text field

✦ Age : A Number field

✦ Salary [in thousands] : A Number field

✦ Summary : A Summary field

The same Summary field appears in two places in the database — in the body and in a trailing subsummary part (at the bottom of each record). That way, you can determine the correct layout part in which to place your own Summary fields. The following figure shows a record from Summary Field Tester in which City is the Sort field.

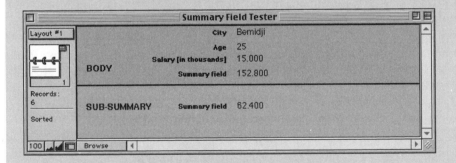

To see how each summary function and option works, open Summary Field Tester and do the following:

1. Choose File ➪ Define Fields (or press Shift+⌘+D/Shift+Ctrl+D).

The Define Fields dialog box appears (as previously shown in Figure 5-1).

2. Select Summary field in the list of defined fields and click Options.

The Options for Summary Field "Summary field" dialog box appears.

3. Choose a different option from the summary function list or alter the status of the check box, if one appears at the bottom of the dialog box.

Make sure that "Salary [in thousands]" remains selected.

4. To dismiss the dialog boxes, click OK and then Done.

If the status area shows that the records are Unsorted or Semi-Sorted, choose the Records ➪ Sort command (or press ⌘+S/Ctrl+S). The Sort dialog box should show that the database will be sorted by City, which is the Sort field set for the subsummary part. Click Sort or press Return or Enter to execute the sort.

Repeat these steps as often as you like, testing a different summary function or option each time. After each definition has been completed, flip through the records to see what the Summary field is summarizing, both in the body and in the subsummary part.

Changing the field order

A field list appears in the Define Fields dialog box. By default, the fields are listed in the order in which you created them. Working with this list can often be easier if you establish a new order for the fields. To change the order, choose one of the following options in the "View by" pop-up menu in the upper-right corner of the Define Fields dialog box (see the accompanying figure):

✦ *creation order:* Fields are listed in the order in which they were defined.

✦ *field name:* Fields names are sorted alphabetically.

✦ *field type:* Fields are grouped by type (Text, Number, and so on). Within each type, the fields are presented in alphabetical order.

✦ *custom order:* You can manually drag fields to new positions in the list. This process is described in the following step-by-step instructions.

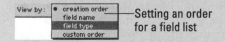
Setting an order
for a field list

You can also sort the Define Fields dialog box by field name or field type by clicking the Field Name or Type column heading. To change between ascending and descending sorts on a Windows PC, click the same heading again. To change between ascending and descending sorts on a Mac, click the tiny triangle above the side scroll bar. (An ascending sort is indicated by an upward-pointing triangle. A descending sort is indicated by a downward-pointing triangle.)

Follow these steps to create a custom field order:

1. In the Define Fields dialog box, move the pointer over the name of the field you want to move. When the pointer moves over the symbol that precedes a field name, it changes to a two-headed arrow.

Continued

(continued)

2. With the two-headed arrow visible, click to select the field, drag the field up or down in the list, and release the mouse button when the field is where you want it to be.

   As soon as you move a single field, the View by pop-up menu automatically shows that the custom order setting has been selected.

3. Repeat these steps for any additional fields you want to move. Note that even if you switch between several different field order views, when you next choose the custom order view, all the manual modifications you made to the field order are restored.

Setting Field Options

The types of options you can set for a field vary with the field type. Options for Global, Calculation, and Summary fields have already been discussed. The options you can set for Text, Number, Date, Time, and Container fields are as follows:

✦ *Data auto-entry*: When you create a new record or modify an existing record, you can have FileMaker Pro automatically enter the creation or modification date or time for each record, the name of the user who created or last modified the record, a serial number, the value from the previous record, a calculated value, a value looked up in another database, or a default value into the chosen field.

✦ *Data validation*: Depending on the options you choose, you can require that a field must not be left blank, the value entered must be unique, the value already exists in another record, the data must be of a particular type, the data is restricted to entries in a value list, the entered value match the result of a calculation, or entries fall within a specific range.

✦ *Look up data values in another file*: When data is entered into a lookup field, FileMaker Pro automatically looks up information in another file and then copies selected data into one or more fields in the current file. Using this option in an inventory database, you could enter a part number into a field. FileMaker Pro would then open the second database file that you specified; find the part name, description, color, and unit cost for the part; and then transfer a copy of that information to the first database. Because of the complexity of this concept, lookups — along with relationships — are discussed separately in Chapter 19.

✦ *Repeating values*: This option enables you to enter multiple values in what normally would be considered a single field. In an invoice database, for example, you can define Quantity, Item Description, Price, and Extended Price fields as repeating, each of which can receive up to ten values. (You determine the maximum number of values.)

✦ *Present a list of values from which to choose*: This option causes a user-defined list of values to appear when someone tabs into or clicks the field. For example, you can create a value list that lists all the payment methods (such as specific credit cards, checks, cash, and traveler's checks) that your store accepts as payment for services and goods. In addition to speeding data entry for the field, this option helps ensure that each entry is spelled correctly and worded consistently. Depending on the formatting option selected (choose Format ➪ Field Format), value lists can be presented as pop-up lists, pop-up menus, check boxes, or radio buttons.

The following steps describe the general procedure for setting options for a Text, Number, Date, Time, or Container field. Instructions for setting specific kinds of field options are explained in the sections that follow.

1. Choose File ➪ Define Fields (or press Shift+⌘+D/Shift+Ctrl+D).

   The Define Fields dialog box appears (as previously shown in Figure 5-1).

2. In the field list, select the Text, Number, Date, Time, or Container field for which you want to set options.

   — or —

   If the field doesn't already exist, define the field by following the instructions presented earlier in this chapter.

3. Click Options (or double-click the name of the field in the field list).

   The Options for Field "*field name*" dialog box appears, as shown in Figure 5-10. Note that the title of the Options dialog box changes to reflect the name of the selected field. The specific options you can set vary with the data type of the field. For example, the only data validation options available for a Container field are "Not empty" and "Validated by calculation."

4. Click a tab at the top of the dialog box and set options as desired.

5. If you want to set other options for the same field, click another tab at the top of the dialog box.

6. Click OK to return to the Define Fields dialog box.

7. To set options for additional fields, repeat Steps 2 through 6. Click Done when you are through setting options.

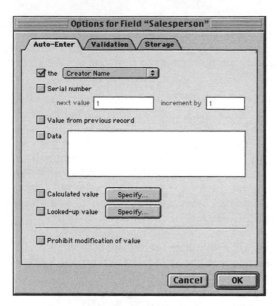

Figure 5-10: The Options dialog box displays auto-entry, validation, or storage options, depending on the tab you click.

Problems with setting field options after the fact

You should note that setting entry options for a field after the field contains data for some records can cause problems. FileMaker Pro does not warn you about existing records that, as a result of the new field options, now contain invalid data. You have to find and correct them yourself. The following table lists Find request symbols that are helpful in performing this task.

Find Symbol or Operation	Action
=	Find empty fields
!	Find duplicate values
value1 . . . value2, and click the Omit check box	Find values that fall outside of the range

You can also search for invalid dates and times by entering a question mark (?) in a Date or Time field. However, because the contents of these fields are automatically restricted to valid dates and times, this type of search is necessary only if you have converted a field to a Date or Time field from some other field type (a Text field, for example).

Auto-Enter options

When you click the Auto-Enter tab at the top of the Options dialog box, you are shown options that provide for the automatic entry of several types of information in a field when you create or modify a record. The various auto-entry options are discussed in the following sections.

Creation Date, Creation Time, Modification Date, Modification Time, Creator Name, and Modifier Name

Click the first check box on the Auto-Enter screen, and choose an option from the pop-up menu to the right (see Figure 5-11). The specific choices you can select in the pop-up menu depend on the type of field for which you are setting options. If you are defining options for a Date field, for example, you can select only the Creation Date and Modification Date options. Other options are *grayed-out* (dimmed).

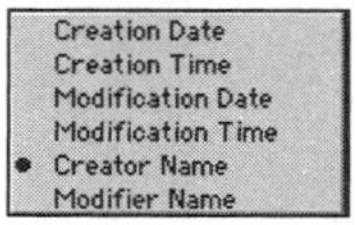

Figure 5-11: Setting an automatic date, time, creator name, or modifier name for a field

Selecting Creation Date or Creation Time causes FileMaker Pro to enter the appropriate data automatically as each new record is created. When these options are set, you can tell how old each record is, so you have an idea of whether the record is up-to-date.

Note   If you define a Creation Date, Creation Time, or Creator Name field after the database already contains records, the field will be blank in existing records. You may want to enter this information manually for the old records.

Modification Date and Modification Time show the date or time that *any* field in a record was last changed. FileMaker Pro automatically enters the appropriate value when you finish editing a record (by pressing Enter or switching to a different record). If you're interested only in how current a record is — as opposed to when it was originally created — use the Modification Date option. When a new record is created, the Modification Date is the same as the Creation Date.

Creator Name and Modifier Name show the name of the person who created or last modified the record, respectively. These field options are extremely helpful in a multiuser environment to determine who is creating or modifying records.

Selecting a creator/modifier name (Windows)

To select the name that FileMaker Pro will use for the Creator Name and the Modifier Name, choose Edit ➪ Preferences ➪ Application. Click the General tab at the top of the Application Preferences dialog box. Enter the name you want to use in the User name box. Then click OK.

Selecting a creator/modifier name (Mac)

To select the name FileMaker Pro will use for the Creator Name and the Modifier Name, choose Edit ⇨ Preferences ⇨ Application. Click the General tab at the top of the Application Preferences dialog box. Near the middle of the dialog box is a section labeled "User Name," as shown in Figure 5-12. You have two options:

✦ Click the System radio button to use the Owner Name that you set up in the File Sharing (OS 8) or Sharing Setup (System 7) control panel. See below for instructions on how to use these control panels to set the Owner Name.

✦ Click the Custom radio button and type a name.

After choosing the option you want to use, click OK.

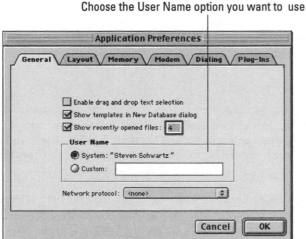

Choose the User Name option you want to use

Figure 5-12: Setting application preferences for User Name

If you choose to use the Owner Name from information entered in the Sharing Setup or File Sharing control panel, you can set or change the Owner Name by following these steps:

1. Open the Sharing Setup or File Sharing control panel by selecting it from the Control Panels section of the Apple menu.

2. In the Network Identity section of the control panel window, type your name or other identifying information in the Owner Name box, as shown in Figure 5-13.

3. Close the control panel window to save your changes.

Enter your name here

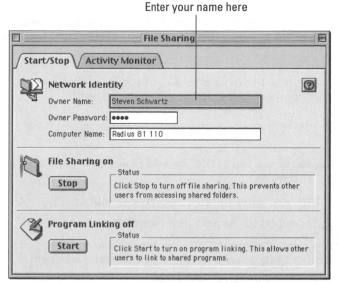

Figure 5-13: Identifying yourself in the File Sharing control panel (OS 8)

Performing automatic time calculations

If you do time billing, you can use the Creation Time and Modification Time auto-entry options to track time spent on the phone with a client or time spent working on a project. For example, you can create a simple database like Time Billing (shown in the figure below). When a client calls, you immediately create a new record. The Creation Date (Date), Creation Time (Start Time), and Modification Time (End Time) values are automatically filled in for you. The Total Time is calculated by subtracting the Start Time from the End Time. When you create the record, the result of this formula is initially zero (0).

Enter the client's name. When the call ends, press Enter (Macintosh) or Enter or Ctrl+Enter (Windows) to complete the record. The Modification Time is then automatically updated to reflect the current time, and the Total Time is recalculated to show the actual length of the call.

Serial number

You use this option to enter a number that automatically increments by a set amount for each new record. For example, you can use this option to create invoice and statement numbers.

The following steps describe how to create a field in which FileMaker Pro automatically enters serial numbers using the increment you specify:

1. In the Define Fields dialog box, select or create a Number or Text field, and click Options.

2. Click the Auto-Enter tab at the top of the Options dialog box, and then click the "Serial number" check box.

3. In the "next value" text box, enter the starting serial number.

   This number will be assigned to the next new record you create.

4. In the "increment by" text box, enter a number for the amount that you want each new serial number to increase over the previous serial number.

5. Click OK to return to the Define Fields dialog box.

Tip   You should note that a serial number does not have to be a simple number. For example, you can set the starting serial number ("next value") as A27B-1000. In a mixed text-and-number entry such as this one, FileMaker increments the serial number by using the right-most number string and ignoring other numbers in the string. In this example, assuming that the increment was 1, the next serial numbers would be A27B-1001, A27B-1002, and so on.

Value from previous record

If you enter data in presorted batches, this auto-entry option can be very helpful. Selecting the "Value from previous record" option instructs FileMaker Pro to use the most recently entered data for this field as the default entry in each new record.

For example, suppose you need to enter warranty card information. If the cards are already sorted by city and you set the "Value from previous record" auto-entry option for the City field, you'll only have to type the city name when you encounter a different city in the card stack.

Data

The Data option enables you to specify a piece of data that you want to have automatically entered for every record. As such, this option creates a default entry for a field. For example, in an employee database, employees often live in the same city. By using the name of this city as auto-entry data, you can save some typing. If you create a record for an employee who lives in a different city, you can edit the name of the city in that record.

Calculated value

This auto-entry option enables you to use a formula to set a default value for any Text, Number, Date, Time, or Container field. Unlike formulas entered for Calculation fields, auto-entered formulas *can* be edited.

When you click the check box labeled "Calculated value" (or click its Specify button), a modified version of the Specify Calculation dialog box appears (as shown previously in Figure 5-6). Create the formula and click OK. Note that the result type of the formula must match the data type of the field. Optionally, you can remove the check mark from the "Do not evaluate…" check box at the bottom of the dialog box.

Looked-up value

This auto-entry option instructs FileMaker Pro to look up information in a second database (or in the same database) and copy it into the current database. When you create several databases that share some common element, such as address information, you can minimize the amount of duplicate data entry that is required by instructing each of these databases to extract the address information from a separate Address database, for example.

A *lookup* is a one-way function in which data is copied into the current file (much like importing field information but affecting only the current record rather than the entire database).

To learn more about lookups and the relational capabilities of FileMaker Pro 5, see Chapter 18.

Follow these steps to create a lookup field:

1. Choose File ➪ Define Fields (or press Shift+⌘+D/Shift+Ctrl+D).

   The Define Fields dialog box appears.

2. Select or create a field to receive the copied (lookup) data, and then click Options or double-click the field name in the field list.

   The field type of the selected field must be Text, Number, Date, Time, or Container.

3. Click the Auto-Enter tab at the top of the Options dialog box, and then click the check box labeled "Looked-up value."

   The Lookup for Field "*field name*" dialog box appears, as shown in Figure 5-14.

4. From the pop-up menu, choose the relationship from which you intend to extract the lookup information.

   If a relationship that links the two files doesn't already exist, choose Define Relationships from the pop-up menu and then define the relationship.

Relationship definition

Field to be copied from   Selected relationship

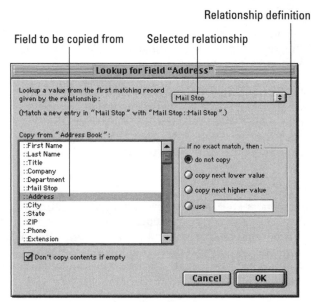

Figure 5-14: The Lookup for Field dialog box

Note   Whenever a lookup is executed, the second file is automatically opened for you as part of the lookup process.

5. In the "Copy from" section of the dialog box, select the name of the field whose data you want to copy into the current database.

When the lookup is executed, the contents of the selected field are copied into the current field, whose name is shown in the title of the dialog box. (In the example shown in Figure 5-14, Address will be copied from the lookup file into the Address field in the current file.)

Note   After a lookup executes, you can still edit the contents of the field into which data was copied. If you ever edit the trigger field (the field in the current database that initiates the lookup), however, the lookup will be executed anew. If a match is found, your edited data will be replaced.

Choose the match field wisely

When selecting a field on which to base a lookup, you'll be much happier if you choose one whose contents will be unique for each record, such as a customer ID number, Social Security number, or telephone number. If, for example, you use the Last Name field, you will run into problems if you have several people who share the same last name. No matter how many times you execute the lookup, you'll find only the first person who has that particular last name.

6. In the section of the dialog box labeled "If no exact match, then," select from the following options to tell FileMaker Pro what to do if it doesn't find an exact match:

   - *do not copy*: This option is the default (and, in most cases, is what you want). Rather than copying erroneous data, the field is left as is.

   - *copy next lower value*: Choose this option to copy the next lower value (numerically or alphabetically, depending on the type of data stored in the field).

   - *copy next higher value*: Choose this option to copy the next higher value (numerically or alphabetically, depending on the type of data stored in the field).

   - *use*: This option enables you to specify a string that will be used if no match is found. For example, if the lookup is based on a phone number and the search comes up empty, you can have Not a current customer inserted into the field.

7. *Optional*: Click the check box labeled "Don't copy contents if empty" to avoid copying information from a blank field into the current file.

   In the example shown in Figure 5-14, if you had hand-entered an address in the Address field, selecting this option would prevent the address from being replaced by a blank address from the external file.

8. Click OK to accept the options you have just set, or click Cancel to ignore the new settings. Click OK again to dismiss the Options dialog box.

9. Repeat steps 2 through 8 to define additional lookup fields, as desired. Click Done when you're ready to close the Define Fields dialog box and return to the database.

Here are some other important factors to keep in mind when you are creating and using lookups:

✦ To determine whether a match has been found, FileMaker Pro compares only the first 20 characters in the match fields. It ignores word order, punctuation, and capitalization, as well as any text that is contained in a Number field.

✦ If the data in the external database changes, a lookup that you previously performed may now contain incorrect data. To correct this situation, you can instruct FileMaker Pro to perform the lookup again by tabbing into or clicking in the field that is used to trigger the lookup and choosing the Records ➪ Relookup command.

✦ You can select any FileMaker Pro file in which to do a lookup, including the current file. This technique can be extremely useful with any database that contains multiple records for the same customer, client, or subject. As an example, an invoice database can look for a customer ID among the existing records and then, if a match is found, fill in the fields of the mailing address for you.

Using lookups to fill in multiple fields

At first glance, you may not think you can trigger a lookup that will copy multiple fields to the original database. As the example in the instructions for creating a lookup field shows, when a match is located, the lookup copies the contents of only one external field into one field in the current database.

The solution is to define a lookup individually for every field you want to copy, using the same trigger field for each lookup. For example, to copy an entire address, begin by identifying a unique field, such as a Social Security number, phone number, or customer ID number field. Then create a separate lookup for each field in the address (First Name, Last Name, Address, City, State, and ZIP) using the same trigger and match fields in each lookup definition (the Social Security number, for example). When you enter the information in the trigger field during data entry, FileMaker Pro will perform all the lookups simultaneously. Although FileMaker Pro will appear to be performing only one lookup, it will, in fact, perform half a dozen of them—pulling all the data from the same record in the lookup file.

Tip   Unlike a regular lookup, which is performed for only the current record, a relookup is performed for all records being browsed. To perform a relookup for only the current record, the easiest method is to cut the data from the trigger field, paste it back into the field, and then tab to the next field. Editing the data in the trigger field automatically causes the lookup to be executed.

Data validation options

Click the Validation tab at the top of the Options dialog box to set or view data validation options. These options govern the types of information that must, may, or may not be entered in a chosen field (see Figure 5-15).

Protecting auto-entered values

To protect auto-entered values, you may want to check the "Prohibit modification of value" option in the bottom section of the Options dialog box. Setting this option prevents you and other users of the database from inadvertently altering the contents of an auto-entry field. You need to set this option for *each* field you want to protect (a serial number field, for instance).

If you later discover that you need to edit one or more of the auto-entered values for a particular field, return to this screen, remove the check mark from the "Prohibit modification of value" option, edit the field contents as necessary, and then restore the check mark.

Custom validation message   **Figure 5-15:** Validation options

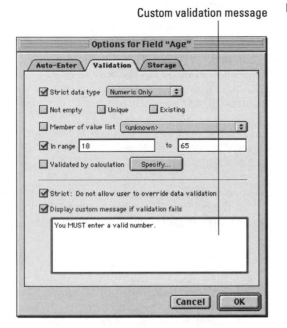

You need to keep two things in mind when you set validation options for a field. First, you can set validation options only for Text, Number, Date, Time, and Container fields. Second, even with a validation option set, unless you also set the option labeled "Strict: Do not allow user to override data validation," FileMaker Pro gives you (or any other person who may be using the database) the option of overriding the validation requirements. If you leave a required field blank, for example, you see a dialog box like the ones shown in Figure 5-16.

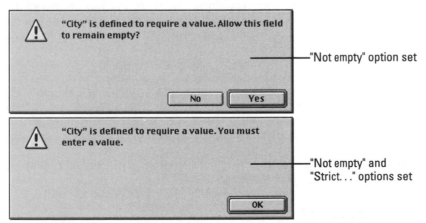

Figure 5-16: These alert boxes warn the user that a required field has not been filled in. The top alert box appears if only "Not empty" is chosen; the bottom one appears if both "Not empty" and "Strict: Do not allow..." are chosen.

The following sections describe the validation options.

The "Strict data type" option

Use this option to indicate that only a number, a date with a 4-digit year, or a time is an acceptable entry for the field. Assigning this option is the way to ensure that only numbers are entered in Number fields, for example. (A number can include a decimal separator, thousands separator, sign, and parentheses.)

As with the other data validation options, the user can still override the warning dialog box that appears when the wrong data type is entered—unless you also set the "Strict: Do not allow user to override validation" option.

In previous versions of FileMaker Pro, any legitimate date would satisfy this validation requirement. With year 2000 on the horizon, FileMaker changed this validation option to require that a complete, unambiguous year be entered in the date field, such as 4/23/2001.

The "Not empty" option

Click this check box to create a *required field* (one that must not be empty). In many databases, you will have essential fields that render a record worthless if their data is left blank. In a customer database, for example, you cannot send out bills if the Name, Address, or City field for a customer is blank. If you attempt to switch to another record without filling in a required field, FileMaker Pro displays a warning.

The "Unique" option

This option requires that every record in the database have a different value for the field. FileMaker Pro warns you if you enter a value that already exists in another record. For example, customer or record ID numbers generally must be unique.

When determining whether an entry is unique, FileMaker Pro ignores punctuation, capitalization, and word order. Thus, it considers Steve Schwartz and schwartz, steve to be identical.

The "Existing" option

Use this option to ensure that every value entered in a particular field matches a value in that field in another record. Essentially, this entry option is the opposite of the Unique option. When determining whether one entry matches another, FileMaker Pro ignores punctuation, capitalization, and word order.

The Unique and Existing value entry options are mutually exclusive. For any given field, you can set only one of these options.

The "Member of value list" option

Select this option to restrict data to the items in a value list. For example, you may have a Payment Method field that includes all allowable forms of payment in a value list (such as cash, VISA, and Discover). Linking the validation options to this value list prevents your salespeople from entering (and — presumably — accepting) other forms of payment, such as personal checks or other credit cards.

If a suitable value list hasn't already been created for the database, choose Define Value Lists from the pop-up menu and create the value list. (See "Value lists," later in this chapter, for instructions.)

Note   Value lists in FileMaker Pro 4 and higher are not treated as though they are linked to a specific field. Any value list that you define for a database can be associated with any field in the database — or with several fields, if you like. For example, you could create a single value list that contained the choices: "Yes," "No," and "Don't know," and use this value list with every Yes/No question in a survey database.

The "In range" option

Select this option to specify an allowable range for a Text, Number, Date, or Time field. Enter the lowest acceptable value in the first text box and the highest acceptable value in the second text box. Because text is handled alphabetically, you can enter the letters A and E to restrict acceptable entries to text strings that begin with the letters A, B, C, D, and E, for example.

Tip   For numeric ranges, you may want to set "Numeric only" as the "Strict data type," as well as setting the "In range" option. This ensures not only that the value will be in range, but also that it will be the proper data type — a number. In order to get precisely the type of validation you require, it is not uncommon to select two or more validation options that work in concert with each other.

The "Validated by calculation" option

To set the "Validated by calculation" option, click its check box. A slightly modified version of the Specify Calculation dialog box appears. Enter a Boolean formula (one that returns a true or false result), check or remove the check mark from the check box labeled "Validate only if field has been modified," and click OK.

Note   If necessary, any Text, Number, Date, Time, or Container field can be validated by a Boolean (true/false) formula. As an example, the formula Age ≥ 18 could be used to determine whether the entry in Age is a legitimate one (≥18) or should be flagged (<18).

The "Strict: Do not allow user to override data validation" option

When set in combination with one or more other validation options, this option prevents you or other users from overriding validation warnings (previously shown in Figure 5-16). Thus, if you have specified "Strict data type: Numeric only" for a field and have also chosen the "Strict: Do not allow..." option, users will be prevented from entering anything other than a legitimate number in the field — rather than simply being warned of their error and allowed to override the warning.

The "Display custom message if validation fails" option

This option enables you to present a dialog box with a custom message if the validation fails (refer to Figure 5-15). (This option can only be checked if you have also chosen at least one other validation option.) Rather than rely on FileMaker Pro's standard validation error messages, you may prefer to display a detailed explanation of what you expect from the user.

Repeating fields

Although most fields are intended to handle only one piece of data, you may sometimes want to use a single field to collect multiple bits of information. This type of field is called a *repeating field*.

In older, less capable database programs, you often had to handle repeating fields the hard way. For example, to create an eight-line invoice, you had to define eight separate Quantity, Item Description, Unit Price, and Extended Price fields. Calculations based on these fields were cumbersome to create, as in ExtPrice1 + ExtPrice2 + ExtPrice3... . The FileMaker Pro invoice shown in Figure 5-17, on the other hand, was created by defining a single field for each of the following: I.D. Number, Category, Title/Description, and Price. Then the Repeating field option was assigned to each field. You can set any type of field to repeat, except for Summary fields.

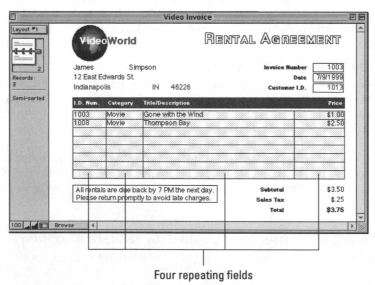

Four repeating fields

Figure 5-17: Repeating fields in an invoice database

Follow these steps to set the Repeating field option for a field:

1. Choose File ➪ Define Fields (or press Shift+⌘+D/Shift+Ctrl+D).

   The Define Fields dialog box appears.

2. From the scrolling field list, select the Text, Number, Date, Time, Container, Calculation, or Global field that you want to define as a repeating field.

3. Click Options.

   An Options for *field type* "*field name*" or Specify Calculation dialog box appears. (The specific dialog box that appears depends on the type of field you chose in step 2.)

4. Locate the Repeating field option.

   If this is a Text, Number, Date, Time, or Container field, click the Storage tab at the top of the dialog box. If this is a Calculation or Global field, the option is at the bottom of the displayed dialog box.

5. Click the "Repeating field with a maximum of *x* repetitions" check box and enter the maximum number of repetitions.

   This number is simply the upper limit of repetitions that the field can store. You set the number of repetitions that are *displayed*, on the other hand, by switching to Layout mode and choosing the Format ➪ Field Format command (described in "Formatting Repeating Fields" in Chapter 6).

6. Click OK to return to the Define Fields dialog box.

7. Repeat steps 2 through 6 for additional fields you want to define as repeating fields.

8. Click Done to record the changes and return to the database.

Note   Several built-in functions are provided expressly for the purpose of performing computations on repeating fields. You are already familiar with many of them, such as Total and Average, from the discussion in this chapter concerning summary functions (see "Defining Calculation, Summary, and Global fields"). For calculation purposes, you can use the Extend built-in function to treat a nonrepeating field as though it repeats.

You need to be aware of some important facts about repeating fields:

✦ Regardless of the number of repetitions that are visible on the current layout, FileMaker Pro uses *all* repetitions in calculations.

   For example, if you alter an invoice layout that was originally designed to show eight line items so that it now shows only five, FileMaker Pro will also consider the other three line items when it calculates the Sum function. If you really want to keep the additional entries from being included in the calculation, you must delete them.

✦ When you conduct a sort that is based on a repeating field, only the first repetition is used in the sort.

✦ Other database programs will not correctly handle a FileMaker Pro export that contains repeating fields.

Value lists

If you have been impressed by the pop-up menus used in many programs, you will be equally impressed to learn that FileMaker Pro enables you to create the same type of choice lists for your database fields.

You determine the values that appear in the list. Depending on the format you select for a field, the list can be presented as a pop-up menu, a pop-up list, a set of check boxes, or a set of radio buttons. When you tab into a field that is formatted as a pop-up list, the list automatically appears. When you click a field that is formatted as a pop-up list or a pop-up menu, the list or menu appears. Even if a field has an associated value list, you can still type different information in the field (unless you also set the "Member of value list" validation option, as described previously in this chapter).

There are two ways to create a value list for a field: The first — setting "Member of value list" as a validation option — was described earlier in this chapter. Although that approach enables you to create a value list, it does not associate it with the field. The second method of creating value lists has the advantage of both defining the list and associating it with the field. To use this method, follow these steps:

1. Switch to Layout mode (⌘+L/Ctrl+L), select the field to which you want to attach a value list, and choose Format ➪ Field Format.

   The Field Format dialog box appears, as shown in Figure 5-18.
2. To define the format for the field as a value list, click the second radio button in the Style section of the dialog box (as shown in the figure) and choose a format from the first pop-up menu (Pop-up list, Pop-up menu, Check boxes, or Radio buttons).

3. If an appropriate value list has already been defined, choose it from the pop-up menu to the right. Go to step 7.

   — or —

   To define a new value list that you intend to use with this field, choose Define Value Lists from the pop-up menu to the right.

   The Define Value Lists dialog box appears, as shown in Figure 5-19.

Choose this option to display a value list in a field

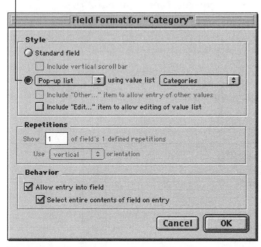

Figure 5-18: Choose a format for the value list in the Field Format dialog box.

Defined value lists

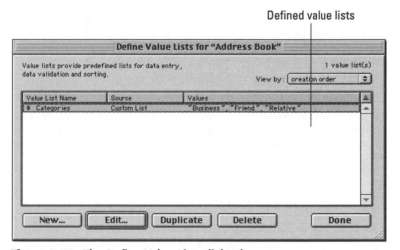

Figure 5-19: The Define Value Lists dialog box

4. Click the New button.

The Edit Value List dialog box appears (see Figure 5-20).

5. Type a name for the new list in the Value List Name text box.

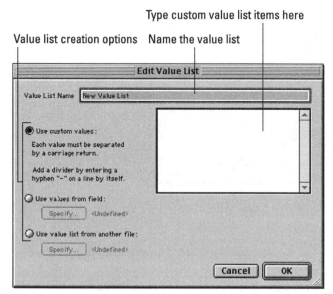

Type custom value list items here

Value list creation options   Name the value list

Figure 5-20: Create or edit value lists in the Edit Value List dialog box.

6. Click the "Use custom values" radio button (if it is not already selected), and type entries for the value list, pressing Return/Enter after each entry except the last one. (If you press Return/Enter after the final entry, you will end up with an extra blank line at the end of the list.)

— or —

Click the radio button labeled "Use values from a field."

The Specify Fields for Value List dialog box appears, as shown in Figure 5-21.

Choosing this option instructs FileMaker Pro to create a value list based on the contents of another field — in this or another database. By default, FileMaker Pro lists all fields in the current file. Choose a field on which to base the value list from the scrolling list on the left. (Optionally, you can select a second field from the list on the right.)

To view fields in a different file, click the Specify File button. To restrict field choices to those in a related file, click the "Only related values" radio button and choose a relationship from the drop-down list.

Select a field

Click to specify fields from a different file

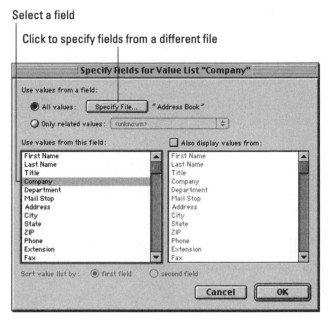

Figure 5-21: The Specify Fields for Value List dialog box

— or —

If you want to use a value list that you've created in a *different* database, click the radio button labeled "Use value list from another file." The Specify External Value List dialog box appears (see Figure 5-22). Click the Specify File button, and then select the database from the file dialog box that appears. Choose a value list from the pop-up menu and then click OK.

Choose a file

Choose a value list from the other database

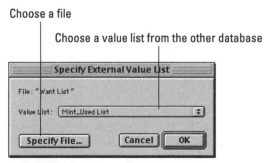

Figure 5-22: The Specify External Value List dialog box

7. Click OK when you are finished creating the value list.

8. Click Done to record the changes.

Tip   You can type a hyphen (-) on any line to create a dashed line in pop-up menus and pop-up lists or an empty space between radio buttons and check boxes.

FileMaker Pro doesn't have an option to alphabetize the values in a value list. If you want them in a particular order, you have to type them in that order. However, you can change their order by cutting and pasting.

Tip   Displaying the values from a second field in the database can help you determine which of the values in a value list to choose. For example, if you have a list of customer IDs (constructed from the Customer ID field), the corresponding customer's name would be helpful in deciding which ID to pick from the list. However, FileMaker Pro only enables you to display one other field from the database. So you could, for example, display the customer's last name — but not the last name, first name, and city together — which is what you'd probably need to figure out if the chosen ID belonged to the customer you wanted. The solution is to create a Calculation field that combines all the fields you want to see, and use that Calculation field as the additional field in the value list.

When formatting a field with a value list (in the Field Format dialog box), if you select any format other than Pop-up list, you can click the check box for "Include 'Other...' item to allow entry of other values." This adds a choice marked "Other..." to the pop-up menu, check boxes, or radio buttons. An "Other..." choice facilitates the entry of data that is not present in the field's value list.

If you've created a custom value list by typing its entries and selected either of the pop-up formats (list or menu), you can click the check box for "Include 'Edit...' item to allow editing of value list." This adds an "Edit..." choice to the pop-up list or pop-up menu. Any choices you add during editing will be available whenever you use the value list in the future.

New Feature   FileMaker Pro 5 also lets you create another type of value list in which only a subset of data in a given field (based on a relationship) is used as the values. To define such a value list, chose File ⇨ Define Value Lists, click the New button, choose the option to "Use values from field," select "Only related values," choose a relationship, and then select the related field.

Selecting multiple radio buttons or check boxes

If you format a value list field as a set of check boxes (in the Field Format dialog box), you can select multiple options when you enter data in the field. And although radio button options are mutually exclusive in most programs (you can normally choose only one radio button from a set), you can select multiple radio buttons by holding down the Shift key as you click each one.

Indexing and storage options

In FileMaker Pro 4 or higher, you decide whether any or all fields are indexed, as well as whether calculation results are stored with the data file or are calculated only as needed.

Indexing improves the speed with which find and sort operations are performed. Any fields that you regularly sort the database by or use as the basis of Find commands are good candidates for indexing.

Indexing options can be set for any Text, Number, Date, Time, or Calculation field. (Indexing cannot be set for Container, Global, or Summary fields.) In addition to indexing options, you can also set storage options for Calculation fields.

To set indexing options for a Text, Number, Date, or Time field, follow these steps:

1. Choose File ➪ Define Fields (or press Shift+⌘+D/Shift+Ctrl+D).

   The Define Fields dialog box appears (refer to Figure 5-1).

2. Select the field and click Options. (If the field has not yet been created, create it first and then click Options.)

   An Options dialog box appears.

3. Click the Storage tab at the top of the Options dialog box (see Figure 5-23).

Indexing options

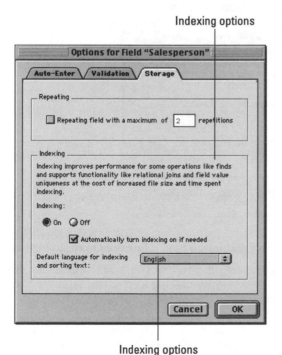

Indexing options

Figure 5-23: Storage options for a Text, Number, Date, or Time field

4. To turn on indexing for a field, click the On radio button.

If you decide to leave indexing off, you can still enable FileMaker Pro to index the field if it becomes necessary by placing a check mark in the box marked "Automatically turn indexing on if needed."

5. *Optional (for Text fields only)*: You can select a particular language to be used in determining sort and index orders from the pop-up menu at the bottom of the dialog box.

6. Click OK to return to the Define Fields dialog box.

To set indexing or storage options for a Calculation field, follow these steps:

1. Choose File ➪ Define Fields (or press Shift+⌘+D/Shift+Ctrl+D).

The Define Fields dialog box appears (refer to Figure 5-1).

2. Select the Calculation field for which you'd like to set storage options and click Options.

The Specify Calculation dialog box appears (refer to Figure 5-6).

3. Click the Storage Options button.

The Storage Options for Field "*field name*" dialog box appears, as shown in Figure 5-24.

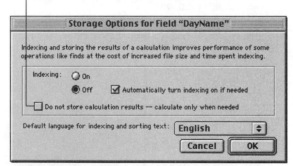

Figure 5-24: The Storage Options dialog box for a Calculation field

4. To turn indexing on for a Calculation field, click the On radio button.

If you decide to leave indexing off, you can still enable FileMaker Pro to index the field if it becomes necessary by placing a check mark in the box marked "Automatically turn indexing on if needed."

5. To instruct FileMaker Pro to store calculated results for this field as part of the file's data, leave the "Do not store calculation results..." check box unchecked (this is the default setting). If you want to reduce storage requirements for the database (at the expense of increased time to perform recalculations), place a check mark in the check box.

6. *Optional (for Calculation fields that return a Text result only)*: You can select a particular language to be used in determining sort and index orders from the pop-up menu at the bottom of the dialog box.

7. Click OK to return to the Define Fields dialog box.

Tip If a Calculation field needs to be frequently recalculated (such as one that computes the number of days until a project is due), check the "Do not store calculation results..." box.

Modifying Field Definitions, Names, and Options

A few capabilities of the Define Fields dialog box still remain unexplored (and unexplained). As previously mentioned, FileMaker Pro enables you to add, change, or delete field definitions and options whenever you like. You can also rename fields. And to speed the process of creating fields, FileMaker Pro enables you to duplicate existing field definitions. The step-by-step instructions in the following sections explain how to perform these tasks.

Changing field names

Unless you give a lot of thought to field names when you design databases, you'll find that some of the names can stand a little improvement. Feel free to change them to names that are more appropriate. FileMaker Pro automatically corrects field labels, sort instructions, and other references to the field (in formulas and scripts, for example).

Follow these steps to rename a field:

1. Choose File ➪ Define Fields (or press Shift+⌘+D/Shift+Ctrl+D).

   The Define Fields dialog box appears (refer to Figure 5-1).

2. Select the field you want to rename.

   The field name appears in the Field Name text box.

3. Type a new name in the Field Name box and click Save.

FileMaker Pro renames the field and automatically adjusts any references to the field in Calculation field formulas, Summary fields, and scripts to reflect the new field name. If, when you originally created the field, you accepted and placed the default label for the field in a layout, FileMaker Pro also changes the label to match the new field name. Field labels that you've manually edited or typed from scratch, on the other hand, are unaffected.

4. To rename additional fields, repeat Steps 2 and 3. Click Done when you are through renaming fields.

Actually, field names aren't all that important. As long as the field name clearly indicates to you what each field is meant to hold, it doesn't matter whether you name a field Sale Amount, Sale, Amount, Amt, or S1. However, because each field's default label is identical to the field name, you may well want to edit the label to something more descriptive. Remember, a field label is just a piece of static text and can be changed as you like, whenever you like.

Tip   Developers sometimes use a simple naming trick that enables them to quickly tell the field type of any field. Begin every field name with a lower-case letter that indicates its type. You could use t for Text, n for Number, d for Date, i for Time, o for Container, c for Calculation, s for Summary, and g for Global, for example. Follow the letter with the remainder of the file name, such as nSales or tAddress.

Deleting a field and its data

The more you work with a particular database, the more familiar you become with the data it was designed to collect. If you decide that you no longer need a particular field (or perhaps that you should never have created it in the first place), follow these steps to delete the field and the data it contains:

1. Choose File ➪ Define Fields (or press Shift+⌘+D/Shift+Ctrl+D).

   The Define Fields dialog box appears (refer to Figure 5-1).

2. Select the field you want to delete and then click the Delete button.

   One of three dialog boxes appears:

   • The normal dialog box simply asks whether you're sure you want to delete the field and its contents (see Figure 5-25, top).

   • If the field is referenced in a Calculation or Summary field, another dialog box appears (see Figure 5-25, middle), explaining that you cannot delete the field. To delete such a field, you first have to edit the appropriate Calculation and Summary field formulas and options so they no longer reference the field that you want to delete.

   • If the field defines a current relationship with another database, it cannot be deleted (see Figure 5-25, bottom) unless you first delete the relationship definition.

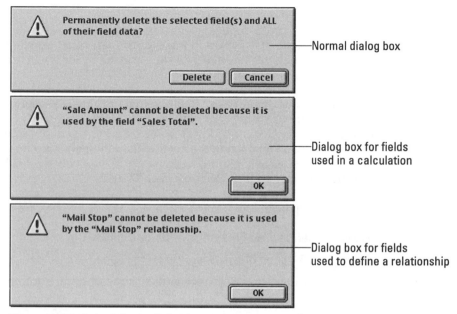

Figure 5-25: Any of these dialog boxes may appear when you attempt to delete a field.

3. Click the Delete button in the dialog box to delete the field, or click Cancel if you change your mind.

4. To delete additional fields, repeat steps 2 and 3. Click Done when you are ready to return to the database.

 Caution As the topmost dialog box in Figure 5-25 warns, deleting a field eliminates the field and all data for the field. You cannot undo a field deletion. If there is a chance that you may later need the data, you should make a backup copy of the file by choosing the File ➪ Save a Copy As command before deleting the field.

An alternative to deleting fields

Instead of deleting a field, you can simply remove it from all layouts. Removing a field in this manner does not delete it. All data previously entered in the field remains intact. To be able to see the data, all you have to do is put the field back onto a layout. This approach makes the database larger than necessary, however, because it is still storing information you may never use again. If you're certain that you no longer need to continue collecting the data for a field, the best approach is to make a backup copy of the original database, delete the field in the current version of the file, and then move on.

Duplicating fields

To save time, you may want to duplicate some existing fields — particularly fields that have complex options that you don't want to re-create. After you duplicate a field, editing and renaming the new field is a simple matter. (See the instructions for renaming a field, earlier in this section.)

For example, in an invoice or statement database, you might have a series of repeating fields that you use to record each line item (such as Quantity, Description, Unit Cost, and Extended Cost). You would use separate Calculation fields to compute the total for each of the cost fields. After defining a formula for the first Calculation field as Sum (Unit Cost), you could duplicate the field definition and, in the formula, simply replace Unit Cost with Extended Cost.

To duplicate an existing field, follow these steps:

1. Choose File ➪ Define Fields (or press Shift+⌘+D/Shift+Ctrl+D).

   The Define Fields dialog box appears (refer to Figure 5-1).

2. Select the field you want to duplicate and click the Duplicate button.

   FileMaker Pro creates an exact duplicate of the field and appends the word *Copy* to its name. For example, if the field to be duplicated is named Comments, the duplicate is named Comments Copy. Additional duplicates of the same field are named Comments Copy2, Comments Copy3, and so on.

3. To rename the duplicate field, select the field in the scrolling field list, type a new name in the Field Name box, and click Save.

4. *Optional*: To change any of the options for the duplicate field, select the field and click Options.

5. To duplicate additional fields, repeat Steps 2 through 4. Click Done when you are through duplicating fields.

Setting options for existing fields

You don't have to set field options when you first define a field. You can set or change them later as the need arises. (However, if you enter data before setting options for a field, you may need to go back and correct some of the earlier entries for the field.)

Follow these steps to set options for fields you have already defined:

1. Choose File ➪ Define Fields (or press Shift+⌘+D/Shift+Ctrl+D).

   The Define Fields dialog box appears (refer to Figure 5-1).

2. Select the field for which you want to set options and click the Options button. (You can also double-click any field in the list to move directly to the Options dialog box for that field.)

3. In the dialog box that appears, set options as described in "Setting Field Options," earlier in this chapter.

4. To accept the new options, click OK. To ignore the options you have selected, click Cancel.

5. To set options for other fields, repeat steps 2 through 4. Click Done when you are through setting options.

Changing a field definition

The following steps describe how to change a field definition:

1. Choose File ➪ Define Fields (or press Shift+⌘+D/Shift+Ctrl+D).

   The Define Fields dialog box appears (refer to Figure 5-1).

2. Select the field you want to change.

3. To change the field's type, select a new type and click Save.

   If changing to the new field type involves any potential problems, FileMaker Pro presents a dialog box, such as the ones shown in Figure 5-26. (The particular dialog box displayed is related to the type of change you want to make.) This warning box contains information that you should consider before proceeding with the conversion. If such a warning box appears, you may want to use the Save a Copy As command to make a backup copy of the database before you proceed.

Replacing one field with another

Has this ever happened to you? After carefully selecting, placing, resizing, and setting attributes for fields on a layout, you discover that one of the fields wasn't the right one. Rather than deleting the errant field and then adding the correct one, you can use the following trick to redefine the field as a different field:

1. Switch to Layout mode, and double-click the field you want to redefine.

   The Specify Field dialog box appears, listing the fields for this database, as well as the fields available in any defined relationships.

2. Select a replacement field and click OK.

Redefining the field preserves its original placement on the layout, as well as its dimensions and formatting attributes.

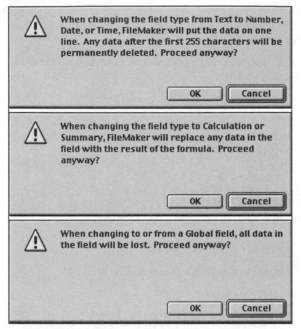

Figure 5-26: Warning boxes like these may appear when you are changing a field's type.

— or —

If you are changing the field to a Summary or Calculation field, click the Options button, select a summary function or create the formula for the Calculation field, and click OK to accept the changes or Cancel to revert to the original settings. Similarly, if you are switching to a Global field, choose a data type for the field (in the Options dialog box that appears) and then click OK.

4. To change additional field definitions, repeat Steps 2 and 3 for each field. When you are through, click Done to leave the Define Fields dialog box.

Changing or deleting options for a field

To change or delete options for a field, follow these steps:

1. Choose File ➪ Define Fields (or press Shift+⌘+D/Shift+Ctrl+D).

   The Define Fields dialog box appears (refer to Figure 5-1).

2. Select the field whose options you want to change, and then click the Options button or double-click the field name in the field list.

   An Options dialog box appears, appropriate to the data type of the selected field.

3. Change the options you want to modify and then click OK to return to the Define Fields dialog box.

   The means of changing options is always obvious. You can add or remove options by clicking check boxes, clicking buttons, making selections from pop-up menus, and using normal editing techniques (to change formulas, for example).

4. To change options for other fields, repeat steps 2 and 3. Click Done when you are through changing field options.

Summary

✦ FileMaker Pro 5 includes eight field types: Text, Number, Date, Time, Container, Calculation, Summary, and Global. The type you choose for a field determines the kinds of information you can enter in the field.

✦ The Global field type enables you to record a single value that is used for every record in the database. A Global field value is stored only once in the entire database (rather than storing a separate copy of the value for every record).

✦ You can set auto-entry options for a field to instruct FileMaker Pro to enter a value for a field whenever you create a new record or, in some cases, when you edit a record. By selecting the option labeled "Prohibit modification of value," you can protect the auto-entered data from inadvertent (or deliberate) modification.

✦ Any value list that has been defined for a database can be associated with many fields in the database. You can also associate value lists from *other* databases with fields in the current database.

✦ You can store multiple values in a single field using repeating values. This is very handy for fields that normally have multiple values, such as line items on an invoice. Using calculation functions, you can easily sum the multiple values that appear in a repeating value field.

✦ Data validation options help ensure that only acceptable values are entered for a field. By selecting the option labeled "Strict: Do not allow user to override data validation," you can protect the integrity of the field's data and ensure that only the right kind of information is accepted.

✦ You can alter the fields for a database at any time by changing their names, definitions, or options. You can also add new fields or delete existing fields.

✦   ✦   ✦

Layouts

I f you've used other database programs — particularly
any of the simpler ones, such as AppleWorks or Microsoft
Works — before you switched to FileMaker Pro, you may have
become used to creating every field that was needed for a
database and then dutifully arranging the fields all on a single
form. That, however, is not the way FileMaker Pro works.

Although you can create dozens or even hundred of fields
for a FileMaker Pro database, it's unlikely you'd ever want or
need to display them all on the same form. To print envelopes
or mailing labels, for example, you only need the name and
address fields for each client in your database. You don't need
information about the products that each client has ordered. If
you're preparing a summary of recent sales figures, client
address information is of little importance. Even though all this
data may be collected in the same database, you only need to
display it where it's appropriate. The FileMaker Pro feature that
makes this possible is called the layout.

A *layout* is a particular arrangement of all, or a subset of, the
fields that have been defined for a database. You choose the
fields that are included in each layout — as many or as few
fields as you like. You can arrange the fields in each layout to
address a specific need (such as printing labels, entering data,
or presenting a report). You can add layout parts (for example,
a header and footer to make some information repeat on every
page). And you can include special items to help identify your
layouts or make them more attractive (such as titles, 3D field
borders, graphics, and buttons). You can have as many layouts
for a given database as you like — one to suit every need. (For
a quick introduction to creating and modifying layouts,
see Chapter 4.)

Layout Basics

A FileMaker Pro layout is composed of layout *parts* (the
sections of the layout, such as the body, header, and footer),

fields (in which data is entered and displayed), and static objects (such as graphics, titles, and field labels).

When you design a new database and define its initial set of fields, FileMaker Pro automatically creates a default layout for you named Layout #1. The default layout is a one-column arrangement of all fields that have been defined for the database in the order they were defined. To create the initial layout for a new database, follow these steps:

1. To create a new database when launching FileMaker Pro, choose "Create a new empty file" from the New Database dialog box that automatically appears.

   — or —

   If FileMaker Pro is already running, choose File ➪ New Database. Then choose "Create a new empty file" from the New Database dialog box that appears.

   The Define Fields dialog box appears.

2. Define the initial fields for the database by following the procedures outlined in Chapter 5. Click Done when you are finished.

   A default layout entitled Layout #1 appears (see Figure 6-1), ready for you to begin entering data. The first record is automatically created for you, and the database switches to Browse mode.

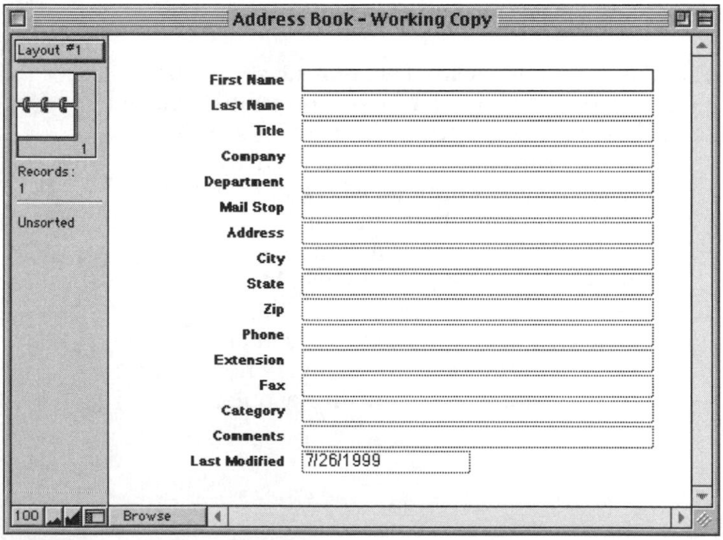

Figure 6-1: A new default layout

For many data collection purposes, the initial layout is all you'll need. If you have other layout requirements, such as printing labels or generating reports, you will want to create additional layouts that present the data in other ways.

Note

You aren't locked into using Layout #1 as is — or at all, for that matter. You may find that it can serve as the basis for a custom layout. Simply change the formatting and arrangement of its fields. On the other hand, if you don't even want to use it as the starting point for a custom layout, you can delete it — provided you have created at least one more layout. (The Layouts ⇨ Delete Layout command is not available if you have only a single layout in your database.) Modifying and deleting layouts are explained later in this chapter.

You create new layouts and modify existing ones in Layout mode — one of FileMaker Pro's four operational modes. (The others are Browse, Find, and Preview.) Switch to Layout mode, and you'll see a screen similar to Figure 6-2.

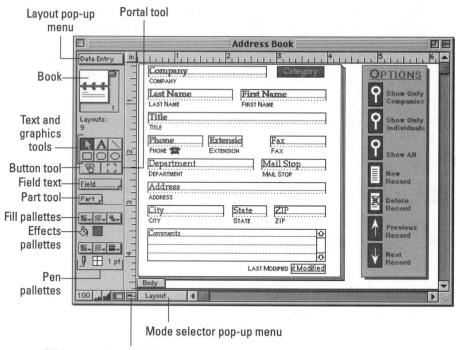

Figure 6-2: The Address Book database in Layout mode

At the upper-left corner of the Address Book database is a pop-up menu, listing the layouts that have been defined. This menu enables you to choose an existing layout to edit. Below the pop-up menu is a book icon that also gives you access to available layouts. You click the book to switch between the available layouts. Beneath the book icon are the tools that you use to add or modify elements on a layout. You use the field and part icons to create new layout parts and to add fields to the layout.

You'll find important Layout mode features and options in the View, Insert, Format, Layouts, and Arrange menus. These menus contain commands that enable you to add items to layouts, arrange items, and specify how to display the items.

To switch to Layout mode, follow these steps:

1. Launch FileMaker Pro, if it isn't already running.

2. Open the database in which you want to add, modify, or view layouts.

3. Choose View ➪ Layout Mode, press ⌘+L/Ctrl+L, or choose Layout from the mode selector pop-up menu at the bottom of the document window (as shown previously in Figure 6-2).

4. From the layout pop-up menu in the upper-left corner of the window, choose the layout you want to view.

   — or —

   Click the book icon to page through the available layouts until the one you want appears.

Creating New Layouts

As previously explained, after you define fields for a new database, FileMaker Pro creates your first layout for you. You can immediately use this layout for data entry and browsing if you like.

To view data in other ways, you must create more layouts. FileMaker Pro 5 includes six predefined layout styles you can use as starting points. The supported layout styles are described in Table 6-1.

Table 6-1	
FileMaker Pro Predefined Layout Styles	
Layout Name	**Purpose**
Standard form	Shows one record per screen, with all fields displayed in the order in which they were defined; similar to the default layout used when creating a new database.
Columnar list/report	Fields are displayed left to right in columns. Fields that don't fit the current page width are either wrapped to the next line or extend beyond the page break (depending on the option you choose).
Table View	Data is displayed in spreadsheet fashion, in which each record is a row and each column is a field.
Labels	Fields are formatted for use with mailing and other types of labels.
Envelope	Fields are formatted for use with business (#10) envelopes.
Blank layout	Used to create custom layouts.

FileMaker Pro 4/4.1 offered seven layout types. The changes to layout types in FileMaker Pro 5 are as follows:

✦ Columnar report and Extended columnar have been combined into the new Columnar list/report.

✦ The Single page form layout has been removed.

✦ Table View is a new report style — in support of FileMaker Pro 5's new data view. (The three data views are View as Form, View as List, and View as Table.) As in previous versions of FileMaker Pro, you can freely switch among the data views — regardless of the layout style you choose.

New Feature To make it simpler to create layouts, FileMaker Pro 5 steps you through the process with its New Layout/Report assistant. All new layouts (beyond the initial one) are created using this assistant.

Follow these steps to create a new layout based on any of the predefined layout styles:

1. Determine what sort of layout you want and the fields you need to display.

2. Switch to Layout mode by choosing View ➪ Layout Mode (or by pressing ⌘+L/Ctrl+L).

3. Choose Layouts ⇨ New Layout/Report (or press ⌘+N/Ctrl+N).

The New Layout/Report assistant appears, as shown in Figure 6-3.

Include the layout in the layout pop-op menu

Name the layout   Layout sample

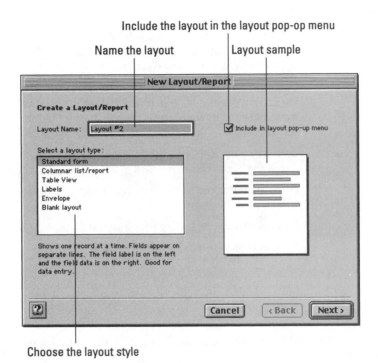

Choose the layout style

Figure 6-3: The New Layout/Report assistant

4. Type a name for the new layout.

5. Choose the layout style you want to use by clicking the appropriate radio button in the "Select a layout type" section. (Do not choose the Blank layout type unless you want to create a layout from scratch, as described later in this chapter.)

6. Determine whether the layout should appear in the layouts pop-up menu by leaving or removing the check mark in the "Include in layout pop-up menu" check box.

7. Click Next (or, if you chose the Blank layout, click Finish).

If you choose the Blank layout, FileMaker Pro creates your layout immediately. The Blank layout contains no fields (it consists of just a blank page).

Additional steps follow, depending on the layout style chosen.

Hiding layouts

Being able to display or hide the name of a layout in the layout pop-up menu can be very useful. For example, if you are distributing a shareware template, you may want to reveal certain layouts only after users have paid the shareware fee. Similarly, there may be some layouts that you never want users to see. Hiding a layout by removing the check mark from the "Include in layout pop-up menu" check box (previously shown in Figure 6-3) makes it impossible to see the layout in Browse mode. (It can still be seen in Layout mode, however.) Hiding the layout in this manner and setting appropriate access options can make it completely invisible to the user.

You can also hide any layout to which you don't want users to be able to switch. In a database that is entirely script controlled, for example, you might list only the layout for the main menu or the data entry screen, and leave the task of switching to other layouts to scripts attached to navigation buttons. This way, you can keep users from inadvertently messing up the database by directly selecting layouts that should normally be reached only as part of a script.

The remaining layout types use a limited set of the fields. Additional dialog boxes appear in which you select fields and set options, as explained in the following layout-specific sections.

Note

Regardless of the type of layout you choose, the sections included in the layout (called *layout parts*) are restricted to a body (where the fields are generally placed) and, in some cases, a header and a footer. You'll learn all about adding, removing, and modifying layout parts in "Understanding layout parts," later in this chapter.

Standard form layouts

A Standard form layout is similar to the one FileMaker Pro creates as the default data entry layout (Layout #1) when you define fields for a new database. That is, the fields are automatically placed on the layout, one above the other, and each has a label that matches the field name. There are two differences from the initial default layout. First, rather than using all the fields in your database, only the ones you choose are added to the layout. Second, you can choose a layout *theme* (a set of coordinated colors applied to the layout parts and fields).

In a Standard form layout, one record is displayed at a time. In addition to the body area, where the fields are displayed, the layout includes blank header and footer parts. To create a Standard form layout, follow these steps:

1. Switch to Layout mode by choosing View ➪ Layout Mode (or by pressing ⌘+L/Ctrl+L).

2. Choose Layouts ➪ New Layout/Report (or press ⌘+N/Ctrl+N).

   The New Layout/Report assistant appears, as previously shown in Figure 6-3.

3. Type a name for the new layout.

4. Choose "Standard form."

5. Determine whether the layout should appear in the layouts menu by leaving or removing the check mark in the "Include in layout pop-up menu" check box. Click Next to continue.

The Specify Fields screen appears (see Figure 6-4).

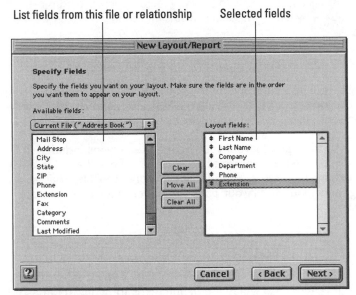

Figure 6-4: Select fields to be placed on the layout.

6. Select fields to be included in the layout by clicking the Move or Move All button. (The wording of the button changes, depending on whether you have one field selected (Move) or no fields selected (Move All). Click Next to continue.

Note   The order in which fields appear in the Layout fields list is the order in which they will appear in the layout. You can rearrange the fields by dragging them up or down in the Layout fields list.

7. Choose a layout theme. Note that every theme is available in two versions: one for on-screen viewing and another for printed output. Click Finish.

The new layout is created and displayed (see Figure 6-5). Make any necessary changes (changing fonts and adding static text to the header and footer parts, for example).

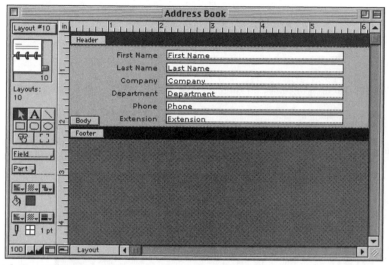

Figure 6-5: A Standard form layout for the Address Book database

Columnar list/report layouts

Previous versions of FileMaker Pro offered two kinds of columnar layouts (in which fields are displayed in columns across the page). In the Columnar report layout, FileMaker Pro attempted to fit all fields on a single line but wrapped excess fields to the next line. In the Extended columnar layout, FileMaker Pro displayed all fields on a single line, no matter how wide the line was. In FileMaker Pro 5, you can create either type of report layout by choosing "Columnar list/report." In addition, a columnar list/report can now be a simple columnar arrangement of fields or a complex report (with record groups, subtotals, and totals.)

Creating a simple columnar layout

Follow these steps to create a simple columnar layout or report:

1. Switch to Layout mode by choosing View ➪ Layout Mode (or by pressing ⌘+L/Ctrl+L).

2. Choose Layouts ➪ New Layout/Report (or press ⌘+N/Ctrl+N).

   The New Layout/Report assistant appears, as previously shown in Figure 6-3.

3. Type a name for the new layout.

4. Choose "Columnar list/report."

5. Determine whether the layout should appear in the layouts menu by leaving or removing the check mark in the "Include in layout pop-up menu" check box. Click Next to continue.

   The Choose Report Layout screen appears (see Figure 6-6).

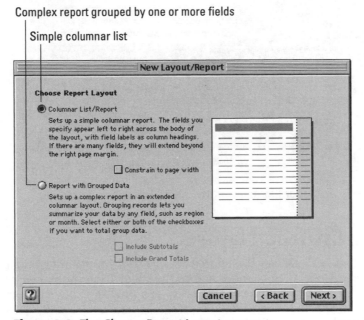

Figure 6-6: The Choose Report Layout screen

6. Choose "Columnar List/Report" to create a simple columnar report.

7. If all columns of your report are meant to fit the width of a normal page, click the check box to "Constrain to page width." (Note that if the fields do not initially fit, some will be placed in a row beneath the other fields.) This corresponds to the "Columnar report" layout in previous versions of FileMaker Pro.

   — or —

If you don't want to restrict the initial width of the layout, do not check the "Constrain to page width" check box. (Note that you can always resize fields later to fit within a normal page, if you like.) This corresponds to what was known as an "Extended columnar report" layout in previous versions of FileMaker Pro.

8. Click Next to continue.

9. In the Specify Fields screen, select the fields you want to include in the report and click Move to add them (one at a time) to the Layout fields list. Click Next to continue. Note that the order that fields appear in the Layout fields list (on the Specify Fields screen) is the order in which they will appear in the report layout. To change a field's position in the list, you can click and drag it to a new position.

Because FileMaker Pro 5 is a relational database program, you can also add related fields to layouts. To choose fields from any currently defined relationship, choose the name of the relationship from the pop-up menu located above the Available fields list. If necessary, you can also define a new relationship at this time by choosing Define Relationships from the pop-up menu. (For information about relationships, see Chapter 18.)

The Sort Records screen appears (see Figure 6-7).

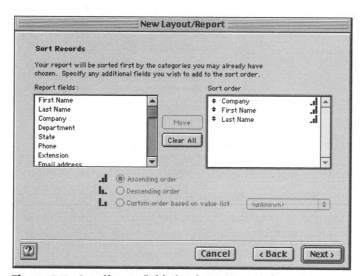

Figure 6-7: Specify sort fields for the report on the Sort Records screen.

10. If the report requires that records be arranged in a particular order, select the appropriate sort field or fields (on the Sort Records screen) and click Move to add them to the Sort order list. Click Next to continue. (For additional information on sorting records, see Chapter 10.)

Note If you don't intend to use the New Layout/Report assistant to create a script that you can use to generate the report, the choices you make for sort fields are irrelevant.

The Select a Theme screen appears (see Figure 6-8).

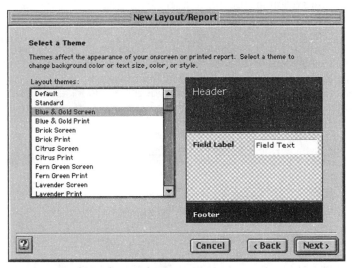

Figure 6-8: The Select a Theme screen

11. Depending on whether you want the current layout to be used for on-screen or printed reports, select a "screen" or "print" theme (based on the examples that appear in the right side of the screen). Click Next to continue.

The Header and Footer Information screen appears (see Figure 6-9).

12. Select header and footer elements and the locations in which each element will appear. Click Next to continue.

The Create a Script for this Report screen appears.

13. If you want to automate the report-generation process, click "Create a script" and enter a name for the script (or accept the default name). Click Next to continue. (For additional information on creating and editing scripts, see Chapter 15. To learn what this specific script does, see the paragraph immediately following these steps.)

Choose header and footer elements from these pop-up menus

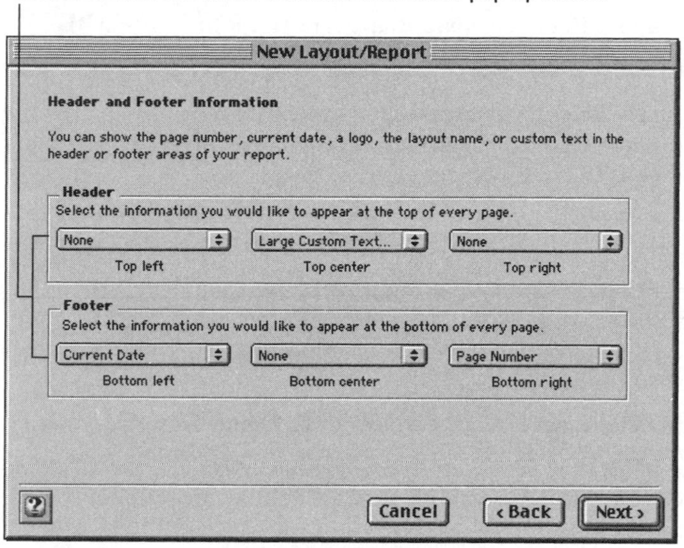

Figure 6-9: The Header and Footer Information screen

Note If you create a script, it is automatically added to the Scripts menu.

14. You can either view the report layout in Preview mode or go to Layout mode to make any necessary changes. Select an option and click Finish.

After cleaning up the layout (changing field widths and placements, for example), if you created a script in step 13 to generate the report, you'll want to examine it in ScriptMaker. You'll see that this basic script changes to the report layout, performs a sort (if specified in step 10), enters Preview mode, and pauses until you click the Continue button. Then it switches to Browse mode and displays whichever layout was active when you executed the script. You might want to modify this script so that it includes appropriate Find instructions, maximizes the screen, and prints, for example. See Chapter 15 for instructions concerning working with scripts.

Creating a complex columnar report

As mentioned earlier, you can also create more complex reports that are grouped according to some criterion, such as city, job classification, month, or the like. This is referred to as a *complex columnar report*.

Follow these steps to create a complex columnar report:

1. Switch to Layout mode by choosing Views ➪ Layout Mode (or by pressing ⌘+L/Ctrl+L).

2. Choose Layouts ➪ New Layout/Report (or press ⌘+N/Ctrl+N).

   The New Layout/Report assistant appears (refer to Figure 6-3).

3. Name the report and choose "Columnar list/report" as the layout style.

4. Determine whether the layout should appear in the layouts menu by leaving or removing the check mark in the "Include in layout pop-up menu" check box. Click Next to continue.

   The Choose Report Layout screen appears (refer to Figure 6-6).

5. Choose "Report with grouped data." If you want to compute totals for the groups, click one or both of the check boxes ("Include Subtotals" and "Include Grand Totals"). If you elect to include subtotals or grand totals, you will specify the summary fields to use to generate these totals in steps 9 and 10. Click Next to continue.

   The Specify Fields screen appears (refer to Figure 6-4).

6. Select the fields that you want to include in the report, and click Move to add them to the Layout fields list. Be sure to include any fields by which the database will be sorted. (Note that you cannot select the summary fields until step 9.) Click Next to continue.

   The order that fields appear in the Layout fields list is the order in which they will appear in the report layout. To change a field's position in the list, simply click and drag it to a new position.

Note   Because FileMaker Pro 5 is a relational database program, you can also add related fields to layouts. To choose fields from any currently defined relationship, choose the name of the relationship from the pop-up menu located above the Available fields list in the Specify Fields screen. If necessary, you can also define a new relationship at this time by choosing Define Relationships from the pop-up menu. (For information about relationships, see Chapter 18.)

   The Organize Records by Category screen appears.

7. Select one or more grouping fields and move them to the Report categories: list, as shown in Figure 6-10. Click Next to continue.

Tip   Be sure to examine the sample report layout on the right side of the screen. It shows how the selected field(s) will be grouped. As in the other parts of the New Layout/Report assistant, you can change the order of the grouping fields by dragging them up or down.

   The Sort Records screen appears (refer to Figure 6-7).

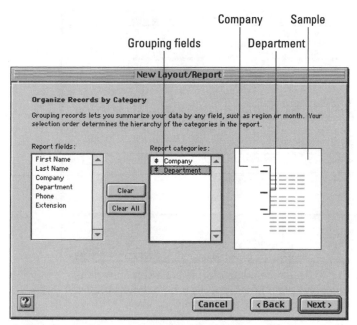

Figure 6-10: Choose grouping fields. (In this example, records are grouped by Company and — within each Company — by Department.)

8. By default, the database will be sorted by the grouping fields selected in step 6. If you want to sort by additional fields, select and move them to the Sort order list. Click Next to continue.

Note   You can neither remove nor change the order of the grouping fields. The database is always sorted by them first, in the order specified in step 6. Any additional sort fields must appear lower in the Sort order list. To change the grouping fields or their order in the list, click the Back button to return to the Organize Records by Category screen.

The Specify Subtotals screen appears (see Figure 6-11) — unless you elected not to generate subtotals in step 5.

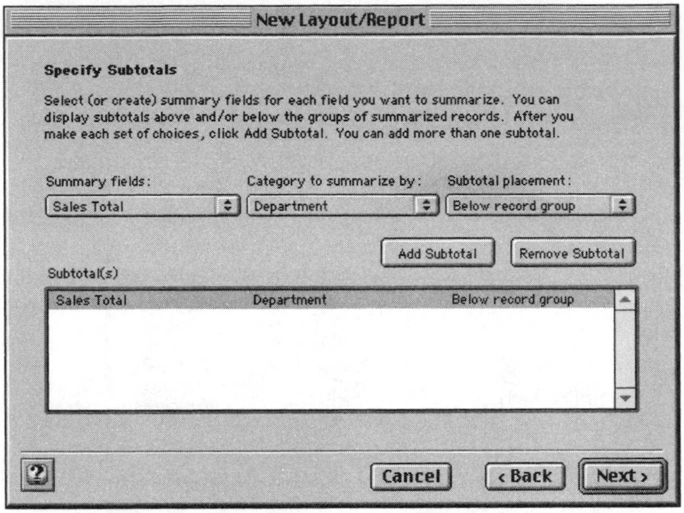

Figure 6-11: To designate a subtotal, select a summary field, choose a category (break) field, specify where the subtotal will appear, and click the Add Subtotal button.

9. Choose one or more Summary fields to use to calculate the subtotals for each record group. For each Summary field, specify the grouping field to be subtotaled and the location of the subtotal (above the break field, below it, or both above *and* below it). (If you haven't already defined the necessary Summary fields, you can do so by choosing "Create Summary field" from the first pop-up menu.) Click Next to continue.

   The Specify Grand Totals screen appears (see Figure 6-12) — unless you elected not to generate grand totals in step 5.

10. Choose one or more Summary fields to use to calculate a grand total across all records in the report, and choose a location for each grand total. (If you have not already defined the necessary Summary fields, you can do so by choosing "Create Summary field" from the first pop-up menu.) Click Next to continue.

    The Select a Theme screen appears (refer to Figure 6-8).

11. Depending on whether you intend the current layout to be used for on-screen or printed reports, select a "screen" or "print" theme (based on the examples that appear in the right side of the screen). Click Next to continue.

    The Header and Footer Information screen appears (refer to Figure 6-9).

12. Select header and footer elements and the locations in which each element will appear. Click Next to continue.

    The Create a Script for this Report screen appears.

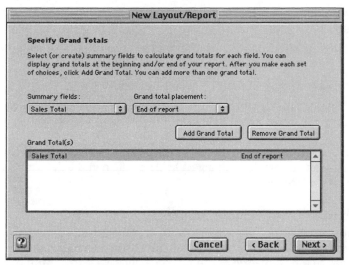

Figure 6-12: To designate a grand total, select a summary field, indicate where you want the total to appear, and click the Add Grand Total button.

13. If you want to automate the report-generation process, click "Create a script" and enter a name for the script (or accept the default name). Click Next to continue.

Note If you create a script, it is automatically added to the Scripts menu. (For information on creating and editing scripts, see Chapter 15.)

14. You can either view the report layout in Preview mode or go to Layout mode to make any necessary changes. Select an option and click Finish.

Table View layouts

A Table View layout (new in FileMaker Pro 5) displays selected fields in a spreadsheet-style table. Each row is a record and each column is a field.

To create a Table View layout, follow these steps:

1. Switch to Layout mode by choosing View ➪ Layout Mode (or by pressing ⌘+L/Ctrl+L).

2. Choose Layouts ➪ New Layout/Report (or press ⌘+N/Ctrl+N).

   The New Layout/Report assistant appears (refer to Figure 6-3).

3. Type a name for the new layout, and choose "Table View" as the layout type.

4. Determine whether the layout should appear in the layouts menu by leaving or removing the check mark in the "Include in layout pop-up menu" check box. Click Next to continue.

   The Specify Fields screen appears (refer to Figure 6-4).

5. Select the fields you want to include in the report and click Move to add them (one at a time) to the Layout fields list. Click Next to continue.

Note   The order that fields appear in the Layout fields list is the order in which they will appear in the report layout. To change a field's position in the list, simply click and drag it to a new position.

   The Select a Theme screen appears (refer to Figure 6-8).

6. Depending on whether you want the current layout to be used for on-screen or printed reports, select a "screen" or "print" theme (based on the examples that appear in the right side of the screen). Click Next to continue.

7. You can either go directly to Browse mode or switch to Layout mode to make any necessary changes. Select an option and click Finish.

If you examine a Table View layout in Layout mode, you'll note that it looks nothing like a table. In fact, the field arrangement is exactly what you'd see if you'd created a Standard form layout. The chosen fields are displayed one above the other. However, when a Table View layout is displayed in Browse mode, the View ➪ View as Table command is automatically selected—causing the layout to take on its expected spreadsheet-style appearance.

You can rearrange the fields (columns) of a Table View layout by selecting any column heading and dragging it to a new position. You can also change the width of any column. Move the pointer over the column heading's right edge until it turns into a double-headed arrow. Then click and drag to the left or right to change the column's width.

Because you are working in a table, it's not uncommon to want to rearrange the data so it's sorted by one of the fields or columns. To quickly accomplish this, Ctrl+click/right-click the column heading you want to sort by and choose a Sort command from the pop-up menu that appears (see Figure 6-13). If you prefer to sort by merely clicking a column heading in Table View, you can set this Table View property by switching to Layout mode, choosing Layouts ➪ Layout Setup, clicking the Views tab, clicking the Table View check box, clicking the Properties button, and then clicking "Sort data when selecting column."

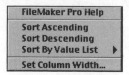

Figure 6-13: This menu appears when you Ctrl+click/right-click a column heading in a Table View.

Previewing and printing layouts in columns

If you merely want to print data in a multi-column format (similar to the column formatting in advanced word processing programs), you don't need to create a separate columnar layout. Using the Layout Setup command, you can instruct FileMaker Pro to print or preview any layout in two or more columns. The columns are visible only in Preview mode or when you print the database; Browse mode still shows the original layout.

To view the Layout Setup dialog box shown in the follownig figure, choose Layouts ⇨ Layout Setup.

Print the selected layout in multiple columns

Click the "Print in" check box to choose to display columns and then indicate how many columns you want to use by typing a number in the text box. Finally, specify how records will fill the columns by clicking the radio button that corresponds to the desired option:

✦ Across first: Fills each column across the page before proceeding to the next row. This option is good for printing labels, and it helps you conserve paper.

✦ Down first: Fills an entire column on a page and then moves to the top of the next column. This option is appropriate for phone directory listings and sheets of mailing labels (3-Up, for example).x

If you use Apple's LaserWriter 8 printer driver or Adobe's PSWriter driver, you can create a similar effect in the Page Setup or Print dialog box (which command you use depends on the version of system software installed). In the Layout section of the dialog box, choose 2-Up, 4-Up, or a specific number of "Pages per sheet." Instead of printing a single record per page, multiple records will now appear on every page.

Tip

Strictly speaking, it isn't necessary to create a separate layout for viewing records as a table. You can view any existing layout (a data entry layout, for example) as a table whenever you wish by choosing View ⇨ View as Table. The only advantage to creating separate table layouts is that you can specify the fields to use and set a premanent display order for them.

Label layouts

FileMaker Pro's Labels layout style is designed specifically for printing labels. You can specify any of the supported Avery or CoStar label formats, or you can create your own label format. Simply follow these steps:

1. Switch to Layout mode by choosing View ⇨ Layout Mode (or by pressing ⌘+L/Ctrl+L).

2. Choose Layouts ⇨ New Layout/Report (or press ⌘+N/Ctrl+N).

   The New Layout/Report assistant appears (refer to Figure 6-3).

3. Type a name for the new layout, and choose "Labels" as the layout type.

4. Determine whether the layout should appear in the layouts menu by leaving or removing the check mark in the "Include in layout pop-up menu" check box. Click Next to continue.

   The screen shown in Figure 6-14 appears.

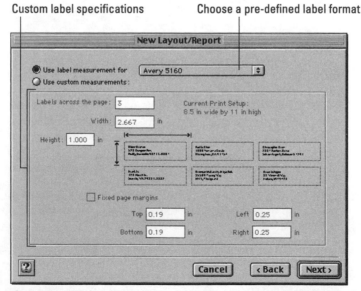

Figure 6-14: Choose an Avery label or create a custom label layout.

5. If you will be printing on an Avery label (or its equivalent), click the "Use label measurements for" radio button, and select the Avery part number from the pop-up menu. Click Next to continue.

— or —

Click the "Use custom measurements" radio button. The dimmed area at the bottom of the dialog box becomes active. Enter the height and width for a single label, as well as the number of labels across. If required for your printer, use the "Fixed page margins" option to specify the offsets (in inches) from the edges of the label sheet to the printable area of the sheet. Click Next to continue.

The Specify Label Contents screen appears, as shown in Figure 6-15.

Select fields   Label contents, including spacing and punctuation

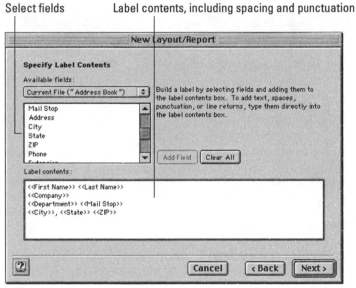

Figure 6-15: Select fields and design the label layout in the Specify Label Contents screen.

6. Add fields to the layout by double-clicking them or by selecting them and clicking the Add Field button. Add space between fields and punctuation marks, as necessary. Be sure to press Return/Enter to end each label line (except the last one). Click Next to continue.

Note

Because FileMaker Pro 5 is a relational database program, you can also add related fields to layouts. To choose fields from any currently defined relationship, choose the name of the relationship from the pop-up menu located above the Available fields list. If necessary, you can also define a new relationship at this time by choosing Define Relationships from the pop-up menu. (For information about relationships, see Chapter 18.)

7. You can either view the label layout in Preview mode or go to Layout mode (see Figure 6-16) to make any necessary changes. Select an option and click Finish.

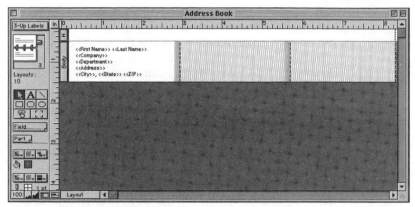

Figure 6-16: A label layout viewed in Layout mode

Note If your database contains no records, viewing this layout in Preview mode — as well as any other layout that doesn't have a "theme" — will present a blank page.

As you can see, when defining a Labels layout, the choice and placement of fields is all handled in the Specify Label Contents screen, rather than on the layout itself. And the entire label is placed as a block of merge fields. (Merge fields are surrounded by angle bracket symbols, as shown in Figure 6-16.) Unlike a normal field,
a merge field does not have to be resized; it automatically expands as needed to handle the data it must contain. In fact, when you finally see the layout that has been generated, the only thing you may want to change is the formatting (selecting a different font or size, for instance).

To format a merge field, select the Text tool (the capital A) from the Tools panel and use it to select both a field name and its surrounding brackets. You can then apply formatting commands to the field, such as choosing a different font, style, or size. If you want to apply the same formatting to *all* merge fields, use the Pointer tool to select the entire block of fields and then choose formatting commands.

Caution When you apply styles and fonts to merge fields, be careful to select the entire field, including the brackets (<< and >). If you select just part of a merge field when making a style change, FileMaker Pro will ignore it.

Tips for creating custom label formats

If you buy labels from a company other than Avery and don't know which, if any, Avery label is compatible, you can choose the "Use custom measurements" option to create your own label format.

If you know a couple of fairly simple rules, you can design labels from scratch. First, the height of the header in your layout should equal the distance from the top of the label sheet to the top of the first row of labels. Second, when entering the dimensions, set the height to match the label's *vertical pitch* (the distance from the top of the first row of labels to the top of the second row). Set the width to match the label's *horizontal pitch* (the distance from the left edge of one label to the left edge of the next label).

After dismissing the New Layout/Report assistant, switch to Layout mode. Click the Header part label to select it. Then, in the Size windoid (chose View ➪ Object Size), click the bottom text box and enter the distance from the top of the label sheet to the top of the first row of labels.

An essential detail that isn't covered by the New Layout/Report assistant is the handling of blank fields within labels. When printing address labels, for example, it's not uncommon for some records to include a company name, while others do not have this information. Similarly, if you provide two address lines for each label, some records may only have a single address line. To keep such records from printing with blank lines, you must tell FileMaker Pro how to handle this situation using the Set Sliding/Printing command:

1. Change to Layout mode and use the Pointer tool to select the block of merge fields.

2. Choose Format ➪ Sliding/Printing.

   The Set Sliding/Printing dialog box appears (see Figure 6-17).

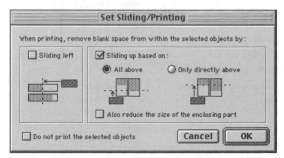

Figure 6-17: The Set Sliding/Printing dialog box

3. If at least one line of the label layout contains multiple fields and one or more of the fields could be missing in some records, click the "Sliding left" check box.

— or —

If one or more entire label lines might be blank for some records, click the "Sliding up based on" check box and the "All above" radio button.

4. Click OK to dismiss the dialog box.

Envelope layouts

The process of creating an Envelope layout is very similar to that of creating a Labels layout. Simply follow these steps:

1. Switch to Layout mode and choose Layouts ➪ New Layout/Report (or press ⌘+N/Ctrl+N).

   The New Layout/Report assistant appears (refer to Figure 6-3).

2. Enter a name for the layout and select the Envelope layout type.

3. Determine whether the layout should appear in the layouts menu by leaving or removing the check mark in the "Include in layout pop-up menu" check box. Click Next to continue.

   The Specify Envelope Contents screen appears (see Figure 6-18).

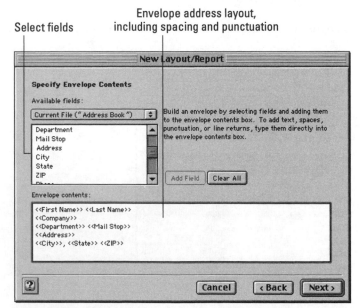

Figure 6-18: Select fields and design the Envelope layout in the Specify Envelope Contents screen.

4. Add fields to the Envelope layout by double-clicking them or by selecting them and clicking the Add Field button.

   Add space between fields and punctuation marks, as necessary. Press Return/Enter to end each address line. Click Next to continue.

5. You can either view the Envelope layout in Preview mode or go to Layout mode (see Figure 6-19) to make any necessary changes. Select an option and click Finish.

Address block

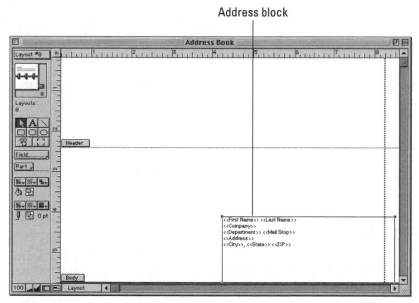

Figure 6-19: An Envelope layout prepared for use with the Address Book database

FileMaker Pro 5 uses merge fields to format the body of an Envelope layout — just as it does with a Label layout. Rather than place normal, resizable fields on the layout, the entire envelope address is a single text object with the field names embedded in it. If you attempt to click any of the address information, you'll see that four *handles* (black dots) surround the field. If you want to change the formatting of the address, you can use the Text tool to select individual field names and their surrounding brackets (<< >) and then choose commands from the Format menu.

An essential detail that isn't covered by the New Layout/Report assistant is the handling of blank fields within addresses. When printing envelopes, it's not uncommon for some records to include a company name, while others do not have this information. Similarly, if you provide two address lines, some records may only have a single address line. To keep such records from printing with blank lines, you must tell FileMaker Pro how to handle this situation using the Set Sliding/Printing command:

1. Change to Layout mode and use the Pointer tool to select the block of merge fields.

2. Choose Format ⇨ Sliding/Printing.

   The Set Sliding/Printing dialog box appears (refer to Figure 6-17).

3. If at least one line of the envelope layout contains multiple fields and one or more of the fields might be missing in some records, click the "Sliding left" check box.

   — or —

4. If one or more envelope lines might be blank for some records, click the "Sliding up based on" check box and the "All above" radio button.

5. Click OK to dismiss the dialog box.

As with any other type of layout, you can add static graphic and text items (such as your logo or the return address). These operations are detailed in the section called "Designing Your Own Layouts."

Note When printing an Envelope layout, be sure to set Page Setup/Print Setup for landscape mode printing. See your printer manual for instructions on envelope feeding procedures. Refer to Chapters 2 and 13 for additional information on printing within FileMaker Pro.

Blank layouts

As its name suggests, the Blank layout style presents you with a blank form — devoid of fields and field labels. The layout contains header, body, and footer parts. Choose the Blank layout style when you want to create a layout entirely from scratch.

Tip As an alternative, you may find it easier to edit an existing layout (a standard form layout, for example), or to duplicate an existing layout and then edit the duplicate.

Designing Your Own Layouts

There's often more to creating layouts than just choosing a layout style and tossing in a few fields. For example, you may want to put fields in different positions in the layout; or you may want certain fields to print only at the top or bottom of a page or only after a group of sorted records. You also may want to apply formatting to different fields and add extra objects, such as field labels and graphics. Layout mode has tools and commands that enable you to do all these things and more.

Specifying layout views

In previous versions of FileMaker Pro, any layout could be displayed in Form or List View. FileMaker Pro 5 adds a new display format called *Table View*, in which records are shown as a spreadsheet-style table. In addition, you can now specify which of the three views are enabled for a given layout. Switch to Layout mode, choose Layouts ⇨ Layout Setup, and click the Views tab in the Layout Setup dialog box. Add or remove check marks, as desired, to enable or disable the views. When you later examine the layout in Browse or Find mode, you can switch between all enabled views by choosing commands from the View menu.

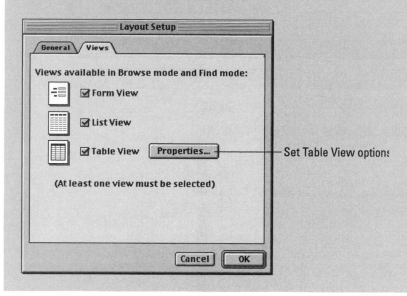

Set Table View options

Understanding layout parts

All FileMaker Pro layouts are divided into parts that control how and when data appears. When you change to Layout mode, each layout part is labeled. Figure 6-20 shows many of the available layout parts as they appear when you're in Layout mode and Preview mode. The various layout parts are described in the following sections.

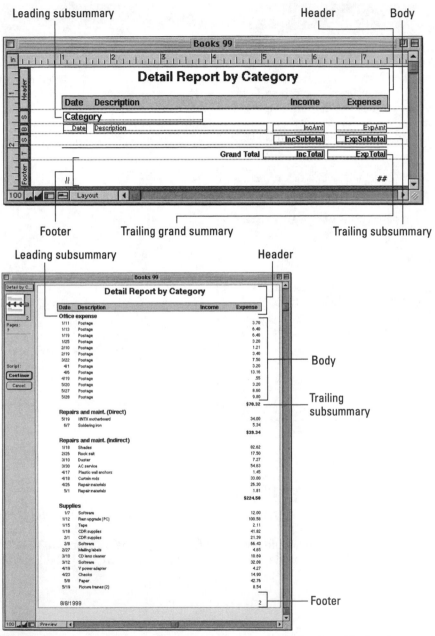

Figure 6-20: Layout parts as they look in Layout mode (top) and in Preview mode or when printed (bottom)

Body

In general, every layout has a body. The layout body is displayed once for each record. If you have fields that you want to see in every record you view, you should place those fields in the layout body. If you open several databases from the *FileMaker Pro 5 Bible* CD-ROM and then switch to Layout mode, you'll note that the bulk of the fields usually appear in the body of the layout. (If you don't want to see detailed data for each record, you can remove the body from the layout — as long as you leave some other part, such as a subsummary or summary part.)

Header

FileMaker Pro displays the header at the top of every page. The header is visible in all modes. At printing time (or in Preview mode), the header is printed (or shown) at the top of each page. You can use headers for column headings, report titles, logos, and so on. Layout navigation buttons are commonly placed in the header area, too. You can also create a title header part that is visible only on the first page of a printed or previewed report.

Footer

FileMaker Pro displays the footer at the bottom of every page. The footer is visible in all modes. At printing time (or in Preview mode), the footer is printed (or shown) at the bottom of each page. You can also create a special title footer part that prints only on the first page of a report.

Subsummary and grand summary parts

Subsummary and grand summary parts are used to print information that summarizes the *found set* of records (the current subset of records you are browsing). You use these parts to display information calculated by Summary fields that have been placed in these parts. A Summary field, in effect, computes a statistic (such as a total or average) across all records in the found set.

Subsummary parts are used to display or print a summary of values for records sorted by a specific field. A subsummary of total sales by salesperson, for example, would show the sales subtotal for each salesperson in the current found set. In this example, you must first sort the database by the Salesperson field. The field on which the database is sorted is also referred to as a *break field* (it breaks the database into groups). You must select a break field when you create the subsummary part.

A grand summary part is used to display or print summary figures for the entire found set (rather than for each subgroup in the found set, as is done in a subsummary part). For example, you could display the grand total of sales for all salespeople in a database.

You can place a subsummary or grand summary part before or after the body. The former is called a leading subsummary or leading grand summary, and the latter is called a trailing subsummary or trailing grand summary. To learn more about using Summary fields and summary parts, see Chapter 5.

Note   The report layout previously shown in Figure 6-20 includes two subsummary parts. Each uses the Month field as the break field; that is, the database must first be sorted by the Month field in order to generate a report that groups records by month. The leading subsummary part is used to display a single field containing the name of the month. The trailing subsummary part displays the summary data (income and expense totals for each month). A trailing grand summary is used to display the total income and expense amounts for the entire found set.

Adding a layout part

You use the Layouts ⇨ Part Setup command to add a part to a layout. The Part Setup dialog box appears, as shown in Figure 6-21.

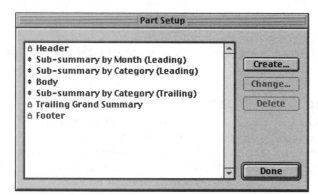

Figure 6-21: The Part Setup dialog box

This dialog box shows all parts that are currently used in the layout. To add a new part, click the Create button. The Part Definition dialog box appears, as shown in Figure 6-22.

Tip   You can go directly to the Part Definition dialog box—without seeing the Part Setup dialog box first—by clicking the part icon in the Tools palette and dragging it onto the layout. You can also open this dialog box by double-clicking any part label in the layout (the Body label, for example).

To specify the type of part you're creating, click the appropriate radio button. (Buttons are dimmed for parts that already exist or that aren't appropriate for the type of layout you're modifying.) Below the radio buttons are check box options for page numbering and page break options. The specific options that can be set vary with the type of part you're creating.

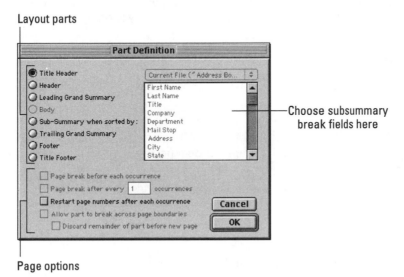

Figure 6-22: The Part Definition dialog box

Follow these steps to add a new part to a layout:

1. In Layout mode, choose the appropriate layout from the layouts pop-up menu.

2. Choose Layouts ⇨ Part Setup and, when the Part Setup dialog box appears (as previously shown in Figure 6-21), click Create.

    — or —

    Drag the Part tool onto the layout.

    In either case, the Part Definition dialog box appears (as previously shown in Figure 6-22).

3. Click the radio button for the part you want to add.

    If the button is dimmed, the part already exists or isn't appropriate for the layout you're modifying.

4. *Optional*: Set page numbering and page-break options.

5. If the part is a subsummary, choose the sort field from the field list on the right side of the dialog box.

    The sort field can also be selected from any file that is related to the current database. To display these fields, choose the name of the relationship from the pop-up menu.

6. Click OK.

If you began this process by dragging a part onto the layout, you are immediately returned to Layout mode.

If you began this process by choosing the Part Setup command, you return to the Part Setup dialog box. Click Done to return to Layout mode.

Modifying parts

You can change existing parts in several ways. For example, you can do any of the following:

✦ Change a part's size.

✦ Change the order in which parts appear on a page—within limits. (You can't place a header below the body or a footer above it, for instance.)

✦ Change the part types and options.

✦ Move the part labels out of your way.

✦ Delete a part.

These procedures are explained in the following sections.

Resizing layout parts

To change the height of a part, drag its label. Part labels appear on the left side of the layout area. The name of the part appears in its label.

Follow these steps to make a layout part larger or smaller:

1. Switch to Layout mode and choose the appropriate layout from the layouts pop-up menu.

2. Locate the label for the part that you want to resize. (The label contains the part's name.)

3. Click and drag the part label in the appropriate direction: up to make the part smaller, or down to make it larger.

4. Release the mouse button when the part is the size you want.

Note

FileMaker Pro enables you to drag a part until you come to some other object—a field in another part, for example. To drag past an object (text, a graphic, or a field), hold down the Option/Alt key as you drag.

You can also set the height of a part by choosing the View ➪ Object Size command. This command enables you to set the part's height precisely. Choosing the Object Size command brings up a small window (called a *windoid*) like the one shown in Figure 6-23.

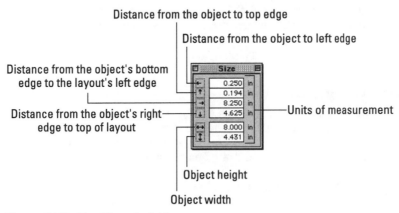

Distance from the object to top edge

Distance from the object to left edge

Distance from the object's bottom edge to the layout's left edge

Distance from the object's right edge to top of layout

Units of measurement

Object height

Object width

Figure 6-23: The Size windoid

The Size windoid displays the part's distance from the left, top, right, and bottom margins, as well as the part's width and height.

To specify a part's size precisely, follow these steps:

1. In Layout mode, choose the appropriate layout from the layouts pop-up menu.

2. Choose the View ➪ Object Size command.

   The Size windoid appears.

3. Click the label of the part that you want to resize.

   The part label turns dark to show that it is selected.

4. Enter the desired height for the selected part in the bottom text box. Press Tab or Enter to put the new height into effect.

Tip

You can also *color* any layout part, if you like. In Layout mode, click to select the part label (Body, for instance) and choose a color from the Fill Color palette.

Multipage layouts

If you like, you can extend a single layout body over two or more pages. To do so, simply make the body very long, changing its length by dragging its part name (Body) downward on the layout. FileMaker Pro then displays a dashed line to show where the page breaks. Place the fields that you want to appear on the first page above the dashed line; place fields for the second page below the dashed line. Of course, pages can be broken left to right (the wide way) as well.

Reordering layout parts

Within certain logical limitations, you can change the order in which parts appear in a layout. Headers always go at the top and footers at the bottom, for example. You can change part order in two ways: by using the Part Setup dialog box or by holding down the Shift key while you drag a part's label.

To use the Set Layout Order command to change the order of parts, follow these steps:

1. In Layout mode, switch to the appropriate layout.

2. Choose Layouts ⇨ Part Setup.

   The Part Setup dialog box appears (refer to Figure 6-21).

3. Drag part names up or down in the part list to set their new order.

Note

A part name with a lock icon next to it (such as a trailing grand summary) cannot be moved.

4. Click Done.

Changing part types and options

You can change a part's type, and you can reset certain options for the parts. (For example, you might want to choose a different break field for a subsummary part.) You do both of these in the Part Definition dialog box. Follow these steps to change a part's type and/or options:

1. In Layout mode, switch to the layout that contains the part you want to modify.

2. Double-click the label for the part you want to change.

   — or —

   Choose Layouts ⇨ Part Setup, select the part name, and click the Change button.

   In either case, the Part Definition dialog box appears for the chosen part (refer to Figure 6-22).

3. Click options to make the necessary changes. (Options that are dimmed are not available or are not allowed.)

4. Click OK.

If you began this process by double-clicking a part label on the layout, you immediately return to Layout mode.

If you began this process by choosing the Part Setup command, you return to the Part Setup dialog box. Click Done to return to Layout mode.

Deleting layout parts

The method you use to delete a layout part depends on whether the part contains objects (fields, labels, or graphics). If the part is empty, you can drag it upward on the layout until it disappears. Otherwise, you can select the part's label and press the Delete key. You can also delete a part from the Part Setup dialog box in Layout mode by choosing Layouts ⇨ Part Setup, selecting the name of the part, and clicking the Delete button.

If a part contains objects, you'll see an alert box when you try to delete it, because any objects in the part will be deleted with the part. Any fields that are removed from the part when you delete it can be added back to the layout using the Field tool. However, other objects, such as graphics or static text, will have to be re-created if you find that you still need them.

Caution To recover a part that you deleted with the Delete key, choose Undo from the Edit menu (or press ⌘+Z/Ctrl+Z) immediately after deleting it. Part deletions accomplished within the Define Parts dialog box, on the other hand, cannot be recovered with the Undo command.

Adding items to a layout part

You now know enough about layout parts to create well-ordered, appropriately sized blank layout parts. However, the purpose of a layout part is to display information rather than blank space. You must add objects to the parts. Objects include fields, field labels, text, graphics, portals, and buttons. To add objects, you use the tools in the Tools palette on the left side of the document window. Additional options for placing, arranging, and formatting objects are available in the View, Insert, Format, and Arrange menus.

Adding fields

Fields are generally the most important objects in any layout. You've seen how to add fields at layout creation time. The initial default layout automatically places every field you've defined for the database. When you design a new layout with the New Layout/Report assistant, you specify which fields to place, as well as the order in which they are placed. You can also add a field to any layout at any time, even if the field didn't exist when you created the layout.

You add fields to an existing layout by clicking the Field tool. This tool is in the center of the Tools palette. Follow these steps to add fields to a layout:

1. In Layout mode, switch to the layout to which you want to add fields.

2. Click the Field tool and drag the field object into the appropriate layout part to the position where you want to place the field.

   The Specify Field dialog box appears, as shown in Figure 6-24.

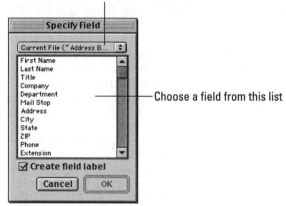

Figure 6-24: The Specify Field dialog box

3. Click the name of the field you want to add.

   You can choose any field that has been defined for the database, as well as any field in a related file. To view fields in related files, choose the name of the relationship from the pop-up menu at the top of the Specify Field dialog box.

4. If you want a matching field label to be created, make sure there is a check mark in the "Create field label" check box. (If you don't want a label, remove the check mark.)

5. Click OK.

   The field appears in the layout part in which it was placed.

Toggling the positions of part labels

Part labels are used in Layout mode to resize, move, or modify parts. These labels can get in your way, however, obscuring the fields and labels beneath them. To switch labels to a vertical position, click the part label control at the bottom of the Layout window. You'll find this control just to the left of the mode selector pop-up menu, as previously shown in Figure 6-2. You can also toggle part label orientation by ⌘/Ctrl+clicking any part label.

6. Move and resize the field as necessary.

To move a field within a layout, select the Pointer tool, click once within the field to select it, and then drag the field to a new location. To resize a field, select the Pointer tool, click once within the field to select it, and then drag any of the field's *handles* (the black dots in the four corners of a field).

To delete a field from a layout, click to select it and then press the Delete or Backspace key.

Tip

If you find that you've simply added the wrong field to a layout, there's a better approach to correcting this problem than deleting the errant field and then adding the correct one: You can swap one field for another. In Layout mode, double-click the field. The Specify Field dialog box appears and presents a list of all fields that have been defined for the database. Choose the replacement field from the field list. All formatting options that were set for the old field are automatically applied to the new field.

You can use a similar technique to duplicate the formatting of an existing field. Just quickly press Option/Ctrl as you drag the field. When you release the mouse button, the Specify Field dialog box appears. Choose a field from the field list.

Adding merge fields

In most database programs, the process of performing a mail merge involves two steps: exporting the merge data from a database program and then merging it with a word processing document that includes field placeholders (to show where the merge data should be inserted). Although you can do it this way in FileMaker Pro, too, you can perform a merge without leaving FileMaker by embedding one or more merge fields in any text block, as follows:

1. In Layout mode, switch to the layout to which you want to add the merge fields.

2. Create or select an existing text element in the layout, and then set the text insertion point by clicking or pressing the arrow keys.

3. Choose Insert ➪ Merge Field (or press ⌘+M/Ctrl+M).

The Specify Field dialog box appears (as previously shown in Figure 6-24).

4. Choose a field to insert by selecting it and clicking OK.

The merge field is added at the current text insertion point. A merge field is always surrounded by bracket symbols, as in <<Last Name>>. Figure 6-25 shows a form letter that contains three merge fields. As illustrated in the figure, merge fields can also be selected from any related file, as well as from the current database. To view the fields in a related file, choose the name of the relationship from the pop-up menu at the top of the Specify Field dialog box.

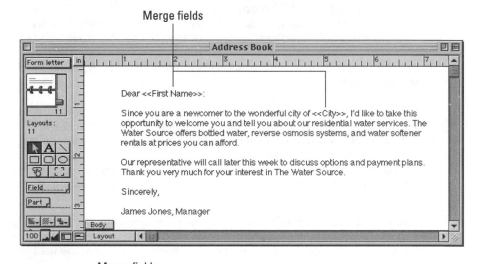

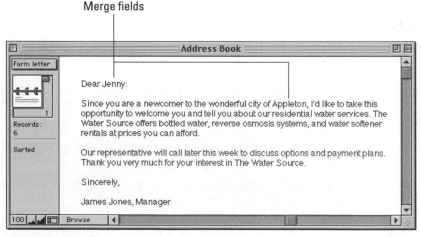

Figure 6-25: A layout with two merge fields in Layout mode (top) and Browse mode (bottom)

Note Like any other text, you can format merge fields by changing the font, style, size, color, and so on. When formatting a merge field, you *must* also apply the formatting to the surrounding brackets.

Adding graphics

FileMaker Pro provides several ways for you to add graphic elements to layouts. You can create simple graphics — including ovals, squares, and lines — directly in the program by using the Line, Rectangle, Rounded Rectangle, and Oval tools in the Tools palette (see Figure 6-26). An icon that shows the result of using that tool identifies each tool.

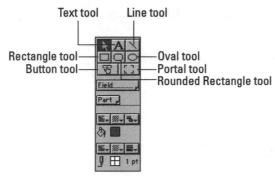

Figure 6-26: The Tools palette in Layout mode

To add a simple graphic element to a layout, follow these steps:

1. In Layout mode, switch to the layout to which you want to add the element.

2. Use the Fill, Border, Effects, and Line Width palettes to select the appropriate formatting for the new element. (Note that if you preselect options in any of these palettes when no element is currently selected in the layout, they become the new default settings and are automatically applied to the next layout element you create.)

New Feature The Effects palette is a new feature in FileMaker Pro 5. By selecting options from its pop-up menu, you can add engraving, embossing, or a drop shadow to any layout object.

3. Click the tool that represents the type of graphic element you want to add (line, rectangle, rounded rectangle, or ellipse).

4. Position the tool over the spot where you want to add the graphic, and then click and drag until you create an element of the desired size.

You can create special objects by holding down the Option/Ctrl key as you drag with any of the tools. When Option/Ctrl is pressed, the Rectangle and Rounded Rectangle tools create squares; the Oval tool creates circles; and the Line tool is restricted to straight horizontal, vertical, or 45-degree lines.

To change the formatting for an object, click the object to select it and then choose options in the Fill, Border, Effects, and Line Width palettes. You can also drag an object to change its position and drag its handles to change its size.

Complex graphics, such as logos or elaborate illustrations, are better created in a dedicated graphics program. To bring graphics in from other programs, use the Insert command as follows:

1. In Layout mode, switch to the layout to which you want to add the graphic.

2. Choose Insert ⇨ Picture.

   A modified file dialog box appears, as shown in Figure 6-27.

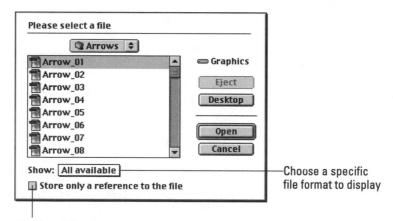

Figure 6-27: Select a graphic file to insert.

3. *Optional*: To limit the file list to only those graphic images saved in a particular format, choose a format from the Show/Files of type pop-up menu.

4. Find the graphic's name in the list and click to select it.

5. *Optional*: To store a reference to the graphic file in the database (rather than the actual graphic), click the check box at the bottom of the dialog box.

6. Click Open.

   The graphic appears in the current layout.

7. Drag the graphic to the appropriate position in the layout. Drag the graphic's handles to change its size, if necessary.

Graphics can also be added to a layout via copy-and-paste. Simply open the graphic file in its original program, select it, issue the Copy command, and then — in FileMaker Pro — issue the Paste command.

To remove any graphic on a layout, select it with the Pointer tool and press the Delete or Backspace key.

Tip

FileMaker Pro 5 supports drag-and-drop. Using drag-and-drop, you can move a graphic or text object from one program to another by simply selecting it in the original program's document and then dragging it to the other program's document. If you have a graphics program that supports drag-and-drop, such as AppleWorks (formerly known as ClarisWorks and ClarisWorks Office), for example, you can drag a graphic directly onto a FileMaker Pro layout.

Adding OLE objects (Windows only)

FileMaker Pro enables you to add OLE objects directly to a layout. You can create these OLE objects with any application that can behave as an "OLE Server." The kinds of objects you can add depend on the applications you have installed on your PC.

To add an OLE object to a layout, follow these steps:

1. Switch to Layout mode by choosing View ➪ Layout Mode or pressing Ctrl+L.
2. Choose the layout into which you want to insert an OLE object.
3. Choose Insert ➪ Object.

   The Insert Object dialog box appears (see Figure 6-28).

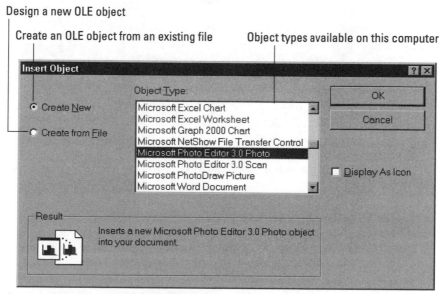

Figure 6-28: The Insert Object dialog box

4. Click the Create New radio button to create a new OLE object.

5. Select the *object type* (the application for creating the OLE object) from the Object Type list and click OK.

FileMaker Pro opens the selected application.

6. Create the OLE object in the application and then close the application.

The new OLE object appears in the layout as text (for textual objects), graphics (for graphic documents), or an icon (for nondisplayable objects, such as sounds).

Note   An OLE object created in this way is "embedded" in the database—you can only access the object through FileMaker Pro—and the object is included with the database if you give the database to someone else. (See Chapter 8 for more information on embedding, linking, and editing OLE objects.)

—or—

7. Click the Create from File radio button to create the OLE object from an existing file. The dialog box changes to display new options (see Figure 6-29).

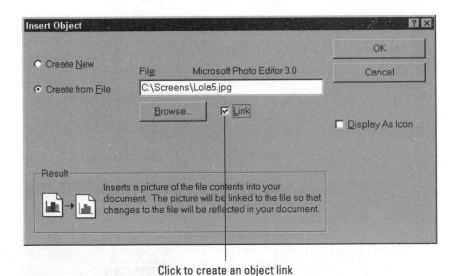

Click to create an object link

Figure 6-29: Select the filename of the OLE object that you want to embed.

8. Type the full pathname of the file in the File text box, or click the Browse button and choose the filename from the dialog box that appears.

9. If you want to link the file as an OLE object rather than embedding it, click the Link check box.

   The new OLE object is displayed in the layout as text (for textual objects), graphics (for graphic documents), or an icon (for nondisplayable objects like sounds).

Once you add an OLE object to a layout (as opposed to adding it to a Container field in a record, as discussed in Chapter 8), you can only modify the OLE object — either edit or play it — when you are in Layout mode. In Browse mode, you can *see* the object, but you can't access it. Also, you can modify links for OLE objects (choose Edit ➪ Object ➪ Links) only in Layout mode. For additional information on working with OLE objects, see "OLE objects" in FileMaker Help.

Note

An OLE object created as a link can be accessed from the original application just like any other file. If you change the file from outside FileMaker Pro, you have the option to configure the link so the OLE object in the layout is automatically updated to show the latest version. However, this flexibility comes with a price — if you give your database to someone else (or even move it to another computer), you must move the linked file as well and reestablish the link.

Adding buttons

Ever since scripting was introduced in FileMaker Pro, you could make the program perform special tasks for you in response to a button click. Any object — text or graphic — can be made to function as a button.

Follow these steps to create a new button with the Button tool:

1. In Layout mode, switch to the layout to which you want to add the button.

2. Click the Button tool in the Tools palette to select it. (The Button tool looks like a finger pushing a button.)

3. On the layout, drag the pointer to set the height and width of the button, and then release the mouse button.

   The new button becomes visible and the Specify Button dialog box appears, as shown in Figure 6-30.

Select a button shape

Button action

Options, if any, are listed here

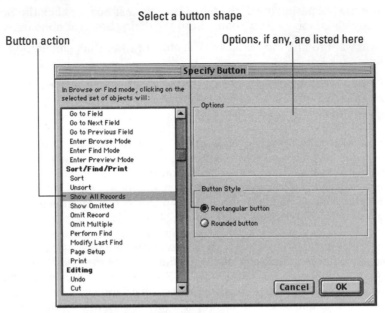

Figure 6-30: The Specify Button dialog box

4. Select the script step to be assigned to the button, set any necessary options, and choose a button shape (rectangular or rounded).

New Feature

In previous versions of FileMaker Pro, button shape was determined by a Preference setting. In FileMaker Pro 5, you designate a button shape (in the Specify Button dialog box) each time you create a new button.

If you want to associate an existing script with the button (rather than just a single script step), choose the Perform Script step in the Control section. For more information about scripting, see Chapter 15.

5. Click OK.

The Specify Button dialog box is removed and a text insertion point appears in the center of the blank button.

6. Type a name for the button.

7. Press Enter or click anywhere outside the button to end the button definition process.

To remove a button from a layout, select it with the Pointer tool and press the Delete or Backspace key. If you simply want to move the button to a different layout in the same database, select it, choose the Edit ➪ Cut command (or press ⌘+C/Ctrl+C), switch to the target layout, and then choose Edit ➪ Paste (or press ⌘+V/Ctrl+V).

More about buttons

When choosing an action for a button (Step 4 in the button creation procedure), you can select Do Nothing for any button for which a final script doesn't exist. To later assign a permanent action to the button, simply select the button and choose the Format ⇨ Button command.

Also, because a button is like any other object in a FileMaker layout, you can change its formatting. Features that you may want to alter include the button label (changing its font, size, style, or color); the button's fill color, pattern, or border; and the size of the button.

Adding portals

Fields from related databases can be placed directly onto a layout (as described previously in "Adding fields"). However, related fields placed in this manner can show only the value from a single matching record. If you want to display values from *multiple* matching records, you place the related fields in a portal.

Think of a *portal* as a window into a related file. All fields placed within a portal must be from a previously defined relationship. Any record that meets the requirements of that defined relationship will display its data in the portal.

For example, Figure 6-31 shows a portal that contains the full names and companies of a series of people (the fields placed in the portal were Company, First Name, and Last Name). The relationship was defined as matching the City fields in the current and the related database. Thus, when **San Mateo** is entered in the City field of the current record, the portal displays the names and associated companies of all records in the related file that have San Mateo in the City field.

Company	First Name	Last Name	
Anderson Construction	Betty	Anderson	⬆
Anderson Construction	William	Anderson	
Berkshire Motors	Adrian	Jones	
Physicians Center	Dr. Mark	Conners	⬇

Figure 6-31: A portal that displays three fields from a related file

To create a portal in a layout, follow these steps:

1. If you haven't already done so, define the relationship that will be used for the portal's data by choosing File ⇨ Define Relationship. (See Chapter 18 for information about defining relationships.)

2. In Layout mode, switch to the layout to which you want to add the portal.

3. Click the Portal tool in the Tools palette to select it. (The Portal tool looks like a square that is missing the center section on each side.)

4. On the layout, drag the pointer to indicate the height and width of the portal, and then release the mouse button.

   The portal becomes visible and the Portal Setup dialog box appears, as shown in Figure 6-32.

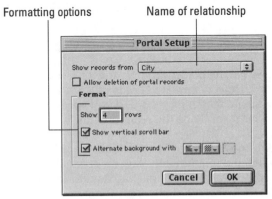

Figure 6-32: The Portal Setup dialog box

5. Choose a relationship from the pop-up menu at the top of the dialog box.

6. In the "Show rows" text box, enter the number of rows that the portal will display.

7. Change any of the other options you want, as follows:

   • Click the check box labeled "Allow deletion of portal records" if you want to be able to delete records in the related file by selecting them in the portal.

   • If you think the number of records will sometimes exceed the number of portal rows set in step 6, click the check box for "Show vertical scroll bar." Doing this will enable you to scroll through all the records in the portal.

   • To make it easier to distinguish each portal record from the next, click the check box labeled "Alternate background with" and then choose a color and/or fill pattern. When you switch to Browse mode, you'll see that the portal row colors alternate between white and the selected color/pattern combination (much like "green bar" printer paper or some types of ledger paper).

8. Click OK to dismiss the Portal Setup dialog box.

9. Click the Field tool in the Tools palette and drag a field into the portal.

   When you release the mouse button, the Specify Field dialog box appears (refer to Figure 6-24).

10. Choose a related field and then click OK.

    The field and its label appear in the portal.

11. Drag the field into the top row of the portal. Move the field's label so it is above the field's position (outside the portal) or, if you prefer, you can delete the field label.

12. Repeat steps 9 through 11 for additional related fields that you want to display in the portal.

Fields inside the portal, as well as the portal itself, can be resized as needed. If you later need to modify the portal settings, you can select the portal and choose the Format ➪ Portal command or simply double-click the portal. In either case, the Portal Setup dialog box appears.

For more information about portals and relationships, see Chapter 18.

Formatting fields and other objects

Newly placed fields are seldom exactly as you want them. A field may be too small or too large, or it may be in the wrong position. The field's formatting — text attributes, borders, and so on — may not display the field in the manner you had intended. Other objects, such as buttons and graphics, may also be in the wrong place, be the wrong size, or need additional formatting. Fortunately, you can easily correct these problems. FileMaker Pro includes a variety of tools that make the placement and formatting of fields and other objects as simple as possible.

Although this section concentrates on the size, placement, and formatting of fields, the majority of the commands and procedures apply to any object on a layout, such as buttons, field labels, graphics, and static text.

Using the measurement and alignment tools

The View menu (shown in Figure 6-33) includes many tools that make it easy to place or arrange fields, labels, graphics, and other objects accurately on the layout — even when you're doing it manually by dragging the objects.

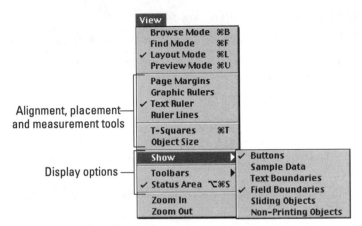

Figure 6-33: The View menu

The alignment, placement, and measurement tools listed in the View menu provide the following functions:

✦ *Page Margins*: Choose the Page Margins command to see where layout objects will appear in printouts in relation to the page margins.

✦ *Graphic Rulers*: Graphic rulers can be shown at the top and left edges of the layout area. Choose the Graphic Rulers command to toggle these rulers on and off. When you select and drag any object, its dimensions and location are indicated on the rulers.

✦ *Text Ruler*: FileMaker Pro 5 includes a text ruler and an associated ruler bar that can be displayed at the top of the document window. Although the main purpose of the text ruler is for formatting fields and text objects (such as field labels), it is also useful for showing and checking an object's horizontal location on the layout. Choose the Text Ruler command to toggle this ruler on and off.

✦ *Ruler Lines*: You can display dotted lines that correspond to lines on the rulers. You can use these lines to check layout spacing and positioning of objects. Choose the Ruler Lines command to toggle the lines on and off.

✦ *T-Squares*: These are solid vertical and horizontal lines. You use T-square lines to precisely position an object relative to the rulers. (You can move the lines by dragging them.) Choose T-Squares or press ⌘+T/Ctrl+T to toggle the T-square lines on and off.

✦ *Object Size*: As described earlier in this chapter, you can type entries in any of the Size windoid's six text boxes to change the dimensions and location of the currently selected object in a layout. To display the Size windoid (illustrated previously in Figure 6-23), choose View ➪ Object Size.

The View ➪ Show submenu contains additional options to make objects visible or stand out while in Layout mode. You can choose any of the following helpful options:

✦ *Buttons*: Surrounds all buttons in the layout with a gray border.

✦ *Sample Data*: Displays sample data of the correct type in each field, rather than the field name.

✦ *Text Boundaries*: Surrounds all static text in the layout (such as field labels and title text) with a black border.

✦ *Field Boundaries*: Surrounds each field in the layout with a black border.

✦ *Sliding Objects*: Shifts the remaining objects (if any of the objects originally defined in the layout are missing). Sliding objects — commonly found in label layouts — are indicated by tiny left-pointing and upward-pointing arrows to indicate the direction that they will be shifted. In an address label, for example, you normally want fields to move up to remove blank lines if an entire record line (such as a company name or department) is missing.

✦ *Non-Printing Objects*: Surrounds all objects that have been designated as non-printing with a gray border. These objects are visible only on-screen and will not appear in printouts or in Preview mode.

New Feature

In order to be Microsoft Office-compliant, FileMaker Pro 5 now includes a series of toolbars that provide quick access to common commands and procedures. In Layout mode, you can display up to four toolbars: Standard (not relevant to formatting), Text Formatting (for choosing font, size, style, color, and alignment options), Arrange (for issuing Arrange menu commands), and Tools (duplicates the commands in the Tools panel). To enable or disable any of the four toolbars, choose its name from the View ➪ Toolbars submenu. (The names of enabled toolbars are preceded by a check mark.)

FileMaker Pro maintains an invisible grid that corresponds to current ruler settings. If the grid is on, objects being moved or resized move in increments, snapping to the nearest grid intersection. Choose Arrange ➪ Object Grids to toggle the grid on and off.

To change the spacing and units for the grid and rulers, choose Layouts ➪ Set Rulers and select new settings in the Set Rulers dialog box, as shown in Figure 6-34.

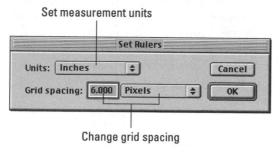

Figure 6-34: The Set Rulers dialog box

Tip If the graphic rulers are enabled, you can quickly change ruler and grid measurement units by clicking the Units box in the upper-left corner of the document window. Each time you click it, the box switches to a different measurement unit, such as inches or centimeters.

Moving and resizing fields and objects

It is simple to change a field's or object's position on a layout. Click the field or object to select it, and then drag it to a new location. (The tools described in "Using the measurement and alignment tools" can be very helpful in this task.)

It's often necessary to alter a field's size, too. If a Text field is too small, part of the text may be hidden until you click or tab into the field. A Number field that is too small to show its contents displays only a question mark. On the other hand, the default width for some fields, such as a State field that is designed to hold a two-letter abbreviation, may be much too wide.

To change a field's size or position, follow these steps:

1. In Layout mode, switch to the layout that contains the field you want to modify.

2. Click the Pointer tool in the Tools palette.

3. To move the field, click and drag the field to the desired location.

   To restrict the movement of the field to straight horizontal or vertical, hold down Shift as you drag.

4. To change the field's size, click to select the field and then click and drag a *handle* (any of the four black dots) until the field is the desired size.

   You can press Shift as you resize any field to restrict changes to only the vertical or horizontal size of the field.

Setting field formatting

When you define fields for a database (in the Define Fields dialog box), you must specify a type for each field, such as Text, Date, Time, or Number. Although the field type determines the kind of data that the field will store, it does not determine how that field's data will be displayed in a layout. To set a display format for a field, change to Layout mode and do any of the following:

✦ Choose formatting options from the Format menu.

✦ Choose settings from the fill, pen, effects, or line palettes in the Tools palette.

Any formatting options that you set for a field while in Layout mode will be applied to the field and its data when viewed in Browse mode, as described in the following sections.

Using the Format menu

To set formatting options for a field, switch to Layout mode, select a field, and then choose commands from the Format menu (see Figure 6-35). Regardless of the type of the selected field, these commands at the top of the Format menu can be chosen: Font, Size, Style, Align Text, Line Spacing, and Text Color. (These same commands can also be issued from the Text Formatting toolbar. If you Ctrl+click/right-click a field, a variety of formatting commands appear, as shown in Figure 6-36.)

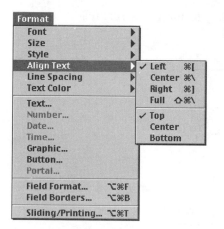

Figure 6-35: The Format menu (in Layout mode)

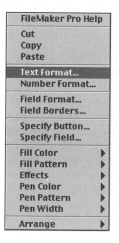

Figure 6-36: Ctrl+clicking/right-clicking a field displays this pop-up menu.

The commands available in the second section of the Format menu depend on what is currently selected: a graphic object, a field of a particular type, a field label, and so on. For example, if a Date field is selected, the Text, Date, and Button formatting commands are available in the Format menu. Text can be chosen because the field contains alphanumeric characters, as do most field types; Date can be chosen because the field is a Date field; and Button can be chosen because virtually any object on a layout can be made into a button.

The Text command

As shown in Figure 6-37, choosing the Format ⇨ Text command is an easy way to assign multiple text formatting commands to a field, field label, or piece of static text. Rather than having to select multiple commands from the Format menu, you can set all text formatting options in the Text Format dialog box. (The Paragraph button is grayed out unless you are currently formatting a Text field.)

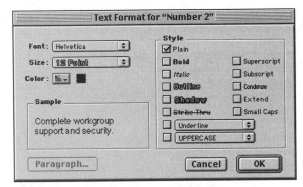

Figure 6-37: The Text Format dialog box

The Date and Time commands

When formatting a Date or Time field, choose Format ⇨ Date or Format ⇨ Time. The Date Format or Time Format dialog box appears, as appropriate (see Figure 6-38). Rather than enabling you to set text attributes for the fields — as the Text Format dialog box does — these dialog boxes let you assign a particular date or time display format for the field. You can either display the dates and times as they were typed into the field (by clicking the "Leave data formatted as entered" radio button), or format them by setting options for the field (such as leading characters and separators). The Sample box at the bottom of the dialog box shows the effects of your choices. (Note that if you also want to set general text-formatting options for a Date or Time field, you can click the Text Format button at the bottom of the Date Format or Time Format dialog box.)

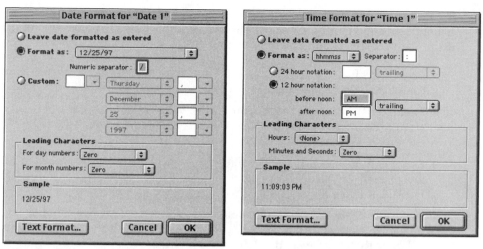

Figure 6-38: The Date Format (left) and Time Format (right) dialog boxes

New Feature

To avoid Y2K confusion, all Date fields in FileMaker Pro 5 are always displayed with 4-digit years — regardless of the formatting specified for the field.

The Graphic command

When you select a graphic or a Container field on a layout, you can choose the Format ➪ Graphic command. The Graphic Format dialog box appears, as shown in Figure 6-39. By choosing options in the dialog box, you can change the size of the graphic or its alignment.

Alignment options

Select a resizing option

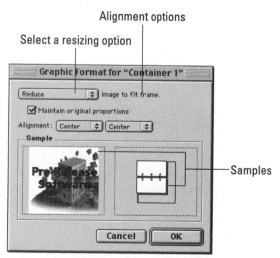

Samples

Figure 6-39: The Graphic Format dialog box

The most important options are contained in the pop-up menu at the top of the Graphic Format dialog box. These options determine how the image will be sized to fit the frame in the layout. The options are:

✦ *Crop*: If the image is larger than the frame, it will be cropped (edges removed) to fit. If the image is smaller than the frame, no modifications will be made.

✦ *Reduce*: If the image is too large to fit the frame, FileMaker Pro will reduce the size of the image to fit within the frame. If the image is already smaller than the frame, FileMaker Pro will not modify the image.

✦ *Enlarge*: If the image is smaller than the frame, FileMaker Pro will enlarge the image to fit the frame. However, if the image is already larger than the frame, FileMaker Pro will not modify the image.

✦ *Reduce or Enlarge*: This is a combination of the previous two options. If the image is smaller than the frame, it will be enlarged. Alternatively, if the image is larger than the frame, it will be shrunk to fit.

Be sure to also choose Alignment options from the remaining two pop-up menus. Check the images in the Sample box to see the effects your choices will have.

Note   In most cases, you will want to enable the option to "Maintain original proportions." When disabled, the graphic will be stretched or shrunk to fit the frame — frequently resulting in an odd picture (squished, for example).

The Portal command

If you select a *portal* (a rectangular area that holds a group of related fields), the Portal Setup dialog box appears (as previously shown in Figure 6-32). In the Format portion of the dialog box, you can set the number of rows to be displayed, whether a vertical scroll bar appears on the right side of the portal (so you can scroll through all related records in the portal), and whether every other row of the portal should be colored and/or patterned (to distinguish records from one another). Formatting portals is discussed in "Adding portals," earlier in this chapter.

The Button command

You can select the Button command if the current object could conceivably be defined as a button. Because virtually every element on a layout can be made into a button — including normal fields — the Button command is always present.

When you choose Format ➪ Button, the Specify Button dialog box appears (as previously shown in Figure 6-30). To define the object as a button, simply choose the script or script step that will execute whenever the button is clicked. Options (when available) are set in the right side of the dialog box.

Tip   If you hold down the Option/Alt key as you double-click fields and other objects on a layout, an appropriate Format dialog box is automatically presented to you.

Adding borders

Although fields are frequently displayed in Layout mode with boxes around them, these boxes appear only for your convenience in moving and resizing the fields. If you want borders to appear around a field when you browse or print (that is, when you are actually *using* the database), you must create the borders with the Field Borders command.

Follow these steps to add borders to a field:

1. In Layout mode, switch to the layout that contains the field to which you want to add borders.

2. Click to select the appropriate field.

   If there are additional fields to which you'd like to apply the same border options, you can Shift+click or drag a selection rectangle around them.

3. Choose Format ⇨ Field Borders.

   The Field Borders dialog box appears, as shown in Figure 6-40.

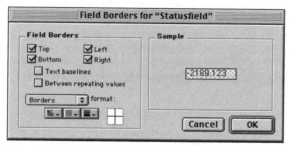

Figure 6-40: The Field Borders dialog box

4. Click the appropriate check boxes for the borders you want to add.

5. Choose Borders from the "format" pop-up menu.

6. Choose the desired color, pattern, and line width for the borders from the pop-up palettes at the bottom of the dialog box.

   The effects of your choices appear in the Sample box on the right side of the dialog box.

7. Click OK.

Adding baselines

You may want the contents of a field to be underlined. FileMaker Pro refers to such an underline as a *baseline*. As with borders, you add baselines by using the Field Borders dialog box (previously shown in Figure 6-40).

Choose Baselines from the Field Borders dialog box's pop-up menu. Then choose the desired color, pattern, and line width for the baselines from the pop-up palettes at the bottom of the dialog box. The effects of your choices appear in the Sample box on the right side of the dialog box.

Setting fill colors and patterns

You can add a fill color and/or pattern to a field—whether the field has a border or not. In Browse mode, the color and/or pattern appears behind the field's data.

You can specify fill colors and patterns in two ways. The first way is to use the Fill tools (the two pop-up palettes above the bucket icon in the Tools palette, as previously shown in Figure 6-26). If a field is currently selected, its fill color and/or pattern take on the new settings. If no field is currently selected when you choose a color or pattern with these tools, the color and pattern become the default fill color and pattern. If you now add a field, it is automatically formatted with the selected fill pattern and color.

Tip   You can also set default formatting options by simply pressing ⌘/Ctrl and clicking any field or object. Then, whenever you create a new field or text object, the clicked field or object's format settings will automatically be applied.

Alternatively, you can use the Field Borders command to select a fill for a field. Choose Fill from the dialog box's pop-up menu and then choose the desired color and pattern for the fill from the pop-up menus at the bottom of the dialog box. The effects of your choices appear in the Sample box on the right side of the dialog box.

Adding 3D effects

You can quickly add 3D effects to fields (or any other object) by choosing commands from the Effects pop-up menu in the Tools palette (refer to Figure 6-26). Choose "Embossed" to make the field or object look like it's raised off the page. Choose "Engraved" to make the field or object appear sunken into the page. Choose "Drop Shadow" to make the field or object appear engraved with a drop shadow on its bottom and right edges.

New Feature   The Effects pop-up menu is a new feature in FileMaker Pro 5.

Adding scroll bars

If you don't make a field large enough initially, the entire contents of the field may not always be visible. Although you could simply make the field bigger, this method may not produce the effect you want—especially if the available space in your layout is limited. To make it possible to view the additional contents of a field, you can add scroll bars to the field. These scroll bars enable you to scroll a field and view its additional contents—just as you can with many document windows. You add scroll bars by using the Field Format dialog box, as follows:

1. In Layout mode, switch to the layout that contains the field to which you want to add scroll bars.

2. Click to select the field.

3. Choose Format ⇨ Field Format.

   The Field Format dialog box appears, as shown in Figure 6-41.

Add a scrollbar to the chosen field

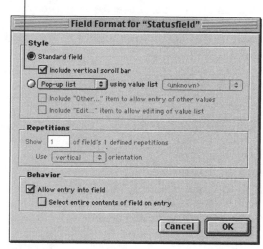

Figure 6-41: The Field Format dialog box

4. Click the "Include vertical scroll bar" check box.

5. Click OK.

Rotating text and objects

You can rotate any layout object in 90-degree increments. Rotating comes in handy when you need to add a label that runs up or down the side of a portal, for example. You can also label a block of fields with vertical text, taking up little of the valuable room in your layout.

To rotate an object, follow these steps:

1. In Layout mode, switch to the layout that contains the object you want to rotate.

2. Click to select the field.

3. Choose Arrange ⇨ Rotate.

Each time you issue the Rotate command, the selected object rotates 90 degrees clockwise.

Note When you click or tab into a rotated field in Browse mode, the field is temporarily displayed in its unrotated form. Once you tab out of the field or click elsewhere in the layout, the field resumes its rotated form.

Formatting repeating fields

As you learned in Chapter 5, some fields can contain more than one entry. These fields are called *repeating fields*. In an invoice database, for example, you might have a repeating field named Price that contains a series of prices — one for each item in an order. Use the Field Format dialog box to set options for repeating fields by following these steps:

1. In Layout mode, select the field you want to format.

2. Choose Format ➪ Field Format.

   The Field Format dialog box appears (as shown previously in Figure 6-41).

3. Enter the number of repetitions to show for the field.

4. Choose an orientation from the pop-up menu as follows:

   • Choose "Vertical" to display repetitions in a single column.

   • Choose "Horizontal" to display repetitions in a row.

5. Click OK.

Adding and modifying text

To make it easy to identify items in a layout, you can add extra text. For example, you can add a title to a report layout and place it in the header, place an automatic page number and a date stamp in the footer, and create custom labels for fields.

You add text by using the Text tool (the letter A in the Tools palette). When you click this tool, the mouse pointer changes to an insertion bracket. Click to position the bracket where you want the text to appear and then type the text. Text appears with the current settings for font, size, color, and so on, but you can change these attributes at any time.

To change the formatting of existing text, switch to Layout mode, use the Pointer tool to select the text object you want to change, and then select the desired Font, Size, Style, Align Text, Line Spacing, and Text Color options from the Format menu or the Text Formatting toolbar.

To edit existing text, use the Text tool to select the text, position the insertion point inside the text box, and use the standard editing keys to modify the text.

Besides adding standard text items, you can paste special items onto a layout, such as the current time and date, an automatic page number, or your user name. To insert special text of this type, follow these steps:

1. In Layout mode, click the Text tool.

2. Click to position the insertion point where you want the special text to appear.

3. Choose one of the following options from the Insert menu: Current Date, Current Time, Current User Name, Date Symbol, User Name Symbol, Page Number Symbol, or Record Number Symbol.

Applying the finishing touches

Even after you add all the desired elements to a layout, the layout may still need minor adjustments. If object alignment is a problem, you can easily correct it. You can also group objects so you can move or format them as a unit. You can even set the order in which fields are filled during data entry.

Aligning objects

The Align and Set Alignment commands in the Arrange menu enable you to align objects with other objects on the layout. If you have a vertical list of fields, you can use these commands to align one edge of each of the fields and field labels, for example.

Follow these steps to align two or more objects:

1. In Layout mode, select the objects you want to align. (You can hold down the Shift key to select additional objects after the first object or simply drag a selection rectangle around all the objects.)

2. Choose Arrange ➪ Set Alignment (or press Shift+⌘+K/Shift+Ctrl+K).

   The Set Alignment dialog box appears, as shown in Figure 6-42.

The sample shows how the selected objects will be aligned

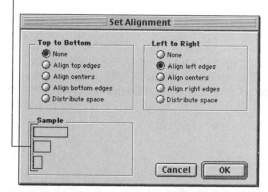

Figure 6-42: The Set Alignment dialog box

3. Choose the Top to Bottom and Left to Right options that you want to use.

The effects of your choices appear in the Sample box in the lower-left corner of the dialog box.

4. Click OK.

The alignment settings are applied to the selected objects. If you find that you have made an error, you can correct it by immediately selecting the Edit ➪ Undo Align command.

If you later want to apply the same alignment settings to a different group of objects, simply select the objects and choose the Arrange ➪ Align command (or press ⌘+K/Ctrl+K).

You can also have FileMaker Pro automatically snap objects to a grid by enabling Object Grids (choose Arrange ➪ Object Grids or press ⌘+Y/Ctrl+Y). This option makes field and label placement extraordinarily simple because each placed or moved object snaps to the nearest grid intersection. (Grid increments are based on the current ruler settings, as described previously in this chapter.)

Grouping objects

To make it easier to move several aligned objects to a new position without messing up their alignment, you can group the objects. FileMaker Pro treats grouped objects as though they were a single object.

To group several objects, follow these steps:

1. In Layout mode, select the objects you want to group. (Hold down the Shift key to select additional objects after the first object or simply drag a selection rectangle around all the objects.)

2. Choose Arrange ➪ Group (or press ⌘+G/Ctrl+G).

FileMaker Pro groups the objects, displaying them with a single set of handles.

To ungroup objects, select the group and then choose Arrange ➪ Ungroup (or press Shift+⌘+G/Shift+Ctrl+G).

Other object commands

You can also change the layering order in which objects are displayed (back to front) with the Bring to Front (Shift+Option+⌘+F), Send to Back (Shift+Option+⌘+J), Bring Forward (Shift+⌘+F/Shift+Ctrl+F), and Send Backward (Shift+⌘+J/Shift+Ctrl+J) commands in the Arrange menu. These commands are particularly useful for placing background graphics behind fields or other graphics.

If you want to make sure a particular object isn't moved by mistake, you can lock it in place by choosing the Arrange ➪ Lock command (or pressing ⌘+H/Ctrl+H). To unlock an object (so you can change its size, position, and attributes, for example), choose Arrange ➪ Unlock (or press Shift+⌘+H/Shift+Ctrl+H).

New Feature

If you frequently use the Arrange commands, you may find it beneficial to enable the Arrange toolbar. Choose View ➪ Toolbars ➪ Arrange to enable or disable this toolbar.

Setting the tab order for data entry

You can set the order in which you move from field to field on a layout when you press the Tab key. Although this has no effect on the appearance of the layout, it can often be the difference between an easy-to-use layout and one that is annoying to use. The default tab order is from left to right and top to bottom. You can change this order and even omit fields from the tab order, if you want.

To change the tab order, use the Set Tab Order command. Follow these steps:

1. In Layout mode, choose Layouts ➪ Set Tab Order.

   The Set Tab Order dialog box appears (see Figure 6-43). A numbered arrow marks each field in the layout (see Figure 6-44).

Create a tab order from scratch

Edit current tab order

Figure 6-43: The Set Tab Order dialog box

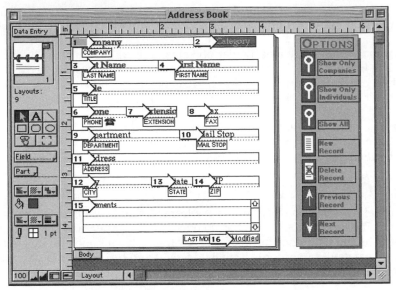

Figure 6-44: Setting the tab order for a layout

2. Click the appropriate radio button to specify whether you want to edit the existing tab order or create a new one.

3. To edit the tab order for fields, change the numbers in the arrows that appear next to each field in the layout. Enter **1** in the arrow for the field that you want first, and so on.

— or —

If you selected "Create a new tab order," click the arrows in the order in which you want the related fields to appear.

Note

To omit a field from the tab order, leave its arrow blank. When the user presses the Tab key, omitted fields are skipped.

4. Click OK to save the new tab order, or click Cancel if you change your mind.

Note

At any time during this process, you can revert to the tab order that FileMaker Pro originally set for the layout by clicking Revert to Default.

Duplicating, Renaming, Reordering, and Deleting Layouts

There are several additional operations that you can perform on layouts. You can use an existing layout as the basis for a new one, preserving the old while modifying the new. You can change the display order for layouts, and you can give any layout a new name. You can also get rid of layouts that are no longer needed. These layout operations are discussed in the following sections.

Duplicating a layout

To create a new layout that differs only slightly from an existing one, the easiest method is to duplicate the existing layout and make small changes to the copy. As an example, when you write letters, you may at times use preprinted envelopes that include your return address and at other times use plain, unprinted envelopes. If you already have a layout for printing on one type of envelope, you can duplicate the layout, make a couple of small changes, and handle the other type of envelope, too.

To duplicate a layout, switch to Layout mode, choose the layout you want to duplicate by selecting it from the layouts pop-up menu, and choose Layouts ➪ Duplicate Layout. By default, the layout is named *layout name Copy*. You can change its name by following the instructions in "Renaming a layout," later in this chapter.

Reordering layouts

In the layouts pop-up menu, layouts are displayed in the order in which you created them. However, this order may not be what you want. For example, you may want to display the layouts you use most frequently at the top of the layouts pop-up menu or arrange them in order of importance or function.

To change the order in which layouts are displayed in the pop-up menu, follow these steps:

1. In the appropriate FileMaker Pro database, switch to Layout mode.
2. Choose Layouts ➪ Set Layout Order.

   The Set Layout Order dialog box appears, as shown in Figure 6-45.

Drag a layout up or down in the list
to change order in the layout pop-up menu

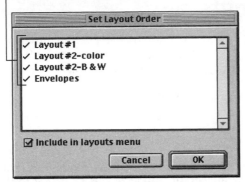

Figure 6-45: The Set Layout Order dialog box

3. Drag layout names into the desired order.

To make a layout first in the list, for example, click and drag its name to the top of the list.

4. Click OK to put the new order into effect.

You return to the Layout Options dialog box.

As Figure 6-45 shows, you can also change whether a layout's name appears in the layouts pop-up menu. A check mark in front of a layout name signifies that it will be listed in the layouts pop-up menu. The check mark works as a toggle—you can click in front of any layout name to add or remove the check mark.

Tip   If you like, you can add separator lines to the layouts pop-up menu. Simply create a new blank layout and name it "-" (hyphen).

Renaming a layout

The default names assigned to new and duplicated layouts (such as Layout #1 and Data Entry Copy) aren't very informative. You can use the Layout Setup dialog box to give a layout a new name.

Follow these steps to rename a layout:

1. In the appropriate FileMaker Pro database, switch to Layout mode.

2. Choose the layout that you want to rename from the layouts pop-up menu.

3. Choose Layouts ⇨ Layout Setup.

   The Layout Setup dialog box appears, as shown earlier in this chapter in the "Previewing and Printing Layouts in Columns" sidebar.

4. Type a new name for the layout in the Name text box.

5. Click OK.

Deleting a layout

A layout may no longer be useful for several reasons. For example, the layout may not have been exactly what you wanted, you may have created it just to test certain FileMaker Pro layout features with no real intention of putting the layout to use, or you may no longer require the kind of report for which the layout was designed.

You can eliminate layouts you no longer need by following these steps:

1. In the appropriate FileMaker Pro database, switch to Layout mode.

2. Choose the layout you want to delete from the layouts pop-up menu.

3. Choose Layouts ⇨ Delete Layout (or press ⌘+E/Ctrl+E).

   An alert box appears, asking you to confirm the deletion.

4. Click the Delete button in the alert box.

   FileMaker Pro removes the layout from your database. Keep in mind that at least one layout must remain in every database.

Summary

✦ FileMaker Pro databases can have multiple layouts. The particular fields placed in each layout and their formatting are up to you.

✦ Layouts can be based on any of six predefined layout styles, including columnar lists/reports, Avery labels, and business envelopes. All new layouts (after the initial one) are designed with the help of the New Layout/Report assistant.

✦ Layouts can have multiple sections (called *parts*), including headers, footers, a body, subsummaries, and a grand summary.

✦ Layout parts can include fields, text, and graphics. Objects of any type can be aligned and moved as a group.

✦ FileMaker Pro includes many tools that enable you to size and place fields and objects on a layout precisely. You can apply powerful formatting commands to fields and objects to make them look as you want.

✦ If you're a Microsoft Office user, you may want to enable one or more of FileMaker Pro 5's toolbars. If you're comfortable with toolbars, you can choose common formatting commands from the icons and pop-up menus on the toolbars.

✦ Any layout—regardless of its style—can be displayed in the new Table View. Table View takes all fields from the current layout and arranges them in a spreadsheet-style grid in which each row is a record and the columns are fields.

✦　　✦　　✦

Setting Preferences

Not everyone likes to work the same way (some of us are morning people, and others are night owls, for example). The same holds true for using FileMaker Pro. The way you prefer to create database layouts, enter data, and work with a database may differ significantly from the way your coworkers perform the same tasks. Fortunately, you can set preferences to customize the way you work with the program and the way you work with specific databases.

It's important for you to learn what the available preferences are, how to set them, and how to change them when necessary. For example, you may find yourself working on someone else's computer or with a database that another person created. If the other person's computer or setup behaves differently from yours, you benefit from knowing that the differences are likely due to alternative preferences and that you can easily change them to match your normal way of working. (Be considerate, though. If you change the preferences on someone else's computer, put them back as you found them when you're through.)

There are two types of FileMaker Pro preferences. *Application preferences* are global settings that affect the way FileMaker Pro operates — regardless of what database you are using. *Document preferences* are specific to one particular database. Every database can have its own set of document preferences.

Setting Application Preferences

You set all application preferences from the Application Preferences dialog box (shown in Figure 7-1). To access this dialog box, choose Edit ➪ Preferences ➪ Application.

Macintosh

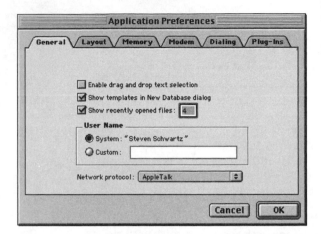

Windows

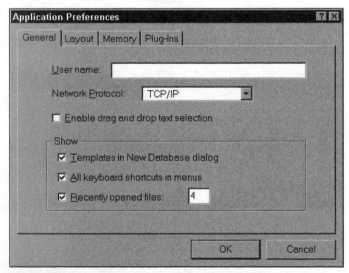

Figure 7-1: The Application Preferences dialog box for the Mac (top) and Windows (bottom)

The preference categories are as follows:

✦ *General preferences* refer to those preferences that govern how FileMaker Pro behaves as a whole. They also enable you to specify a network protocol, if appropriate.

✦ *Layout preferences* affect only actions that occur in Layout mode.

✦ *Memory preferences* enable you to adjust the frequency with which FileMaker Pro saves data to disk.

✦ *Modem preferences* enable you to configure FileMaker Pro to work with a modem. (Windows users must set modem preferences in the Modems control panel, rather than in FileMaker Pro).

✦ *Dialing preferences* enable you to specify prefixes and suffixes to use when dialing phone numbers from various locations. (Windows users must set dialing preferences in the Modems control panel, rather than in FileMaker Pro).

Plug-Ins are add-ins that increase FileMaker Pro's functionality. For example, FileMaker Pro 5.0 comes with a Web Companion plug-in that helps you publish your database on the World Wide Web or on a corporate Intranet. (See Chapter 20 for more information on Web Companion.)

Follow these general steps to set Application preferences:

1. Choose Edit ⇨ Preferences ⇨ Application.

   The Application Preferences dialog box appears (as previously shown in Figure 7-1).

2. Determine which category of preferences you want to set and choose the corresponding option from the tabs at the top of the dialog box.

   The preference settings change to those appropriate to the selected category.

3. Make the desired changes.

4. Choose another category for which you want to make changes.

   — or —

   Click OK to put your changes into effect and dismiss the Application Preferences dialog box.

 New Feature
The Application Preferences dialog box in FileMaker Pro 5 now sports a Cancel button. Clicking Cancel discards all changes and dismisses the dialog box. In previous versions of FileMaker Pro, if you set some options in the Application Preferences dialog box and then changed your mind, you had to manually restore the options to their previous settings.

The following sections discuss the specific options that you can set in each category.

Setting General program preferences

The General preferences (previously shown in Figure 7-1) govern overall program behavior. The General preference options are as follows:

✦ *Enable drag-and-drop text selection*: FileMaker Pro supports the drag-and-drop feature found in Windows and Macintosh System 7.5 and later. When enabled, you can select and drag information from one field to another, from one FileMaker Pro database to another, and between FileMaker Pro databases and documents created in other programs (such as word processing, spreadsheet, and graphics programs).

Note   To drag text or objects between FileMaker Pro and another application, the other application must also support drag-and-drop.

✦ *Show templates in New Database dialog*: FileMaker Pro 5 includes a variety of business, home, and educational templates that you can use to create ready-to-use databases. Check this option if you want these templates to be listed and selectable in the New Database dialog box that appears when you launch FileMaker Pro or choose the File ➪ New Database command.

✦ *Show recently opened files*: You can have FileMaker Pro display the most recently opened files at the bottom of the File menu, making it simple to reopen them. Select this check box and type the number of files you want to list.

✦ *All keyboard shortcuts in menus* (Windows only): Check this check box if you want FileMaker Pro to display all available keyboard shortcuts in the various menus (File, Edit, and so on).

✦ *User Name* (Macintosh): This option governs whether FileMaker Pro for the Macintosh uses the system user name or a name you supply in the Application Preferences dialog box. The default is to use the system name (System), which is set in the Sharing Setup control panel in System 7 and in OS 8's File Sharing control panel. Click the System button to use the name that appears in quotes, or click the Custom button and enter another name in the text box. (Note that if the system name is currently blank—shown as an empty pair of quotation marks—you haven't identified yourself to the Mac. Step-by-step instructions in Chapter 5 show you how to set the system user name.)

After you've specified a user name, you can enter it into a field with the Insert ➪ Current User Name command, automatically enter it in a field by setting an appropriate auto-entry option, or use it in scripts. In a networked database, for example, you could automatically enter the current user's name as the person who created or most recently modified each record.

✦ *User Name* (Windows): In the Windows version of FileMaker Pro, you only have the option to enter a User Name.

After you've specified a user name, you can enter it into a field with the Insert ⇨ Current User Name command, automatically enter it in a field by setting an appropriate auto-entry option, or use it in scripts. In a networked database, for example, you could automatically enter the current user's name as the person who created or most recently modified each record.

Tip You can also create scripts that employ the custom user name. For example, you may want to create a script that finds data specific to a given individual, such as all telephone orders taken by a particular telemarketer. Instead of creating a separate script for every user, you can have FileMaker Pro use the custom user name. To find information for a different person (another telemarketer, for instance), you merely change the custom user name in the Application Preferences dialog box before running the script. (See Chapter 15 for more information about scripts.)

✦ *Network protocol*: If you are going to use FileMaker Pro over a network or the Internet, choose the appropriate network protocol from this drop-down list. (If you aren't sure of the correct choice, ask your network administrator.) Internet users will normally choose TCP/IP.

Setting Layout preferences

Layout preferences (shown in Figure 7-2) apply solely to actions that can take place while you're in Layout mode — either designing a new layout or editing an existing one. Settings chosen in the Layout section of the Application Preferences dialog box affect *all* databases, not merely the database that is active when the Application Preferences command is chosen.

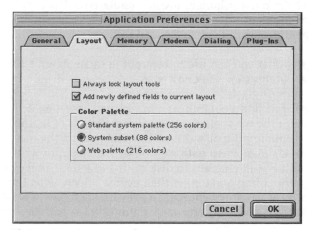

Figure 7-2: Layout preferences

The Layout preferences perform the following functions:

✦ *Always lock layout tools*: This option determines how tools behave when you're designing or modifying layouts. By default, FileMaker Pro automatically switches back to the Pointer tool after you perform an operation with any other tool. Although this way of operating enables you to select an item quickly after you modify it, it can be annoying if you routinely perform several operations in a row with the same tool. When "Always lock layout tools" is checked, FileMaker Pro keeps the same tool selected until you choose a different tool or press the Enter key.

✦ *Add newly defined fields to current layout*: This option determines whether new fields that you define will automatically be added to the current layout. By default, FileMaker Pro is set to add them. If you want to define new fields without automatically placing them on the current layout, remove the check mark from this option. You will then have to add newly defined fields manually (by dragging them onto the layout).

✦ *Color palette*: When adding colors to objects, you can now specify one of three color palettes to use. (If you are creating cross-platform databases or ones you intend to publish with the Web Companion, choose the "Web palette.")

Setting Memory preferences

Memory preferences control the manner in which FileMaker Pro saves data to disk (see Figure 7-3). As you work, FileMaker Pro saves data in two ways: by using the memory cache and by copying new data to the disk that contains the original database document. The cache is a special part of RAM (random access memory) that is set aside for FileMaker Pro's use. Changes are accumulated in the cache until it is full or until an opportune moment arises (that is, when the system is idle). At this point, changes are flushed from the cache and saved to disk.

Note   ScriptMaker includes a step that you can use to control the cache directly: Flush Cache to Disk. To learn about this step, see Chapter 15.

This way of operating is fine for desktop computers. On laptops, however, it can waste battery power. One of the most energy-consuming aspects of laptop operation is powering up and running the disk drives. For this reason, the drives on a laptop are frequently powered down when data isn't being read from or written to them. If FileMaker Pro is set to save all changes to disk during idle time, however, it can keep the drives running more often and longer than normal, decreasing the amount of work time you get from a battery charge. To prevent such power waste, you can specify that FileMaker Pro save only after a given interval — perhaps once every 30 minutes.

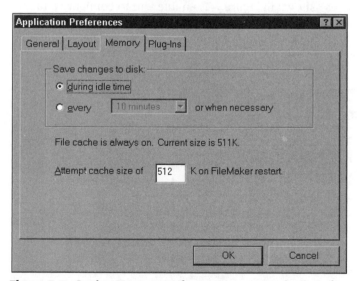

Figure 7-3: Setting Memory preferences on a Mac (top) and a Windows PC (bottom)

Setting a save interval involves a significant trade-off. The longer the interval you choose, the less battery power is consumed, but the more data you put at risk. If you suffer a crash between saves, you may lose everything in the cache. This problem is not significant if you're only using the database to look up information or if you're making only limited changes. Note, however, that even if you set a relatively long save interval, FileMaker Pro will still save if the cache fills before the interval is reached.

To set a save interval in the Memory section of the Application Preferences dialog box, click the button labeled "every ... or when necessary" and choose the desired interval from the pop-up menu. Remember that longer intervals are riskier to data, but they save more power. If you decide that you'd rather save new data as soon as possible, click the button labeled "during idle time" (the default).

The size of FileMaker Pro's cache is fixed in the Macintosh version. Under Windows, however, you can change the amount of memory used for the cache by entering a new number (refer to Figure 7-3, bottom).

Setting Modem and Dialing preferences

The Modem and Dialing options are available for all Macintoshes and for some versions of Windows, as indicated in the following sections. The Modem and Dialing preferences work together to enable FileMaker Pro scripts to dial telephone numbers through a modem or the computer's speaker.

Modem preferences

The Modem preferences (shown in Figure 7-4) enable you to configure a modem to work with FileMaker Pro. If you do not have a modem, you can configure the Modem preferences to use the computer's speaker for dialing. (When dialing a number, you'll have to put your telephone handset up to the speaker.)

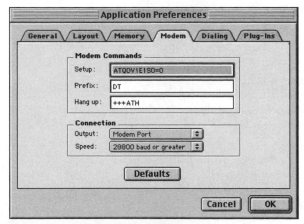

Figure 7-4: Modem preferences

Note   Modem preferences can be set for all Macs and users of Windows 3.1, Windows for Workgroups, and Windows NT 3.51. If you use Windows 95, 98, or Windows NT 4.0 or later, refer to the sidebar in this section for help using the Phone Dialer utility to set modem and dialing preferences.

Use the Modem Commands section of the dialog box to specify a setup string for the modem, a dialing prefix, and a hang-up command. For most modems, the default entries for these commands can be left alone. If you decide to change them, refer to your modem manual for the appropriate commands.

Use the Connection section of the dialog box to specify the port to which your modem is connected and the speed with which the modem should operate. In the Output pop-up menu, choose the port to which your modem is attached. Choose Speaker if you don't have a modem or if you don't want to use your modem for dialing.

The Speed pop-up menu is used to set the modem speed for dialing. Normally, you should select the highest speed that your modem is designed to handle.

Note   If — after experimenting with the Modem preferences — you want to return to FileMaker Pro's original modem settings, simply click the Defaults button at the bottom of the dialog box (refer to Figure 7-4).

Setting modem and dialing preferences with Phone Dialer

If you are running Windows 95, 98, or Windows NT 4.0 (or later), there are no Modem or Dialing tabs in the Application Preferences dialog box. Instead, you must set these preferences using the Phone Dialer. Click the Start button on the Taskbar, and choose Programs ➪ Accessories ➪ Phone Dialer.

To configure Phone Dialer so FileMaker Pro and other applications can dial through your modem, choose Tools ➪ Connect Using. In the Connect Using dialog box (shown below), select your modem from the Line pop-up menu, and be sure that "Use Phone Dialer to handle . . ." is checked. To create or set the properties for different dialing locations (home, office, and so on), choose Tools ➪ Dialing Properties.

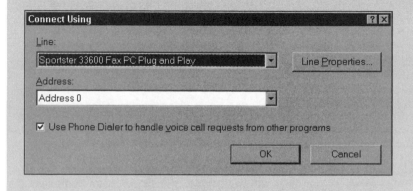

Dialing preferences

The Dialing preferences (see Figure 7-5) are used to create sets of dialing configurations based on your current location (Home, Office, Road, and Other). You can create different preferences for each location.

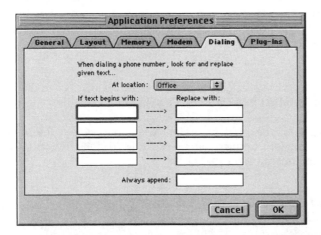

Figure 7-5: Dialing preferences

In the Dialing preferences, you can establish substitution strings to be dialed, depending on the composition of different phone numbers. Table 7-1 gives some examples of Dialing preferences when the local area code is 617.

	Table 7-1	
	Substitution Strings for Dialing Preferences	
If Text Begins with:	*Replace with:*	*Comments*
617		If your area code (617) is found, do not dial the area code as part of the number; that is, replace 617 with nothing (blank).
617	9,	Dial local calls by replacing the area code with 9, followed by a two-second pause (represented by the comma).
	1	Regardless of the number found, treat it as long distance by preceding it with a 1.

Optionally, you can also specify a dialing suffix in the "Always append" text box. Some long-distance services can track different types of calls (various business projects, for example) if you append extra digits to the phone number.

To set the Dialing preferences for this and future sessions, select a location from the "At location" pop-up menu. When you are at another location (taking your laptop on the road, for example), choose a different location. Each defined location can have a different set of dialing preferences.

Note   To dial from a FileMaker Pro database, you must use a script that contains the Dial Phone step. Also, unless the script step enables the "Use dialing preferences" option, the Dialing preferences are ignored.

Setting Plug-Ins preferences

FileMaker Pro versions 4.0 and higher support *plug-ins* — small applications that add functionality to FileMaker Pro. FileMaker Pro includes ODBC data access plug-ins and a Web Companion plug-in that enables you to publish your database on the World Wide Web. You use the Plug-Ins preferences (see Figure 7-6) to enable and disable plug-ins or to configure enabled plug-ins.

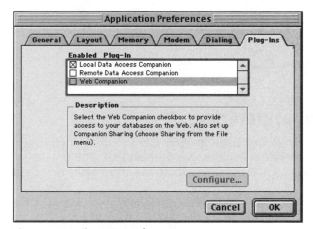

Figure 7-6: Plug-Ins preferences

To enable a plug-in, click in the check box beside the plug-in. Once the plug-in has been enabled, you can click the Configure button to set options that are specific to the plug-in.

To learn about configuring and using the Web Companion plug-in, see Chapter 20.

Note   FileMaker Inc. is not the sole source of plug-ins. Some FileMaker Pro developers — such as Troi Automatisering — offer plug-ins that extend FileMaker Pro's functionality. (See the Troi folder on the *FileMaker Pro 5 Bible* CD-ROM for some examples.)

Setting Document-Specific Preferences

In addition to setting preferences for FileMaker Pro as a whole, you can set document preferences (shown in Figure 7-7) individually for each database. For instance, you can set a start-up action for a given database by setting a preference that directs it to open to a particular layout or automatically run a script.

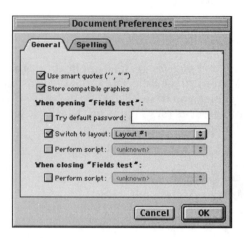

Figure 7-7: Document preferences — General

General document preferences

Every database can have different document preferences. To view or change document preferences, choose Edit ⇨ Preferences ⇨ Document. The Document Preferences dialog box appears. Click the General tab to set the following General document preferences.

✦ *Use smart quotes*: This option instructs FileMaker to use curved open and closed quotation marks rather than straight quotation marks (' ' and " " versus ' ' and " "). The former characters are commonly referred to as curly or "smart" quotes and are generally favored because they look more professional.

FileMaker Pro contains a set of rules that determines when it uses a left quote and when it uses a right quote. When the "Use smart quotes" option is selected, the appropriate curly quote character is typed each time you press the single or double quotation mark key. Note that this preference option has no effect if the font you're using doesn't contain symbols for the curved quotes — straight quotes will be used instead.

✦ *Store compatible graphics*: This option instructs FileMaker Pro to store compatible graphics in both Mac and Windows formats. If this option is not enabled, the graphics are stored only in the format native to your platform.

✦ *When opening, try default password*: In addition to normal and blank passwords (discussed in Chapter 19), FileMaker Pro enables you to specify a default password that is automatically tried when a user opens a particular database. You can associate specific privileges with the default password (such as allowing the user to only browse through records, but not edit, create, or delete them). One advantage of establishing a default password rather than using an ordinary password is that the user is never confronted with a request to enter a password. The database opens automatically (just like most other databases), and only the FileMaker Pro features specified by the person who developed the database are enabled.

You set the default password option by clicking the "Try default password" check box and then typing the default password in the text box.

Tip　If this option has been set for a database and you want to force the password dialog box to appear (so you can enter a different password), hold down the Shift key (Windows) or the Option key (Mac) as you open the database.

✦ *When opening, switch to layout*: This option specifies a particular layout to display whenever the database is opened. If you do not set this option, the database opens to whatever layout was active when the database was last closed.

This option is especially helpful in two situations: First, many databases are menu-driven. Instead of a normal data-entry screen, a database might contain a menu of buttons that enables the user to select which portion of the database or function he/she wants to perform (data entry, report printing, or label generation, for example). By selecting the menu layout as the opening layout, you can ensure that new users won't be confused by starting in a different (possibly foreign) section of the database each time.

Second, many databases are designed so that they revolve around one basic layout. For example, the Address Book database discussed in Chapter 4 has a data-entry layout as the central layout. Because most of the work a user will do is on that layout, it makes sense to have FileMaker Pro open automatically to it.

✦ *When opening, perform script*: This option automatically performs a selected script when the database is opened. For instance, you can perform a script that opens to a particular record (other than the first one), sorts the database, or sets a particular display option, for example.

✦ *When closing, perform script*: This option automatically performs a selected script when the database is closed (when you click the document's close box, choose File ➪ Close, press ⌘+W/Ctrl+W, or quit FileMaker Pro while the database is still open). For example, you may want to execute a script that prints a daily report. Setting this script as a closing action — rather than as an opening action — enables you to avoid a lengthy delay at the beginning of your work session.

Manually entering curly quotes (Mac only)

In some databases (ones that contain measurements in feet and inches, for example), using smart quotes may not be to your advantage. If the "Use smart quotes" option is selected, you cannot type straight quotation marks (' and "). If you find that you frequently need to use straight quotes in a particular database, the best approach is to remove the check mark from the "Use smart quotes" setting. When you need curly quotes, you can enter them manually in the Mac version, as explained in the following table. (As a bonus, you can also use the instructions in the table to produce curly quote characters in other programs that don't provide a smart quotes option.)

Type This . . .	To Produce This Curly Quote Character
Option+[	" (double left quote)
Shift+Option+[	" (double right quote)
Option+]	' (single left quote)
Shift+Option+]	' (single right quote)

Spelling document preferences

You can also set document preferences for the spelling checker. Choose Spelling from the tab at the top of the Document Preferences dialog box (see Figure 7-8).

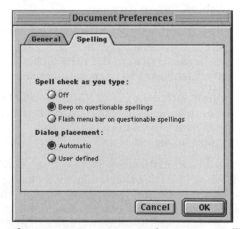

Figure 7-8: Document preferences — Spelling

The power user's guide to preferences

Setting a start-up or closing script with the "Perform script" document preference is a great way to exert control over a database. Scripts can instruct FileMaker Pro to perform any of the following actions automatically when a database is opened or closed:

✦ Make sure the database is sorted in a particular order.

✦ Select a subset of records with which to work or make certain all records are visible.

✦ Perform a Relookup procedure so all lookup fields contain current data.

✦ Open a report layout and automatically print a current copy of the report.

You can set these options:

✦ *Spell check as you type*: Click the appropriate radio button to make your selection. If you turn on this feature, FileMaker Pro will either beep or flash the menu bar when you type a word that it isn't in its spelling dictionary. If you click the Off radio button, FileMaker Pro will not spell check as you type. However, you can still perform manual spelling checks by choosing commands from the Edit ➪ Spelling submenu.

✦ *Dialog placement*: When you enable spell checking, FileMaker Pro will pop up a dialog box whenever it finds a potential error. You can choose to have the dialog box appear in a location determined by FileMaker Pro ("Automatic") or in the location to which you last dragged the dialog box ("User defined").

Summary

✦ You can customize how FileMaker Pro operates, as well as the start-up and closing actions of individual databases, by choosing the Application or Document command from the Edit ➪ Preferences submenu.

✦ Selecting the "Use smart quotes" option instructs FileMaker Pro to substitute curved left and right quotation marks for straight quotation marks. However, using this option makes entering foot and inch symbols (straight quotation marks) difficult.

✦ You can save battery power on a portable Macintosh (a PowerBook, for example) or portable PC by specifying the frequency with which FileMaker Pro saves data to disk.

✦ FileMaker Pro plug-ins can be enabled, disabled, or configured in the Application Preferences dialog box.

✦　　✦　　✦

Working With Databases

◆ ◆ ◆ ◆

In This Part

◆ ◆ ◆ ◆

Working with Records

As a FileMaker Pro user, you will spend most of your time in Browse mode, one of the four FileMaker Pro operational modes discussed in Chapter 1. Whenever you want to view, enter, or edit data, add new records, or delete records, you must first switch to Browse mode.

Browse Mode Basics

As the name suggests, you can use Browse mode to flip through a database record by record, examining, creating, and modifying records as you go. You also have to be in Browse mode to omit records (temporarily hide them) or to sort records. Because you usually omit records in conjunction with a find request, this topic is discussed in Chapter 9. Sorting is covered in Chapter 10.

You can be in only one mode at a time. Determining which mode you are in is easy. In the View menu, the current mode has a check mark next to it, as shown in Figure 8-1. The name of the current mode also appears in the mode selector pop-up menu at the bottom of the database window (also shown in Figure 8-1).

Select a mode

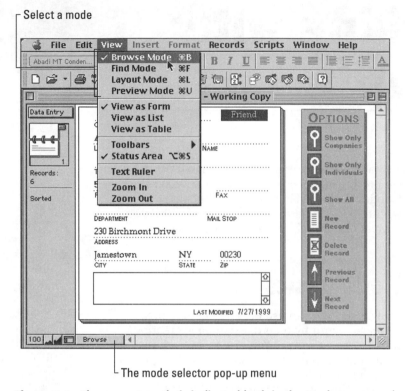

The mode selector pop-up menu

Figure 8-1: The current mode is indicated both in the Mode menu and in the mode selector pop-up menu.

Switching to Browse mode

Regardless of the mode you're currently in, you can switch to Browse mode in two ways:

✦ By choosing the View ➪ Browse Mode command (or pressing ⌘+B/Ctrl+B)

✦ By choosing Browse from the mode selector pop-up menu at the bottom of the database window

You can also switch to other modes (Find, Layout, and Preview) by selecting the mode from one of these menus.

Note

When you first open a database, FileMaker Pro automatically displays it in Browse mode. This is convenient, because browsing is what you do most.

Using Browse mode controls

As shown in Figure 8-2, fewer controls are available in Browse mode than in Layout mode — the mode in which database layouts (arrangements of fields, graphics, and static text) are designed. The available controls are all related to record navigation and data viewing.

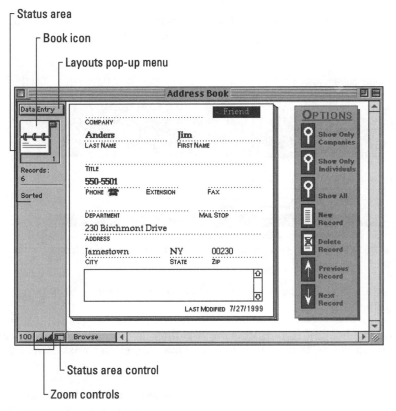

Figure 8-2: Browse mode controls

Using the Layouts pop-up menu to switch layouts

As I have emphasized throughout this book, layouts are extremely important in FileMaker Pro. A *layout* is a particular arrangement of database fields. Because no single way of displaying fields is equally useful for all tasks, many databases have multiple layouts. For example, a layout that makes it easy to enter data may not be the best one for displaying a report. You can change layouts in Browse mode at any time.

In the upper-left corner of the window, at the top of the status area, is the *layouts* pop-up menu (previously shown in Figure 8-2). You use this menu to determine which layout is currently displayed and to switch between available layouts for the database (by selecting a layout from the menu). For example, follow these steps to switch the Address Book database from one layout to another and then back again:

1. With the Address Book database displayed, choose the Phone Directory layout from the layouts pop-up menu.

   The display changes to show the Phone Directory layout (see Figure 8-3). The layouts pop-up menu shows that you have changed to a new layout.

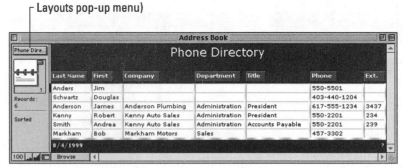

Figure 8-3: The Phone Directory layout in the Address Book database

2. Choose the Data Entry layout from the layouts pop-up menu to switch back again.

Keep in mind that different layouts may require different amounts of screen space. When changing from one layout to another, you may sometimes need to resize the database window.

Tip   If you want, you can specify an opening layout for each database. Instead of opening to the layout that was displayed when you last closed the database (which is the default), FileMaker Pro displays the opening layout that you set in the Document Preferences dialog box. For instructions on setting an opening layout, see Chapter 7.

Using the book icon to navigate among records

Below the layouts pop-up menu is the *book icon* (see Figure 8-4). In Browse mode, you use the book to navigate among records and select the next one you want to work with or view.

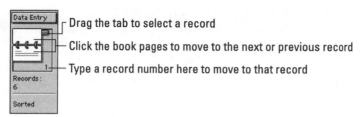

Drag the tab to select a record

Click the book pages to move to the next or previous record

Type a record number here to move to that record

Figure 8-4: The book icon

Note The book has different functions in other modes. In Find mode, you use it to switch between multiple find requests. In Layout mode, each book page represents a different layout. In Preview mode, you click the book to view different report pages.

In Browse mode, the navigation operations you can perform by using the book include the following:

✦ Flipping from one record to the next or the previous record (by clicking the bottom or top pages of the book, respectively)

✦ Quickly moving to the first or last record (by dragging the tab on the side of the book to the top or bottom)

✦ Moving to an approximate position in the database (by dragging the tab on the side of the book)

✦ Moving to a specific record (by typing a record number in the area below the book)

The tab on the side of the book shows the approximate position in the database of the currently displayed record. The number below the book shows the exact position of the current record. The first record in the database is record #1, the second is record #2, and so on. The area below the book shows the total number of records that are currently in the database, the number of records that are being browsed (if all records aren't presently visible), and whether the database has been sorted (arranged in a particular order). In the example previously shown in Figure 8-4, the first record out of six is currently displayed, and the database is in sort order.

The following sections explain the various methods of navigating through the database. If you want to experiment with the different methods, you can use the Address Book database or any other database that's handy.

Browsing suggestions

Looking up individual records is a common thing to do with a database. After all, the purpose of a database is to store information for later retrieval. Although you can locate and examine records in several ways (many of which are discussed in later chapters), frequently you'll just flip through records one at a time until you find the one you want.

However, flipping through records can be time-consuming when you are working with a large database. (See Chapter 9 for quicker, more efficient search methods.) One thing you can do to make this process easier is to switch to a layout that shows more than one record at a time (such as the Phone Directory layout for the Address Book database) or display the records in the current layout as a list or table. (See the section, "Navigating without using the book," later in this chapter.)

Moving to the next or previous record in a database

You can use the book icon or keyboard shortcuts to move forward and backward in a database one record at a time. Follow these steps:

1. To move forward in a database, click the lower half of the book.

   Each click switches to the next record in the current sort order, making it the current record. The book tab moves down slightly, and the new record is displayed.

   — or —

   To move backward through a database, click the upper half of the book. Each click switches to the previous record in the current sort order, making it the current record. The book tab moves up slightly, and the new record is displayed.

2. Continue clicking until the desired record appears.

Tip   FileMaker Pro 5 also provides keyboard shortcuts that you can use to move to the next or previous record. To go to the next record, press Ctrl+down arrow. To go to the previous record, press Ctrl+up arrow. (In previous Macintosh versions of FileMaker Pro, the equivalent commands were ⌘+Tab and ⌘+Shift+Tab.)

Moving to the first record in a database

Follow these steps to move to the first record in a database:

1. Click the book tab and drag upward until it reaches the top of the book.

2. Release the mouse button.

   — or —

1. Click the record number indicator directly below the book to select it.

2. Type **1** and then press Return/Enter.

You can type any number to move directly to a particular record. Although you normally won't know specific record numbers, you will always know the first one.

The first record in the database becomes the current record.

You can tell when you're at the first record of a database because the top half of the book icon is blank. As usual, the record number (1, in this case) is displayed below the book.

Tip

If you want to go to a specific record, you can select the record number indicator (beneath the book icon) by pressing the Esc key. You may find this faster than clicking to select the record number indicator. Note that this only works if no record is currently selected.

If the current layout displays one record per screen (such as the Data Entry layout in the Address Book database), only the first record is visible. If you have chosen View as List or View as Table from the View menu, as is often done in reports, a small vertical bar on the left side of the record display area marks the current record in the list (as previously shown in Figure 8-3).

Moving to the last record in a database

Follow these steps to move to the last record in a database:

1. Click the book tab and drag downward until it reaches the bottom of the book.

2. Release the mouse button.

The last record in the database becomes the current record.

— or —

1. Click the record number indicator directly below the book to select it.

2. Type a number greater than or equal to the number of records in the database (displayed below the book area) and press Return/Enter.

As long as the number is greater than or equal to the number of records that are currently being browsed, the last record is displayed, and it becomes the current record.

When the last record is selected, the bottom of the book is blank — showing that no records follow the current one. As always, the record number is displayed immediately below the bottom book page.

Note

Regardless of the record navigation method you use, if you attempt to move up past the first record or down past the last record, nothing happens.

Who's on first?

The particular database record that is displayed as first and the one that is last depends on whether the database has been sorted, and if so, by which field or fields. For example, the first record originally entered in Address Book may have been the one for Don Smith.

If you sort the database by the Last Name field, the new first record may be that of Jim Abrams. (See Chapter 10 for more information on sorting and how it affects a database.)

Moving to a specific record in a database

You can also move to a specific record number if you happen to know, for example, that the desired record is the fourth one down.

Follow these steps to move to a specific record number:

1. Click the record number indicator below the book to select it.

   — or —

   If no record is currently selected, press the Escape key (Esc).

   In either case, the record number indicator changes to inverse video to show that it is selected.

2. Type the number of the record you want to examine, and press Return/Enter.

   The corresponding record appears on the screen and becomes the current record.

Note

When you are browsing a database, you usually have all of its records at your disposal. Sometimes, however, you may want to view only a subset of the records. To view a subset, you can issue a find request. A find request restricts visible records to those that match the find criteria (Salary < 50000, for example). For more information about searching for record subsets, see Chapter 9.

Navigating without using the book

By choosing View ➪ View as List, you can bypass the book icon when browsing records. In List View, all records are displayed as a continuous, scrolling list. You use the scroll bar at the side of the database window to change records in view. Reports and data-entry screens that have limited fields are often displayed and worked with in List or Table View. If you have an appropriate keyboard, you can also use the keys in Table 8-1 to move through the database in List View.

In addition to Form and List views (available in previous versions of FileMaker), FileMaker Pro 5 offers a third way to view records: Table View. Choose View ➪ View as Table to display the fields from the current layout in a spreadsheet-style grid (see Figure 8-5). The navigation commands available in List View can also be used in Table View.

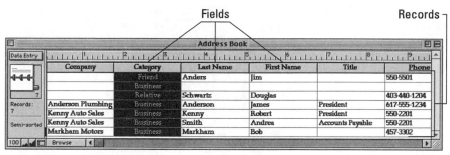

Figure 8-5: View as Table

<table>
<tr><td colspan="2" align="center">Table 8-1
Navigational Shortcuts for View as List and View Table Modes</td></tr>
<tr><td>*Key*</td><td>*Effect*</td></tr>
<tr><td>Home</td><td>Move to the first record</td></tr>
<tr><td>End</td><td>Move to the last record</td></tr>
<tr><td>Page Up</td><td>Move up one screen</td></tr>
<tr><td>Page Down</td><td>Move down one screen</td></tr>
</table>

Note that these keys are purely for viewing and navigating through records. If you want to add data to or edit the current data in a record, you must select the record by clicking somewhere inside it.

If List View or Table View aren't the views you normally use for the current layout, choose View ➪ View as Form. The display reverts to one record per screen.

Changing the magnification level

Below the status area (at the bottom of the database window) are three tools that enable you to change your view of the database: the *magnification level*, *zoom out*, and *zoom in controls*. For example, you can decrease the magnification (or zoom out) to get a bird's-eye view of a layout or report (as shown in Figure 8-6); you can also increase the magnification (or zoom in) to concentrate on a particular section of a record. Although these tools are more useful in Layout mode, you can use them in Browse mode, too.

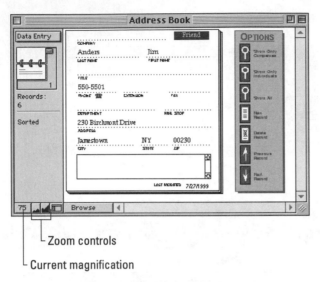

Zoom controls

Current magnification

Figure 8-6: Address Book zoomed to 75 percent

The current magnification is shown as a percentage: 100 means that the database is shown actual size, 200 means that it's twice the usual size, and so on. Clicking the number toggles the display between 100 percent and the most recently selected zoom level. You use the pair of buttons to the right of the magnification percentage to zoom out (decrease magnification) and zoom in (increase magnification), respectively. Each time you click one of the buttons, the magnification is decreased or increased, to a maximum of 400 percent and a minimum of 25 percent.

Showing and hiding the status area

To the right of the zoom controls is the status area control (previously shown in Figure 8-2). This button works as a toggle, enabling you to hide or show the status area. Hiding the status area gives you more room in which to display the database. When you click the status area control to hide the status area, the current layout fills the entire window. Click the status area control again to display the status area and regain access to the tools.

Finally, to the right of the status area control button is the mode selector pop-up menu. As mentioned earlier in this chapter, you can use this menu to switch from one operational mode to another.

Working in different views

When browsing, you can display records in any of three views: Form View (one record per screen), List View (all records displayed in a scrolling list using the current layout), or Table View (all fields from the current layout displayed as a spreadsheet-style grid). You can switch freely among the different views — depending on your current needs — by choosing a "View as" command from the View menu.

Form View is frequently used for entering data. List View is commonly used for on-screen and printed reports. Table View (a new feature in FileMaker Pro 5) is useful for examining the entire database or all records of a found set. You can specify which of the three views are available for a given layout — enabling one view and disabling the other two, for example. To do this:

1. Choose a layout from the Layouts pop-up menu in the upper-left corner of the status area.

2. Switch to Layout mode (press ⌘+L/Ctrl+L, choose View ➪ Layout Mode, or choose Layout from the Mode pop-up menu at the bottom of the database window).

3. Choose Layouts ➪ Layout Setup.

   The Layout setup dialog box appears.

4. Click the Views tab (see Figure 8-7).

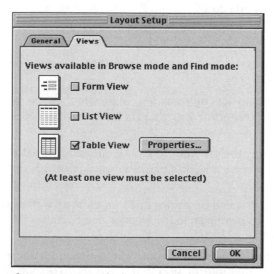

Figure 8-7: Specify the enabled views for the current layout

5. Add and remove check marks to enable and disable views for this layout, as desired.

6. *Optional*: If Table View is enabled, click the Properties button to set Table View options. Otherwise, go to step 11.

The Table View Properties dialog box appears (see Figure 8-8).

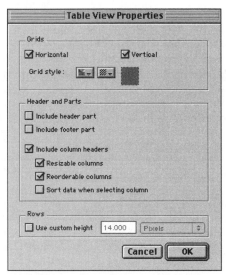

Figure 8-8: The Table View Properties dialog box

7. Set grid display options in the Grid section of the Table View Properties dialog box:

   • The Horizontal and Vertical options determine whether the table is shown with horizontal and/or vertical gridlines between records and fields, respectively.

   • If you want to display the gridlines in a different color or pattern than solid black, select a color and/or a pattern from the Grid Style pop-up palettes.

8. Specify the layout parts that will be shown in Table View, as well as the behavior of column (field) headings, in the Header and Parts section of the Table View Properties dialog box:

   • Check the boxes to "Include header part" and/or "Include footer part" if you have text or other information that you want to display in these parts. It is common to have a header and/or footer part in a report layout or when you want to display a layout title, for example.

- Check "Include column headers" to display the field names at the top of the columns.

- Check "Resizable columns" if you want to be able to manually resize columns by clicking and dragging the right edge of any column heading.

- Check "Reorderable columns" if you want to be able to change the column order by clicking and dragging column headings to new positions.

- Check "Sort data when selecting column" if you want to be able to sort the browsed set by the contents of a clicked column. (This can be extremely useful. Note that, by default, this feature is *not* enabled.)

9. To set a custom height for rows (records), check "Use custom height" and enter a row height in pixels, centimeters, or inches.

10. Click OK to dismiss the Table View Properties dialog box.

11. Click OK to dismiss the Layout Setup dialog box.

Data Entry and Editing

Perhaps the most important uses of Browse mode are entering and editing data. As you work with FileMaker Pro, you'll discover that a wealth of commands and techniques have been provided to make data entry and editing as simple as possible.

Creating new records

Few databases are static entities that you just browse through now and then. Whether you've just finished designing a database or are working with one that you've had around for years, you'll want to add new records to it at some point. For example, a new business or personal contact requires a new record in your Address Book database. After you create the new record, you can enter the appropriate information in each of the record's fields.

The exact way in which you add a record to the database can sometimes depend on the way in which the database was designed. For example, in the Data Entry layout for Address Book (previously shown in Figure 8-2), you can click a New Record button to activate a script that adds a new record to the database. Most database layouts, however, don't have such a button. Instead, you switch to Browse mode and choose the Records ➪ New Record command (or press ⌘+N/Ctrl+N).

The new record appears on-screen, and it is added in the database immediately after the current record. Unless you have set auto-entry options for some fields (see Chapter 5), the record is blank.

Note   If adding the new record disrupted an existing sort order (the indicator below the book icon reads "Semi-sorted"), you can restore order to the database by sorting again, as discussed in Chapter 10.

Entering data

A blank record isn't very useful. After adding a record, you need to enter appropriate information in it. First, however, you need to select the field in which you want to enter data, either by clicking in the field or tabbing into it.

You enter information one field at a time. The *current field* is the one in which you can immediately enter and edit data. A solid border surrounds the current field; borders around all other fields are dotted. The current field also contains the *insertion point*, a blinking vertical line that is sometimes called the *cursor*. Figure 8-9 shows a new record's current field and insertion point.

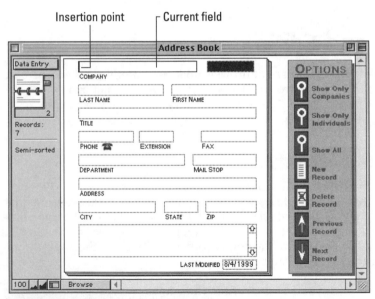

Figure 8-9: A new record

Note   The position of the insertion point in a blank field is determined by the alignment that has been set for the field (using the Align Text submenu of the Format menu). When a field is left aligned, the insertion point appears on the left side of the field. When a field is right aligned — as Number fields frequently are — the insertion point is on the right side of the field.

To enter data in another field, you first need to make it the current field. You can either click the field with the mouse or tab into the field by pressing the Tab key. Pressing Tab moves you forward through a record one field at a time. Pressing Shift+Tab moves you back to the previous field.

You cannot tab into a Summary or Calculation field because you cannot edit or manually enter data in these types of fields. (The only permissible action in these fields is copying the contents.) To select a Summary or Calculation field for copying, you must click the field with the mouse.

Note

By default, when you press the Tab key, the insertion point moves through the fields from left to right and top to bottom. However, you can create a custom tab order by changing to Layout mode and choosing the Set Tab Order command from the Mode menu. (See Chapter 6 for details.)

When you are finished entering data in the record, press the Enter key, choose New Record again, or use the book icon to switch to a different record. The record is immediately evaluated by FileMaker Pro and examined for data validation failures (such as leaving a required field blank). If you have committed any errors, FileMaker Pro will let you know.

Keep in mind that you can enter data in any layout in which fields are displayed — report or mailing label layouts, for example. Of course, because some layouts show different sets of fields, data entry is more convenient in some layouts than in others. Regardless of which layout you use when entering or editing data, the new data for a field is recorded in all layouts in which that same field appears. For example, the Address Book database has two layouts: Data Entry and Phone Directory. Adding or changing the text in a record's Company field in the Phone Directory layout simultaneously changes the text in the Company field in the Data Entry layout. (Remember — every layout is simply a different arrangement of the data contained in the database.) However, because the Phone List layout doesn't provide a place to enter the Category (which is required), FileMaker Pro will present an error message that the category is missing if you try to complete a new record in the Phone List layout.

Using the data-entry and cursor-control keys

As you're entering data, some keys actually enter data (*data-entry keys*) and others merely move the insertion point (*cursor-control keys*) — either within a field or between fields. The differences between the data-entry and cursor-control keys are explained in the following sections.

The data-entry keys

Data-entry keys do what their name suggests. When you press a data-entry key, a corresponding character is entered in a field at the insertion point. The data-entry keys consist of the letters *a* through *z*, the numerals *0* through *9*, and the punctuation keys, as well as these same keys pressed in combination with Shift (Mac/Windows), Option (Mac only), and Shift+Option (Mac only). Return also acts as a data-entry key. Pressing Return/Enter ends the current line and adds a new line to the field.

Note   Number fields do not accept a Return. You need to enter all numbers on a single line within the field.

You can embed a tab character within any Text field by pressing Option+Tab/Ctrl+ Tab. By default, tab stops are set every half-inch. To insert a new tab stop for a Text field, choose View ➪ Text Ruler, and then click the appropriate position on the ruler. A left tab appears at the spot you clicked, as shown in Figure 8-10. To change the new tab to a right, center, or decimal-aligned tab, double-click the tab stop. The Tabs dialog box appears (see Figure 8-11), in which you modify or change the tab stops for the current field.

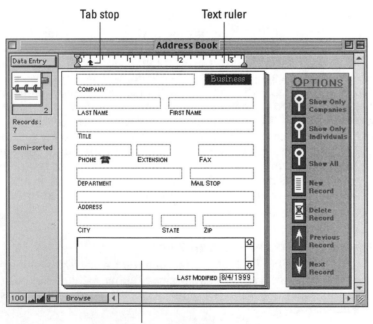

The text ruler always shows
settings for the current field

Figure 8-10: With the text ruler displayed, you can set tab stops for the current field.

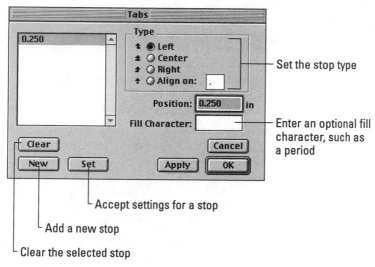

Set the stop type

Enter an optional fill
character, such as
a period

Accept settings for a stop

Add a new stop

Clear the selected stop

Figure 8-11: The Tabs dialog box

Note When setting a tab stop in Browse mode, you are only setting it for the active field
in the current record. If you want to set tabs for another field in the same record or
for the same field in a *different* record, you must set them again. To permanently
set tab stops for a field and have it affect *all* records, switch to Layout mode, select
the field, choose Format ➪ Text, click the Paragraph button, and then click the
Tabs button.

The cursor-control keys

You use the cursor-control keys to move within and between fields. As the name
suggests, a cursor-control key merely moves the cursor. Table 8-2 lists the cursor-
control keys and their functions.

After you master the cursor-control keys, entering data is relatively
straightforward. FileMaker Pro supports the text-entry, cursor-control, and
editing functions that you have already learned in other programs (such as
pressing Delete/Backspace to remove the previous character and using the
Cut, Copy, and Paste commands). Keep in mind, however, that some field types
and definitions may restrict the range of acceptable data that you can enter, as
described in the next section.

Table 8-2
Cursor-Control Keys

Key or Key Combination	Function
Tab	Move to the next field
Shift+Tab	Move to the previous field
Up arrow	Move up one line in the current field, if possible; otherwise, do nothing
Down arrow	Move down to the next line in the current field, if possible; otherwise, do nothing
Left arrow	Move one character position left in the current field, if possible; otherwise, do nothing
Right arrow	Move one character position right in the current field, if possible; otherwise, do nothing

Typing special characters

On a Mac

On a Mac, you use the Option and Shift+Option key combinations to type special characters, such as symbols and foreign language characters. For example, to type a bullet (•), you press Option+8. If you want to find out where those special characters are hiding—the ones that aren't visible on the keyboard—you can use a desk accessory such as Key Caps from Apple Computer (included with every copy of the system software).

As you hold down Shift, Option, or Shift+Option, Key Caps shows the characters you can type by pressing a particular letter, number, or punctuation key in combination with the modifier key or keys that you're holding down. A *modifier key* is any key that changes the meaning of a normal key. In regular typing, the modifier keys are Shift and Option. The Ctrl and ⌘ modifier keys—if supported—are under program control and are usually reserved for issuing commands from the keyboard and similar functions. You can copy any character created in Key Caps and then paste it into the current document.

In Windows

In the Windows version, you can use an accessory included with every copy of Windows called Character Map. Like the Mac's Key Caps, this accessory shows all the characters available in all of your installed fonts.

Beware: If you need to move a database between the Macintosh and Windows versions of FileMaker Pro, or you are using a database on a mixed PC and Mac network, be sparing with your use of special characters. In most cases, these characters will not translate appropriately from one platform to the other. (See Chapter 16 for details.)

Entering different types of data

In FileMaker Pro, each defined field is one of eight different data types: Text, Number, Time, Date, Global, Container, Calculation, and Summary. (You cannot enter or edit data in Calculation and Summary fields.) The following sections describe data entry and editing procedures that you can use with the other six types of fields. (If you need additional help in determining what kinds of information can and cannot go into the different field types, see Chapter 5.)

Note   Any formatting that you set for a field is applied after you enter the data and move to another field.

Text fields

Text fields can contain any kind of character data, including text, numbers, and other characters. A single Text field can accept up to 64,000 characters of text.

If you exceed the size of a Text field (as designed in Layout mode) when entering information into it, the field automatically expands downward to accommodate the excess text. When you leave the field, it reverts to its original size, and the extra text is hidden from view. To see all the information that's stored in the field, you have to click or tab into the field (see Figure 8-12). If you want to use the field's contents in a printed report, be aware that whatever you normally see on-screen is also what will appear in the report. If the contents of the entire field are not visible in Preview mode, you should expand the field in Layout mode or edit the field's contents before printing.

New Feature   If you have a valid Web address in a Text field (such as `http://www.filemaker.com`), you can view the referenced Web page in your default browser. Ctrl+click/right-click the field and choose Open URL from the pop-up menu that appears. You must have an Internet connection for this feature to work.

Creating multiword index entries

As part of its record-keeping routine, FileMaker Pro creates a separate index for each database field for which the indexing storage option has been turned on. The index consists of every word or value entered in each Text, Time, Date, Number, and Calculation field. If you want an entire phrase from a Text field to serve as an index entry (such as "Jim Knowles"), press Option+Spacebar/Ctrl+Spacebar between each word in the phrase. This unseen character is called a *nonbreaking space* and can be used to separate words with a space but still treat the entire phrase as a single word for spell checking, indexing, line wraps, and so on. (See Chapter 5 to learn about field indexing.)

All text is displayed only when
the field is selected

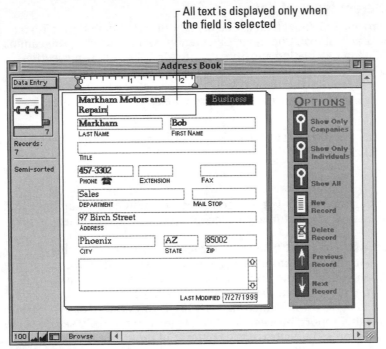

Figure 8-12: Text overflow in a field

Number fields

FileMaker Pro ignores nonnumeric data in a Number field when it is performing calculations based on the field, executing find requests based on the field, and recording index entries for the field. Number values can consist of up to 255 characters, typed on a single line (no Returns are allowed). Any numeric formatting you have set for the field (with the Format ⇨ Number command) is applied only to the numeric parts of data within the field.

If a number exceeds the width of its field, it displays as a question mark. (This also applies to Global fields of type Number.) You can see the entire number by clicking the field or tabbing into it. A question mark also appears in a Calculation or Summary field if the formula cannot be evaluated or if it results in a divide-by-zero error.

Tip   Although you can enter any kind of character in a Number field, restricting the field to numeric data may be helpful — particularly if someone else will be doing the data entry. To restrict the field to numeric data, choose the validation option labeled "Strict data type: Numeric Only" when you are defining the Number field. (See Chapter 5 for instructions on how to set field validation options.)

You use the Format ➪ Number command (in Layout mode) to set a display format for the field.

Time fields

When entering data in a Time field, you can use either the standard 12-hour format or the 24-hour military time format. When you type values, you need to use colons to separate the hours, minutes, and seconds (for example, 1:00 PM or 13:00:00). In 12-hour format, if you leave off the AM or PM designation, FileMaker Pro assumes that you mean AM. If you simply enter the number 7, for example, FileMaker interprets it as 7:00 AM.

Unlike with Number fields, you must leave any extraneous, non-time-related data out of a Time field. FileMaker Pro accepts only legitimate times.

You use the Format ➪ Time command (in Layout mode) to set a different display format for the date. Note that this formatting command affects only how the time is displayed in the record, not how you enter it.

Date fields

Date fields are similar to Time fields. The maximum length of a Date field is ten characters — up to eight characters for the month (two), day (two), and year (four), plus two separators. You can separate the parts of the date with any nonnumeric character, such as a slash or dash.

If you enter only two digits for the year (10–99), FileMaker assumes that you mean a year between 1910 and 1999. If you enter two digits between 00 and 09 for the year portion of a date, FileMaker assumes that you mean a year between 2000 and 2010. If you omit the year altogether, FileMaker assumes that you mean the current year (per the system clock). (Note that if you want to be sure that a year in a date is interpreted correctly, you can always enter it as a 4-digit string.)

You use the Format ➪ Date command (in Layout mode) to set a different display format for the date. This command affects only how the date is displayed in the record, not how you enter it. Regardless of the date format, leading zeros (as in 04/07/98) are optional. As with Time fields, you must leave any extraneous, non-date-related data out of a Date field. Only legitimate dates are accepted.

In Time and Date fields, you can edit auto-entry times or dates (information that's taken from the system clock) unless the "Prohibit modification of value" option is set as part of the field's definition. (See Chapter 5 for details on setting auto-entry options for fields.)

Note If the database was created on a computer that uses U.S. date formats, you enter dates in month-day-year format (12/31/98, for example). If the database was created on a system that uses an international format for dates (day-month-year, for example), you have to use that same format when you enter dates. You can use the Date & Time control panel to set an international date or time format for programs such as FileMaker Pro.

Global fields

You use a Global field to store a single value that is shared across all records in a database. For example, in an invoice database, you might use a Global field to record the state sales tax percentage or a flat-fee shipping charge that is added to all orders. Global fields are also useful in scripts.

When creating a Global field, you have to decide whether it will hold Text, Number, Date, Time, or Container (sound, picture, or movie) data, as shown in Figure 8-13. The data type selected for the field determines the type of information the field can hold, as well as the rules that apply to entering data in the field (as described in this chapter).

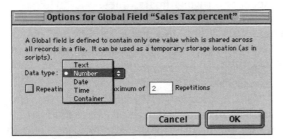

Figure 8-13: Setting the data type for a Global field

Container fields

Container fields can contain still images, sounds, QuickTime movies, or QuickTime audio clips.

> In the Windows version of FileMaker Pro, Container fields can also store OLE objects. See "Container fields" in Chapter 5 for instructions on working with OLE objects.

Working with Container fields is a little more complicated than working with Text or Number fields. In the case of movies, audio clips, and sounds, the Macintosh or PC needs to have special capabilities that are provided in software, hardware, or a combination of the two (described later in this section).

Table 8-3 lists the most popular graphics and sound file formats that FileMaker Pro 5 supports. (A *format* is a specific method for storing a particular kind of data.) For a complete list of supported formats, see "About working with graphics, sounds, and movies" in FileMaker Pro Help.

Table 8-3
Supported Graphics and Sound Formats

Format	Description
AVI (Audio Video Interleave)	A popular format for Windows-based video clips.
BMP (Bitmap)	Windows Bitmaps are the default graphics format for Windows. They are extremely wasteful of space.
EPSF (Encapsulated PostScript)	A graphics format for detailed drawings; favored by illustrators. The quality of the graphic depends on the output device.
GIF (Graphics Interchange Format)	A compressed image format popular for storing Web graphics and graphics downloaded from online services. Limited to 8-bit (256 color) images.
CGM (Computer Graphics Metafile)	CGM files are vector-based graphics that can have a considerable amount of detail, yet take up little space and can be stretched or shrunken without distorting the image.
JPEG (Joint Photographic Experts Group)	Another compressed image format used for Web graphics. Some image information may be lost during compression.
Lotus PIC	The native graphics format for pictures stored in Lotus 1-2-3 spreadsheets. Although this format is not very common, it is the default choice for exporting graphic charts.
MacPaint	An older Macintosh black-and-white graphics format, now seldom used.
PaintBrush PCX	A format that originated with a very popular drawing program called PaintBrush, PCX is still the most common image format in Windows. It uses space efficiently, without losing any image information.
PICT	A Macintosh-specific graphics format. This is a common format for Mac graphics.
QuickTime Movie (MooV)	QuickTime movie format. Note that QuickTime VR (Virtual Reality) clips can also be stored in Container fields, as well as a variety of movie clips, audio clips, and still pictures that are supported by QuickTime 3.0 and higher.

Continued

Table 8-3 *(continued)*	
Format	**Description**
TIFF (Tag Image File Format)	A common Mac and PC graphics format. Images can be color or grayscale. Compressed versions are supported, but they may not be compatible with all programs. Between the Mac and PC, there are many varieties of TIFF, but not all are supported.
WAV	The most popular sound format for Windows.
SND 1 and SND 2	Macintosh sound formats. These formats require a microphone (to record sounds) and the Monitors & Sound control panel.
WMF (Windows Metafile)	Windows Metafiles are often used in conjunction with Microsoft Office. The clip art supplied by Microsoft and other vendors is in WMF format.
DRW	DRW is the native format for Micrografx Designer, a sophisticated Windows drawing and painting package.

You can use a variety of methods to insert pictures, sounds, and movies into a Container field:

✦ You can import pictures and movies by using commands in the Insert menu.

✦ If you have an appropriate program or system utility that can open a picture, movie, or sound, you can copy or cut the picture, movie, or sound to the Clipboard and then paste it into the Container field. Current versions of Apple's Scrapbook desk accessory, for example, can be used to store all three types of material.

✦ If your Mac or PC has a microphone, you can record sounds directly into the field.

The remainder of this section describes how to use each of these methods to insert data into a Container field.

Follow these steps to insert a picture or a movie into a Container field:

1. Switch to Browse mode by choosing View ➪ Browse Mode (or by pressing ⌘+B/Ctrl+B).

2. Make the Container field the current field by clicking or tabbing into it.

About QuickTime

QuickTime is an Apple system extension that provides a set of tools and standards for creating, editing, storing, and playing moving pictures with sound on Macs and PCs. An important part of QuickTime is its ability to play movies on any Mac and most PCs. QuickTime movies require a great deal of disk space. For example, a 19-second movie that I created occupies over 6MB of space!

Getting video data into a Macintosh or PC requires special hardware, such as a video capture card. Although you can use simple utility programs to capture and edit movies, serious QuickTime work requires serious software, such as Adobe Premiere. Because of the storage, hardware, and software requirements, movie making is out of the reach of many users. If you don't want to create your own movies, many prerecorded QuickTime movies are available as commercial products.

3. To insert a still picture, choose Insert ⇨ Picture.

4. To insert a movie or QuickTime audio clip, choose Insert ⇨ QuickTime.

    One of the dialog boxes in Figure 8-14 appears.

    If the desired picture or movie isn't shown in the file list, use normal navigation techniques to move to the appropriate disk and folder. For help with file navigation, see Chapter 2.

Standard file dialog boxes accompany the Insert Picture and Insert QuickTime commands in Windows. No previews are available to help you select files.

5. Select the picture or movie that you want to insert.

If you are inserting a movie, you can click the Show Preview check box in the dialog box to see a frame of the movie before you import it.

6. Click Open to place the picture or movie in the field.

When a movie is inserted into a Container field, only a reference to the movie file is actually stored in the database (rather than the movie itself). This means that if you move the database (for example, giving it to someone else or copying it onto a removable medium such as a disk cartridge), the references to the movies become unresolved. Such unresolved references will result in a prompt to the user to find the associated referenced file. When importing a picture, on the other hand, the actual picture is stored in the database — unless you check the check box labeled "Store only a reference to the file" (as previously shown in Figure 8-14).

Insert a picture (Macintosh)

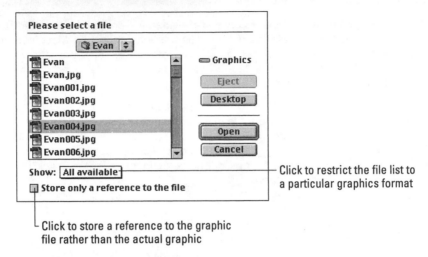

Click to restrict the file list to a particular graphics format

Click to store a reference to the graphic file rather than the actual graphic

Insert a QuickTime Movie (Macintosh)

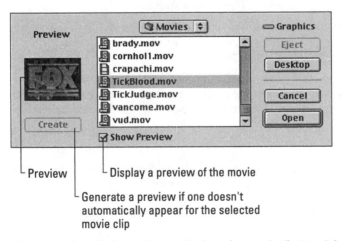

Preview

Display a preview of the movie

Generate a preview if one doesn't automatically appear for the selected movie clip

Figure 8-14: Inserting a picture (top) and a movie (bottom) into a Macintosh database

You can also copy a picture, movie, or sound and paste it into a Container field. Follow these steps:

1. Open the program that contains the picture, sound, or movie that you want to copy.

Dealing with lost movies

When you copy or insert a QuickTime movie into a Container field in FileMaker Pro, a link is created to the original movie. The actual movie data is not copied into the database. Using this method saves disk space, but it also has important consequences. If you delete the original movie or move the database to another computer without also supplying a copy of the movie, the link will be broken, and FileMaker Pro won't be able to play the movie. However, you will be given an opportunity to insert the disk that contains the movie.

If you think that the movie is on a disk that is already mounted (displayed on the desktop), you can tell FileMaker Pro where to find the movie or ask the program to search for the movie. If the movie is nowhere to be found, the contents of the Container field are changed to a still picture. If you eventually locate the movie or transfer a new copy of it to your hard disk, the next time you open the database that references the movie, the link is reestablished.

2. Within the program, open the item that you want to copy, select it, and then choose Edit ⇨ Copy (or press ⌘+C/Ctrl+C) to copy the item to the Clipboard.

3. Open the FileMaker Pro database into which you want to copy the picture, sound, or movie.

4. Select the Container field into which you want to copy the picture, sound, or movie (making that field the current field).

5. Choose Edit ⇨ Paste (or press ⌘+V/Ctrl+V).

You can record sounds directly into a Container field if you have a Macintosh or PC that is equipped with a microphone, audio CD, TV/radio tuner card, or other audio-capable devices.

If you're using a Mac, you need to make sure the Sound (or Monitors & Sound) control panel, which is part of the Macintosh system software, is installed and properly configured. If you're using Windows, you can record sounds with the Sound Recorder accessory.

Follow these steps to record a sound directly into a field:

1. Double-click the Container field into which you want to record.

A dialog box appears, as shown in Figure 8-15.

Click the control buttons at the top of the dialog box to record, stop recording, pause the recording, and play back the recording. A bar below the buttons indicates the length of the recording. The icon that looks like a speaker indicates the sound level.

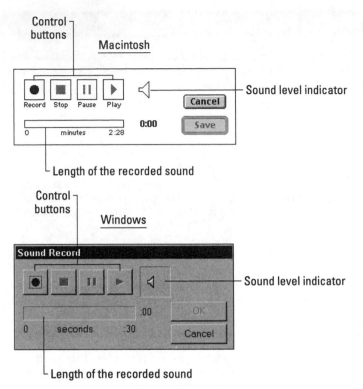

Figure 8-15: Recording a sound on a Mac (top)
or a Windows PC (bottom)

2. When you are ready to record, click Record (the first button).

3. Speak or otherwise direct sound into the microphone.

4. When you are done recording, click Stop (the second button).

5. Click Play (the fourth button) to listen to the sound that you recorded.

Playing back stored sounds or movies is simple. To play a sound, simply double-click the field in which it is stored. To play a movie, click the Play/Stop button on the movie's frame (see Figure 8-16) or double-click the movie itself. To stop playback, click the movie once or click the Play/Stop button again. Other movie controls enable you to change the playback volume and step forward or backward through the movie one frame at a time.

Inserting existing sounds into a Container field (Windows)

If you have sounds already stored on your PC that you would like to insert into a Container field, follow these steps:

1. Open the Sound Recorder accessory. You can open this accessory from the Accessories ➪ Multimedia submenu.

2. Choose File ➪ Open. From the Open dialog box, choose the sound file you want to use in your FileMaker Pro database.

3. To copy the entire contents of the sound file, simply choose Edit ➪ Copy (or press Ctrl+C).

4. Switch to FileMaker Pro and select the Container field in the desired record.

5. Choose Edit ➪ Paste (or press Ctrl+V). The sound is pasted into the field.

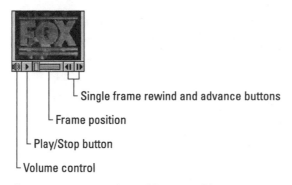

Single frame rewind and advance buttons

Frame position

Play/Stop button

Volume control

Figure 8-16: A movie and its control bar

Working with value lists

Not all data has to be typed or imported. Using the Format ➪ Field Format command (in Layout mode), you can format fields to display as pop-up lists, menus, radio buttons, or check boxes (see Figure 8-17). These formats help speed data entry by providing a list of user-defined choices from which you can select. The list of choices is called a *value list.* Any of these formats (except pop-up lists) can also have an Other choice appended to it. (For information on creating value lists and attaching them to fields, see Chapter 5.)

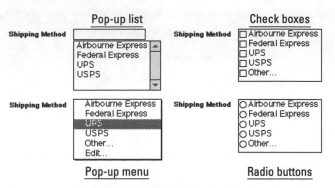

Figure 8-17: Examples of fields formatted as a pop-up list, a pop-up menu, radio buttons, and check boxes

The following sections describe how to make a choice from different kinds of value lists.

Choosing an item from a pop-up list

When you click or tab into a field formatted as a pop-up list, a scrolling list of values appears, similar in appearance to a list you often find in dialog boxes. To choose an item from a pop-up list, follow these steps:

1. Click or tab into the field that contains the pop-up list.

   The list automatically expands.

2. Select the item of interest by clicking it once.

   The choice is registered and the insertion point moves to the next field.

   — or —

   If you want to enter a response that is not included in the value list, ignore the list and click once in the field, type a different response, and then press the Tab key to move to the next field.

You can also use the arrow keys to choose a particular item. The up arrow and left arrow move up in the list; the down arrow and right arrow move down in the list. In addition, you can type the first letter or two of a value to select that item quickly. Complete your selection by pressing Return.

A pop-up list can also have an Edit choice. Include such a choice when you want the user to be able to edit the value list on which the field choices are based. (See Chapter 5 for instructions.)

Choosing an item from a pop-up menu

When you click a field formatted as a pop-up menu, a traditional pop-up menu appears. Unlike using a pop-up list, you cannot manually enter a value that is not in the menu unless you have included an Other menu choice. To choose an item from a pop-up menu, follow these steps:

1. Click or tab into the field that contains the pop-up menu.

   Initially, the field is blank.

2. Click the blank box to expose the pop-up menu and then drag to select your choice.

   —or—

   If an Other value was included in the original field format, you can record a choice that is not listed in the menu by choosing Other from the pop-up menu. Type your choice in the Other dialog box that appears (see Figure 8-18) and click OK.

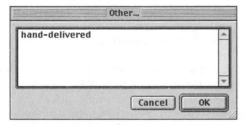

Figure 8-18: The Other dialog box

To clear an Other choice from a record, choose Other again and then delete the text that you previously entered in the Other dialog box.

Note   As Figure 8-17 illustrated, a pop-up menu can also have an Edit choice. Include such a choice when you want the user to be able to edit the value list on which the field choices are based. (See Chapter 5 for instructions.)

Choosing an item from a group of check boxes

Check boxes can be used to enable users to choose multiple options from a value list. To choose an item from a group of check boxes, follow these steps:

1. Click or tab into the field that contains the check boxes.

2. To select a particular check box, do one of the following:

- Click the check box once.

- Select the check box by using the arrow keys and then press Return or the Spacebar.

- Select the check box by typing the first letter or two of the check box label and then press Return or the Spacebar.

When selected, a check box is marked with an X.

— or —

If an Other value was included in the original field format, you can record a choice that is not listed as an option by clicking or otherwise selecting the Other check box. Type your choice in the Other dialog box (previously shown in Figure 8-18) and click OK.

To clear an Other choice from a record, click the Other check box again and then delete the text that you previously entered in the Other dialog box.

Although an alternate choice is recorded, you cannot see it on the layout. You just see that Other has been selected. To determine the exact wording of the choice, click the Other check box again. The Other dialog box appears, showing what you originally typed as your choice.

Caution

Multiple choices are frequently found in market research surveys. You often see a set of check boxes preceded by the statement, "Check all that apply." No special procedure is necessary to check several check boxes; simply click all the ones that you want. Note, however, that sorts, calculations, and summaries that are based on a field with multiple choices can produce unusual results.

Choosing an item from a group of radio buttons

To choose an item from a group of radio buttons, follow these steps:

1. Click or tab into the field that contains the radio buttons.

2. To select a particular button, click the button once or select the radio button by using the arrow keys, and then press Return/Enter or the Spacebar. Or, you can select the radio button by typing the first letter or two of the button's label, and then press Return/Enter or the Spacebar.

When selected, the radio button blackens.

— or —

If an Other value was included in the original field format, you can record a choice that is not listed as an option by clicking or otherwise selecting the Other radio button. Type your choice in the Other dialog box (previously shown in Figure 8-18) and click OK.

To clear an Other choice from a record, click the Other radio button again and then delete the text that you previously entered in the Other dialog box.

Although an alternate choice is recorded, you cannot see it on the layout. You just see that Other has been selected. To determine the exact wording of the choice, click the Other radio button again. The Other dialog box appears, showing what you originally typed as your choice.

Note

Although radio buttons are normally used in most programs to present mutually exclusive choices, you can select multiple radio buttons if you want. Just press Shift as you make your selections. Note, however, that sorts, calculations, and summaries that are based on a field with multiple choices can produce unusual results.

Changing a value in a value list

To change a value that you have previously selected from a value list, use the following procedures:

✦ *Pop-up lists* and *pop-up menus*: Select a different item from the pop-up list or menu.

✦ *Radio buttons*: Click a different radio button. The previously selected button or buttons become deselected.

✦ *Check boxes*: Each check box works as a toggle. Click to reverse the state of any given check box.

To change a value that you have manually typed in a pop-up list field or an Other choice that you've selected in a pop-up menu, radio button, or check box field, use normal editing techniques.

Copying and reusing data

If you have already typed a particular piece of data somewhere else — either within or outside the current database — you can use it again without retyping it. The simplest method is to select the data that you want to use from another record, another field, or another program (such as a word processor or graphics program), copy it to the Clipboard, and then paste it into the database field where you want it. (If you'd rather *move* data from one field or record to another, use the Edit ➪ Cut command rather than the Copy command.)

You can also copy the contents of a field that is formatted as a value list (a pop-up list, a pop-up menu, radio buttons, or check boxes). Simply select the field and choose Edit ➪ Copy (or press ⌘+C/Ctrl+C). Then, in the field where you want the value to appear, choose Edit ➪ Paste (or press ⌘+V/Ctrl+V). The appropriate information will appear in the field.

Copying data from a field index

You can reuse data that you previously typed in the database by selecting it from the index that FileMaker Pro maintains for the field (assuming, of course, that you have turned on the indexing storage option as part of the field's definition, as explained in Chapter 5). Each index consists of all of the words and numbers you have entered in that field. You can use the index to make sure a particular value is always entered in the same form in every record in which it appears. In a customer database, for example, you can use this technique to ensure that you don't have half a dozen different entries for the same company name (such as Apple, Apple Inc., Apple Computer, and Apple Computer Inc.).

To enter data from a field index, follow these steps:

1. Select the field into which you want to enter data, making it the current field.

   If the field is currently empty, skip to step 3.

2. If the field currently contains data, you can either replace all or part of that data or append the new information to the existing data as follows:

   • To replace the existing data, select the data.

   • To append the new information to the existing data, click in the field to position the insertion point where you want the new data to be pasted.

3. Choose the Insert ➪ From Index command (or press ⌘+I/Ctrl+I).

   The View Index dialog box appears, as shown in Figure 8-19.

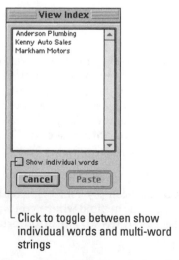

Click to toggle between show individual words and multi-word strings

Figure 8-19: The View Index dialog box

4. Select the item that you want to insert by typing the first few characters of the item's name, using the arrows and other navigation keys (Home, End, Page Up, Page Down), or using the mouse to select the item directly.

5. Click the Paste button to insert the item in the current field.

The View Index dialog box has a check box at the bottom that determines whether individual indexed words are listed or multiword text strings are displayed as they were originally typed. As Figure 8-19 illustrates, showing multiword strings is preferable when working with some fields, such as the Company field from the Address Book database. Note, too, that punctuation is not recorded in the index and every indexed word is capitalized, so you may still have to do some minor editing after pasting from the index.

Duplicating a field from the previous record

If data in the current field will be exactly the same as in the corresponding field in the last record you entered or edited, you don't have to retype it. You can copy the data directly into the new field by using the Insert ⇨ From Last Record command. (Think of this as a "ditto" command.)

To duplicate a field from a previous record, follow these steps:

1. Make sure the last record that you entered or changed has the data you want to duplicate.

2. Select the field in the new record into which you want to copy the data.

3. Choose Insert ⇨ From Last Record (or press ⌘+' [apostrophe] /Ctrl+' [apostrophe]).

   The data from the corresponding field in the last record you modified is immediately entered in the current record.

Creating a duplicate record

Sometimes working with a duplicate record is preferable to creating a whole new record and copying fields, especially if you want to enter a new record that is very similar to an existing one. In the Address Book database, for example, you may have a new contact at a company that is already in the database. Your previous contact still works there, so you don't want to modify that person's record. Instead, you can duplicate the record and then edit the duplicate.

To create a duplicate record, follow these steps:

1. Select the record that you want to duplicate.

2. Choose Records ⇨ Duplicate Record (or press ⌘+D/Ctrl+D).

   A duplicate record is added to the database and becomes the current record. You can now edit the duplicate.

Entering the current date, time, or user name

You can insert the current date, current time, or the current user's name into a field by choosing the appropriate menu command. Follow these steps:

1. Select the field into which you want to insert data, making it the current field.

2. Choose one of the following commands from the Insert menu:

   • *Current Date* (⌘ — [hyphen]/Ctrl — [hyphen]) inserts the current system date.

   • *Current Time* (⌘+; [semicolon]/Ctrl+; [semicolon]) inserts the current system time.

   • *Current User Name* (Shift+⌘+N/Ctrl+Shift+N) inserts the current user name. (See Chapter 7 for information on setting the user name in Application Preferences.)

Editing records

Data is seldom static; information needs to be updated from time to time. In the case of the Address Book database, for example, people move, change jobs, and get new titles or phone numbers. You can edit the records for these individuals to keep them up-to-date. You can also eliminate records if you no longer need the data they contain.

In a nutshell, editing an existing record involves locating the record, moving into the first field that you want to edit, changing the data in it, and then repeating this process until you have made all desired changes. The procedures discussed previously in this chapter, as well as the way the data-entry and cursor-control keys work, apply to the process of editing data, too.

Note   You can also edit data that is entered automatically, such as the date, time, or a default value, unless you have set the option for "Prohibit modification of auto-entered values" as part of the field's definition. (See Chapter 5 for details.)

The usual editing keys that are supported in most programs are also supported in FileMaker Pro. In addition to the data-entry keys discussed previously, you can use the keys, commands, and procedures listed in Table 8-4 while entering and editing data.

The following steps describe the general procedure for modifying a record:

1. With the database open, find the record that you want to modify and make it the current record.

2. Tab into or click to select the first field you want to modify.

Table 8-4
Editing Techniques

Key, Command, or Procedure	Function
Delete (Mac) or Backspace (PC)	Deletes the character to the left of the insertion point or, if text is selected, deletes the selection; also deletes contents of Container fields.
Del (Apple extended or equivalent keyboards only) or Del or Delete (PC)	Deletes the character to the right of the insertion point or, if text is selected, deletes the selection; also deletes contents of Container fields.
⌘+X/Ctrl+X or Edit ➪ Cut	Deletes the current selection within a field and places a copy of it on the Clipboard.
Clear or Edit ➪ Clear	Deletes the current selection within a field without placing a copy of it on the Clipboard.
⌘+C/Ctrl+C or Edit ➪ Copy	Copies the current selection within a field and places it on the Clipboard.
⌘+V/Ctrl+V or Edit ➪ Paste	Pastes the contents of the Clipboard into a field at the current insertion point.
⌘+A/Ctrl+A or Edit ➪ Select All	Selects the entire contents of the current field.
Double-click	Selects the current word within a field.
Triple-click	Selects the current line within a field.
Quadruple-click	Selects all text within the current field.

3. Edit the data using normal editing procedures.

4. Tab into or click the next field that you want to modify, and edit the data. Continue editing in this manner until you have made all changes that you want to make.

As you edit and move from field to field, FileMaker Pro evaluates the changes. FileMaker will notify you if it discovers an error.

5. When you have finished editing the current record, press Enter or switch to another record.

If you make an inadvertent change to a field, you can often correct it by choosing the Edit ➪ Undo command (or by pressing ⌘+Z/Ctrl+Z). The wording of the Undo command changes to reflect the most recent "undoable" action, such as "Undo Typing." Note that Undo is available only for the most *recent* action you performed. For example, if you type some text and then press the Delete key to remove a character, you can only undo the single character deletion—not the typing.

Replacing data in multiple records

You can replace data in several records at the same time with the Records ➪ Replace command. One handy use of this command is to reorder and renumber serialized records that have been mixed up after records were imported from other sources. Because the Replace command is best used on a limited group of records (rather than on a whole database), coverage of this topic is postponed until the next chapter, where finding and selecting groups of records are discussed.

FileMaker Pro 5 has a powerful form of Undo. To undo all changes made to the record since it was last worked on, choose Records ➪ Revert Record.

Tip   Changing the format of a field is also editing (applying italics or boldface to a word for emphasis, for instance). If you can't remember the keyboard shortcuts or don't feel like dragging the mouse pointer all the way to the top of the screen to choose the appropriate command, you can use the miniature pop-up menu.

Within any field, select the characters of interest, press the Mac's Control key, and click the mouse button. A miniature pop-up menu appears from which you can choose character formatting commands and standard editing commands. (This is a system software feature that requires Mac OS 8.x.) Under Windows, click the right mouse button to display the same menu. Note that other commands, such as the Insert commands, are also available from these pop-up menus.

Deleting records

Follow these steps to get rid of old or unneeded records:

1. Locate the record that you want to delete and make it the current record.

2. Choose Record ➪ Delete Record (or press ⌘+E/Ctrl+E).

   An alert box appears, asking you to confirm that you want to delete the record.

3. Click Delete to remove the record or click Cancel to dismiss the alert box without deleting the record.

Caution   Before you delete a record, think carefully about whether you need the information it contains. After you delete the record, it is gone for good. You cannot get it back by using Undo.

Mass deletions are often performed on *found sets* (groups of records that are identified by one or more find requests). For example, in a client database, you may want to delete records for any person or company that hasn't done any business with your firm in the last several years. After performing the appropriate find operation, you can choose the Records ➪ Delete All Records command to eliminate those records. The Delete All Records command is also discussed in Chapter 9.

Tip   If you plan on wholesale deletions (via the Delete All Records command), making a backup copy of the database before you delete the records is a good idea. Old data is sometimes useful, so erring on the conservative side is often best.

Using the spelling checker

Depending on the type of database with which you are working, FileMaker Pro's spelling checker may be helpful. You can instruct the program to check spelling as you type or to check it on command (to examine a particular layout, record, group of records, or a text selection). You access the spelling checker and spelling options by choosing commands from the Edit ➪ Spelling submenu. The spelling checker is discussed in Chapter 11.

Summary

✦ You use Browse mode to view records within an existing database, to enter new records, and to modify or delete existing records.

✦ Databases can have multiple layouts to serve different purposes, such as data entry and reports. You select layouts in Browse mode from the layouts pop-up menu.

✦ You can display the records within a database one per screen or as a continuous, scrolling list or spreadsheet-style table. The book icon enables you to move from one record to another, to an approximate position within the database, or to a specific record number. When a database is displayed in list form (View as List) or table form (View as Table), the scroll bar functions in much the same way as the book icon.

✦ FileMaker Pro databases can store still-picture, sound, and moving-picture data in several file formats. Only one copy of a given sound or picture is stored in the particular database's library, no matter how many records contain that sound or picture. You can specify whether each sound or picture is stored within the database or whether only a pointer to the element's location on disk is recorded.

✦ FileMaker Pro maintains an index for each database field in which the indexing storage option has been turned on. The index contains every word and number that has been entered in the field. To improve consistency, entries can be made into fields directly from the index.

✦   ✦   ✦

Searching for and Selecting Records

In the last chapter, you learned about using the book to browse through records in a database. While this works well when browsing a small database, it's tedious and cumbersome when dealing with a large database. And Browse mode is no help at all when you want to identify groups of records. In working with the Address Book database, for example, you may want to examine all your business contacts, excluding friends and relatives. At best, Browse mode will show your records displayed in a list or table.

Find mode provides a way to locate individual records and to group records that share some characteristic. Within Find mode, you can quickly search all records in a database for information that matches the contents of a field (such as a particular last name or a known telephone number). You can also have FileMaker Pro create groups of records that share a characteristic (such as all your business contacts or everyone within a certain ZIP code). Going well beyond simple searches, Find mode provides powerful tools for locating and working with individual records and groups of records.

Find Mode Basics

Find mode does much more than make browsing through records easier. The immediate effect of a find request is to change the set of records that you're currently browsing — that is, the ones that are visible. When you want to see only one particular record, you can search using a field that contains unique data, such as a Social Security number, phone number, inventory code, or customer ID number. You will also discover that performing a find operation is often an important part of preparing reports. For example, in a prospective customer database, you may want to see only your successes or clients for whom you've scheduled a follow-up. To produce such a list, you execute a find request prior to printing the report.

Switching to Find mode

As with Browse mode, you can switch to Find mode in two ways — regardless of the mode you're currently in:

✦ Choose the View ➪ Find Mode command (or press ⌘+F/Ctrl+F).

✦ Choose Find from the mode pop-up menu at the bottom of the database window.

Using Find mode tools and functions

Figure 9-1 shows the Address Book database (introduced in Chapter 4 and provided on the *FileMaker Pro 5 Bible* CD-ROM) in Find mode. As you can see, Find mode has more tools available than Browse mode, but fewer tools than Layout mode.

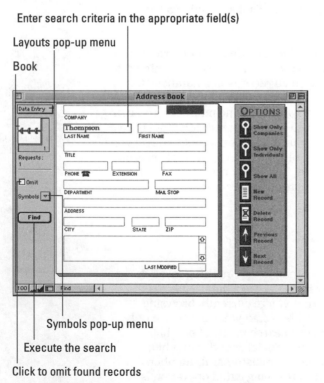

Figure 9-1: The Address Book database in Find mode

The Browse mode tools are also available in Find mode. You can switch to a different layout by clicking the layouts pop-up menu in the upper-left corner of the window. You can change the current magnification at which the database is displayed by clicking the zoom in and zoom out buttons below the status area. You can also toggle the status area by clicking the status area control button at the bottom of the document window. All of these controls work as they do in Browse mode (described in Chapter 8).

The Symbols pop-up menu (see Figure 9-2) plays an important role in Find mode. This menu contains special symbols that enable you to easily execute custom searches. Using these symbols, you can search for values that are less than, equal to, or greater than a specified value, for example. For instance, you can search for all records that have an entry in the Last Name field that begins with the letter *H* or later in the alphabet. You can also look for ranges of values and for invalid values. (You'll learn more about using these symbols in "Matching all criteria," later in this chapter.)

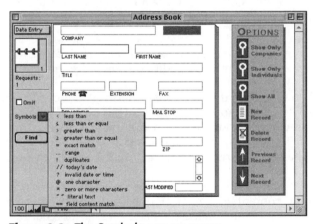

Figure 9-2: The Symbols pop-up menu

Finding Records

Suppose you work in the marketing department of a small company. While you were at lunch, your receptionist took a message for you and then left for lunch, too. Unfortunately, you can't make out anything other than that the caller's last name is Thompson and the call was urgent. You don't want to wait until the receptionist returns from lunch to find out who called and what the phone number is. What do you do?

Using your Address Book database, you can search through all your contacts for a Thompson. An examination of the found records ought to give you an idea about who this anxious person is. Here's how you do it:

1. First, launch FileMaker Pro and open the Address Book database.

   The Data Entry layout appears, showing names and phone numbers. (If the database opens to a different layout, use the layouts pop-up menu to switch to the correct layout.)

2. Switch to Find mode by using the mode pop-up menu, choosing the View ⇨ Find Mode command, or pressing ⌘+F/Ctrl+F.

   A blank find request appears on the screen (as previously shown in Figure 9-1). You enter search criteria into the find request.

3. Type **Thompson** in the Last Name field.

4. Click the Find button.

   FileMaker Pro searches for all records that certain the last name *Thompson* and displays one record with that name.

   Because only one record was found that matched your criteria, you call Mr. Thompson back to discover that he needs to place a large rush order with you and would have called a competitor if you hadn't responded so quickly.

This example of using Find mode shows the basic steps involved in locating specific records within a database. With the database open, you switch to Find mode and choose a layout that shows the information for which you want to search. You then enter the search criteria into fields on the layout and click the Find button. Finally, you examine the *found set* (the set of all records that are identified as the result of a find operation).

Searches are performed on the contents of one or more fields in every record in the database. You can look for an exact match in a given field, such as all records that contain Thompson in the Last Name field. You can also look for records that contain only partial matches (matching one set of criteria or another), as well as for records that contain specific pieces of information in two or more fields.

As soon as you click the Find button, FileMaker Pro locates any matching records and then switches to Browse mode, displaying only the found set. The number of records in the found set is shown beneath the book icon. The rest of the records in the database are temporarily hidden from view. You then browse — as well as sort or print — the found set as you would normally browse the entire database. To make all the records visible again, choose Records ⇨ Show All Records (or press ⌘+J/Ctrl+J).

Matching all criteria

The simplest kind of find operation consists of searching for records that match all of one or more specific criteria. The preceding scenario — in which you combined a single-field search with manual browsing of the found set — is an example of using a single search criterion. You can also conduct multiple-field searches — all you need to do is enter information in each field on which you want to search.

For example, to locate all Thompsons in the state of Washington, you would use two criteria. You would enter **Thompson** in the Last Name field and **WA** in the State field. To further narrow the search, you can enter information in as many fields as you like.

Note
This type of multifield search is called an AND search. When you type search instructions in multiple fields, you are asking FileMaker Pro to identify only those records that match *all* the criteria (Last Name = Thompson AND State = WA, for example).

When you enter search criteria by simply typing some text or numbers into a field, FileMaker Pro not only locates records that exactly match the specified information, but also finds records that contain the search string at the beginning of any word within the field. Thus, if you enter Smith, FileMaker Pro finds not only Smith, but also Smithy, Smithers, and Bobby Joe Smith. You can restrict searches to exact matches if you want (only a real Smith, for example). Refer to the section on "Matching text exactly," later in this chapter.

If FileMaker Pro doesn't locate any records that satisfy all of your search criteria, a dialog box appears that informs you of this fact (see Figure 9-3). You can click Modify Find to return to the find request and enter different criteria, or click Cancel to return to Browse mode.

Click to change the search criteria and try again

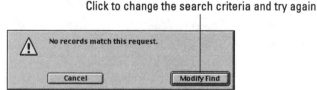

Figure 9-3: No matches were found.

Using symbols in search criteria

To help narrow a search, you can include special symbols in any or all of the search criteria. You can select symbols from the Symbols pop-up menu (in the status area), or you can type them directly into the appropriate fields on a find request. As Table 9-1 illustrates, some symbols must precede the search string, others must surround it, and still others must be embedded within it. The proper use of each kind of search symbol is discussed later in this chapter.

Table 9-1
Find Symbols

Symbol	Meaning	Example
<	Less than	<50000 (Find persons who make less than $50,000 per year.)
≤	Less than or equal to	≤5 (Find cities with annual rainfall less than or equal to 5 inches.)
>	Greater than	>7/4/94 (Find any date after July 4, 1994.)
≥	Greater than or equal to	≥10:43 (Find any time that is equal to or later than 10:43 a.m.)
=	A partial match	Match a portion of the field's contents (for example, =Toys will find "Toys R Us").
==	An exact match	Match the exact contents of the field (for example, == Toys will only match "Toys," not "Toys R Us").
...	Data within a range	80210...80218 (Find Zip codes that fall within that range.)
!	Duplicate values	! (Entered in an ID field, selects all records with duplicate ID numbers.)
//	Current date	// (Selects all records with today's date in the chosen Date field.)
?	Invalid dates or times	? (Entered in a Date or Time field, finds all records or times with invalid dates or times.)
@	Wildcard for a single character	B@nd (Finds Band, Bend, Bind, and Bond.)
*	Zero or more characters	B*S (Finds BS, bus, bats, and BUSINESS.)
" "	Literal text	"Homer" (Finds Homer Simpson, Homer's Iliad, and Hi there, Homer! within the field.)

Matching one criterion or another

At times, you may want to search for all records that match any of two or more criteria. This kind of search is known as an OR search — as in "Find all records that match this set of criteria OR that set." For example, you may want to find all Smiths who live in either California or New York. The manner in which you specify an OR search is quite different from trying to match all of several criteria (that is, an AND search). To create an OR search, you must fill out a separate find request for each criterion by choosing Request ⇨ Add New Request. FileMaker Pro combines the results of the find requests into a single found set. This set combines all records that match *any* of the search criteria.

Use the following steps to perform a search for data that satisfies the criteria of at least one of several find requests (an OR search):

1. In the database you want to search, switch to a layout that shows the fields you want to use for the search.

2. Switch to Find mode by using the mode pop-up menu, choosing View ⇨ Find Mode, or pressing ⌘+F/Ctrl+F.

   A blank find request appears.

3. Enter the first criterion into the appropriate field.

4. If you want to use additional criteria for this find request (Last Name = Jones and Salary < 25000, for example), tab to the appropriate fields and enter the criteria.

5. Choose Requests > Add New Request (or press ⌘+N/Ctrl+N).

   The database window is cleared, and a new blank find request form appears.

6. Enter the criteria for this find request into the appropriate field or fields.

7. Repeat steps 5 and 6 until you have created all necessary find requests.

8. Click the Find button.

   All find requests are evaluated. The found set is presented, consisting of all records that satisfied the criteria in at least one find request.

Note Whenever you click Find, all previous searches are cleared. If you want to repeat the most recent search, choose Records ⇨ Modify Last Find (or press ⌘+R/Ctrl+R). You will learn more about performing multiple find requests later in this chapter.

Individual Finds aren't the same as multiple Find requests

Each time you switch to Find mode and issue one or more find requests, two important things happen. First, regardless of which records are currently visible, FileMaker Pro considers all records in the search. Second, if you have created multiple find requests (to conduct an OR search), all requests are carried out at the same time.

Every find request starts from square one; the effects are not cumulative. For example, if you conduct two separate find operations—the first searching for Smiths from California and the second searching for Smiths from New York—when you execute the second search, only the Smiths from New York appear in the found set. On the other hand, if you conduct a single find operation that contains two find requests—one for California Smiths and another for New York Smiths—the found set shows you all Smiths who are from California or New York.

Matching different kinds of text

By using one of the special Find symbols (refer to Table 9-1), you can make FileMaker Pro do more than locate matches for single words. You can look for a specific text string, accepting no substitutes ("Smith," but not "Smithers," for example). You can also look for text that contains certain words or phrases. As an example, you can search a Notes field for all instances of the word *email*—regardless of where the word falls within the field. You can also use this technique to look for pieces of text that aren't in a field's index, such as consecutive groups of letters ("mith," for example). However, such nonindex searches can take longer to perform, especially in large databases.

Matching text exactly

In a find request, using the equal sign (=) in a field tells FileMaker Pro to look only for an exact match to the text that you have entered somewhere in the contents of the field. That is, the text you enter must match all or a portion of the contents of the field in order for a match to be found. For example, to find all customers whose last name is Schwartz, you enter **=Schwartz** in the Last Name field. This search will also find customers with the last name of Schwartz-Brown.

Using the double-equal sign (==) in a field tells FileMaker Pro to look for only those records where the search criteria you have entered matches the contents of the field exactly. To find all customers whose last name is Schwartz but *not* those with a last name of Schwartz-Brown (or any other variation), you enter **==Schwartz** in the Last Name field.

To locate an exact match to a phrase, enter the phrase but precede each word with an equal sign (for example, **=Sinbad =Schwartz**).

Finding text alphabetically above or below a value

You can also look for records that contain values that are less than, less than or equal to, greater than, or greater than or equal to a given value by using the appropriate mathematical symbols. For example, entering ≥**Schwartz** in a Last Name field searches for all last names that are either Schwartz or come alphabetically after Schwartz. To identify only those records for persons with a last name greater than but not including Schwartz (that is, those that come after Schwartz), use the greater than symbol instead—as in >**Schwartz**.

Using wildcard characters for partial matches

You can search for records that contain a specific group of letters. To do so, use wildcard characters to represent the missing letters. FileMaker Pro supports @ and * as wildcards. The @ symbol stands for a single character, and the * symbol represents a group of characters that is any length—including zero characters.

If, for example, you want to find all seven-letter names that begin with John, use three @ signs in the last three positions of the search criterion (**John@@@**). Searching for this string of letters finds Johnson and Johnley, but not Johnston (because it contains eight letters rather than seven). To find all values that start with a particular group of letters (such as John), you merely need to enter the exact group without any wildcards following it. Searching using **John** will find John, Johnson, Johnley, and Johnston. (You can also include the asterisk wildcard, if you like — such as **John*** — although it isn't necessary.)

You can also use wildcard characters in the middle of a word. For example, to find all last names that begin with Smith and end with the letter *n*, enter **Smith*n** in the Last Name field. FileMaker Pro finds Smithson, Smithsonian, and so on. To find words that differ only by a single character, use the @ sign. For example, searching for **Sm@th** finds both Smith and Smyth.

Searching for nonindexed (literal) text

The preceding text search methods find only indexed text items. You will recall that FileMaker Pro can create an index for any Text, Number, Date, Time, or Calculation field, keeping a record of each word or value in the field for all records in the database. If you want to look for information that isn't part of a field's index (including phrases whose component words aren't separated by Option+Space/Ctrl+Space characters), you have to enclose the search text in double quotes. (When entering data, you can press Option+Spacebar/Ctrl+Spacebar between words to force FileMaker Pro to index a phrase rather than the individual words that make up the phrase.) If punctuation marks need to be included in your search string, you must use this method to search for them — as in **"Johnson, Jr."**

You can type the quotation marks directly if you want, but FileMaker Pro provides a simpler method. Choose " " *literal text* from the Symbols pop-up menu. Doing so immediately enters both a pair of quotation marks and places the insertion point between them.

More about Find Requests

Whenever you switch to Find mode and enter information on the blank form that appears, you're creating a find request. FileMaker Pro lets you manipulate find requests in several ways. You can delete requests or repeat requests, perhaps editing them slightly to alter the search criteria. For example, if you looked for all Smiths from California one time, you could repeat the request and change **CA** to **NY** to find all Smiths from New York.

Creating find requests

Creating a new find request is easy. FileMaker Pro creates the first find request automatically when you switch to Find mode. You may want to create additional requests, however, when searching for information that matches one of several criteria (an OR search).

You have two options when creating additional find requests. You can create an entirely new find request (by choosing Requests ➪ Add New Request or pressing ⌘+N/Ctrl+N), or you can duplicate the current find request and edit its contents (by choosing Requests ➪ Duplicate Request or pressing ⌘+D/Ctrl+D). Until you click the Find button to execute the find requests, you can use the book icon to page through all current find requests — just as you use it in Browse mode to flip through records.

Repeating and editing find requests

When you finish entering all the search criteria and click the Find button, FileMaker locates all matching records and displays them in Browse mode as the found set. If FileMaker Pro does not find any matches, you can either modify and repeat the search, or you can cancel the search and return to Browse mode.

If you switch to Find mode again, FileMaker Pro presents you with a new blank find request form. In some cases, however, you may want to use your previous find requests as the basis for a new search. For example, if a search for Smiths in California doesn't yield results, you may want to go back and look for Smiths in Oregon. By using the Modify Last Find command, you can repeat the last search, preserving all find requests that you defined within it. You can edit any or all of these find requests to match any new search requirements that you have.

To repeat or modify the previous set of find requests, follow these steps:

1. From Browse mode, choose Records ➪ Modify Last Find (or press ⌘+R/Ctrl+R).

   FileMaker Pro displays the previous set of find requests.

2. To simply repeat the last find request(s), go directly to step 5.

   — or —

   If there are multiple find requests, use the book icon to move to the request(s) that you want to edit.

3. Use normal editing procedures to change the search criteria.

4. *Optional*: You can also add more requests to the set, duplicate any of the requests, or delete requests (as long as at least one still remains) by choosing the appropriate command from the Requests menu (Add New Request, Duplicate Request, or Delete Request, respectively).

5. Click the Find button.

The find request or requests are executed.

Tip If you find that you've made a mistake when entering search criteria (particularly while modifying the most recent request), you can choose Requests ⇨ Revert Request to restore the request to its prior state.

Deleting find requests

If one or more requests within the current set of find requests don't meet your needs, you can get rid of them.

To delete find requests, use one of the following methods:

✦ To specify search criteria from scratch (effectively deleting all current find requests), choose View ⇨ Find Mode again (or press ⌘+F/Ctrl+F).

✦ To delete a specific find request, use the book icon to move to the request that you want to delete and choose Requests ⇨ Delete Request (or press ⌘+E/Ctrl+E). Repeat this procedure for each request that you want to delete.

Note that you can only delete find requests when you have created more than one. If a Find consists of only a single request, the Delete Request command is disabled. Rather than delete the request, you can simply change it to reflect the correct criteria.

Tip If you think you'll be using a particular find request over and over again, you can create a script that "remembers" your find request and performs the find automatically. Scripts are excellent for finds with multiple requests or complex criteria. (See Chapter 15 for more details on writing scripts.)

Matching Special Items

As mentioned earlier in the chapter, you can enter special symbols as part of your search criteria by selecting them from the Symbols pop-up menu (as previously shown in Figure 9-2 and described in Table 9-1). By using these symbols, you can find all records that have values between two extremes, such as two dates, times, or salaries. You can also use symbols to perform database maintenance by searching for erroneous or duplicate values and then editing or eliminating the records that contain them.

Matching values in a range

You use the ellipsis symbol (...) to indicate values within a range. You can look for alphabetic values between two text strings, numeric values between two calculated or numeric items, or chronological values between two times or dates. For example, you can search for all records that have last names between Smith and Zane or for all records created between January 1 and December 31, 1999. In the former case, you enter **Smith...Zane** in the Last Name field; in the latter case, you type **1/1/99...12/31/99** in the Date field.

To enter a range in a search field, separate the two values by typing three periods, by pressing Option+; (Macintosh), or by choosing the ... symbol from the Symbols pop-up menu.

Matching the current date

Assuming the system clock in your Macintosh or PC is set correctly, you can easily search for records that match the current date, even if you don't happen to know it yourself. This feature is especially handy in scripts because you don't need to enter specific information. Instead of having to re-create the script each time (changing the date from 10/5/99 to 10/18/99, for example), you can just instruct the script to find today's date—whatever the date happens to be. (See Chapter 15 for more information on scripts and their uses.)

Note   To check or set your computer's system clock, open the Date & Time control panel (Mac) or the Date/Time control panel (Windows).

To find all values that contain the current date, follow these steps:

1. In Find mode, move the cursor to the Date field in which you want to search.

2. Choose the "today's date" option from the Symbols pop-up menu or type a pair of slashes (//).

3. Click Find to execute the search.

Searching for empty fields

Occasionally, errors creep into a database. For example, you may create extra records and forget to fill them in, or you may get interrupted and neglect to complete the current record. FileMaker Pro provides a way for you to look for all records that have no information in one or more fields. You simply enter an equal sign (=)—and nothing else—in that field. You can then correct or delete the errant records.

If you want to find all records that contain one or more blank fields, you need to create a separate find request for each potentially blank field and then click Find. If you enter all potentially blank fields in a single find request, FileMaker Pro will find only records in which *all* of these fields are blank. (Remember, when you specify multiple criteria in one find request, you are conducting an AND search. All criteria must be satisfied in order for a match to be found.) Thus, records that have some fields blank and other fields filled in will not be identified.

The correct procedure is to create multiple find requests—one for each field that you want to check for blanks. Although this procedure may sound as if it requires a great deal of work, it usually doesn't. In most cases, you want to search for blanks in a small set of critical fields—those that, if left blank, would render the record useless.

Searching for values greater or less than a given value

In the discussion of text searches, you saw that you can use the <, ≤, >, and ≥ symbols to find text that is alphabetically greater or less than a particular value. You can also use these symbols to find numeric, date, or time values. For example, to find all records dated on or after January 1, 1996, you enter **≥1/1/96**.

To find values that exceed or are less than a given value, follow these steps:

1. Switch to Find mode.

2. Move to the field that you want to use in the search.

3. Choose the appropriate symbol from the Symbols pop-up menu (or type it directly into the field):

   > (greater than) to find all items that exceed the value entered

   ≥ (greater than or equal to) to find all items that exceed or are exactly equal to the value entered

   < (less than) to find all items that are smaller than the value entered

   ≤ (less than or equal to) to find all items that are smaller than or exactly equal to the value entered

To type the ≤ or ≥ symbols, press Option+, (comma) or Option+. (period), respectively.

4. Following the symbol that you entered in step 3, type the search value.

5. Click Find to execute the search

The greater than or equal to symbol (≥) and the less than or equal to symbol (≤) are not legitimate characters in Windows. Instead, they appear in the Symbols pop-up menu as >= and <=, respectively. If you wish to manually enter either symbol, you should type it the same way.

Searching for duplicate records

Find mode can also be used to help you perform another form of database maintenance: You can use it to identify records that have the same information in several fields. Although some people do have the same last names, for example, some of these records may be duplicates. If you checked your mail recently, you probably noticed that some direct mail firms are sending you multiple copies of their catalog. They have a problem with duplicate database records — the ones that contain *your* name. FileMaker Pro has a special symbol that enables you to find all records that have duplicate information in one field. You can then browse these records and eliminate any exact duplicates.

To search for records that have identical contents in a given field, follow these steps:

1. Switch to Find mode.

2. Move to the field whose contents you suspect is shared by two or more records.

3. Choose "duplicates" from the Symbols pop-up menu or type a single exclamation point (!).

4. Click Find to execute the Find.

As when looking for empty fields (discussed previously), if you want to find all records that have duplicate values in one or more of several different fields, you need to create a separate find request for each of these fields. Otherwise, you will find only records that match in *all* potential fields. (Check those catalog mailing labels again. In most cases, you will find that the labels aren't exactly the same. Your name or address may be slightly different, for example.) As a rule, you should include only one "duplicates" criterion in each find request.

Note   There are three restrictions when searching for duplicates. First, when determining if data in Text fields is duplicated, FileMaker Pro only examines the first 20 alphanumeric characters of each word in the field. A maximum of 60 characters, including spaces, are examined per field. Second, for two records to be considered duplicates, the word order in the chosen field must be identical. Third, you can only search for duplicates in indexed fields.

Searching for invalid information

Sometimes, you may find that time or date calculations don't yield valid results, particularly when working with data imported from another database or program. To search for records that have invalid dates or times, enter a question mark (?) into a Date or Time field (or choose "invalid date or time" from the Symbols pop-up menu).

Finding records that don't match the criteria

When you are trying to narrow down a search for very specific kinds of records, you may find that a little "negative logic" is easier to apply than the conventional kind. For example, suppose you want to find all your contacts in every state except California. You can create a separate find request for each of the other 49 states, but doing so is a lot of work. As an alternative, you can enter **California** in the State field and then elect to omit from the found set all records that contain California. FileMaker Pro makes this task easy. Find mode has an Omit check box in the status area (as previously shown in Figure 9-1). You click this check box to turn a conventional find request into one that hides the found records and shows only the records that are left.

In a series of find requests, if you use the Omit option in some but not in others, you should put all find requests that include the Omit option at the end of your list. FileMaker Pro works through all find requests in the order that you specify. If you put Omit requests first, subsequent find requests will tend to wipe out their results. For example, if you want to find all records of employees who are older than 25, or have a salary greater than $27,000, or are not from Houston, you create the following three find requests, making sure you create the request that uses the Omit option last:

```
>25 (in Age field)
>27000 (in Salary field)
=Houston (in City field) and Omit check box checked
```

Remember that whenever you issue multiple find requests, you are conducting an OR search—looking for records that satisfy any one or more of the find requests.

If you later want to look at just the records that the Find request(s) omitted, choose Records ⇨ Show Omitted. Essentially, this command instructs FileMaker Pro to show all records *except* those that are currently being browsed; that is, it reveals all the hidden records, while hiding those that are currently visible.

You can also omit records after conducting a find request, as described in "Omitting records from a found set," in the next section.

Working with Found Records

You can do many things besides just browsing through a found set. Many operations you can perform are directly related to the reason you searched for the records. For example, if you searched for duplicate records, you probably did so because you wanted to delete the duplicates. Another thing you can do with found records is copy them to the Clipboard and then paste them into another database or even into another program.

Omitting records from a found set

When working with a found set, you may sometimes want to temporarily hide some of the found records. For example, if you have just done a search to find duplicate records, the found set contains both the original records that you want to keep and the duplicates. Before you can delete the duplicate records, you need to omit the originals from the found set by using the Omit Record or Omit Multiple commands. (Omitting records merely hides them from view, removing them from the found set. The records still remain in the database, however, and can be revealed with the Records ➪ Show All Records command.) After omitting the originals from the found set, you can delete the duplicates with the Delete All command (discussed in "Deleting found sets," later in this chapter).

To omit a specific record from a found set, follow these steps:

1. Select the record that you want to omit.

   If you're in form view (View as Form), use the book to select the record. If you're in list view or table view (View as List or View as Table), you can click in any field of the record to select it.

2. Choose the Records ➪ Omit Record command (or press ⌘+M/Ctrl+M).

   The current record is removed from the found set; that is, it is hidden.

3. Repeat steps 1 and 2 for each additional record that you want to omit from the found set.

If a found set contains several consecutive records that you want to omit from the found set, you can omit all of them with one command — Omit Multiple. Follow these steps:

1. *Optional*: If the records to be omitted are not grouped consecutively, you may be able to use a Sort command (⌘+S/Ctrl+S) to group them in the desired manner. See Chapter 10 for information on sorting.

2. Use the book icon to select the first record you want to omit from the found set.

   If the layout is displayed in list view (View as List), you can click in any record to select it.

3. Choose the Records ➪ Omit Multiple command or press Shift+⌘+M/Shift+Ctrl+M.

   The Omit Multiple dialog box appears, as shown in Figure 9-4.

Figure 9-4: The Omit Multiple dialog box

Omit can be used with or without a found set

Although the Omit command is most frequently used with a found set (following a find request), you can use it at any time to hide records temporarily. In effect, such use of the Omit command manually creates the equivalent of a found set. Suppose, for example, that you are using a database to prepare a list of stamps that you want to purchase from a mail-order dealer. After preparing the want list, you can use the Omit command to eliminate several stamps selectively—either because buying them will put you in the poorhouse or because you think they are currently overpriced.

4. Enter the number of consecutive records to omit.

5. Click the Omit button.

The records are omitted; that is, they are hidden from view.

If you want to restore all records omitted from a found set, simply use the Modify Last Find command to repeat the last find request. You cannot restore omitted records directly (there is no Reveal or "Un-omit" command), but you can use other methods to get the records back, as you will learn in the next section.

Swapping found sets with omitted records

In the want list example presented in the previous sidebar, you learned that you can use the Omit command to handpick records that you want to remove from a found set. On the other hand, these omitted records may be the ones that really interest you at the moment. Suppose, for example, that you want to prepare a list of all stamps that you have no interest in buying. Perhaps you want to take the list to stamp shows and to meetings with dealers to prevent yourself from buying something that you don't want or need. By using the Show Omitted command, you can make the omitted records the new found set. Show Omitted swaps the remaining records in the found set with all omitted ones. The omitted records then become the new found set.

Follow these steps to swap a found set with records omitted from it:

1. Use the Omit Record or Omit Multiple command to mark records in a found set that you actually want to keep.

2. Choose the Records ⇨ Show Omitted command.

Omitted records become the new found set, and the remaining records are omitted in their place.

Tip   Show Omitted can also be used after issuing a normal find request. For instance, after examining the records of all club members whose dues payments are delinquent, you can use Show Omitted to display the records of the members whose payments are up to date.

Copying found sets

You can copy an entire found set of records to the Clipboard. From there, you can paste the data elsewhere — into documents from other applications, for example. Each field is separated from the next by a Tab character, and each record is ended with a Return character. (This is commonly known as a tab-delimited text file.) To copy a found set to the Clipboard, press Option-⌘+C/Shift+Ctrl+C.

Note This procedure is a quick-and-dirty version of the Export command with "tab-delimited" as the selected format. The main difference is that you have less control over the particular fields that are copied and the order in which they are copied. Whatever layout is in effect when you issue the command determines the selected fields and their order.

Deleting found sets

As mentioned previously, one major use for Find mode is to locate records that you want to delete from a database. After you have omitted records that you want to save from a found set, removing the remainder of the records from the database is simple.

Follow these steps to delete records in a found set:

1. Enter Find mode (⌘+F/Ctrl+F) and create the find requests that are necessary to identify the records that you want to delete.

2. *Optional*: Examine the found set and use the Omit command to leave out records that you do not want to delete from the database.

Note The Delete All command that you use in this procedure affects only the visible (browsed) records, not all of the records in the database.

3. Choose Records ⇨ Delete All Records.

An alert box appears, asking you to confirm that you want to delete the records in question.

4. Click Delete to proceed or click Cancel to dismiss the alert box without deleting the records.

Caution As with other Delete commands in FileMaker Pro, you cannot use the Undo command to undo the Delete All Records command. Because you risk significant data loss if you make a mistake when using this command, you may want to make a backup copy of the database by using the File ⇨ Save a Copy As command (described in Chapter 2) before you use the Delete All Records command.

Replacing values in a found set

Another thing you can do with a found set is replace the contents of a single field in all found records simultaneously (in much the same way as you use a word processor's global Replace commands). After using find requests to locate the particular records in which you want to make the replacement, you can use the Replace command to replace the contents of any single field with data that you specify.

This global replacement procedure is often useful. For example, either of the following situations would be prime candidates for the Replace command:

✦ A company in one of your databases has recently changed its name or moved. Search for the original name of the company, and then use Replace to enter the new name or new address in all found records. If the company has changed both its name and address, use two Replace procedures on the same found set: first the company name and then the address. (You can use this same procedure to ensure consistent wording for text in selected fields. By identifying all records that contain Apple in the Company field, for instance, you can use Replace to change all entries to read "Apple Computer, Inc.")

✦ A major kennel association reclassifies a particular breed of pooch as a "working dog." Search for all instances of that breed and then use Replace to change the classification for each of the found dogs.

Use the following procedure to replace the contents of one field in all records in the found set:

1. Switch to Find mode (⌘+F/Ctrl+F) and use one or more find requests to select the group of records whose contents you want to replace.

   This creates the found set.

2. In Browse mode, select the field you want to replace by tabbing into or clicking the field.

   It does not matter what record is currently displayed; any record in the found set will suffice.

3. Type the replacement text or value in the field.

4. Choose Records ➪ Replace (or press ⌘+=/Ctrl+=).

   The Replace dialog box shown in Figure 9-5 appears.

5. Select the "Replace with" option.

   The replacement text or value is shown within quotes. (For example, the replacement string is "SA Schwartz Associates" in Figure 9-5.)

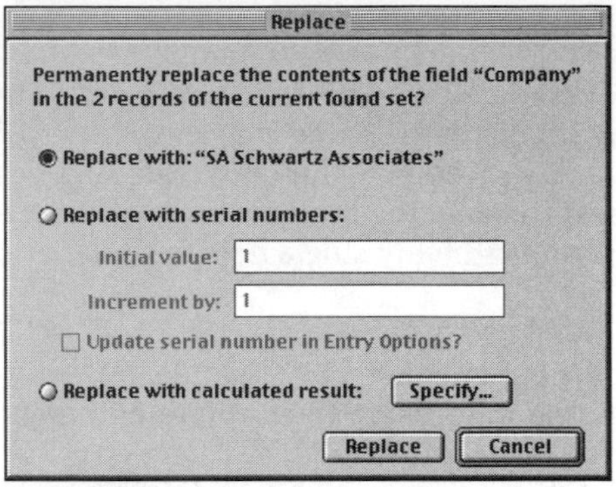

Figure 9-5: Use this dialog box to replace the contents of a field with a single text string or value.

6. Click Replace.

The contents of the current field are replaced with the specified text string or value in all records in the found set.

Replacing the contents of a field with a serial number

As you can see by looking at the dialog box in Figure 9-5, you can also use the Replace command to replace the contents of a field in the found set with serial numbers. This option is useful when, for example, you've imported records into a database and have left gaps or otherwise thrown off the existing numbering scheme.

To replace the contents of a field in a found set with serial numbers, do the following:

1. Switch to Find mode (⌘+F/Ctrl+F) and use one or more find requests to select the group of records that you want to renumber.

   This creates the found set.

2. In Browse mode, select the field that you wish to reserialize by tabbing into or clicking the field.

3. *Optional*: Sort the database.

   When the records are reserialized, numbers are assigned according to each record's position within the found set. The first record will get the first new serial number, the second record will get the second number, and so on. Using the Sort command, you can change the order of the records to a more meaningful arrangement. (See Chapter 10 for more information on sorting records.)

4. Choose Records ➪ Replace (or press ⌘+=/Ctrl+=).

   The Replace dialog box appears (as previously shown in Figure 9-5).

5. Click the "Replace with serial numbers" radio button.

6. In the "Initial value" text box, enter the value for the new first serial number for the found set. In the "Increment by" text box, enter the value by which each successive serial number should increase over the previous number.

7. Click Replace.

Remember that a serial number can contain more than just numbers. If your serial number is a mix of numbers and text, only the numeric portion of the field will change when the field is reserialized. Also, if the selected field was initially defined as an auto-entry field that would receive a serial number, you may wish to click the "Update serial number in Entry Options?" check box in the Replace dialog box. When reserializing the found set, this option instructs FileMaker Pro to note the last serial number used and to make sure that the next new record created continues the serialization sequence. (It updates the Next Value figure in the Entry Options dialog box for the serial number field.)

Tip   You can also use the Replace command to create a record-numbering system where none existed before. Simply define a new field to hold the serial numbers, add it to a layout, issue a Records ➪ Show All Records command (⌘+J/Ctrl+J), sort the records (if necessary), select the field, and then issue the Replace command.

Replacing the contents of a field with a calculated result

You can also use the Replace command to replace the contents of a field with a calculated result. Suppose, for example, that you want to increase the salary of a group of employees by five percent. After using a find request to select the set of employees, you would choose the Replace command, click the radio button for "Replace with calculated result," and — in the Specify Calculation dialog box that appears — enter either of these formulas:

```
Salary + (Salary * .05)
```

— or —

```
Salary * 1.05
```

The result type for the Replace formula must be the same as the replaced field's type (as set in the Define Fields dialog box when the field was created). If the field is a Text field, for instance, only a formula that returns a text string is allowed. (To learn about defining fields, refer to Chapter 5.)

Note   When defining a replacement formula, the Specify Calculation dialog box that appears works exactly the same as when you are defining a formula for a Calculation field. (See Chapter 5 for more information.)

Working with all records again

When all is said and done, you will probably want to go back to working with all the records in the database. To do so, switch to Browse mode (⌘+B/Ctrl+B) and choose Records ➪ Show All Records (or press ⌘+J/Ctrl+J). All records that were previously hidden or omitted will instantly become visible again.

Some live examples

I realize that after you move beyond a simple one-field search, you can easily get confused. Remembering how to do AND and OR searches, how to look for duplicates, and so on may be difficult for you. Reading about Find mode isn't necessarily the best way to learn about it. You may find it easier to understand if you just create a series of find requests and see what happens. The *FileMaker Pro 5 Bible* CD-ROM contains a Find Examples database (in the FileMaker Pro Bible folder) where you can see examples of many typical find requests, each prepared as a script that you can execute with a button click.

To use the Find Examples database, click any of the text buttons on the menu screen.

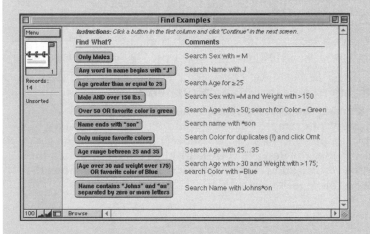

FileMaker Pro enters Find mode and displays another screen that shows the appropriate find request. Because the requests are displayed in list view (each line represents a separate find request), you can see all the necessary requests on this single screen. After examining the requests, click the Continue button in the status area. The find requests execute, and the results are displayed. To return to the menu screen, click the Return to Menu button at the bottom of the page.

Find Criterion

Summary

✦ In Find mode, you can locate records that match specific criteria.

✦ FileMaker Pro performs find operations on one or more fields in a database. Such operations compare the contents of the fields in each record in order to find matches to the search criteria. Each set of criteria is known as a find request.

✦ Any layout can be used when creating a find request. Before creating a find request, you can select the layout you'd like to use by choosing it from the layouts pop-up menu.

✦ All records that match the search criteria are grouped into a found set, which you can then browse in the same manner that you would normally browse the entire database. Records that do not match the criteria are temporarily hidden.

✦ You can have multiple find requests, each of which is evaluated in order.

✦ Find mode supports the use of special symbols that enable you to search for records within a range of values, for invalid or blank values, for duplicate values, and so on.

✦ A request to find records that match certain criteria can be changed to a request to omit these records from the found set. To do so, click the Omit check box on the appropriate find request.

✦ Other useful activities that you can perform with a found set include manually omitting certain records, swapping the omitted records for those that remain in the found set (creating a found set from the previously omitted records), and deleting the found set. You can also copy a found set to the Clipboard for use outside the original database.

✦   ✦   ✦

Sorting Records

Issuing find requests (discussed in Chapter 9) is one way to locate information in a FileMaker Pro database, but it isn't always the most convenient way. And although flipping through records to find information is easy, it can be very time consuming when working with a large database. The primary reason this method takes so long is based on the way that FileMaker stores records. Records are stored in the order in which they are entered. Unless you are importing or hand-entering data from an existing database (as described in Chapter 16), your records may be in no discernible order whatsoever.

About Sorting

Consider the Address Book database that you created in Chapter 4. On the first day, you record the information for James Johnson when he sends you a letter. Your next few contacts are with Susan Brown, Tom Ziegler, and Paula Short. If you create records for every new person in the order in which the contact is made, the records are stored in that order. What you need is a way to change the order of the records so browsing through them is easier and you don't need to issue a find request every time you want to locate a specific record. You can change the order of the records by *sorting* the database.

In life, we are used to seeing information in a particular order. Phone books are organized alphabetically, entries in check registers are arranged by the date of transaction, and so on. In FileMaker Pro, sorting is the process of ordering the records that are being browsed, according to the values contained in one or more of the database fields. Both the fields used and the kind of sort order imposed on each field (ascending or descending, for example) are up to you. For instance, you can sort the Address Book database in ascending order by the Last Name field. After FileMaker Pro completes the sort, the database is arranged so records with last names beginning with A appear first in the database, those beginning with H are near the middle, and records with last names beginning with Z are at the end. If you choose descending order, last names beginning with Z appear first, and so on.

Even if you have never performed a sort in a database program before, you have probably done so in the Finder. The View⇨Sort List submenu (see Figure 10-1) provides a number of commands that enable you to sort the files and folders in any window by name, size, kind, label, or date. Each time you choose a different command from the View menu, the files and folders are sorted according to the new criterion.

Even if you have never performed a sort in a database program before, you have probably done so in Windows Explorer or in a folder (with Active Desktop enabled). The View⇨Arrange Icons submenu (see Figure 10-1) provides a number of commands that enable you to sort files and folders in any window by name, type, size, and date.

Macintosh

Figure 10-1: The View menu in Mac OS 8.5 (left) and Windows 95 (right)

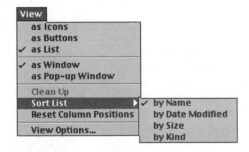

Windows

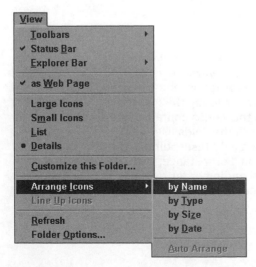

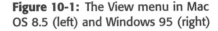

More about sorting

All computer systems contain data that has to be located from time to time. The rapidity with which this information can be found is of critical importance to the system's overall speed and efficiency. Because searching through ordered information is easier than searching through random information (both for the computer and for the computer's users), the process of sorting continues to be an important topic in computer science research.

One of the simplest sorting methods—frequently taught to beginning computer science students—is the *bubble sort*. In this sort method (or algorithm), each record is compared with the first record. If the two records are out of order, they are swapped, causing the record that was being compared with the first record to become the new first record.

After all records have been compared with the first record, the sort moves on to the second record and repeats the process. Every subsequent record is then compared with the second record. Swapping occurs if the two records are found to be out of order. The procedure continues for the third and every subsequent record down to the next-to-last record. Records are said to bubble up into the correct order (hence, the name of the algorithm).

The bubble sort works, but it consumes copious amounts of computing power and is very slow, especially when used with a large database. A more efficient method is the *binary sort*, which involves making comparisons within increasingly small subdivisions of the list that is being sorted. The binary sort uses far fewer steps than does the bubble sort. Other sort methods also exist.

You should note that the true storage order for a FileMaker Pro database is rarely (if ever) changed by a sort operation. Physically moving records to reflect a new database order is inefficient and unnecessary. Instead, the current sorted order of the database is often maintained within a separate list. This list shows which record is currently first, second, and so on. Normally, only this list (or *index*) is physically changed when a database is sorted.

Sorting in FileMaker Pro works in much the same way that sorting in the Finder or Windows Explorer works. Depending on your needs at the moment, you may decide to sort by last name and then later re-sort by Zip code. Just as you can change your choice in the View menu whenever you like, you can sort any FileMaker Pro database as often as you want and by any field or fields that currently interest you.

When people first use sorting, they usually keep it simple, restricting each sort to a single field. They might sort an employee list by last name only, for example. Unfortunately, an important limitation of single-field sorts is that ties (cases in which more than one record has the same value for the sort field) are not broken. If you sort only by last name, all the people who share the same last name are listed in whatever order their records were originally entered into the database, perhaps as follows:

```
Jones, Evan
Jones, Marcia
Jones, Bobby
Jones, Abbie
```

Improving sorts by indexing

In FileMaker Pro 5, indexing is optional. In fact, the default is to index nothing. If you want to index a particular field, you must specifically set that option for the field (choose a field in the Define Fields dialog box, click Options, and then click Storage Options, as described in Chapter 5). Fields that are the best candidates for indexing are those on which sorts or finds will be based, as well as those for which you intend to use the Insert ➪ From Index command to fill the field.

FileMaker Pro, however, can sort by more than one field, solving the problem of what to do when two or more records contain identical information in the primary sort field. In the last example, you can have FileMaker Pro sort the database by the Last Name and First Name fields. Records with identical last names are then arranged in order according to their first name. Thus, performing an ascending sort on the Last Name and First Name fields would arrange the Jones records like this:

```
Jones, Abbie
Jones, Bobby
Jones, Evan
Jones, Marcia
```

As you can see, adding First Name as the second sort field re-sorts all records that have the same last name.

After you apply the proper sorting options, browsing the database can be much easier — just as the alphabetic ordering of entries makes finding words in a dictionary or names in a phone book easier. In this chapter, you learn how to sort a database, set sorting options, and — if need be — restore the records to their original order.

Creating a Sort Order

Prior to sorting a database, you need to make three basic decisions:

✦ *Whether to sort the entire database or only part of it*: By using find requests or Omit Record, Omit Multiple, or Show Omitted commands (see Chapter 9), you can restrict the visible portion of any database to a selected set of records. As with most FileMaker Pro commands, sorting affects only records that are currently visible.

✦ *The field or fields on which to sort:* Which fields you sort on depend on how you want to use the database. Use the field or fields that are presently of greatest importance to you as the sort fields. For example, in a customer database, you may be concerned with sales totals. Sorting on the Total field enables you to see which customers are big buyers and which ones have recently bought little or nothing from you.

Note

You can also sort on fields from another related database; that is, one for which a relationship with the current database has been defined. Related fields can appear anywhere within the list of sort fields. Note that if several records in the related file match a record in the current file, the sort will use the first matching record found in the related file.

✦ *Whether records should be arranged in ascending, descending, or a custom order:* Text data is usually more useful when sorted in ascending order. That is, you normally want to see the A entries first, rather than the Z entries. Numeric information, on the other hand, is frequently more useful when you view it in descending order (largest number to smallest). When you examine file sizes or cost figures, for example, your primary interest will often be in the largest files or the biggest dollar amounts.

If you have defined one or more value lists for the database, you can sort according to the order set in any of these value lists. This is a great way to organize records in a specific order that is neither alphabetic nor numeric. For example, you may have a value list that consists of the department names of your company organized in a specific order. When you sort according to this value list (rather than alphabetically, as you normally might), you can make sure that people in Administration will be listed before those in Accounting, for instance. See the section, "Additional Sorting Options," at the end of this chapter for details.

You sort by choosing the Records ⇨ Sort command (or by pressing ⌘+S/Ctrl+S). The Sort Records dialog box appears, in which you specify sorting options, as shown in Figure 10-2.

In the field list area (on the left side of the Sort Records dialog box) is a list of the fields by which you can also sort the database. Eligible sort fields include all fields that you have defined for the database—not just the ones that appear on the current layout. By choosing a previously defined relationship from the pop-up menu at the top of the field list, you can also sort the database by any field in a related file, if you prefer. (If no relationships have been defined for the current database, you can create them by choosing Define Relationships from the same pop-up menu.) For information about relationships, see Chapter 19.

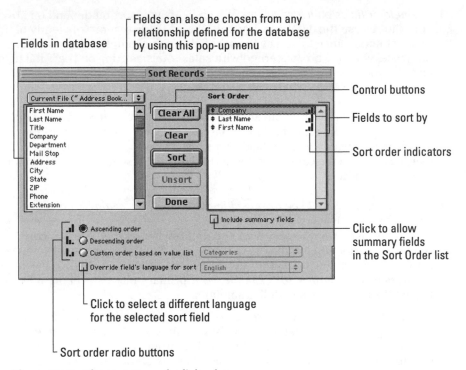

Figure 10-2: The Sort Records dialog box

You can also use Summary fields as sort fields if you check the "Include summary fields" check box. For details, see the "Sorting by Summary fields" section, near the end of this chapter.

In the Sort Order area on the right side of the dialog box is a list of the currently chosen sort fields. The order in which the fields appear corresponds to the order in which the database will be sorted. In Figure 10-2, for example, the database will first be sorted by the Company field. Within each company, records will be re-sorted by each person's last name and then by first name. An icon following each field name in the Sort Order list indicates the sort order (ascending, descending, or custom) for that field. The meanings of the icons are shown at the bottom of the dialog box. To rearrange the sort fields, click a double-headed arrow next to a field name and drag the field name to its new place in the Sort Order list.

The buttons in the center of the dialog box enable you to control the Sort Order list. At the bottom of the dialog box are three radio buttons you can use to specify, for each sort field, whether you want an ascending sort, a descending sort, or a sort based on a value list.

Following are brief explanations of the components in the Sort Records dialog box:

✦ *Clear All*: Click this button to remove all fields from the current Sort Order list. Use Clear All when you want to define a sort order from scratch and ignore any fields that are presently selected.

✦ *Move*: Click this button to copy the selected field from the field list to the Sort Order list. Use Move to choose each field by which you intend to sort.

✦ *Clear*: When you select a field in the Sort Order list, this button replaces the Move button. Click Clear when you want to remove the selected field from the Sort Order list. (Clear enables you to remove fields from the Sort Order list selectively. Use Clear All to remove all fields from the Sort Order list.)

✦ *Sort*: Click this button to sort the database according to the current settings.

✦ *Unsort*: This command "undoes" any current sort operation and restores the records to the order in which you entered them into the database. You seldom need to restore records to the original order—unless, of course, you created or imported the records in some meaningful order that you cannot duplicate by using a Sort command.

✦ *Done*: This command dismisses the Sort Records dialog box without sorting but preserves any changes you have made to the sort specifications.

✦ *Include summary fields*: This check box specifies whether Summary fields are listed as eligible sort fields. If this option is not checked, Summary field names are grayed out (dimmed)—meaning you cannot use them as sort fields.

✦ *Ascending order*: Click this radio button to sort the selected field from the lowest value to the highest value (from A to Z, for example).

✦ *Descending order*: Click this radio button to sort the selected field from the highest value to the lowest value.

✦ *Custom order based on value list*: If you have prepared one or more value lists for the database (see Chapter 5), click this radio button and select the name of the value list from the pop-up menu. This action instructs FileMaker Pro to use the order of the value list as the sort order for the field. (If an appropriate value list doesn't already exist, you can choose Define Value Lists from the pop-up menu.)

As an example, the days of the week in chronological order might constitute a value list. Using this value list, records would appear in the order Sunday, Monday, Tuesday, and so on, rather than in ascending or descending alphabetical order.

The "Override field's language for sort" check box and associated pop-up menu at the bottom of the dialog box enable you to specify an international sorting convention, if desired, for any selected field. (See "Setting an international sort order," later in this chapter.)

Sorting on one field

The simplest and most common kind of sort is one based on a single field — sorting only by the Zip Code, Invoice Total, Age, or Grade Point Average field, for example. Depending on the complexity of your databases, you may find that the majority of your sorts use only a single sort field.

Follow these steps to sort on one field:

1. Decide whether you want to sort the entire database or only selected records. FileMaker sorts only those records that are currently visible (those being browsed).

2. Use the Find, Omit Record, Omit Multiple, and related commands and options to select the records of interest (see Chapter 9 for instructions).

   — or —

   If you are currently browsing only a subset of records and want to sort the entire database, choose Records ➯ Show All Records (or press ⌘+J/Ctrl+J).

3. Choose Records ➯ Sort (or press ⌘+S/Ctrl+S).

   The Sort Records dialog box appears (as previously shown in Figure 10-2).

4. If the Sort Order list includes fields you don't want to use in this sort operation, click Clear All to remove them all or individually select each field and click Clear.

Note   If you have not sorted the database before, the Sort Order list will already be clear. Otherwise, it will contain the fields used in the most recent sort.

5. In the scrolling field list on the left side of the dialog box, click the name of the field by which you want to sort.

6. At the bottom of the dialog box, click the radio button that corresponds to the sort order you want to use for the field:

   • Click "Ascending order" to start with the smallest numeric value and end with the largest, to sort words alphabetically (from A to Z), or to arrange times and dates chronologically.

   • Click "Descending order" to start with the largest numeric value and end with the smallest, to sort words in reverse alphabetic order (from Z to A), or to arrange times and dates from the most recent to the oldest.

   • Click "Custom order based on value list" to use a value list that you have defined for the database.

7. Click Move to transfer the field to the Sort Order list.

— or —

Double-click the field name to select it in the field list and simultaneously move it to the Sort Order list.

8. Click Sort to sort the database in the specified order by the selected field.

When the sort is finished, the status area changes to show that the database has been sorted, as shown in Figure 10-3. The new first record in the sorted database appears in the document window.

Figure 10-3: The status area for a sorted database

Sorting on multiple fields

As mentioned earlier in the chapter, sorting by a single field isn't always sufficient, particularly in a database in which several records may have the same value in the sort field. In such a case, you may want to further organize the records by specifying additional sort fields.

As an example, you may have several records for people who have the same last name. Sorting only by the Last Name field will leave the first names in whatever order the records were in when you created them. (Can you imagine what a mess a metropolitan phone directory would be if it were sorted only by last name? Try finding Jake Johnson in a 20-page listing of Johnsons!) Selecting First Name as the second sort field is often a smart move. And if you believe (or know) that some people have the same last names and the same first names, you can consider adding a third sort field, such as Middle Initial, Phone Number, Address, or Age.

Canceling a sort operation

Sometimes, in the middle of a sort operation, you may decide that you want to sort on fields other than the ones you have chosen. Instead of waiting for FileMaker Pro to finish sorting the database, you can cancel the sort by pressing ⌘+. (period)/Esc. This feature is especially helpful when the database is large and the sort operation is lengthy.

When specifying multiple sort fields, select them in the order of their importance. Fields further down in the Sort Order list are merely tiebreakers, as illustrated in Figure 10-4. Working with the Address Book database, you may decide that your main interest is in companies, rather than in people, and choose Company as the first sort field. If you have multiple contacts at various companies, you can use Last Name or Department as the second sort field. If the companies are very large, you may also want to select a third sort field, such as First Name.

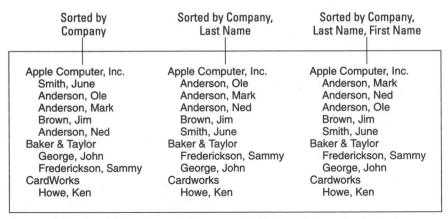

Figure 10-4: As additional sort fields are added, the ordering of records becomes progressively more useful.

The only difference between sorting by one field and sorting by multiple fields is the presence of the additional fields in the Sort Order list. (For instructions, refer to the steps previously presented in "Sorting on one field.")

Tip   If you discover that the fields in the Sort Order list are in the wrong order, you don't have to clear them and start over. You can rearrange the fields by simply dragging them to new positions in the list. To do this, move the pointer over the field you want to relocate in the Sort Order list. When the pointer changes to a double-headed arrow, click and drag the field to its new position in the list, and then release the mouse button.

Sorting on multiple fields versus performing multiple sorts

Performing a sort that includes multiple sort fields is not the same as performing several successive sorts that use those same fields. Every sort always starts from the original record order—not from the order that is currently displayed on-screen.

For example, if you sort a database by the Company and Last Name fields, the records are arranged in order according to company. Within every company, records are further arranged alphabetically by the employees' last names. On the other hand, if you perform two sorts—the first by the Company field and the second by the Last Name field—each sort works independently of the other; the effects are not cumulative. The first sort arranges records in company order. The second merely arranges the records according to last names, completely ignoring the results of the initial sort.

Modifying Sort Specifications

After you define a sort for a database and set options, you may later decide that you want to change some of the options or perhaps sort on different fields. Although you can click Clear All in the Sort Records dialog box and then specify new sorting instructions from scratch, changing the options is often easier. For example, you can do any of the following:

- ✦ Clear unnecessary fields from the Sort Order list (by clicking Clear All or selecting individual fields in the Sort Order list and then clicking Clear).

- ✦ Add new sort fields (by selecting them in the field list and clicking Move).

- ✦ Change the order of fields in the Sort Order list (by dragging them to new positions).

- ✦ Change to an ascending, descending, or custom sort order for a field (by selecting the field in the Sort Order list and then clicking a different sort order radio button).

Sorting Data in Portals

In FileMaker Pro 4.0 and higher, related data that is displayed in a portal can be sorted. In the absence of a sort order, FileMaker Pro displays the records in a portal in the order in which they were entered. For example, if you have a database of video rental invoices, each customer invoice record could have a portal that shows video rental details: the movie ID, category, title/description, and price. The video rentals in the portal are displayed in whatever order they were entered.

To change the sort order for records in a portal, you must set the sort order as part of defining the relationship between the main file (Invoices, in this example) and the related file (Customer Rentals, in this example).

To establish a sort order for portal records, follow these steps:

1. Choose the File ➪ Define Relationships command. (You can also choose Define Relationship from any dialog box where it is available, such as the Portal Setup dialog box and the Specify Field dialog box.)

   The Define Relationships dialog box appears.

2. Create a new relationship by clicking the New button, or select an existing relationship and click the Edit button to open the Edit Relationship dialog box (see Figure 10-5).

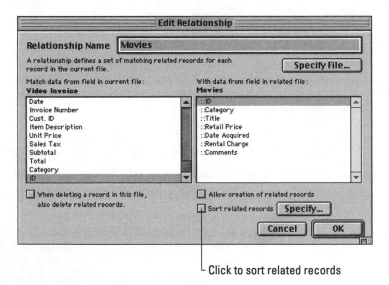

Click to sort related records

Figure 10-5: The Edit Relationship dialog box

3. Check the "Sort related records" check box.

   The Specify Sort dialog box appears (see Figure 10-6).

4. As with any other sort, select the fields in the related file that you want to sort on and click the Move button to add them to the Sort Order list. For each sort field, choose "Ascending order," "Descending order," or "Custom order based on a value list."

Related field list

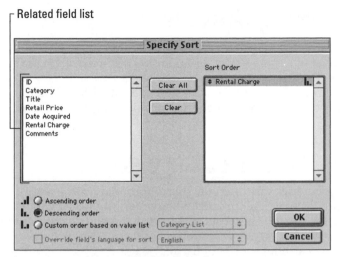

Figure 10-6: The Specify Sort dialog box

5. Click OK in the Specify Sort dialog box, and then click OK in the Edit Relationship dialog box. Finally, click Done to close the Define Relationships dialog box.

FileMaker Pro will now display the records in the portal in the specified sort order. For example, if you chose to sort the portal records in order of Rental charge (descending), the most expensive item in the video invoice would be listed at the top of the portal.

The need for re-sorting

FileMaker Pro tries to maintain the current sort order for a database, even when you add new records to a previously sorted database. Because it doesn't do a perfect job, however, you see "Semi-sorted" (rather than "Sorted") in the status area. To ensure that all records are correctly sorted, you need to use the Sort command again after you add new records. FileMaker Pro records the last set of sort instructions that you use, so re-sorting the database is as simple as choosing the Sort command and then immediately pressing Return/Enter (the equivalent of clicking the Sort button).

Executing a find request, on the other hand, has a more profound effect on the current sort order: It obliterates it. The new condition of the database is reported as "Unsorted" in the status area. (This follows logically from the fact that a sort operates only on the found set, rather than on the entire database. A new Find results in a new found set.) Thus, you will usually want to re-sort the database following a find request.

Additional Sorting Options

You can sort a database in more than one way. The Sort command offers additional capabilities, many of which are useful for tasks such as preparing reports. You can sort a database in the order defined by a value list, sort by Summary fields, sort in a way that makes the organization of records more useful for individuals in a different country, and restore the records to the order in which they were entered in the database.

Using a value list to set a sort order

Ascending and descending sorts aren't always appropriate. For example, if you sorted the months of the year in ascending order, you would end up with an alphabetized list that started with April and August and ended with September — probably not what you had in mind. Sorting according to the order defined in a value list offers a way around such problems.

A value list displays the acceptable values for a field in a preset order. You can sort the database by any value list that has been defined for the database, substituting the order defined in the value list for the normal alphabetic, numeric, and chronological orders used by ascending and descending sorts.

To sort according to a value list, select a field in the Sort Order list and click the "Custom order based on value list" radio button (previously shown in Figure 10-2). Then select a value list from the pop-up menu — in most cases, a value list that has been associated with the chosen sort field. (FileMaker Pro 4.0 and higher, however, does not impose this restriction. For example, you could use a value list composed of day-of-the-week names — even if that value list has never been associated with the chosen sort field.)

When you select the value list sort option, the order used for the sort matches the order in which the various values appear in the value list. As shown in the example in Figure 10-7, a value list for a Payment Method field may list various payment methods according to their frequency of use. When the field is sorted, cash transactions will appear first, checks will follow next, and individual credit card charges will be last.

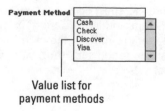

Value list for
payment methods

Figure 10-7: Sorting by a value list is appropriate when you want records sorted in a special, predetermined order, rather than alphabetically, numerically, or chronologically.

Setting an international sort order

Different countries follow different conventions for sorting information. Many countries use a non-Latin alphabet, for example, and some differences also exist among countries that use the Latin alphabet. FileMaker Pro enables you to select an international sorting convention for any field by choosing a language.

To choose a sorting convention for a field, select the field in the Sort Order list, click the check box for "Override field's language for sort," and choose a language from the pop-up menu at the bottom of the Sort Records dialog box (see Figure 8-10). The sort language affects only the selected field. To sort additional fields by the same or a different language, repeat this procedure for those fields.

Figure 10-8: Setting an international sort order for a field

The handling of "other" choices

When you create a value list, providing an "Other..." choice as a catch-all is often helpful. In a value list to be used with a Shipping Method field, for example, you might list choices for Federal Express, UPS, and USPS. Because your company occasionally uses other carriers, you can add an "Other..." choice to the value list so they, too, can be recorded.

In performing an ascending or descending sort on such a field, FileMaker Pro arranges the records in which the "Other..." choice was selected according to the actual contents of the field (Yellow Cab, Jimmy's Messenger Service, and so on). That is, it does not group all of the records together as though they all contained the same value ("Other"). On the other hand, when FileMaker Pro performs a custom sort based on a value list (rather than a simple ascending or descending sort), all "Other..." choices are grouped together at the end of the database, followed only by records in which nothing at all was chosen or entered for the field. (The procedure for adding an "Other..." choice to a value list is explained in Chapter 5.)

Sorting by Summary fields

As you may recall from Chapter 5, a Summary field summarizes information from a single field across a series of records. For example, a Sales Total field may combine individual orders into one sales figure for all records that you are currently browsing.

When placed in a data entry layout, the data in many Summary fields is the same, no matter which record you're currently viewing. For example, any Total or Average Summary field always shows the same total or average, regardless of which record is currently visible. For this reason, sorting by a Summary field makes more sense in a report layout than in a data entry layout.

Here's an example: Suppose you want to create a report that shows total sales for each member of your company's sales force. To accomplish this task, all you need to do is create a layout that contains a subsummary part, define the part as "Subsummary when sorted by Salesperson," and then place the Sales Total Summary field in the subsummary part. When you want to see the summary figures, sort by the Salesperson field and then print or preview the report. (As explained in Chapters 5 and 6, you must sort before printing or switching to Preview mode if you want the information in the subsummary part to display correctly.)

This accomplishes two things. First, the sort specifications group sales by salesperson. All of Bob's sales are listed together, for example, instead of being scattered throughout the database. Second, adding the Summary field enables you to see an individual sales total for each salesperson. The report is shown in Figure 10-9.

Figure 10-9: This report is generated when the database is sorted by the Salesperson field.

Note, however, that what you have accomplished so far has been done without sorting by the Summary field. Although the salespeople are effectively grouped (for example, all of Marjorie's sales are listed together), arranging the groups in alphabetical order is not necessarily the most informative manner of presenting the data. If you add the Sale Total Summary field to the Sort Order list and sort the database again, the report becomes even more useful. As Figure 10-10 shows, not only are the records still grouped by salesperson, they are arranged in order of increasing sales (Marjorie, Bob, and Jim).

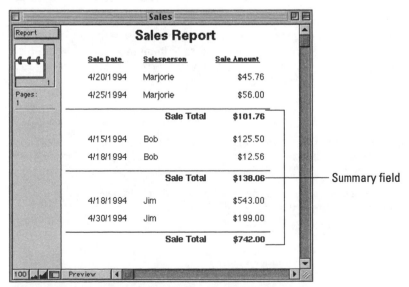

Figure 10-10: A report sorted by a Summary field

To sort by one or more Summary fields, you need to set the "Include summary fields" option in the Sort Records dialog box. Choose Records ⇨ Sort (or press ⌘+S/Ctrl+S) and then click the "Include summary fields" check box in the Sort Records dialog box. Any Summary fields that are visible in the field list change from dimmed to selectable fields, and you can move them into the Sort Order list. As with other sort fields, you can sort a Summary field in ascending or descending order. However, because you cannot associate a value list with a Summary field, you cannot select the "Custom sort" option for such a field. Similarly, you cannot select a different language for a Summary field.

If you want to sort by a Summary field, you also need to include at least one non-Summary field among the sort fields. Note that although the Summary fields always appear at the bottom of the Sort Order list, they are treated as the primary sort fields. (That is, they have a higher precedence than non-Summary sort fields.)

Unsort: Restoring the original record order

If you want to restore the records in a database to the order in which you entered them, click the Unsort button in the Sort Records dialog box. The records are then displayed in the order in which you entered them. (This is the actual order in which records are stored, even after you sort them.)

Tip   You do not need to issue an Unsort command before issuing a new Sort command. Every sort operates on the records in their original order (as you entered them in the database), not on the currently visible order.

Special sorting tips and considerations

Although the examples in this chapter concentrate on sorting the contents of Text and Number fields, you can sort records based on the contents of any field other than a Container or Global field. For example, sorting by date is frequently useful (when you are organizing a check register, for example). And if you were recording harness racing results, you might want to sort by finish time. Calculation fields, such as sales totals, are also often useful as sort fields.

Here are some additional sorting tips you may find helpful:

✦ If you need to sort on a Container field, create an additional field (normally a Text field) that describes or names the picture, movie, audio clip, or sound in the Container field and then sort on that Text field instead.

✦ If you sort on a field that has been declared a repeating field, FileMaker bases the sort only on the contents of the first entry in the field.

✦ When you include a sort in a FileMaker Pro script, you don't need to sort the database before you define the script. Just set sort options and click Done in the Sort Records dialog box. This dismisses the dialog box without sorting, but saves the sorting instructions. (However, if you want to be certain that the sort results are as you intended, you may want to perform the sort anyway, and then examine the results in Browse mode.)

Summary

✦ Sorting is the process of arranging a group of records into a specific display order. The mechanics of sorting is an important topic in computer science.

✦ A sort operation is based on the value of one or more fields in the records to be sorted.

✦ You can use any field type other than a Container or Global field as the basis for a sort.

✦ Sorting does not change the physical location of records in a database. It merely changes the order in which records are displayed. Records are always stored in the order in which you entered them. As a result, you can easily restore the display order of records in a database to the order in which you entered them (by clicking the unsort button in the Sort Records dialog box).

✦　　✦　　✦

Using the Spelling Checker

The spelling checker provided with FileMaker Pro 5 includes a Main Dictionary file. This file contains the spellings of approximately 100,000 words.

Of course, no dictionary designed for general use will contain the spellings of all words that are relevant to your business or your life. For example, you are not likely to find company names, people's names, or technical terms in the main dictionary. Rather than having the spelling checker flag each of these items as a *questionable spelling* (the spelling checker's term for a word not found in its dictionary), you can create user dictionaries that contain additional words that are important to you. When you install FileMaker Pro, it creates the first user dictionary for you, which is called User.

Setting Spell-Checking Options

FileMaker Pro provides two ways for you to check spelling:

✦ *On request*: FileMaker Pro examines the current record, set of found records, text selection, or layout only when you choose the appropriate command from the Edit ⇨ Spelling submenu.

✦ *On the fly*: As you type, FileMaker Pro automatically checks each word against the words in the current main dictionary and user dictionary.

Note The manner in which spell checking is performed is document-specific. That is, you must set spell-checking preferences individually for each database.

Follow these steps to set spell-checking options:

1. Launch FileMaker Pro and open the database for which you want to set spell-checking preferences.

2. Choose Edit ➪ Preferences ➪ Document.

   The Document Preferences dialog box appears.

3. Click the Spelling tab.

   The Spelling preferences are shown (see Figure 11-1).

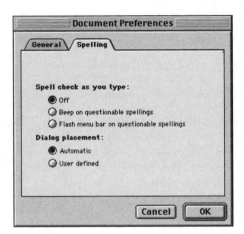

Figure 11-1: The Spelling preferences dialog box

4. To initiate on-the-fly spell checking, click either of these buttons:

   • Beep on questionable spellings

   • Flash menu bar on questionable spellings

   The advantage of this type of spell checking is that you can react immediately and correct errors as the spelling checker discovers them. And you're still free to ignore the beeps or flashes if you prefer to continue typing and make corrections later.

   If FileMaker Pro is currently set to check spelling on the fly (as you type), you can switch to checking spelling on request by clicking the Off button. (Note that even if you've enabled on-the-fly spell checking, you can still request a normal spell check whenever you wish.)

5. Click the radio button labeled "User defined" in the "Dialog placement" option to specify a preferred location for the Spelling dialog box. After placing the

Spelling dialog box where you want it, it will be positioned at the same location every time it appears.

— or —

Click the Automatic radio button to let FileMaker Pro determine the location for the Spelling dialog box.

6. When you have finished making changes to the Spelling options, click OK.

Checking Your Spelling

Spell checking on request (discussed below) is more commonly used than spell checking on the fly. If you prefer to use the other method, you can skip ahead to the "On-the-fly spell checking" section.

Spell checking on request

By selecting the appropriate command from the Edit ➪ Spelling submenu (see Figure 11-2), you can request that spelling be checked for any of the following:

✦ Currently selected text

✦ The current record

✦ The current set of found (visible) records

✦ Labels in the current layout (available only in Layout mode)

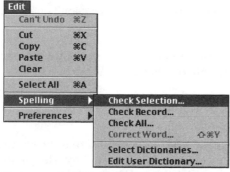

Figure 11-2: The Spelling submenu

In preparation for a spell-checking session, you need to decide what you want to check, as follows:

✦ *To check selected text*: In Browse mode (press ⌘+B/Ctrl+B), use normal text-selection techniques to select text within a field. The amount of text can be as little as a single word or the entire contents of a field. To begin the spelling check, choose Edit ⇨ Spelling ⇨ Check Selection. The Check Selection command is particularly useful when you want to restrict a spell check to a single field rather than examine the entire record.

✦ *To check the current record*: In Browse mode, choose Edit ⇨ Spelling ⇨ Check Record. The spelling of all text in all fields is checked. If you've just added a new record, for example, this command enables you to check just that record.

✦ *To check a subset of records or all visible records*: Issue a Find, Omit, Omit Multiple, or a related command to select a group of records. Or, if you prefer to check all records in the database, choose Records ⇨ Show All Records (or press ⌘+J/Ctrl+J). Following the find request, the database automatically switches to Browse mode, at which time you can choose Edit ⇨ Spelling ⇨ Check All. FileMaker Pro checks the spelling of all text in all fields of the visible (found) records. (For more information on using Find mode and omitting or selecting records, refer to Chapter 9.)

✦ *To check the current layout*: Select the layout of interest by choosing it from the layouts pop-up menu in the upper-left corner of the database window, change to Layout mode (press ⌘+L/Ctrl+L), and then select Edit ⇨ Spelling ⇨ Check Layout. (The Check Layout command appears in the menu only when you are in Layout mode.) This command is useful after you've designed a new layout or altered an existing one. Using it enables you to make certain that all field labels and other static text on the layout are spelled correctly.

After you decide what you want to check, proceed with the spell-checking operation by following these steps:

1. Choose the appropriate command from the Edit ⇨ Spelling submenu (Check Selection, Check Record, Check All, or Check Layout).

   The Spelling dialog box appears (see Figure 11-3). The spelling checker identifies the first questionable spelling it finds and displays it in the Word box of the Spelling dialog box.

   If you prefer to see questionable words in context (within the sentence or phrase in which each one is embedded), click the tiny triangle in the lower-right corner of the Spelling dialog box (Mac) or the Context button (Windows). In addition to appearing in the Word box, the word also appears in context at the bottom of the dialog box.

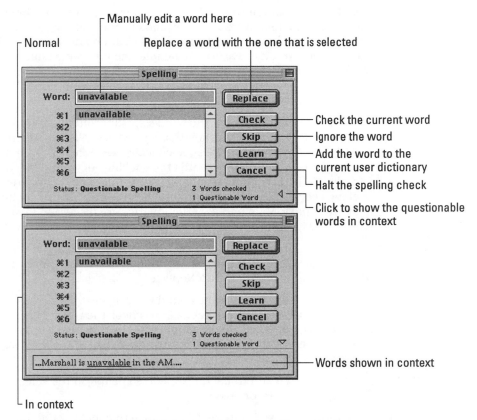

Figure 11-3: The Spelling dialog box (normal and in context)

2. For each questionable spelling that is found, click one of these buttons:

- *Replace*: Click Replace to use a replacement word from the list of words that is provided. Highlight the appropriate word and click Replace, type the word's keyboard equivalent (⌘+1 through ⌘+6 on the Mac, Alt+1 through Alt+6 in Windows), or double-click the replacement. The questionable word is replaced by the selected word, and the spelling check continues.

  Note that in some cases, the spelling checker offers more replacement words than can fit on a single screen. You can use the scroll bar to see the additional word choices. Each time you scroll, the new words are assigned their own Command (⌘)+key (Mac) or Alt+key (Windows) equivalents.

- *Skip*: Click the Skip button to ignore the questionable word here and throughout the rest of text to be examined. You usually use Skip when you know that a word is spelled correctly but do not want to add it to the current user dictionary. For example, the last name Lundeen is not in the Main Dictionary file, but unless it's your last name or the name of an associate with whom you frequently correspond, you probably have no reason to add it to a user dictionary.

- *Learn*: Click Learn to accept the word's spelling and add it to the current user dictionary. If you're certain that a word is spelled correctly and you want it to be known in future spell-checking sessions, click the Learn button. (A user dictionary records the spellings of words that you've added with the Learn command. By supporting user dictionaries, the spelling checker is not limited to just those words that are included in its main dictionary. Main and user dictionaries are discussed in more detail later in this chapter.)

- *Check*: As an alternative, if you know the correct spelling of the questionable word, you can edit it within the Word box. Make the necessary edits and then click Replace.

  If you want, you can check the edited word against the current dictionaries before clicking Replace. To check the word, finish your editing and click Check. Most people edit questionable words manually when they're in a rush or when the spelling checker does not suggest the correct replacement word.

3. Repeat step 2 for each additional questionable spelling in the selected text, record, group of records, or layout.

4. After all words have been examined, click Done to conclude the spelling check.

   Keep in mind that you can click Cancel at any time during a spelling check to halt the process immediately.

Note If you're working in a password-protected file or in a file in which you don't have access privileges for all fields, you may not be allowed to replace some questionable words. In those cases, the Replace button is labeled Next. Click Next to continue.

On-the-fly spell checking

If you have set the spell-checking options to notify you of suspected spelling errors as they occur, FileMaker Pro automatically checks each word the moment you press the spacebar or type a punctuation mark (these actions signify the completion of a word). You can quickly check the most recent questionable spelling by doing one of the following:

✦ Choose Edit ➪ Spelling ➪ Correct Word.

✦ Press Shift+⌘+Y/Shift+Ctrl+Y.

The normal Spelling dialog box appears (as previously shown in Figure 11-3), providing a list of possible replacements for the questionable word. Respond to the dialog box as you would in on-request spell-checking mode (described previously). After you deal with the word, the dialog box disappears, and you can continue typing.

If you're sure that a flagged word is correct and you have no desire to add it to the current user dictionary (by clicking the Learn button), you're free to ignore the spelling checker's beep or flash. Similarly, if you know the correct spelling of a word, making the correction directly in the field is much faster than summoning the Spelling dialog box.

Note that you cannot rely on on-the-fly spell checking to catch all errors. For example, if you move the mouse back into a word that has already been checked and edit it but make a spelling error in the process, FileMaker does not notify you that you have made an error. Thus, if you are unsure of your spelling skills, using both checking methods is a smart idea: Check as you type and then recheck the entire record by choosing the Check Record command.

Installing a Dictionary

When you run a spelling check, you can have only one main and one user dictionary active. However, you can create as many additional user dictionaries as you like.

The Select Dictionaries command enables you to switch between different main and user dictionaries, as needs dictate. You can also use this command to let FileMaker Pro know that you've moved one or more dictionaries to a new location on your hard disk. Follow these steps:

1. Launch FileMaker Pro and open a database.

   Unless a database is open, the Spelling commands are disabled.

2. Switch to Browse or Layout mode.

   The Spelling commands are only available in these modes.

3. Choose Edit ➪ Spelling ➪ Select Dictionaries.

   The Select Dictionary Type/Select Dictionaries dialog box appears, as shown in Figure 11-4.

Macintosh

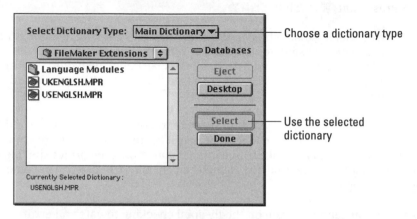

Choose a dictionary type

Use the selected dictionary

Windows

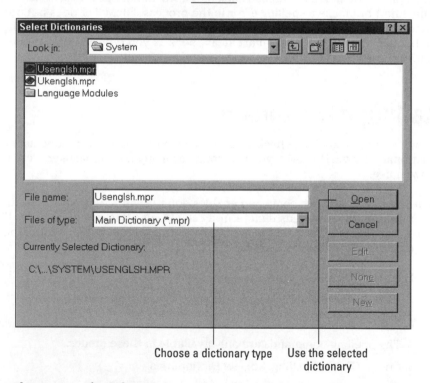

Choose a dictionary type   Use the selected dictionary

Figure 11-4: The Select Dictionary Type (Mac) dialog box and the Select Dictionaries (Windows) dialog box

4. To install a main dictionary, choose Main Dictionary from the pop-up menu at the top of the dialog box on the Mac, or choose Main Dictionary (*.mpr) from the "Files of type" drop-down list at the bottom of the dialog box in Windows. The currently installed main dictionary is indicated below the file list. (By default, Macintosh dictionaries are stored in the FileMaker Extensions folder inside the FileMaker Pro 5 folder; Windows dictionaries are stored in the System folder inside the FileMaker Pro 5 folder. Change to this folder, if necessary.) Select a main dictionary from the file list and click Select/Open.

Note Most users leave the main dictionary supplied with FileMaker Pro as the installed one. The only times you might have to install a main dictionary are after you've moved it to a different location on disk, or if you want to use a different dictionary supplied by FileMaker, such as the UK English dictionary.

5. To install a user dictionary, choose User Dictionary from the pop-up menu at the top of the dialog box on the Mac or choose User Dictionary (*.upr) from the "Files of type" drop-down list at the bottom of the dialog box in Windows. The currently installed user dictionary, if any, is indicated below the file list. Select the user dictionary you want from the file list and click Select/Open. (Or click None to avoid using a user dictionary.)

If the dialog box does not close automatically, click Done.

Any user dictionary or main dictionary that you installed is now used rather than the previous one. To return to the main dictionary or user dictionary that you previously used, repeat these steps and select the old dictionary (or dictionaries).

The steps you need to follow to create a new user dictionary are presented in "Creating a user dictionary," later in this chapter.

Once chosen, the main dictionary is used for all databases. User dictionaries, however, do not work the same way. Every database can have a different user dictionary. When you install a user dictionary, it affects only the current database. Whenever you close a database, FileMaker Pro notes the last user dictionary installed for the file and automatically makes it available the next time you open the database.

Working with User Dictionaries

As discussed earlier in the chapter, user dictionaries contain spellings of words that you want FileMaker Pro to recognize as being spelled correctly. Although only one user dictionary can be active at a time, you can create as many user dictionaries as you like. This section discusses the procedures for working with user dictionaries: creating user dictionaries, adding words to a user dictionary, and merging the contents of two or more user dictionaries.

Creating a user dictionary

FileMaker Pro automatically creates the first user dictionary for you during the installation process. For many of you, this initial dictionary—called User—will be the only user dictionary you'll ever need. Every new "Learned" word can automatically be added to that user dictionary, and the same word will be recognized when encountered in other databases.

However, you may prefer to create several special-purpose user dictionaries instead of simply jamming all your unique words into a single user dictionary. If you dedicate a user dictionary to a special purpose or type of terminology, you may find it easier to maintain. For example, you could create separate user dictionaries for medical, legal, and insurance terms, and another that contains the names of companies with which you regularly do business. This approach works best when a single user dictionary (just the legal one for database A, just the medical one for database B, and so on) can service each of your databases. If you find that many databases need to be checked with more than one user dictionary, you're better off combining them into one large dictionary.

Follow these steps to create a new user dictionary:

1. Launch FileMaker Pro and open a database.

   Unless a database is open, the Spelling commands are disabled.

2. Switch to Browse or Layout mode.

   The Spelling commands are only available in these modes.

3. Choose Edit ➪ Spelling ➪ Select Dictionaries.

   The Select Dictionary Type/Select Dictionaries dialog box appears (as previously shown in Figure 11-4).

4. Choose User Dictionary from the pop-up menu (Mac) or the drop-down "Files of type" menu (Windows).

5. *Macintosh*: Click New to create a new user dictionary. In the file dialog box that appears, enter a name for the dictionary and click Save. The new dictionary is created and becomes the current user dictionary.

   —or—

   Windows: Enter a name for the new dictionary and click New. Select the newly created user dictionary and click Open.

Whenever you want to use one of your user dictionaries, follow the instructions in the section, "Installing a Dictionary," earlier in this chapter, to make the dictionary of your choice the current user dictionary. In the next section, you will learn to add words to the new dictionary.

Adding words to a user dictionary

You can add words to a user dictionary in several ways:

✦ *Adding words as you go*: As you work with a database and perform on-the-fly or on-request spelling checks, you can click Learn whenever FileMaker Pro finds an important word that it doesn't know. The advantage of this approach is that you add only words that are essential, because, by definition, they have already been encountered at least once in a spell-checking session. The disadvantage is that until you have used FileMaker Pro for a fair amount of time, you may be adding words quite frequently, interrupting the flow of the spelling checks.

✦ *Manually adding words*: You can use the Edit ⇨ Spelling ⇨ Edit User Dictionary command to add new words. This option enables you to add key terms to a user dictionary without waiting for them to be encountered in a spell-checking session.

✦ *Importing a word list*: You can also use the Edit ⇨ Spelling ⇨ Edit User Dictionary command to import a list of words (in Text-Only format) that you want to add to a user dictionary *en masse*. This approach makes the most sense when you already have a list of terms prepared, perhaps as a user dictionary that you created in another program. Because such a list can contain many words, this is easily the fastest way to build a user dictionary. To be useful, however, you should carefully screen the contents of the word list beforehand to avoid having to delete unnecessary terms later.

You already know how to use the Learn button to add words to a user dictionary. Follow these steps to manually add or remove words from the current user dictionary:

1. Launch FileMaker Pro and open a database.

   Unless a database is open, the Spelling commands are disabled.

2. Switch to Browse or Layout mode.

   The Spelling commands are only available in these modes.

3. Choose Edit ⇨ Spelling ⇨ Edit User Dictionary.

   The User Dictionary dialog box appears and presents a list of the words that the dictionary contains, as shown in Figure 11-5.

Note

If a user dictionary is not currently installed or chosen, the Edit User Dictionary command cannot be selected. See "Installing a Dictionary," earlier in this chapter, for instructions on installing a user dictionary.

Name of currently installed dictionary

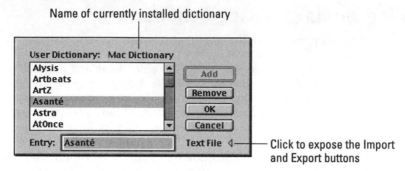

Click to expose the Import
and Export buttons

Figure 11-5: The User Dictionary dialog box

   4. To add a word to the user dictionary, type the word in the Entry box
   and click Add.

   If the word already exists in the user or main dictionary, FileMaker Pro
   informs you. Otherwise, the word is added to the user dictionary.

   5. To remove a word from the user dictionary, select the word in the word list
   and click Remove.

Note

You cannot *edit* words in the user dictionary. You must remove the old word and
then add the replacement (spelled correctly, of course). As an alternative, you can
select the misspelled word in the word list, edit it, choose Add, and then use the
Remove command to eliminate the original word.

   6. Repeat steps 4 and 5 as desired.

   7. To accept the additions and deletions, click OK. Or, to ignore all changes,
   click Cancel.

Importing a word list is another way to add words to a user dictionary. FileMaker
Pro can also export the contents of a user dictionary so it can be used in other
programs. Whether you are importing or exporting a word list, the files are always
in Text-Only format. On import, FileMaker Pro doesn't require that the words be set
up in any particular way. As long as a space, tab, or Return character separates
every word from the next word, FileMaker will consider the word for inclusion in
the user dictionary. On export, a user dictionary is written as a single, alphabetized
paragraph, with every word separated from the next word by a space.

Note

Importing and exporting work hand-in-hand. You export data from one program
so it can be imported into and used by another program. (Other FileMaker Pro
import and export capabilities are discussed in Chapter 16.)

Follow these steps to import or export a word list:

   1. Launch FileMaker Pro and open a database.

Unless a database is open, the Spelling commands are disabled.

2. Switch to Browse or Layout mode.

The Spelling commands are only available in these modes.

3. Choose Edit ➪ Spelling ➪ Edit User Dictionary.

The User Dictionary dialog box appears and presents a list of the words that the dictionary contains.

4. Click the tiny triangle in the lower-right corner of the dialog box (Mac) or the Text File button (Windows).

The dialog box expands, and Import and Export buttons appear, as shown in Figure 11-6.

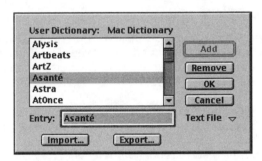

Figure 11-6: The User Dictionary dialog box with importing and exporting enabled

5. To import a word list, click Import, select a text file to import from the file dialog box that appears, and click Open.

The words in the text file are compared to those in the main and user dictionaries. Any words that are not found are added to the current user dictionary; words that already exist in either of the dictionaries are ignored. A dialog box notifies you when the import is complete.

— or —

To export a word list, click Export. In the file dialog box that appears, type a name for the file (or accept the one that is suggested), select a destination disk and folder, and click Save.

The entire contents of the user dictionary are saved as a one-paragraph text file. Each word is separated from the next word by a space. A dialog box notifies you when the export is complete.

6. Click OK to dismiss the notification dialog box and click OK a second time to dismiss the User Dictionary dialog box.

Importing word processing documents into a dictionary

As mentioned in the previous procedure, during an import, FileMaker Pro ignores words that are already contained in its main dictionary or in the current user dictionary. Other than requiring Text-Only format, FileMaker isn't picky about the setup of the word list. You can use this fact to your advantage. You can take *any* word processing document, save a copy of it in Text-Only format, and then import the entire new document into the user dictionary. Any new terms that are encountered will be added to the dictionary; words that are already in the main or user dictionary (the bulk of them, in most cases) will be ignored.

Merging user dictionaries

Although being able to create as many special-purpose user dictionaries as you like is nice, switching from one dictionary to another can be a pain. And if you aren't keeping careful track of which one you used last, chances are better than average that the wrong dictionary may be currently installed.

If your user dictionaries aren't gigantic, you can make life simpler by merging them into a single user dictionary that you can use for most spell-checking sessions.

Note   In the following procedure, the new dictionary is referred to as the *primary user dictionary*.

Follow these steps to merge dictionaries:

1. Begin by creating a new user dictionary to hold the merged user dictionaries. Follow the steps listed in the section, "Creating a user dictionary," earlier in the chapter.

   — or —

   If you want to merge dictionaries into a user dictionary that already exists, go on to step 2.

2. Choose Edit ➪ Spelling ➪ Select Dictionaries.

   The Select Dictionary Type/Select Dictionaries dialog box appears (as previously shown in Figure 11-4).

3. Choose User Dictionary from the pop-up menu at the top of the dialog box (Mac) or from the "Files of type" drop-down menu (Windows), select the first user dictionary that you want to merge with the primary user dictionary, and click Select. Then click Done to close the dialog box.

   The selected user dictionary becomes the current one.

4. Choose Edit ➪ Spelling ➪ Edit User Dictionary.

   The User Dictionary dialog box appears (as previously shown in Figure 11-5).

5. Click the tiny triangle at the bottom of the User Dictionary dialog box (Mac) or the Text File button (Windows).

   Import and Export buttons appear.

6. Click Export.

   A standard file dialog box appears.

7. Select an output location and enter a name for the export file.

Tip

After you merge the export file with the primary user dictionary (after completing step 15), you will have no further use for the export file. Although you can save it here to any disk and folder that you choose, you may want to save it to a location where it's easy to find and delete, such as the root (top) level of the start-up hard disk or to the desktop.

8. Click Save.

   The export commences. A dialog box notifies you when the export process is complete.

9. Click OK to dismiss that dialog box, and then click OK again to dismiss the User Dictionary dialog box as well.

10. Choose Edit ➪ Spelling ➪ Select Dictionaries, and then select the primary user dictionary (see Step 1) from the Select Dictionary Type/Select Dictionaries dialog box that again appears.

11. Choose Edit ➪ Spelling ➪ Edit User Dictionary.

    The User Dictionary dialog box appears once again.

12. Click the tiny triangle at the bottom of the User Dictionary dialog box (Mac) or the Text File button (Windows).

    Import and Export buttons appear.

13. Click Import.

    A standard file dialog box appears.

14. Navigate to the disk and folder in which you saved the export file in Step 7, select the export file, and click Open.

    The import commences. After FileMaker Pro has successfully merged the two user dictionaries, a dialog box will notify you.

15. Click OK to dismiss the dialog box, and then click OK again to dismiss the User Dictionary dialog box as well.

    If you want to merge additional user dictionaries with the primary user dictionary, repeat steps 2 through 15.

Spelling Tips and Tricks

This section examines several easily mastered tricks for creating useful user dictionaries and working with the spelling checker.

Creating a spelling list from existing FileMaker Pro databases

Having a spelling checker that questions most company names, unusual last names, and technical terms wastes considerable time. Worse still, it encourages you not to use the spelling checker at all! (This is precisely why most people go "Huh?" when they discover that a database program has a spelling checker. Because databases are often filled with proper nouns, spell-checking sessions can take forever.)

If you've been using FileMaker Pro for awhile, you may have already completed the first step toward creating one or more useful user dictionaries. In an address database (Address Book, for example), you may have collected dozens of company names and people's last names. In an inventory database, you may already have entered the precise spellings of most of the important items that your company sells. A medical records database may contain the names of the majority of diseases that you treat. By using FileMaker Pro's Import/Export command, you can export the contents of these fields and create a text file that you can then import into a user dictionary.

Follow these steps to create a word list from an existing database:

1. Open the database from which you intend to extract the word list.

2. Choose File ➪ Export Records.

    A file dialog box appears, as shown in Figure 11-7.

Macintosh

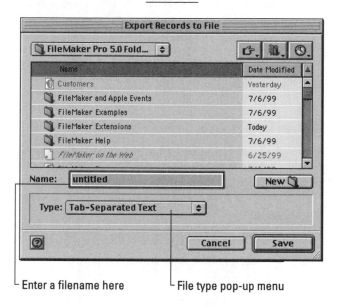

Enter a filename here　　　　File type pop-up menu

Windows

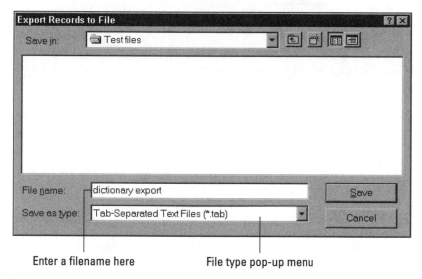

Enter a filename here　　　　File type pop-up menu

Figure 11-7: Exporting data from a FileMaker Pro database

3. Select a location for the export file, type a filename for it, set the type to Tab-Separated Text (Mac) or Tab-Separated Text Files (Windows), and click Save.

The Specify Field Order for Export dialog box appears, as shown in Figure 11-8. This dialog box works much like the Sort dialog box. The left side contains a list of all fields that have been defined for the database; the right side contains a list of the fields that are currently chosen to be exported (in the order in which they will be exported).

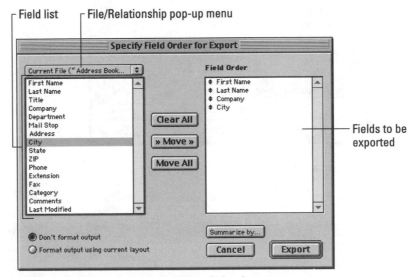

Figure 11-8: The Export Field Order dialog box

4. Add fields to be exported to the Field Order list by selecting them in the left-hand list and clicking Move.

Note   Because FileMaker Pro databases can be relational, you may have defined one or more relationships between the current database and other databases. You can export fields from a related database by choosing the name of the relationship from the pop-up menu above the field list.

5. Remove unnecessary fields from the Field Order list (on the right) by clicking Clear All or by selecting individual fields and clicking Clear.

6. Make sure the "Don't format output" radio button is selected, and then click Export.

The export file is created.

7. Choose Edit ➪ Spelling ➪ Select Dictionaries. In the Select Dictionary Type/Select Dictionaries dialog box that appears (as previously shown in Figure 11-4), choose User Dictionary from the pop-up menu, select the appropriate user dictionary from the file list, and click Select/Open.

   These actions make the selected user dictionary the one that will receive the word list.

8. Choose Edit ➪ Spelling ➪ Edit User Dictionary.

   The User Dictionary dialog box appears.

9. Click the tiny triangle at the bottom of the User Dictionary dialog box (Mac) or the Text File button (Windows).

   Import and Export buttons appear at the bottom of the dialog box.

10. Click Import.

    A standard file dialog box appears.

11. Navigate to the disk and folder in which you saved the export file in Step 3, select the export file, and click Open.

    The import commences. When FileMaker Pro has successfully imported the word list, a dialog box will notify you.

12. Click OK to dismiss that dialog box, and then click OK again to dismiss the User Dictionary dialog box.

Restricting spelling checks to a subset of fields

Depending on the types of fields you have created for a database, you may have no desire to check the spelling in every field (by using Check Record). Unfortunately, the only other option is to select and check one field at a time. Performing this task manually is time consuming. However, you can simplify the process by creating a FileMaker Pro script that selects and checks only the desired fields one by one.

Figure 11-9 shows a sample script that checks the contents of a series of fields in a database. When the script executes, it selects the entire contents of the first field (Company) and executes the Check Selection command. After the first field is checked, the second field (Last Name) is selected, and the same procedure is used to check that field, and so on. Note that this script performs the spelling check for only the current record, and you must click the Done button to move from one field to the next.

To add more fields to such a script, simply include additional Check Selection script steps. Be sure that the "Select entire contents" option is checked for each Check Selection script step.

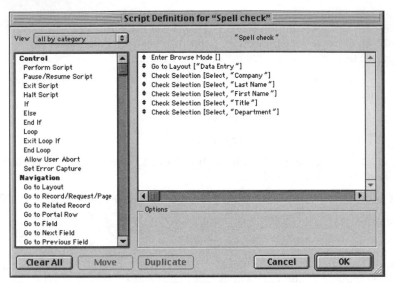

Figure 11-9: Steps for the Spelling Check script

Summary

✦ You can have spelling checked as you type, on request, or both. You can check the spelling of any record, group of records, text selection, or set of field labels and static text.

✦ Only one main and one user spelling dictionary can be active at any given moment, but you may have more than one of each stored on disk and switch among them as the need arises.

✦ Each database remembers the last user dictionary that was used. The next time you open the database, the same user dictionary will be active again.

✦ User dictionaries contain the special or unusual words that you've added to them. You add words by clicking the Learn button during a spelling check, by editing the user dictionary and typing the words, or by importing words from a standard text file.

✦ When FileMaker Pro imports a word list into a user dictionary, it checks each word against the contents of the current main dictionary and user dictionary and ignores words that are already included.

✦ You can import a user dictionary that was created in another program if the dictionary can be saved as a text file.

✦   ✦   ✦

Reports

◆ ◆ ◆ ◆

In This Chapter

Designing a
typical report

Creating reports
with the New
Layout/Report
assistant

Tips for designing
attractive, useful
reports

◆ ◆ ◆ ◆

Perhaps the main reason you enter data into a database
is so you can eventually get it back out in an attractive,
organized, and informative fashion. You've seen how to locate
information in a database using Find mode and how to
organize that information with the Sort command. You've even
learned about using layouts to view different arrangements of
your data. What's been missing up to this point is a discussion
of putting these procedures together to produce reports that
you can keep and share.

Report Design Essentials

A *report* is a summary of the data entered into a database, or
an organized, collated view of the data. You don't necessarily
have to print a report (you can use Preview mode to view it
on-screen), but the process of creating a report is much the
same whether you choose to print or not. (You will learn more
about printing in Chapter 13.)

Preparing a report involves four steps:

1. *Designing a report layout:* Create a layout that displays
   only the fields you want to see. Make sure the layout
   takes advantage of available page space and that the
   data is clearly presented. You use Layout mode to create
   and modify layouts (as explained in Chapter 6).

2. *Selecting records to include in the report:* You don't
   always want to see the entire database in a report. Your
   needs for the report will dictate the particular records to
   select. You may want to include only records in a given
   time frame, records associated with certain individuals
   or organizations, or records with some specific property,
   such as overdue invoices. Records are selected in Find
   mode by creating find requests or using related
   procedures, such as the Omit Record command.

3. *Sorting the records:* If they've never been sorted, records are displayed in the order in which they were entered into the database. For report purposes, records often need to be arranged in some other order so readers can locate particular records and make sense of the information. You arrange records in FileMaker Pro using the Sort command.

4. *Printing:* When designing a report layout, it's important to keep your printing requirements and capabilities in mind (unless you intend to view the report only on-screen). The type of printer you have can affect the layout you use and how information must be arranged within that layout. Finally, certain kinds of information (such as Summary fields) appear only when you display a print preview or print the report.

The following sections provide more information about these four essential steps in the report preparation process.

Designing a report layout

When designing a report layout, you should ask yourself these questions:

✦ *What is the purpose of this report?* This is the key to determining what information to display in the report layout. To begin, you should exclude any fields that are not needed. In a phone directory created from an employee database, for example, you would not want to display information about employees' ages or Social Security numbers — even though that data is routinely collected for the database. If current layouts include extraneous information, you will either have to edit a duplicate of the most appropriate layout or design a new one especially for the report.

✦ *How much information can — and should — I put on a page?* You should make optimal use of the print area, but not at the expense of the report's clarity. Provide an adequate amount of white space between records, as well as between fields in each record. It's also important to recognize that when printing or displaying records, FileMaker Pro truncates data that doesn't fit within a field. This is not a problem in Browse mode because the field expands the moment you click in it. In Preview mode or when printing, on the other hand, there is no opportunity to click within fields. You may have to resize some fields in the report layout so their data displays completely.

✦ *Is the report layout clear?* A report should be self-explanatory. Report recipients should be able to recognize its purpose without having to ask for explanations. Fields and summary sections should be clearly labeled. And don't underestimate the importance of headers and footers for labeling and numbering report pages. The report's purpose can be further reflected in its title, which is normally printed in the header.

Once you create an appropriate report layout, you can change to that layout at any time by selecting its name from the layouts pop-up menu at the top of the status area. Because creating a report is a multistep process (described previously), you may want to design a FileMaker Pro script that does the necessary preparatory work, changes to your report layout, and then prints the report for you. (Scripts are discussed in detail in Chapter 15.)

New Feature

In prior versions of FileMaker Pro, all layout design was done manually. When you chose the New Layout command, the only part of the design that you could automate was to select an appropriate layout style (such as Standard or Columnar Report) and choose the fields to be included. What inevitably followed was extensive tweaking (rearranging and moving fields, changing fonts and sizes, and so on). In FileMaker Pro 5, on the other hand, you use an assistant to create all new layouts. When you choose Layouts ➪ New Layout/Report, you are presented with a series of dialog boxes that enable you to design an attractive report with minimal tweaking. (Of course, you can still modify any assistant-generated layout, if needed.) To learn how to use the New Layout/Report assistant to design reports, see "Creating New Layouts" in Chapter 6.

Selecting records to include in the report

Selecting records is perhaps the subtlest part of creating a report. What records do you need to display? Your choice will likely be based on the content of one or more fields in the database. You may want to choose all records that have a certain value or range of values in a field — for example, all invoice records prepared the third quarter of the current calendar year.

After you decide which records to include in the report, you can create one or more find requests that locate those particular records — and *only* those records. After performing a find or using other related commands (such as Omit Record and Omit Multiple), the remaining visible records are referred to as the *found set*. Whether you intend to print your report or just preview it on-screen, the records included in the report are always drawn exclusively from the found set. (Refer to Chapter 9 for more information on finding records and working with found sets.)

Tip

Some reports need to display every record in the database. To include all records in a report, simply choose the Records ➪ Show All Records command (or press Ô+J/Ctrl+J). Show All Records instantly adds every record to the found set.

Sorting the found set

Unless the found set has previously been sorted, the records appear in the order in which they were entered into the database. To create a more meaningful order for the data, you can sort the found set.

You may want to sort on the same fields you used to create the found set. If a field contains names, it is usually best to sort alphabetically (from A to Z). For a sales report in which you want to highlight the performances of your best salespeople, you may want to sort a Sales field numerically in a descending order (showing highest sales first and lowest ones last).

Keep in mind that you can sort by more than one field. In the sales report example, you could sort records first by salesperson name and then by the amount of each sale. This produces a report in which each salesperson's sales are grouped with the most prominent sale appearing at the top of the group. (Refer to Chapter 10 for more information on sorting records.)

If you're using a layout that includes a subsummary part, you must sort by the field that you designated when you created the subsummary; otherwise, the summary information won't appear in the report. Sorting by the specified field has the result of dividing the records into groups based on that field. For example, if a City field were the designated sort field, the report would have separate sections for each city. (For more information on this subject, refer to Chapters 5 and 6.)

Printing or previewing the report

After preparing the report, you can view your work on-screen. Switch to Preview mode (choose View ➪ Preview Mode, press ⌘+U/Ctrl+U, or choose Preview from the mode pop-up menu at the bottom of the document window.

Tip   Sometimes, printing is a waste of paper. Many reports only need to be seen once and then never again. It's often more convenient — and faster — to review the report on-screen.

To produce a report that is easily shared with others, however, you will probably need to print it. When designing a report that you intend to print, you should consider the following issues:

✦ *What type of paper will I be using?* This consideration is especially important when you're working with odd paper sizes or with special stock, such as mailing labels. You want your layout to fit and to print properly on that paper. The paper you use can dictate the size of the layout body, the distribution of fields in the layout, and whether you will include headers and footers.

✦ *How much information will the report contain?* Short reports can use large type sizes, while smaller type sizes help conserve paper in longer reports as well as increase the number of fields that can fit across the page. Don't choose type so small that it's difficult to read, though.

✦ *Do I have all the fields I need?* If you want to summarize information in certain fields across records or within individual records, you may need to define Summary and/or Calculation fields. You can also use a Calculation field to convert data from one format to another format that is more appropriate for your report (see Chapter 14).

✦ *Which orientation should I use: portrait or landscape?* Because many columnar reports require multiple fields, it's sometimes better to print the report in landscape mode (that is, sideways) than it is to reorganize and resize the fields so they'll fit in portrait mode. To set the display and printing of the report to landscape or portrait, choose the appropriate orientation icon from the Page Setup/Print Setup dialog box.

✦ *Is data being fully displayed?* The amount of data that can be displayed in any field in a printed report or in Preview mode is limited to the size of the field on the layout. Before printing, switch to Preview mode and flip through the report pages. That way, you can quickly determine if some of the fields are too small to display the information they hold. You can then change their sizes on the layout, as necessary.

Refer to Chapter 13 for instructions on printing from FileMaker Pro.

Keeping selected objects from printing

Occasionally, there will be items (buttons, static text, and so on) that are part of your report layout that are not meant to be printed as part of the report. To keep one or more items from printing, change to Layout mode, select the item(s), and choose Format ➪ Sliding/Printing. The Set Sliding/Printing dialog box appears (see the figure below). Click the check box labeled "Do not print the selected objects" and then click OK.

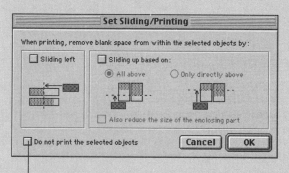

Click to avoid printing the selected objects

Modifying and Reusing Layouts

Even with the capable help of the New Layout/Report assistant, there's inevitably some clean-up that remains to be done. You may find, for example, that some layout parts (such as a footer) are unnecessary or that you wish to add other parts. Or you may have already designed a similar layout that—with minor changes—would meet your needs for a particular report.

Working with layout parts

Some of the major parts of a report layout can be seen in Figure 12-1. Every layout part that you've defined for your report appears in a particular place when the layout is printed or viewed in Preview mode.

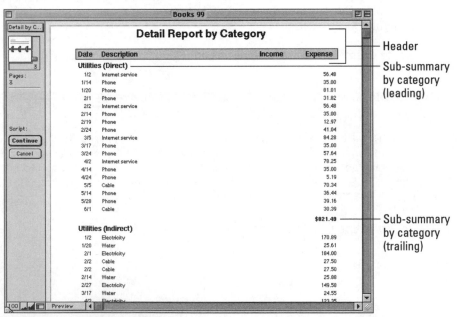

Figure 12-1: An example of a report layout, as viewed in Preview mode

Keep the following facts in mind when choosing parts for a report layout:

✦ A *title header* (if any) is printed once, at the top of the first page. If you make the title header a full page long, you have effectively created a cover sheet. A field placed in the title header displays data from the first record in the found set.

✦ A regular *header* (if any) prints at the top of every page. If you also included a title header, the title header takes the place of the regular header on the first page. A field placed in the header displays data from the first record on that page.

✦ If a *leading grand summary* is part of the report, it prints above the body, before the contents of any records are printed. (For more information on grand and subsummaries, see Chapter 5.)

✦ All of the found and sorted records are printed in the *body* of the report. You can exclude the body part from a report if you want to print only summary information. This method is useful for getting total sales information from an invoice database, for example, when you have no interest in seeing the data from individual invoices.

✦ If you have placed *subsummary parts* above or below the body, each subsummary prints once for each group of records. You must sort the database with the "Sort by" field for a subsummary part to appear. If you like, you can specify a page break before or after a subsummary, forcing a break after each new group has been printed, for example.

✦ If the report contains a *trailing grand summary*, the summary prints below the body once, after the contents of all records are printed.

✦ A *title footer* (if any) is printed once, at the bottom of the first page. A field placed in the title footer displays data from the last record in the found set.

✦ The regular *footer* (if any) prints at the bottom of every page. If you also included a title footer, the title footer takes the place of the regular footer on the first page of the report. A field placed in the footer displays data from the last record on that page.

Duplicating a report layout

When you design a layout for a report, you can begin in either of two ways. You can start from scratch by choosing an appropriate predefined layout, such as the "Columnar report" or "Extended columnar," or you can duplicate and then modify an existing layout. The method you choose will depend on whether you already have a layout that is close to the final report that you envision.

For example, the Want List database on the *FileMaker Pro 5 Bible* CD-ROM successfully reuses a report layout to present two different arrangements of the same data: purchases sorted by catalog number and purchases sorted by purchase date. After creating the first report layout, these steps were used to create the second report layout:

1. Create a duplicate of the layout by switching to Layout mode and choosing Layouts ⇨ Duplicate Layout.

2. Edit the title in the header part of the duplicate layout to reflect the new sort order that will be used.

3. Create a duplicate copy of the script that produces the original report, and then modify the duplicate script so it uses the correct sort instructions.

4. Copy the button that is used to execute the original script, edit the button's name, and then attach the new script to the button.

Because many reports are often only a minor variation of another report, you'll find that using this approach enables you to generate informative reports with minimal effort.

Transferring layouts between databases

You may already have a perfect report layout, but that layout may reside in a different FileMaker Pro database. If you used the same field names in both databases, you can transfer layout elements from the first database to the second.

Follow these steps to move layout elements from one database to another:

1. Open the database that contains the layout elements you want to copy.

2. Choose View ➪ Layout Mode (or press ⌘+L/Ctrl+L).

3. Choose the appropriate layout from the layouts pop-up menu.

4. Choose Edit ➪ Select All (or press ⌘+A/Ctrl+A), and then choose Edit ➪ Copy (or press ⌘+C/Ctrl+C).

   All objects on the layout are selected and then copied to the Clipboard.

5. Open the database in which you want to use the layout.

6. Choose View ➪ Layout Mode (or press ⌘+L/Ctrl+L).

7. Choose Layouts ➪ New Layout/Report (or press ⌘+N/Ctrl+N).

   The New Layout/Report assistant appears, as shown in Figure 12-2.

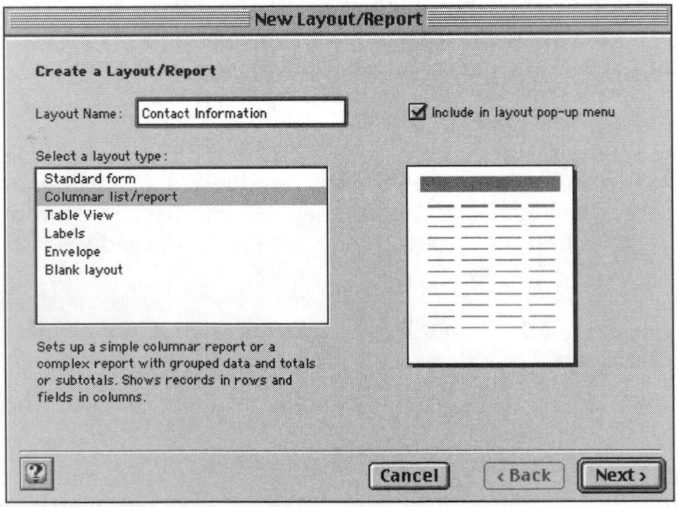

Figure 12-2: The New Layout/Report assistant

8. Enter a name for the layout, choose the Blank layout type, and click Finish.

9. Drag the Body label so the body is the same length, or longer, than the body of the original layout.

10. Choose Edit ➪ Paste (or press ⌘+V/Ctrl+V).

11. Adjust layout parts and objects to the correct positions and sizes.

Any fields from the first (source) database that don't already exist in the second database are pasted but are undefined. Because they don't represent real fields, data cannot be entered into them. To assign actual fields to the undefined fields, double-click each one. The Specify Field dialog box appears, as shown in Figure 12-3, enabling you to assign an existing field (in this database or a related one) to the undefined field. You can eliminate the fields you don't care to define by selecting them and pressing Delete. (See Chapter 6 for more information on editing layouts.)

Figure 12-3: Assigning a field name to an undefined field

Duplicating a layout using drag-and-drop

FileMaker Pro 5 supports a system software feature called drag-and-drop. Drag-and-drop enables you to move graphics, text, and data between documents and applications by simply dragging them from one document to the other. (When you are using two different applications, both must support drag-and-drop in order for this to work.)

To duplicate a layout that's in two different FileMaker Pro databases, you can drag fields, static text, and graphics from one layout to the other. If Copy and Paste is one step too many for you, give drag-and-drop a try.

Note that buttons can also be dragged between layouts, but you will have to redefine the attached scripts.

Summary

✦ A report is a printed or on-screen copy of a selected group of records sorted in a specific order, arranged in a way that provides information that viewing individual records does not (and cannot).

✦ The process of preparing a report typically includes selecting or designing an appropriate layout, choosing records to include using Find mode commands, arranging the records in a meaningful fashion with the Sort command, and then displaying the report on-screen with Preview mode or printing it with the Print command.

✦ Before committing a lengthy report to paper, it's a good idea to examine it first in Preview mode. Because Preview mode shows exactly what a report will look like when printed, you can quickly identify problems — such as field data that is being truncated, header information that is improperly aligned, and so forth.

✦ Many reports can be created almost entirely in the New Layout/Report assistant.

✦   ✦   ✦

Printing

Having mastered the art of designing and producing reports from databases, you are no doubt eager to see your work realized on paper. This chapter takes you step by step through the printing process — from setting up your computer to work with a particular printer to resolving problems that may crop up as you print.

Throughout this chapter, I discuss printing "reports." Although some of the procedures are indeed specific to reports, most can be applied equally to any type of FileMaker document you want to print, such as individual records, script definitions, and field definitions. And many of the printing procedures can be applied to printing documents in other programs, too.

Printing a Report

Printing a report involves three or four basic steps:

1. *Setting up*: You use Apple's Chooser desk accessory or the Windows Page Setup/Print Setup or Print command to select the printer you want to use. After you select a printer, you set print options in the Page Setup/Print Setup dialog box within FileMaker Pro. (You can omit the first part of this step if you always use the same printer. Frequently, you can omit choosing the print options as well.)

2. *Readying a report for printing*: With the database open, select the appropriate layout, find the records you want to include in the report, and sort the records. You can then preview the report to make sure it will print correctly. (Previewing a report before printing is a good way to save paper.)

3. *Printing*: After you are satisfied with the way a report looks in Preview mode, you send it to the printer using the Print command.

If all goes well, the end result of this process is a neatly printed report that contains just the information you need. Unfortunately, things do not always go well, which sometimes leads to a fourth step.

4. *Troubleshooting*: If you don't get the results you want, you need to adopt a systematic approach to isolate and correct the problem.

Note The Page Setup and Print dialog boxes shown in this chapter are from Macintosh System 7.5, OS 8, and Windows 95. If you are using a different version of system software or if you have a different printer than the ones discussed here, the dialog boxes you see may be slightly different.

Step 1: Setting Up

Before printing, you must choose a printer and use the Page Setup command (Mac) or Page Setup, Print Setup, or Printer Setup command (Windows) to enable FileMaker to print correctly.

If you are running System 7.5.*x* or higher and also have the Desktop Printing system software installed, you can select a printer to use without opening the Chooser (as described in "Selecting a printer for a Macintosh"). Simply drag the database's file icon onto the printer's icon on the desktop. The next thing you see is FileMaker Pro's Print dialog box for the chosen printer. Set options as desired and click Print.

Selecting a printer for a Macintosh

Depending on your work environment (a stand-alone computer versus a network, for example), many printers may be available to you, but the Mac doesn't know which one you want to use until you tell it. Before you can print anything, whether in FileMaker Pro or any other program, you need to use the Chooser to select the printer you want to use. (Yes, this is also the case if you have only one printer.)

Tip If your main printer supports desktop printing, you can Ctrl+click the printer's icon on your desktop and choose Set as Default Printer.

The Chooser is a desk accessory, a program you'll find in the Apple menu at the left side of the screen. The Chooser enables you to choose special pieces of software called print drivers that your system uses to control different printers. A print driver is a set of instructions that enables the Macintosh to communicate with a printer.

Selecting the Chooser from the Apple menu displays a desk accessory window similar to the one shown in Figure 13-1. (The appearance of the Chooser on your system may be slightly different, depending on the print drivers installed and the version of system software you are using.)

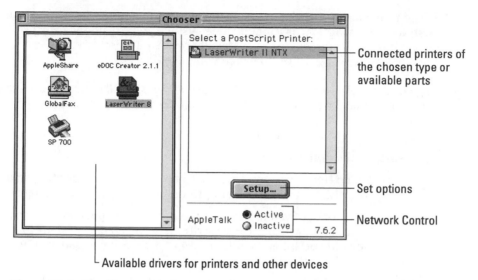

Connected printers of the chosen type or available parts

Set options

Network Control

Available drivers for printers and other devices

Figure 13-1: The Chooser desk accessory

On the left side of the window, you see icons that represent the print drivers that are currently installed on your Mac. Click the icon for the type of printer you want to use. If you are connected to a network, a list of network zones is also displayed. Select a zone to see what printers are currently on line.

To the right is an area that contains icons for all printers that can use the selected print driver. (Only printers that are turned on and connected are shown.) After you select a printer, printer-specific options are displayed below this area. Options may include specifying the port to which your printer is connected (modem or printer) and turning background printing on or off. AppleTalk control is another common option. AppleTalk is a networking system — a way of stringing together computers and peripherals (such as printers) so they can share information. Many laser printers require the use of AppleTalk.

To select a printer, follow these steps:

1. Select the Chooser from the Apple menu.

   The Chooser window appears (refer to Figure 13-1).

2. In the left side of the Chooser window, choose the print driver that is appropriate to the printer you want to use.

Note

For some printers (such as the Epson SP 700 shown in Figure 13-1), choosing a printer driver is sometimes all that is required. There is no specific printer in the right side of the Chooser for you to select, as suggested in step 3. If this is the case with your printer, go directly to step 4.

3. In the right side of the window, click the icon for the particular printer you wish to use. If your Mac is a stand-alone system, you can choose any printer that is connected directly to your Mac. If you are on a network, you can choose any network printer to which you have access.

In general, to select a printer, the printer must be turned on. If necessary, close the Chooser, turn on the printer, and let it warm up. Then open the Chooser again.

4. Set options for the chosen print driver.

Following are the options available for three popular printers:

- *LaserWriter.* Under System 7.x, click to turn background printing on or off. (Under OS 8, all LaserWriter options are set in the Print dialog box.)

- *StyleWriter.* Under System 7.x, click the name of the port on the back of the Macintosh to which the StyleWriter is connected. (Ports are labeled jacks you plug peripheral cables into.) Under OS 8, you can also turn background printing on or off.

- *ImageWriter.* Click the name of the port on the Macintosh to which the ImageWriter is connected.

5. If an AppleTalk section appears in the Chooser and the selected printer is directly connected to your Macintosh by a serial cable, click to indicate that AppleTalk is Inactive.

— or —

If the selected printer is on a network or always requires the AppleTalk option, click the Active button in the AppleTalk section of the window. If you're unsure whether your printer requires AppleTalk, refer to the printer's documentation.

Other than LaserWriters and similar printers, many printers do not require AppleTalk. However, you should check your printer manual and software to determine whether your printer can be shared over an AppleTalk network.

6. Click the close box in the Chooser window to put your choices into effect and dismiss the window.

Until you select a different printer in the Chooser, all future print jobs — regardless of the program you're in — will be directed to the chosen printer.

If your Macintosh print driver is missing

When using the Chooser, you should see an icon for the printer you want to use. If there is no icon for your printer type, you need to install the appropriate print driver. This software normally comes on a disk with your printer, and the printer's documentation should tell you how to install the software. The following procedure describes this task in general terms; consult the printer documentation for specifics.

Note that drivers for Apple printers are included with each version of system software. You can install additional Apple drivers by following the directions in your system software manual. You can download the latest Apple driver's from the Internet at:

```
ftp://ftp.info.apple.com/Apple_Support_Area/Apple_Software_Upda
tes/English-North_American/Macintosh/Printing/
```

You should also note that Apple printer drivers are generally backwards compatible; that is, you can install the newest drivers into older versions of the Macintosh system software.

To install a manufacturer-provided print driver, follow these steps:

1. Locate the print driver disk that accompanied the printer and insert it into the Macintosh floppy disk drive or CD-ROM drive.

2. Double-click the disk's icon to open it.

3. Locate the print driver icon for the printer and drag it to the System Folder on your start-up hard disk.

   An alert box appears, informing you that the driver must be copied into the Extensions folder. Click OK to do so.

   — or —

   If the printer disk comes with an installer program, use it. The installer's job is to make sure everything goes where it is supposed to.

4. Turn on the printer, select Chooser from the Apple menu, and choose the newly installed print driver and your printer.

Using Chooser on a network

If your Mac is connected to a network, you can select any printer that is on the network and currently turned on. For example, when you choose a LaserWriter print driver, you see the names of all LaserWriters on the network. Select whichever one you want to use.

If you are connected to a network that is divided into AppleTalk zones, the Chooser window you see looks somewhat different from the one shown in Figure 13-1. An AppleTalk Zones area appears on the left side of the window beneath the installed print drivers. Before selecting the particular printer to which you intend to print, you must select the AppleTalk zone in which the printer is located. As you click each zone name, the names of the printers available in that zone appear in the printer list on the right side of the window.

Selecting a printer for a PC

Each time you print from a program running under Windows, you can send the print job to any installed printer. You can choose a printer to use from the Print dialog box (see Figure 13-2, top) or Print Setup dialog box (see Figure 13-2, bottom).

Note   Under Windows, there is no standard name for the dialog box in which you specify printer and page settings. It may be called Print Setup, Printer Setup, or Page Setup, depending on the program you are currently running. In FileMaker Pro, it is called Print Setup.

If you do not see your printer listed (perhaps you recently purchased a new printer, for example), you can add a print driver for it by opening the Printers control panel and double-clicking the Add Printer icon.

Note   When you install FileMaker Pro 5 for Windows, it initially uses the default Windows printer. If you later choose a different printer in FileMaker Pro's Print setup dialog box, the chosen printer becomes the new default — but only for FileMaker Pro. The default Windows printer and the default FileMaker Pro printer are independent from one another.

Using the Page Setup dialog box on a Macintosh

You can choose Page Setup from the File menu — in FileMaker Pro, in another program, or from the Finder desktop. The Page Setup dialog box contains controls and options you use to adapt your printer to the kind of output you want to produce. Different printers and different versions of the Macintosh system software present different versions of the Page Setup dialog box. Options that are listed depend on the printer's capabilities and on the types of paper the printer supports.

Print dialog box

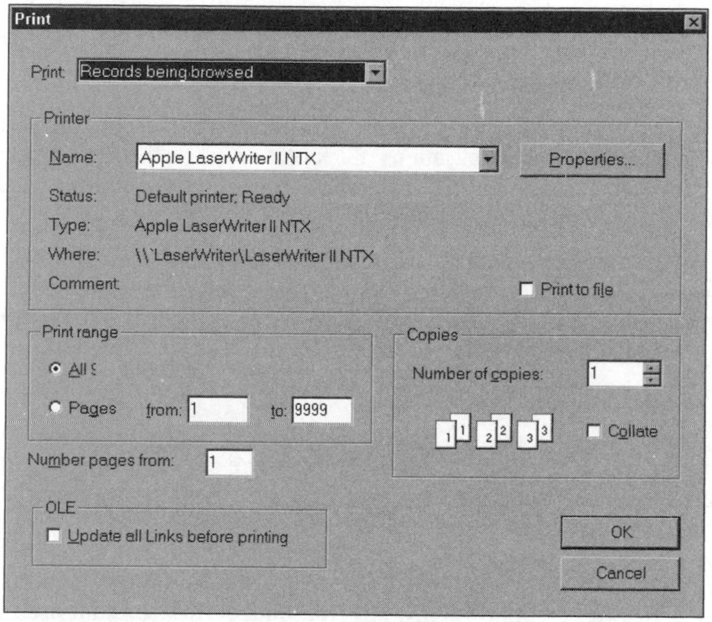

Print Setup dialog box

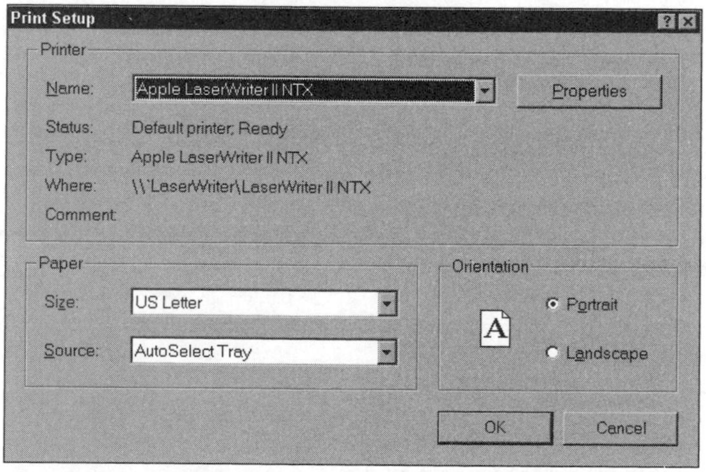

Figures 13-2: Both the Print (top) and Print Setup (bottom) dialog boxes contain a Name drop-down list from which you can choose a printer.

Page Setup options are document-specific rather than global. Even if you always want to print in landscape mode, for example, you will have to set that option individually for each document. Luckily, however, the most recent Page Setup settings used with a given document are stored along with the document when it is saved.

Note

Whenever you change printers in the Chooser, an alert box appears, telling you to change Page Setup for all open applications. Click OK to dismiss this alert box, and do as it suggests. This ensures that any differences between the currently chosen print driver and the previous one are taken into account when you print.

Using a LaserWriter

Choosing Page Setup when you are working with any laser printer that uses the LaserWriter print driver brings up a dialog box similar to the one shown in Figure 13-3.

Whether you are using System 7.*x* or OS 8.*x*, the Page Setup dialog box for a LaserWriter has two pages. In System 7.*x*, you can view the second page by clicking the Options button. In OS 8.*x*, you choose a page to view (Page Attributes or PostScript Options) from the pop-up menu at the top of the dialog box.

The dialog box contains a Paper pop-up menu that lists the predefined paper sizes you can use with the printer. (A4 and B5 are international standards that are not widely used in the United States.) The sizes of paper you can use depend on which printer you choose.

Note

If you are running a recent version of the Mac OS and have multiple LaserWriter printers, you can select the one you wish to use from the "Format for" pop-up menu.

The Layout pop-up menu (only available in later versions of System 7) enables you to print multiple document pages on each piece of paper (in a reduced size). Choices include 1 Up (one document page per printed page), 2 Up (two document pages on each printed page), or 4 Up (four document pages on each printed page). For normal printing, choose 1 Up.

Note

Under OS 8.*x*, the Layout pop-up menu is found in the Print dialog box, rather than the Page Setup dialog box.

You can also enter a magnification factor by typing a number in the Reduce or Enlarge box (System 7.*x*) or the Scale box (OS 8.*x*). You may find this option handy if you are having trouble fitting records on a page.

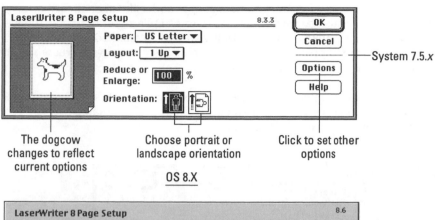

The dogcow changes to reflect current options

Choose portrait or landscape orientation

Click to set other options

System 7.5.x

OS 8.X

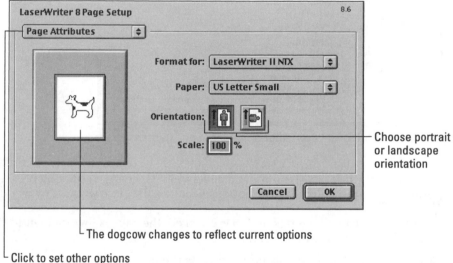

Choose portrait or landscape orientation

The dogcow changes to reflect current options

Click to set other options

Figure 13-3: The Page Setup dialog box for a LaserWriter under System 7.5.x (top) and OS 8 (bottom)

Tip

For best results, you should restrict your Reduce or Enlarge/Scale choices to values that are divisible by two. Such values work best because most laser printers have resolutions of 300 or 600 dots per inch (dpi). If you scale by an odd factor, the dots will have to be apportioned fractionally, occasionally yielding poor results.

Click one of the Orientation buttons to set the orientation of the paper. Click the icon on the left for portrait mode, in which text prints in the normal way. Click the icon on the right for landscape mode, in which text prints across the long dimension of the paper (sideways). Landscape mode, like magnification, is handy for fitting wide records or reports onto a single sheet of paper. You also print envelopes in landscape mode. (Doing so pulls them through the printer lengthwise. Trying to print them in portrait mode is generally not recommended, since it frequently results in paper jams.)

To set special printer effects, click the Options button (System 7.x) or choose PostScript Options from the pop-up menu at the top of the dialog box (OS 8.x). The dialog box shown in Figure 13-4 appears.

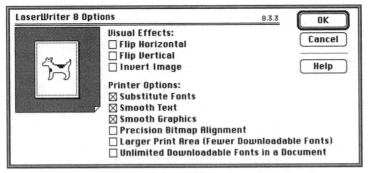

Figure 13-4: Additional LaserWriter printing options (System 7.x)

You set most of these options once and never change them, but nothing prevents you from fiddling with some of the options occasionally. Here's how they work:

✦ *Flip Horizontal*: When this option is checked, the page is inverted left to right, producing a mirror image of the original.

✦ *Flip Vertical*: Choosing this option inverts the page top to bottom.

✦ *Invert Image*: This option swaps black to white and white to black. It produces a negative image of the original.

✦ *Substitute Fonts*: This option enables the Macintosh to supply a different font to the laser printer if the laser version called for in a document isn't available in the system or in the printer's set of built-in fonts. If this box isn't checked, the Mac will use the bitmap version of the font (the one you see on-screen). The text may appear "jaggy," and printing will take longer.

✦ *Smooth Text*: With this option checked, the Mac applies a special algorithm to text to smooth "jaggies" — those diagonal, staircase-looking edges that mar the appearance of text. Checking this option slows printing slightly.

✦ *Smooth Graphics*: This option is similar to Text Smoothing, but it applies to graphics.

Moving up to LaserWriter 8

If you haven't already switched to a version of LaserWriter 8, there are several excellent reasons for doing so. For example, the Print dialog box enables you to select black-and-white, color/grayscale, or calibrated color/grayscale printing. And, unlike earlier versions of the LaserWriter print driver, LaserWriter 8 can display messages (either on-screen or in a printed report) when a PostScript error occurs. LaserWriter 8 can be downloaded for free from most online information services and from Apple's Web site.

✦ *Precision Bitmap Alignment*: This option attempts to reconcile the mathematical difficulties of printing a 72dpi bitmap (that is, a screen image) on a 300dpi printer. In essence, it causes printing at 288dpi (a 4-percent reduction). Note, however, that only the printing of bitmaps is affected. Surrounding text, for example, is printed at the printer's normal resolution.

✦ *Larger Print Area (Fewer Downloadable Fonts)*: This option expands the area available for printing under System 7.*x*. Laser printers, as a rule, aren't capable of printing all the way to the edge of a page, nor within a certain distance from the top or bottom. Checking this option enlarges the print area, at the expense of printer memory, and hence, decreases the number of fonts that can be used.

Note

To achieve the Larger Print Area effect when using LaserWriter 8.4.3 or a more recent driver, choose "US Letter" from the Page Size pop-up menu.

✦ *Unlimited Downloadable Fonts in a Document*: This option enables the Macintosh to supply as many fonts to the printer as the current print job requires. It can slow down printing considerably for documents that use a large number of different fonts in different styles.

After you set all the Page Setup options for a document, you are ready to print.

Tip

At the left side of the initial Page Setup dialog box—as well as the Page Setup Options dialog box—is a small icon of an animal called a *dogcow*. As you set different options, the dogcow shows the effects of your choices. You can click it to see additional information, such as the paper size and margins.

Using a StyleWriter

Choosing Page Setup when you have selected a StyleWriter printer displays a dialog box similar to the one shown in Figure 13-5. Note that the options listed in the dialog box depend on the particular model of StyleWriter you have and the version of system software in use.

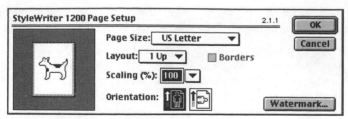

Figure 13-5: The Page Setup dialog box for the StyleWriter 1200 (OS 8)

The three Page Setup options that can be set for all StyleWriter printers are page size, scaling, and orientation. At the top of the dialog box is a Page Size pop-up menu from which you choose the type of paper you will use for the coming print job. In the center is a text box and pop-up menu that you use to set scaling or magnification. You can choose any of the preset scaling options from the pop-up menu, or you can type a setting directly into the text box. Acceptable values range from 5% to 999%.

At the bottom are a pair of orientation icons. Click the icon on the left for portrait mode, in which text prints in the usual way. Click the icon on the right for landscape mode, in which text prints across the long dimension of the paper (sideways). The latter choice is good for fitting wide records or reports onto a single sheet of paper.

Print drivers for the more advanced StyleWriters may also offer layout and watermark options. Choose an option from the Layout pop-up menu to specify the number of document pages to be printed on each piece of paper. The default is 1 Up.

To print a watermark in the background of the document — similar to one you might make with a rubber stamp — click the Watermark button and choose a text string from the pop-up Watermark menu, such as Draft, Confidential, or Proposal (see Figure 13-6). If you pick a watermark, the Density and Scaling options can also be set — enabling you to specify the darkness and print position of the watermark.

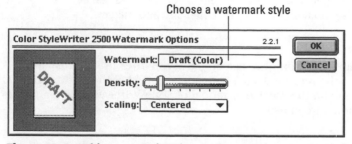

Figure 13-6: With some StyleWriters, you can print a watermark or rubber stamp image in the background of documents.

Using an ImageWriter

Choosing the Page Setup command when you're using an ImageWriter, or another dot-matrix printer that uses the same driver, brings up the dialog box shown in Figure 13-7.

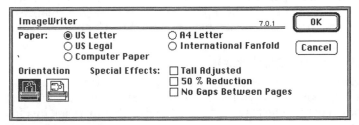

Figure 13-7: The Page Setup dialog box for an ImageWriter

Note   Unlike print drivers for many of the other Apple printers, the ImageWriter driver in OS 8 has exactly the same options as it had in System 7.x.

At the top of this dialog box are radio buttons that you click to indicate the kind of paper you want to use. Note, in particular, the Computer Paper option. Choose this option when you're working with fanfold, tractor-feed paper. This type of paper has perforated, detachable edges with holes that guide the paper through the printer.

Below the paper radio buttons are icons that control the paper's orientation. Click the icon on the left for portrait mode, in which text prints in the usual way. Click the icon on the right for landscape mode, in which text prints across the long dimension of the paper (sideways). The latter is good for fitting wide records or reports onto a single sheet of paper.

To the right of the paper orientation icons are three check boxes for special printer effects:

✦ *Tall Adjusted*: Choose this option whenever you are printing graphics. It tells the printer to print the same number of dots per inch horizontally and vertically. If you neglect to choose this option, circles will print like elongated ovals or eggs, for example.

✦ *50% Reduction*: This is the only magnification option that is available for most ImageWriters. It reduces everything to half its normal size.

✦ *No Gaps Between Pages*: This option is useful only when you are using continuous-feed computer paper. It eliminates top and bottom margins, printing everything on one long sheet. This option is especially good for printing banners or spreadsheets in landscape mode.

Click OK to put your changes into effect. Click Cancel to take no action and dismiss the dialog box.

Note   The ImageWriter printer is no longer in production and was discontinued in favor of the StyleWriter, which is quieter, produces higher-quality printouts, and costs about the same. Even so, many ImageWriters are still in service, and Apple includes print drivers for them with every new release of its system software. (One reason for the continued popularity of the ImageWriters is that they are *impact* printers—that is, they print by striking a printhead against a ribbon. ImageWriters are the only type of Apple-native printer that can print through multipart forms.)

Setting page options on a Macintosh

No matter what printer you're using—whether it's the latest model or an old standby—you set page options for your printer in the same way. The following procedure describes in general terms how to use the Page Setup dialog box for almost any printer:

1. Open the document you want to print (a FileMaker Pro database, for example).

2. Choose File ⇨ Page Setup.

   A Page Setup dialog box appears that corresponds to the printer last selected in the Chooser.

3. Select the size of paper you are using (from a pop-up menu or set of radio buttons).

   The standard choice in the United States is US Letter (System 7.*x*) or US Letter Small (OS 8.*x*).

4. Choose a paper orientation.

   Click the left icon, which has an image of an upright torso, to choose portrait mode. Click the right icon to choose landscape mode.

5. Select a magnification level or leave this option at 100% to print at the standard size.

6. Set any special printer effects that are relevant to the print job.

7. Click OK.

If you always intend to print information from this document or database on the same kind of paper, in the same orientation, and at the same size, you need to configure Page Setup only once—these settings are saved when you save the document. Remember, however, that the Page Setup options you just selected are specific to this document or database; they have no effect on how any *other* document or database will print.

Using the Print Setup dialog box on a PC

When you choose Print Setup, Printer Setup, or Page Setup from the File menu of any Windows program, a dialog box similar to the one shown in Figure 13-8 appears. The primary dialog box displays four options:

✦ *Name*: The printer you intend to use to print the current document. (All printers for which you have installed print drivers are listed in the Name pop-up menu.)

✦ *Size*: The size and type of the paper that will be used

✦ *Source*: Where the paper will be fed from, such as a tractor or a default paper tray.

✦ *Orientation*: Whether the document will be printed right-side up (Portrait) or sideways (Landscape).

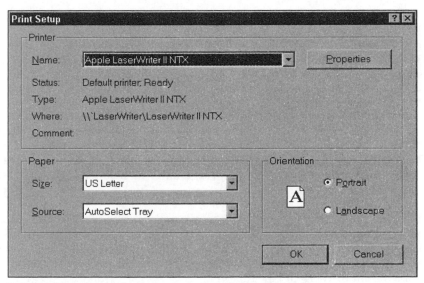

Figure 13-8: Choose basic setup options in this dialog box.

To view and set additional printer-specific options, click the Properties button. Depending on the capabilities of the printer, the Properties section of the dialog box may contain one or several pages of options, such as Paper and Graphics. To view different classes of printer properties, click a tab at the top of the dialog box.

Tip Although the options that you will always want to check are presented on the first page of the Print Setup/Page Setup dialog box, you should familiarize yourself with the options in the Properties section of the dialog box, too. If you want to print multiple copies of a document on a LaserWriter printer, for example, you *must* click the Properties button.

Step 2: Readying a Report for Printing

With the preliminaries out of the way, you can get down to brass tacks. Before you can print a report, you need to prepare the report. You learned all about reports in Chapter 12, but you can refresh your memory by reading the following sections.

Selecting and sorting

You will seldom print the entire contents of a database. To print many company databases, you would hog a printer the whole day and spend most of your time feeding it paper. And you wouldn't be too popular with your coworkers and whoever orders supplies.

Printing only a selection of the information that is contained in a database is much more common than printing the entire database. (Actually, the only reason to print the entire contents of most databases is to have a paper backup copy of the file's contents in case disaster strikes. Even then, several strategically located disk copies of the database are probably more useful.) The records you choose to print depend on the nature of your report.

Consider this example. Susan is head of sales at a small company, and she has access to a FileMaker Pro database that contains records for every sales transaction. The database includes a field that shows which salesperson is responsible for each transaction. Susan wants to see how Guy Smith — a member of her sales team — has been doing lately.

All Susan needs to do is open the database and issue a find request to locate all records in which Guy's name appears in the Salesperson field. She switches to Find mode and enters **=Guy =Smith** into the Salesperson field on the find request. To restrict things further, she also places **>1/1/99** in the Date field to limit the search to sales from the current calendar year.

After using Find mode to select a relevant group of records, the next step is to arrange them in a useful order. Susan uses the Sort command to arrange the records in descending order based on the amount of each sale. This sort puts the largest transaction first. Finally, Susan chooses a layout that shows only the information she needs. In this case, she selects a layout that includes a Summary field — one that shows Guy's total sales this year (so she won't have to add them manually).

Following are the general steps necessary to prepare a report from a database:

1. Within FileMaker Pro, open the database that contains the information from which you want to prepare a report.

2. Use Find mode to issue one or more find requests to locate the records you want to use as part of the report.

3. Choose the Records ⇨ Sort command to arrange the found set in a meaningful order.

4. From the Layout pop-up menu (in the upper-left corner of the database window), choose an appropriate layout from which to create the report.

5. *Optional*: Preview the report on-screen.

6. Print the report.

Previewing before printing

More paper has been wasted because of minor problems with a document's appearance than because of any other problem. Much of this paper waste could be avoided by previewing documents on-screen prior to printing them. Admittedly, checking them isn't always easy (or even possible) in all Macintosh and Windows applications. FileMaker Pro, however, has a Preview mode that enables you to see how a job will print.

To switch to Preview mode, choose it from the mode selector pop-up menu at the bottom of the database window or from the View menu (or press ⌘+U/Ctrl+U). You see a view similar to that shown in Figure 13-9.

In Preview mode, output is divided into pages. To see additional pages, click the book icon. Use the scroll bars to move around in the view and check its contents. If you want to determine the total number of pages in the report, drag the bookmark to the bottom of the book icon. (FileMaker Pro doesn't know how many pages the report contains until you perform this action or click through all the book pages.)

If your report looks satisfactory and you want a permanent copy of it, you can print it by choosing File ➪ Print.

If problems are detected in Preview mode, you have several options. If the problem is just a case of getting everything to fit, you may be able to correct it by adjusting the scaling or magnification in the Page Setup dialog box or by switching from portrait to landscape printing. This may not be the best solution if you're preparing presentation copies of reports, however.

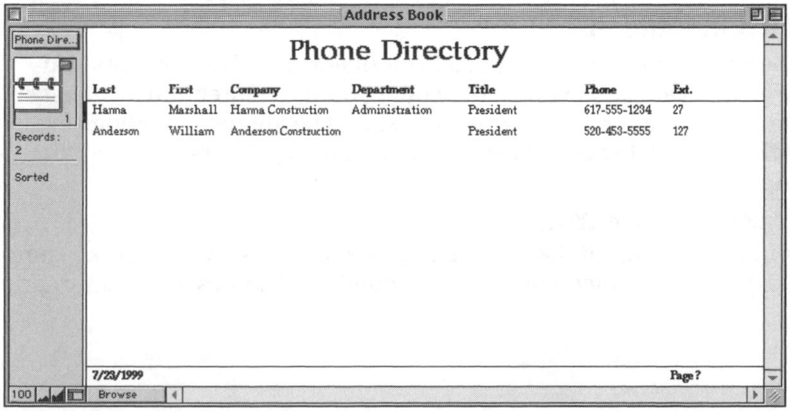

Figure 13-9: An Address Book layout in Preview mode

For more serious Preview problems, you may need to go back to Layout mode and make adjustments. Omitting unnecessary fields is often a good idea — doing so provides more room for relevant data. (Consult Chapter 12 for more information on the art of preparing reports, including tweaking the layout and creating new, report-specific layouts.)

The following steps explain how to use Preview mode and what to do if a report is less than perfect:

1. Prepare a report according to the steps presented in "Selecting and sorting," earlier in this chapter.

2. Choose View ➪ Preview Mode (or press ⌘+U/Ctrl+U).

3. Use the scroll bars to move around on each page if the screen isn't large enough to display the entire page. (You can also drag the window's size box to increase the viewing area.)

4. Click the book icon to view any additional pages of the report.

5. Carefully review each page to ensure that all data fits without running off the edge. Also check for other problems, such as data that is truncated within fields.

6. Correct errors in Layout mode or by setting different options in the Page Setup/Print Setup dialog box.

When the report appears satisfactory, you are ready to print.

Step 3: Printing

Printing should seem like a breeze after all this preparatory work. To print records, reports, field definitions, or scripts in FileMaker Pro, choose the File ➪ Print command (or press ⌘+P/Ctrl+P), and then set options in the Print dialog box that appears.

Printing on a Macintosh

Choosing the Print command presents a Print dialog box. The contents and appearance of the dialog box varies, depending on the printer you have chosen and the version of the system software you are using. The following sections explain how to use the Print dialog boxes for several common printers.

The Print command – LaserWriter

Near the upper-left corner of the Print dialog box for a LaserWriter (see Figure 13-10) is a text box into which you enter the number of copies you want to print.

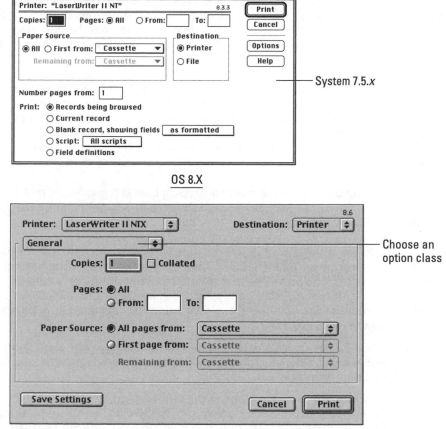

Figure 13-10: The Print dialog box for a LaserWriter in System 7.5.x (top) and OS 8 (bottom)

Next are controls for designating the particular pages to print. Click the All radio button to print the entire report. On the other hand, if you want to print a range of pages, enter the appropriate page numbers in the From and To text boxes. For example, enter **2** in the From box and **4** in the To box to print pages 2 through 4.

Use the Paper Source option to designate whether paper will be drawn from the printer's internal paper cassette or fed by hand. The Manual Feed option is not useful for long reports, but you can use it to print a single envelope or piece of letterhead, for example. Manual feed is also useful for printing label stock, transparencies, and any other paper types that tend to cling together (creating misfeeds and paper waste).

Depending on the particular operating system and version of the LaserWriter driver you are using, you can view and set additional print options by clicking the Options button (System 7.x) or choosing a class of options from the pull-down menu at the top of the Print dialog box (OS 8.x). Following are a few of the other important print options:

✦ *Destination*: Choose Printer to send the job directly to the printer you have chosen. Choose File to create a PostScript file into which the print job is spooled. You can send such a file to a service bureau for printing on a high-end imagesetter. (Note, however, that this is seldom done with a database. Generating print files is more commonly done with illustrations and desktop publishing files.)

Note   If you are using OS 8.x, you can create a PostScript, an EPS graphic, or an Adobe Acrobat file by choosing Save as File from the second pop-up menu on the left side of the Print dialog box.

✦ *Cover Page*: You use this option to designate whether to include a cover page as part of the print job and whether to place the cover page at the beginning or end of the report. A cover page is useful if you're printing on a network printer and want to make sure your print job is properly identified. Your user name, the name of the document you're printing, and the number of pages appear on the cover page.

✦ *Print* (System 7.x) or *Print Color* (OS 8.x): Choose Black & White for text-only reports — it's faster. Choose Color/Grayscale or Calibrated Color/Grayscale if you're including graphics.

✦ *PostScript Errors*: You can select one of the following notification methods to be used if an error occurs during a print job: No Special Reporting (nothing happens), Summarize on Screen (a dialog box appears), or Print Detailed Report (an error report is sent to the printer).

✦ *Layout* (System 7.6 and higher): This option, which enables you to print multiple report pages on each piece of paper, is the same option that is found in the System 7.5.x Page Setup dialog box. See "Using the Page Setup dialog box on a Macintosh," earlier in this chapter.

✦ *Background Printing* (OS 8.x only): Under System 7, background printing is set in the Chooser and is simply off or on. In the Background Printing section of the OS 8.x Print dialog box, you can turn background printing off by choosing *Foreground (no spool file)* or on by choosing *Background*. By clicking an option in the Print Time section, you can control when the current document will print, or you can specify its importance. Choose Urgent, for example, to move the document ahead in the print queue — if there happen to be multiple jobs waiting to be printed.

At the bottom of the Print dialog box (System 7.x) or on the FileMaker Pro page of the Print dialog box (OS 8.x) are options that are specific to FileMaker Pro (see

Figure 13-11). The "Number pages from" text box enables you to enter the number to use for the first page of the printout. For example, you would enter a number other than 1 if you were preparing one grand document from several smaller reports. In this case, you would let FileMaker Pro know to begin numbering each report section where the previous section left off. To make the current print settings the defaults for all subsequent print jobs (in FileMaker Pro and other programs), click the Save Settings button.

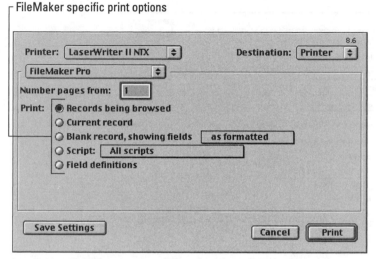

Figure 13-11: FileMaker-specific print options (OS 8.x)

There are also radio buttons that control what will be printed:

✦ *Records being browsed*: Prints the current found set in the current sort order.

✦ *Current record*: Prints only one record — the one currently visible on-screen.

✦ *Blank record, showing fields*: Prints an empty record. Choose a style of border, if any, to put around each field (as formatted in the current layout, boxed, or underlined).

✦ *Script*: Prints a particular script or all scripts. Choose the script you want to print from the pop-up menu of all currently defined scripts for the database, or choose All Scripts to print all currently defined scripts for the database.

✦ *Field definitions*: Prints the field definitions for the database.

Note

The latter three Print options are excellent tools for documenting a database and its logic.

When you have finished setting options in the Print dialog box, click Print to print the material; or click Cancel if you change your mind.

The Print command – StyleWriter

When you are using a StyleWriter and choose the Print command, you see the dialog box shown in Figure 13-12. Many options are the same as those for the LaserWriter (see "The Print command — LaserWriter"). In addition, the StyleWriter enables you to set the print quality. Use Best for high quality and Normal for lower quality but speedier printing. The StyleWriter also offers a Draft option that uses a built-in font for very fast printing (but often with strange results).

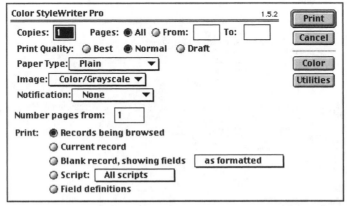

Figure 13-12: The Print dialog box for a Color StyleWriter Pro (OS 8.x)

You can also choose between black-and-white, grayscale, and — on some models — color printouts. If you click the Options button, you can instruct the printer to clean its cartridge before beginning the print job.

Note   As shown in Figure 13-12, under OS 8 you can indicate the type of paper you will be using for the print job by choosing an option from the Paper Type pop-up menu. This option is not available using the driver that shipped with System 7.x.

Bypassing the Print dialog box

As is evident in this chapter, using the Print dialog box involves many steps. However, FileMaker Pro also enables you to print without even bringing up the Print dialog box. In this case, all the Print dialog box's default choices are used.

To bypass the Print dialog box, press Option+⌘+P/Shift+Ctrl+T. An alert box appears briefly, telling you what will be printed.

The Print command – ImageWriter

When you are using an ImageWriter and choose the Print command, you see the dialog box shown in Figure 13-13. (Note that the ImageWriter print driver used in OS 8.*x* is the same as the one for System 7.5, so the Print dialog boxes are identical.)

```
┌─────────────────────────────────────────────────────────────┐
│ ImageWriter                          7.0.1    ┌──────────┐    │
│                                               │  Print   │    │
│ Quality:     ○ Best     ◉ Faster   ○ Draft    └──────────┘    │
│ Page Range:  ◉ All      ○ From: [   ] To: [   ] ┌─────────┐   │
│ Copies:      [1]                                │ Cancel  │   │
│ Paper Feed:  ◉ Automatic  ○ Hand Feed           └─────────┘   │
│                                                               │
│ Number pages from: [1]          ☐ Color ribbon installed     │
│                                                               │
│ Print:  ◉ Records being browsed  ☐ Enable Print Spooling     │
│         ○ Current record                                     │
│         ○ Blank record, showing fields [ as formatted    ]   │
│         ○ Script: [ All scripts                         ]     │
│         ○ Field definitions                                  │
└─────────────────────────────────────────────────────────────┘
```

Figure 13-13: The Print dialog box for an ImageWriter

Many options are the same as those shown for the LaserWriter (see "The Print command—LaserWriter"). In addition, the ImageWriter enables you to set the print quality. Use Best for high quality and Faster for lower quality but speedier printing. The ImageWriter also offers a Draft print quality option. Draft uses a built-in font and is very fast, but it can produce strange results. In general, this setting is not appropriate for most FileMaker Pro documents.

The Print dialog box also has options you can use to indicate whether you are using a color ribbon and whether you want the computer to spool documents prior to printing (that is, whether you want the job to print in the background so you can continue to do other work on your Mac).

New Feature The formatting of printed scripts has been improved in FileMaker Pro 5, making them much easier to read (and debug).

Printing on a PC

Choosing the File ⇨ Print command (or pressing Ctrl+P) presents a Print dialog box (see Figure 13-14).

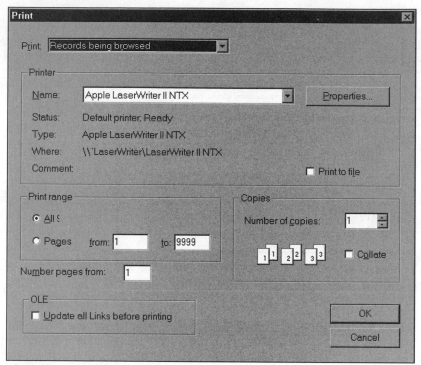

Figure 13-14: A Windows 95/98 Print dialog box

Regardless of the printer chosen from the Name list, the options remain the same. The most important ones are as follows:

✦ *Name*: Select the printer that will receive the print job. (If you want to change some of the print options for the current print job only, click the Properties button. After printing, the properties will revert to their previous settings.)

✦ *Print range*: Specifies the particular pages to print. Click the All radio button to print the entire report. On the other hand, if you want to print a range of pages, enter the appropriate page numbers in the From and To text boxes. For example, enter **2** in the From box and **4** in the To box to print pages 2 through 4.

✦ *Copies*: Specifies the number of copies you want to print. If you are making multiple printouts, click the Collate check box to request that each copy be printed separately.

✦ *Number pages from*: Sets the page number to be used on the first page of the printout. For example, you would enter a number other than **1** if you were preparing one grand document from several smaller reports. In this case, you would let FileMaker Pro know to begin numbering each report section where the previous section left off.

✦ *OLE*: If the current database contains OLE objects, you can elect to print them in their current state (*unchecked*) or only after they have all been updated (*checked*). Note that updating OLE links can be time consuming.

The most important print option is chosen from the Print menu at the top of the dialog box—in which you specify what you want printed:

✦ *Records being browsed*: Prints the current found set in the current sort order.

✦ *Current record*: Prints only one record—the one currently visible on-screen.

✦ *Blank record, showing fields*: Prints an empty record. You choose from the pop-up menu to determine what kind of border to put around each field (as formatted in the current layout, boxed or underlined).

✦ *Script definition for*: Prints a particular script or all scripts. Choose the script you want to print from the list of all currently defined scripts for the database, or choose All Scripts to print all currently defined scripts for the database.

✦ *Field definitions*: Prints the field definitions for the database.

Once all options have been set, click OK to begin printing or Cancel if you change your mind.

Step 4: Troubleshooting

Things go wrong. Here are some common printing problems and what to do if you encounter them:

✦ *My printer doesn't do anything*: Is it turned off (the #1 cause of missed print jobs)? Are cable connections snug and secure? On a Mac, if you are using a printer that does not require AppleTalk, be sure that the correct port is selected in the Chooser. On a PC, make certain that your chosen printer is indeed connected to the port specified in the Where line of the Print or Print Setup dialog box. (Serial printers connect to COM: ports; parallel printers connect to LPT: ports.)

✦ *The laser printer isn't visible in the Chooser*: Is your printer properly hooked up? Again, make sure all cables are secure and tight. If you are printing to a network laser printer, see if it is connected correctly to the network. Is the printer online (turned on) and warmed up? Has the network gone down?

✦ *Print quality seems poor*: Does your laser printer need more toner; does your ink-jet need more ink; or does your dot-matrix printer need a new ribbon? Failure to print dense, even, black tones can be caused by any of these situations. You can temporarily correct this problem on a laser printer by gently rotating the toner cartridge a few times or increasing the print density setting (if the printer has one). If you are using a Mac connected to a StyleWriter or ImageWriter, change the Print Quality setting to Best.

✦ *Laser printing is taking too long*: Try turning off the printer, waiting a few seconds, and then restarting it. You will have to use a desktop printer or PrintMonitor to restart the job.

Occasionally, some print jobs may simply be too complex for your laser printer to handle. Try reprinting them with different print options, printing a smaller set of pages, or turning off background printing. This may help you isolate the cause of the problem.

Effective Printing Tips

Every type of printer has some quirks. Understanding the more common idiosyncrasies and knowing how to deal with them can not only save you some grief, it can also help you achieve better results. The following basic hints apply to the most common types of printers.

Laser printers

✦ *Sunny side up.* Not many people are aware that most laser paper and copier paper has a good side and a so-so side. (The same holds true for inkjet papers.) The paper's manufacturer intends for the paper to be printed only on the good side. You can achieve the best results by making sure you print on the correct side.

Sometimes, you cannot easily determine which side is the good side by just looking. Although the good side may be shinier, looking at the paper package is a better way to tell. In many cases, you'll see an arrow or a similar indicator that shows which side is meant to be printed on. When inserting the paper into your printer, be sure that the correct side is up. (Some printers expect paper to be inserted face up, while others print on the side of the paper that is face down. If you aren't sure which way you should insert paper into your printer, refer to the printer manual.)

✦ *We be jammin'.* Everybody hates paper jams and misfeeds. You can't avoid them all, but you can cut down on their number and frequency. When you load a printer, grasp the paper firmly and "riffle" the edges with your thumb. (Draw your thumb down the edges.) This action loosens the sheets from each other, lessening the chance that two or more sheets will be drawn into the printer together.

✦ *Fontasies can come true.* A laser printer takes a long time to do two things: construct a font for use in a document and prepare a graphic. You can save time by using only fonts that are built into the printer or are available on a printer's dedicated hard disk. (The printer doesn't have to construct these fonts.) Also, try to limit the number of different text styles you use. Using too many fonts makes documents print slowly and can, in extreme cases, crash the system or the printer.

✦ *You only go 'round once.* Several companies (such as Avery) make special labels for use in laser printers. Resist the temptation to use only a few labels from one sheet and then reuse the sheet later. After a few passes, the heat of the printing process can cause the remaining labels to peel off during printing, resulting in expensive trouble. Try to do label printing jobs in large batches and throw away the unused labels from each batch (or find another use for them).

✦ *Is it just me, or is it warm in here?:* If your printer has been turned off, be sure to allow enough time for it to warm up. If you try to print immediately after you turn the printer on, you will likely see a message telling you the printer isn't responding. Give it a minute or so before you try again.

Dot-matrix printers

✦ *Don't be uptight:* When you are using tractor-fed computer paper, make sure the tension is adjusted correctly between the two feed mechanisms. Too little tension can cause the paper to jam and misfeed; too much tension can tear off the perforated edges and cause another kind of misfeed. Getting the tension exactly right is an art.

✦ *Back in the black:* Use only new ribbons and keep them well inked. Old ribbons can fray, resulting in ugly printouts and possible damage to the print head.

Ink-jet printers

✦ *Ink-a-dink:* Avoid printing long reports that have a large number of graphics. Graphics consume a great deal of expensive ink and take longer to print.

✦ *Time on my hands:* To speed up printing, limit the number of fonts in the report. You may also want to select a lower print quality for jobs that will not be used for presentations.

Summary

✦ Before you can print on a Mac, you need to use the Chooser desk accessory to tell the computer which print driver and printer you want to use. (If you have the desktop printing software installed, you can designate a default printer by Ctrl+clicking the printer's icon on your desktop.) Once selected, all future print jobs will be sent to that printer. If you have just one printer, you will only need to use the Chooser again if you reinstall or update your system software, buy a new printer, or obtain a newer version of a print driver.

✦ If your Mac is on a network and there are multiple LaserWriters connected, you can also use the Chooser to select a particular printer to receive each print job.

✦ On a PC, you can print to any printer that has been installed under Windows. You can select a printer to use for the current print job from either the Print Setup or the Print dialog box.

✦ In the Page Setup/Print Setup dialog box, you set page options for the document you're about to print. On a Mac, these options include the type of paper you want to use, the amount of scaling (if any), page orientation, and whether to employ special effects, such as inversion or printing continuous sheets. Page Setup settings are document-specific and are saved along with the other information contained in the document. On a PC, options include the printer to be used, the size and type of paper, the source of the paper, and the page orientation.

✦ Prior to printing a FileMaker Pro report, you should select the records you want to include, sort them in an appropriate order, and choose a layout in which to display them.

✦ You can use Preview mode to view a report on-screen. This mode shows how the report will look when you print it. You can correct problems at this stage before you waste time and paper.

✦ Printing is accomplished via the Print dialog box. You can use it to set the number of copies to print; which pages to print; whether to use color or grays (if your printer can handle them); and exactly what database contents to print, including the current record, the found set, scripts, or field definitions.

✦ To print directly (bypassing the Print dialog box), press Option+⌘+P/Shift+Ctrl+T.

✦ You can avoid many potential printing problems by setting up your printer correctly before you print. Checking the integrity of all cable connections, loading paper the right way, and restricting the use of fonts and graphics can ensure better results.

✦   ✦   ✦

Putting FileMaker Pro to Work

◆ ◆ ◆ ◆

◆ ◆ ◆ ◆

Calculations and Computations

The ability to perform calculations on the contents of
database fields gives modern database programs such as
FileMaker Pro extraordinary power and flexibility. For example,
in an invoice database where each record is an order, you can
total all the item prices and compute the sales tax. If the cost
of shipping varies according to distance, you can determine
how much to charge each order, based on its state of
destination. FileMaker Pro offers a variety of computational
capabilities to make these and similar tasks easy.

You use a Calculation field to perform a specific operation or
group of operations on specific data within a record (and in
related records). The operations you can perform include the
standard arithmetic functions, logical operations, and even
special operations that perform complex calculations on
numbers and text.

About Calculation Fields

The data in a given Calculation field consists of whatever
result is obtained when the field's definition is evaluated
for that particular record. The definition specifies, in
mathematical form, what manipulations to perform on the
contents of one or more other fields in the current record.
The results of these manipulations (or operations) are then
displayed as the field's contents.

Here's an example: Suppose you have an invoice database that
has a field named Merchandise Total. You want to compute
the sales tax on this total and display the grand total for the
bill (the merchandise total plus the sales tax). You could use

Calculation fields for both the sales tax and the grand total. The field definitions might look like this:

```
Sales Tax = Merchandise Total * .06 [Multiply total by tax
rate]
Grand Total = Merchandise Total + Sales Tax [Add tax to total]
```

If the current record shows a Merchandise Total of 23.75, the Sales Tax field would display 1.425, and the Grand Total would display 25.175. Of course, you would want to round this figure off to the nearest cent before presenting a bill. FileMaker Pro enables you to round numbers easily, as you will see shortly.

Calculation fields are similar to Summary fields. There is one important difference, however. Summary formulas are calculated across all browsed records, while the Calculation field formulas apply only to data in each individual record. For example, if you want to compute the total sales for all the invoices issued over a certain span of time, you define a Summary field, but to calculate the merchandise total within an invoice, you use a Calculation field.

Calculation fields can do much more than just add or multiply the contents of other fields. Calculation fields can also manipulate the contents of Text fields and can perform tests on the contents of fields to determine which alternative course of action to select.

A formula in a Calculation field can contain several components: field references, operators, constants, and built-in functions. You should have a basic understanding of these components before you begin creating Calculation fields.

Note   FileMaker Pro does not restrict the use of formulas to Calculation fields. Formulas can also be used to validate field data as it is entered or edited, as information to be "auto-entered" into fields, and as components of scripts. For information on using formulas for data validation or auto-entry, see Chapter 5. For details on using formulas in ScriptMaker scripts, refer to Chapter 15.

FileMaker Pro uses *operators* to specify how to manipulate data items. Operators fall into three categories:

✦ *Arithmetic operators* are used to perform computations on numbers.

✦ *Logical operators* test whether specified conditions are true or false; this information can then be used to determine a course of action.

✦ *Text operators* work with text, extracting information from it or converting it to another form.

Arithmetic operators

The arithmetic operators in Table 14-1 perform the basic functions of arithmetic.

Operator	What It Means
	Table 14-1 **Arithmetic Operators**
+	The plus sign performs addition (for example, 2 + 3 yields 5).
-	The minus sign performs subtraction (for example, 3 - 2 yields 1).
*	The asterisk indicates multiplication (for example, 2 * 3 yields 6).
/	The slash indicates division (for example, 3 / 2 yields 1.5).
^	The caret indicates exponentiation, raising a number to a power (for example, 3 ^ 2 is three to the second power, or 9).

Logical operators

The logical operators perform comparisons. If necessary, you can combine the results into more complex tests. Basically, the logical operators are used to test whether a statement is true or false. Here's an example:

```
1 = 2 [one equals two]
```

This statement is false; one does not equal two.

Here's a more practical example:

```
Bob's Sales > Anne's Sales [Bob's sales exceed Anne's sales]
```

You don't know whether this statement is true because you don't know how much Bob or Anne sold. If Bob's sales equaled 1,500 and Anne's sales equaled 1,000, then the statement would be true. If the figures were reversed, or if their sales were equal, the statement would be false.

Why should you care? Because you can have a Calculation field perform additional steps that are based on whether a statement is true or false. For example, you might use the following formula in the Calculation field to present a different message (a Text result) depending on which salesperson had the most sales:

```
If (Bob Sales = Anne Sales, "", If (Bob Sales > Anne Sales,
"Nice going, Bob!", "Nice going, Anne!"))
```

If Bob's sales equal Anne's, no message is displayed. If Bob's sales total more than Anne's sales, the Calculation field displays the true condition for the nested IF test (that is, the message "Nice going, Bob!"). On the other hand, if Bob's sales were not greater than Anne's, the field displays the false condition for the nested IF test (that is, the message "Nice going, Anne!"). You will learn more about using logical operators to perform tasks such as this as the chapter progresses. (Pay particular attention to the section on the IF function.)

Table 14-2 lists the logical operators and their meanings.

Table 14-2 Logical Operators	
Operator	*What It Means*
=	Means "equals." The test is true if the items on both sides of the sign are exactly equal in value. For example, the statement $1 + 1 = 2$ is true.
◇ or ≠ (Mac); ◇ (PC)	Means "not equal to." The test is true if the items on both sides of the sign are not equal in value. For example, "Bob"◇ "Anne" is true. [To create the ≠ symbol on a Macintosh, press Option+= (equals).]
>	Means "greater than." The test is true if the value of the item at the left of the sign exceeds the value of item to the right. For example, $3 > 2$ is true.
<	Means "less than." The test is true if the value of the item at the left of the sign is smaller than the value of the item to the right. For example, $2 < 3$ is true.
≤ or <= (Mac); <= (PC)	Means "less than or equal to." For example, $2.9 + 0.1 \leq 3$ is true. [To create the ≤ symbol on a Macintosh, press Option+, (comma).]
≥ or >= (Mac); >= (PC)	Means "greater than or equal to." For example, $2.9 + 1.5 \geq 3$ is true. [To create the ≥ symbol on a Macintosh, press Option+. (period).]
AND	Used to combine the results of two separate tests. The result is true if, and only if, the results of both tests are true. For example, $3 > 2$ AND $2 < 3$ is true.

Operator	What It Means
OR	Used to combine the results of two separate tests. The result is true if either, or both, of the tests are true. For example, 3 > 2 OR 2 > 3 is true.
XOR	Used to combine the results of two separate tests. The result is true only in the case where just one of the tests is true. If both tests are true or both are false, the result is false. For example, 3 > 2 XOR 2 > 3 is true. (In computer parlance, this is known as an "exclusive OR.")
NOT	Used to switch a test's result to its opposite. For example, NOT 2 > 3 is true.

You can type the less than or equal to (≤), greater than or equal to (≥), and not equal (≠) symbols by pressing Option-, (comma), Option-. (period), and Option-= (equals), respectively. These symbols do not exist on a PC, as noted in Table 14-2.

Text operators

Table 14-3 lists the three basic text operators.

Table 14-3 Basic Text Operators	
Operator	What It Means
&	Used to combine (or *concatenate*) two Text fields into one. For example, "market" & "place" yields marketplace.
" "	Used to indicate a text constant. If you enter a text item without quotes, FileMaker assumes that you mean the name of a field. "Anne" + Last Name returns Anne Markham, if the Last Name field contains Markham.
¶	Used to indicate a paragraph break within a text constant. If you want a constant to have more than one line, use this operator to separate the lines. (The symbol must be enclosed within the quotation marks of the text constant.) For example, "Anne¶Markham" yields the following: Anne Markham To type this symbol on a Mac, press Option-7. On a Windows PC, you can select this character from the Character Map utility (click Start ➪ Programs ➪ Accessories ➪ Character Map).

Creating an expression

Operators are combined with constants (numeric or text) and field names to create expressions. Think of an expression as a mathematical statement. From an earlier example, both of the following are statements:

```
Sales Tax = .06 * Merchandise Total
Grand Total = Merchandise Total + Sales Tax
```

The sales tax rate (.06) is a numeric constant; that is, its value does not change. Merchandise Total represents the contents of that field in the current record; it can change from record to record. If you recall your high school algebra, you will recognize Merchandise Total (or any valid field name) as a variable. Expressions consist of constants and variables that are separated by operators.

You can build complicated expressions in FileMaker Pro. For example, consider the following expression:

```
1 + 2 * 3
```

FileMaker Pro evaluates expressions according to the standard algebraic order of operations, which specifies that all multiplications are done before any additions. The result for this expression is 7, not 9, which you might expect if all operations were performed strictly in left-to-right order.

To force FileMaker Pro to perform operations in the order you want, you can use parentheses. Operations within parentheses are performed first, from innermost to outermost. You can nest operations within parentheses to gain further control. For example, the following expression yields 18:

```
((( 1 + 2 ) * 3 ) * 2 )
```

Without parentheses, it would equal 13.

The standard order of operations is as follows:

1. Exponentiation
2. Multiplication and division
3. Addition and subtraction

You can also use parentheses with logical expressions. For example, the following expression is true:

```
(3 > 2 OR 2 > 3) AND 2 > 1
```

Creating a Calculation Field

To create a Calculation field, you decide what type of results you want, determine the necessary expression, and then define the field. After you create the Calculation field in the Define Fields dialog box, the Specify Calculation dialog box appears (see Figure 14-1).

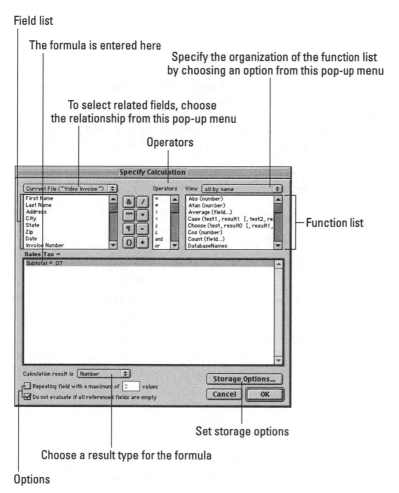

Figure 14-1: Defining a Calculation field

The fields available in the current database appear in a scrolling list at the left. If you want to use fields in a related file in this equation, choose the relationship from the pop-up menu above the field list.

In the center of the dialog box are the available operators. To the right are the FileMaker Pro functions. You'll learn more about functions in the next section. For now, you only need to know that a function is a predefined set of operations that work with specific kinds of data. A function operates on the data, known as the function's *arguments,* and then returns a *result*.

Beneath these sections is a large blank area. As you create the formula for the Calculation field, it appears in this area. You can type the formula directly or simply choose the appropriate field names, operators, and functions (by clicking or double-clicking them). Below this area, a pop-up menu indicates what type of data the field's result should be. You must select the correct result type. The check boxes and buttons in this section of the dialog box enable you to set storage options for the field, designate it as a repeating field (used in invoice line items, for example), and tell FileMaker Pro what to do if all fields referenced in the formula are empty.

As an example, the following steps show how to define a new Calculation field named Sales Tax that calculates a 7 percent tax:

1. Choose File ➪ Define Fields.

   The Define Fields dialog box appears.

2. Type **Sales Tax** as the field name, click the Calculation field radio button, and then click Create.

   The Specify Calculation dialog box appears (as previously shown in Figure 14-1).

3. Double-click Subtotal in the field list (or type it), and then type * .07 to complete the formula.

4. Using the "Calculation result is" pop-up menu, set the result type to Number.

5. Click OK.

   You return to the Define Fields dialog box, and the new Calculation field appears in the list of defined fields.

In addition to these two required procedures (specifying a formula and setting a result type), there are several options that you can set (shown at the bottom of the Specify Calculation dialog box):

✦ *Repeating field with a maximum of [x] values*: You can define the Calculation field as a repeating field by clicking this check box. An Extended Price field that multiplies the Item Price by the Quantity Ordered for each line item in an invoice is one example of a repeating Calculation field. When defining a field as repeating, you must also specify the maximum number of times it can repeat within each record.

✦ *Do not evaluate if all referenced fields are empty*: When checked, this option prevents the calculation of a result for the current record when all fields referenced in the formula are blank or have no values.

✦ *Storage Options*: Click the Storage Options button to display the Storage Options for Field "*field name*" dialog box (see Figure 14-2). This dialog box enables you to turn indexing on or off for the field, as well as specify whether FileMaker Pro will store the results of the calculations as part of the database.

If you intend to sort by the results of this field frequently, or perform find requests using this field as the search criterion, you may want to turn on indexing by clicking the On radio button. If disk space is at a premium or this field must be recalculated often, click the "Do not store calculation results — calculate only when needed" check box.

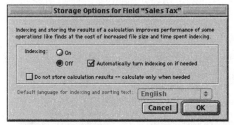

Figure 14-2: Setting storage options for a Calculation field

 Note You can examine a range of already-defined Calculation fields by looking at the templates and example files that are included with FileMaker Pro 5 or on the *FileMaker Pro 5 Bible* CD-ROM. With any of the unlocked templates open, choose File ➪ Define Fields. The dialog box will show the definitions for all fields in the database. If you can't see the entire formula for a Calculation field, simply select the field and click the Options button.

About FileMaker Pro's Built-In Functions

FileMaker Pro includes dozens of predefined functions that you can use to define formulas for Calculation fields. The purpose of each of these functions is described in Table 14-4. For a detailed explanation of each function and example formulas, see Appendix E.

 Note If you previously used FileMaker Pro 4.0, there's very little new material for you to learn. The only new function introduced since FileMaker Pro 4.0 is Status (CurrentRecordModification).

Table 14-4
FileMaker Pro's Built-In Functions

Function Name	Purpose
Abs	Calculates the absolute value of an expression
Atan	Calculates the arc tangent of an expression, in radians
Average	Computes the average value (the arithmetic mean) of all values in one or more fields
Case	Performs a series of tests and selects one answer (or the default answer, if no test is found to be true)
Choose	Selects one answer from a series
Cos	Calculates the cosine of an argument expressed in radians, returning a value between −1 and 1
Count	Counts the number of valid, nonempty entries in one or more fields
DatabaseNames	Returns the filenames of all currently open FileMaker Pro databases
Date	Converts a numeric value into a valid date
DateToText	Converts a value in a Date field to text
Day	Displays the day of the month, 1–31, for a given date
DayName	Displays the weekday name for a given date
DayofWeek	Displays the number of the day within a week, 1–7, for a given date
DayofYear	Displays the number of the day within a year, 1–366, for a given date
Degrees	Converts a value in radians into degrees
Exact	Returns "true" if two text expressions match exactly (including case)
Exp	Returns the antilog (base *e*) of an expression
Extend	Makes a nonrepeating field into a repeating field (with the identical value in each place) for use in calculations with other repeating fields
External	When the Web Companion plug-in is enabled, these functions return information about the individuals who access your database on the World Wide Web or an Intranet
FieldBounds	Returns the location and rotation angle of a given field in a particular layout of a database
FieldNames	Returns the names of all fields used in a particular layout (or in all layouts) of a specified database

Function Name	Purpose
FieldRepetitions	Returns the number of repetitions of a given repeating field as it is formatted on a particular layout of a database
FieldStyle	Returns information about how a field in a particular layout is formatted, as well as whether the field has a value list associated with it
FieldType	Returns the field definition for a specified field in a particular database
FV	Computes an investment's future value for a given payment amount, interest rate, and number of periods
GetRepetition	Presents the contents of a particular repetition in a repeating field
GetSummary	Calculates the value of a particular Summary field when the database has been sorted by the specified break field
Hour	Displays the number of hours in a time expression
If	Performs a logical test and completes one action if it is true, another if it is false
Int	Returns the integer portion of a numeric value
IsEmpty	Determines whether a value or field is blank
IsValid	Determines whether a related field can be found and contains valid data, and whether a related file can be found
Last	Shows the last valid, nonempty entry in a repeating field
LayoutNames	Returns the names of all layouts in a specified database
Left	Returns the specified number of characters of a text string, counting from the left
LeftWords	Returns the specified number of words from a text string, counting from the left
Length	Finds the number of characters in a given text string
Ln	Computes the natural (base e) logarithm of an expression
Log	Computes the common (base 10) logarithm of an expression
Lower	Converts a text string to all lowercase
Max	Displays the greatest value among those in specified fields
Middle	Returns the middle portion of a supplied text string, starting at a given position and extending a specified number of characters
MiddleWords	Returns the specified number of words from a text string, counting from the specified starting word
Min	Displays the smallest value among those in specified fields

Continued

Table 14-4 *(continued)*

Function Name	Purpose
Minute	Returns the minute portion of a time expression
Mod	Returns the remainder when an expression is divided by a given number
Month	Displays the number of the month in a date expression, within the range 1–12
MonthName	Displays the name of the month in a date expression
NPV	Finds the net present value of an investment, using values in repeating fields as unequal payment values and a given interest rate
NumToText	Converts a numeric expression to text format
PatternCount	Returns the number of instances of a specified text string found within another text string or field
Pi	Returns the value of the mathematical constant *pi*
PMT	Calculates a loan payment, using a given principal, interest rate, and term
Position	Scans text for the specified string starting at the given position; returns the location of the first occurrence of the string
Proper	Converts the first letter of each word in the text string to uppercase (used to capitalize names, for example)
PV	Calculates the present value of an investment, using a given payment amount, interest rate, and periods
Radians	Converts a degree value to radians (for use with trigonometric functions)
Random	Generates a random number
RelationInfo	Returns information about a particular relationship that has been defined for the current database
RelationNames	Displays the names of all relationships that have been defined for the specified database, separated by Returns
Replace	In a text string, starts at the given position, moves the specified number of places, and replaces the existing text with the specified new text string
Right	Counting from the right, returns a given number of characters in a text expression
RightWords	Returns the specified number of words from a text string, counting from the right

Function Name	Purpose
Round	Rounds off a numeric expression to the specified number of decimal places
ScriptNames	Returns the names of all scripts that have been created for a given database, separated by Returns
Seconds	Displays the seconds portion of a time expression
Sign	Examines a numeric expression and returns 1 for positive, – 1 for negative, or 0 for 0
Sin	Computes the sine of an angle expressed in radians
Sqrt	Computes the square root of a numeric expression (the same as expression ^ 0.5)
Status	Displays status information about the current time, operating system in use, version number of FileMaker Pro, name of the selected field, and so on (*Note:* There are currently 37 different status tests. See Appendix E.)
StDev	Examines all values in any repeating or nonrepeating field and gives the sample standard deviation
StDevP	Examines all values in any repeating or nonrepeating field and gives the population standard deviation
Substitute	Substitutes one set of characters in a text string for another
Sum	Totals all values in specified fields
Tan	Computes the tangent for a given angle expressed in radians
TextToDate	Converts a text string into date format
TextToNum	Converts a text string to numeric format, ignoring alphabetic characters
TextToTime	Converts a text string to time format
Time	Converts three given numeric values into a time equivalent
TimeToText	Converts a time value into text format
Today	Returns the current date from the system clock
Trim	Strips the specified text expression of leading and trailing spaces
Truncate	Truncates a number to the specified number of decimal places
Upper	Converts a text expression to all uppercase
ValueListItems	Returns the items in a particular value list for a given database
ValueListNames	Returns the names of all value lists that have been defined for a given database

Continued

	Table 14-4 *(continued)*
Function Name	**Purpose**
WeekofYear	Determines the number of the week in the year, 1–52, for the specified date expression
WeekofYearFiscal	Determines the number of the week in the year, 1–53, for the specified date expression (in accordance with the particular day that is considered the first day of the week)
WordCount	Returns the total number of words found in a text expression or field
Year	Returns the year part of the specified date expression

All functions work the same way. A function performs operations on data (the arguments to the function) and then returns a result. The arguments are enclosed in parentheses directly after the function name. For example, in the following expression:

```
Round(Sales Tax, 2)
```

Round is the function name, and Sales Tax and 2 are the arguments.

A function expects certain types of data for each argument: numbers, text, or logical tests. Failure to provide the correct types of arguments will result in errors. For example, although you can choose a Text field as an argument to the Round function, the calculation doesn't make any sense and results in a blank field. The kinds of data expected for each argument appear to the right of the function's name in the Specify Calculation dialog box (previously shown in Figure 14-1).

Functions don't have to be the only component in an expression. They can be combined with constants or references to fields, as shown in the following example:

```
Product Total + Round(Sales Tax, 2)
```

This example shows an expression to define a Grand Total field, obtained by adding the Product Total to the results of rounding off the Sales Tax field's contents to two decimal places.

The following example demonstrates that an expression can also be used as the argument to a function:

```
Round(Product Total * .07, 2)
```

In this example, the Sales Tax field is replaced by an expression that yields the same result. The result of this expression is Sales Tax rounded to two decimal places.

The functions are divided into 13 categories: text, number, date, time, aggregate, summary, repeating, financial, trigonometric, logical, status, design, and external.

Cross-Reference

Appendix E provides a detailed explanation for each of FileMaker Pro's built-in functions. The functions are listed alphabetically within the category to which they belong. In addition to an explanation of each function's purpose and an example of how the function is used, the sections include a statement that shows how to phrase the function and its arguments. (The order for arranging the function and its arguments is called the *syntax* of the function.) Special notes and cautions, as well as references to other related functions, are included in the explanations of some of the functions.

To use a function in a Calculation field definition, double-click its name in the function list in the upper-right section of the Specify Calculation dialog box (previously shown in Figure 14-1). Then replace the function's arguments with the appropriate field names or expressions.

If you don't know the specific name of the function you need, click the View pop-up menu in the upper-right corner of the Specify Calculation dialog box (see Figure 14-3). Depending on your selection from this menu, you can view an alphabetical list of all functions (by selecting "all by name"), an alphabetical list of all functions grouped by type (by selecting "all by type"), or just a particular category of functions (by selecting "Text functions," "Logical functions," and so on).

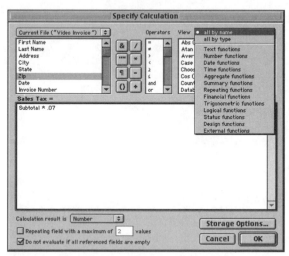

Figure 14-3: Use the View pop-up menu to specify how the functions are listed.

Summary

✦ FileMaker Pro supports the use of Calculation fields. These fields can perform operations on data in other fields.

✦ A Calculation field's definition consists of a formula made up of mathematical expressions and functions. Calculation fields can combine data from other fields and can also contain constant values.

✦ An expression consists of one or more operators that join fields or constant values. Database fields are similar to algebraic variables.

✦ An expression for a Calculation field can include arithmetic, logical, and text operators.

✦ FileMaker Pro 5 includes over 130 built-in functions. These functions perform data conversion, and also date, logical, mathematical, financial, statistical, summary, text, time, and trigonometric calculations. They can also be used to determine the status of important system and database properties, as well as return information about users who are accessing your database on the World Wide Web.

✦   ✦   ✦

Automating FileMaker Pro

When most people — particularly new computer owners — see the terms *script* or *scripting*, they think of programming. And when they think of programming, they quickly skip to the next section of the manual, assuming that this feature was not meant for them. Unfortunately, in many cases, they're right. But FileMaker Pro provides an easier, kinder way to create scripts:

✦ Rather than type scripts in a word processing program or text editor, you design scripts in FileMaker Pro by choosing script steps from a list. Step options are set by clicking buttons and check boxes.

✦ You can create many scripts simply by executing sort instructions, find requests, and similar commands and then telling FileMaker Pro that you want to use the identical procedures in a script. When you perform these important steps just before creating the script, FileMaker Pro includes them for you as part of the default script. The general philosophy is "Set it up and then save it as a script."

To make it easy to design scripts, FileMaker Pro provides a built-in script-creation utility called ScriptMaker. Using ScriptMaker, you can automate almost any FileMaker Pro function that you usually execute manually by selecting commands from menus. Once defined, a script can be added to the Scripts menu and/or attached to a button in any layout, making it simple to execute the script any time you like. To make it simpler to reuse existing scripts, FileMaker Pro 5 now allows you to import scripts from other FileMaker databases.

Although this chapter is devoted primarily to explaining how to create and use scripts, you can automate FileMaker Pro functions in other ways as well, such as:

✦ Creating auto-entry fields that are filled in for you whenever a new record is created or a record is edited (refer to Chapter 5)

✦ Setting a start-up script for a database (discussed in Chapter 7)

✦ Using a macro utility (QuicKeys, for example) to automate functions (Mac only)

✦ Using Apple Events and AppleScript (Mac only) or DDE (Windows only) to enable FileMaker Pro to interact with other programs

✦ Controlling FileMaker Pro for Windows using ActiveX components (see "ActiveX Automation" in the FileMaker Pro Help file)

Using ScriptMaker

FileMaker Pro scripts are created in ScriptMaker. The commands used in the script are called *steps*. In many cases, the steps duplicate FileMaker Pro menu commands. (See the "Script Step Reference" section, later in this chapter, for information about specific steps.) As you read through this chapter, however, you will learn that script steps are often more powerful than the menu commands they represent. For example, you can use a Clear script step that makes a particular field the active one, selects the entire contents of that field, and then clears its contents. To clear a field without such a script, you must click the field and then manually select its contents (or use the Select All command) before choosing the Clear menu command. Thus, many steps can frequently be reduced to one.

The real power of FileMaker Pro scripts becomes apparent when you design a sequence of steps to carry out a complex function. With a script, you can be sure that the steps are executed in precisely the same manner each time. If you prefer, the same script can be designed so that the user can select different options each time it runs. For example, you could create a Find script that selects a particular group of records (such as all people in the database who are younger than 30) and then displays information about those records in a different layout. With only a minor modification, the same script can be designed so that the find criteria can be changed by the user each time the script is performed. Similarly, a script designed to act on a specific field can be modified so it simply acts on whatever field happens to be current. In that way, the script can be used with any field in the database.

Note   Scripts are not available when you publish a database on the Internet or an Intranet using Instant Web Publishing.

Creating a script is not a complex process. Simply follow these steps:

1. Open the database for which you want to define a script.

   Scripts are stored with the database in which they are created.

2. Choose the Scripts ➪ ScriptMaker command.

The Define Scripts dialog box appears, as shown in Figure 15-1.

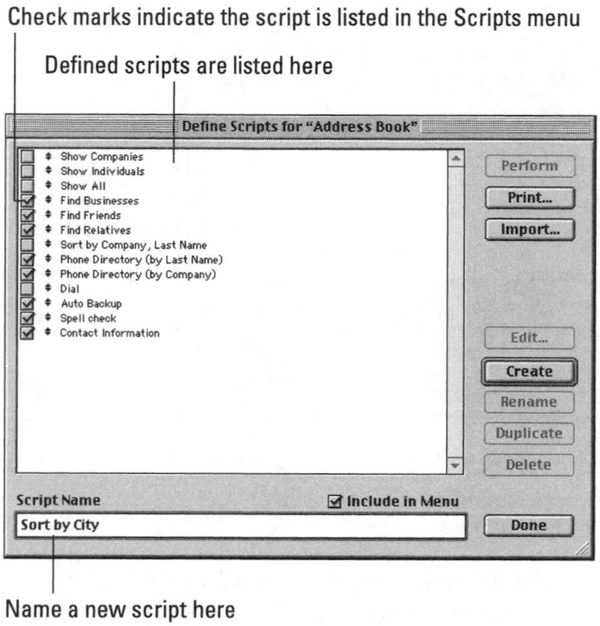

Check marks indicate the script is listed in the Scripts menu

Defined scripts are listed here

Name a new script here

Figure 15-1: The Define Scripts dialog box

3. In the Script Name box, type a name for the script.

As soon as text is entered in the Script Name box, the Create button is enabled (that is, the button is no longer dimmed).

4. If you do not want to list the script in the Scripts menu, click to remove the check mark from the "Include in Menu" check box. (If you *do* want to list the script in the Scripts menu, be sure that "Include in Menu" is checked.)

You can change the status of this check box at any time during the script creation or editing process. A maximum of 52 scripts can be listed in the Scripts menu for any database. For additional information about this option, see "Listing scripts in the Scripts menu," later in this chapter.

5. Click Create.

The Script Definition dialog box appears, as shown in Figure 15-2. A standard set of script steps, based on FileMaker Pro's best guess of what you might want to do, is presented on the right side of the dialog box. This is the initial version of the script.

Select steps from this list

Current script definition is shown here

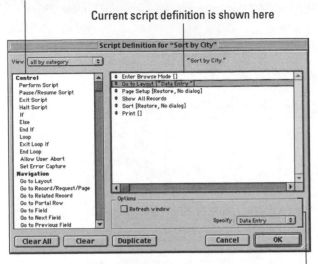

Options for the selected step appear here

Figure 15-2: The Script Definition dialog box

6. Edit the contents of the script so that it contains only the steps you need and lists them in the correct order. You can perform any of the following actions:

   • To remove all steps from the script, click Clear All.

   • To remove individual unwanted steps, select them in the current script (in the right side of the dialog box) and then click Clear. (The Clear button replaces the Move button when a step is selected.)

   • To add a step to the script, select it in the steps list (on the left side of the dialog box) and then click Move — or double-click the step.

   • To rearrange the order of steps in the script, click the step you want to relocate and drag it to the desired position.

   • To set options for a script step, begin by selecting the step in the script. Options that can be set for the step appear at the bottom of the dialog box.

7. To accept the script definition, click OK. To ignore the changes you made, click Cancel.

Tip

If a script consists of only one step, you may be able to avoid the script-definition process by assigning the step to a button. (See "Attaching a Script to a Button" later in this chapter.)

Learning by example

Learning to create scripts can be facilitated by looking at examples. In this and other chapters in this book, as well as in the databases included on the *FileMaker Pro 5 Bible* CD-ROM, you'll find plenty of scripts that you can use as starting points. Want to understand an interesting action that you've seen in someone else's database? Choose Scripts⇨ ScriptMaker, select the script you want to examine, and click Edit. You'll see the list of steps that the author of the database selected for the script. (Be aware, however, that some databases—including some that you can buy, those that are available for downloading from popular online services, and many of the databases on this CD-ROM—are protected. Unless you know the necessary password, you may not be allowed to see or modify the scripts.)

Listing scripts in the Scripts menu

As mentioned earlier, if the "Include in Menu" check box is checked for a defined script, the script is assigned a place in the Scripts menu. Up to 52 scripts can be listed in the Scripts menu. The first ten such scripts are also shown in the Define Scripts dialog box with a check mark in front of their names. These ten scripts are special in that they are assigned keyboard shortcuts (⌘+1 through ⌘+0 for the Mac or Ctrl+1 through Ctrl+0 for Windows) so you can also execute them from the keyboard. You can position the scripts that you need to use most often among the first ten to make them easily accessible.

To change the position of a script in the Define Scripts dialog box, click the double-headed arrow that precedes its name in the script list. The pointer changes to a larger version of the double-headed arrow. Then, while continuing to hold down the mouse button, drag the script up or down in the script list. When the script is in the correct position in the list, release the mouse button. Repeat this process for other scripts that you want to move.

Note   You can assign a script to the Scripts menu, attach the script to a button, make the script the start-up script, or set none of these options. The decision is entirely yours. You can also change a script or button assignment at any time by following the procedures outlined in this chapter. Note that the Perform button can be used with any script, regardless of the other ways in which the script can be accessed.

Choosing script names

When you name or rename a script, it's always best to choose a descriptive name. Although you could follow the same naming conventions that FileMaker Pro uses for layouts (instead of Layout #1, Layout #2, and so on, you could use Script #1, Script #2, and so on), you'll have a miserable time later trying to determine what each script does. On the other hand, there will be little possible confusion if you name your scripts descriptively — for example, Sort by State, Find Recent Purchases, and Print Aging Report.

Note, too, that there is no practical limit to the length of each script name. However, before going overboard and naming a script "Aging Report (designed for an ImageWriter printer in landscape mode) — to be printed only on the last day of the month," keep two things in mind:

✦ The Define Scripts dialog box does not expand to show all characters in an extremely long script name. FileMaker Pro displays only as much text as fits in the script list; the remainder is shown as ellipses.

✦ If a long script name is included in the Scripts menu, the width of the Scripts menu will expand as much as possible to display the longest script name — an arrangement that can result in a ridiculous-looking pull-down menu. (I used to have two monitors attached to my Mac. When I assigned the long script name described earlier to the Scripts menu, the resulting pull-down menu extended off my main monitor and halfway onto a nearby two-page display!)

Running a script

After you finish defining a script, you can run it in any of several ways:

✦ Select the name of the script in the Define Scripts dialog box and then click the Perform button.

✦ Choose the script name from the Scripts menu (only if "Include in Menu" was checked when you defined the script).

✦ Press the ⌘+key/Ctrl+key combination assigned to the script (only if "Include in Menu" was checked when you defined the script and if the script is one of the first ten scripts defined for the database).

✦ Click a button to which you have attached the script (if you've assigned the script to a button).

✦ Open the database (if you defined the script as a start-up script that runs automatically each time you open the database) or close the database (if you defined the script as a closing script that runs automatically each time you close the database). See Chapter 7 for more information on this option.

If you need to stop a script in progress, press ⌘+. (period)/Esc. If a script is paused by using a Pause step option or the Pause/Resume Script step, you can stop the script by clicking the Cancel button (instead of the Continue button, as you normally would).

Modifying a script

FileMaker Pro provides several methods for altering scripts, including renaming, duplicating, deleting, editing, and changing their order. These important script-editing techniques are discussed in the following sections.

Renaming a script

If you add a script to the Scripts menu by clicking the "Include in Menu" check box in the Define Scripts dialog box (previously shown in Figure 15-1), whatever name you give the script is what appears in the Scripts menu. (Otherwise, script names are visible only when you are editing scripts, assigning scripts to buttons, or setting a start-up action. In such cases, the specific script names aren't nearly as important because they are normally hidden from the user's view.)

If you decide to change the name, select the script in the Define Scripts dialog box, type a new name in the Script Name text box (or edit the existing name), and then click the Rename button.

Make your own command-key equivalents

The first ten scripts you create that have the "Include in Menu" check box checked are automatically assigned a Command-key equivalent (⌘+1 through ⌘+0) on the Mac or a Control-key equivalent (Ctrl+1 through Ctrl+0) in Windows. You can also use any of these first ten script slots to create Command-key-equivalent (Mac) or Control-key-equivalent (Windows) menu commands for which FileMaker Pro does not provide keyboard shortcuts.

For example, you may want to create a one-step script that simply executes the normal Page Setup command (Page Setup [] or Page Setup [Restore]). As long as this script is one of the first ten scripts added to the Scripts menu, you can issue its command by pressing its new Command-key or Control-key equivalent (⌘+3 or Ctrl+3, for example). You can use this trick to add all your frequently used menu commands to the Scripts menu, such as View As [toggle] (to switch between viewing records normally or as a list), Save a Copy As (to make a backup copy of the current database), and Check Record (to check the spelling of the current record).

Duplicating a script

Rather than create every new script from scratch, you will sometimes find it easier to edit a copy of an existing script. For example, you may already have created a script that prints a certain report for you. If you want a similar script that displays the report on-screen, just create a duplicate of the script and change the Print step to an Enter Preview Mode step in the duplicate script.

To create a duplicate of a script, follow these steps:

1. From the script list in the Define Scripts dialog box (previously shown in Figure 15-1), select the name of the script that you want to duplicate.

   When selected, the name of the script appears in the Script Name box.

2. Click the Duplicate button.

   A copy of the script is created and is listed as *script name* Copy (for example, Print Sales Report Copy).

3. *Optional*: Change the name of the duplicate script to something more descriptive by selecting the script in the script list, editing its name in the Script Name box, and clicking the Rename button.

4. Click the Edit button and edit the new script as desired.

5. Click Done when you finish working with the script.

Deleting a script

If you no longer need a script, or if you are approaching the limit of 52 scripts in the Scripts menu and need to make room for more, you can delete scripts or stop them from showing in the Scripts menu. As an alternative, of course, you can activate the script from a button.

To delete a script, follow these steps:

1. In the Define Scripts dialog box, select the name of the script that you want to delete.

2. Click Delete.

3. In the confirmation dialog box that appears, click Delete to remove the script or click Cancel if you change your mind.

To remove a script from the Scripts menu without deleting it, remove the check mark from the "Include in Menu" check box.

Editing a script

Other editing actions that you can perform on a script include adding, removing, or changing the order of steps and altering the options for steps. To change a script's listing in — or omission from — the Scripts menu for the database, you can either click the "Include in Menu" check box in the Define Scripts dialog box or click the check mark (or space) in front of the script's name. This acts as a toggle; each click reverses the state of the option.

If any steps relevant to the Page Setup, Sort, Find, Import, and Export commands are used in a script, their settings are saved as part of the script. If you set the database for landscape printing and include a Page Setup step, for example, that setting is saved with the script. Whenever you edit an existing script that includes a step that performs a Page Setup, Sort, Find, Import, or Export operation, FileMaker Pro presents the dialog box shown in Figure 15-3.

Figure 15-3: You can either keep the previous settings or replace them with the current settings.

You use this dialog box to determine whether you want to continue to use the previous settings that were saved with the script (the Keep radio buttons) or replace those settings with the ones that are in effect at the moment (the Replace radio buttons). For example, the Page Setup and Sort Order settings in Figure 15-3 can be kept or replaced. (The other options are dimmed because those steps were not used in the script.) If one of the reasons you are editing this script is that you just set a different sort order, click the Replace button for Sort Order and then click OK.

Printing scripts

If you want a permanent record of a script, you can print it by issuing the Print command, clicking the Script radio button in the FileMaker Pro section of the Print dialog box (Mac) or selecting "Script definition for" from the drop-down Print list (Windows), and then choosing the script you want to print from the pop-up menu (see Figure 15-4). If you want to print every script for a database, choose "All scripts" from the pop-up menu.

New Feature You can also print any script by selecting its name in the Define Scripts dialog box (refer to Figure 15-1) and clicking the Print button.

Filemaker Pro print options

Macintosh

Choose a script to print

C hoose a script to print

Windows

Figure 15-4: Printing a script

Importing scripts from other databases

If you regularly use ScriptMaker, you'll probably create some general-purpose scripts that you'd like to reuse in other databases. Rather than creating them again from scratch, you can use FileMaker Pro 5's new script importing procedure to copy any script from one database to another.

To import scripts, follow these steps:

1. Open the database that will receive the imported script(s).

2. Choose Scripts ➪ ScriptMaker.

   The Define Scripts dialog box appears.

3. Click the Import button.

   A standard file dialog box appears.

4. Select the database that contains the script(s) you want to import and click Open.

   The Import Scripts dialog box appears (see Figure 15-5).

Checked scripts will be imported

Figure 15-5: Select scripts to import from the Import Scripts dialog box

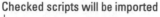

5. Check each script that you want to import and then click OK.

   FileMaker processes each of the scripts, mapping them as closely as possible to the field names, relationships, and so on that are present in the receiving database. To distinguish imported scripts from any others you've defined, their names are listed as *script name* imported.

6. Select each imported script, click Edit, and make any necessary changes.

During the import process, when matches aren't found for referenced fields, relationships, layouts, script names, and so on, the script step will include the word *<unknown>*. Be sure to correct all such incorrect references.

Tip   Rather than trying to keep track of where your general-purpose scripts are stored, you might want to create a special database that serves as a repository for such scripts.

Script Step Reference

Each element of a script is called a step. In this section, the step explanations are presented in the same order in which you'll encounter them in the left side of the Script Definition dialog box.

Note   The Windows version of FileMaker Pro 5 includes several script steps that are not supported by the Macintosh version of the program, and vice versa. These steps are related to support for system software features, such as AppleEvents and AppleScript (on the Macintosh) and OLE, DDE, and messaging capabilities (Windows). If any of your scripts rely on platform-specific steps, users on the other platform will not be able to run them. (If the scripts are examined on the other platform, these steps are shown in italic.)

Script step options

As you examine the different script steps in ScriptMaker, you'll notice that many of them include options that you can set. The options are individually explained within each step definition (as presented in "Script step definitions" in this chapter), but here's a rundown of the effects of the most common step options:

✦ *Perform without dialog.* Many script steps that are normally performed with an accompanying dialog box (enabling you to select a particular file, for example) can be performed without displaying the dialog box. Set the "Perform without dialog" option when, as part of the script step, you have already specified the file to be opened or other options to be performed, and there is no need for the user to examine or change those options.

✦ *Specify file.* Click "Specify file" when you always want the current script step to operate on a particular file. This option is often used in conjunction with the "Perform without dialog" option. (Because you have already selected the file, there is no reason to present a file dialog box that enables you to choose a file.)

Debugging a script

When a script doesn't do what you intended it to do, you should check several things:

✦ Are the steps in the proper order?

A script is not executed *en masse*—its steps run in the order in which they're listed. If you need to set a printout for landscape mode, for example, you would place a Page Setup step before the Print step.

✦ Should you have performed a preparatory action before executing the script?

If a step acts on a field, for example, you must somehow make the field the current one. If no field is selected, the step does nothing. Use a Specify Field option as part of the step (if one is allowed); include a Go to Field, Go to Next Field, or Go to Previous Field step; or manually select the desired field before running the script.

✦ Have scripts, layouts, or fields been renamed or deleted?

Reexamine your scripts in ScriptMaker. If any Perform Script, Go to Layout, or Go to Field step now reads "unknown," it means the database does not know what script or sub-script it is supposed to perform, the layout to which it is supposed to switch, or the field it is supposed to select. This is often the case when you copy buttons from one database and paste them into another.

✦ Are you in the proper FileMaker Pro mode?

Although a script can be run from any mode, it cannot operate in Layout mode. For example, a Delete Record/Request step cannot be used to delete a layout. If you're in Layout mode when you execute a script, the script will switch to the mode that the step requires (Browse, Find, or Preview) before continuing.

✦ *Specify record.* Click "Specify record" when you want the current script step to always operate on a particular record. If you do not click this option, FileMaker Pro assumes that you (or another script step) will make the desired record the active one before executing this script step.

✦ *Specify field.* Some script steps operate on the contents of a field. Click "Specify field" if the script should always operate on a particular field. If you do not click this option, FileMaker Pro assumes that you (or another script step) will make the desired field the active one before this script step is executed.

Note   You can choose an appropriate field from the current file or from any related file.

✦ *Select entire contents.* In script steps that deal with field contents (particularly the editing steps, such as Copy, Paste, and Clear), this option causes the entire contents of the chosen field to be selected. Otherwise, only the portion of the field that has been preselected by the user before executing the script will be affected.

✦ *Restore (import order, sort order, setup options, find requests, and so on).* The wording of the Restore option varies depending on the step to which it is attached. For example, in conjunction with a Sort step, it reads "Restore sort order." Set this option when you want FileMaker Pro to execute whatever settings were in effect for this procedure at the time the script was created. If neither Restore nor "Perform without dialog" is chosen, FileMaker Pro displays the appropriate dialog box when the script step is executed (enabling you to set options as you like).

✦ *Refresh window.* This option causes the screen to be redrawn when the step is reached.

✦ *Pause.* This option adds Continue and Cancel buttons to the associated script step. The purpose of this option is to give the user an opportunity to perform an action (entering criteria in a find request or browsing through the report information that is currently displayed, for example) before continuing the current script.

✦ *Exit after last.* This option is available for relative record navigation steps (Go to Record/Request/Page). When this option is selected and the script tries to select a record that is outside the range of record numbers (choosing a record before the first record or after the last record in the current browsed set), the step is not performed and either the script ends (if the record navigation command is executing outside a loop structure) or the loop is exited and the rest of the script is executed (if the record navigation command is executing inside a loop structure). When this option is not selected and the script tries to select a record that is outside the range of record numbers, the step is performed on a record that it *can* reach (either the first or last record in the database).

✦ *On/Off.* Use the On or Off options to toggle a script feature on or off. In many cases, such a script step is used in pairs — the first instance turns on a feature (such as error capture) and a second instance turns it off.

Script step definitions

FileMaker Pro 5 provides 103 steps that you can use individually or in combination with other steps to form a script. (No new script steps were introduced in FileMaker Pro 5, although several have new names.) The following sections provide detailed explanations of each step, including the ways in which the available options affect the step. For additional information on a menu-related script step, refer to the chapter in which the equivalent menu command is discussed.

Control script steps

The following script steps are used to execute sub-scripts and external scripts, control script execution, provide conditional branching and looping, and enable or disable FileMaker Pro's normal error-handling mechanism.

Perform Script

Purpose: Use Perform Script to execute another script from within the current script. When the execution of the other script concludes, the original script resumes automatically.

Options: Perform sub-scripts

Use the Specify pop-up menu to select the script that you want to perform. The name of every script that is currently defined for the database is listed in this pop-up menu. The first option in the Specify pop-up menu is External Script. Choose External Script if you want to execute a script in another FileMaker Pro database. When an external script is executed, its database is automatically opened in FileMaker Pro and then the script runs.

If you choose the "Perform sub-scripts" option, any scripts used by the chosen script are also executed.

Example: Suppose you have two databases: Invoices and Addresses. You could create a script in Invoices that — using the Perform Script command — executed a find request in Addresses (enabling you to locate a particular customer address or all addresses that include "San Francisco" in the City field, for example).

Pause/Resume Script

Purpose: Use this script step to pause a script, enabling the user to perform some nonscript action during the execution of a script.

Options: Specify

A script can be paused indefinitely, for a duration specified by a field value, or for a specific amount of time (see Figure 15-6). When a Pause/Resume Script step is executed, the status area of the document window changes to show Continue and Cancel buttons — indicating that the script has been paused. If Indefinitely (the default choice) is selected, the script will remain paused until the user clicks Continue. If a pause duration is specified (either by the contents of a specific field or by entering a particular pause time), the script will continue when the user clicks Continue or when the specified time period has elapsed.

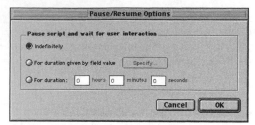

Figure 15-6: The Pause/Resume Options
dialog box

Example: You can alternate Go to Field steps with Pause/Resume Script steps to
walk a novice user through a data-entry routine.

Exit Script
Purpose: The Exit Script step is used to immediately end the execution of any sub-
scripts or external scripts, and then resume executing the main script.

Options: None

This script step is particularly useful when executed in conjunction with the If step
to test for error conditions or another reason to end a sub-script or external
script prematurely.

Halt Script
Purpose: When encountered in a script, the Halt Script step immediately ends the
execution of the current script, as well as any sub-scripts or external scripts. Like
the Exit Script step, a conditional test (an If step) is often used to determine when it
is necessary to end the script.

Options: None

If
Purpose: Use the If step to evaluate a calculation (set with the Specify option) and
perform a conditional action based on the result. If the calculation evaluates as true
(a nonzero result), the additional steps are performed. If the calculation evaluates
as false (zero), the remaining steps associated with the If script structure are
skipped.

Note   Every If structure must end with an End If step (added automatically by FileMaker
Pro). You can specify an additional condition by including an Else step.

Options: Specify the calculation

See also: Else, End If, Loop.

Else

Purpose: The Else step is used in conjunction with the If step to perform an alternate course of action.

Options: None

Example: The following script moves to Field 1 if the current record contains "Redmond" in the City field (true); otherwise, it moves to Field 2 (false):

```
If ["City = "Redmond""]
  Go to Field ["Field 1"]
Else
  Go to Field ["Field 2"]
End If
```

See also: If, End If, Exit Loop If.

End If

Purpose: The End If step ends every If script structure. When you insert an If statement into a script, an End If is automatically added by FileMaker Pro.

Options: None

See also: If, Else.

Loop

Purpose: The Loop step is used to repeat a series of script steps. (In the BASIC programming language, loops are performed by combining For/Next, Do/Until, and Repeat/While statements.) An End Loop statement must be the final step in the loop, and FileMaker Pro automatically adds it.

The loop repeats as directed or until the condition specified in an enclosed Exit Loop If step option within the loop is fulfilled.

Options: None

Examples: Here are two ways to exit from a loop. In the first example, the loop is exited after the first ten records in the database have been processed (the Global field Count is used to keep track of the number of passes made through the loop — one pass per record):

```
Go to Record/Request/Page [First]
Set Field ["Count","0"]
Loop
  ...
statements to be executed go here
...
  Set Field ["Count", "Count + 1"]
  Exit Loop If ["Count = 10"]
End Loop
```

In the second example, the loop automatically ends when the last record in the file is encountered (an Exit Loop If step is unnecessary). The first record to be processed as part of the loop is specified in the first script step. Rather than using a Global field as a counter, the [Next] option (near the bottom of the loop) is used to step through the records. The loop is exited after reaching the end of the found set, as instructed by the [Exit after last] option:

```
Go to Record/Request/Page [First]
Loop
   ...
statements to be executed go here
   ...
Go to Record/Request/Page [Exit after last, Next]
End Loop
```

See also: Exit Loop If, End Loop.

Exit Loop If

Purpose: This step specifies the condition that, when tested, determines if a loop has been completed. The calculation is evaluated on each pass through the loop. If the result of the calculation is true (nonzero), the loop is exited; otherwise, another pass is made through the loop.

For an example of how the Exit Loop If step works, see the Loop step (described previously).

Options: Specify the calculation

See also: Loop, End Loop.

End Loop

Purpose: The End Loop step is the final step in every Loop structure. When you insert a Loop step into a script, FileMaker Pro automatically adds an End Loop step.

Options: None

See also: Loop, Exit Loop If.

Allow User Abort

Purpose: This script step either enables or prevents the user from halting the script to which it is attached. Scripts can be stopped by pressing ⌘+. [period] (Mac) or Esc (Windows). The default setting is On.

Options: On or Off

Examples: In continuous running demos, it is a good practice to set Allow User Abort to Off and make it the first step in the script. When Allow User Abort is set to Off for such a script, not only do you prevent the script from being halted, you effectively prevent the user from quitting the program, too.

As another example, if a script contains a critical section that must never be interrupted, you can precede the section by Allow User Abort [Off] and then conclude the section with Allow User Abort [On] — restoring the ability to halt the remainder of the script.

Set Error Capture

Purpose: By default, FileMaker Pro presents alert boxes when an error that it is designed to handle is detected. (This is the equivalent of Set Error Capture [Off].) By adding this step and setting its option to On, you tell FileMaker Pro to suppress all error messages while the script is running — usually because you intend to do the error trapping yourself by using the Status (CurrentError) function.

Options: On or Off

Note A list of the error codes that Status (CurrentError) generates can be found in the FileMaker Pro Help listing for that function.

Navigation script steps

The navigation script steps enable FileMaker Pro to switch to or select a particular layout, record, field, and so on, as well as change to a specific mode (Browse, Find, or Preview).

Note There are no script steps that change to Layout mode because scripts can't be executed when FileMaker Pro is in Layout mode.

Go to Layout

Purpose: Use this step to switch to a particular layout that has been created for the current database (which is the same as choosing a specific layout name from the layout pop-up menu in the upper-left corner of the document window).

Options: Refresh screen

The Specify pop-up menu must be used to select the layout that you want to display. In most cases, you will want to change to a particular layout; to do so, choose its name (Menu or Data Entry, for example) from the Specify menu.

You can also switch to a layout based on a number in a chosen field. (You must specify the field name if you choose this option.) If you choose to switch to the layout given by the contents of a chosen field, the specified field must contain a number.

The number corresponds to the order of the layouts in the file. For example, if you use the field "Layout Number," and that field contains **1**, the script will switch to the first layout in the file (as specified in the Set Layout Order dialog box).

The Specify pop-up menu also has a special option called "Original layout" that is useful for ending a script. This option tells FileMaker Pro to switch back to whatever layout was current when the script was executed. For example, a Print Report script could be invoked from a layout named Data Entry. The script might switch to a report layout, print a copy of the report, and then — using the "Original layout" option — end by switching back to the Data Entry layout. The advantage of using "Original layout" rather than specifying the exact layout name (Data Entry, in this case) is that the script could conceivably be invoked from any layout and still return the user to that layout.

Tip

Go to Layout is one of the most frequently used script steps. It's not unusual to begin a script with this step (to ensure that the correct layout is displayed, for example). In many databases (such as those found on the *FileMaker Pro 5 Bible* CD-ROM), this step is attached to navigation buttons that display a help or report layout.

Go to Record/Request/Page

Purpose: This step is used to display a particular record in the current found set or to enable the user to select one of these records to display. Go to Record/Request/Page is frequently used to move directly to the first or last record in the database. (Specify First to go to the first record; specify Last to go to the last record.) When executed from Find mode, Go to Record/Request/Page displays a find request page instead of a record. When run from Preview mode, Go to Record/Request/Page displays the specified report page.

Options: Specify First, Last, Previous, Next; Specify By Number; Specify By Field Value; Exit after last; Perform without dialog

Depending on the Specify option you select, this step can display the previous, next, first, or last record, request, or page. It can also display a particular record, request, or page (if you choose "By Number"), or it can select a record, request, or page according to the contents of a field that you specify (if you choose "By Field Value").

Records can only be selected from the current found set. If you are using the By Number option to point to a specific record, and it is conceivable that the record could be hidden, you will usually want to precede this script step with a find request to ensure that the record of interest will indeed be available. If the record to be displayed could be different for each execution of the script, leave the "Perform without dialog" check box unchecked.

When the By Number option is chosen and "Perform without dialog" is unchecked, the dialog box in Figure 15-7 appears.

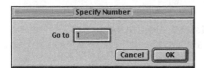

Figure 15-7: The Specify Number dialog box

When "Perform without dialog" is checked, no dialog box appears, and the script immediately displays the specified record, find request, or report page.

When the By Field Value option is chosen, the field selected must contain a number that corresponds to the record number in the database.

Tip   The contents of the referenced field can be the result of a calculation. For example, you could use the customer number of a particular customer to refer to another record based on a calculation that includes the customer number.

The "Exit after last" option can be used in conjunction with the Previous or Next option. When chosen, "Exit after last" keeps the script or loop from wrapping around when the last or first record, request, or page is encountered (when Next or Previous is chosen, respectively). This is of special concern when you are using a script to step through the records of a database, for example.

See also: Go to Related Record.

Go to Related Record

Purpose: This script step is used to display a record in a related file, based on the current relationship and the field that is presently active. If either a field in a portal or a related field that has been placed directly on the layout is selected, executing the Go to Related Record step displays the matching record from the related database. If the field that defines the relationship is selected, the first matching record from the related file is displayed.

Options: Specify relationship, Show only related records

Use the Specify pop-up menu to select a relationship (or define one, if none currently exists). The "Show only related records" option can be very useful. Choose it to limit the visible records (the found set) in the related file to those that meet the criteria of the relationship.

See also: Go to Record/Request/Page, Go to Portal Row.

Go to Portal Row

Purpose: This step enables you to move to a particular row in the active portal. If a portal isn't active, the step is applied to the first portal encountered in the layout's stacking order (that is, the front-most, highest one).

When changing portal rows, this step attempts to keep the same field active (if one is currently active). If no field in the portal is active, the step activates the first field that it can enter.

Options: Select entire contents; Specify First, Last, Next, Previous; Specify By Number; Specify By Field Value; Exit after last; Perform without dialog

Choose "Select entire contents" if you want the entire portal row to be selected, rather than just making a single field active. You must use the Specify pop-up menu to choose a target portal row.

The Next and Previous options include an "Exit after last" option that enables this script step to end if you attempt to select a portal row that is before the first or after the last row. If you do not include this option, the step simply wraps around and goes to the last or first portal row, respectively.

Choose the By Number option to specify a particular portal row by its number. When executed, this step can present a dialog box in which you choose a row number, or it can go directly to a particular row when "Perform without dialog" is checked.

To choose a portal row based on the current value in a particular field, choose "By Field Value" and select a field. The field must contain a number corresponding to a row in the portal.

See also: Go to Related Record, Go to Field.

Go to Field

Purpose: Use this step to go to a particular field in the current layout or in a layout for a related file.

Options: Select/Perform, Specify field

When a script includes steps that copy, cut, or paste information, you can use Go to Field to specify the appropriate field for each editing operation. Use the "Specify field" option to tell FileMaker Pro the field to which you want to go. (You must specify a field; otherwise, the script fails at this step.)

Set the Select/Perform option if you want to select the contents of a field (usually as a prelude to editing). If you set Select/Perform and choose a Container field that contains a sound or a movie, the sound or movie plays.

If you choose a field that contains an OLE object, FileMaker Pro activates the application that created the object and loads the OLE object into the application, ready for editing. When you exit the creating application, you will have the option to update the contents of the OLE object in the FileMaker Pro field to reflect the editing changes you made.

See also: Go to Next Field, Go to Previous Field.

Go to Next Field

Purpose: Use this step to move to the next field in the current layout. If no field is selected when a Go to Next Field step executes, you move to the first field in the current layout. FileMaker Pro uses the tab order that is set for the layout to determine what the "next" field is.

Options: None

Example: After starting a script with a Go to Field step to set the first field, you could use a series of Go to Next Field steps — each followed by a Pause/Resume Script step — to walk a new user through a data-entry layout. The beginning of the script might look like this:

```
Go to Field ["Last Name"]
Pause/Resume Script
Go to Next Field
Pause/Resume Script
Go to Next Field
```

See also: Go to Previous Field, Go to Field.

Go to Previous Field

Purpose: Use this step to move to the preceding field in the current layout. If no field is selected when a Go to Previous Field step executes, you move to the last field in the current layout. FileMaker Pro uses the tab order that is set for the layout to determine what the "previous" field is.

Options: None

See also: Go to Next Field, Go to Field

Enter Browse Mode

Purpose: Regardless of the active mode of the current database, this step switches to Browse mode (which is the same as choosing View ➪ Browse Mode or pressing ⌘+B/Ctrl+B). You use Browse mode to enter and edit data.

Options: Pause

Select the Pause option if you want to pause the script temporarily to enable the user to enter or edit data.

See also: Enter Find Mode, Enter Preview Mode.

Enter Find Mode
Purpose: This script step switches the current layout to Find mode, enabling you to execute find requests (which is the same as choosing View ➪ Find Mode or pressing ⌘+F/Ctrl+F).

Options: Restore find requests, Pause

Select "Restore find requests" to start each find request with the criteria that were in effect when the script was created. If you prefer to start the find request from scratch, leave this option unchecked. If additional steps follow Enter Find Mode, you should also select the Pause option — assuming you want an opportunity to modify the find requests.

See also: Perform Find, Enter Browse Mode, Enter Preview Mode.

Enter Preview Mode
Purpose: This step switches the current layout to Preview mode (which is the same as choosing View ➪ Preview Mode or pressing ⌘+U/Ctrl+U).

Options: Pause

Preview mode is often used to display on-screen reports or to examine a layout before printing (commonly called a *print preview* in many programs). When other steps follow the Enter Preview Mode step, you may want to use the Pause option so users of the database will have an adequate opportunity to examine the preview.

See also: Print, Enter Find Mode, Enter Browse Mode.

Sort/Find/Print script steps
The Sort/Find/Print script steps enable you to execute Sort, Find, and Print commands in scripts, as well as set options for these procedures.

Sort
Purpose: Use the Sort step to sort the browsed records in a particular order (which is the same as choosing Records ➪ Sort or pressing ⌘+S/Ctrl+S).

Options: Restore sort order, Perform without dialog

If "Restore sort order" is checked, the sort order defaults to the sort instructions that were in effect at the time the script was created. If "Restore sort order" is not checked, the sort order defaults to the most recently executed sort instructions for the database.

If you want to be able to set different sort instructions each time the step executes, make sure you do not check the "Perform without dialog" option. If, on the other hand, the sort instructions will not change from one execution of the script to another, or if you want to keep users from modifying the instructions, check "Perform without dialog."

See also: Unsort.

Unsort

Purpose: Use Unsort to restore records to the order in which they were entered into the database (which is the same as clicking the Unsort button in the Sort Records dialog box).

Options: None

Example: This script step is most useful when you have a database with records that were created in a purposeful order but now are sorted in some other order. Records in a checkbook database, for example, are normally created in date order; records in an invoice database are entered in order of invoice number. Unsort restores the records to their original order.

See also: Sort.

Show All Records

Purpose: This step makes all records visible (which is the same as choosing Records ➪ Show All Records or pressing ⌘+J/Ctrl+J). Use Show All Records when you want to work with all records in the database, rather than with just the current found set.

Note   In previous versions of FileMaker Pro, this step was named Find All.

Options: None

See also: Enter Find Mode, Perform Find Request, Modify Last Find, Omit Record, Omit Multiple, Show Omitted.

Show Omitted

Purpose: This step swaps any records that are currently not included in the found set for those that are in the found set (which is the same as choosing Records ⇨ Show Omitted). The omitted records become visible, and the previously browsed records are hidden. Note that if all records are currently being browsed, this step has no effect.

Note   In previous versions of FileMaker Pro, this step was named Find Omitted.

Options: None

See also: Enter Find Mode, Perform Find Request, Show All Records, Modify Last Find, Omit Record, Omit Multiple.

Omit Record

Purpose: This step omits (hides) the current record from the found set (which is the same as choosing Records ⇨ Omit Record or pressing ⌘+M/Ctrl+M).

Note   In previous versions of FileMaker Pro, this step was named Omit.

Options: None

See also: Enter Find Mode, Perform Find Request, Show All Records, Modify Last Find, Omit Multiple, Show Omitted.

Omit Multiple

Purpose: This step omits (hides) the next *x* consecutive records from the found set (which is the same as choosing Records ⇨ Omit Multiple or pressing ⌘+Shift+M/Ctrl+Shift+M).

Options: Specify record, Perform without dialog

When an Omit Multiple step executes, a dialog box normally appears (see Figure 15-8), which asks for the number of records you want to omit, beginning with the current record.

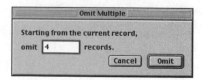

Figure 15-8: This dialog box appears when the Omit Multiple script step executes.

If the "Perform without dialog" option is checked, the step defaults to omitting only the current record, just as though you had used the Omit Record step described earlier.

The "Specify record" option enables you to set the number of records that you want to omit (as always, beginning with the record that is current at the time the step is performed). If "Perform without dialog" is also selected, the specified number of records are automatically omitted. Otherwise, the normal dialog box appears, and it uses the number of records that you specified as the default entry.

See also: Enter Find Mode, Perform Find Request, Show All Records, Modify Last Find, Omit Record, Show Omitted.

Perform Find
Purpose: Use this step to execute the current find request or requests (which is the same as clicking the Find button on a find request screen).

Options: Restore find requests

You must already have defined one or more find requests to use this script step. You can do so by using the Enter Find Mode step earlier in the script, by manually setting up the find request (or requests) just before executing the script, or by executing a find request just before creating the script and then checking the "Restore find requests" option.

See also: Show All Records, Modify Last Find, Enter Find Mode.

Modify Last Find
Purpose: This step presents the most recently executed find request, which you can re-execute or use as the basis for a new find request (which is the same as choosing Records ⇨ Modify Last Find or pressing ⌘+R/Ctrl+R).

This script step is always performed by displaying a normal find request on-screen.

Options: None

See also: Enter Find Mode, Perform Find Request, Show All Records, Omit Record, Omit Multiple, Show Omitted.

Page Setup (Mac) or Print Setup (Windows)
Purpose: Use this script step to specify Page/Print Setup options, such as paper size and orientation, for a print job (which is the same as choosing File ⇨ Page Setup or File ⇨ Print Setup).

Options: Restore setup options, Perform without dialog

See also: Print.

Print

Purpose: Use this step to send data to a printer or other output device (such as a fax-modem) according to the options set in the Print dialog box (which is the same as choosing File ➪ Print or pressing ⌘+P/Ctrl+P).

Options: Perform without dialog

By default, FileMaker Pro assumes you want to use the Print options that were in effect when you last printed the database. If you want the capability to specify different Print options each time the script runs, leave the "Perform without dialog" option unchecked. When the script runs, you see the normal FileMaker Pro Print dialog box. I recommend this option, because, if the user has a different printer or driver than you do, the output could be rendered useless. On the other hand, if you always want to print with the same set of Print options (or you don't want to give users an opportunity to select other Print options — inappropriate ones that might ruin the print job, for example), click "Perform without dialog."

> **Tip**
> If special Page/Print Setup options are necessary for a print job to print correctly (such as printing labels on a dot-matrix printer or printing in landscape mode), you will want to include Page/Print Setup as an earlier script step. Before creating the script, start by printing the job correctly. Then, when you enter the Print and Page/Print Setup steps in the script, FileMaker Pro will note the options that are set for these two steps and use those options whenever the script executes.

See also: Page/Print Setup, Enter Preview Mode.

Editing script steps

The editing script steps enable you to execute standard editing commands within scripts and apply them to selected fields.

Undo

Purpose: This step reverses the most recent action performed in the database (which is the same as choosing Edit ➪ Undo or pressing ⌘+Z/Ctrl+Z). The "most recent action" could have been another script step.

Options: None

> **Caution**
> Not all actions can be undone. Any command associated with deleting records, for example, cannot be reversed. When a command cannot be undone, the Undo command reads Can't Undo, and the Undo script step has no effect.

Cut

Purpose: This step cuts the selected contents of a field to the Clipboard (which is the same as choosing Edit ➪ Cut or pressing ⌘+X/Ctrl+X). Information that is cut with this step is available for pasting elsewhere in the record, in a different record (enabling you to move existing information from one record to another), or in another program.

 Tip Cutting removes the selected text from the field. If your intent is merely to duplicate the information, use the Copy step instead.

Options: Select entire contents, Specify field

Using the options alone or in combination, you can cut the entire contents of the current field ("Select entire contents"), cut the selected contents of a particular field ("Specify field"), or cut the entire contents of a particular field ("Select entire contents" and "Specify field").

 Note Like the other editing script steps, Cut must be directed to a specific field in order for it to work. You can use a Go to Field script step to move to a particular field or the "Specify field" option. If you want this step to apply to *any* field on a layout, you must tab into or click the field before executing the step.

See also: Clear, Copy, Paste.

Copy

Purpose: This step copies the selected contents of a field to the Clipboard (which is the same as choosing Edit ➪ Copy or pressing ⌘+C/Ctrl+C). Information that is copied with this step is available for pasting elsewhere in the record, in a different record (enabling you to duplicate existing information), or in another program.

Options: Select entire contents, Specify field

Using the options alone or in combination, you can copy the entire contents of a field ("Select entire contents"), copy the selected contents of a particular field ("Specify field"), or copy the entire contents of a particular field ("Select entire contents" and "Specify field").

See also: Cut, Paste.

Paste

Purpose: This script step pastes the current contents of the Clipboard into the current field (which is the same as choosing Edit ➪ Paste or pressing ⌘+V/Ctrl+V) or into a specified field.

Options: Select entire contents, Paste without style, Specify field, Link if available (Windows only)

Data can be pasted into a field that is specified as a script step option or into the current field, depending on whether the "Specify field" option is used. Pasted data can replace the entire contents of the field (with "Select entire contents" checked) or can be added to the field at the insertion point (with "Select entire contents" unchecked). If "Paste without style" is checked, any style formatting applied to the text (bold or italic, for example) is ignored. Otherwise, the pasted text includes whatever styles originally were applied to the text.

You should be aware of several common-sense restrictions when you use the Paste step. First, if the Clipboard is empty, nothing is pasted. Second, if the Clipboard contains data that is inappropriate for the selected field (such as a sound, picture, or movie that you are attempting to paste into a Text field), nothing is pasted. Third, if no field is selected in the current layout and a field is not specified as an option for the script step, nothing is pasted.

Because the Clipboard is shared among all programs, the material pasted can come from a program other than FileMaker Pro. For example, you could use a macro utility such as QuicKeys (discussed elsewhere in this chapter) to copy some text in a word processing program and then use the Paste step to transfer a copy of the text to a database field.

 The "Link if available" option is for Windows users only. It is grayed out in the Macintosh version of FileMaker Pro 5. When you "paste a link" in Windows, the contents of the field are then linked to the original material (such as word processing file, graphic, sound, and so on). If the original material is modified by the creating program, the contents of the field can be updated in the FileMaker Pro field either automatically or manually, depending on how the link was set up.

See also: Insert Text, Insert from Last Record, Insert from Index, Insert Current Time, Insert Current Date, Paste Current User, Cut, Copy.

Clear

Purpose: The Clear step removes data from the current field (which is the same as choosing Edit ⇨ Clear) or removes it from the particular field specified in the script step. Depending on the option selected, this step can delete all the data from a field or only the data that is currently selected.

Options: Select entire contents, Specify field

Clear can be used either on the currently selected field (by leaving the "Specify field" option unchecked) or on a particular field (by clicking "Specify field" and then choosing a field in the current file or in a related file). To clear all data from a field, click the "Select entire contents" check box. To clear only the currently selected data from the field, leave "Select entire contents" unchecked. If the script step does not use the "Select entire contents" option, you must preselect text in the field before executing the script; otherwise, the step has no effect.

Tip Unlike Cut, the Clear step does not save a copy of the data that has been removed—the data is not available for pasting. If you make a mistake, however, you can correct the Clear operation by immediately choosing the Edit ⇨ Undo Clear command.

See also: Cut.

Select All

Purpose: The Select All step selects the entire contents of the current field (which is the same as choosing Edit ⇨ Select All, pressing ⌘+A/Ctrl+A, or quadruple-clicking a field). If no field is currently selected, nothing happens.

Options: None

Fields script steps

These steps are used to paste or place information of various types into a selected field.

Set Field

Purpose: Use the Set Field step to set the contents of a particular field, based on the result of a calculation. The result of the calculation must be of a type that is appropriate for the target field.

Options: Specify field, Specify the calculation

If the "Specify field" option is not used to select a field to be set, the currently active field (if any) is set. The Specify button is used to create the formula used by the step.

Example: The Set Field step can be used to set the value for a Global field. For example, when using a loop to move through all records in a database and calculate a value, you can create the following Set Field step to initialize the value (held in a Global field named Insurance Total):

```
Set Field ["Insurance Total", "0"]
```

Then you can use the Set Field step again within a loop to update the value in Insurance Total, as follows:

```
Go to Record/Request/Page [First]
Loop
   If ["Insurance = "Yes""]
        Set Field ["Insurance Total","Insurance Total +
        Insurance Amount"]
   End If
   Go to Record/Request/Page [Exit after last, Next]
End Loop
```

Thus, if there is a Yes entry in the Insurance field for a record, the value of Insurance Total is updated by adding the amount in the record's Insurance Amount field.

See also: Insert Calculated Result.

Insert Text

Purpose: Use this step to paste a specific string (text or number) at the insertion point within the current field. Click Specify to indicate the string that you want to paste.

This script step assumes that you have selected a field and positioned the insertion point before the step is executed. You can do this manually or by choosing the appropriate options for the step.

Note   In previous versions of FileMaker Pro, this step was named Paste Literal.

Options: Select entire contents, Specify field

Insert Text can be used either on the currently selected field (by leaving the "Specify field" option unchecked) or on a particular field (by clicking "Specify field" and then choosing a field in the current file or in a related file). To replace all data in the field, click the "Select entire contents" check box. To replace only the currently selected data from the field or paste at the insertion point (if no text is selected), leave "Select entire contents" unchecked.

See also: Paste.

Insert Calculated Result

Purpose: This step pastes the result of a calculation (specified as part of the Insert Calculated Result step) into a particular field on the current layout in the current record.

Note   In previous versions of FileMaker Pro, this step was named Paste Result.

Options: Select entire contents, Specify field, Specify the calculation

Click Specify to create the calculation. You can then use the "Specify field" option to choose a field in which to paste the result. If no field is specified, the result is pasted into the active field (if any) on the current layout. If no field is active, or if the target field is not available on the current layout, this step has no effect.

Click "Select entire contents" to replace the entire contents of the target field. If this option is not chosen, only the selected contents of the field are replaced, or the paste is made at the current insertion point. (If there is no current insertion point, the result is pasted at the end of the contents of the target field.)

Both the Insert Calculated Result and Set Field steps take the result of a calculation and use it to change the contents of a field. However, there are two notable differences, as follows:

✦ Insert Calculated Result can only change fields that are on the currently selected layout. Set Field doesn't care what layout is active or even if the field has been placed on a layout.

✦ Set Field automatically replaces the entire contents of the selected field. Insert Calculated Result can be directed to replace just the currently selected portion of the target field, or it can insert the result at the current text insertion point.

See also: Set Field.

Insert from Index

Purpose: This step enables you to paste information into a field by selecting the data to be pasted from the index for that field (which is the same as choosing the Insert ⇨ From Index command or pressing ⌘+I/Ctrl+I). When this script step is executed, FileMaker displays the index for the current field (see Figure 15-9) and allows you to select the index entry that you want to paste. This step is very helpful for ensuring the correct spelling and consistent wording of field entries.

Current index entires for the selected field

Click to split index entries into their components

Figure 15-9: The current field's index is presented in the View Index dialog box.

Note   In previous versions of FileMaker Pro, this step was named Paste from Index.

Options: Select entire contents, Specify field

If you do not set the "Specify field" option, FileMaker assumes that you will preselect a field before executing this script step.

Caution   The Insert from Index step does nothing if the chosen field doesn't exist in the current layout. The same is true if no index has been created for the field and "automatically turn indexing on if needed" is not part of the field's definition.

See also: Paste.

Insert from Last Record

Purpose: This step pastes information from the same field in the most recently modified record into the selected field of the current record (which is the same as choosing Insert ➪ From Last Record or pressing ⌘+'/Ctrl+').

Note   In previous versions of FileMaker Pro, this step was named Paste from Last Record.

Options: Select entire contents, Specify field

If the field to be used is not set with the "Specify field" option, FileMaker Pro assumes that you will select the field manually or as a previous script step before executing the Insert from Last Record step. Because you will generally want to replace whatever is in the chosen field with the entire contents of that field from the last modified record, the "Select entire contents" option is the one you will most often need to use with this step.

See also: Duplicate Record/Request.

Insert Current Date

Purpose: This step pastes today's date (according to your system clock) into the current field (which is the same as choosing Insert ➪ Current Date or pressing ⌘–/Ctrl–) or in a field specified as a step option.

Note   In previous versions of FileMaker Pro, this step was named Paste Current Date.

Options: Select entire contents, Specify field

The date can be pasted into a field that is specified as a step option or into the current field, depending on whether the "Specify field" option is used. The pasted date can replace the entire contents of the field (with "Select entire contents" checked) or can be added to the field at the insertion point (with "Select entire contents" unchecked). For the step to work, the chosen field must be of a proper type to accept a date.

Example: If you do not already have an auto-entry field that automatically receives the current date when a new record is created or edited, you can use this script step to add a date stamp — such as a step in a data-entry or report-preparation script.

See also: Paste, Insert Current Time.

Insert Current Time

Purpose: This step pastes the current time (according to your system clock) into the current field (which is the same as choosing Insert ➪ Current Time or pressing ⌘+;/Ctrl+;) or in a field specified as a step option.

> **Note** In previous versions of FileMaker Pro, this step was named Paste Current Time.

Options: Select entire contents, Specify field

The time can be pasted into a field that is specified as a step option or into the current field, depending on whether the "Specify field" option is used. The pasted time can replace the entire contents of the field (with "Select entire contents" checked) or can be added to the field at the insertion point (with "Select entire contents" unchecked). For the step to work, the chosen field must be of a proper type to accept a time.

Example: If you do not already have an auto-entry field that automatically receives the current time when a new record is created or edited, you can use this script step to add a time stamp — as a step in a data-entry or report-preparation script.

See also: Paste, Insert Current Date.

Insert Current User Name

Purpose: This step pastes the name of the current user — according to the setting in the General section of the Application Preferences dialog box — into the current field or in a field specified as a step option. This is the same as choosing Insert ➪ Current User Name or pressing Shift+⌘+N/Ctrl+Shift+N. (See Chapter 7 for instructions on setting or changing the current user name.)

> **Note** In previous versions of FileMaker Pro, this step was named Paste Current User Name.

Options: Select entire contents, Specify field

The user name can be pasted into a field that is specified as a step option or into the current field, depending on whether the "Specify field" option is used. The pasted name can replace the entire contents of the field (with "Select entire contents" checked) or can be added to the field at the insertion point (with "Select entire contents" unchecked).

See also: Paste.

Insert Picture

Purpose: Use this script step to insert a graphic from a disk file into a Container field (which is the same as choosing Insert ⇨ Picture).

Note   In previous versions of FileMaker Pro, this step was named Import Picture.

Options: Specify file

For Insert Picture to work, a Container field must be selected before the step is executed — by clicking or tabbing into the field before executing the script or by adding a Go to Field step to the script that specifies the name of a Container field.

Click "Specify file" if you always want the script step to insert the same picture. If you do not specify a file as a step option, a standard file dialog box appears when the step is executed. Use normal navigation techniques to select the drive and/or folder in which the graphic file is stored. By clicking the "Show/Files of type" pop-up menu at the bottom of the dialog box, you can restrict the files displayed to those of a specific graphic type, such as JPEG or TIFF.

See also: Go to Field, Insert Movie.

Insert Movie

Purpose: This script step is used to insert a QuickTime movie, QuickTime VR clip, or a QuickTime audio clip into a Container field in the current record (which is the same as choosing Insert ⇨ QuickTime). When executed, this step displays a dialog box in which you can select a movie file to be imported (see Figure 15-10). If the Show Preview check box in the file dialog box is checked (Macintosh only), you can see a scene from each movie to help you choose the correct one. When choosing a movie to insert under Windows, previews are not available.

Note   In previous versions of FileMaker Pro, this step was named Import Movie.

Options: None

Macintosh

Movie previews appear here

Figure 15-10: Selecting a QuickTime movie to insert (Macintosh)

For Insert Movie to work, a Container field must be selected before the step is executed — by clicking or tabbing into the field before executing the script or by adding a Go to Field step to the script that specifies the name of a Container field. The QuickTime software must also be installed and enabled.

See also: Go to Field, Insert Picture.

Insert Object

Purpose: This step enables you to insert an OLE object into a Container field. This is the same as choosing Insert ⇨ Object. This command does nothing if the selected field is not a Container field.

Options: Specify

To specify the OLE object to insert into the Container field, click either the Specify check box or the Object button. FileMaker Pro opens the Insert Object dialog box (see Figure 15-11).

Create an OLE object from scratch

Windows

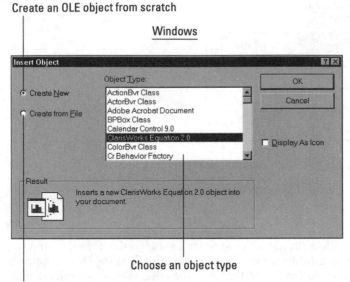

Choose an object type

Use an existing file as an OLE object

Figure 15-11: The Insert Object dialog box enables you to create a new object type or use an existing object type as the contents of a Container field.

In the Insert Object dialog box, you can create a new OLE object or create an OLE object from a file. To create a new OLE object, follow these steps:

1. Click the Create New radio button.

2. Choose the type of OLE object from the Object Type list. The options available in the list depend on the OLE server applications you have installed on your PC.

3. If you want the final result displayed as an icon (rather than the actual contents of the OLE object), click the Display As Icon check box. Showing the contents as an icon speeds up the display of the FileMaker Pro layout.

4. Click OK.

   FileMaker Pro opens the application that can create the selected object type. For example, if you selected Corel Quattro Pro 8 Chart, Corel Quattro Pro 8 opens.

5. Create the OLE object in the selected application.

6. When you have created the OLE object, exit the application and choose to update FileMaker Pro. If you change your mind, you can select the option in the other application to not update FileMaker Pro.

To create an OLE object from a file, follow these steps:

1. Click the Create from File radio button.

   A File text box replaces the Object Type menu.

2. Type the name of the file you want to use as the OLE object into the File text box, or click the Browse button to choose the file from the Browse dialog box.

3. If you want to create a link to the file, rather than embed the file in the FileMaker Pro Container field, click the Link check box.

   If you choose to link, any changes you later make to the file using the original application can be automatically updated in the FileMaker Pro Container field. However, if the linked file is not available (for example, if you delete it or open FileMaker Pro on another computer that doesn't have the file), the Container field will be empty.

See also: Update Link.

Update Link

Purpose: Updates the link to the OLE object in the Container field. Updating a link displays the most recent version of the OLE object in the FileMaker Pro layout.

Options: Specify

To specify the field for which you want to update the link, click the Specify check box or click the Field button. Although the field list includes all fields in the database (with access to linked databases as well), this script step does nothing if:

✦ You choose a field that is not a Container field.

✦ You choose a Container field that does not contain an OLE object.

✦ You choose a Container field that contains an OLE object that is not linked (in other words, one that is embedded).

See also: Insert Object.

Records script steps

These steps enable you to create, delete, and duplicate records, as well as issue other record-related commands.

New Record/Request

Purpose: Use this script step to create a new blank record or find request. When used in Browse mode, this step has the same effect as choosing Records ➪ New

Record (or pressing ⌘+N/Ctrl+N). When used in Find mode, this step has the same effect as choosing Requests ➪ Add New Request (or pressing ⌘+N/Ctrl+N).

Options: None

Example: When scripting a data-entry routine to be used by novice computer users, you might begin the script with a New Record/Request. In the Address Book database, this single step is attached to the New Record button (in the Data Entry layout) so users can create additional records without having to know the Command/Control key sequence or the menu in which the command is located.

Duplicate Record/Request

Purpose: When executed in Browse mode, this step makes a duplicate of the current record (which is the same as choosing Records ➪ Duplicate Record or pressing ⌘+D/Ctrl+D). When executed from Find mode, the step makes a duplicate of the current find request (which is the same as choosing Requests ➪ Duplicate Request or pressing ⌘+D/Ctrl+D).

Options: None

Example: Making a duplicate record and then editing the duplicate is a common data-entry shortcut for working with records that contain similar information. In a home-expenses database, for example, you undoubtedly would record expenses to some companies over and over. If the only items that change are the amount and/or payment date, you can save time by finding a previous record for the same company, duplicating the old record, and then editing the record by typing the new dollar amount and transaction date.

See also: Insert from Last Record.

Delete Record/Request

Purpose: This step is used to delete the current record (which is the same as choosing Records ➪ Delete Record or pressing ⌘+E/Ctrl+E) or the current find request (which is the same as choosing Requests ➪ Delete Request or pressing ⌘+E/Ctrl+E).

Options: Perform without dialog

Select "Perform without dialog" if you don't want the opportunity to confirm the "Permanently delete this ENTIRE record?" query that normally appears. Keep in mind, however, that — as with other FileMaker Pro Delete commands — you cannot undo a record deletion.

See also: Delete All Records.

Delete Portal Row

Purpose: This step is used to delete the selected portal row (and the associated data in the related record).

Options: Perform without dialog

Select "Perform without dialog" if you don't want the opportunity to confirm the deletion. Keep in mind, however, that as with other Delete commands, you cannot undo a record deletion. If a portal record is not selected when this script step executes, nothing happens.

Revert Record/Request

Purpose: This step is used to restore the current record or the current find request to its state before you began editing the record (which is the same as choosing Records ⇨ Revert Record) or the find request (which is the same as choosing Requests ⇨ Revert Request).

Options: Perform without dialog

Exit Record/Request

Purpose: This step exits the current record (in Browse mode) or find request (in Find mode). It is equivalent to clicking outside of the active record or pressing Enter (to complete a record). Following an Exit Record/Request, field data for the record is updated and no field is currently active.

Options: None

Copy Record

Purpose: This step copies the contents of all eligible fields for the current record to the Clipboard (in tab-delimited format). Graphics and sounds are not copied.

Options: None

> **Note** When copying a record that contains repeating fields, ASCII 29 (a nonprinting character) represents the repetitions.

See also: Copy All Records.

Copy All Records

Purpose: This step copies the contents of all eligible fields for all browsed records to the Clipboard in tab-delimited format (which is the same as pressing Option/Shift while choosing Edit ⇨ Copy). Graphics and sounds are not copied.

Options: None

Note   When copying a record that contains repeating fields, ASCII 29 (a nonprinting character) represents the repetitions.

See also: Copy Record.

Delete All Records
Purpose: Use the Delete All Records step to delete all records that are currently being browsed (which is the same as choosing Records ➪ Delete All Records).

Options: Perform without dialog

To make sure that this step is performed on the correct set of records, you should first issue appropriate Find commands or use a Find step, such as Perform Find, to select the group of records to be deleted.

Caution   As with other Delete commands, you cannot undo a Delete All Records step.

See also: Delete Record/Request, Show All Records, Perform Find, Enter Find Mode, Modify Last Find, Omit Record, Omit Multiple, Show Omitted.

Replace
Purpose: This step enables you to replace the same field in all records being browsed with the contents of the current field, a serial number, or a calculated value (which is the same as choosing Records ➪ Replace or pressing ⌘+=/Ctrl+=).

Options: Perform without dialog, Specify field

If you want to automatically use whatever information is in the selected or specified field of the current record, choose "Perform without dialog." If you want to use the Replace step to *reserialize* the records (assign serial numbers to the chosen field) or perform a calculation, do not check "Perform without dialog." When the step executes, the dialog box shown in Figure 15-12 appears, enabling you to specify a calculation or set a starting serial number and an increment.

Replace
Permanently replace the contents of the field "Category" in the 96 records of the current found set?
● Replace with: "Income"
○ Replace with serial numbers:
Initial value: 1
Increment by: 1
☐ Update serial number in Entry Options?
○ Replace with calculated result: Specify...
Replace   Cancel

Figure 15-12: This dialog box enables you to set serial number options, specify a formula to use to calculate replacement values, or replace the contents of the current field with a constant in all browsed records.

Example: The Replace step is useful when you want to ensure consistency in a set of records. For example, you might issue a find request that selects all New York Zip codes, and then use Replace to make sure that all the State fields contain the same information — presumably, **New York** or **NY**.

Relookup

Purpose: This step causes a Relookup operation to be performed for the currently selected trigger field across all records being browsed (which is the same as choosing the Records ⇨ Relookup command).

Options: Perform without dialog, Specify field

Use the "Specify field" option to select an eligible trigger field on which to base the Relookup operation. If you do not set this option, FileMaker Pro assumes that you will select the field manually before executing the script.

Example: If a database relies on lookups to record customer address data, you could create a Relookup start-up script that automatically updates the address information each time the database is opened.

Import Records

Purpose: Use the Import Records step to import data into the current database from another FileMaker Pro database or from a compatible data file (which is the same as choosing File ⇨ Import Records).

Options: Restore import order, Perform without dialog, Specify file

Leave all options unchecked to perform an import operation from scratch. When the step executes, FileMaker Pro displays a standard file dialog box from which you select the file to be imported. To make the file list more manageable, you can select a particular file type from the Show/Files of type pop-up menu at the bottom of the dialog box.

Next, the Import Field Mapping dialog box appears (see Figure 15-13). To execute the import operation, match the fields in the two databases (as explained in Chapter 16), and click a radio button to indicate that you want to "Add new records," "Replace data in current found set," or "Update matching records in found set." If the latter option is chosen, you can optionally "Add remaining records" (that is, new records in the target database will be created from all nonmatching records). Click Import to perform the import procedure.

Matched fields (with arrows) will be imported

Click to view records in the import file

Figure 15-13: The Import Field Mapping dialog box

If you previously selected the import file and the matching fields, you can click the "Restore import order" option to repeat the same import operation each time.

Example: Suppose that you periodically export new address records to a tab-separated text file called New Addresses. After importing these records into the Address Book database once, you can create a script that uses the Import Records step to import the new records automatically by using the same data file (click "Specify file" in the Script Definition dialog box to select the New Addresses file) and the same import order ("Restore import order") each time. In this case, you could also add the "Perform without dialog" option because nothing would change that might require user intervention.

See also: Export Records.

Export Records
Purpose: Use the Export Records step (which is the same as choosing File ⇨ Export Records) to export data from the current FileMaker Pro database so the data can be imported (read) into another FileMaker Pro database or another program.

Note Export Records automatically exports data from all records currently being browsed. If you want to limit exports to a subset of records, use find requests or related commands (or script steps) to select those records beforehand. See Chapter 9 for details on finding and selecting records.

Options: Restore export order, Perform without dialog, Specify file

Leave all options unchecked to perform an export from scratch. When the step executes, FileMaker Pro displays a dialog box in which you name the new export data file and select a file type for the export file (Tab-Separated Text, for example). Next, the Specify Field Order for Export dialog box appears (see Figure 15-14). To execute the export, choose the fields that you want to export, set options (as explained in Chapter 16), and then click Export.

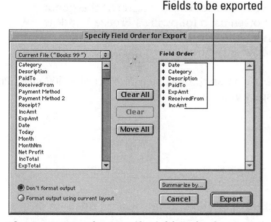

Figure 15-14: The Specify Field Order for Export dialog box

If you have performed the export operation before, you can click the "Restore export order" option to repeat the same export operation each time.

Example: Suppose that you periodically export new address records to a tab-separated text file called Addresses. After performing this export operation once, you can create a script that uses the Export Records step to export the new records to the same output file automatically. In this case, you could also add the "Perform without dialog" option because nothing would change that might require user intervention.

See also: Import Records

Windows script steps

The windows script steps enable you to control the appearance of the document window.

Freeze Window

Purpose: The Freeze Window step instructs FileMaker Pro to perform the current script without updating information in the document window until either the script ends or a Refresh Window script step is executed.

Options: None

See also: Refresh Window.

Refresh Window

Purpose: This step causes FileMaker Pro to redraw (or refresh) the document window. A Refresh Window step is often used following a Freeze Window step to force a screen refresh to occur. Check the "Bring to front" option if you want to make sure that the document window is the front-most database window.

Tip   It is unnecessary to include this step as the last step of a script—FileMaker Pro automatically refreshes the display when a script ends.

Options: Bring to front

See also: Freeze Window

Scroll Window

Purpose: This step scrolls the document window to the desired position or in the indicated direction.

Options: Home, End, Page Up, Page Down, To selection

Choose Home to scroll the document to the top of the window, End to scroll to the bottom of the window, Page Up to scroll up one page, or Page Down to scroll down one page. If you have an extended keyboard, choosing any of these options has the same effect as pressing the key of the same name.

Choose "To selection" to scroll the window so that the current field is visible.

Note   Unlike most other script step options, you *must* choose one of the scrolling options.

Toggle Window

Purpose: Depending on the option chosen from the Specify pop-up menu, this step can be used to zoom, unzoom, or maximize the current database document, or to hide the document window (which is the same as choosing Window ➪ Hide Window).

Options: Zoom, Unzoom, Maximize, Hide

The Specify pop-up menu is not optional for the Toggle Window step; you *must* choose an option. Choose Maximize to expand the document window to the full size of the current display. Choose Zoom to resize the document window to the most recent size and location that has been set for it. Choose Unzoom to return the document to its normal size and position on the screen.

Choosing Hide results in hiding the current database. The name of the database is shown surrounded by parentheses in the Window menu, as in "(Sales)." To make the database visible again, select its name from the Window menu.

Note

Repeated execution of either the Zoom or Unzoom option has no additional effect — the screen stays zoomed or unzoomed, as appropriate. To reverse the effect of a Toggle Window [Zoom] or a Toggle Window [Unzoom], add the opposite command as a new script step.

Toggle Status Area

Purpose: This step enables you to toggle the state of the *status area* (the section of the document window that contains FileMaker Pro controls, such as the book icon and the Tools panel) between visible and hidden, or to hide or show the status area. The Toggle option has the same effect as clicking the status area control at the bottom of the document window.

Options: Specify Toggle, Show, or Hide; Lock

To toggle the state of the status area (switching from Hide to Show or from Show to Hide), choose Toggle from the Specify pop-up menu. To switch to a specific state, whether the status area is currently shown or hidden, choose either Hide or Show from the Specify pop-up menu.

Click the Lock check box if you want to prevent the user from changing the status area display.

See also: Set Zoom Level.

Toggle Text Ruler

Purpose: This step hides or shows the text ruler.

Options: Specify Toggle, Show, or Hide; Refresh screen

Choose Toggle from the Specify menu to switch the state of the text ruler from Hide to Show and vice versa. Choose Show or Hide to set the text ruler to a specific state (regardless of its current state).

Set Zoom Level

Purpose: This step sets the zoom level to any of the normally supported magnification percentages, or instructs FileMaker to zoom the display in or out (using the default zoom increase or decrease). The latter script step options (Zoom In and Zoom Out) are the same as choosing the View ⇨ Zoom In and View ⇨ Zoom Out commands.

Options: Lock, Specify

Clicking the Lock check box grays out the zoom controls in the document window, freezing the display at the chosen zoom level.

Tip   In many cases, Set Zoom Level steps are used in pairs — one step (or script) to zoom the screen to a particular level and a second step (or a second script) that restores the window to the original zoom level. Similarly, after locking the zoom level (to prevent the user from changing what you want to show him or her), you must also execute a script step to unlock the zoom level — otherwise, it will continue to be frozen for the database.

By using the Set Zoom Level step in combination with the Scroll Window step, you can display a particular section of a database window at a specific magnification.

See also: Toggle Window.

View As

Purpose: This step can be used to specify the way records are displayed (as one record per screen, as a continuous scrolling list, or in spreadsheet form) or to switch from the current display mode to another display mode.

New Feature   FileMaker Pro 5 offers three display modes: View as Form, View as List, and View as Table. When browsing records, these commands can be selected from the View menu.

Options: Cycle; View as Form, View as List, View as Table

To cycle through the three display modes, choose Cycle. Each time a script is executed (or a button clicked) that contains the View As [cycle] step, the view changes to the next viewing method. The order in which the views cycle is form, list, and table.

To set the display mode to a specific state, regardless of the current display mode, choose View as Form, View as List, or View as Table from the pop-up menu.

Files script steps

These steps are used to open, close, and save database files; create new files; and set file-related options.

New

Purpose: This step displays the New Database dialog box (which is the same as choosing File ➪ New Database), enabling the user to create a new empty file or one based on any of the FileMaker-supplied templates.

Options: None

Open

Purpose: This step enables the user to select a FileMaker Pro database to open (which is the same as choosing File ➪ Open or pressing ⌘+O/Ctrl+O) or to open a specific database file automatically.

Options: Specify file; Open hidden

If a file is specified, that file is opened when the step executes. If no file is specified, a standard file dialog box appears, enabling you to select a database to open. In either case, a database opened with this script step becomes the current database.

If you enable the Open hidden option, the database opens but is not displayed on-screen. To view open but hidden databases, look in the Windows menu for filenames surrounded by parentheses — **(Addresses)**, for example.

Note that if you intend to perform a script in another database, you don't have to open the other database first. Simply use the Perform Script step, specify that an external script is to be used, and then select the database to open and the particular script you want to perform.

See also: Close.

Note

If you assign the Open step to a button, you cannot set options for it; clicking the button automatically presents the Open File dialog box. If you want to set options for the Open step (open hidden and/or specify the file to open), you must include the step as part of a script. (Of course, the script can consist of *only* the Open step, if you like.)

Close

Purpose: This step closes the current file (which is the same as choosing File ➪ Close or pressing ⌘+W/Ctrl+W) or closes another specific database file.

Options: Specify file

If no options are set, the Close step simply closes the current file. If the "Specify file" option is checked, you can choose a particular file to close (**Sales.fp5** or **Sales**, for example).

Example: The Close step is useful for ending a script that performs a final action for a database. You could, for example, create a script that sorts the database in a specific way (to be sure that the database is ready for use the next day) and then closes the file. If you have a database that works in conjunction with other databases (see the Callable Help Example folder in the FileMaker Pro Bible folder of the *FileMaker Pro Bible 5* CD-ROM), you can use the Close step to close the other file or files when they're no longer needed. (Closing unnecessary databases frees memory for other FileMaker Pro activities.)

See also: Open, Quit.

Change Password

Purpose: When executed, this script step presents the Change Password dialog box shown in Figure 15-15. This dialog box enables the user to change his or her password for the current database.

Figure 15-15: The Change Password dialog box

Note   If no passwords have been defined for the current database (or if they've all been deleted), this script step does nothing.

Options: None

Set Multi-User

Purpose: This step turns the multi-user status for a database on or off (allowing or disallowing network access to the data).

Options: On, On (Hidden), Off

Choosing the On option is equivalent to choosing Sharing from the File menu and selecting the Multi-User radio button in the File Sharing dialog box; choosing Off is equivalent to selecting the Single User radio button in the File Sharing dialog box.

If a network protocol has not been chosen in the General section of the Application Preferences dialog box, setting the Set Multi-User step to On or On (Hidden) has no effect.

New Feature Choosing On (Hidden) sets the database for multi-user status, but does not list the database in the Hosts dialog box. This is the same as choosing Multi-User (Hidden) in the File Sharing dialog box.

Set Use System Formats

Purpose: Both the Macintosh and the PC have control panels for setting the default formats for displaying dates, times, and numbers. On the Macintosh, two control panels (Date & Time and Numbers) are used, while on the PC, the Regional Settings control panel (with Number, Time, and Date tabs) is used. FileMaker Pro, however, saves its own default settings for displaying dates, times, and numbers as part of each database file. The Set Use System Formats step enables you to choose between using the normal system formats for these entities or the formats that are stored with the database.

Options: On, Off

Choose the On option to use the current system formats. Choose the Off option to use the formats that were saved with the file.

Save a Copy As

Purpose: This step is the same as choosing the File ➪ Save a Copy As command. If no options are set for the Save a Copy As step, the Create a Copy Named/Create Copy file dialog box appears when the script executes the step (see Figure 15-16). The dialog box enables you (or the current user) to name the copy, determine where on disk the file will be saved, and select the type of copy that is made (a duplicate, a compressed copy, or a clone).

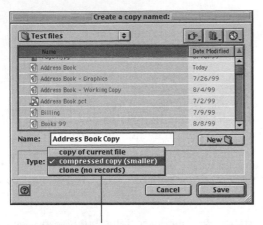

Choose the type of copy you want
to create from this pop-up menu

Figure 15-16: Saving a copy of a database

Options: Specify file

Click the "Specify file" option if you always want the file to be saved in a particular location, with the same filename and type.

Example: An example of using the Save a Copy As script step appears in the "Automatic backups" section in Chapter 2.

Recover

Purpose: The Recover script step performs the same action as choosing the File ⇨ Recover command. Its purpose is to repair damaged database files.

 Caution   There must be enough free space on the disk to recover the file successfully.

Options: Perform without dialog, Specify

If you want to specify the file to recover, choose the Specify File button. FileMaker Pro opens a dialog box that displays a list of files. Choose the file you want to recover. Choose "Perform without dialog" if you don't want the user to have the choice of which file to recover. However, if you select "Perform without dialog" but do *not* specify a file, the Open Damaged File dialog box will still open when this script step is executed because FileMaker Pro won't know which file to recover.

Spelling script steps

The spelling script steps enable you to check the spelling of a field, an entire record, or the browsed set of records.

Check Selection

Purpose: This step uses the spelling checker to examine the selected text in the current field (which is the same as choosing Edit ➪ Spelling ➪ Check Selection).

Options: Select entire contents, Specify field

With no options set, this step can be used to check the spelling of selected text in any field of any layout. However, if no text is selected when the script executes, nothing happens — that is, no spell check is performed.

When only the "Select entire contents" option is set, this step causes a spell check to be executed for the entire contents of the current field (the one that contains the cursor). If no field is current, the spell check is skipped.

If only the "Specify field" option is used, the spell check is restricted to selected text within the particular field specified.

When both options are set, the entire contents of the specified field are checked. This method can be particularly useful for ensuring that the spelling is correct in a long text field (a Comments or Notes field, for example).

See also: Check Record, Check Found Set.

Check Record

Purpose: This step instructs the spelling checker to examine every field in the current record (which is the same as choosing Edit ➪ Spelling ➪ Check Record).

Options: None

See also: Check Selection, Check Found Set.

Check Found Set

Purpose: This step performs a spelling check for every field in all records in the current found set — that is, the records that are currently being browsed. This step is the same as choosing Edit ➪ Spelling ➪ Check All, following a find request.

Options: None

See also: Check Selection, Check Record.

Correct Word

Purpose: This step opens the Spelling dialog box so you can correct a word that FileMaker Pro identified as misspelled. This is the same as choosing Edit ⇨ Spelling ⇨ Correct Word after performing a spell check (for a selection, record, or all current records).

Options: None

To work correctly, the spelling checker must have identified a misspelled word. If there are no misspellings, nothing happens when this script step is executed.

See also: Check Record, Check Found Set, Check Selection

Spelling Options

Purpose: This step opens the Document Preferences dialog box to the Spelling section, enabling the user to set spelling options for the current database. This is the same as choosing Edit ⇨ Preferences ⇨ Document and then clicking the Spelling tab of the Document Preferences dialog box.

Options: None

Select Dictionaries

Purpose: This step opens the Select Dictionaries dialog box so the user can choose either a user dictionary or a main dictionary. This is the same as choosing Edit ⇨ Spelling ⇨ Select Dictionaries.

Options: None

Edit User Dictionary

Purpose: This step opens the User Dictionary dialog box, enabling the user to edit the contents of the user dictionary. This is the same as choosing Edit ⇨ Spelling ⇨ Edit User Dictionary.

Options: None

Open Menu Item script steps

This category contains script steps for modifying preferences, creating database definitions (field and relationships), getting help, accessing ScriptMaker, and changing the network/Internet sharing protocols.

Open Application Preferences

Purpose: This step opens the Application Preferences dialog box. The user can modify different classes of application preferences by clicking tabs at the top of the dialog box. This is the same as choosing Edit ⇨ Preferences ⇨ Application.

Options: None

See also: Open Document Preferences.

Open Document Preferences
Purpose: This step opens the Document Preferences dialog box. The user can modify the document preferences by clicking tabs at the top of the dialog box. This is the same as choosing Edit ➪ Preferences ➪ Document.

Options: None

See also: Open Application Preferences, Spelling Options.

Open Define Fields
Purpose: This step displays the Define Fields dialog box for the current database, enabling you to create new fields, edit definitions for existing fields, delete fields, and set and change options for fields. This is the same as choosing File ➪ Define Fields or pressing Shift+⌘+D/Shift+Ctrl+D. See Chapter 5 for more information about defining fields.

Options: None

Note You must have access privileges to the whole database in order for this script step to work. That is, if passwords have been defined, you must be using a password for which the privileges include the check box marked "Access the entire file."

Open Define Relationships
Purpose: This step displays the Define Relationships dialog box, enabling you to define, delete, or edit relationships between the current database file and others (which is the same as choosing Edit ➪ Define Relationships).

Options: None

Note You must have access privileges to the whole database in order for this script step to work. That is, if passwords have been defined, you must be using a password for which the privileges include the check box marked "Access the entire file."

Open Define Value Lists
Purpose: This step opens the Define Value Lists dialog box so the user can define new value lists or edit existing value lists. This is the same as choosing Edit ➪ Define Value Lists.

Options: None

Open Help

Purpose: This step opens FileMaker Pro Help. This is the same as choosing Help ⇨ FileMaker Pro Help or Help ⇨ Contents and Index.

Options: None

Open ScriptMaker

Purpose: This step presents the Define Scripts dialog box (the opening screen that normally appears when ScriptMaker is chosen from the Scripts menu). Any steps that appear after the Open ScriptMaker step are not performed.

Options: None

The Open ScriptMaker step is useful when you are modifying or debugging scripts. In addition, if you find yourself frequently popping in and out of ScriptMaker, you can attach this step to a button or add it as one of the first ten scripts to the Scripts menu, giving it a ⌘+key/Ctrl+key equivalent.

Open Sharing

Purpose: This step opens the File Sharing dialog box, where you can set up network database sharing and "companion" sharing (for example, for using the FileMaker Pro Web Companion). This is the same as choosing the File ⇨ Sharing command.

Options: None

Miscellaneous script steps

This "catch-all" category includes steps that perform special, less-frequently needed script actions, such as dialing the phone, beeping, displaying messages, and executing AppleScripts.

Show Message

Purpose: This step displays a user-specified message in a dialog box and enables the user to respond by clicking a button. Between one and three captioned buttons can be presented.

Options: Message text, Button captions

Example: The Show Message step can provide data-entry instructions for the user. You might, for instance, attach this step to a Help button. When clicked, an appropriate message could be displayed, such as "Press the Tab key to move from field to field."

In addition, this step can be used to enable a script to take different actions depending on the button the user clicks — determined by using the Status

(CurrentMessageChoice) function. As an example, in the Show Message step that is part of the following script, two buttons were defined (labeled "Once" and "Twice"). The script presents a message to which the user must respond by clicking one of the buttons.

```
Show Message ["How many times should I beep?"]
If ["Status(CurrentMessageChoice) = 1"]
  Beep
Else
  Beep
  Beep
End If
```

If the Once button is clicked [Status (CurrentMessageChoice) = 1], one beep is played; if Twice is clicked, two beeps are heard (see Figure 15-17).

Figure 15-17: Specifying a message and options

 Note To view and use any of the Status functions when defining an If step, choose Status Functions from the View menu in the Specify Calculation dialog box.

Beep

Purpose: This step plays the current sound for the system alert. You can alter the sound that is played by selecting a different alert sound in the Sound or the Monitors & Sound control panel (Mac) or the Sounds control panel (Windows). The Beep step is useful for signaling user errors, script errors, and the conclusion of lengthy scripts.

Options: None

Speak

 Purpose: If the PlainTalk and Speech Manager system software components are installed on your Mac, you can use this step to speak a text string or the contents of a given field in a voice that you select.

Options: Field value, Text to speak, Use voice, Wait for speech completion before continuing

Click the Specify button to set speech options. The Specify Text to Speak dialog box appears (see Figure 15-18). To speak the contents of a field, click the "Field value" radio button and select the field to be spoken. To make the step speak a particular text string, click the "Text to Speak" radio button and type the text string in the text box.

Speak text typed in the dialog box

Speak text in a field

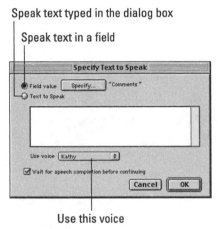

Use this voice

Figure 15-18: The Specify Text to Speak dialog box

If you don't want to use the robotic default voice for the speech, choose a voice from the "Use voice" pop-up menu. (If you intend to combine several Speak steps in a script, you must select a voice for each step. For all Speak steps in which no voice is chosen, the default voice is used.)

The "Wait for speech completion before continuing" option enables you to control the timing of the speech segment. When this option is unchecked, the script continues regardless of whether the speech has been completed.

Dial Phone

Purpose: This step is used to dial phone numbers through an attached modem or the computer's speaker.

Options: Perform without dialog, Specify field, Use Dialing Preferences

Click Specify to set dialing options. The phone number can be taken from a specific field in the current record or can be a constant that always dials the same number, regardless of the record that is currently displayed. Click Use Dialing Preferences if you want this step to take user-defined dialing preferences into account. (See Chapter 7 for instructions on setting dialing, modem, and other preferences.)

Open URL

Purpose: This step enables you to handle different types of Internet URL (*Uniform Resource Locator*) protocols. The text value for the URL can be specified as part of the script step, or the contents of a specified field can be used.

Options: Specify, Perform without dialog

Exactly what happens when the script step executes depends on the contents of the URL (specified as either text or field contents). There are four types of URLs that FileMaker Pro can handle. They are:

✦ *http*: If the text or field contents begin with **http://**, FileMaker Pro will launch your preferred Web browser and navigate to the Web location specified by the rest of the URL. For example, if the URL reads **http://www.filemaker.com**, your Web browser will display the FileMaker, Inc. home page.

✦ *ftp*: If the text or field contents begin with **ftp://**, FileMaker Pro will launch your preferred FTP (file transfer protocol) helper application and retrieve the file specified by the balance of the URL. For example, if the URL reads **ftp://ftp.webnet.com/example.txt**, FileMaker Pro will retrieve the file example.txt from the Webnet ftp site. If the URL doesn't specify a particular file, the ftp helper application opens to the designated directory.

✦ *File*: If the text or field contents begin with **File:**, FileMaker Pro will launch the application that is associated with the file specified by the balance of the URL. For example, if the URL reads **File:C:\Example.txt**, FileMaker Pro will launch the application that is associated with Example.txt (which might be Notepad in Windows) and load the file for viewing.

✦ *mailto*: If the text or field contents begin with **mailto:**, FileMaker Pro will launch your preferred e-mail program and create a new e-mail message addressed to the address specified by the balance of the URL. For example, if the URL reads **mailto:fmprobible@hotmail.com**, your preferred e-mail program will open with a new e-mail message addressed to my Hotmail account.

If you specify that the script step should perform without a dialog box, you must specify a field that contains the URL or supply the text of the URL in the Specify URL dialog box (see Figure 15-19). If you don't check the "Perform without dialog" check box, the user will have the opportunity to supply a field or the URL text when the script step executes. If the field specified for the URL is a repeating field, you can specify which of the repetitions to use by supplying a number in the Repetition box.

Take the URL from the text box

Take the URL from a field

Figure 15-19: Specifying the URL to use with the Open URL script step

Send Mail

Purpose: This script step sends an e-mail message (Internet or intranet) to specified recipients using your preferred e-mail program. You can specify that the recipients (both "To:" and "CC:"), subject, and message contents come from either a text box or from the contents of a field.

Options: Specify, Perform without dialog

For this script step to work, you must have an e-mail application properly installed on your Macintosh or PC. If you choose the Specify option, FileMaker Pro opens the Specify Mail dialog box (see Figure 15-20).

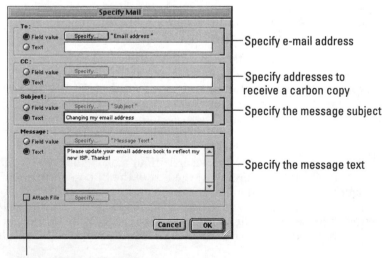

Add an e-mail attachment

Figure 15-20: Use the Specify Mail dialog box to specify the addressees, subject, and message for your e-mail.

Fill out the Specify Mail dialog box as follows:

✦ To address the e-mail message, click the "Field value" radio button or the Text radio button in the To: area of the dialog box. If you selected a field value, choose the field that contains the address information for the primary recipients from the Specify Field dialog box. If the field is a repeating field, you can specify which repetition contains the addressee information by entering a number in the Repetition text box. You can also choose whether to use only the field value in the current record (for a single addressee) or the field values in all records in the found set (for multiple addressees). If you selected the Text option, you can type in the addresses (up to 255 characters).

✦ To add "CCs" (addressees who are "copied" on the e-mail message), choose the "Field value" radio button or the Text radio button in the CC: area of the dialog box. All other options are the same as in the To: section.

✦ To add a subject to the e-mail message, choose the "Field value" radio button or the Text radio button in the Subject: area of the dialog box. If you selected a field value, choose the field that contains the subject information. If the field selected is a repeating field, you can specify which repetition contains the subject information by entering a number in the Repetition text box. Unlike the addressee information, however, the subject is drawn from the specified field in the current record only. Alternatively, you can type a subject in the Text box (up to 255 characters).

✦ To create the message contents, choose the "Field value" radio button or the Text radio button in the Message: area of the dialog box. If you selected a field value, choose the field that contains the message. The message can be up to 64K if you choose the field value option, or 32,760 characters if you choose the text option. If the field is a repeating field, you can specify which repetition contains the message by entering a number in the Repetition text box.

✦ To attach a file to the message, click the Attach File radio button and choose the file to attach.

If you select "Perform without dialog," FileMaker Pro places the composed e-mail message directly into your e-mail program's outbox. If you don't select this option, the composed message is left open in the e-mail application so you can review and change it before sending it (although most e-mail packages enable you to revise messages that are already in the outbox).

In Windows, the Specify Mail dialog box contains an extra button marked "Address" in both the To: and CC: areas of the dialog box. Clicking these buttons opens the address book for your e-mail package, enabling you to choose addressees.

See also: Open URL

Mass mailings via a script

The Send Mail script step is typically used to send e-mail to one person. Using a script, you can instruct FileMaker Pro to send the same message to every member of a found set. To illustrate this, I created a modified version of the Address Book database and named it Email (found in the FileMaker Pro Bible folder on the *FileMaker Pro 5 Bible* CD-ROM). The purpose of Email is to send a catalog file as an e-mail attachment to every customer who requests a catalog.

Email contains four new fields: Email Address, Cat Request, Cat Sent, and Date Sent. When a new record is created, Cat Sent is automatically set to **No**. When entering data for the new record, you enter the person's e-mail address and — if a catalog has been requested — click the "Yes" check box for Cat Request.

To perform a mass e-mailing to all customers who want catalogs, choose the Send Catalog script from the Scripts menu. As shown in the following Figure, the script begins by finding all records where Cat Request is **Yes** and Cat Sent is **No**. The Loop section of the script steps through the records in the found set one by one. It sends a prepared e-mail message with an attached catalog to the record's e-mail address, sets the Cat Sent field to **Yes**, and enters today's date in the Date Sent field. This repeats until all records in the found set have been processed.

Specifying the recipient (the Email Address field), the message text, and the attachment are done by setting options for the Send Mail script step. If you want to test this script, create a single record using your own e-mail address.

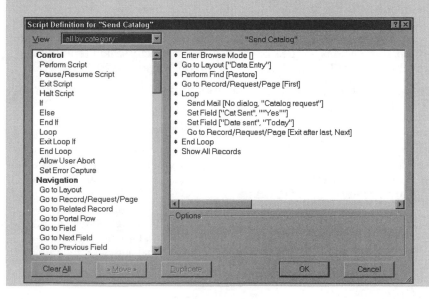

Send Apple Event

Purpose: You use the Send Apple Event step to facilitate interaction between FileMaker Pro and other programs—or even instruct FileMaker Pro to send messages to itself.

Options: Specify

Apple Events—a feature of System 7 and higher—enable you to send messages (commands and data) between programs. Although most users will never personally create a script that uses AppleEvents, anyone can easily use this script step to launch other programs and documents from FileMaker Pro (discussed in "Using AppleEvents," later in this chapter). And if you have QuicKeys (a commercial macro utility from CE Software), you can use this step to execute impressive macros (described in "Using QuicKeys with FileMaker Pro scripts," later in this chapter).

Send DDE Execute

Purpose: This script step sends a DDE (*Dynamic Data Exchange*) command to another application, telling it to execute a series of commands available in that application. The exact commands that can be sent depend on the receiving application.

Options: Specify

For each Send DDE Execute script step, you can specify the following items:

✦ *Service Name*: This is the name of the application that executes the DDE commands. You must check the documentation for the receiving application to find out its service name. You can type the service name into the Text box or use the contents of a field to specify a value for it. If the field is a repeating field, you can choose which repetition contains the service name by typing a value in the Repetition text box.

✦ *Topic*: A topic is used by the receiving application to group a set of commands. Check the documentation of the receiving application for the valid topics. You can choose to specify the topic by typing text in the Text box, selecting a filename, or choosing a field value and specifying the field that contains the topic name. If the field is a repeating field, you can choose which repetition contains the topic by typing a value in the Repetition text box.

✦ *Commands*: Specify the actual commands that instruct the receiving application to perform the tasks you want. Check the documentation of the receiving application for valid commands. You can choose to specify the commands by typing them in the Text box or specifying the field that contains the commands.

Tip

If you use the script step Send DDE Execute following a Send Message step to open another application, you may need to insert a Pause step after the Send Message step to allow the application to open.

See also: Send Message.

Perform AppleScript

Purpose: This step is used to send AppleScript commands to another program. The AppleScript commands must be contained in a designated field on the layout or they can be typed into the Specify AppleScript text box when you add this step to a script.

To use this script step, the AppleScript system software must be installed on your Macintosh. AppleScript is included as a component of the most recent versions of System 7 and OS 8. AppleScript can also be purchased separately.

Options: Specify

When you click the Specify button, the Specify AppleScript dialog box appears. Click the "Field value" radio button (or the Specify Field button to its right) to choose the field that contains the text of the AppleScript to be performed. If the script is not stored in a field, click the "Script text" radio button and enter or paste the AppleScript in the text box.

FileMaker must recompile scripts stored in text fields whenever the script runs. Scripts entered in the text box, on the other hand, are compiled immediately and saved in compiled format. FileMaker always checks for script errors during the compilation process.

Tip

If the AppleScript has already been created elsewhere (as will often be the case), you don't have to retype it in FileMaker Pro. Instead, simply open the script in Apple's Script Editor application, copy it, and then paste it into the appropriate field or the text box in the Specify AppleScript dialog box.

Send Message

Purpose: This step is used to launch another application, open a document in another application, or print a document in another application. You can also create and compile a program and execute that program with the Send Message script step.

Options: Specify

When you click the Specify button, the Specify Message dialog box appears (see Figure 15-21), where you can set the following options:

✦ *Message type*: Choose the type of message you want to send from the drop-down list. The two choices are "open document/application" and "print document."

✦ *File*: You can directly specify the file to open from the Open dialog box. If you choose an application file (for example, Notepad.exe), the application runs. If you choose a document file (for example, Mountain.bmp), the associated application (such as Paint.exe) is run and the document is loaded into the application. If no application is associated with the document type, Windows will require you to specify the application to run before the script step can continue.

✦ *Field value*: You can choose a field that contains the name of the application or document to open, or some other message to send. If the field is a repeating field, you can choose which repetition contains the filename by typing a value in the Repetition text box.

✦ *Text*: You can type the text string that specifies the name of the application or document to open, or some other message to send.

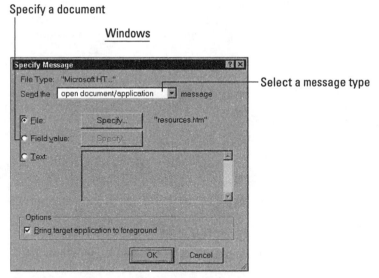

Figure 15-21: The Specify Message dialog box

Click the check box marked "Bring target application to foreground" if you want the application receiving the message to appear in front of FileMaker Pro.

See also: Send DDE Execute.

Comment

Purpose: Use the Comment step to insert nonexecuting comments in your scripts. Comment steps make it easy to explain script logic and assumptions—for your own records and to inform others.

Options: Specify

Click the Specify button to enter the text for the comment. Comments are preceded by a pound sign (#) and are displayed in boldface.

Flush Cache to Disk

Purpose: With this step, you can force the contents of FileMaker Pro's internal cache to be written to disk (rather than waiting for this action to be performed automatically at the designated time).

Options: None

Quit Application

Purpose: This step quits FileMaker Pro and returns the user to the desktop. This is the same as choosing File ➪ Quit or pressing ⌘+Q (Mac) or Ctrl+Q/Alt+F4 (Windows). Any files that are currently open are saved automatically, if necessary.

Options: None

Example: The Quit Application step can be useful as a final command in a cleanup script. If you always print a report from a particular database as the final activity for the day, for example, you could define a script that performs the printing and then ends by quitting FileMaker Pro.

See also: Close.

Attaching a Script to a Button

As mentioned previously, you can attach scripts to buttons. When a button is clicked, the script or script step attached to that button executes instantly—exactly as though you had chosen the script name from the Scripts menu or clicked Perform in the Define Scripts dialog box.

Buttons are frequently added to layouts to make it easy and convenient for users to perform a simple or complex series of commands. By assigning the Go to Layout step to a button, for example, you can quickly navigate to a particular layout, such as a help screen or a report layout. You can also attach a multistep script to a button that executes a find request, performs a sort, prints a report, returns to the data-entry screen, and then restores the database to its state before the button was clicked. For examples of buttons, examine the databases on the *FileMaker Pro 5 Bible* CD-ROM.

Although FileMaker-drawn buttons and graphic icons are frequently used as buttons, you can use any object as a button (including static text strings).

To attach a script step or a script to a button, follow these steps:

1. Switch to Layout mode. (Choose View ➪ Layout Mode, press ⌘+L/Ctrl+L, or choose Layout from the mode pop-up menu at the bottom of the database window.)

2. Select the object that you want to make into a button.

   When selected, an object has a handle (black dot) in each of its corners.

3. Choose Format ➪ Button.

   The Specify Button dialog box appears, as shown in Figure 15-22.

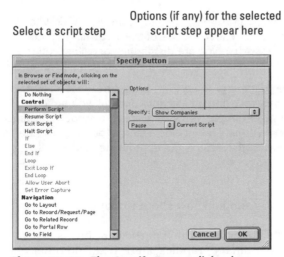

Figure 15-22: The Specify Button dialog box

4. To assign a single script step to the button, select the script step, set any options that appear for that step, and then click OK.

   — or —

   To assign a particular script to the button, select Perform Script, select the script to be executed from the Specify pop-up menu that appears in the Options section of the dialog box, and click OK.

Script-making tips

The following are some useful script-making tips passed on by Max Pruden of FileMaker Technical Support:

✦ The Insert Text step works only if you first specify a target field for the paste by using the Go to Field step.

✦ When you exit a Sort or Find step, you automatically switch to Browse mode, and the first record in the sort order or found set is displayed. Thus, you don't need to include an Enter Browse Mode step or a Go to Record/Request/Page step to go to the first record.

✦ Two types of scripts can be executed by the Perform Script step: internal scripts (scripts in the current file) and external scripts (scripts in other files). When you use Perform Script to execute an external script, you don't need to use the Open step to open the other database.

✦ If you use the Copy step without setting any options, the step copies the contents of all fields in the layout for the current record (which is the same as the Copy Record step).

✦ You can use the Toggle Window [Maximize] step to zoom the window to the full size of the current screen. If you don't know the size of the particular monitor that will be used with the database (as when you are distributing or selling your databases to others), this step can be very useful as part of a start-up (On Opening) script.

✦ A script executes in its own database. To perform procedures that affect two files, such as a Copy from one database and a Paste into another, you need two scripts: one in each database. For this example, you would create a script that copies the contents of a field in the current file and include a step to perform an external script (defined in the other database) that selects the appropriate field and then pastes.

Here are a few more things you should know about working with buttons:

✦ If you're having trouble identifying which particular objects in a layout are buttons (as opposed to ordinary graphics, static text, and other objects), change to Layout mode, and choose View ➪ Show ➪ Buttons. Each button will be surrounded by a gray outline.

✦ When you copy a button in a layout, that button's definition is also copied — that is, any script or script step attached to the button is attached to the copy. If you paste the button into another layout in the same database or a different one, the pasted button will attempt to perform the same function as the original button. You may need to edit the script or script step so the duplicate now refers to the proper layout, field name, and so on.

✦ To delete a button you no longer need, switch to Layout mode, select the button, and then choose Cut or Clear from the Edit menu. Or you can press the Delete/Backspace key.

✦ To remove a script or script step from a button (undefine it), perform steps 1 through 3 in the previous procedure, select Do Nothing, and click OK.

Advanced Scripting Procedures

You can create many perfectly functional scripts by selecting single steps and by combining steps for commands with which you are familiar, such as Go to Layout, Sort, Find, and Print. However, some of the steps, step options, and system software features supported by ScriptMaker can add extraordinary flexibility and power to FileMaker Pro. Although you may not immediately be interested in pursuing these power-scripting features, the following sections discuss them.

Decision-making in scripts

In versions of FileMaker Pro prior to 3.0, the If script step enabled you to perform limited decision-making (that is, "If the conditional test x is true, perform this step. Otherwise, do nothing."). FileMaker Pro 3.0 and higher extend the decision-making capabilities of scripts by adding Else and End If steps. The End If step marks the end of every If structure. When embedded within an If structure, the Else step enables you to select a second alternative in response to a conditional test, as in the following script:

```
If [x]
   Do this if test x is true
Else
   Do this if test x is false
End If
```

Note   Multiple statements can be included in both the true and false sections of an If structure, and Ifs can be nested within other Ifs.

What does this button do?

If you're curious about a script step or script that has been assigned to a button, there's a simple way to determine what the step or script does. Just switch to Layout mode, select the button, and choose the Format ➪ Button command. In the Specify Button dialog box that appears, the step or script that is assigned to the button will be highlighted.

Using loops in scripts

Support for looping enables you to repeat a sequence of commands a set number of times or until a particular condition has been fulfilled. The three Loop commands are Loop, End Loop, and Exit Loop If.

Tip   One interesting use for loops is to step through the records in a database. For example, in a bookkeeping database, I created a layout by scanning an IRS Schedule C. Each line item is represented by a Global field, such as Advertising or Legal Expense. To calculate my year-to-date expenses and income, I use a loop to step though the records in the database – one by one. The income/expense category for each record is examined, and then the total for the appropriate Global field is adjusted by that record's income or expense amount. When the loop is exited (after examining the last record in the database), the Global field amounts are displayed on the Schedule C.

Environment considerations

The Status script steps enable you to determine information about the current state of the database, as well as the environment in which it is being run. Based on the results of the various Status tests, you can use other script steps to change the appearance of the display, branch to appropriate sub-scripts and external scripts (disabling Windows-related steps if the database is being run on a Mac, for example), or display relevant messages. The Status steps are a boon to any developer who intends to offer cross-platform databases.

Executing other scripts from within a script

A FileMaker Pro script can be instructed to perform other scripts, known as sub-scripts. (In programming parlance, sub-scripts are called *subroutines*.) To allow one script to perform another script (or several other scripts, for that matter), you simply set the "Perform sub-scripts" option when choosing the Perform Script step. After running a sub-script, the original (or calling) script continues from where it left off.

Any script that is executed as part of a Perform Script step — whether it is the object of the step or a sub-script — can be an internal or external script. An *internal script* is a script that is defined within the current database. An *external script* is a script in another database. When you run an external script, FileMaker Pro automatically opens the external database and executes the script. When the external script is completed, control returns to the original script and database, just as it does when a sub-script is performed.

To run an external script, follow these steps:

1. When you define the script, choose Perform Script as one of the steps.

2. With the Perform Script step selected in the script, choose "External script" from the Specify pop-up menu.

The Specify External Script dialog box appears, as shown in Figure 15-23.

Select an external script to perform

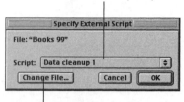

Select an external database file

Figure 15-23: The Specify External Script dialog box

3. Click Change File to select the database that contains the external script you want to execute.

A standard file dialog box appears.

4. Select the database that contains the external script you want to execute, and click Open.

5. Click the Script pop-up menu, and select the script that you want to perform.

6. Click OK to record your choices.

Using Apple Events

The Send Apple Event script step enables you to send messages from FileMaker Pro to itself and other programs. Although not all programs support the required events and "do script" events, most programs should be able to respond to a request to launch or to open a document. This section describes how to perform these simple actions from within a FileMaker Pro database.

To create a program or document launcher by using AppleEvents, follow these steps:

1. Create a new script, choose the Send Apple Event step, and click Specify.

The Specify Apple Events dialog box appears, as shown in Figure 15-24.

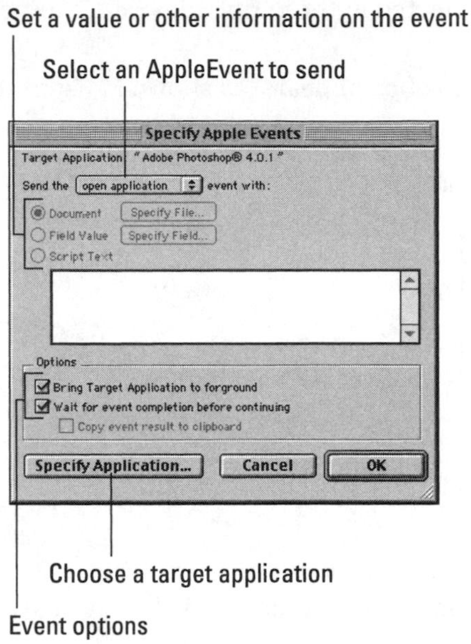

Set a value or other information on the event

Select an AppleEvent to send

Choose a target application

Event options

Figure 15-24: The Specify Apple Events
dialog box

2. From the "Send the" pop-up menu at the top of the dialog box, choose
"open application."

A standard file dialog box appears, in which you select the program that you
want the script to launch.

— or —

From the "Send the" pop-up menu, choose "open document." Click the Specify
File button beside the Document radio button to choose a document.

3. At the bottom of the Specify Apple Event dialog box, set any desired options.

In most cases, you will want to choose "Bring Target Application to
foreground;" otherwise, when the program or document is launched, it may
be hidden behind your FileMaker Pro database window.

4. To save the script step settings, click OK.

To learn more about how FileMaker uses AppleEvents, check out the FileMaker, Inc.
database named Apple Events Reference and the many examples in the FileMaker
and Apple Events folder that is installed as part of FileMaker Pro 5.

Tip   After defining a program- or document-launcher script, you can pretty things up by using a screen-capture utility to capture a picture of the program's or document's icon, paste the icon into your FileMaker Pro layout, and then use the Format⇨ Button command to make the icon into a button that launches the script. If you frequently use several utilities while running FileMaker Pro (such as a calculator, clock, and address book, for instance), you can employ this technique to create a string of buttons. Because these button definitions are not specific to one database, you can copy and paste them into any database. As long as the databases are run on your machine, and you don't change the locations of the programs or documents to be launched, the buttons should work fine.

Using QuicKeys with FileMaker Pro scripts

QuicKeys is a general-purpose macro utility that enables you to automate complex functions in most Macintosh programs, desk accessories, the Finder, and so on. QuicKeys 2 and higher can work in conjunction with Apple Events. Because FileMaker Pro 5 has a Send Apple Event script step, you can use a script to invoke QuicKeys and execute any macro that you have defined.

To use a script to launch QuicKeys and execute a macro, follow these steps:

1. Select the Send Apple Event script step and click Specify.

   The Specify Apple Events dialog box appears (as previously shown in Figure 15-24).

2. Choose the Other... event from the pop-up menu at the top of the dialog box.

   The Specify Event dialog box appears.

3. For Event Class and Event ID, enter the following: **QKy2** and **QPNm**. Click OK.

   Be sure that the capitalization is correct — it must match exactly!

4. If you have QuicKeys 2, click the Specify Application button, and then choose CEIAC in the Extensions folder of your System Folder.

   — or —

   If you have QuicKeys 3, click the Specify Application button and then choose the QuicKeys Toolbox in the Extensions folder of your System Folder.

5. Click the "Script text" radio button, and then type the name of the QuicKeys macro you want to run.

6. Click OK to finish the step definition.

For example, you could create an AppleEvent script that runs a QuicKeys macro called AOL Flash, a multistep macro that runs an America Online flash session. (The macro could connect with AOL, send pending messages, retrieve incoming mail, and then log off.) Because QuicKeys can automate almost any program function, you could also use it to create FileMaker Pro-specific macros — ones that perform a series of field-formatting operations, for example — and then use a Send Apple Event step to activate each macro.

Using AppleScript

Available as part of recent versions of System 7 and Mac OS8 , AppleScript is an English-based programming language you can use to integrate Macintosh programs and customize the way your Mac works. Unlike using the scripting feature in FileMaker Pro, using AppleScript really is programming.

To execute an AppleScript from within FileMaker Pro, follow these steps:

1. In ScriptMaker's Define Scripts dialog box, specify whether you are creating a new script or editing an existing one. (To create a new script, enter a new name in the Script Name box and click Create. To edit an existing script, select its name in the list box and click Edit.)

2. In the Script Definition dialog box, select the Perform AppleScript step.

3. Click the Specify button.

   The Specify AppleScript dialog box appears.

4. Click "Field value."

   The commands in the specified field are compiled each time FileMaker Pro runs the script.

   — or —

   Click "Script text," and then type or paste the AppleScript commands into the text box.

   The commands are compiled and then stored as part of the database.

5. Finish defining the script, and then click OK.

Summary

✦ FileMaker Pro provides a built-in script-creation utility called ScriptMaker. Using ScriptMaker, you can automate almost any FileMaker Pro function that you usually execute manually by selecting commands from menus. Once defined, a script can be added to the Scripts menu and/or attached to a button in any layout, making it simple to execute the script any time you like.

✦ Rather than type scripts in a word processing program or text editor, you design scripts in FileMaker Pro by choosing script steps from a list. Step options are set by clicking buttons and check boxes.

✦ You can create many scripts simply by executing sort instructions, find requests, and similar commands and then telling FileMaker Pro that you want to use the same procedures in a script. When you perform these important steps just before creating the script, FileMaker Pro includes them for you as part of the default script.

✦ FileMaker Pro 5 provides over 100 script steps that you can use individually or in combination with other steps to form a script.

✦ Scripts can now be imported from other FileMaker databases.

✦ You can attach scripts to buttons or icons that you include in a layout. When you click a button, the script or script step attached to that button executes instantly — as though you had chosen the script name from the Scripts menu or clicked Perform in the Define Scripts dialog box.

✦ ✦ ✦

Exchanging Data Between Applications

As nice as it would be, you probably won't spend your computing life happily curled up inside FileMaker Pro. Most likely, you work with many applications, and perhaps you even stored your database information in some other program before you became a FileMaker Pro user. Wouldn't it be great to be able to move all that data into FileMaker Pro? For example, you may want to transfer your address and phone number data directly to FileMaker. Similarly, you may want to move data from a FileMaker Pro Invoices database to a spreadsheet program so you can see how you're doing and make predictions.

There are many reasons why you may want to move data around. The good news is that you can do so without much trouble, as this chapter explains.

Moving Data Between Programs

FileMaker Pro can work with data produced by many other programs. If a program can save or export its data in one of several common formats (such as tab-delimited text), FileMaker Pro can read and use the data. This data exchange is a two-way street: FileMaker can produce data files that other applications can use, and it can take data from other applications for use in a FileMaker Pro database. The former process is called *exporting*; the latter is called *importing*.

About importing and exporting

When you import data into FileMaker Pro, you bring that data in from another program, such as dBASE. FileMaker Pro can import data from many popular Mac and PC programs, such as dBASE, ClarisWorks (now called AppleWorks), and Microsoft Excel. And you can import data from another FileMaker Pro database — even one created on a different type of computer.

You can import data into FileMaker Pro in three ways:

✦ You can open a non-FileMaker file using the File ➪ Open command, automatically converting it *en masse* to a new FileMaker Pro database.

✦ If you already have a FileMaker Pro database, you can use the File ➪ Import Records command to import records from another FileMaker Pro database or from a file created in a different program.

✦ You can take advantage of FileMaker's ODBC support to import data from any ODBC-compliant application, such as Microsoft Access, into an existing FileMaker Pro database.

Note

When you import records, you can choose to append the new records to your existing file, use the new data to replace existing records, or update only the changed records. (The latter capability is a new feature of FileMaker Pro 5.) When you import, FileMaker Pro copies data but does not copy layouts or field definitions. In addition, you cannot import data into Calculation or Summary fields.

You can also make information from a FileMaker Pro database available for use in other applications. You might export the current found set of records to a spreadsheet program for further analysis, for example.

Another common use of exporting is to prepare for a mail merge in a word-processing program. In FileMaker Pro 3.0 and higher, however, you can perform a mail merge completely within FileMaker. See Chapter 6 for details.

FileMaker Pro cannot export to remote sources, nor can it export data directly into another FileMaker Pro file. Instead of exporting directly into the target application file, you simply export the data to a temporary file and then import it using the target application's procedures to import data. The net effect is the same.

FileMaker Pro 5 and ODBC

ODBC is an API (*application programming interface*) that enables disparate database applications to access and use each other's data. Typical ODBC-compliant applications for which this method would be used include Microsoft Access and Oracle.

Beginning in FileMaker Pro 4.1, you could construct SQL (*Structured Query Language*) statements to import data from ODBC-compliant applications into FileMaker Pro databases. In FileMaker Pro 5, you can also use these procedures to import data from FileMaker Pro databases into other ODBC-compliant applications. This is made possible by the following FileMaker Pro components:

✦ *FileMaker Pro ODBC driver.* All SQL queries and data are routed through the ODBC driver.

✦ *Local Data Access Companion.* Enables data to be shared between applications on the same computer (via ODBC).

✦ *Remote Data Access Companion.* Enables data to be shared between applications on different computers across a TCP/IP network (via ODBC).

Learning to query databases is a subject that is beyond the scope of this book. Much like learning to program a computer, if you aren't already working with ODBC databases, it's unlikely that you'll be doing so in the near future—and certainly not after reading a few pages in a manual or a book. If this indeed is something you wish to pursue, you should begin by reading about ODBC in FileMaker's manual and then consult with your database administrator. For other data importing and exporting requirements (as explained in this chapter), you'll find that FileMaker's regular tools will easily meet your needs.

Understanding file formats

Although FileMaker Pro can work with data from many different applications, its capability is limited by the ways in which these applications store their data. The way that data is stored in an application is called the application's *file format*.

A file format specifies how an application's data is organized and interpreted. You can think of a file format as being a recipe for creating the finished file from its raw data (from the text that you type, for example). The instructions for interpreting a file format must be stored within the program in which you want to use the data; otherwise, very strange and unsatisfactory results may occur.

FileMaker Pro supports the file formats discussed in the following sections. Note that some formats are for importing data only and others are solely for exporting data.

Tab-separated text

This format is sometimes called ASCII (pronounced "askee"), but a few differences exist between tab-separated text and ASCII text. ASCII (which stands for American Standard Code for Information Interchange) refers to plain, unformatted text arranged according to an industry-standard coding scheme. In tab-separated text, Tab characters separate fields in a record, and Return characters separate records. Virtually all computer applications can interpret files that are in this format.

Comma-separated text

This format is used for BASIC programming and in some applications. Commas separate field values, and Return characters separate records. All field values except unformatted numbers are surrounded by quotation marks. Many Windows applications use this format, referred to as *CSV*, as a standard interchange format.

SYLK

SYLK stands for symbolic link format, a spreadsheet format in which data is stored in rows and columns. Each field is a column, and each record is a row. Returns are output as spaces, and dates and times are output as text within quotation marks. Non-numeric data in a number field is suppressed, and fields are limited to a maximum of 245 characters.

DIF

DIF (Data Interchange Format) is another spreadsheet format, used by older applications such as VisiCalc and the original AppleWorks (the program for the old Apple II computer). Each field is a column, and each record is a row.

WKS

WKS (Worksheet format) is a spreadsheet format used by Lotus 1-2-3. Each field is a column, and each record is a row.

BASIC

This format is similar to comma-separated text but is designed for use with Microsoft's standard BASIC language.

Merge

Merge is an export format that you use to create special documents for the data portion of mail merges. Commas separate field values, return characters separate records, and the ASCII character 29 separates repeating fields. In this format, the first record is called the header. The header lists the field names contained in the file. Quotation marks surround field data.

ClarisWorks 2–4

FileMaker Pro 5 can import databases created in ClarisWorks 2.0–4.0. When you use the Open command to open a ClarisWorks database in FileMaker Pro, the database is converted to FileMaker format and saved on disk in the location you specify. For more information about importing ClarisWorks databases, see "Opening a foreign data file to create a new database," later in this chapter.

Note   FileMaker Pro 5 cannot import ClarisWorks 5 data (also known as ClarisWorks Office and AppleWorks). Until an import filter is created for this product, you should export the data to a file format that FileMaker Pro 5 supports and then perform the import procedure. You can also use ClarisWorks'/AppleWorks' Save As command and choose ClarisWorks 4 as the file format.

DBF

DBF is the dBASE III (also known as xBASE) database format. Field names can be no more than ten characters long, with a maximum of 254 characters per field and 128 fields per record.

Microsoft Excel

This import-only format enables you to import Microsoft Excel worksheets into FileMaker Pro databases. Mac worksheets created with Excel 5–8, as well as Microsoft Office 98, can be imported. In Windows, Excel 4–8 are supported, as well as Office 97 and 2000.

HTML table

This export-only format is used to translate a FileMaker Pro database into a table that can be published as a page on the World Wide Web. Field names become column headings. Each record is a row in the table; each field is a column. After creating an HTML table, you can open the resulting text file in any text editor or word-processing program, copy it, and paste it into the source code for your Web page (see Figures 16-1a and 16-1b).

Tip   Field names are not always appropriate as column heads. Instead of *Qty*, you may prefer *Quantity*, for example. You can change any of the field names by editing the HTML lines that begin with <TH>, as shown in Figure 16-1a.

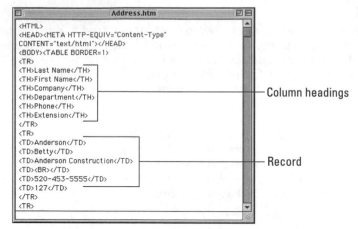

Figure 16-1a: Code produced when exporting to an HTML table

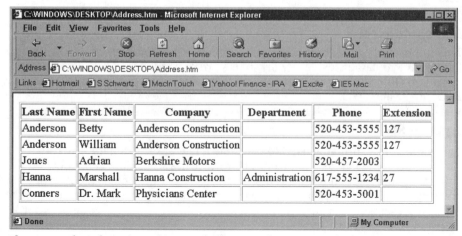

Figure 16-1b: When viewed in a Web browser, the HTML code produces this table.

Edition file

This format, for use with the Macintosh Edition Manager (Publish & Subscribe), is an export-only format similar to tab-separated text. When you export data to this format, you create an Edition file to which other users and programs can subscribe. Exporting in Edition file format is the same as publishing a record in other programs.

FileMaker Pro

FileMaker Pro 5 can import data from any FileMaker Pro database between versions 2 and 5. Exported FileMaker Pro 5 data can be read by FileMaker Pro 5 only.

Importing Data from Other Sources

You have several options when you import data from another source. For example, you can combine information stored in several places into one master file (which might contain only selected fields from several similar files). You can also change the order in which records are stored. Although FileMaker Pro normally stores records in the order in which they are entered, it copies records in their sorted order when they are imported. If you import data that includes repeating fields, you can split the latter values into separate records.

Format selection

When importing data, FileMaker Pro makes it easy to determine whether the import file is in an appropriate format. By default, the Import file dialog box lists only the file types that FileMaker Pro understands (based in part on the files that were copied into the FileMaker Extensions folder as part of FileMaker Pro's installation procedure). If the file that you want to import does not appear in the Open File dialog box's list of files, you may need to check the relevant application's documentation to determine what file format it uses. If FileMaker Pro doesn't support the native file format of your source application, you'll need to use the application to output a new data file in a format that FileMaker Pro can use. Many applications can output tab- or comma-separated text, for example.

FileMaker Pro can import the following types of files:

✦ FileMaker Pro

✦ Tab-separated text

✦ Comma-separated text

✦ SYLK

✦ DIF

✦ WKS

✦ BASIC

✦ Merge

✦ ClarisWorks 2.0–4

✦ DBF

✦ Excel

✦ ODBC

Data clean-up (prior to importing)

Data that you want to import may not be in tip-top shape. You may find, for example, that the match between fields in your source and target files isn't as clean as you had hoped, or that you don't have access to a supported file format. The procedures outlined in the following sections show you how to solve some of these problems.

Cleaning up data in a spreadsheet

If you had your computer for a while before you bought FileMaker Pro, you probably also had one or more address or contacts files that you created in other programs — address data recorded in a desk accessory, utility program, or e-mail program, for example. Rather than keep this information spread across a handful of programs and desk accessories, it's usually preferable to put all the data into one database, program, or desk accessory. Unfortunately, most of us don't plan for (or count on) the difficulties encountered when trying to create one composite file from two or more separate address files. In particular, the various files are likely to contain different fields. This section discusses some simple procedures you can use to clean up your disparate data before importing it into, or exporting it from, FileMaker Pro.

Following are two of the most common problems in importing address data:

✦ Address, phone number, and name fields in the file you want to import are split into two fields (address line 1 and address line 2, area code and phone number, and first name and last name), but the FileMaker Pro database contains only one field for the corresponding items, or vice versa.

✦ When exported, some Zip codes may lose their leading zero (for example, 1276 rather than 01276).

Rather than import the data as it is and clean it up in the database afterward, using a spreadsheet application (such as the one included in ClarisWorks/AppleWorks) to make the necessary transformations to the data is more efficient. To do this, follow these general steps:

1. Export the data from your database or address book program as a tab-delimited ASCII text file.

2. Open the text file in a spreadsheet program, make the transformations to the data (creating new fields as necessary), and save the revised file as a text file.

3. Open the FileMaker Pro database into which you intend to import the data.

4. Use the Import Records command to import the tab-separated text file into the database.

The simplest way to make the transformations in the spreadsheet is to create additional columns on the right-hand side of the spreadsheet. The following text explains how to accomplish this task within the AppleWorks spreadsheet environment. The procedure will be similar in other spreadsheet applications, such as Microsoft Excel.

To make it easy for you to use the formulas discussed in this section, copies of the worksheets in both ClarisWorks/AppleWorks and Excel formats can be found in the FileMaker Pro Bible folder of the CD-ROM.

Each new column must contain a formula that combines or converts one or more columns of the original data. Create the appropriate formula and then use the Fill Down command (⌘+D) to copy the formula into the remaining cells in the column.

The simple spreadsheet shown in Figure 16-2 illustrates the formula needed to convert First Name and Last Name fields into a single Name field. Column A contains first names, column B contains last names, and column C contains the combined first and last names. The formula shown in the entry bar (=A2 & " "& B2) takes the first name in cell A2 (Jody), adds a space (" "), and then adds the last name from cell B2 (Privette) to the end of the text string. As mentioned previously, you use the Fill Down command to copy the formula to all the rest of the cells in column C.

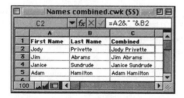

Figure 16-2: A formula to combine first and last names into a single name

Extracting first and last names from a Name field is more complex, but — with a little spreadsheet wizardry — it, too, can be accomplished. Figure 16-3 shows a spreadsheet in which Column A contains a list of names, each having a single first and last name. To extract the first name Steve from the combined name Steve Schwartz in cell A2, you use this formula in cell B2:

```
=LEFT(A2,FIND(" ",A2,0)-1)
```

Figure 16-3: Extracting the first and last name from a Name field

The Find function searches for the first occurrence of a space in the name in cell A2, and then subtracts one from the character position where the space was found. For "Steve Schwartz," the Find returns a result of 5, which is then decremented to 4. The Left function operates on this result, extracting the first four characters from the name in cell A2 — or **Steve**, in this case. (We could extract all five characters, but that would include the trailing space.)

To extract the last name, this complex formula is entered in cell C2:

```
=RIGHT(A2,LEN(A2)-FIND(" ",A2,0))
```

The Len function returns the length of the text string in cell A2; for the name "Steve Schwartz," it returns a result of 14. The result of the same Find function used previously (searching for the first space in the name in cell A2) is subtracted from the Len result — in this case, 14 – 6 for a result of 8. The Right function then extracts the eight right-most characters from the name in cell A2 — **Schwartz**, in this case. To complete the spreadsheet, all you need to do is select the formulas in cells B2 and C2, highlight the blank cells beneath them, and choose Fill Down.

Suppose you have a database or other address file in which address information is split into two lines or fields, and you want to import that data into a file in which Address is only a single line or field. However, some addresses in the original file have only one line, while others in the file have two. In Figure 16-4, the equation =IF (B2 <> "", A2 & ", " & B2, A2) checks to see whether the address has a second line (B2 <> ""). If the address has a second line, the formula combines the two portions, separating them with a comma followed by a blank, as in:

```
251 Rock Road, P.O. Box 116
```

If the address has no second line, the formula simply copies the first address part (A2) into the cell.

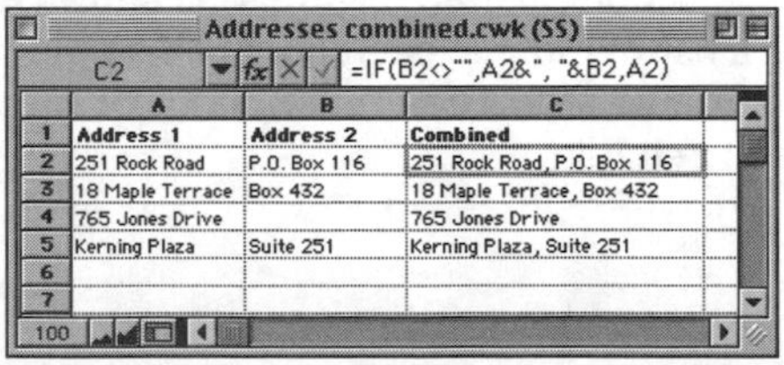

Figure 16-4: A formula to combine two-line addresses into a single address line

Because Zip codes are often treated as numbers, the leading zero may disappear when the data is exported, resulting in an improper four-digit code. The lengthy formula =IF(LEN(A2) = 4,"0"&A2, NUMTOTEXT(A2)) shown in Figure 16-5 checks to see whether the Zip code is four digits long (LEN(A2)=4). If the Zip code contains four digits, a leading zero is appended to the Zip code ("0"&A2), which is then converted to text. If the Zip code does not contain four digits, the Zip code is converted to text and passed through unaltered (NUMTOTEXT(A2)).

Converting Zip codes to text is necessary to display leading zeros and to handle blank Zip code fields. If the formula ended simply with A2 rather than NUMTOTEXT(A2), a blank Zip code would translate as **0** (zero).

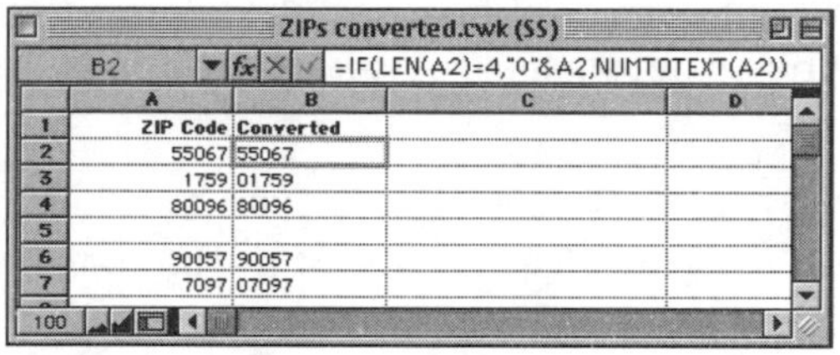

Figure 16-5: A formula to check the length of the Zip code

Converting return-delimited text

Another clean-up problem you may encounter is data that has been exported in return-delimited format. In this format, Return characters separate fields, and records are separated by two Returns. You can convert this format to tab-delimited format if you have access to a word-processing program that can search for and replace hidden characters, such as the ASCII Return and Tab characters. Microsoft Word and ClarisWorks can perform this task, as can other applications.

To convert return-delimited text, follow these steps:

1. Open the return-delimited file in your word-processing program.

2. Choose the application's Find/Change command.

   In Microsoft Word, for example, you would choose Replace from the Edit menu.

3. Perform the following change operations:

   • Find all occurrences of two returns (^p^p in Word, for example) and change these characters to something else, such as XXXX.

   • Find all occurrences of a single return (^p in Word) and change these characters to tabs (^t in Word, for example).

   • Find all occurrences of XXXX and change these characters to single returns.

4. Save the result as a text file.

The file is now in tab-delimited format.

Importing records

When your data is cleaned up (if clean-up was needed), you're ready to import. To add new records to a FileMaker Pro database or to replace the current found set with imported records, follow these steps:

1. Open the destination database file in FileMaker Pro and switch to Browse mode.

2. *Optional*: If you intend to *replace* records in the current database with imported records, you can use Find procedures to select the records to be replaced. (This assumes that you do not wish to replace *all* records in the database.)

3. Choose File ➪ Import Records.

The Open File dialog box shown in Figure 16-6 appears. At the bottom of the dialog box is a Show/Files of type pop-up menu where you can select the format of the file that you want to import.

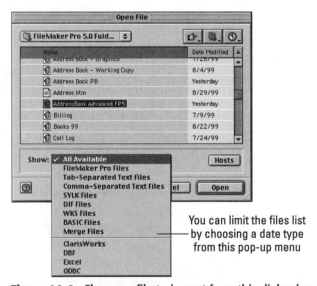

Figure 16-6: Choose a file to import from this dialog box.

4. *Optional*: To limit the listed files to only those of a particular type, choose the appropriate file format from the Show/Files of type pop-up menu.

The default option in the pop-up menu is All Available. This tells FileMaker to list in the file dialog box every file that it can read. In most cases, this is fine. However, if you're having a hard time finding the particular file you want to import, you can choose its specific type from the Show/Files of type pop-up menu.

5. Select the name of the file you want to import.

6. Click Open. (If the chosen database is password protected, you will be asked to enter a password.)

The Import Field Mapping dialog box appears (see Figure 16-7). The purpose of this dialog box is to match fields in the source file with those in the destination file, as well as to pick the fields you want to import and the ones you want to ignore.

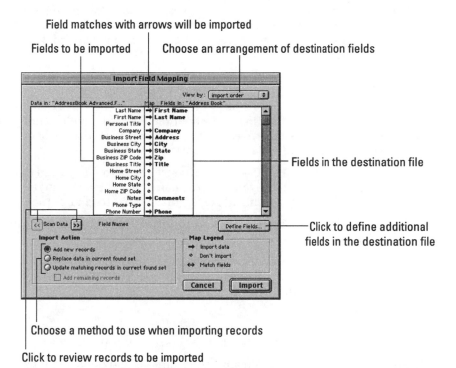

Figure 16-7: The Import Field Mapping dialog box

7. *Optional*: To import fields for which there are currently no matching fields, click Define Fields.

   The Define Fields dialog box appears, enabling you to create the additional fields in the current database. See Chapter 5 for details.

8. Click the appropriate radio button to specify whether you want to add new records or replace data in the current found set.

New Feature

Notice that there is now a third radio button labeled "Update matching records in current found set." This new import option allows you to synchronize two databases and is described in the next set of steps.

The "Add new records" option simply appends the imported records to the destination file, while the "Replace data in current found set" option overwrites the records in the current found set. If you intend to use the latter option, you should first make a backup copy of the destination file.

Caution

The Import command cannot be undone, so a mistake can have serious consequences for your data. Note, too, that if the destination file has fewer records in it than the imported file, the leftover records will not be imported if you use the Replace option.

9. Match the fields that you want to import.

   An arrow following a field name in the Map column indicates that the field will be imported into the field in the destination file. If you don't want to import a particular field, click its arrow. The indicator changes to a slashed circle (()), showing that the field will not be imported.

   Because fields in the two files can be in any order, you may need to rearrange them manually so that they match. You can drag field names in the destination file (on the right side of the dialog box) to change their order.

10. *Optional*: Click the Scan Data buttons to review the matching fields in several records.

    This is mainly a sanity check. By scanning several records, you can assure yourself that the fields do indeed match properly and that you have not omitted an important field.

11. Click Import.

    The Import Options dialog box appears (see Figure 16-8).

12. Specify the manner in which auto-enter options and imported repeating fields should be handled, and click OK.

Note When importing data, there are some restrictions you should understand. First, you cannot import data into Calculation, Summary, Global, or related fields. To import data into related fields, open the database in which they are stored and then perform the import. Second, you can only import data into Container fields if you're importing from a FileMaker Pro database.

Perform auto-enter options when importing records

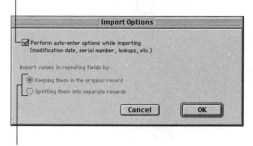

Specify how data in imported repeating fields is handled

Figure 16-8: The Import Options dialog box

As was seen in Figure 16-7, FileMaker Pro 5 has a new import option. You can update changed records, merging two databases. This option enables you to synchronize two copies of a database. For example, you might have a master copy of a Contacts database on your desktop computer (or on a network) and periodically need to update it with changes you made to a copy on your laptop. Follow these steps to update a database:

1. Perform steps 1 through 7 from the previously described import procedure.

2. In the Import Action area of the Import Field Mapping dialog box, click the radio button to "Update matching records in the found set."

3. *Optional*: Click the "Add remaining records" check box. All records for which no match is found will be added as new records in the destination database.

4. In the Map column of the Import Field Mapping dialog box (see Figure 16-9), click to select match fields.

   Match fields are used by FileMaker Pro to determine which records from the two databases are matches and, hence, should be updated during the import procedure. You can specify one or several match fields. (Match fields should be unique, such as a Social Security number or client ID.) A double-headed arrow designates a match field.

Match fields

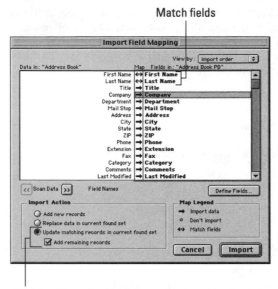

Update changed records

Figure 16-9: Specifying match fields

5. *Optional*: Click the Scan Data buttons to review the matching fields in several records.

6. Click Import.

   The Import Options dialog box appears (refer to Figure 16-8).

7. Specify the manner in which auto-enter options and imported repeating fields should be handled, and click OK.

   FileMaker examines the two databases and determines which pairs of records are matches, based on the match fields chosen in step 4. All fields that you have marked for importing overwrite the fields in the destination database.

Opening a foreign data file to create a new database

If you want to change an existing file from some other program directly into a new FileMaker database, you can do so without first creating the database fields and layouts in FileMaker Pro. That is, you don't need to have a FileMaker Pro database to receive the new data — one can be created for you automatically.

To create a new database from a file in another program, follow these steps:

1. Choose the File ⇨ Open command.

   A standard file dialog box appears.

Changing the field order when importing data

In the upper-right corner of the Import Field Mapping dialog box is a View By pop-up menu that you can use to make it easier to match fields between the two databases. The option that you choose from this menu determines the order of display for the fields in the current database (on the right side of the dialog box). The Matching Names option is particularly useful for quickly selecting all matching field names in the two files. Note, however, that this option is only available when the import file contains a header record that lists the file's field names.

2. From the Show/Files of type pop-up menu, choose All Available or the specific type of file you want to open.

The list of file types is identical to the list displayed when you import data using the Import Records command.

3. Select the file and click Open.

A new file dialog box appears in which you are asked to save the converted file, as shown in Figure 16-10.

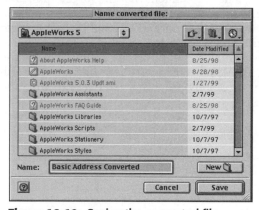

Figure 16-10: Saving the converted file

4. Accept the proposed name for the converted file or type a new name in the Name text box. Click Save.

The new database is converted to FileMaker Pro format and then opens in a new window. Fields are presented in the default vertical format and are named using the convention f1, f2, f3, and so on. You can now clean up the database by using the Define Fields command to rename and define additional fields, and change the layout as necessary by switching to Layout mode.

Tip

Opening a ClarisWorks 2–4 database presents you with several bonuses. Field names and definitions carry over into the new FileMaker Pro database. Also, if you have defined multiple layouts in the ClarisWorks database, you'll find that they now exist in the FileMaker Pro database as well.

Other file types in which the field names carry over to FileMaker include Excel, DIF, DBF (dBASE/xBASE), and Merge files. FileMaker Pro 5 correctly translates field types when opening the following file types: Excel, ClarisWorks, and DBF (dBASE/xBASE). When importing a dBASE/xBASE database, two FileMaker Pro layouts are automatically created: a standard layout and a columnar layout in Table View.

Exporting Data

When you export records from FileMaker Pro, you change FileMaker Pro data to a format that another program can use. The process is virtually the same as importing, except it operates in reverse.

Format selection

When you export records, you don't save directly into a document in another application — you simply create a new document that the target application can open. As you do when importing records, you need to determine the file format of the destination program before you export data to be used by that program. You may need to check the relevant application's documentation to determine what file formats it can use. If FileMaker Pro doesn't support the application's standard file format, you'll have to instruct FileMaker to export a new data file in a format that the destination application can use. Many programs can read tab- or comma-separated text files, for example.

FileMaker Pro supports the following formats for export purposes:

✦ FileMaker Pro

✦ Tab-separated text

✦ Comma-separated text

✦ SYLK

✦ DBF

✦ DIF

✦ WKS

✦ BASIC

✦ Merge

✦ HTML table

✦ Edition File (Macintosh only)

Data clean-up

As you do when you import, you may need to clean up your data — either before exporting it or prior to opening it in the destination program. In particular, you may find unnecessary returns and spaces at the end of some records. These unneeded characters are usually the result of careless data entry and can cause trouble in your target file when you export data to it.

As a solution, you can define a new Calculation field for each field to be exported. The definition of this field is a procedure that strips spaces and returns. Use the following definition:

```
If(Position(FieldName,"¶",1,1), Trim (Left(FieldName,
Position(FieldName,"¶",1,1)-1)),Trim(FieldName))
```

Replace "FieldName" with the name of the field that you want to strip. (To insert the ¶ symbol into the formula, click its button to the left of the Operators list in the Specify Calculation dialog box.) You must define a separate Calculation field for each potential source field. Then export the Calculation fields rather than the originals.

Caution If you use this formula on a field that contains intentional returns (for example, in a Comments field that contains several paragraphs), the formula truncates the field contents at the end of the first paragraph — effectively deleting all paragraphs that follow.

Exporting records

With data clean-up behind you (in the event that clean-up was necessary), you are ready to export the data. Follow these steps to export FileMaker Pro data for use in another application:

1. Open your source FileMaker Pro database.

2. Use Find mode to locate the set of records to export.

   An export always consists only of records in the current found set. You can also use the Sort command to sort these records, if you want.

3. In Browse mode, choose File ➪ Export Records.

   A standard file dialog box appears, similar in appearance to the dialog box previously shown in Figure 16-6.

4. Type a name for the destination file.

5. Choose a file format for the destination file from the Type/Save as type pop-up menu.

6. Click Save.

   The Specify Field Order for Export dialog box appears, as shown in Figure 16-11.

Click the pop-up menu to export fields from a related file

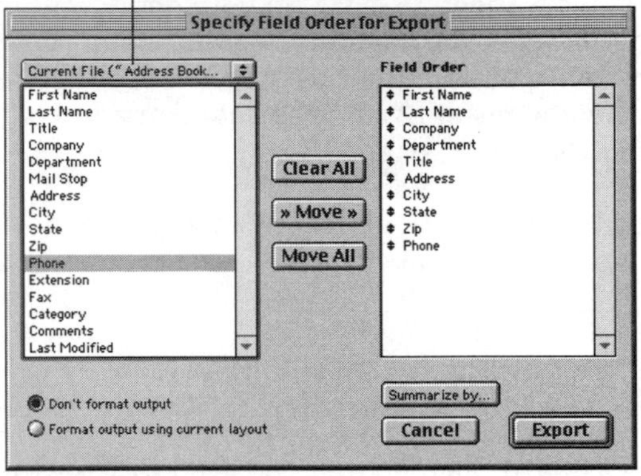

Figure 16-11: The Specify Field Order for Export dialog box

7. In the left side of the dialog box, select the fields that you want to export.

As each field is selected, click the Move button to transfer it to the Field Order section of the dialog box.

8. Drag field names up or down to change the export order, if necessary.

Click to select the name of the field you want to move and then drag it to a new position in the Field Order list. In most cases, you will want the order of the fields to match the order in which they appear in the destination file (assuming the destination file already exists).

9. Click the appropriate radio button to specify whether you want to format the output.

Click the "Don't format output" radio button if you want the export file to contain unformatted text. Click "Format output using current layout" if you want the data to be formatted to match the number, date, and time formats you have assigned to the fields in the current layout.

10. Click Export.

The target data file is created in the chosen format.

Note   If you have defined one or more relationships for the current database, you can also export fields from any of the related files. To view the field names in any related file, just choose the name of the relationship from the pop-up menu at the top of the dialog box. In the export field list, fields from the current file and from related files can be mixed.

It's also possible to export summary data from a FileMaker Pro database. Follow these steps:

1. Open your source FileMaker Pro document.

2. Repeat steps 2 through 6 described previously in the export procedure.

3. Sort the file on the break field that groups the records (that is, the "sub-summary when sorted by" field).

4. In the Specify Field Order for Export dialog box, click the Summarize by button.

   The Summarize by dialog box shown in Figure 16-12 appears, listing the fields by which you can summarize the data.

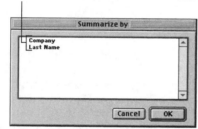

Figure 16-12: The Summarize by dialog box

5. Choose one or more of the listed sort fields and then click OK.

6. Click Export.

Moving Data Using Drag-and-Drop

FileMaker Pro 5 can import and export selected text strings using a system function called *drag-and-drop*. With drag-and-drop enabled, you can copy data by selecting and then dragging it from one field to another, from one database to another, or from a database to any other drag-and-drop–enabled application — such as a spreadsheet or word-processing program — or vice versa.

To enable drag-and-drop in FileMaker Pro, choose Edit ➪ Preferences ➪ Application. Click the General tab at the top of the Application Preferences dialog box, and then click the check box for "Enable drag and drop text selection," as shown in Figure 16-13.

Enable/disable drag-and-drop

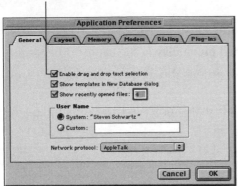

Figure 16-13: Drag-and-drop is enabled or disabled in the Application Preferences dialog box.

You can also use drag-and-drop to convert foreign data files into FileMaker Pro databases. For example, if you drag the file icon for a Microsoft Excel worksheet onto the FileMaker Pro 5 icon, FileMaker launches (if it isn't already running) and immediately initiates the procedure to convert the worksheet into a database. The First Row Option dialog box appears (see Figure 16-14). If the worksheet contains column labels in its first row, you can instruct FileMaker to use them as field labels in the new database (rather than using the default f1, f2, f3 . . . field-naming system).

The first worksheet row contains labels (field anmes)

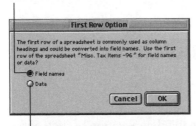

The first row contains data

Figure 16-14: When converting an Excel worksheet to a FileMaker Pro database, the labels in the first row can be treated as field names.

Note   The First Row Option dialog box appears whether you are converting a worksheet via drag-and-drop or simply opening it directly in FileMaker Pro.

Exchanging Data with PCs

Because FileMaker Pro 5 also runs under Microsoft Windows 95, 98, and NT, you can move data to and from PCs as well. Keep two things in mind when you exchange data with a PC. First, you actually have to get the data from your Mac to a PC, and vice versa. Second, you need to understand the differences between the Macintosh and PC versions of FileMaker Pro. The following sections explain both of these concepts.

Moving data to and from FileMaker Pro for Windows

You can share files between a Mac and a PC in three ways. You can use a network (which provides direct access to files), you can use the time-honored "sneaker net" (moving files physically — on floppy disks or another removable medium — between machines), and you can transfer files electronically (using a modem or the serial ports on both computers). Here's how the three methods work:

✦ *Network*: Setting up a mixed network of Macs and PCs is a task for the experts. You can use AppleShare to make the task easier. For AppleShare, you need something like Farallon's PhoneNet Talk software, with a PhoneNet or Ethernet card for each PC. You can place the FileMaker Pro database files on an AppleShare server, on a host Mac, or on a host PC. FileMaker Pro 5 also supports IPX/SPX and TCP/IP networking for multi-user file sharing. (See Chapter 20 for more information about using FileMaker Pro on a network.)

✦ *Floppy disk*: You need a Macintosh with an Apple SuperDrive floppy drive. (All Macs sold since the late 1980s have these high-density, 1.44MB floppy drives.) Use PC-formatted floppies to exchange databases between the two types of computers. (A Mac can read PC floppies, but a PC can't read Mac floppies unless it's outfitted with special software.)

When moving a FileMaker Pro database from a PC to the Mac, you can use the Mac's PC Exchange extension to transfer a readable copy of the database to your Mac's hard disk. When moving files from a Mac to the PC, you can use the same utilities to enable you to transfer a copy of your Mac databases to a PC-formatted floppy disk. (Remember to add a .fp5 extension to the end of the filename, so Windows can identify it as a FileMaker Pro 5 database.) Then simply take the disk over to the PC and load the database into FileMaker Pro for Windows.

✦ *Serial communications*: You can transfer files by using a modem and the appropriate communications software. Alternatively, you can transfer files directly between the serial ports of the two machines by using a program such as MacLinkPlusPC (DataViz).

Tip   Microsoft Internet Explorer (Mac and PC) and Mac OS 8 include software that can turn your computer into a personal Web server. You can use this software to make files on your hard disk available over the Internet or a local Intranet. Similarly, by creating and posting ordinary Web pages with file links, you can use the Internet or an Intranet as a repository for files that you wish to make available to others — regardless of their computer platform.

After you have transferred the files, both the Mac and PC versions of FileMaker Pro can work with the databases without any further ado — importing and exporting are unnecessary. You may, however, run into some problems caused by the differences between Macs and PCs, as well as minor differences between the two versions of FileMaker Pro (as explained in the following section).

Note   When running on a mixed PC/Mac network, it isn't necessary for each user to have a separate copy of a FileMaker database. Any FileMaker Pro user can host a database on the network, making it available to other network users.

Understanding the compatibility issues

In general, you should watch out for eight potential problem areas when you move a Macintosh FileMaker Pro document to Microsoft Windows (or vice versa):

✦ Character sets

✦ Fonts

✦ Filenames

✦ Colors

✦ Graphics formats

✦ Printing

✦ OLE support

✦ Platform-specific capabilities

Character sets

Characters with ASCII values 0 through 127 (low ASCII) are the same in both systems. Characters with ASCII values greater than 127 (high or extended ASCII) may be different, depending on the Windows font you're using. Some Macintosh high-ASCII characters such as the bullet character (Option+8) — do not translate properly in Windows. Thus, if you enter text with special characters (the *é* characters in *résumé*, for example) on your Mac, you may get unexpected results that require cleaning up on the PC.

Fonts

TrueType and Adobe fonts are available for both systems. However, you should use the same technology on both computer systems, if you can. Otherwise, you're likely to encounter text-alignment problems in your layouts. You may find, for example, that the comparable font on the other platform is too large, causing text to spill into adjacent areas in your otherwise attractive layout. As a result, it may be necessary to tweak the layout when moving a database between platforms.

The Macintosh version of FileMaker Pro substitutes PC fonts, as summarized in Table 16-1.

Table 16-1
A Comparison of PC and Macintosh Fonts Used in FileMaker Pro

PC	Macintosh
MS Serif	Times
Times New Roman	Times
Times	New York
Tms Rmn	Times
Courier New	Courier
Courier	Monaco

Filenames

Macintosh filenames can have up to 32 characters, but PC filenames under Windows 95 or 98 can now contain over 200 characters. And filenames in FileMaker Pro 5 for Windows now end with a .fp5 extension (as in SALES.fp5), rather than .fp3 (FileMaker Pro 3.0–4.1). Thus, databases that you want users to be able to run on either platform should be named according to the lowest common denominator: 32 characters maximum, including the .fp5 extension.

Colors

Colors are organized into palettes. Colors are not necessarily mapped the same way on the two systems, so you may see strange color effects on your PC when you open a Mac document. However, you can avoid color-related incompatibilities by choosing the 216-color Web palette in the Layout section of Application Preferences.

Graphics formats

FileMaker Pro 5 for Windows uses a variety of PC file formats to store pictures. Some of these formats are not supported by the Macintosh version of FileMaker Pro. You can, if you want, change this preference setting for any database so FileMaker Pro for Windows stores all non-portable graphic images in PICT (Macintosh) format. (Images in GIF, TIFF, JPEG, or EPS format are compatible across the two platforms, so they are not converted.) To do so, open the database in FileMaker Pro 5 for Windows and choose Edit ➪ Preferences ➪ Document. In the General section of the dialog box that appears, click the option for "Store compatible graphics."

For a list of all supported Windows graphics formats, see "File formats: About working with graphics, sounds, and movies" in FileMaker Pro Help.

Printing

Depending on the print driver you use on your PC, your PC results may differ from your Mac results, even when using the same printer. You may have to create two versions of each report layout: one tailored to the PC and the other for your Macintosh.

OLE support

Only Windows users can insert or edit OLE objects in a FileMaker Pro database. Although Mac users can view, cut, copy, and paste OLE objects, they cannot insert or modify them in any way.

Platform-specific capabilities

Several capabilities of the two operating systems are platform-specific; that is, they are available only in Windows or only on the Mac. If such features are used in designing a script, the script will not run on the other platform. Some examples of platform-specific capabilities are listed here.

Mac-specific features

✦ AppleTalk support

✦ Ability to play Macintosh .snd (sound) files

✦ AppleScript and AppleEvents support

Windows-specific features

✦ Microsoft Registry support

✦ DDE messaging

New Feature

Previous versions of FileMaker Pro for the Macintosh could not play Windows WAV files—a popular format for audio clips. QuickTime 3 and higher now recognizes such files. To insert a WAV file into a Container field, you can open the file in MoviePlayer (a free QuickTime player from Apple Computer), choose Edit ➪ Select All, and then paste it into the Container field. The Container field then displays a QuickTime control bar that you can use to play the audio clip.

Summary

✦ You can exchange FileMaker Pro data with other applications and with FileMaker Pro for another platform (Windows or Macintosh). FileMaker Pro supports a variety of popular import and export file formats.

✦ FileMaker Pro can import data created in other programs, such as spreadsheets and other database applications.

✦ When importing FileMaker Pro data into an existing FileMaker database, you can now merge (or synchronize) the files by using the new "Update matching records in current found set" option.

✦ Macintosh users can directly share databases with users of the Windows version of FileMaker Pro, but layouts may differ, especially in terms of fonts, graphics, and colors.

✦   ✦   ✦

Creating and Using FileMaker Pro Templates

You've already learned a lot about designing and using databases. However, it isn't necessary to reinvent the wheel. You may find a template that has been developed by someone else that you can use as is or easily modify to meet your needs. A *template*, in the case of FileMaker Pro, is a ready-to-use database into which you can enter your own data. More specifically, a template is a database without any records.

The FileMaker Pro 5 Templates

When you install FileMaker Pro 5, a series of FileMaker Pro templates is copied to your hard disk. You can use any of them by choosing File ⇨ New Database, clicking the radio button labeled "Create a new file using a template" (in the New Database dialog box), choosing a template from the list (see Figures 17-1 and 17-2), and clicking OK.

To find out more about any of the templates that are included with FileMaker Pro 5, click the Template Info button.

These templates serve two purposes: First, they give you some databases with which you can safely experiment. Second, they are full-featured databases that you may be able to use in your business, home, or school.

Templates pop-up menu

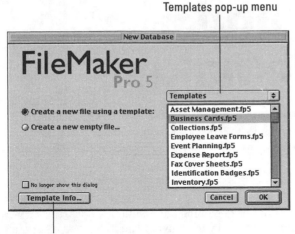

Click to get information about the selected template

Figure 17-1: In the New Database dialog box, you can create a database from any of the provided templates.

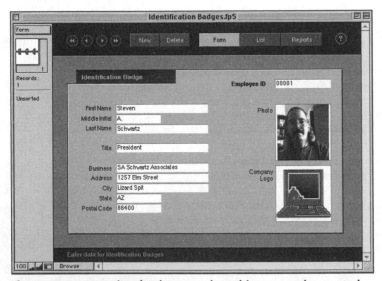

Figure 17-2: Attractive databases such as this one can be created from the templates provided in FileMaker Pro 5.

Tip You can also make your own templates available in the New Database dialog box. Simply use the Save a Copy As command to make a clone of your database and save it in the Templates folder. On a Mac, this folder can be found by opening the FileMaker Pro 5 folder and then opening the FileMaker Templates Folder. Under Windows, it can be found by opening the Program Files folder and then opening the following folders in sequence: FileMaker ⇨ FileMaker Pro 5 ⇨ Templates.

This chapter discusses the techniques and commands you will need to know in order to work with any FileMaker Pro template, regardless of whether you receive it from an online information service or off the Internet, from a friend or a colleague, purchase it as a commercial product from a member of the FileMaker Solutions Alliance (see Appendix D), or get it from the *FileMaker Pro 5 Bible* CD-ROM. For details on creating your own templates with the intent of giving or selling them to others, see Chapter 21.

Installing a Template

When you obtain a FileMaker Pro template, there are several different methods that the database designers may provide to help you install their templates. Here are some of the most common procedures used to install templates or databases:

✦ *Run a special installer program.* This method is often associated with commercial packages, such as FileMaker Pro. When you run the installer program, you may be given an option to install all or selected parts of the software—usually to any disk and folder you choose.

✦ *Double-click a self-extracting archive.* To save disk space, templates (and other software) are frequently compressed into self-extracting archives. A self-extracting archive contains a compressed copy of the template—conserving disk space and reducing download time (for templates that are distributed through online information services or the Internet). A self-extracting archive is called self-extracting because it includes a built-in file extraction program. When you double-click a self-extracting archive, a dialog box appears asking where you wish to install the files. After you select a destination, the files are extracted from the archive, expanded to their normal size, and copied to the destination disk and folder.

✦ *Extract the templates from a normal archive.* This is a variation of the previous distribution method. Instead of creating self-extracting archives, normal archives are sometimes created. The only difference is that you need a separate file-extraction utility (such as StuffIt Expander or StuffIt Deluxe on the Mac; WinZip on the PC) in order to extract the files. This distribution method (as well as the previous one) is commonly used with templates, programs, and other materials that you'll find on the Internet and online services, such as America Online.

Because either Macintosh or Windows users can use FileMaker Pro template and database files, there will be occasions when Windows users will need to "unstuff" Macintosh StuffIt archives. To handle this situation, there is a copy of StuffIt Expander for Windows in the Aladdin Systems folder on the *FileMaker Pro 5 Bible* CD-ROM.

If you do not have file extraction utilities, you can find many of the most popular ones in the Aladdin Systems folder (StuffIt Expander) and the Nico Mak Computing folder (WinZip) of the *FileMaker Pro 5 Bible* CD-ROM.

✦ *Use the Finder or Windows to make a copy of the template*. Many database templates are distributed as normal, uncompressed files. To install these templates, all you need to do is copy them to your hard disk — just as you would any other file or program.

Reinstalling a Fresh Copy of a Template

Like any other FileMaker Pro database, any changes you make to a template (entering or editing data, changing field definitions, rearranging fields on a layout, and so on) are instantly saved and become a permanent part of the file. Thus, when you are finished experimenting with a new template and are ready to begin entering your own data, you may want to start with a fresh copy of the template. There are two safe ways you can accomplish this:

✦ Re-run the installation program, double-click the self-extracting archive, or run the necessary file-extraction utility.

✦ For templates that are distributed as normal uncompressed files, drag a fresh copy of the template from the distribution disk to your hard disk.

As an alternative, it may be simpler to just think ahead. Whenever you receive a template, make a backup copy of the uncompressed templates. When you're through trying it out and are ready to commit your own data to the template, you can use the Finder or Windows to make a new copy of the template from your backup copy. This is always a good idea.

Saving a Database as a Template

FileMaker Pro templates are also referred to as clones (the terms template and clone are interchangeable). A *clone* is an exact copy of a database but without any records. The clone contains the same field definitions, layouts, buttons, and scripts as the original database. Because all the records have been removed, however, it is in the perfect state to receive fresh data.

In several instances, you might want to create a clone of an existing database:

✦ *To create an archival copy of the structure of an important database — just in case.* Many of us tend to "tweak" a database as we use it: moving fields around, trying out new layouts, and testing scripts, for example. Because FileMaker Pro automatically saves any change that you make to a database, these little experiments can sometimes wreak havoc — causing scripts to stop functioning, Calculation fields to present the wrong results, and so on. If you've created a clone of the original database, you can get back to square one by simply importing the data from your current database into the clone.

Tip   An even simpler method of protecting the structure of a database and its data is to make an exact copy of the database. Choose File ➪ Save a Copy As, and then choose "copy of current file" from the Type:/Save a: pop-up menu.

✦ *To begin a new weekly, quarterly, or other time-based database.* Many databases are designed to be used only for a certain period of time and then started over with new records. For example, I created a database in which I do my bookkeeping. The IRS expects me to turn in an annual Form 1040 and Schedule C, so I need a fresh copy of this database at the beginning of each year. Another example would be if you were to make a call-tracking database to be used by your department's receptionist to make a permanent record of incoming calls. You might want to start a fresh copy on a more frequent basis (monthly, weekly, or even daily, depending on the call volume).

✦ *To remove sample records and prepare a commercial or shareware database for your own data.* Some templates — including some of the ones on the *FileMaker Pro 5 Bible CD-ROM* — contain a small set of sample records, enabling you to get a feel for how the database works without having to enter (or risk) your own data. As long as you restrict your experimentation to adding, deleting, and editing records, you can strip out all the sample records by simply making a clone of the database; then you're ready to begin entering your own data.

✦ *To enable you to give the template away or sell it.* Unless your records are meant to be used as a sample, you probably don't want to include your personal or business data in a template. Making a clone strips out that data in one easy step.

To make a template or clone from any existing database, follow these steps:

   1. Open the database in FileMaker Pro.

   2. Choose File ➪ Save a Copy As.

   A standard file dialog box appears.

   3. Choose "clone (no records)" from the Type:/Save a: pop-up menu.

   4. Select a destination disk and folder using normal file navigation procedures.

   5. Type a name for the clone in the "Create a copy named"/"File name" text box.

   If you're saving the file in a different folder and/or disk than the one where the current database is stored, you can use the same name as that of the original database. If you're storing it in the same folder and/or disk, you will want to use a new name or the default name proposed by FileMaker Pro (*filename* Clone).

   Under no circumstances should you use the same name as the original database when saving the template in the same folder and/or disk location! Doing so replaces your original database with an empty template.

   6. Click Save.

   The clone is created but not opened. The original template file remains open. If you want to immediately begin working with the clone, close the original database (choose File ➪ Close or press ⌘+W/Ctrl+W) and then open the clone (choose File ➪ Open or press ⌘+O/Ctrl+O).

The other two Save a Copy As options presented in the pop-up menu are:

   ✦ "copy of current file," which creates a backup copy of the current database with all records intact

   ✦ "compressed copy (smaller)," which creates a compressed backup copy of the current database with all records intact

   Although they aren't used to create clones, these two additional Save options are very useful in their own right. For more information about these options, see Chapter 2.

Working with a New Template

As mentioned previously in this chapter, the only difference between a database and a template or clone is that the latter contains no records. This presents one immediate problem for many users: When a template is first opened, the database window may be blank (see Figure 17-3). Because there are no records, there may be nothing for FileMaker Pro to display—other than an empty database window.

Figure 17-3: A blank database window

To begin working with the template, choose Records ➪ New Record (or press ⌘+N/Ctrl+N). The opening layout immediately appears, and you can get down to business.

Avoiding that blank look (in your templates and on users' faces)

There's nothing so potentially confusing to a new user as a blank screen. To avoid causing a panic, you can make one small modification to your template before handing or selling it to a user: Add a single new record and then close the file. When users open the file, they will see whatever you originally intended them to see, such as a blank data-entry form for record #1 or an opening menu.

Summary

✦ There are a number of methods you can use to install FileMaker Pro templates and databases that you obtain from others. The most common methods include running a special installation or file-extraction program, running a separate file-extraction utility, and making a copy from the Finder or Windows.

✦ To adapt a database for use as a template, you clone it by using the Save a Copy As command. The file dialog box has a "clone (no records)" option that omits records from the new copy. In FileMaker Pro, the terms *template* and *clone* are used interchangeably.

✦ When working with a clone or template, you may have to create the first record in order to make the various layouts appear.

✦ ✦ ✦

Mastering
FileMaker Pro

Linking Databases: Relationships and Lookups

Versions 3.0 and higher of FileMaker Pro are fully relational. Any database can draw information from any other *related database* (one with matching data in a key field, such as a customer identification number, a part number, or a Social Security number). This has some important implications for how you create databases.

First, many databases will be smaller and easier to maintain than they were in the early versions of FileMaker Pro. Rather than stuffing every possible field into each database, you can divide the information among several smaller databases. For example, address information for your customers, clients, or suppliers can be kept in an Address database that is separate from an Invoices database. In that way, a person's address need only be entered once (in the Address database) and then simply referenced by the Invoices database. Related data stays in the database in which it is entered — regardless of how many different related files refer to it. When you request data that is in a related file, it is only displayed on-screen rather than being copied into the target database.

As with previous versions of FileMaker Pro, lookups are still supported as an alternative to relationships. A lookup works like a relationship, but instead of merely displaying the related data, it is actually copied into the target database. Because lookups are actually preferable in some cases, you should be sure to read the following section so you understand the differences between lookups and relationships.

Lookups versus Relationships

Here's how a lookup works: When you make an entry in a key field in the primary database, a search is done in a secondary database. FileMaker Pro locates the first record that contains a match for the key field, and data is then copied from a selected field in the secondary database into a selected field in the primary database.

For example, suppose you have two databases named Orders and Addresses. Both databases have a Customer ID field. Three lookups are defined as being dependent on the Customer ID field: Name, Mailing Address, and Phone. When a new order is taken, you create a new record in the Orders database and type a number into the Customer ID field. This triggers the three lookups, causing FileMaker Pro to search the Addresses database for a matching Customer ID number. When the ID number is found, the customer's name, address, and phone number are copied into the appropriate fields in the primary database.

Lookups have some drawbacks:

✦ The looked-up data is physically copied from the secondary database into the primary database, resulting in data duplication and additional storage requirements.

✦ If the data in the secondary file changes, the primary data does not change unless you execute the lookup again.

✦ Even if multiple matches exist for the key field, FileMaker only identifies the first match that it finds.

On the other hand, lookups have one feature that's occasionally very useful. Looked-up data that is copied into the primary file will not change unless you trigger the lookup a second time or do a blanket relookup for the found set (described later in "Performing a relookup"). Sometimes this is exactly what you want. For example, looked-up price information in an invoice shouldn't change when the prices are changed. (You can't pass on an after-the-fact price increase.) Lookups are discussed in the second part of this chapter.

When lookups aren't the answer to your development needs, you can define relationships instead. The advantages of relationships include the following:

✦ Related data is not copied into the primary file; it is merely referenced. This avoids unnecessary duplication.

✦ Related data is automatically updated whenever it changes. You don't have to do anything to trigger an update.

✦ In addition to the one-to-one correspondence between records that is offered by lookups, relationships can be one-to-many. By using a general field, such as Department as a key field, multiple matching records can be drawn from the related file (all personnel in the Accounting Department, for instance).

✦ You can define relationships so there is two-way communication between the files. For example, deletions in the primary file can be carried through to the related file.

Perhaps the easiest way to understand the differences between relationships and lookups is by looking at an example. Figure 18-1 shows three databases used by a hypothetical video rental store to create and print customer invoices.

Related information   Lookups

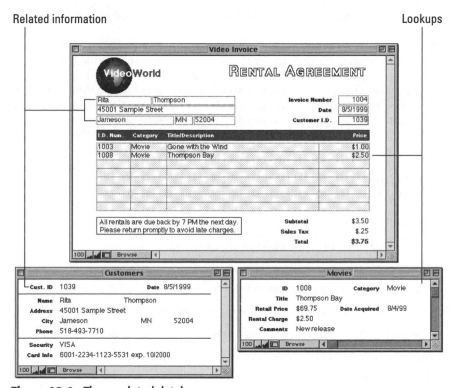

Figure 18-1: Three related databases

You'll find these three related databases in the FileMaker Pro Bible folder on the *FileMaker Pro 5 Bible* CD-ROM. You may find it helpful to have them open in FileMaker Pro while reading the remainder of this section.

In this example, Video Invoice (top) is the main database. When a customer wishes to rent a movie, game, or piece of equipment, a clerk creates a new record in Video Invoice and then completes this form.

The Customers database (bottom left) contains only customer information, such as the name and address, phone number, customer identification number, and security deposit/credit card information. When a customer opens an account with Video World, the clerk records this information. Similarly, if the customer moves, changes his or her name, or wants to change the security deposit information (switching to a different credit card, for instance), the changes are made in the customer record. As the figure shows, the name and address are displayed in the Video Invoice file as relations. Thus, if a customer's address changes in the Customers database, the owner can be assured that every invoice for the customer displays the current address (making it easy to locate overdue rentals, if the need arises).

The Movies database (bottom right) contains a separate record for each rental item (movies, video games, and equipment). Each item has a unique identification number, as well as its current rental price. As indicated in the figure, items in the Movies database are copied into each appropriate record in the Video Invoice file via lookups. This makes each invoice line item a permanent entry. When the rental charge for an item changes (because of a sale or a change in policy, for example), only new invoices will reflect the new price. Outstanding invoices will retain their original rental charges — as, of course, they must.

After defining the fields for the three databases and creating layouts for them, it is a simple matter to define the relationships between the files, as follows:

1. In the Video Invoice file, choose File ⇨ Define Relationships.

   The Define Relationships dialog box appears.

2. Click New to define the first relationship.

   A standard file dialog box appears.

3. Select the first related file (in this case, Customers) and click Open.

   The Edit Relationship dialog box appears (see Figure 18-2).

4. *Optional*: If you wish, you can change the relationship name.

   By default, the name of the related file is used.

5. Select the pair of fields in the two databases that defines a set of matching records (in this case, Cust. ID and Cust. ID).

   There is no requirement that the matching fields have the same name — although in this instance, they do.

6. *Optional*: To enable the user to delete or create records in the related file (Customers) by making changes in the primary file (Video Invoice), click the appropriate check boxes at the bottom of the dialog box.

Relationship name

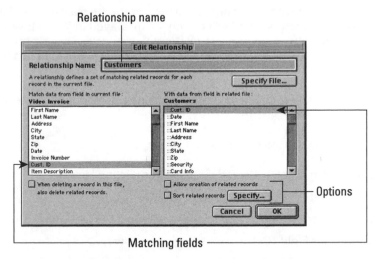

Figure 18-2: You can define or revise relationships in the Edit Relationship dialog box.

7. Click OK to record the first relationship.

8. Repeat steps 2 through 7 to define the relationship with the Movies database. (In this example, the two matching fields are both named ID.)

After the two relationships have been defined, the Define Relationships dialog box looks like Figure 18-3.

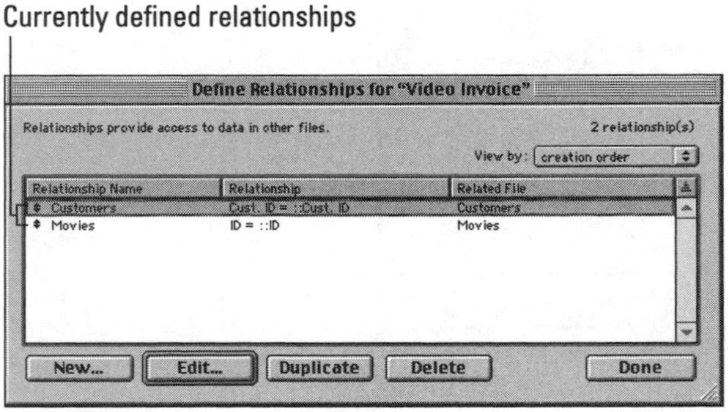

Currently defined relationships

Figure 18-3: The two relationships defined for the Video Invoice database

These steps establish that there are two separate relationships between the Video Invoice database and the Customers and Movies databases, each based on different match fields (Cust. ID and ID, respectively). To specify the fields whose data will be copied to Video Invoice when matches are identified (in the case of rental item lookups) and the fields whose data will merely be displayed in Video Invoice (in the case of the customer name and address relations), options are set for the lookup fields in the Define Fields dialog box and the related fields are placed in a layout for Video Invoice.

The Category, Item Description, and Unit Price fields will be defined as lookups, based on the Movies relationship.

To define these lookups, follow these steps:

1. Select the Video Invoice file and choose File ➪ Define Fields.

   The Define Fields dialog box appears.

2. Select the Category field in the field list, and click the Options button.

   The Options for Field "Category" dialog box appears.

3. In the Auto-Enter section of the dialog box, click the "Looked-up value" check box.

   The Lookup for Field "Category" dialog box appears, as shown in Figure 18-4.

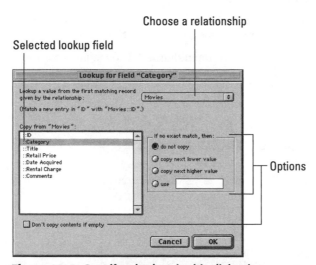

Figure 18-4: Specify a lookup in this dialog box.

4. In the pop-up list at the top of the dialog box, choose the Movies relationship.

5. In the field list, choose "::Category" as the field to copy from in the Movies database. Then click OK twice to return to the Define Fields dialog box.

6. Repeat steps 2 through 5 to define the lookups for Item Description and Unit Price.

The fields to copy from the Movies database are Title and Rental Charge, respectively.

7. Click Done to close the Define Fields dialog box.

If you were to examine the Video Invoice file in Layout mode, you'd note that the field names in the line item section of the invoice are unchanged. They still appear as Category, Item Description, and Unit Price, even though they will now be filled in via lookups triggered by typing an item's ID number at the beginning of each invoice line.

Related fields are defined a little differently from lookups. You have two options:

✦ Place the fields directly on the layout.

✦ Use the Portal tool to draw a rectangle on the layout and then place the fields in the portal.

In this example, you'll place the individual related customer name and address fields directly onto the Video Invoice layout. (Using a portal is explained later in this chapter.)

To add related fields to a layout, follow these steps:

1. Bring the Video Invoice database to the front, and choose View ➪ Layout Mode.

2. Select the Field tool from the Tools palette and drag a blank field onto the layout.

The Specify Field dialog box appears, as shown in Figure 18-5.

Choose a relationship   **Figure 18-5:** The Specify Field dialog box

3. Choose Customers from the pop-up menu at the top of the dialog box.

   This indicates that you are basing the selected field on the previously defined Customers relationship and that you will be choosing a field from the Customers file.

4. Choose the First Name field, click to remove the check mark from the "Create field label" check box, and click OK.

   The field you just placed on the layout is now labeled "::First Name." (The pair of colons that precedes the name indicates that it is a related field.)

5. Repeat steps 2 through 4 to create and place additional fields for Last Name, Address, City, State, and Zip. Arrange the fields so they form the address section of the layout (as previously shown in Figure 18-1).

If you were defining one-to-many joins rather than the one-to-one joins used here, you would place the related fields in a portal on the layout (drawn with the Portal tool). Related fields in a portal display *all* matches rather than just the first one found. For example, you could use a portal to show the names and rental charges of all inventory items of a given type (new movies or comedies starring Chevy Chase, for example).

Now that all the necessary fields have been defined and placed in the data entry layout for Video Invoice, here's what happens when a clerk creates a new customer invoice:

1. FileMaker Pro automatically fills in the invoice number and today's date.

2. The clerk asks for the customer's membership number, enters it in the Customer ID field, and presses Tab to move to the first line item.

3. The act of tabbing out of the Customer ID field causes FileMaker Pro to search for a matching ID number in the Customers database. When one is found, the customer's name and address information is automatically filled in on the invoice. If a match is not found, the clerk creates a new record in the Customers database for this customer.

   If the "Allow creation of related records" check box was checked for this relationship definition, the clerk could enter the name and address information directly on the invoice form — simultaneously generating a new record for the customer in the Customers database.

 Tip   It sometimes isn't a good idea to allow creation of a record for a related database, as was suggested above (creating a customer record from the Video Invoice form). Most of the time, not all the fields you want to record are displayed and enterable on the related database form. For example, the Video Invoice form does not include the customer's phone number — clearly an important field. Instead, it may be better to create a button with a script (see Chapter 15) on the Video Invoice form that takes you directly to the Customer form, where you can enter all the customer information. Then come back to the Video Invoice form and enter this customer's ID (which now exists).

Here are some additional details concerning the design and use of the three related databases (Video Invoice, Customers, and Movies):

✦ The Video Invoice database has a single layout that is devoted to creating the rental statements that customers receive when they rent movies, games, or video-related equipment (such as VCRs, DVD players, and video game systems).

✦ The Customers database contains customer-specific information, including a customer identification number, the date the customer record was created or last modified, name and address data, and information on the security deposit. The deposit information includes the form of the deposit (cash or a specific credit card) and a credit card number (if the deposit was made with a credit card). A unique customer identification number is automatically assigned whenever a new record is created, that is, when this information is taken from a new customer.

Note

The Cust. I.D. field is an auto-entry field. A new serial number is assigned to each record by incrementing the previous record's serial number by 13. The numbers assigned to the sample records are 1013, 1026, 1039, 1052, and 1065. (For more information on creating auto-entry fields, see Chapter 5.)

✦ The Movies database contains a separate record for every movie, video game, and piece of equipment the store rents. Every item gets its own identification number which, like Cust. I.D., is automatically assigned when the record is created.

Note

The I.D. field in the Movies database is an auto-entry field. The I.D. numbers begin with 1000, and the number is incremented by 1 for each new record. The numbers assigned to the sample records are 1000 to 1009.

✦ Other information that can be recorded for each movie, game, or piece of equipment includes a category (Movie, Game, or Equipment) that is chosen from a pop-up menu, a title, the retail price, the date acquired, the current daily rental charge, and comments. (Equipment can optionally be identified by a serial number.)

All lookups and relationships are performed from the Video Invoice database. When a customer selects one or more items to rent, the clerk chooses Records ⇨ New Record or presses Ô+N/Ctrl+N to create a new rental statement in Video Invoice. FileMaker Pro generates a new invoice number, and today's date is automatically entered on the form. Next, the clerk asks for the individual's customer number and enters it in the Customer I.D. field. (If you want to try out the database, you can enter any of the following numbers into this field: 1013, 1026, 1039, 1052, or 1065.)

Customer I.D. is the field that is used to define the relationship with the Customers database. The moment the clerk tabs out of the Customer I.D. field or presses Enter, FileMaker Pro searches the Customers database for a record that contains a match in the Cust. I.D. field. If it finds a match, the customer's name and address information are automatically filled in. On the other hand, if a match is not found, the clerk knows that the customer has an invalid number or that a search of the Customers database must be performed.

After FileMaker Pro has copied the address data onto the form, it automatically positions the cursor in the first I.D. Num. field. When the clerk types the first item's identification number (a movie I.D., for example) and tabs to the next field, this action triggers a lookup. (To ensure that a match is found in the sample data, you can enter any number between 1000 and 1009.) FileMaker Pro searches the Movies database for a record that has a matching I.D. When it locates that record, it fills in the rest of the information for that item (category, title, and daily price).

If the customer wants to rent additional items, the clerk enters them in the same manner as the first item. Because the body of the rental agreement is composed of repeating fields, every entry in the I.D. Num. field triggers a lookup for that particular rental item. As the clerk enters items, the subtotal, sales tax, and total are instantly updated. (In this example, the sales tax is set as 7 percent on all video rental items, so it is calculated by multiplying the subtotal by .07.)

After checking the rental statement to make sure it contains no errors, the clerk prints the customer's copy by choosing the File ➪ Print command and selecting "Current record" as the data to be printed. (If this database were used by an actual rental store, it would undoubtedly include a printing script that automatically chose "Current record.")

Whenever the rental price of an item changes (charging less for older movies than for current ones is a common practice, for example), the store owner simply opens the Movies database, locates the record, and then enters the new rental price. Similarly, if a customer moves or loses rental privileges, the owner or a clerk can edit or delete a customer's record in the Customers database.

Among other things, these databases demonstrate the following:

- ✦ A relationship can cause multiple related or lookup fields to be displayed. When a Customer I.D. is typed into a record in the Video Invoice database, all of the following lookups are triggered: First Name, Last Name, Address, City, State, and ZIP.

- ✦ A database can have multiple relationships, each one triggering one or several lookups and/or relations. The Video Invoice database contains two such fields: Customer I.D. (which displays the customer's name and address) and I.D. Num. (which looks up the category, title, and price information for each rental item).

- ✦ A single database can be linked (via relationships) to multiple databases. Video Invoice is linked to both the Customers database and the Movies database.

✦ When a repeating field is used as a match or key field, every repetition triggers another lookup or relationship. In Video Invoice, an entry in any of the eight repetitions of I.D. Num. triggers a lookup for that invoice line.

✦ When databases are linked by a relationship, you do not have to open the other files before you use them. As long as the databases have not been moved and the necessary disks are mounted, FileMaker Pro can access data in them.

Going Relational with FileMaker Pro

For end-users and developers who need the functionality afforded by FileMaker Pro's relational capabilities, there may no longer be a reason to choose another database program. These features make FileMaker Pro a ready match for all but a few very expensive, high-end database management systems.

If you don't think you're ready for relational databases — many of us are very comfortable with FileMaker Pro's flat-file capabilities — there's nothing new you have to learn. The relational features are there if you need them and stay out of the way if you don't.

Defining a relationship

To work with related files in FileMaker Pro, you need to do just two simple things:

✦ Define the relationship (or relationships).

✦ Place the related fields in a layout in the current database.

Follow these steps to define a relationship:

1. Choose File ➪ Define Relationships.

   The Define Relationships for "*file name*" dialog box appears (as shown previously in Figure 18-3). If any relationships are already defined for the database, they are listed in this dialog box.

2. Click New.

   A standard file dialog box appears, and you are asked to "Specify a file to relate to *current database name*."

3. Choose a database file and click Open.

   The Edit Relationship dialog box appears, as shown in Figure 18-6.

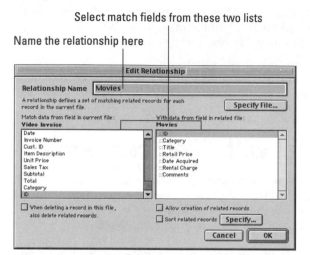

Name the relationship here

Select match fields from these two lists

Figure 18-6: The Edit Relationship dialog box

4. Enter a name for the relationship in the Relationship Name box.

   By default, the name of the related file is proposed.

5. Choose a pair of match fields that will define the relationship — one from the left-hand field list (from the current database) and one from the right-hand field list (from the related database).

   When FileMaker Pro later uses the relationship to check for related records, it matches data from the first field with data in the second field.

6. *Optional*: To create a two-way link between the current database and the data in the related file, you can click the check boxes labeled "When deleting a record in this file, also delete related records" and/or "Allow creation of related records."

7. Click OK to save your changes and dismiss the Edit Relationship dialog box. Otherwise, click Cancel to ignore all changes.

8. Repeat steps 2 through 7 for any additional relationships you wish to define.

9. When you are through defining relationships, click Done.

If you later want to change a relationship (modifying its name, the match fields, or the options), choose File ➪ Define Relationships, select the name of a current relationship in the Define Relationships dialog box, and then click Edit. You can also duplicate or delete existing relationships by clicking the appropriate buttons (Duplicate and Delete) in the Define Relationships dialog box.

In addition to using the Define Relationships command to specify relationships for a database, note that you can create them on the fly in almost any dialog box that contains a field list. Just choose Define Relationships from the pop-up menu above the field list, as shown in the example in Figure 18-7.

Figure 18-7: Defining a relationship from the Specify Field dialog box

Placing related fields in a layout

There are two ways you can make data from a related file appear in a layout for the current database:

✦ Place related fields directly on the layout.

✦ Create a portal on the layout and then place the related fields in the portal.

The decision concerning which approach is best for a given relationship is not an arbitrary one, however. If records in the two databases have a one-to-one correspondence with each other (only one customer has the same I.D. number, for example), you should place the related fields directly onto the layout. On the other hand, if you are establishing a one-to-many relationship (you may have many contacts at a particular company, for example), you should place the related fields in a portal. Only a portal can display multiple matching records for the same key field.

Placing related fields directly on the layout

Follow these steps to place a related field directly onto a layout:

1. Open the database for which a relationship has been defined.

2. Switch to Layout mode by choosing View ⇨ Layout Mode (or by pressing ⌘+L/Ctrl+L).

3. From the Layouts pop-up menu, select the name of the layout in which you want to display the related information.

4. Select the Field tool from the Tools palette and drag a field icon onto the layout.

   The Specify Field dialog box appears (as shown previously in Figure 18-7).

5. From the pop-up menu above the field list, select the name of the relationship.

   The field list changes to display only fields that have been defined for the related file (rather than for the current database). A pair of colons precedes the names of related fields (for example, "::Last Name").

6. Select the name of the related field that you want to place on the current layout.

7. If you want a field label to be created for the field automatically, check the "Create field label" check box.

8. Click OK to place the chosen field on the layout, or click Cancel if you change your mind.

The related field appears on the layout. You can now resize it, alter its formatting, or change its position, as necessary.

Placing related fields in a portal

Follow these steps to create and use a portal:

1. Open the database for which a relationship has been defined.

2. Switch to Layout mode by choosing View ➪ Layout Mode (or by pressing ⌘+L/Ctrl+L).

3. From the Layouts pop-up menu, select the name of the layout in which you want to display the related information.

4. Select the Portal tool from the Tools palette, and then click and drag to create the portal. Release the mouse button when the portal is the correct size and shape. (Every portal is a rectangle.) FileMaker Pro opens the Portal Setup dialog box (see Figure 18-8).

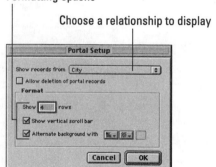

Figure 18-8: The Portal Setup dialog box

5. In the Portal Setup dialog box, use the "Show records from" pop-up list to choose the relationship that specifies the related database from which the portal fields are coming. If no relationship is correct, choose Define Relationships from the list to create a new relationship (as discussed earlier in this chapter).

6. Use the options in the Format section of the Portal Setup dialog box to choose the number of rows you want to show and whether to allow a vertical scroll bar.

   You can choose to alternate the rows of the portal with a background color and/or a pattern. Distinguishing the rows makes them easier to read.

7. Select the Field tool from the Tools palette and drag a field icon into the white, top row of the portal.

   The Specify Field dialog box appears (as shown previously in Figure 18-7).

8. From the pop-up menu above the field list, select the name of the relationship.

   The field list changes to display only fields that have been defined for the related file (rather than for the current database). A pair of colons precedes the names of related fields (for example, "::Last Name").

9. Select the name of a related field to place on the current layout.

10. If you want a field label to be created for the field automatically, check the "Create field label" check box.

11. Click OK to place the chosen field on the layout, or click Cancel if you change your mind.

12. Repeat steps 7 through 11 to add other related fields to the portal, as required.

Figure 18-9 shows what a portal looks like in Layout mode and in Browse mode. To make it easy to determine which fields are being displayed in the portal, their field labels have been dragged above the portal. As you can see, each related record is displayed on a separate line in the portal. If there are many related records, the scroll bar at the right can be used to view records that are currently off-screen.

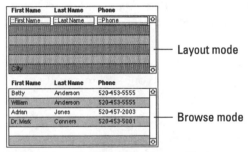

Figure 18-9: A fully defined portal in Layout mode (top) and Browse mode (bottom)

Working with Lookups

In order to execute a lookup, you need to have a pair of matching fields in two databases. (As described previously in this chapter, you specify the matching fields by defining a relationship—just as you do when working with related data rather than lookups.) Both fields must store the same kind of information, such as customer I.D. numbers. In general, the information in the matching fields should be unique.

The moment you enter or edit information in the field on which the lookup is based, FileMaker Pro automatically performs any lookups you have associated with that field. Often, only a field triggers a single lookup. For example, typing an inventory part number could result in a lookup of the part's price. You can also associate multiple lookups with the same field. Entering an inventory part number could trigger lookups of the part name, color, description, and price, for instance.

Here's an extended example: Suppose you have two databases that you want to link via lookups. The first is an Orders database. The order form that serves as the main layout for Orders has a field in it called Customer Code. Customer information (including names and addresses) is kept in a separate database called Customers. A unique identification code, which is assigned when a customer first places an order, identifies each record in the Customers database. You define each of the name and address fields in Orders as lookup fields that are triggered by an entry in the Customer Code field.

Whenever a customer calls in a new order, a salesperson creates a new record in Orders and enters the customer's I.D. number into the Customer Code field. FileMaker Pro then checks the Customers database for a record that contains a matching I.D. If it finds a matching I.D., it automatically copies the name and address information for that customer into the current order form. As this example shows, nothing prevents you from defining several lookup fields that are all activated by the same match field—in this case, Customer Code.

Figure 18-10 shows an example of the Lookup for Field "*field name*" dialog box in which you set options for a field that you're defining as a lookup field. To reach this dialog box, choose File ⇨ Define Fields (or press Shift+⌘+D/Shift+Ctrl+D), create or select the lookup field, and click the Options button. In the Options dialog box that appears, click the Auto-Enter tab at the top of the dialog box, and then click the "Looked-up value" check box. (Clicking the Specify button to the right of "Looked-up value" also works.)

By examining this figure, you can learn several important things about lookups. First, when you define a field as being a lookup field, you need to specify only two pieces of information:

- ✦ The name of the relationship on which the lookup is based. (The relationship specifies the names of the two fields to be matched in the databases.)
- ✦ The field in the lookup file whose contents FileMaker Pro will copy into the current field.

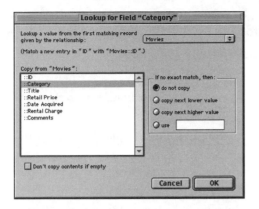

Figure 18-10: The Lookup for Field *"field name"* dialog box

Second, the Lookup for Field dialog box enables you to specify what will happen when FileMaker Pro does not find a match (see the right-hand side of the dialog box). The default choice is to do nothing ("do not copy"). The next two choices ("copy next lower value" and "copy next higher value") are often useful when you are performing lookups of numeric values. For example, when you want to determine the amount of postage that is necessary for a package, you could trigger a lookup in a postage rates database by entering a weight in the current database. Because postage is based on full ounces, you would use the "copy next higher value" option to take care of any weight that included a fraction of an ounce. Thus, entering **7.4** would return the value for 8 ounces.

The final option ("use") enables you to specify a particular value or text string to enter when FileMaker Pro doesn't find a match. For example, if the lookup is supposed to return a consulting rate and you entered a new consulting code in the trigger field, you could instruct the lookup to return **100** (your usual hourly rate, right?). In the case of missing customer information, you could set this option to copy a message, such as "New Customer" or "Client not found," into the field.

Finally, sometimes FileMaker Pro finds a match, but the field that's to be copied into the current file is blank. You can click the check box for "Don't copy contents if empty" (at the bottom of the dialog box) to indicate what FileMaker Pro should do if it finds a match but the field to be copied is blank. This option is useful if you have hand-entered information into the current file and want to avoid having it replaced by blank data.

Defining lookup fields

Follow these steps to define a lookup field in your own database:

1. Open the database in which you want to define lookup fields.

2. Choose File ➪ Define Fields (or press Shift+⌘+D/Shift+Ctrl+D).

   The Define Fields dialog box appears.

3. In the field list, select the first field that you want to define as a lookup field and then click the Options button.

   The Options for Field "*field name*" dialog box appears.

4. Click the Auto-Enter tab at the top of the dialog box.

5. Click the "Looked-up value" check box (or the Specify button to the right of the check box).

   The Lookup for Field "*field name*" dialog box appears (as shown previously in Figure 18-10).

6. From the pop-up menu, select the name of the relationship that you want FileMaker Pro to use.

   The relationship defines the matching fields in the two files that will be used for the lookup. If you haven't already defined a relationship (as described in "Defining a relationship," earlier in this chapter), you can define one now by choosing Define Relationships from the pop-up menu.

7. From the "Copy from" list, choose the field to be copied.

   The name of the chosen field does not need to be the same as the name of the field you're defining. What's important is that the fields contain similar contents.

8. Click a radio button in the right side of the dialog box to indicate how you want to handle instances in which FileMaker Pro does not find an exact match.

   • Select "do not copy" if you want FileMaker Pro to do nothing at all. (This option is the default.)

   • Select "copy next lower value" or "copy next higher value" if you want FileMaker Pro to use the closest value it can find — either lower or higher (numerically or alphabetically). Be sure to use these options only in appropriate instances. (If FileMaker Pro can't find a matching I.D. number, for example, would you really want it to copy data from the closest I.D. it can find?)

   • Select "use" and type a value or text string (up to 254 characters) into the text box to specify default data to be copied into the field.

9. To tell FileMaker not to copy a blank field into the current file, check the "Don't copy contents if empty" check box.

   Normally, if a lookup is performed and a match is found, FileMaker Pro copies the contents of the appropriate field into the field in the current file. Sometimes, however, the field to be copied from is blank. If the field in the current file already contains data, copying an empty field into it would delete the contents of the current field. Clicking the "Don't copy contents if empty" option leaves the original data intact.

10. To accept the options you have set for the lookup field, click OK. To ignore any changes you have made to the field definition, click Cancel.

    Either way, you return to the Options dialog box.

11. To accept this field as a lookup field, click OK.

The Define Fields dialog box appears.

12. When you have finished defining fields and setting field options, click Done.

If you ever want to change a field from a lookup field back to a normal field, choose File ➪ Define Fields (or press Shift+⌘+D/Shift+Ctrl+D), select the field in the field list, click Options, and then uncheck the "Looked-up value" check box. To edit the options for any lookup field, just click the Specify button to the right of "Looked-up value."

Another idea for creating matching fields

When FileMaker Pro executes a lookup, it presents data from the first matching record it finds. If, for example, you use Last Name as the trigger field and the lookup file contains five people who have the last name Hamilton, FileMaker simply selects the first Hamilton record that it finds. Other Hamiltons in the database would never be located by the lookup. For this reason, a match field should normally contain unique data, such as an I.D. number, Social Security number, or phone number.

Unfortunately, many databases contain no such field. With a little imagination, however, you can create trigger and match fields that are composites of other fields. To do so, you can create a Calculation field that *concatenates* two or more fields (adds them together). In an address database, for example, you could create an I.D. number by combining an individual's last name with the last four digits of his or her phone number (as in "Jones1247"). Although this approach is not guaranteed to produce a unique I.D., the only people you would normally expect to share the same composite number would be members of the same family.

In the file that triggers the lookup, you would need to ask for two pieces of information: the last name (Last Name) and the last four digits of the person's phone number (Last4). The Calculation formula for the I.D. field would read as follows:

```
Last Name & Last4
```

The result type should be set to Text.

Because a matching field must also exist in the lookup file, you could create an I.D. Calculation field by using the following formula:

```
Last Name & Right (Phone, 4)
```

As in the first formula, the result type should also be Text. This formula assumes that you are already collecting a complete phone number (Phone) in the lookup file. The part of the formula that reads "Right (Phone, 4)" tells FileMaker Pro to consider only the last four digits of the phone number. Thus, you do not need to be concerned about whether some phone numbers in the database contain an area code while others do not. Similarly, it doesn't matter whether the phone number was typed with parentheses, dashes, spaces, or as a continuous string—because only the final four digits are used, and they will always be digits.

Opening lookup files

When FileMaker Pro checks for a match in a related file (whether you are working with lookups or related data), it doesn't actually open the file. The file's name is displayed in the Window menu, surrounded by parentheses to indicate that a link has been established to it. If you want to examine the file, you can choose it from the Window menu. The file opens just as it does when you choose the File ➪ Open command.

Therefore, when you are working with lookup or relational fields, you need to open only the file for which the relationship(s) have been defined. You never need to open the related files themselves unless you have some other reason for opening them (to enter or edit data, for example).

More about lookups

As you can see, defining and using lookup fields is not difficult. When you are doing so, however, keep the following features and restrictions in mind:

✦ You can use the *current* file as the lookup file. That's right. Rather than looking in an external file, you can copy values from other records in the same file. In the Video Invoice database, for example, the lookup field definitions could be changed so that when a Customer I.D. is entered, FileMaker Pro searches Video Invoice (rather than Customers) for a record with a matching Customer I.D. As long as a previous invoice for that customer exists, FileMaker can simply copy the address information from that invoice into the current one. If no match is found, you're talking to a new customer, and you can fill in the information by typing it.

✦ When FileMaker Pro is determining whether it has found a match, it compares only the first 20 characters in the trigger and match fields. Be sure that no I.D. number or text is longer than 20 characters — or that the match doesn't rely on any characters beyond the twentieth. If you have two or more records that differ only in the twenty-first character or later, FileMaker will simply select the first one that it finds. Also, FileMaker Pro ignores the order of words, capitalization, and punctuation when it is performing the comparison. Thus, it considers "crosby" and "Crosby!" to be the same, just as it considers "Steve Simms" and "Simms, Steve" to be the same. Finally, FileMaker Pro ignores text in Number fields when it is checking for a match (just as it does when indexing a Number field).

✦ If possible, entries in a match field should be unique. When FileMaker Pro checks for a match, it simply reports the first one that it finds. If there are several matches, the others will never be used. (This is precisely why it is dangerous in most databases to use Last Name as a match field.) You can avoid duplication in match fields by defining the field as an automatically generated serial number and/or specifying that the field must be unique. (For more information about setting field definition options, see Chapter 5.)

✦ You can edit the information in a lookup field just as you can in any other field. However, a new lookup will occur only when you execute the Relookup command (discussed in the next section) or edit the data in the match field.

✦ If possible, avoid selecting a repeating field as one from which you are copying (looking up) data. FileMaker Pro simply copies the first entry from the repeating field.

✦ You may have some older FileMaker Pro databases that rely on lookups. When you use these old databases with FileMaker Pro 3.0 or higher, the secondary files are converted as needed — either when you open and convert the primary file or as the files are referenced while using the primary file. However, a new lookup will occur only when you execute the Relookup command (discussed in the next section) or edit the data in the match field.

Note

During the conversion process, FileMaker Pro 5 automatically defines the relationships that were specified by the lookups in the original files.

Performing a relookup

Sometimes information in your lookup file changes. You update part descriptions and prices; contact names, addresses, and phone numbers can change. You can bring any values in the current file up to date by simply tabbing into or clicking in a match field and then issuing the Relookup command.

As an example, imagine that you have a small mail-order business that sells tropical fish. You create a database called Catalog that can print an on-demand catalog that lists the fish you have on hand and their prices. Catalog performs its lookups by searching an Inventory database that contains description and price information for each type of fish that is currently in stock. As a small, specialized business, prices on particular fish may vary on a daily basis (depending on who your supplier happens to be today or what you recently caught). Whenever a customer requests a catalog, you perform a relookup to make sure that the prices are current.

You need to keep several important things in mind when executing a relookup:

✦ A relookup is performed for all records that are currently being browsed. You can restrict the affected records by first selecting a particular record or group of records.

✦ Just as each match field in the current file triggers its own lookups, relookups are done only for the current match field (the one that contains the cursor when you choose the Relookup command). Thus, if a file has several match fields, you can decide to perform a relookup for all or just some of the match fields.

✦ You cannot use the Undo command to undo a relookup. You may want to protect the integrity of the database by using the File ⇨ Save a Copy As command to create a backup of the database before you perform a relookup.

To perform a relookup, follow these steps:

1. Open the database that contains the match field (or fields) and display the appropriate layout.

2. Select the records that you want to affect with the relookup.

   Use normal record selection techniques (such as the Find, Show All Records, and Omit commands) to select the appropriate records.

3. Tab into or click the first match field.

4. Choose the Records ⇨ Relookup command.

   The dialog box in Figure 18-11 appears, showing the number of records that are currently being browsed.

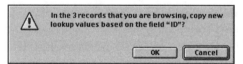

Figure 18-11: This dialog box appears when you are performing a relookup.

5. Click OK to replace the old values with new ones or click Cancel to leave the original values unchanged.

6. If you want to perform a relookup for additional match fields, repeat steps 2 through 5.

You should always think carefully before executing a relookup. For instance, in an invoice database that pulls price information via a lookup field, performing a relookup on that field would effectively change the amounts due on outstanding invoices! Normal business practices dictate that you would seldom want to do a relookup on such a field.

If you want to see how the Relookup command works (rather than just read about it), you can try it out with the three databases in the Relational Example folder of the *FileMaker Pro 5 Bible* CD-ROM (discussed previously in this chapter). First, select an existing invoice in the Video Invoice database. Then, open the Movies database and change some of the values in the records that are currently being looked up. Finally, follow the relookup procedure previously described.

Forcing a relookup for a single record

As mentioned previously, a relookup normally affects all records that are currently being browsed, as well as all lookup fields that are associated with the current match field. Sometimes, however, you may want to update only a single record, rather than the entire database or a subset of it. Although you can use find requests to limit browsing to the one record of interest and then choose the Relookup command, there is an easier method you can use if you are updating only one record.

To perform the equivalent of a single-record relookup, display the appropriate record, select the data in the trigger field, cut it (by choosing Edit ➪ Cut or by pressing ⌘+X /Ctrl+X), and then immediately paste it back into the same field (by choosing Edit ➪ Paste or by pressing ⌘+V/Ctrl+V). Remember that editing the contents of a match field always causes a lookup to be performed. Because FileMaker Pro knows only that something has been done to the field, this cut-and-paste procedure forces a lookup to occur. If the data that is looked up has changed, the new values will appear in the lookup fields. (Another way to force a lookup is to delete a single character and then retype it.)

Summary

✦ A relationship (a pair of matching fields in two files) must be defined when working with related data and lookups. The names of the match fields in the two databases need not be the same.

✦ Relational joins can be one-to-one or one-to-many.

✦ When converting a set of older FileMaker Pro files that are joined together by lookups, the secondary files are converted as needed—either when you open and convert the primary file or as the files are referenced while using the primary file. If you prefer, you can simply open and convert all the files before using the databases.

✦ By defining a field as a lookup field, you can copy its information from another database file. Related data, on the other hand, is merely referenced; it is not copied into the database.

✦ To trigger a lookup or to display related data, simply type data into the match field or edit existing data in that field. Then exit the field by pressing Tab or Enter.

✦ You can have one or many lookup and related fields that are associated with a single match field in the primary database.

✦ To bring records in the current file up to date, you can select the appropriate records and issue the Relookup command. Doing so causes a lookup to be executed for each of the records that are being browsed. (On the other hand, because related data is always up to date, there is no similar command you have to choose.)

✦ Every relookup is associated with a single match field. Only lookup fields that use that particular match field are affected by the relookup. Thus, if you have multiple match fields, you need to use multiple relookups to bring an entire record or found set up to date.

✦   ✦   ✦

Using FileMaker Pro in Workgroups

◆ ◆ ◆ ◆

In This Chapter

Sharing databases
on a network

Protecting databases

Setting user access
privileges

Working with
password-protected
databases

◆ ◆ ◆ ◆

Not only is FileMaker Pro network-compatible, it also includes features that enable it to manage network traffic and to control who sees which databases and who can modify them (regardless of whether the database is on a network or running in a single-user environment). This chapter explains how to use FileMaker Pro on a network, as well as how to password-protect and assign access privileges to sensitive data.

Running FileMaker Pro on a Network

Having your personal FileMaker Pro databases at your beck and call is great, but some data—particularly business information—is meant to be shared with others. Back in the old days (before networks), employees spent an inordinate amount of time unnecessarily duplicating and hand-distributing data. When a colleague down the hall needed a copy of your sales spreadsheet, for example, you made a copy of it on disk and carried the disk to his or her desk. Now that computer workstations can be linked via a company's network, you can share data without physically having to move or copy it. Files can stay right where they are, regardless of whether they're located on your hard disk or on a file server.

New Feature There are two ways you can share a database over a network. If no more than ten users will ever need to simultaneously access the database, the built-in file-sharing features of FileMaker Pro will suffice. If more than ten users will ever need to simultaneously access the database, then it *must* be hosted using FileMaker Server.

Right out of the box, FileMaker Pro 5 is a network-ready program. FileMaker Pro databases can be shared among the users of any AppleTalk (Macintosh), IPX/SPX (Windows), or TCP/IP network. Using Farallon PhoneNET Talk network software and a compatible network connector card, PCs can be part of an AppleTalk network, enabling users of Macintosh and Windows versions of FileMaker Pro to share the same databases. A solution for creating a mixed Mac/Windows Ethernet network is to install PC MacLan (Miramar Systems) on a Windows server, enabling Ethernet-capable Macs to connect to the network.

To select a network protocol, choose Edit ➪ Preferences ➪ Application. Pick a protocol from the pop-up menu in the General section of the Application Preferences dialog box, as shown in Figure 19-1. (See Chapter 7 for more information about setting preferences.)

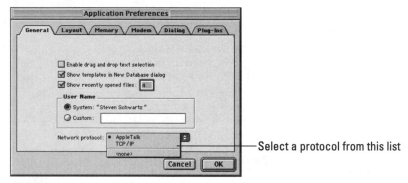

Select a protocol from this list

Figure 19-1: Selecting a network protocol

Note that if you select TCP/IP as the network protocol, FileMaker Pro must be connected to the Internet or a TCP/IP-based Intranet. If an appropriate connection is not active when you launch your copy of FileMaker Pro, the program will automatically attempt to create the connection.

 When FileMaker databases are hosted on an AppleTalk network, file sharing does not have to be enabled in the File Sharing control panel.

 When discussing file sharing in the remainder of this chapter, I am talking about individual users on the network hosting databases, rather than having them served by FileMaker Server.

FileMaker Pro Server

In 1994, Claris announced the first version of FileMaker Pro Server; a special hosting program designed to support up to 100 concurrent licensed FileMaker Pro Macintosh and Windows users over a network. FileMaker Pro Server 3.0 is capable of simultaneously hosting up to 100 databases. (A newer version of FileMaker Pro Server — called FileMaker Server 5 — is being created and will be released some time after FileMaker Pro 5 ships. Because it will have different features and capabilities than 3.0, I will make additional material about it available on IDG Books' Web site — www.idgbooks.com.)

If you have — or are thinking about getting — FileMaker Server, here are some useful bits of information:

✦ There are separate Macintosh and Windows versions of FileMaker Server.

✦ FileMaker Server can be installed on any computer that is connected to your network. However, for optimum performance, install it on a dedicated computer — one that is not used for other tasks.

✦ The purpose of FileMaker Server is to host databases. To *use* any of the hosted databases, each person must have his or her own copy of FileMaker Pro installed on their computer.

✦ When you start FileMaker Server, it automatically opens all multiuser FileMaker Pro files found in the FileMaker Pro Server folder. (All databases to be hosted should reside on the computer on which FileMaker Server is installed.) To manually open other databases, choose File ➪ Administer and click the Open Database button. Other administrative tasks, such as closing databases and disconnecting guests, are also performed in the administer window.

✦ You can remotely administer FileMaker Server from any workstation on which FileMaker Pro is installed. In FileMaker Pro's Open dialog box, click Hosts and choose the server.

✦ Any database containing fields that use the Today function must be closed and reopened in FileMaker Pro each day in order for the fields to be updated. Closing and reopening them in FileMaker Server will *not* accomplish this.

Hosts and guests

The person who opens a FileMaker Pro database and then declares it to be a multiuser database becomes the *host* for that database for the current session. To open a database for sharing, choose File ➪ Sharing and then choose Multi-User from the File Sharing dialog box (see Figure 19-2). The shared database can be located on your personal hard disk or on any hard disk on the network. (Some networks use special file-sharing software, such as AppleShare from Apple Computer, to enable files to be used by others on the network. Contact your network administrator for details.)

Multi-user settings

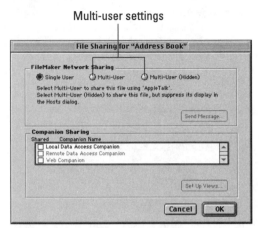

Figure 19-2: Setting the sharing status for a database

While the database is open, as many as ten other users on the network can access it. (In FileMaker Pro 4.0/4.1, the limit for simultaneous users was 25.) These users are referred to as *guests*. The designer of the database or, in some cases, the database administrator, determines the specific privileges of each guest.

If the previous host was someone other than you, you will see the changes made by that person, as well as any changes made by guests. Because the host is in charge, only that person's changes to Sort, Find, and Page Setup commands are saved with the file. When you, as the new host, close the database, your commands are saved.

New Feature

As shown in Figure 19-2, sharing status can also be set to Multi-User (Hidden). Choose this setting for databases which need to be shared, but need not be visible to guests. One common situation in which the Multi-User (Hidden) setting is useful is when you have related databases from which information is being drawn. Although the related databases must be open, you may not want users to be able to access them directly.

The host is in charge

Hosts and guests have different privileges and responsibilities. The following are some guidelines for being a host:

✦ Any lookup files required by the database must be opened by the host.

✦ To avoid bringing the network to a standstill, the host should try to avoid running additional programs while he or she is serving as host.

✦ Only the host can define fields, change the order of layouts, save copies of the file, define groups, set access privileges, or change the database back to single-user status.

As you can see, the host is in charge of the big stuff: making certain that the database is ready to use, ensuring that his or her personal computer is not overburdened, and making major changes to the structure of the database. Reserving these major privileges for the host makes good sense. If any of these actions were available to all users, no one would be able to get any work done. Imagine trying to enter a new record while several individuals were simultaneously shifting around the fields in a key layout.

In fact, if the host attempts any of these actions, FileMaker Pro automatically asks all guests to close the file. After the host completes the necessary changes and reopens the database as multiuser, guests can reopen the file and resume their work.

When you—as host—finish using the file and want to close it, you can choose File ➪ Close, File ➪ Quit, or select Single User in the File Sharing dialog box. If any guests are using the database, FileMaker Pro asks that you notify them, requesting that they close the database as well.

To close a database as a host, follow these steps:

1. Choose File ➪ Sharing, and then click the Single User radio button in the File Sharing dialog box.

   —or—

   Choose Close (⌘+W/Ctrl+W) or Quit (⌘+Q/Ctrl+Q) from the File menu.

   If any guests are using the database, a dialog box appears on the host's screen, as shown in Figure 19-3.

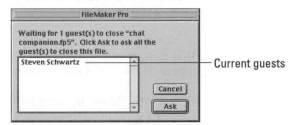

Figure 19-3: This dialog box shows that others are still using the database.

2. Click Ask to send each guest a message asking him or her to close the file.

A message appears on each guest's screen (see Figure 19-4), stating that the host wants to close the file and that guests must relinquish access to it.

To acknowledge the message and relinquish the file, guests click the Close Now button.

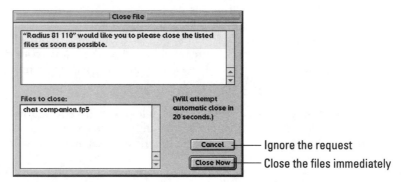

Figure 19-4: This message appears on guests' screens.

3. After 20 seconds, FileMaker Pro automatically attempts to close the file.

If the file can be closed safely, FileMaker does so, regardless of whether guests have responded to the message. If the file cannot be closed safely, it remains open.

Guest activities

To open a shared (multiuser) database as a guest, choose the File ➪ Open command (or press ⌘+O/Ctrl+O), click the Hosts button in the file dialog box that appears, and then choose a file and click Open. Only files that have been opened by a host appear in the file list. (FileMaker Pro also has a keyboard shortcut that you can use to go directly to the Hosts dialog box: Option+⌘+O/Shift+Ctrl+O.)

If your network is divided into zones, the zones will be listed in a separate section at the bottom of the Hosts dialog box. In that case, you first must select a zone and then choose one of the shared files that appear at the top of the dialog box.

Tip   If you're certain that a particular file has been opened as multiuser, but you don't see it in the file list for the appropriate network zone, press the Option/Ctrl key as you click the zone name. This action allows FileMaker Pro more time to check for shared files. (Note that files set for Multi-user (hidden) still will not appear in the file list.)

Setting a file as single user or multiuser

When a host changes the status of a file from multiuser to single user, or vice versa, that new status is saved along with the other database settings. If, for example, a host closes a file while it is still set as multiuser, the next time the file is opened, the file is automatically marked as sharable and is ready to receive guests. On the other hand, if the file is set to single-user status when it is closed, the next host — whoever that might be — must reset the file to multiuser (assuming that the file is still meant to be shared).

To specify a local TCP/IP host, click Local Hosts and then choose one from the hosts shown in the upper list. To specify a host outside of your local TCP/IP area, click Specify Host. In the dialog box that appears, enter a domain name or an IP address. You can add this host to the lower list by clicking "Permanently add entry to Host list." (This feature enables you to connect to the same database again later — without having to search for the domain name or address.)

Each guest may perform any action on the database that his or her privileges allow. At a minimum, each guest can browse the file (they can examine records but cannot change data in them). Other normal activities, such as editing, adding, and deleting records, also may be permitted. For details, see "Protecting Databases and Setting Access Privileges," later in this chapter.

Notes on cross-platform database sharing

As mentioned earlier in this chapter, both Macs and PCs can share FileMaker Pro databases on a network. In general, any typical task (such as entering and editing data, creating and deleting records, and sorting or issuing find requests) can be performed on either platform (Mac or Windows). Data, graphics, and other elements that appear on one machine also appear on the other. In addition, the program commands used to work with databases are the same whether the user is running the Macintosh or Windows version of FileMaker Pro. However, there are a few important differences, as follows:

✦ Platform-specific tasks can be performed only on the appropriate platform. A Windows user, for example, cannot execute a script that relies on Apple Events or AppleScript, and a Mac user can't execute scripts that execute DDE commands.

✦ Fonts occasionally can pose a problem. Common fonts, such as Times and Helvetica, are mapped to compatible fonts when viewed on a different platform from the one on which the database was created. Unusual fonts may not translate so well and can cause field labels to spill over into fields or wrap to a new line, for example.

✦ Special symbols used in entering data or creating layout text can produce unusual or unexpected results when viewed on the other platform.

✦ File-naming conventions differ between the two platforms.

✦ Container fields may exhibit differences between the two platforms. For example, Windows users can embed or link a Container field to an OLE object.

For information concerning other differences between the Mac and Windows versions of FileMaker Pro, as well as the mechanics of sharing databases between these two platforms without a network, see Chapter 16.

Protecting Databases and Setting Access Privileges

Some databases are designed to be shared equally by all users on a network. It is not uncommon for a department to have a shared business contacts database, for example. Allowing such a database to be shared can save considerable time and energy compared to having every person maintain her or his own version of a contacts file.

However, not all company information is intended to be shared among all employees or even all members of the same department. A database that contains employee salary information, for example, may well be available only to members of the Accounting Department. And within that database, certain layouts and data may properly be modified or viewed only by the head of the department.

Other information is often meant for no one other than the person who designed the database. A manager, for example, may create a database that he uses to record comments about employee performance. Although the contents of this file may be extremely useful when the manager writes his annual employee evaluations, this sensitive information is not meant to be viewed or edited by anyone else in the company.

FileMaker Pro anticipates the need for security and for assigning different types of privileges to different users. To this end, you can create passwords for databases, create groups, and associate access privileges and database resources with specific groups.

The following information may help you better understand how these elements interact and how to use them:

✦ *Passwords and privileges.* Each password is associated with a particular set of privileges (what users can or cannot do with the database). Users without a password can be prevented from even opening the file or can be granted minimal privileges, such as only viewing the data.

✦ *Groups and resources.* All group members are assigned passwords, which restrict the privileges of members of that group. Groups can be associated with particular database resources (layouts and fields). You can prevent group members from seeing a sensitive report layout, for example, or stop them from modifying data in certain fields.

Creating passwords

Passwords are used to restrict the types of activities a user can perform on a database. (Examples of activities include browsing, adding, deleting, and editing records.) The *master password* — normally held by the database designer or database administrator — provides complete access to the file, enabling the password holder to perform any desired design activity, including creating or changing layouts and editing scripts. The master password is also required when a user wants to set or change the access privileges of other individuals or groups who use the database.

The database designer or administrator may also create additional passwords that allow fewer privileges. Depending on the content of a database, you may want to create a password that allows the user only to view the data (browse records), for example. This access is the minimum access any user can be given and is available to anyone who is able to open the database. You can also set privileges for users who have no password or have forgotten their passwords (described later in this section).

To create passwords for a database, follow these steps:

1. Open the database for which you want to create passwords.

Note Every database must have its own passwords. There is no command with which you can create a "universal" password that works with all of your databases.

2. Choose File ⇨ Access Privileges ⇨ Passwords.

   The Define Passwords dialog box appears, as shown in Figure 19-5.

3. If you have not yet created a master password for this database, do so now by following these steps:

   In the Privileges section of the Define Passwords dialog box, check the box labeled "Access the entire file." Type a new password in the Password box, and then click Create.

4. To specify the menus that users with the current password will see, choose an option (Normal, Editing Only, or None) from the Available menu commands pop-up menu.

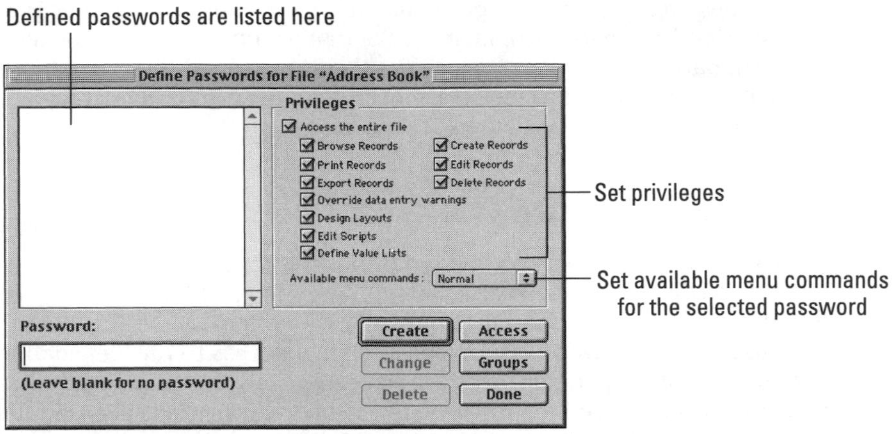

Defined passwords are listed here

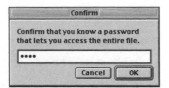

Figure 19-5: The Define Passwords dialog box

5. If this is the only password you want to create at this time, click Done.

— or —

Create the next password by typing it in the Password box, set privileges to be associated with the password by clicking check boxes, and then click Create.

6. Click Done to save the new passwords for the file.

Before closing the Define Passwords dialog box, FileMaker Pro makes sure that you know the master password (and hence, have the right to assign and modify passwords) by displaying the dialog box shown in Figure 19-6.

Figure 19-6: Enter the master password in this dialog box.

7. Type the master password, and click OK.

Note

To access fields from related files in the current database, you must have access privileges for the related file. If the related file uses the same password, FileMaker Pro will automatically reuse the password.

Creating default passwords

FileMaker Pro 5 includes a feature called the *default password*. If you declare a particular password to be the default password for a database, FileMaker Pro automatically uses that password whenever a user opens the database. No password dialog box appears, and the privileges associated with the default password are automatically set.

Note

Setting a default password can sometimes create an interesting problem. Because the default password is used automatically each time you open the database, you are never given the opportunity to enter a higher-level password (in the event you want to have different privileges or make major changes to the database). You can force the password dialog box to appear by pressing Option/Shift as you open the database.

Any password that has been defined for a database can be set as the default password. To establish a default password, follow these steps:

1. Open the database for which you want to set a default password.

2. If an appropriate password doesn't already exist, create a password as previously instructed in "Creating passwords."

3. Choose Edit ⇨ Preferences ⇨ Document.

The Document Preferences dialog box appears, as shown in Figure 19-7. Click the General tab at the top of the dialog box.

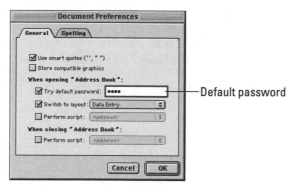

Figure 19-7: Setting a default password for a database

4. In the "When opening" section of the dialog box, click the "Try default password" check box. Then type the password in the text box to the right.

5. Click Done to save your changes and close the dialog box.

In all future sessions — regardless of who is using the database — the default password will automatically be invoked when the database is opened. You can eliminate a default password by returning to the Document Preferences dialog box and removing the check mark from the "Try default password" check box.

Passing out passwords

When the database designer or administrator hands out the passwords, the distribution is handled on a group basis (see "Creating and deleting groups," later in this chapter). If the major groups are defined as departments, for example, the administrator is responsible for ensuring that every salesperson receives the same password. By distributing the passwords, the administrator is defining the group membership.

The group names, as well as their very existence, are of no concern to employees; only the person with the master password ever actually sees the group names. All users know is that they have a password that gives them particular rights — not whether others also have the same password and privileges. Individuals with any password other than the master password have the Change Password command displayed in the File menu rather than the Access Privileges submenu, which only the administrator can use to view and change passwords, groups, and access privileges. For information about changing your assigned password, see "Changing a password," later in this chapter.

Modifying passwords

If you have the master password, you can change or delete any password for the database. To alter a password, open the database by using the master password, and choose File ➪ Access Privileges ➪ Passwords. When the Define Passwords dialog box appears (as previously shown in Figure 19-5), you can do the following:

✦ Delete a password by selecting a password and clicking Delete.

✦ Change a password by selecting a password, typing a new password in the Password box, and clicking Change.

After deleting or altering passwords, it is your responsibility to let the affected individuals know about the changes.

Even if you do not have the master password for a database, you can change any password that has been assigned to you. For details, see "Changing a password," later in this chapter.

Passwords for shareware tem˜plates

One handy use for passwords is when you are developing shareware or commercial templates that you intend to sell to others. Before distributing the templates, you can create several levels of passwords that address different customer needs. Here are some examples:

✦ *No password:* Create a blank password with limited privileges (browse records, print/export records, and edit records, for example). This technique enables a prospective customer to examine the database, print reports, and so on, but he or she is restricted to using the records you included in the database.

✦ *Default password:* FileMaker Pro enables you to set a default password for any database that will automatically be tried whenever the database is opened. (The user never even sees a dialog box asking for a password.) By using this approach, you can set privileges for the database and save the user from dealing with the annoying prompt for a password that accompanies the "no password" setting described in the previous point.

✦ *Second-level password:* In addition to the privileges available when no password or a default password is used, this password can enable a user to create and delete records. Offer to provide this password in exchange for a basic shareware fee. If they like your product, most customers will prefer this option.

✦ *Master-level password:* Check the "Access the entire file" option when specifying privileges for this password. This password gives customers complete freedom to modify the template as they see fit, as well as the capability to remove the password protection. Because using this option is the equivalent of selling the code for a computer program, you will usually want to offer this master password for a higher fee. (Recognize, of course, that giving a user full access means that he or she has more opportunity to revise your scripts or to use the template in ways you never intended, which can lead to technical support nightmares.)

Unless you see a reason to restrict access to certain layouts or fields, you probably don't need to create groups (see the following section).

Creating and deleting groups

After you define passwords, the next step is to define groups and assign at least one password to each group. Because each password has specific privileges associated with it, you can be sure that all members of the group have identical privileges.

Tip   You are not *required* to create groups. If you simply want to prevent anyone else from opening a database that you designed, for example, all you need to do is create a master password with full access privileges. In this case, groups would serve no purpose.

Each group is a cohesive class of users. Group membership can be based on employee rank, departments in your company, or anything else you like. In most cases, "need to know" is the most critical factor in determining group membership. The key thing to remember is that in addition to sharing a password, members of any given group have the same privileges in the database and can work with the same layouts and fields.

To define a group, follow these steps:

1. If the database is not open, open it now and supply the master password when prompted for it.

   Only a person who knows the master password can create or modify groups.

2. Choose File ➪ Access Privileges ➪ Groups.

   The Define Groups dialog box appears, as shown in Figure 19-8. (Note that you can also reach this dialog box by clicking the Groups button in the Define Passwords dialog box.)

Defined groups are listed here

Create a new group

Figure 19-8: The Define Groups dialog box

3. Type a name for the group in the Group Name box and click Create.

4. To associate privileges and resources with the group name, click Access.

   The Access Privileges dialog box appears, as shown in Figure 19-9.

5. Select the current group in the Groups column.

Selected group

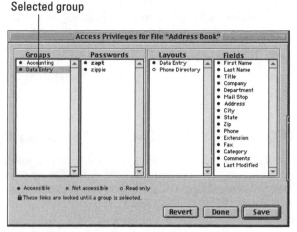

Figure 19-9: The Access Privileges dialog box

6. In the Passwords column, click the bullet next to each password that you want to associate with the group.

Whatever privileges were assigned to the selected passwords are now associated with that group.

A solid bullet beside a password means that the password is associated with the currently selected group. A dimmed bullet means that the password is not associated with the currently selected group.

You can assign multiple passwords to one group, as well as associate multiple groups with the same password, if you like.

7. To restrict access to particular layouts or fields, click the bullets that precede them in the Layouts and Fields columns.

A solid bullet means that the resource is accessible to the currently selected group. An open bullet means that the resource can be read but not altered by the group. A dimmed bullet means that the resource is not accessible by the group. (If a user attempts to display an inaccessible layout or a layout that contains an inaccessible field, FileMaker Pro covers the entire layout and displays the message "Access Denied.")

8. Click Save to save the current settings, or click Revert to restore the original settings.

9. If you want to set passwords and resource privileges for other groups, select another group and repeat steps 6 through 8; otherwise, click Done to return to the Define Groups dialog box.

10. When you finish defining groups in the Define Groups dialog box, click Done to save your changes and return to the database.

You can delete any group by selecting the group's name in the Define Groups dialog box and then clicking Delete. Before you delete or modify groups for a database that is currently being shared, however, users must close the file. When you choose File ➪ Access Privileges ➪ Groups, the Ask dialog box appears immediately if other people are using the file (as previously shown in Figure 19-3). Click Ask, wait until the other users close the file or until FileMaker Pro closes it, and then delete or modify the group.

Setting, changing, and examining access privileges

FileMaker Pro provides another method of setting, changing, and examining the relationships between assigned passwords, groups, and database resources. If you have the master password, you can choose the File ➪ Access Privileges ➪ Overview command. The Access Privileges dialog box appears, as previously shown in Figure 19-9. (This is the same dialog box that appears when you set group privileges, as described in the previous section.)

If you examine the various dialog boxes that appear when you choose a command from the Access Privileges submenu, you'll notice that you can click buttons that take you to any step in the protection-specification process: working with passwords, creating groups, or selecting available resources.

Another use for the Access Privileges dialog box

Regardless of how you reach the Access Privileges dialog box, you can also use it for the following tasks:

✦ Determining which fields are displayed in any layout

✦ Determining all layouts in which a specific field appears

To see the fields used in a particular layout, select the layout name in the Layouts column of the dialog box. As shown in Figure 19-9, a solid bullet in the Fields column precedes all fields that appear in the selected layout. To see all layouts that display a particular field, select the field in the Fields column. A solid bullet precedes associated layouts.

This information can make it easier for you to assign resources to different groups. In the Address Book database shown in the figure, for example, you may want to keep a certain group from seeing the contents of a particular field. If you click the field in the Fields column, you can quickly determine which layouts use that field and, hence, will be dimmed when a user from that group attempts to display those layouts. If the group members must see or work with a layout that currently includes a restricted field, you can modify the layout by removing the field, or you can make a new version of the layout that does not include the field.

Using a protected file

When you attempt to open a password-protected database—whether that database is on a network or only on your personal computer—you immediately see the dialog box shown in Figure 19-10. As you type, the characters are shown as bullets in the dialog box. This extra bit of security keeps passersby from taking a gander at your password. If you make a mistake while typing the password, just press the Delete/Backspace key to remove the incorrect characters and then retype them.

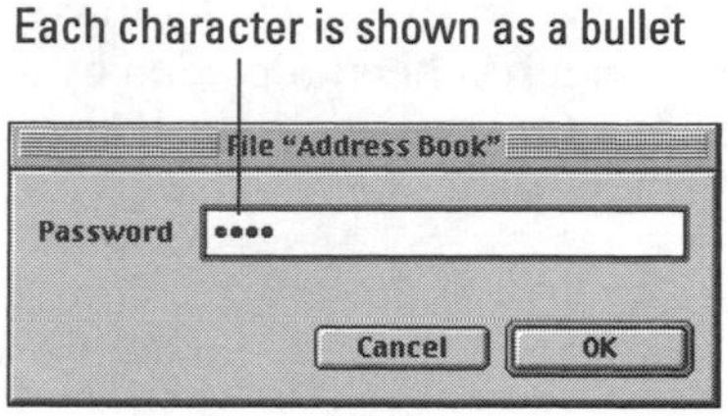

Each character is shown as a bullet

File "Address Book"

Password ••••

Cancel   OK

Figure 19-10: Entering a password

When you finish, click OK, or press Return or Enter. If the password is correct, the database opens, and you are assigned the access privileges that are associated with the password.

If you type the password incorrectly (or are simply entering a guess), FileMaker Pro displays a dialog box informing you that the password is incorrect. If you click the OK button in this dialog box, the original password dialog box reappears, and you can try again. If you don't know or remember the password, click Cancel. FileMaker Pro remains open, and you can select a different database with which to work.

Opening a database without a password

If the person who assigned passwords also created a no-password option that enables users to open the database without entering a password, a slightly different version of the password dialog box appears (see Figure 19-11). If you don't have a password, you can open the database by clicking OK or by pressing Return or Enter. As with actual passwords, a no-password user also has specific access privileges that have been assigned by the database designer or administrator.

File "Address Book"

Password [   ]

(Leave blank for limited access) — This database can be opened
Cancel   OK   without a password

Figure 19-11: A password dialog box
with a "no password" option

Note   If you have assigned a default password to the database (as described in "Creating default passwords," earlier in this chapter), no password dialog box appears. Instead, FileMaker Pro transparently uses the default password for you (or any other user) and opens the database with the specific privileges that were associated with that password. (Note that you can force the password dialog box to appear by holding down Option/Shift when the database is opened. Use this technique when you have another password that offers privileges beyond those of the default password.)

Changing a password

After using any password other than the master password to open a database, you'll notice that the File ⇨ Access Privileges submenu has been replaced by a new command: Change Password. Although you cannot alter your access privileges for the file, you can change your password whenever you want.

To change a password, follow these steps:

1. Choose File ⇨ Change Password.

   The Change Password dialog box appears, as shown in Figure 19-12.

Figure 19-12: The Change Password dialog box

2. Type your current password in the "Old password" box.

3. Press the Tab key, and type the new password in the "New password" box.

4. Press the Tab key, and type the new password a second time (to verify it) in the "Confirm new password" box.

5. Click OK to save the new password.

Caution   Although security experts suggest that you change your password regularly, this FileMaker Pro procedure has one big drawback. When you change a password for yourself, you are also changing it for everyone else who uses the same password — that is, all members of the group or groups to which the password has been assigned. It is your responsibility to see that all affected users of the database are informed of the password change.

Unless you are the sole user of a particular password, a better approach is to leave password changes to the database administrator. Because that person has complete access to the database and can view or alter passwords at any time (even if a user has already changed the password), the administrator is in a perfect position to handle this task. And because the administrator also knows which users share each password, he or she can make sure that the new password is communicated only to the right people.

Summary

✦ If you are working on an AppleTalk, IPX/SPX (Windows), or TCP/IP network, FileMaker Pro 5 databases can be shared among users. Up to ten users can simultaneously work in any shared database. However, each user must have his or her own copy of FileMaker Pro. If more than ten users will ever need to simultaneously work in the database, you must use FileMaker Server to host the database.

✦ The first person to open a database for sharing during a computing session is called the host. Although guests (other users) can view and edit data in the file, only the host's Page Setup, Find, and Sort changes are saved when the file is closed. The host is also responsible for closing the database.

✦ If they are on the same network, users of the Windows version of FileMaker Pro can share their databases with Mac users, and vice versa.

✦ To protect a database or assign different privileges to different classes of users, you can assign passwords to the database, define groups that are associated with each password, and limit access to particular resources (layouts and fields).

✦ ✦ ✦

Web Publishing with FileMaker Pro

✦ ✦ ✦ ✦

In This Chapter

Using Instant Web
Publishing

Using Custom Web
Publishing

✦ ✦ ✦ ✦

T he biggest change introduced in FileMaker Pro 4.0 was that you could publish your databases on the World Wide Web or on a corporate Intranet. By using a Web browser such as Internet Explorer or Netscape Navigator, users around the globe can view and interact with any FileMaker Pro database that you open as multiuser — just as they could if they were connected over a local area network. FileMaker Pro 5 builds on the Web publishing capabilities of 4.0/4.1, enabling your published databases to look very similar to their design in FileMaker Pro.

Publishing Methods and Views

Unlike Web pages you post on an ISP's (Internet service provider) Web server, when you use the FileMaker Pro Web Companion plug-in to host a database, your computer acts as the server. People viewing and editing the database are actually interacting directly with your computer and its hard disk over a TCP/IP connection.

Note   Unlike normal Web pages, users can only view your published databases when you are online and have the databases opened as multiuser. The IP (*Internet Protocol*) address of your computer serves as the URL for the databases you are hosting. Thus, unless you have a permanent connection to the Internet, Web publishing may be impractical because modem connections are fragile and your IP address probably changes each time you reconnect to your ISP. See the "About IP addresses" sidebar later in this chapter for additional information.

FileMaker Pro provides two methods for publishing databases on the Web: Instant Web Publishing and Custom Web Publishing. *Instant Web Publishing* enables you to put your database on the Web without programming or knowledge of HTML (*Hypertext Markup Language*, the language used to create pages for the World Wide Web). All you need to do is select a handful of options from FileMaker Pro dialog boxes.

New Feature

In FileMaker Pro 5, Instant Web Publishing has been enhanced to make Web-published databases more closely resemble their appearance as designed in FileMaker Pro, offer support for cascading style sheets, and provide additional security options.

Two views of the database are available to all users: a *Table View* (listing all fields in a columnar table) and a *Form View* (for creating, editing, and viewing individual records). Users can execute Find requests to locate particular records and — at your discretion — can sort the database to suit their needs. There is also a built-in home page from which users can choose a database to browse, as well as a Help page that provides instructions for using and interacting with the databases.

New Feature

When you use Instant Web Publishing with FileMaker Pro 5, you no longer relinquish control of the layout and the appearance of the data as you did with 4.0/4.1. You can choose one of several layout themes; your Form View layout is embedded within it. Buttons that execute the Go to Layout script step will still function on the Web, enabling users to switch layouts when in Form View. The only restriction is that users viewing the database must have a Web browser that supports cascading style sheets. All of the following browsers (or later versions) offer cascading style sheet support: Internet Explorer 4.5 (Macintosh), Internet Explorer 5 (Windows), Netscape Communicator 4.5 (Windows), and Netscape Communicator 4.6 (Macintosh and Windows).

If you want your published database to be viewable in older browsers (Internet Explorer 3, for example), you can still use the FileMaker Pro 4.0/4.1 themes. Such databases do not use your existing layouts, however. Standard Table and Form Views are created automatically.

You can set different permissions for individuals and groups, and employ advanced features such as value lists and data validation. Figure 20-1 shows a typical database created with Instant Web Publishing.

Custom Web Publishing is for users who want greater control over the capabilities of their Web-based databases. By using HTML and CDML (*Claris Dynamic Markup Language,* a set of proprietary extensions to HTML), you can serve up database information within the context of normal Web pages that incorporate clickable buttons and Java applets, for example.

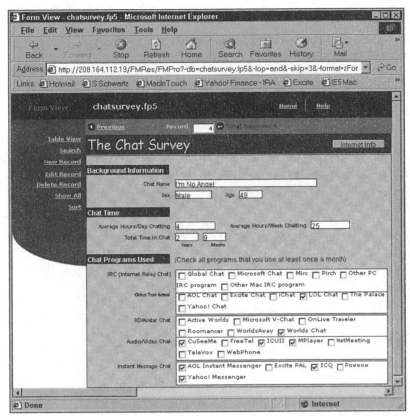

Figure 20-1: A Form View of a database published with Instant Web Publishing

In addition to using CDML to create Web pages, FileMaker Pro 5 also supports database access via XML and Java applets (using a JDBC driver).

New Feature

If you anticipate more than sporadic traffic on your published databases (more than ten guests in any 12-hour period), you should consider an upcoming product from FileMaker, Inc. called FileMaker Pro Unlimited. Like FileMaker Pro Server (and most likely the soon-to-be-released FileMaker Server 5), the purpose of Unlimited is to host (or serve) databases on the Web or an intranet, rather than on a network.

Instant Web Publishing

The quickest way to publish a FileMaker Pro database on the World Wide Web or an Intranet is by using Instant Web Publishing. And with FileMaker's new support of cascading style sheets, Instant Web Publishing will now satisfy the needs of most users.

Publishing a database with Instant Web Publishing

Follow these basic steps to host a database with Instant Web Publishing (additional details are provided in the sections that follow):

1. Open the existing database you want to publish (or create a new one).

2. Choose Edit ➪ Preferences ➪ Application. Set TCP/IP as the network protocol (General preferences) and enable the Web Companion plug-in (Plug-Ins preferences).

3. With the Web Companion plug-in selected, click the Configure button. In the dialog box that appears (see Figure 20-2), enable Instant Web Publishing and set other options (such as the method of security control and whether to use the built-in home page or your own custom page).

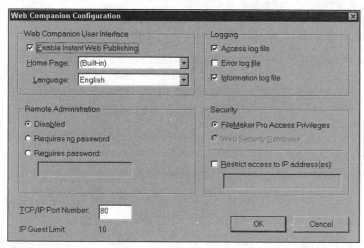

Figure 20-2: The Web Companion Configuration dialog box

4. Choose File ➪ Sharing. In the File Sharing dialog box that appears, choose Multi-User and set Web Companion as the sharing method.

5. Click the Set Up Views button. In the Web Companion View Setup dialog box, choose a Web style, and select the fields you want to present in Table View, Form View, and Search by choosing layouts from the database. (All fields from the chosen layout are used, displayed in the order in which they appear in the layout.) Specify a sort method.

Step 1: Database considerations

When you use Instant Web Publishing, you cannot select specific database fields to display. The layouts you select for Table and Form Views dictate the fields that appear — that is, *all* fields from the chosen layout(s) are used. Thus, if you want to omit some fields (Summary fields, for example), you must do so by creating new layouts that contain only the desired fields.

Step 2: Choosing a network protocol and enabling the Web Companion plug-in

TCP/IP (*Transmission Control Protocol/Internet Protocol*) is the protocol used to send and receive information over the Internet. When publishing a database on the Internet, you must set TCP/IP as your network protocol. To do so, choose Edit ➪ Preferences ➪ Application. Click the General tab, as shown in Figure 20-3. Choose TCP/IP as the network protocol.

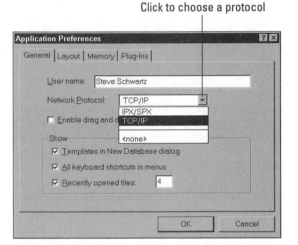

Figure 20-3: Choosing TCP/IP as the network protocol

To enable the Web Companion plug-in, choose Edit ➪ Preferences ➪ Application. The Application Preferences dialog box appears. Click the Plug-Ins tab, as shown in Figure 20-4. Click the check box for Web Companion.

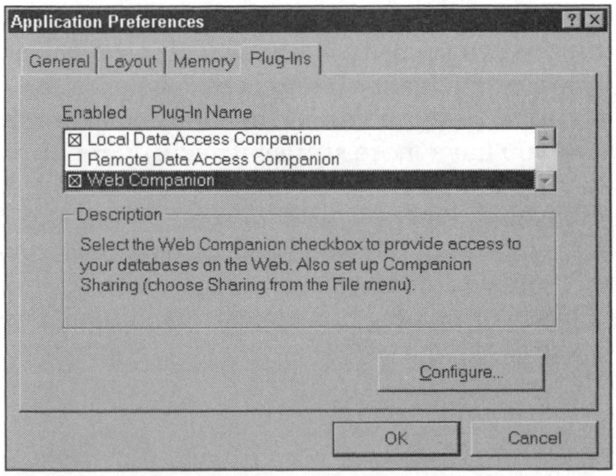

Figure 20-4: Enabling the Web Companion plug-in

Note Before you enable the Web Companion plug-in, make sure your Mac or PC is ready to connect to the Internet or to an Intranet. If a connection is not already active, enabling the plug-in instructs FileMaker Pro to immediately attempt a connection. (If you are using FileMaker Pro locally, you may want to disable the plug-in.)

Step 3: Setting Web Companion configuration options

Go to the Plug-Ins section of the Application Preferences dialog box — if it is not already on-screen. Select Web Companion and click the Configure button to view or change the configuration settings (refer to Figure 20-2). (For most users, the default settings suffice.)

The only critical setting in this dialog box is labeled "Enable Instant Web Publishing." When checked (as it should be in this instance), Instant Web Publishing is selected; when unchecked, Custom Web Publishing is selected. Other settings have the following functions:

✦ *Home Page*: Users access your published databases by clicking links on your home page. You can use the built-in home page (see Figure 20-5) or create one of your own. If you prefer to use your own home page, place its HTML file in the Web folder (inside the FileMaker Pro 5 folder). Only HTML files in the Web folder can be designated as home pages in the Web Companion Configuration dialog box.

✦ *Language*: Choose the language you want to use to present your database to users.

✦ *Remote Administration*: Select a Remote Administration option if you want to maintain the database from your Web browser using HTTP commands (for downloading and uploading files). This option is useful when you must make changes to the database from a remote location.

✦ *Logging*: You can instruct FileMaker Pro to create one or more text files (Activity.log, Error.log, and Info.log) in the FileMaker Pro 5 folder that track user interactions with your published databases. The primary information is recorded when the database is opened, including the date and time the request was made.

✦ *Security*: You can employ either of two security methods to control access to the published database. Choose "FileMaker Pro Access Privileges" to use the passwords and group privileges you've specified in FileMaker Pro (as explained in Chapter 19). If you have more stringent security requirements (for example, different passwords and privileges for each individual) and will be using Custom Web Publishing to host your database, choose the Web Security Database option. Refer to "Using the Web Security database," later in this chapter, for instructions. If passwords have been assigned using either security method, a standard password dialog box appears each time a user attempts to access the database (see Figure 20-6).

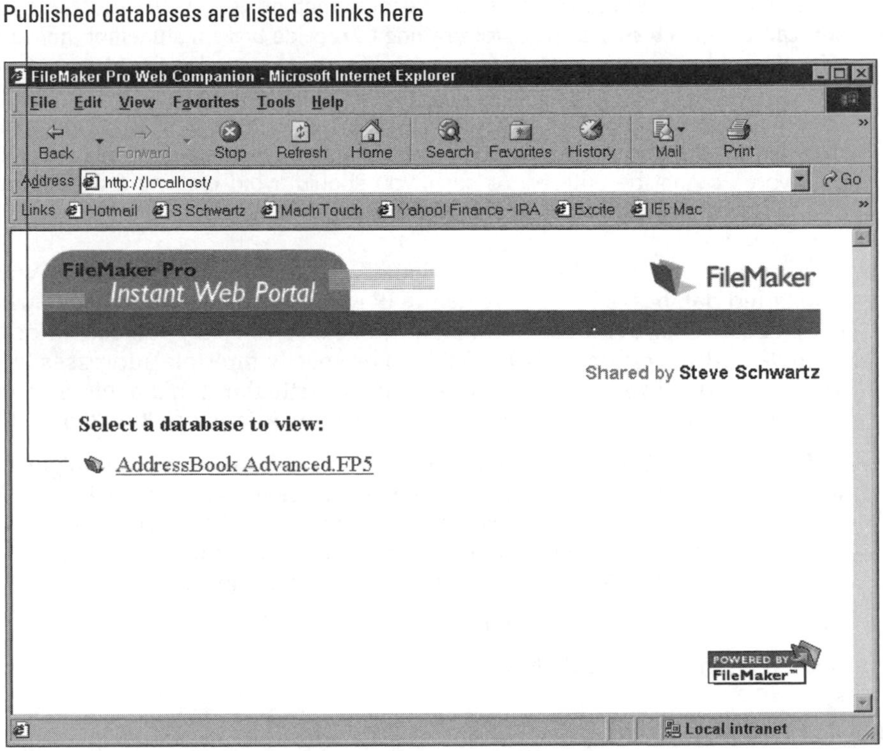

Published databases are listed as links here

Figure 20-5: To open any of your published databases, users click links on this built-in home page (known as the "Instant Web Portal").

Figure 20-6: When security is enabled, users must enter a name and password to gain access to the database.

Caution

When you use Access Privileges as the security method (set within FileMaker Pro), you can assign a blank/no password setting to provide basic features for individuals who do not have a password. Unfortunately, the no password option does not work as you might expect when you publish the database with Instant Web Publishing. Even if other passwords have also been defined, the "no password" condition is automatically invoked for all users; a password dialog box never appears and higher-level passwords cannot be entered. As such, you should avoid creating a no password option unless you want to apply it to all users of the database.

✦ *Restrict access to IP address(es)*: Optionally, you can restrict access to your published databases by specifying the IP addresses of the individuals who can access them. (This feature is new in FileMaker Pro 5.) You can enter a single address (such as 220.205.68.18) or specify multiple addresses by separating them with commas. To specify a particular domain, enter the first three parts of the address, followed by an asterisk (such as **220.205.68.***).

✦ *TCP/IP Port Number.* If you are already running a Web server, you might want to use port number 591, which has been reserved for use with the Web Companion. Note that if you use any port other than 80 (the default port), the port number must be appended to the URL in the following manner when you log on to (or specify the link for) your home page:

```
http://IP address:port number
```

for example, **http://206.223.50.7:591**

Step 4: Enabling sharing

If you are hosting a database on a LAN (local area network), you must set the database's status as multiuser in order to enable others to view and interact with it. The same holds true if you are hosting a database on the Web or an Intranet. To turn on sharing for the database, choose File ➪ Sharing and click the Multi-User radio button.

Tip

To publish a database but prevent users from accessing it (as you might do with a critical related file, for example), choose Multi-User (Hidden) in the File Sharing dialog box. Another alternative is to add an underscore as the last character in the filename, such as **Sales_** or **Sales_.fp5**.

Step 5: Selecting a display style, fields, and sort options

Select Web Companion in the File Sharing dialog box and click the Set Up Views button. The Web Companion View Setup dialog box appears, as shown in Figure 20-7. The View Setup dialog box has five sections: Web Style, Table View, Form View, Search, and Sort.

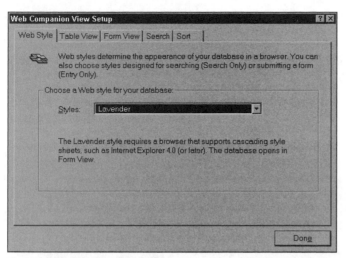

Figure 20-7: Setting up different views for the database

New Feature

You use the Web Style tab of the View Setup dialog box to specify how you want the database to appear when viewed in a browser. The first three styles (Lavender, Wheat, and Blue and Gold 1) display the database in Form View and require a browser with cascading style sheet support. The Blue and Gold 2 and Fern Green styles display the database in Table View and can be viewed with older browsers. (This was the way that published databases were displayed in FileMaker Pro 4.0/4.1.) Choose "Search only" to publish a database in which users can only search and view records, or "Entry only" to publish a database in which users can only create new records. Search-only and Entry-only databases require Internet Explorer 4.5 (Macintosh), Internet Explorer 5 (Windows), or Netscape Communicator 4.5 or later (Windows).

For each of the next three sections (Table View, Form View, and Search), choose an existing layout to use when users view and edit data. The layouts chosen determine the fields that will be presented and the order in which they appear in that particular view. The available fields in each layout are listed in the scrolling Field Name box.

Note

Unless you've selected a Web style that supports cascading style sheets, the actual layouts are not used.

Click the Sort tab to set sort options for the database, as follows:

✦ *Do not sort records.* Users may not specify a sort order for the database. Records are presented in the order in which they were created.

✦ *User defines sorting by specified fields in the browser.* Users may specify a sort order for the database by selecting from a set of fields that you specify. (Click the Specify button to create the list of allowable sort fields.) While this option has the greatest utility for users, it is also the slowest option. Selecting this option displays a Sort button in Table View. (To see how sorting is accomplished, see Figure 20-8.)

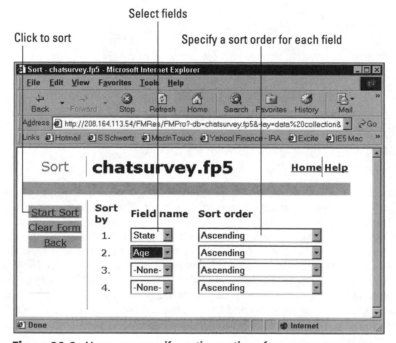

Figure 20-8: Users can specify sorting options from pop-up menus.

✦ *Predefine sorting by specified fields before downloading to the browser.* Choosing this option enables you to specify the sort order for the database. Click the Specify button to select one or more fields by which to sort. The same options are available as when you sort the database within FileMaker Pro, including ascending and descending sorts, sorting on multiple fields, and sorting based on value lists.

About IP addresses

The *IP address* is the URL to which users connect when they go to your Web publishing home page. Every computer connected to the Internet or an Intranet has a unique IP address in the form:

  xxx.xxx.xxx.xxx

where the *x*s represent numbers that contain from one to three digits, separated by periods (such as 207.254.25.117, for example). To open the home page for your Web publishing site, the user launches a Web browser, clicks in the browser's Address box, and types **http://**, followed by the full IP address of your home page, such as **http://207.254.25.117** or **http://207.254.25.117:591**. (The latter method is used in the event that the special FileMaker Pro IP port has been designated instead of 80 — the default port number.)

Computers that have a full-time connection to the Internet or a company Intranet typically have a *static IP address*; their IP address never changes — not even if the computer is temporarily disconnected from the Internet or Intranet. The same IP address is assigned for each new connection.

If you're like most Internet users, on the other hand, you are in a less enviable position. Most typically have a *dynamic* IP address; a new IP address is assigned each time you log on to your Internet account. A dynamic address makes it extremely difficult for users to find your home page because its address changes each time you connect.

Nevertheless, if you still want to publish databases on the Web, all you need to do is find out what your IP address is when you log on and then communicate it to potential users. *How* you determine your IP address, however, may be a mystery to you. Regardless of whether you have a dial-up or a permanent Internet connection, here are some methods you can use to find out your current IP address:

✦ *Macintosh users*: After connecting to the Internet, open the TCP/IP control panel and click the Info button. In more recent versions of the system software, you must choose File ➪ Get Info. The current IP address is shown on the line labeled "This Macintosh." If you use FreePPP as your dialer, you can get the same information by opening FreePPP Setup and clicking the blue *i* (the Info button).

✦ *Windows users*: Windows 95, 98, and NT have built-in utilities that can show your current IP address. The Windows 95/98 program is called WINIPCFG (see the figure below). The equivalent program for Windows NT is IPCONFIG. To make it convenient to run WINIPCFG or IPCONFIG, create a desktop shortcut to the program, add a shortcut for it in the Start menu, or assign a shortcut key to it.

✦ *All platforms*: After logging on, send yourself an e-mail message. Open the returned message and examine the full header. You will find your current IP address there.

Continued

(continued)

_ *All platforms*: Many Internet applications—with the notable exception of browsers and e-mail clients—show the current IP address somewhere within the program.

Current IP address

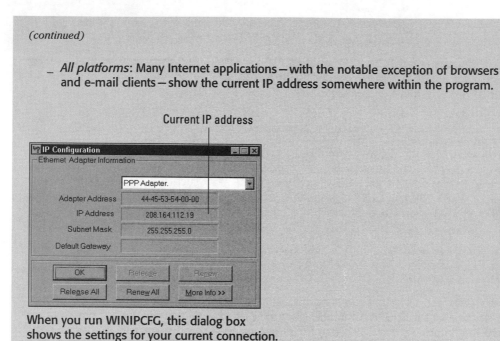

When you run WINIPCFG, this dialog box shows the settings for your current connection.

Note   The method of viewing the full header varies from one e-mail program to the next. For example, in Claris Emailer 2.0 (Mac), choose Show Long Headers from the Mail menu. In Outlook Express (Windows), select the message, choose the File ➪ Properties command, and click the Details tab in the dialog box that appears. To make the information easier to read, you can click the Message Source button. If you use Microsoft Outlook 2000 (Windows), open the message and choose View ➪ Options.

Testing your published database

To examine and interact with your database, you'll do what any other user would do—open it in your browser. Follow these steps to test your Web-published databases:

1. Launch FileMaker Pro and open the database you wish to publish. Make sure that the Web Companion plug-in is enabled and that the database is set for multiuser sharing.

2. With an active connection to the Internet or an intranet, launch your Web browser and type **http://** in the Address box, followed by your current IP address (such as **http://206.184.180.16**).

Note If you are using any port other than 80, the port number must be appended to the IP address (for example, **http://206.184.180.16:591**).

—or—

If you don't have an active Internet connection, simply launch your browser and type http://localhost in the Address box. This method enables you to test the database while working offline. [If this doesn't work, refer to "Testing the Web Companion without a network connection (Windows)" in FileMaker Pro Help.]

Offline testing on a Mac is more complex. For instructions, see "Testing the Web Companion without a network connection (Mac OS)" in FileMaker Pro Help.

3. When the home page appears, click the link for your database. As you modify, add, and delete records on the Web pages, the changes are made to the FileMaker Pro database.

Instant Web Publishing limitations

Although Instant Web Publishing is indeed a quick and easy way to get your databases onto the Web, there are some FileMaker Pro features and controls you must give up:

✦ In Table View, field names are automatically used as field labels. If you want different labels, you must change the field names.

✦ Users cannot run scripts. (There is one exception to this rule, however. If you attach a Go to Layout script step to a button and have chosen a Web style that supports cascading style sheets, the button appears on the layout and is functional.)

✦ If a field validation criterion is not met, a generic error message appears. Even if you have created custom error messages, they are not shown. For example, if data entered into a field fails a range test, there is no provision to explain to the user what the allowable range is.

✦ If a selected layout contains related fields and you are using the built-in home page, the related file is automatically listed and can be opened by users. However, you can prevent users from accessing the related files by opening them as Multi-User (Hidden) or by adding an underscore character at the end of the filename, such as **Sales_** or **Sales_.fp5**.

Interacting with a database published with Instant Web Publishing

When a user enters the URL for your home page (whether it's the built-in home page or one you designed), the current list of published databases appears. When a user clicks a link to a published database, the selected database appears. (If passwords have been assigned to the database, however, a password dialog box appears first.) What appears next depends on the Web style you've chosen for the database.

No support for cascading style sheets

If you've chosen a Web style that doesn't require cascading style sheets, a Table View of the database appears (see Figure 20-9). Down the left side of the table are links that users can click to control the database and access various features. The Table View and Form View links determine whether multiple records (Table View) or single records (Form View) are displayed.

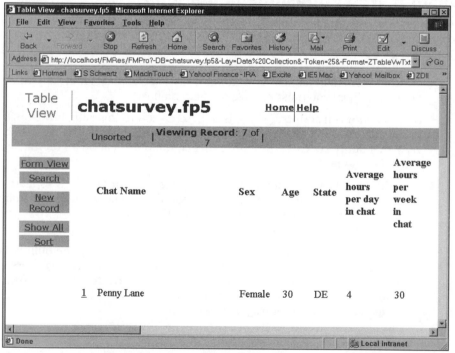

Figure 20-9: A standard database in Table View

Clicking the Search link displays a form with features similar to those available in a FileMaker Pro find request (see Figure 20-10). Searches are limited to those that can be conducted with a single request. Users can perform AND or OR searches by clicking the appropriate radio button and entering criteria as they would in FileMaker Pro.

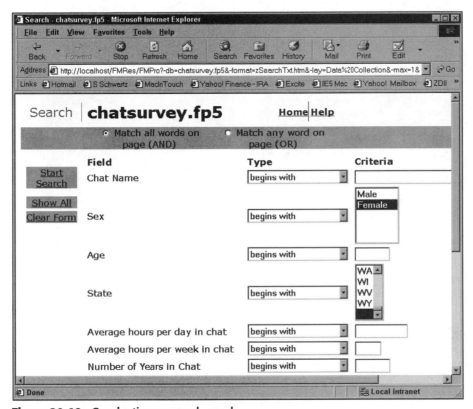

Figure 20-10: Conducting a record search

Clicking the Help link (at the top of the Web page) displays a page of detailed instructions for using and interacting with the database. Clicking the Home link returns users to your home page where other databases—if any—can be opened and examined.

The other available commands (shown as text links) depend on the access privileges assigned to the user. For example, there may be links for creating records, sorting, and executing a Show All Records command.

To view or work with individual records displayed in Table View, the user can either click a specific record number to the left of the desired record or click the Form View link (refer to Figure 20-9). In Form View (see Figure 20-11), a new set of links appears. The links presented depend on the access privileges assigned to the user, and whether the user is editing an existing record or creating a new one (or whether he/she is simply viewing multiple records).

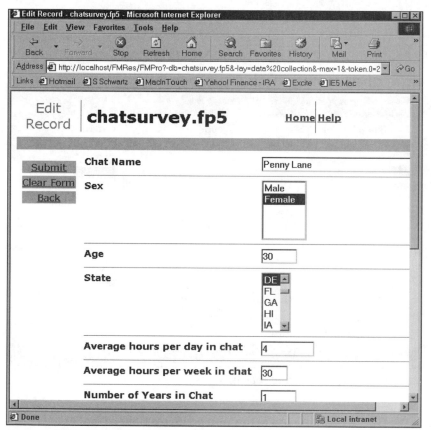

Figure 20-11: Editing a record in Form View

Support for cascading style sheets

If you've selected a Web style that supports cascading style sheets, the database opens in Form View, as shown in Figure 20-12. The layout displayed is the one chosen in the Form View section of the Web Companion View Setup dialog box. (If you also wish to be able to display other layouts in Form View, add buttons that execute the Go to Layout step.) Depending on the permissions set, text links and buttons are provided that enable the user to edit or delete the current record, create new records, show all records, search, sort, summon help, and switch to Table View.

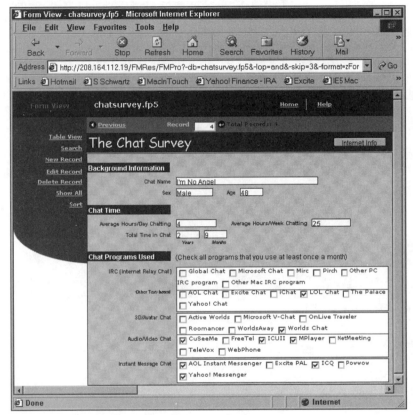

Figure 20-12: Viewing a record in Form View

Table View with cascading style sheets operates in the manner described previously in "No support for cascading style sheets." The main difference is that the same Web style interface is used as when viewing records in Form View. In addition, you can restrict the records displayed to any contiguous range (such as 5–12) by typing numbers into the Record Range box and clicking the arrow beside the box.

Using the Web Companion external functions to extract user information

If you want to gather information on the people who are viewing your published databases, the Web Companion external functions make it simple to do so. As shown in the figure below, you can assign these functions to Calculation fields. As each user connects with your published database, the external functions automatically obtain the desired information and record it in the Calculation fields. By analyzing this information, you can quickly determine what the most popular browsers are, for example, and redesign your site to take advantage of those browsers' features. To learn about using the Web Companion external functions, see Appendix E.

Fields that use the Web external functions

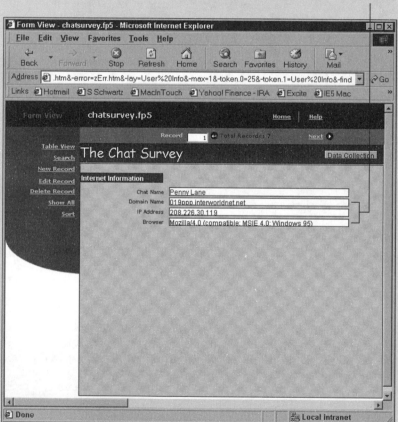

Using the Web Companion external functions to gather user data

Custom Web Publishing

In order to use Custom Web Publishing, you create Web page *format files* that contain a combination of HTML and CDML tags. The format files tell the user's browser how to display each Web page and enable users to interact with data in the published database. You can create format files in any text editor or Web-page design program.

Steps for Custom Web Publishing

Perform these steps to publish a database on the World Wide Web or an Intranet with Custom Web Publishing:

1. Open the existing database that you want to publish (or create a new one).

2. Create format files containing HTML and CDML tags that dictate the appearance of the pages as well as how users will interact with the database. Place the format files and any necessary image files inside the Web folder.

3. Open a connection to the Internet (if one isn't already open).

4. Choose Edit ➪ Preferences ➪ Application. Enable the Web Companion plug-in (Plug-Ins preferences).

5. Select the Web Companion plug-in and click the Configure button. In the Web Companion Configuration dialog box, disable Instant Web Publishing and set other options, such as a method of security control and the home page to use. The home page should contain a link to the IP address of your computer (the one hosting the published database), as well as the name and path of the format file.

6. Choose the File ➪ Sharing command. In the File Sharing dialog box that appears, choose Multi-User. Set Web Companion as the sharing method.

Note   Direct support for Custom Web publishing has been removed from the standard FileMaker Pro 5 package. It isn't discussed in the documentation or help files. Instead, users are encouraged to purchase FileMaker Developer 5 and/or refer to FileMaker's Web site for additional information.

Using the Web Security database

The Web Security database is meant to be used only in conjunction with databases published using Custom Web Publishing. For details, refer to the Web Security.pdf file, found in the Web Security folder. Those who use Instant Web Publishing, on the other hand, can protect their published databases by setting access privileges within FileMaker Pro 5.

Summary

✦ FileMaker Pro 5's Web Companion plug-in enables you to publish databases on the World Wide Web or Intranets. Two publishing methods are provided: Instant Web Publishing and Custom Web Publishing. You host published databases directly from your computer, turning it into a Web server. Users connect to your computer by typing your IP address in their Web browser's Address box.

✦ Working with a published database is similar to using a database in FileMaker Pro. Data can be displayed in tables (for viewing multiple records) or forms (for working with a single record at a time). Users can add, edit, or delete records — depending on the privileges assigned to them — and can execute find requests, for example.

✦ When you use Instant Web Publishing, you determine which fields will be displayed for the database by selecting a layout that contains the necessary fields. All fields of the selected layout are presented in the same order as they are specified in that layout.

✦ The TCP/IP network protocol is used to publish and work with FileMaker Pro databases on the Internet.

✦ You can set Web Companion configuration options to specify whether you will use the built-in home page or a custom home page; choose a language for the interface; permit administrative uploading and downloading of data with a Web browser; specify allowable user IP addresses; and set a different port for the Web server.

✦ If the majority of your users have a recent browser that supports cascading style sheets, records examined in Form View will employ the original layout(s) you designed in FileMaker Pro.

✦ Published databases can be presented in record-creation order, presorted according to criteria you establish, or sorted by the user (but restricted to sort fields of your choice).

✦ For additional control not afforded by FileMaker Pro security settings, you can use the Web Security database to assign permissions on a user-by-user basis. Note that the Web Security Database is intended for use only with databases published with Custom Web Publishing.

✦ If you use Custom Web Publishing, you must create format files that tell browsers how to display the data, graphics, buttons, and other elements on each Web page. The format files are a mixture of standard HTML tags and CDML tags. Refer to FileMaker Developer 5 or the FileMaker Web site for information on using CDML.

✦　　　✦　　　✦

Developing Databases for Others

No database is an island . . . actually, this statement is only sometimes true. You might create plenty of databases for personal use only—for example, a home financial database or one that contains information about friends and business associates. At times, however, you may want to share your examples of database wizardry with friends, colleagues, or the public at large. Here are a few examples:

✦ *Sharing in-house business templates*: Your company doesn't have a network, so employees can't access a central shared database. However, when someone in the company constructs a database that might be useful to other people in your department or to the company as a whole, you can distribute the template to everyone who needs it.

Suppose that as a sales associate, John creates a contact database that he uses to track sales leads, make follow-up calls, and record his successes and failures with each customer. The department decides to standardize, providing a copy of John's template to all salespeople so they can install it on their own computers.

✦ *Sharing with friends*: Sam's club has an ongoing membership drive. Because several people on the membership committee use FileMaker Pro, Sam creates a template to record information about each prospective or new member and then passes the template out to the other people on the committee. Every month, each member hands Sam a disk containing his or her current version of the database. Sam clicks a button on the template to execute a script that identifies which records have been added or modified during the past 30 days, exporting those records to a file. Sam then opens his master copy of the database and imports the records.

✦ *Sharing with the world*: After you develop a database to organize the contents of your wine cellar, to record the results of your biweekly gambling treks to Atlantic City, or to track your huge CD and cassette collection, you may decide that the database is too good to keep to yourself. Because you have an Internet account or are a member of an online information service (such as America Online or CompuServe), you decide to offer the template to others. Depending on your personal philosophy or degree of entrepreneurial spirit, you can post the template as *freeware* (free to anyone who wants it) or *shareware* (software for which you request a fee from all users who decide to keep the template after trying it).

FileMaker Pro provides two means of sharing templates. The usual method is to use the Save A Copy As command to create a clone of the finished database, stripping it of all records. Each user has access to the scripts and layouts you have painstakingly created, but your personal data stays with you.

The second approach is reserved for members of the FileMaker Solutions Alliance (FSA): third-party developers of commercial templates, add-ons, and training materials based on FileMaker, Inc. products. FileMaker offers FSA members a special product called FileMaker Developer 5. Database templates that have been processed by Developer can be run as standalone programs; the templates can be used on any Mac or Windows-based PC — even without FileMaker Pro installed. For anyone who develops commercial templates, Developer provides the enormous benefit of vastly expanding the potential market for those templates. Instead of being able to address only the needs of other individuals who already own FileMaker Pro — or who can be convinced to buy a copy of the program so they can use your template — you can provide ready-made database solutions to virtually anyone who has a computer.

Chapter 17 introduces you to the procedures for creating a database template. This chapter carries the discussion further in four specific ways:

✦ Suggesting techniques that you can use to improve the user interface for your templates

✦ Showing how to protect the structure of a template

✦ Discussing different ways you can provide Help information for your databases

✦ Explaining methods of restricting access to certain template features (for example, distributing templates with some key features disabled as a way of encouraging users to send in the shareware fee so they can obtain full access to features)

You can use the following techniques and strategies to improve the appearance, functionality, and marketability of your work:

✦ Simplify the interface with menus

✦ Include buttons and scripts to handle common functions

✦ Design for monitors of various sizes

✦ Distribute shareware templates as demos or with selected features disabled

✦ Provide help files and other documentation that explain how your database works

✦ Consider developing the template using FileMaker Developer 5

Simplify the Interface by Using Menus

For any database that contains more than just a simple data entry layout, providing a menu to guide users to the different parts of the database is often a good idea. Menus can be particularly helpful for computer novices and individuals who are unfamiliar with the database, ensuring that they can easily find their way around and readily access the functions they need to use.

Menus are most useful when the database is divided into several different modes, each associated with a particular layout or set of layouts. In a parts inventory database, for example, you may have separate layouts for entering parts sales, generating order forms when the inventory for a part drops below a critical level, and printing a status report that shows the optimal number, number on hand, and reorder level for every part. A simple menu with three choices (Sales Entry, Order Parts, and Status Report) can help users move directly to the section of interest.

Of course, the more logical sections your database contains, the more helpful (and appropriate) a menu can be. In databases that include dozens of layouts, you can create additional submenu screens as needed. For example, if you have created layouts for half a dozen different types of reports and labels, you may want to design separate Report and Label menus, placing each set of menus on a separate layout.

Tip   Don't overdo menu nesting, however. Although additional menus are helpful to novices and new users, the added time and button-clicking required to navigate through unnecessary menu layers can get old very quickly.

Figure 21-1 shows a menu created as a separate layout in the New Buttons database. In this example, clicking any of the three buttons carries the user to a different layout in the database. Separate layouts are devoted to blank buttons, over-sized (large) buttons, and navigational buttons. (New Buttons is included on the Macintosh version of the *FileMaker Pro 5 Bible CD*.) This same type of menu could enable users to select from several types of reports or to switch between several primary database functions, such as executing a find request, generating mailing labels, or opening an associated database.

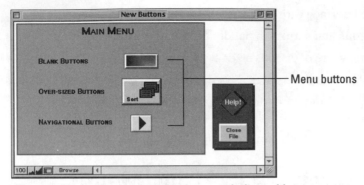

Figure 21-1: A menu created in its own dedicated layout

In the Address Book database, the menu is incorporated into the Data Entry layout (see Figure 21-2). Because users spend the majority of their time in this layout, the menu palette enables them to click a button to perform a variety of functions that are related to data entry. Several of the buttons duplicate menu commands in order to help novice users execute commands without having to remember the menu in which the command is located.

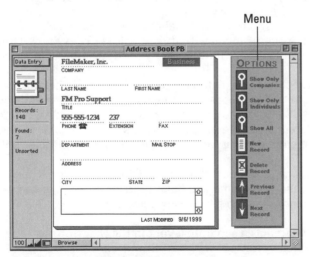

Figure 21-2: A menu palette

Creating a main menu

If you want to use a main menu to control access to the different parts of a database, you can set the menu layout to be displayed automatically whenever the database is opened. To accomplish this, choose Edit ➪ Preferences ➪ Document. In the section labeled "When opening *database name*," click the check box marked "Switch to layout" and choose the name of your menu layout from the pop-up menu. To save the new Preferences setting, click the Done button. From this point on, anyone who opens the database will immediately see the menu rather than the last layout used (the normal FileMaker Pro default).

The menu at the bottom of the database shown in Figure 21-3 is a variation of the menu palette displayed in Address Book. Instead of restricting itself to data-entry functions, it presents all major functions that a user might want to perform with the database. Such functions include selecting important subgroups, generating on-screen and printed reports, clearing out old records, and summoning help. Although this type of menu could easily have been created as a separate layout (as was the one for New Buttons FM), placing it in the most common layout (Data Entry) eliminates having to add an additional layer of complexity to a full-featured database. Parsimony is a good thing!

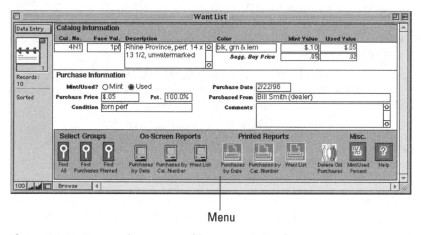

Menu

Figure 21-3: A menu incorporated into an existing layout

Avoid button clutter

After you understand how easily you can assign actions to buttons, you may be tempted to go button crazy. If you check the bulletin boards and online information services, you'll find many templates that have layouts that contain two or even three full rows of buttons. Just as using a dozen fonts in a document can make a desktop publishing effort look like a ransom note, presenting too many buttons in one place can slow the user down (because finding the correct button for a function is difficult). Bad programming . . . .

If you really need that many buttons, either find a logical way to group them by function (as was done in the Want List database in Figure 21-3) or think seriously about creating a series of menu layouts rather than just a single menu.

Creating a Navigation Menu

As mentioned throughout this book, buttons — such as those used in the menu examples — gain their functionality by having ScriptMaker scripts or a script step attached to them. The following series of steps explains how to design a navigation menu like the one used by the New Buttons FM database.

To create a navigation menu, follow these steps:

1. Open the database and switch to Layout mode (by choosing View ➪ Layout Mode or by pressing ⌘+L/Ctrl+L).

2. Create a new layout to hold the menu by choosing Layouts ➪ New Layout/Report (or by pressing ⌘+N/Ctrl+N). Choose the "Blank layout" style, name the layout, and allow the New Layout/Report assistant to create the layout.

   — or —

   If you like, you can create the menu as part of an existing layout (as previously shown in Figures 21-2 and 21-3). If you decide to do so, switch to the appropriate layout and go to step 3.

3. In Layout mode, use the Button tool to create text buttons. If you prefer graphic buttons, you can paste, import, or draw the graphics in FileMaker Pro that will serve as the buttons.

4. Arrange the buttons on the layout as desired.

5. Select a button by clicking it once and then choose the Format ➪ Button from command.

   The Specify Button dialog box appears, as shown in Figure 21-4.

6. Choose the Go to Layout step from the scrolling list and, from the Specify pop-up menu on the right, select the layout to which you want to go.

Specify a layout to switch to when the button is clicked

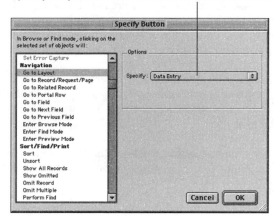

Figure 21-4: Defining a button

7. Repeat steps 5 and 6 for each menu button you want to define, selecting a different layout to go to for each button.

8. *Optional*: If you always want the menu layout to appear immediately when you open the database, see the "Creating a Main Menu" sidebar, earlier in this chapter.

Not all buttons must be icons

Although buttons are cool and lend a professional appearance to most databases, not everyone is a graphics wizard. Nor is everyone an icon lover. In FileMaker Pro, *any* object can be a button.

In Layout mode, you can use the Button tool to create 3D buttons with standard text labels. The following figure shows an example of a text button. You can use normal editing procedures to change the size of the button, as well as the font, style, size, and color of the button text.

Providing Instant Access via Buttons and Scripts

Anything that increases ease of use simultaneously increases the worth of your template. Why ask users to do things the hard way (manually selecting sets of sort instructions, for instance), when you can create scripts and buttons that do the tasks for them when they choose a command from the Scripts menu or click a button?

Think carefully about how others will want to use your template. If you know that many users will perform common sort procedures, focus on specific subgroups, or generate the same kinds of reports, you should create layouts and appropriate scripts to automate these elements.

To make the scripts accessible, assign them to buttons, list them in the Script menu, or do both. See Chapter 15 for more information on creating scripts and defining buttons.

Label those buttons!

Although the Mac and Windows PCs are graphicallyoriented computers and icons are a common part of the user interface, you may frequently be tempted to design buttons as unlabeled icons. Resist at all costs! Although the meaning of a button may be obvious to you, it may not be apparent to other people who will use your database or template. (A new computer user may not even understand the use of a question mark as a Help button.)

When you are designing a template for others, you should avoid anything that slows people down by making them guess what you had in mind, search for the help file, or reach for a manual. As the examples in Figures 21-1 through 21-3 clearly show, adding a label to a button takes little screen space.

Consider Screen Real Estate

When you are designing templates for others, you may want to consider the size of the user's display. For example, users with a full-page or two-page display commonly design layouts that fill the screen. Unfortunately, when such templates are opened on a laptop, significant portions of the window will be off-screen.

You have several options:

✦ Restrict the template dimensions to fit the smallest screen size that you want to support.

✦ Assume that a user who has a small screen will be willing to scroll to reach parts of any layout that are off-screen.

✦ Provide several versions of the template, each optimized for a particular display.

✦ Divide a large layout into several smaller ones and switch between the different layouts using menus or buttons.

Tip

If you just want to expand the window to completely fill whatever screen the user has, you can use the following step in an opening script:

```
Toggle Window [Maximize]
```

You can determine the resolution (in pixels) of any user's display by using the Status (CurrentScreenHeight) and Status (CurrentScreenWidth) functions.

Protecting a Template

When you design a template for in-house use, you may want to prevent others from changing it. For example, regardless of whether the person who is changing the locations of fields in a data layout is an expert or a novice who selected Layout mode by mistake, you may want to prevent changes to the field locations or formatting. Similarly, if a database contains sensitive information, such as salaries, you may want to prevent other users from accessing the database at all or restrict who has access rights to such layouts.

By choosing commands from the File ➪ Access Privileges submenu, the designer of any FileMaker Pro database can set passwords, define specific groups of users for the database, and set privileges that are granted with each password. Figure 21-5 shows the basic process of setting a password for a database.

Note

Although access privileges are more commonly associated in people's minds with products installed on a network, you can set access privileges for *any* FileMaker Pro database — including databases that will be run on standalone Macs or PCs. For more information, refer to Chapter 19.

Choose an option to restrict the available menu commands

Figure 21-5: Setting access privileges

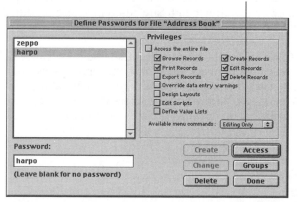

In addition to protecting your template from unwanted changes, you can restrict access to some of its features when you create a demo or shareware version. To restrict access, you assign one or more passwords for the database, each limiting the particular features that are available to the user (as shown previously in Figure 21-5). By taking this approach, you give users an added incentive to buy the full version or to pay the requested shareware fee.

For example, you could define three different passwords for a database. At the lowest level, access could be limited to basic features, allowing users to do no more than browse and edit the sample records included in the database. This level of access provides the equivalent of a demo, giving the user a feel for the database's capabilities but not enabling any of its real functionality. This password could be supplied in the documentation included in the version of the template or set as a default password that would automatically (and transparently) be used by FileMaker Pro every time the database was opened. (For instructions on setting a default password, see Chapter 19.)

As an alternative, FileMaker Pro also enables you to define a "no password" password. To do this, you simply leave the Password box (previously shown in Figure 21-5) blank, select privileges, and then click Create. When new users open the file, they can leave the Password text box blank and be granted access to the minimal privileges that you assigned to this condition. However, this approach is not as elegant as using a default password, as previously described.

Figure 21-5 also shows another Privileges option: Editing Only. By choosing Editing Only from the "Available menu commands" pop-up menu, you can simultaneously restrict users to Browse mode and allow them to do no more than edit existing records and execute scripts.

On receipt of a basic shareware fee, you can supply a second password that enables the user to print and export records, create new records, delete records, and override data-entry warnings. Assuming the user is happy with the way the database is designed (as you hope they will be), this level of functionality will be all the person requires. For an additional charge, you could offer a master password that enables the user to also modify the structure of the database (changing and designing layouts, as well as editing scripts). Advanced users may want to take advantage of this ultimate password so they can freely customize and modify the template in ways that make it more useful to them.

FileMaker Pro provides an additional level of protection that can sometimes be useful. By defining *groups* (collections of users who share the same password), you can restrict access to particular fields and layouts. If you are making a demo, for example, you could use this feature to keep users from ever seeing certain reports. For more information on creating groups, see Chapter 19.

On the CD-ROM

One of my own shareware templates — Family Medical Expenses — is included on the *FileMaker Pro 5 Bible* CD-ROM. This template illustrates yet another approach to creating shareware templates.

Family Medical Expenses already contains a small set of sample records. Users can freely try out any basic operation in the template (executing scripts, viewing and printing reports, and replacing the sample data). However, they cannot add new records, modify or create scripts, or change the layouts. After the shareware fee is received, the user is sent the master password — enabling her or him to remove the password protection and change the template in any way desired. This approach to "crippling" a shareware template has the advantage of leaving all functions intact while still giving the user an important reason for sending the shareware fee.

Creating Help Systems for Your Databases

Do any of the following scenarios sound familiar?

✦ You've just spent half an hour downloading an interesting-sounding FileMaker Pro template from America Online or the Internet. You discover that it contains no instructions whatsoever — no Read Me file, no help screens, no descriptive text. Now what?

✦ Bill, one of your coworkers at XYZ Corp., is on vacation. While he's away, the boss asks whether you can fill in by entering customer orders, printing mailing labels, and generating daily reports. Although you know that Bill accomplishes these tasks with extraordinary ease using a FileMaker Pro database that he designed, you haven't got a clue as to how he does it.

✦ A couple of years back, you designed an elaborate database with dozens of scripts and buttons. Recently you realized that — with just a few modifications — you could put the database to work for a new task. Unfortunately, when you designed the database, documenting how it worked didn't seem important. Now you can't remember what half the scripts do or what data the field named "Extra" was meant to collect. (It's surprising how easily you can forget . . . .)

✦ You've created a whiz-bang FileMaker Pro template that you think every Mac and Windows user will want. In your rush to share it with the world, you deposit copies of it on half a dozen bulletin boards and ask for a $10 shareware fee. Because you didn't bother to explain how the template works, it doesn't sell as well as you'd hoped, and the people who *are* sending you the shareware fee are also pestering you with questions.

Of course, not every database needs elaborate documentation. But if you spend a little time creating a simple help system or Read Me file, you can avoid some headaches later on. The following sections discuss appropriate (and sometimes essential) topics that you should include and suggests several approaches that you can use to create help systems.

Suggested help topics

A help system that is carefully thought out anticipates the user's needs. The better you anticipate, the happier the user will be and the less time you will need to spend supporting or explaining the template. Here is a brief list of some material that is appropriate for inclusion in a help system or a Read Me file:

✦ A description of the purpose of the database

✦ An explanation of the purpose of each field, the type of data it should contain, and any restrictions and/or validation options that have been set (see Chapter 5 for information on data validation options)

✦ An explanation of the purpose of each layout, as well as any special preparations that the user must make before using the layout (changing the Page Setup or printer selection, for example)

✦ An explanation of what each script does and how to execute the script (by selecting it from the Scripts menu or pressing a button)

✦ Suggestions for customizing the template (for example, selecting different fonts, changing screen colors, creating new reports and mailing labels, and adding features)

If you want people to treat your template as a serious business product rather than as something you just knocked together in a free moment, you need to make it look like a business product. Documentation and/or a help system are a must.

Choosing help topics

Need and common sense should dictate the types and quantity of help you provide. If you are writing a help system for a database that will only be used by the accounting department in your company, for example, you should offer help with common data-entry and report-generation questions you expect to occur. Because everyone will be using the same version of the database, you can omit information about customizing the database.

When deciding the types of help to offer, try to put yourself in the place of a new user. Think about field labels you've used that might not be immediately understood. When it could be unclear what type of information should be entered in a field, explain it. (If you're really smart, you'll give the database to some people to test — and ask them to tell you what kind of help they need — *before* you distribute it.)

To get more ideas about the types of help to include, you may want to download some of the shareware templates available from FileMaker, Inc, America Online, and other sources on the Internet. You're sure to find several excellent (as well as many horrid) examples of help information.

Different approaches to providing help

You can present help information and documentation in several ways. In choosing a method, consider who is the intended reader of the information (you, other developers and technical people, or end users and customers) and how often you expect the reader to refer to the information. For example, does it make sense to create an elaborate, context-sensitive online help system for information that the reader may need to see only once?

Approach 1: A Read Me file

Creating a separate Read Me file in a word-processing program or text editor is obviously the easiest way to document a template. And having the full text-formatting capabilities of a word processor at your disposal can make the writing go quickly.

Arguably, the Read Me approach is best for providing information needed only once — such as installation instructions and minor customization notes — or when you create a database only for personal or limited in-house use. In the case of a personal template, if you later decide to share it with others, your notes can form the basis of an in-template help system.

If you intend to distribute your database as shareware, a Read Me is certainly better than no documentation, but it is not the best method. See Approaches 2 and 3, later in this chapter, for more appropriate means of providing help information for shareware.

If you want others to be able to read and print your Read Me file, you should give careful thought to which word processor or text editor you use when you create the file. Obviously, if you write the documentation in an obscure program, you will prevent many people from being able to open and read the file. The following sections offer some suggestions for creating a Read Me file.

Text editors

Text editors — such as BBEdit (Macintosh) and Notepad (Windows) — are essentially bare-bones word processing programs. Fancy formatting commands usually are not provided, nor is there support for multiple fonts and styles. As the name implies, a *text editor* is a program for editing text. Files created in a text editor are stored in Text-Only format and, as such, can be opened by any other text editor or word processing program. This is precisely the reason why so many Read Me files are created in text editors.

If you intend to distribute a template on the Internet, online information systems, and computer bulletin boards, you can keep your documentation compact by creating it in a text editor. (No one wants to waste half an hour downloading a few pages of documentation that — because of the format selected — grew to several hundred K. This is sometimes a problem with standalone documents, as you will see in the following section.)

Caution

When it comes to cross-platform documentation, Text-Only isn't necessarily only text. Current versions of SimpleText (Macintosh), for example, now store font information in documents, and Return characters appear as solid blocks when viewed in a PC text editor. If you want your Read Me file to be readable on both systems, it is critical that you *test* it on both systems. Do not *assume* compatibility.

Standalone documents

If the primary method of distribution will be on disk or CD, you can afford the luxury of using a program that can produce *standalone documents* (that is, documents that work just like programs). You don't need a separate program to open them—they're double-clickable! If you scrounge around online, you're sure to find several utilities of this sort.

DOCMaker, a shareware program from Green Mountain Software, is one of the best-known examples for the Macintosh. It enables you to create standalone documents that include graphics and multiple fonts, styles, and colors (see Figure 21-6). Not only can you type and edit text within DOCMaker; you can use it to import text that was created in a variety of popular word processing formats. You can organize DOCMaker documents into chapters, print them, and search them. DOCMaker's only weaknesses are that the documents it creates tend to be large (over 100K) and that the program does not support tabs.

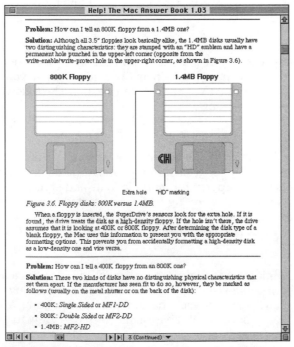

Figure 21-6: A DOCMaker standalone document

eDOC is another Macintosh-only shareware program for creating impressive documentation files. eDOC documents can be read by anyone who has the free eDOC Reader application. They can also be distributed as standalone documents that can be read *without* the Reader application.

You can also use a commercial program called Adobe Acrobat to convert existing formatted documents into PDF (Portable Document Format) files. Such files can readily be opened on a Mac, a Windows PC, or even a Unix workstation with a free Adobe program called Acrobat Reader. To create a PDF file, you can print the document to disk (using a special print driver); you can generate it in Adobe PageMaker, Quark Xpress, or many other popular desktop publishing programs; or you can generate a PostScript file and then convert it to .pdf format with Acrobat Distiller. Acrobat offers several advantages: It supports all normal formatting, graphics, and fonts; its files can be published on the World Wide Web; and documents can include features such as a live, clickable table of contents or multimedia clips.

Word processing programs

If you are creating documentation that will be distributed, the least desirable method is to use a standard word processing program (Microsoft Word or WordPerfect, for example). One exception to this general rule is when you develop a template solely for in-house use and everyone in the company uses the same word processing program. Although many word processing programs can read documents created in other such programs, a sizable number of people may still be unable to read the file. However, authors who distribute documentation in a word processing format can increase the odds that users can read it by including copies of the documentation in several formats. Microsoft Word and Text-Only are the most common choices.

If you're considering distributing files created in a word processor, do your research when it comes to which version of a program is best for your audience. For example, many Macintosh owners have steadfastly refused to upgrade their copy of Microsoft Word to Version 6.0 or Office 98 and have stayed with Version 5.0/5.1. Because Version 6 files are incompatible with Version 5, you might consider distributing Word Read Me files as Version 5. (As an alternative, you can direct readers to Microsoft's Web site where they can download free "importers" that enable Word 5 to open documents created in later versions of Word.) Whether you're using Word or another word processor altogether, be sure to refer to the program's documentation for information about saving files in earlier formats, and carefully consider what version is appropriate for the most users.

Paper-only documentation

Of course, you may want to skip the compatibility issues altogether and simply include printed instructions with the template. You can distribute the template on information services but offer the printed documentation only to users who send in the shareware registration fee. Most authors who take this approach, however, are obliged to also include at least a stripped-down version of the documentation in a Read Me file. If you don't give users some idea of how the template works, they may not explore it enough to determine whether it does something useful for them.

Approach 2: A help layout

Another method is to include the documentation or help information in the template itself. The advantages of placing this material in a FileMaker Pro template include the following:

✦ *No compatibility problems*: Because users need to have a copy of FileMaker Pro in order to use the template, by definition they have all the software they need to read the help text, too.

✦ *Ready access*: Users who need help don't want to hunt for it. When people need help, they usually want it right away. And because Read Me files take up disk space, users frequently delete them after reading them, so such files aren't immediately accessible (or they may no longer be accessible at all).

Figure 21-7 shows an example of help text in a FileMaker Pro database. All the help information is contained in a single layout. If the information is too long to fit on a single screen (as it is in this example), users can click the scroll bar to see it all.

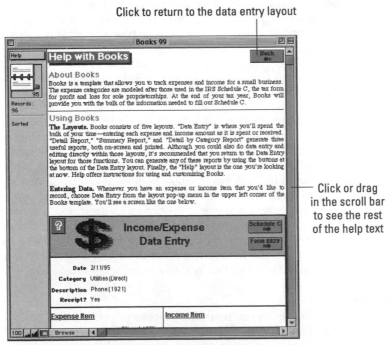

Figure 21-7: Help text as a separate layout

As you can see in this figure, a help layout may contain no fields at all. It can be constructed entirely of static text and graphics, so you never have to worry about the user inadvertently changing what's on-screen. When this layout is displayed, even if the user clicks the book icon to flip from one record to the next, the help screen doesn't change.

To create a help screen similar to the one shown in the figure, follow these steps:

1. In a new or existing database, change to Layout mode.

2. Choose Layouts ⇨ New Layout/Report (or press ⌘+N/Ctrl+N).

   The New Layout/Report assistant appears, as shown in Figure 21-8.

Select a format for the layout

Enter a name for the new layout

```
                    New Layout/Report

  Create a Layout/Report

  Layout Name:  Help              ☑ Include in layout pop-up menu

  Select a layout type:
   Standard form
   Columnar list/report
   Table View
   Labels
   Envelope
   Blank layout

   Contains empty header, body, and footer
   parts. Drag the fields you want onto the
   layout.

   ?                    Cancel    ‹ Back    Finish
```

Figure 21-8: The New Layout/Report assistant

3. Enter an appropriate name for the layout (Help, for example), select Blank layout as the type, and click Finish to create the layout.

   Because you usually don't need to display fields in a help layout, choosing Blank layout saves time. (Including the layout in the layout pop-up menu is optional.)

4. Select the Text tool (the uppercase A) from the Tools palette to add text blocks to the layout. Resize the text blocks as necessary.

   If you have already prepared help text in a word processing document, you can copy and paste it into the layout. And if your word processing program supports it, you can also drag-and-drop the help text into the layout.

Note

Another approach is to take a screen shot of an important layout, edit and embellish it with callouts using your favorite graphics program, and then paste the image into the help layout. (To take a screen shot on a Mac, press Shift-⌘+3. This captures the entire screen and saves it on your hard disk. To capture just a single window, press down the Caps Lock key, press Shift-+4, and then click the window you want to capture. To do the same on a PC running Windows 95, press the Print Screen key. This copies the screen to the Clipboard. Then open a graphics program and choose Edit ⇨ Paste or press Ctrl+V.)

5. *Optional*: Add graphics by copying them from a graphics program and then pasting them into the layout.

You can also import graphics directly into the layout by choosing the Insert ➪ Picture command. (See Chapter 6 for additional information on adding and importing graphics into a layout.) In addition, some graphics programs, such as the graphics environments of ClarisWorks Office/AppleWorks, support drag-and-drop. You can use this feature to drag graphics directly onto FileMaker Pro layouts.

6. *Optional*: Create scripts that switch from the help layout to the data entry layout and vice versa (via the Go to Layout script step).

Although you can place the scripts in the Scripts menu, assigning them to buttons on the layout is more convenient. (See the "Using a Button to Summon Help" sidebar in this chapter.)

As you design the help layout, remember that you can mix fonts, styles, and colors in the same text block. When you are designing for other users, however, getting fancy with fonts doesn't pay. Unless users have the same fonts installed on their computer, different fonts will automatically be substituted. Also, although you can create the help text as one long text block, you may want to break it into a series of smaller, more manageable chunks. When you use this approach, you can easily intersperse graphics (such as screen captures, illustrations, and clip art) in the text.

Using a button to summon help

To make it easy to move from any layout in the database to your help layout (and back again), you can create buttons for the different layouts. The script attached to each navigation button in the database consists of this one line:

```
Go to layout <x>
```

where <x> is the name of the data entry or help layout. (In the data entry layout, use the name of the help layout. In the help layout, use the name of the data entry layout.) To attach the command to a custom button, switch to Layout mode, select the button, and choose Format ➪ Button. Or you can use the Button tool to create and define a button simultaneously. (See Chapter 15 for more information on creating scripts and defining buttons.)

This approach can also be used with multiple help layouts. In a complex database, you may want to have separate help screens for providing help with specific functions — such as data entry, performing find requests and sorts, and printing reports. Having several specific help layouts serves several purposes:

✦ The user doesn't have to scroll through multiple screens of information.

✦ Your help screen more closely approximates the type of specific, context-appropriate help that users have come to expect from programs.

For example, a data entry screen may have separate buttons for data entry and sorting help; a reports screen could have a single button that summons specific help for preparing and printing a report.

Approach 3: Data-entry assistance

Setting data validation options makes it easy to ensure that users enter only the correct type of information for each field. If you want to help them do so, you can present a custom error message whenever incorrect data is entered for a field. As an example, Figure 21-9 shows how to create a custom message that is displayed if a user neglects to enter data into a required field. Thus, if you choose the "Display custom message if validation fails" option, you can create a unique, helpful message for any field whose intended contents may not be immediately obvious. (See Chapter 5 for instructions on setting validation options for fields.)

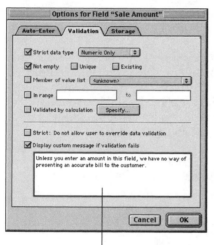

Custom validation message

Figure 21-9: You can set the "Display custom message. . ." option to present an alert box whenever a field's validation fails.

If you don't want to tie a custom message to a field's validation options, you can use the Show Message script step to present field-related help by attaching the script to a button. To enable users to summon such help, you might place a tiny "*?*" button at the end of each field and then associate the appropriate message script with each button. Figure 21-10 shows an example of one type of message associated with a Number field help button.

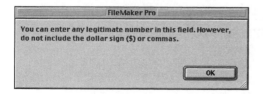

Figure 21-10: The Show Message script step can be used to present custom messages, such as this one.

Approach 4: Script-guided help

FileMaker Pro scripts can make your help system fancier and more helpful. By creating simple scripts and button definitions, you can design a series of help layouts that have the following features:

✦ You can page through the help screens. Each left-arrow and right-arrow button can have an attached script that causes FileMaker Pro to go to the previous — or next — help layout.

✦ You can access the help screens through a menu. Each button or text string in the help menu can cause a different help layout to display.

✦ You can access the help screens through an index. You can link each index entry to a specific help layout.

The *FileMaker Pro 5.0 Bible* CD-ROM has an example of this type of help system in the folder named Callable Help Example (inside the FileMaker Pro 5.0 Bible folder). Instead of forcing the user to jump back and forth between a help layout and other layouts in the database, Callable Help stores the help information in another database file. Because the help information is in a different file, you can view it while you are still working in the main database.

Clicking the Help button in the main database (Help Caller, in this case) opens the help database (Books Help). Figure 21-11 shows the two database files.

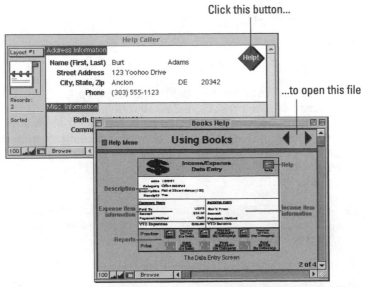

Click this button...

...to open this file

Figure 21-11: The help system consists of two FileMaker Pro databases: the main file (Help Caller) and the help file (Books Help).

Note The help information in Books Help has absolutely nothing to do with the Help Caller database. In fact, it's some help text that I yanked out of one of my own databases and reformatted for this example. Don't let this bother you. What's important is that the files illustrate the mechanics required for you to implement a similar help system of your own.

Here's how the two databases interact. To access help, you simply click the Help button in the main database. Attached to the Help button is a one-line script that reads as follows:

```
Open ["Books Help"]
```

You create the one-line script in ScriptMaker, specifying the name of the help file when you add the Open step to the script (as shown in Figure 21-12). After you create the script, you then use the Format ➪ Button command to link the script to the Help button (with Perform Script *script name*).

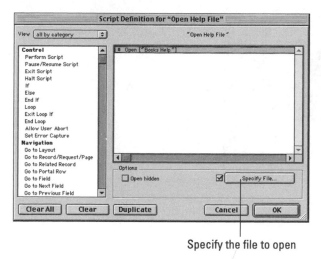

Specify the file to open

Figure 21-12: Creating the script that opens the help file

When the help file opens, several actions that are set in the document preferences automatically occur. The help database displays the first layout (called Help Menu), and then hides the status area (the book pages and Tools palette) by executing the script named "Open Script." (See Chapter 7 for more information on setting Document General preferences.)

In Books Help, you move to a particular help topic by clicking the name of the topic in the Help Menu, which is the first layout (refer to Figure 21-11). In fact, you use a Go to Layout script step to make *every* movement — whether to a help topic, to the main menu, or to a new page in the same help topic. You can then execute a script and make an appropriate layout appear by clicking any of four help-topic text strings in the Help Menu layout.

A set of buttons appears at the top of every help layout. In each layout except that of the Help Menu, the upper-left button (Help Menu) returns the user to the Help menu. In the Help Menu layout, the Help Menu button is replaced with the "Close help file" button, which closes the help file in the same manner as clicking the close box.

In help topics that span two or more layouts (such as Using Books), one or two arrow buttons occupy the upper-right corner of each layout (see Figure 21-13). Clicking an arrow executes a script that switches to the previous or next layout for that help topic. The number of layouts for a help topic appears in the lower-right corner of each layout.

Click to return to the main help screen

Click an arrow to switch to the next or previous page for the help topic

Figure 21-13: Click an arrow to navigate between multiple layouts for the same help topic.

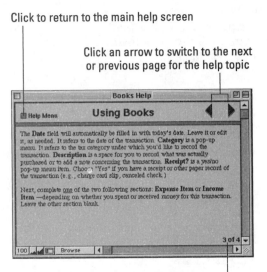

Number of screens in current help layout

More help with help

Regardless of the method you use to incorporate help information into your database, you may find the following tips useful.

Using headers and footers in help screens

If you want some help information to remain on-screen at all times, put it in the help layout's header or footer. As the user scrolls the window, the header and footer stay in place.

Figure 21-14 shows a help layout from the Apple Events Reference database (found in the FileMaker and Apple Events folder in the FileMaker Pro 5.0 folder) in which the header keeps critical information on-screen.

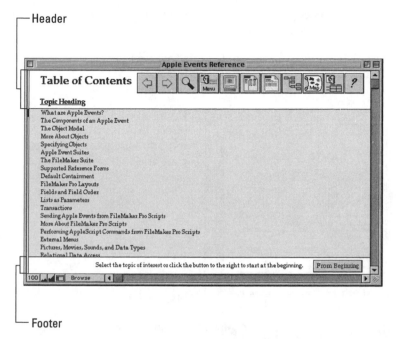

Figure 21-14: You can keep critical help information on-screen by placing it in the header and footer parts.

Checking *riting* and *speling*

Don't forget that FileMaker Pro has a built-in spelling checker. You may be a database whiz, but if your documentation or help text is riddled with spelling errors, your skills as a programmer and/or designer may also be questioned. To check spelling for the entire help layout, change to Layout mode, switch to the help screen layout, and choose Edit ➪ Spelling ➪ Check Layout. (See Chapter 11 for more information on using the spelling checker.)

Creating a credits screen or a registration form

Using the same method you use to provide in-template help, you can create a credits (or copyright) screen or a shareware registration form for a template. Without such a screen, you are likely to lose credit for the work you've done or miss out on shareware fees that are due you. In the case of a shareware template in particular, you want to make it as convenient as possible for the user to pay for your hard work. Creating the registration form as a separate layout ensures that:

✦ When ready to pay, the user never has to search his or her hard disk for a separate file that contains your name and address.

✦ The user is repeatedly reminded that the template is not public domain and that payment is expected.

✦ When the template is copied and given to others, the registration information is also copied.

Figures 21-15 and 21-16 show examples of layouts that provide credit and registration information.

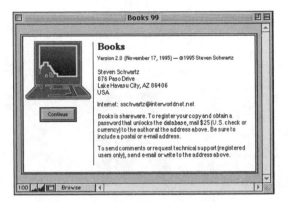

Figure 21-15: This opening screen explains what the user must do to register his or her copy of a shareware template.

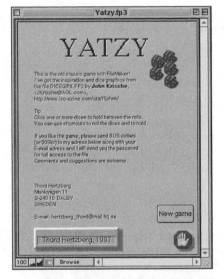

Figure 21-16: An example of a credits screen

Using FileMaker Developer 5

As mentioned at the beginning of this chapter, FileMaker Developer 5 is a special programming tool that compiles FileMaker Pro templates, changing them into standalone programs. If you intend to create commercial templates, using Developer offers two direct benefits when compared to creating normal FileMaker Pro templates:

✦ *It increases the size of the potential market.* To use a normal template, an individual must already own or be willing to buy FileMaker Pro. When you are selling an expensive, vertical-market database (such as a video store rentals database), customers may consider the cost of a copy of FileMaker Pro to be a drop in the bucket. When you are attempting to sell an inexpensive, general-purpose template, on the other hand, you cannot expect customers to shoulder the cost of a program just so they can use the template.

✦ *It protects your investment while preventing tampering.* Providing an unprotected FileMaker Pro template to customers is tantamount to handing them the source code for your product. If you have used special techniques to create the template, Developer keeps them safe from prying eyes and prevents customers from inadvertently or deliberately modifying the way the template works.

When you become a member of the FileMaker Solutions Alliance, you are eligible to purchase FileMaker Developer 5 from FileMaker, Inc. With this CD-ROM, you can produce royalty-free, standalone FileMaker Pro databases that will run on the Mac or in Microsoft Windows.

Summary

✦ Templates that are "good enough" for your personal use may not be ready to market commercially or give to others. You need to consider many factors when designing templates for distribution.

✦ When developing a template for the widest possible audience, you can easily add features that enhance ease of use and enable the template to be used on a variety of monitors.

✦ Shareware and demo templates can use FileMaker Pro's password feature to restrict access to parts or features of the template.

✦ Even if you don't want to implement a formal help system for your database, you can easily create a Read Me file.

✦ You can add help, credit or copyright, and shareware registration screens to any database as separate layouts. You can use the Go to Layout script step to switch between any of these screens and the database's main menu or data entry layout.

✦ When you embed help information in layouts, you can create a single scrolling text screen or break the information into discrete chunks and place it in a series of layouts.

✦ You can attach the Show Message script step to buttons and use it to display custom help messages. A data validation option can display a custom message automatically if a field's validation fails — as when a user neglects to enter information into a required field.

✦ You can use text strings — as well as graphics objects — as buttons. Clicking a text string in a help menu, for example, can cause a specific help layout to display.

✦ To keep a database as small as possible, you can create a separate help database that the user can display and then dismiss when it is no longer needed. Keeping the help separate from the main database also enables users to view the help while they are entering data, creating reports, or constructing new layouts.

✦ If you are interested in becoming a commercial template developer, you should consider joining the FileMaker Solutions Alliance and purchasing a copy of FileMaker Developer 5.

✦   ✦   ✦

About the CD-ROM

About the CD-ROM

Included with this book is a CD-ROM that contains an assortment of handpicked, ready-to-run FileMaker Pro database templates, utilities, and demos. If you are looking for a ready-made solution to a database need, you may be able to save yourself time and effort by browsing through the contents of this CD-ROM. Many of the databases used as examples in the *FileMaker Pro 5 Bible* are also on the CD-ROM, enabling you to follow along with the book and examine the field definitions, layouts, and scripts used to create the databases.

The *FileMaker Pro 5 Bible* CD is a special hybrid CD-ROM, containing separate Macintosh and Windows partitions. When inserted into a Mac CD-ROM drive, only the Macintosh portion of the CD-ROM is visible. When inserted into a PC, only the Windows portion of the CD-ROM appears. Templates, utilities, and demos that are specific to one platform appear only on that platform's portion of the CD-ROM. Cross-platform materials can be found on both partitions.

Supported platforms

FileMaker Pro 5 runs on Macintosh computers and on PCs with the Windows 95, Windows 98, Windows NT, or Windows for Workgroups operating system. (Note that different developers provide varying levels of support for these platforms. Some solutions — such as ones that rely on AppleScript, for example — will run only on a Mac.)

Note Although you must normally have FileMaker Pro 3 or higher to run the FileMaker templates, this is not the case with all the templates on this CD-ROM. Some of them were created with FileMaker Pro 4 Developer's Edition. Such templates are actually stand-alone programs and can be run on computers that do not have an installed copy of FileMaker Pro.

Documentation

The documentation provided for the templates, utilities, and demos may be in a variety of formats. If the template, utility, or demo does not include built-in help, documentation may be provided in the installation program (if one is included). It also may be presented as a separate text or word processing file, a .pdf (Adobe Acrobat) file, or a series of Web pages designed to be viewed in a browser, such as Internet Explorer or Netscape Navigator/Communicator. If you have difficulty opening the documentation files, refer to the following hints:

✦ *.txt files*. These text files can normally be opened by any word processing program and by most text-editing programs. If you do not have a word processor, try opening them with SimpleText or BBEdit on the Mac; on the PC, use Notepad, WordPad, or Word Viewer 97.

✦ *.doc files*. These formatted word processing files are generally Microsoft Word documents. Depending on the version of Word used to create the files, they can be opened on a Windows PC with Word 2000, Word 97, WordPad, or Word Viewer 97. Macintosh Word documents may be formatted for Word 5, 6, or 98.

✦ *.rtf files*. These formatted word processing documents are Microsoft Rich Text Format files. They can be opened with Word 2000, Word 97, WordPad, or Word Viewer 97 on a Windows PC or in most Macintosh versions of Word.

✦ *.pdf files*. These files are intended to be read with Adobe Acrobat Reader. PDF (Portable Document Format) files are cross-platform and can be read on either a Mac or PC.

✦ *.htm and .html files*. These Web page files are intended to be opened and viewed in a Web browser, such as Internet Explorer, Netscape Navigator, Netscape Communicator, Opera, or CyberDog (iCab).

✦ *DOCMaker files*. These are self-contained Macintosh documentation files. Double-click their icons to open and view the information contained within.

Tip Word processing and integrated programs (such as ClarisWorks/AppleWorks, for instance) can often read documents created by other programs. To see if your program can read such a file, use your program's Open, Insert, or Import command.

Installing the Solutions

How you install and try out the various templates, demos, and utilities on the *FileMaker Pro 5 Bible* CD-ROM depends on many factors, including your computing platform (Macintosh or Windows), whether the material is provided as an archive or as ordinary (noncompressed) files, and whether a separate installation program is provided.

Be sure to observe the following precautions when installing material from the CD-ROM:

✦ When using the programs and templates on the CD-ROM, be sure to install, extract, or copy them to a disk other than the *FileMaker Pro 5 Bible* CD-ROM — a hard disk or a removable disk, such as a Zip cartridge or an optical disk, for example. The *FileMaker Pro 5 Bible* CD-ROM is a normal, locked CD-ROM and cannot be written to.

✦ Although installation programs can usually be run from the CD-ROM, if you attempt to run FileMaker Pro templates directly from the CD-ROM, they may not work correctly. FileMaker Pro automatically saves all changes made to a database, such as adding, editing, or deleting records. Because all files on a CD-ROM are locked, FileMaker Pro will not be able to make changes to a database template until you move it *off* the CD-ROM.

✦ It is usually a *bad* idea to rename templates or the folders in which they are contained. Similarly, if a particular FileMaker Pro solution contains folders within other folders, moving the files into the main folder is also often a mistake. Any of these actions may cause scripts to fail or defined relationships to stop working. If a solution contains multiple files but does *not* enclose them in a folder, you may wish to create a new folder in which to store the components.

✦ If a solution or utility includes a Read Me file, a separate copy of that file is located in the solution's folder. You can open these Read Me files directly from the CD-ROM to determine whether a utility or solution might be useful to you. (You do not need to copy these Read Me files to your hard disk. Each archive normally contains a copy of the same file; it will be copied to your hard disk as part of the installation process.)

Note   The majority of the FileMaker Pro solutions on the CD-ROM are in 3.0–4.1 format. As such, after extracting the files from their archives, you will have to convert them to FileMaker Pro 5 format. You convert a FileMaker Pro 3.0, 4.0, or 4.1 database by opening it in FileMaker Pro 5, renaming the old database (when prompted), and then allowing FileMaker to perform the conversion.

Installing normal files

Some of the material on the *FileMaker Pro 5 Bible* CD-ROM may consist of ordinary files and folders. To install such files, merely copy the folder and its contents to a convenient location on your hard disk. If the template, demo, or utility contains multiple files or folders, be sure to leave all files in their respective folders and do not rename either the files or the folders.

Note   Documentation files can be opened directly from the CD-ROM.

Installing archives

Archives are compressed copies of one or more files and/or folders. Most archives are *self-extracting*. By double-clicking or running them, the archive opens, enabling you to specify a location on your hard disk in which to store the extracted files. Archives that are not self-extracting must be opened with a utility program that can extract the files and folders, copying them to a disk and folder of your choosing.

Note   After installing any program, template, or demo, be sure to check the files that have been copied to your hard disk. You may note that some ancillary materials (such as program manuals) are still in archives. To read them, you must extract them as well.

Macintosh archives

The majority of the Macintosh solutions are provided as self-extracting StuffIt archives (see Figure A-1). To install such an archive, double-click its file icon. A file dialog box similar to the one in Figure A-2 appears. Select a drive and/or destination folder on your hard disk, and click Save. All files in the archive are automatically extracted and copied to the designated hard disk.

Figure A-1: A StuffIt self-extracting archive

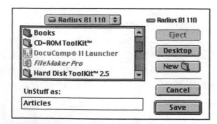

Figure A-2: Select a disk location in which to install the files from the archive, and click Save.

On the CD-ROM
Aladdin Systems also makes a utility for Win-ows users called StuffIt Extractor for Windows, enabling them to extract the contents of Macintosh StuffIt archives. StuffIt Extractor and StuffIt Extractor for Windows can be found in the Aladdin Systems folder on the Macintosh and Windows partitions of the CD.Windows archives.

In most instances, Windows archives are provided as self-extracting WinZip files (http://www.winzip.com) and have a .exe extension (see Figure A-3). To extract the files contained in such an archive, double-click the archive icon. A dialog box appears (see Figure A-4). A default hard disk and folder are proposed as the destination for the extracted files, such as **C:\Windows\Temp**. If you prefer to install the files in a *different* drive and/or folder, edit the text in the Unzip To Folder box to match the drive and folder of your choice. Click the Unzip button to extract the contents of the archive.

Figure A-3: A WinZip self-extracting archive

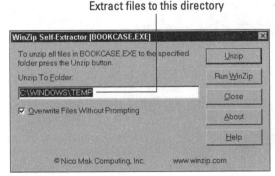

Figure A-4: Enter or choose a disk location in which to install the files from the archive, and click Unzip.

Windows archives that are not self-extracting are generally normal WinZip files — denoted by a .zip extension (see Figure A-5). You can find a copy of WinZip for Windows 95, 98, and NT in the Nico Mak Computing folder of the *FileMaker Pro 5 Bible* CD-ROM.

Ch02.zip

Figure A-5: A normal WinZip (.zip) file icon

To extract a WinZip .zip archive, double-click the file icon or open the archive directly from WinZip (click the Open button on the WinZip toolbar and select the archive's filename). The contents of the Zip file are listed in the document window, as shown in Figure A-6. Click the Extract button on the toolbar. In the Extract dialog box that appears, type or choose a hard disk and folder as a destination for the extracted files (in the Extract To box), click the Extract All radio button, and click Extract.

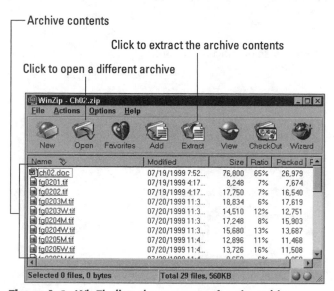

Archive contents

Click to extract the archive contents

Click to open a different archive

Figure A-6: WinZip lists the contents of a .zip archive.

Using installation programs

To make it easy to install multifile templates, demos, or utilities, some of the developers have provided a special installation program. For Windows programs, demos, and templates, the installation program is generally named Setup.exe or Install.exe. Macintosh installation programs often have the word "Installer" in their name. You can run such installation programs by double-clicking them.

In some cases, a program or template's Read Me file is included as part of the installation program. If a particular template or program does not have a visible Read Me file, you may be able to find out more about it by running the installation program.

On the CD-ROM Many of the materials on the CD-ROM are regularly updated by their developers. To determine if you are using the most current version of their files, look for a Web page or site address in their documentation and within the templates. You can periodically visit these Web pages to learn about newer versions. (You can find many of the developer Web site addresses in the Resources.htm file on the *FileMaker Pro 5 Bible* CD-ROM. Double-click the Resources.htm file icon to view the file in your browser.)

Technical Support and Redistribution

The templates, utilities, and demos included on the *FileMaker Pro 5 Bible* CD-ROM are provided as a courtesy of their respective developers. If you need assistance with running or installing them, contact their developers directly. Neither IDG Books Worldwide nor the author of this book can provide support for these materials.

Unless indicated otherwise in the documentation for the various templates, utilities, and demos, you may not distribute or sell (in the original or a modified version) any of the material on this CD-ROM. Contact the various authors for permission.

About shareware and freeware

If you're new to computing, the concept of shareware is probably unfamiliar to you. *Shareware* programs or templates are computer products that you can "try before you buy." If you like the software, you're requested to send a fee to the author of the template or program. To ensure the widest possible distribution of shareware, the authors frequently post copies of their masterpieces on computer information services (such as America Online) and the Internet, enabling users everywhere to download the programs, try them out, and decide for themselves whether the programs are useful.

Shareware is distributed on the honor system. Shareware authors trust you to do the right thing. That is, if you decide to keep and use their program or template, you should send the small fee that's requested. If you decide that the program is not for you, on the other hand, you should remove it from your hard disk. Usually, shareware authors encourage you to share their programs with your friends and colleagues. See each program's documentation for any special distribution instructions that the authors may have included.

Freeware, on the other hand, comes with few strings attached. No fee is requested for keeping and using a freeware program or template, but you must abide by the author's distribution instructions. For example, the author may allow you to give a copy of the program or template to friends on the condition that you make sure the copy has not been altered in any way and that it contains all the original files—including the documentation.

✦   ✦   ✦

Macintosh Keyboard Shortcuts

This appendix contains keyboard equivalents for FileMaker Pro commands and actions on the Macintosh. These commands are organized according to the various kinds of tasks you may want to perform. Note that the tables in this appendix do not contain all the commands the program offers; they merely list the commands for which there are keyboard shortcuts.

Table B-1 General Commands			
Command	**Key**	**Menu**	**Comments**
Cancel any operation	⌘+. (Period)		
Close a file	⌘+W	File ⇨ Close	You can also click the close box on the document window.
Define Fields	Shift+ ⌘+D	File ⇨Define Fields	
Help	⌘+ ? or Help	Balloon Help ⇨ FileMaker Pro Help (System 7.x) or Help ⇨ FileMaker Pro Help (OS 8.x)	You can also Control-click and choose FileMaker Pro Help from the pop-up menu that appears.
Network Access	⌘+Option+O		You can also click Hosts in the Open File dialog box.

Table B-1 (*continued*)

Command	Key	Menu	Comments
Open	⌘+O	File ⇨ Open	
Play a sound or movie in a Container field	Spacebar or double-click the field		
Print	⌘+P	File ⇨ Print	
Print direct	⌘+Option+P		This command bypasses the Print dialog box.
Stop playing a movie in a Container field	Spacebar or single click the field		
Quit	⌘+Q	File ⇨ Quit	

Table B-2
Mode-Selection Commands

Command	Key	Menu	Comments
Browse	⌘+B	View ⇨ Browse Mode	You can also choose this command from the Mode pop-up menu.
Find	⌘+F	View ⇨ Find Mode	You can also choose this command from the Mode pop-up menu.
Layout	⌘+L	View ⇨ Layout Mode	You can also choose this command from the Mode pop-up menu.
Preview	⌘+U	View ⇨ Preview Mode	You can also choose this command from the Mode pop-up menu.

Table B-3
Window Control Commands

Command	Key	Menu	Comments
Close a database	⌘+W	File ➪ Close	
Resize window	Shift+⌘+Z		This command is the same as clicking the window's zoom box.
Scroll to top of current record or preview page	Home		
Scroll to bottom of current record or preview page	End		
Scroll up one page in current record, report, View as List, or View as Table	Page Up		
Scroll down one page in current record, report, View as List, or View as Table	Page Down		
Scroll to first record with View as List or View as Table checked	Home		
Scroll to last record with View as List or View as Table checked	End		
Status area (hide/show)	⌘+Option+S	View ➪ Status Area	You can also click the status area control.

Table B-4
Layout Mode Commands

Command	Key	Menu	Comments
Align selected objects	⌘+K	Arrange ➪ Align	
Bring Forward	Shift+⌘+F	Arrange ➪ Bring Forward	
Bring to Front	Shift+⌘+Option+F	Arrange ➪ Bring to Front	

Continued

Table B-4 (*continued*)

Command	Key	Menu	Comments
Button format	Double-click a button	Format ⇨ Button	
Constrain lines to vertical/ horizontal	Press Shift while drawing		
Constrain lines to 45-degree increments	Press Option while drawing		
Constrain ovals to circles and rectangles to squares	Press Option while drawing or resizing.		
Constrain resizing to vertical/horizontal	Shift+drag a handle		
Copy selected object or text	⌘+C	Edit ⇨ Copy	Copying places a copy of the object or text on the Clipboard.
Cut selected object or text	⌘+X	Edit ⇨ Cut	Cutting places a copy of the object or text on the Clipboard.
Date format	Option+double-click a Date field	Format ⇨ Date	
Delete Layout	⌘+E	Layouts ⇨ Delete Layout	
Display field or object's format	Option+double-click the field or object	See also specific object and field types listed in this table.	
Drag selected layout part past an object	Option+drag		
Duplicate an object	⌘+D (or Option+drag the object)	Edit ⇨ Duplicate	
Field borders	⌘+Option+B	Format ⇨ Field Borders	

Command	Key	Menu	Comments
Field format	⌘+Option+F	Format ⇨ Field Format	
Graphic format	Option+double-click a Container field or graphic object	Format ⇨ Graphic	
Group objects	⌘+G	Arrange ⇨ Group	
Insert Current Date	⌘+- (hyphen)	Insert ⇨ Current Date	
Insert Current Time	⌘+;	Insert ⇨ Current Time	
Insert Current User Name	Shift+⌘+N	Insert ⇨ Current User Name	
Lock object	⌘+H	Arrange ⇨ Lock	
Merge Field	⌘+M	Insert ⇨ Merge Field	
Move an object with Object Grids on	⌘+drag the object		Allows object dragging to positions other than those provided by the grid.
Move selected object	Arrow keys		Moves the object one pixel in the direction of the arrow key.
New Layout	⌘+N	Layouts ⇨ New Layout/Report	
Next layout	Ctrl+down arrow		
Number format	Option+double click a Number field	Format ⇨ Number	
Object Grids	⌘+Y	Arrange ⇨ Object Grids	Works as an on/off toggle.
Paste text or object from Clipboard	⌘+V	Edit ⇨ Paste	
Portal setup	Double-click a portal	Format ⇨ Portal	
Previous layout	Ctrl+up arrow		
Redefine field on layout	Double-click the field		

Continued

Table B-4 (*continued*)

Command	Key	Menu	Comments
Reorder selected layout part	Shift+drag the part		
Reorient part labels	⌘+click a part label		You can also click the control at the bottom of the document window.
Reset default format based on current object	⌘+click the object		
Resize an object with Object Grids on	⌘+drag a handle while resizing		You can create object sizes other than those provided by the grid.
Rotate	⌘+Option+R	Arrange ⇨ Rotate	Rotates a selected text string or object in 90-degree increments.
Select All	⌘+A	Edit ⇨ Select All	
Select objects by type	⌘+Option+A		An object must be selected first.
Send Backward	Shift+⌘+J	Arrange ⇨ Send Backward	
Send to Back	Shift+⌘+Option+J	Arrange ⇨ Send to Back	
Set Alignment	Shift+⌘+K	Arrange ⇨ Set Alignment	
Sliding/Printing	Option+⌘+T	Format ⇨ Sliding/Printing	
Square the object being resized	Option+drag a handle		
Text format	Option+double-click a Text field or label	Format ⇨ Text	
Time format	Option+double-click a Time field	Format ⇨ Time	
T-Squares	⌘+T	View ⇨ T-Squares	Works as an on/off toggle.

Command	Key	Menu	Comments
Undo	⌘+Z	Edit ⇨ Undo	
Ungroup object	Shift+⌘+G	Arrange ⇨ Ungroup	
Unlock object	Shift+⌘+H	Arrange ⇨ Unlock	

Table B-5
Text Formatting Commands†

Command	Key	Menu	Comments
Align Center	⌘+\	Format ⇨ Align Text ⇨ Center	
Align Full	Shift+⌘+\	Format ⇨ Align Text ⇨ Full	
Align Left	⌘+[	Format ⇨ Align Text ⇨ Left	
Align Right	⌘+]	Format ⇨ Align Text ⇨ Right	
Bold	Shift+⌘+B	Format ⇨ Style ⇨ Bold	
Italic	Shift+⌘+I	Format ⇨ Style ⇨ Italic	
Outline	Shift+⌘+O	Format ⇨ Style ⇨ Outline	
Plain	Shift+⌘+P	Format ⇨ Style ⇨ Plain	
Next larger point size in menu	Shift+⌘+ Option+>	Format ⇨ Size	
Next smaller point size in menu	Shift+⌘+ Option+<	Format ⇨ Size	
One point larger	Shift+⌘+>	Format ⇨ Size ⇨ Custom	
One point smaller	Shift+⌘+<	Format ⇨ Size ⇨ Custom	
Select All	⌘+A	Edit ⇨ Select All	
Shadow	Shift+⌘+S	Format ⇨ Style ⇨ Shadow	
Subscript	Shift+⌘+- (hyphen)	Format ⇨ Style ⇨ Subscript	
Superscript	Shift+⌘++	Format ⇨ Style ⇨ Superscript	
Underline	Shift+⌘+U	Format ⇨ Style ⇨ Underline	

†Text-formatting commands can be used in Browse mode (to format user-entered text) or Layout mode (to set default field formatting). Many of these commands can also be chosen from the Text Formatting toolbar or from the pop-up menu that appears when you select and Ctrl+click a text string.

Table B-6
Data Entry and Editing Commands

Command	Key	Menu	Comments
Clear a field	Clear	Edit ⇨ Clear	Clears entire field without storing the material on the Clipboard.
Clear selected Clipboard.	Delete or Backspace		Clears object or selected text within a field without storing it on the text or object
Copy	⌘+C	Edit ⇨ Copy	Copies selected text or object to the Clipboard.
Correct Word	Shift+⌘+Y	Edit ⇨ Spelling ⇨ Correct Word	The Document Preference to "Spell as you type" must be on.
Cut	⌘+X	Edit ⇨ Cut	Cuts selected text or object and stores it in the Clipboard.
Delete next character	del		Not available on all keyboards.
Delete next word (or delete to end of current word)	Option+del		Not available on all keyboards.
Delete previous character	Delete (or Backspace)		
Delete previous word (or delete to beginning of current word)	Option+Delete		
Enter a tab character	Option+Tab		
Insert Current Date	⌘+- (hyphen)	Insert ⇨ Current Date	
Insert Current Time	⌘+;	Insert ⇨ Current Time	
Insert Current User Name	Shift+ ⌘+N	Insert ⇨ Current User Name	
Insert From Index	⌘+I	Insert ⇨ From Index	
Insert From Last Record	⌘+'	Insert ⇨ From Last Record	

Command	Key	Menu	Comments
Insert From Last Record and move to next field	Shift+⌘+'		
Next field	Tab		
Nonbreaking space	Option+Spacebar		
Paste	⌘+V	Edit ➪ Paste	Pastes text or object from the Clipboard.
Paste without text style	⌘+Option+V		
Previous field	Shift+Tab		
Replace a field's values	⌘+=	Records ➪ Replace	
Select All	⌘+A	Edit ➪ Select All	
Undo	⌘+Z	Edit ➪ Undo	

Table B-7
Commands for Working with Records

Command	Key	Menu	Comments
Copy all text in a record†	⌘+C		You must not have anything selected within the record.
Copy found set	⌘+ Option+C		Copies all records in the found set to the Clipboard as text.
Delete Record or Find Request†	⌘+E	Records ➪ Delete Record,or Requests ➪ Delete Request	This command is mode-specific.
Delete immediately	⌘+Option+E		This command bypasses the confirmation dialog box.

Continued

Table B-7 (continued)

Command	Key	Menu	Comments
Duplicate Record or Find Request†	⌘+D	Records ⇨ Duplicate Record, or Requests ⇨ Duplicate Request	This command is mode-specific.
Omit a record	⌘+M	Records ⇨ Omit Record	
Omit Multiple	Shift+ ⌘+M	Records ⇨ Omit Multiple	
Modify Last Find	⌘+R	Records ⇨ Modify Last Find	
New record or Find request†	⌘+N	Records ⇨ New Record, or Requests ⇨ Add New Request	This command is mode-specific.
Next record, Find request, or report page	Ctrl+down arrow		
Previous record, Find request, or report page	Ctrl+up arrow		
Select a record by number	Esc		
Show all records	⌘+J	Records ⇨ Show All Records, or Requests ⇨ Show All Records	
Sort records†	⌘+S	Records ⇨ Sort	

†These commands can also be chosen from the pop-up menu that appears when you Control-click in a blank area of the layout.

✦   ✦   ✦

Windows Keyboard Shortcuts

This appendix contains keyboard shortcuts for FileMaker Pro commands and actions in the Windows environment. These commands are organized according to the various kinds of tasks you may want to perform. Note that the tables in this appendix do not contain all the commands the program offers; they merely list the commands for which there are keyboard shortcuts.

By default, many of the keyboard shortcuts are not displayed in FileMaker Pro's menus. To list them all, choose Edit ⇨ Preferences ⇨ Application, select the General tab in the Application Preferences dialog box, check the option to show "All keyboard shortcuts in menus," and click OK.

Note FileMaker Pro 5 for Windows supports the Microsoft IntelliMouse. You can use it to zoom in or out in all modes and, by using the wheel, you can flip through records in Browse mode. For additional information, refer to Reference ⇨ Keyboard commands ⇨ IntelliMouse support (Windows) in the Help file.

Table C-1
General Commands

Command	Key	Menu	Comments
Cancel a dialog box or operation	Esc		
Close Ctrl+F4	Ctrl+W or	File ⇨ Close	You can also click the close box on the document window.
Define Fields	Ctrl+Shift+D	File ⇨ Define Fields	
Exit	Alt+F4 or Ctrl+Q	File ⇨ Exit	
Help	F1, Shift+F1	Help ⇨ FileMaker Pro Help, Help ⇨ What's This?	
Network Access	Ctrl+Shift+O		You can also click Hosts in the Open dialog box.
Open a database	Ctrl+O	File ⇨ Open	
Play a QuickTime movie or sound	Spacebar or double-click the Container field		
Print	Ctrl+P	File ⇨ Print	
Print without a dialog box	Ctrl+Shift+T		
Stop a QuickTime movie	Spacebar or single-click the Container field		

Table C-2
Mode-Selection Commands[†]

Command	Key	Menu	Comments
Browse	Ctrl+B	View ⇨ Browse Mode	
Find	Ctrl+F	View ⇨ Find Mode	
Layout	Ctrl+L	View ⇨ Layout Mode	
Preview	Ctrl+U	View ⇨ Preview Mode	

[†]You can also choose these command from the Mode pop-up menu at the bottom of any FileMaker document window.

Table C-3
Document Window Control Commands

Command	Key	Menu	Comments
Cascade windows	Shift+F5	Windows ⇨ Cascade	
Close a window	Ctrl+Shift+F4		
Next window	Ctrl+F6		
Previous window	Ctrl+Shift+F6		
Resize window	Ctrl+Shift+Z		
Scroll to top of current record or preview page	Home		
Scroll to bottom of current record or preview page	End		
Scroll up one page in current record/report	Page Up		
Scroll down one page in current record/report	Page Down		
Scroll to first record in View as List or Table mode checked	Home		
Scroll to last record in View as List or Table mode checked	End		
Scroll left in the document window	Ctrl+Page Up		
Scroll right in the document window	Ctrl+Page Down		
Status area (show/hide)	Ctrl+Shift+S		You can also click the status area control at the bottom of the document window.
Tile windows horizontally	Shift+F4	Windows ⇨ Tile Horizontally	
Zoom in	F3	View ⇨ Zoom In	
Zoom out	Shift+F3	View ⇨ Zoom Out	

Table C-4 **Layout Mode Commands**			
Command	*Key*	*Menu*	*Comments*
Align selected objects	Ctrl+K	Arrange ⇨ Align	
Align text to the center	Ctrl+\	Format ⇨ Align r Text ⇨ Cente	
Align text to the left	Ctrl+[	Format ⇨ Align Text ⇨ Left	
Align text to the right	Ctrl+]	Format ⇨ Align Text ⇨ Right	
Align text using full justification	Ctrl+Shift+\	Format ⇨ Align Text ⇨ Full	
Bring Forward	Ctrl+Shift+F	Arrange ⇨ Bring Forward	
Bring to Front Constrain lines to vertical/horizontal	Alt+Ctrl+Shift+F Shift+drag while drawing	Arrange ⇨ Bring to Front	
Constrain lines to 45-degree angles	Ctrl+drag while drawing		
Constrain ovals to circles and rectangles to squares	Ctrl+drag while drawing or resizing		
Constrain resizing to vertical/ horizontal	Shift+drag a handle		
Copy selected	Ctrl+C	Edit ⇨ Copy	Copying places a copy of the object or text on the Clipboard.object or text
Cut selected object or text	Ctrl+X	Edit ⇨ Cut	Cutting places a copy of the object or text on the Clipboard.
Date format	Alt+double- click a Date field	Format ⇨ Date	
Delete Layout	Ctrl+E	Layouts ⇨ Delete Layout	

Command	Key	Menu	Comments
Display object's format	Alt+double-click the object		See also specific object and field types listed in this table.
Drag selected layout part past an object	Alt+drag		
Duplicate selection	Ctrl+D or Ctrl+ drag the object	Edit ➪ Duplicate	
Field Borders	Ctrl+Alt+Shift+B	Format ➪ Field Borders	
Field Format	Ctrl+Shift+M	Format ➪ Field Format	
Graphic format	Alt+double-click	Format ➪ Graphic a Container field or graphic image	
Group objects	Ctrl+G	Arrange ➪ Group	
Insert current date	Ctrl+– (hyphen)	Insert ➪ Current Date	
Insert current time	Ctrl+;	Insert ➪ Current Time	
Insert current user name	Ctrl+Shift+N	Insert ➪ Current User Name	
Lock object(s)	Ctrl+H	Arrange ➪ Lock	
Merge Field	Ctrl+M	Insert ➪ Merge Field	
Move an object with Object Grids on	Alt+drag the object		Allows object dragging to positions other than those provided by the grid.
Move selected object one pixel	Arrow keys		Moves in the direction of the arrow key.
New Layout	Ctrl+N	Layouts ➪ New Layout/Report	
Number format	Alt+double-click a Number field	Format ➪ Number	

Continued

Table C-4 *(continued)*

Command	Key	Menu	Comments
Object Grids	Ctrl+Y	Arrange ⇨ Object Grids	Works as an on/off toggle.
Paste text or object from Clipboard	Ctrl+V	Edit ⇨ Paste	
Portal format	Double-click, Ctrl+double-click, or Alt+double-click a portal	Format ⇨ Portal	
Redefine field on layout	Double-click or Ctrl+double-click the field		
Reorder selected layout part	Shift+drag the part		
Reorient part labels from horizontal to vertical	Ctrl+click any part label		You can also click the label control at the bottom of the document window.
Resize an object with Object Grids on	Alt+drag a handle while resizing		Allows object sizes other than those provided by the grid.
Rotate an object	Ctrl+Shift+R	Arrange ⇨ Rotate	
Select All	Ctrl+A	Edit ⇨ Select All	
Select objects by type	Ctrl+Shift+A		An object must be selected first.
Send Backward	Ctrl+Shift+J	Arrange ⇨ Send Backward	
Send to Back	Alt+Ctrl+Shift+J	Arrange ⇨ Send to Back	
Set Alignment	Ctrl+Shift+K	Arrange ⇨ Set Alignment	
Text format	Alt+double-click a Text field	Format ⇨ Text	
Time format	Alt+double-click a Time field	Format ⇨ Time	
T-Squares	Ctrl+T	View ⇨ T-Squares	Works as an on/off toggle.
Ungroup objects	Ctrl+Shift+G	Arrange ⇨ Ungroup	

Table C-5 Text Formatting Commands†			
Command	**Key**	**Menu**	**Comments**
Unlock object	Ctrl+Shift+H	Arrange ➪ Unlock	
Align center	Ctrl+\	Format ➪ Align Text ➪ Center	Can also be chosen from the text formatting toolbar.
Align left Text ➪ Left	Ctrl+[	Format ➪ Align	Can also be chosen from the text formatting toolbar.
Align right	Ctrl+]	Format ➪ Align Text ➪ Right	Can also be chosen from the text formatting toolbar.
Align with full justification	Ctrl+Shift+\	Format ➪ Align Text ➪ Full	Can also be chosen from the text formatting toolbar.
Bold	Ctrl+Shift+B	Format ➪ Style ➪ Bold	Can also be chosen from the text formatting toolbar.
Italic	Ctrl+Shift+I	Format ➪ Style ➪ Italic	Can also be chosen from the text formatting toolbar.
Plain	Ctrl+Shift+P	Format ➪ Style ➪ Plain	
Next point size larger	Ctrl+>		
Next point size smaller	Ctrl+<		
One point larger	Ctrl+Shift+>		
One point smaller		Ctrl+Shift+<	
Select All	Ctrl+A	Edit ➪ Select All	
Underline	Shift+Ctrl+U	Format ➪ Style ➪ Underline	Can also be chosen from the text formatting toolbar.

†Text formatting commands can be used in Browse mode (to format user-entered text) or Layout mode (to set default field formatting). Many of these commands can be chosen from the Text Formatting toolbar or from the pop-up menu that appears when you select and right-click a text string.

Table C-6
Data-Entry and Editing Commands

Command	Key	Menu	Comments
Clear	Del	Edit ⇨ Clear	Clears selected text or object storing it without on the Clipboard.
Copy	Ctrl+C or Ctrl+Ins	Edit ⇨ Copy	Copies selected text or object to the Clipboard.
Correct Word	Ctrl+Shift+Y	Edit ⇨ Spelling ⇨ Correct Word	Option to "Spell as you type" must be on.
Cut	Ctrl+X or Shift+Del	Edit ⇨ Cut	Cuts selected text or object and stores it in the Clipboard.
Delete next character	Del (or Delete) †		
Delete next word or to the end of current word	Ctrl+Del		
Delete previous character	Backspace		
Enter a tab character	Ctrl+Tab		
Insert Current Date	Ctrl+– (hyphen)	Insert ⇨ Current Date	
Insert Current Time	Ctrl+;	Insert ⇨ Current Time	
Insert Current User Name	Ctrl+Shift+N	Insert ⇨ Current User Name	
Insert From Index	Ctrl+I	Insert ⇨ From Index	
Insert From Last Record	Ctrl+'	Insert ⇨ From Last Record	
Insert From Last Record and move to next field	Ctrl+Shift+'		
Next field	Tab		
Non-breaking space	Ctrl+Spacebar		

Command	Key	Menu	Comments
Paste	Ctrl+V	Edit ⇨ Paste	Pastes text or object from the Clipboard.
Paste without text style	Ctrl+Shift+V		
Previous field	Shift+Tab		
Replace a field's value	Ctrl+=	Records ⇨ Replace	
Select All	Ctrl+A	Edit ⇨ Select All	
Undo	Ctrl+Z or Alt+Backspace	Edit ⇨ Undo	

†Note that the Del and Delete keys perform the same functions when used in FileMaker Pro.

Table C-7
Commands for Working with Records

Command	Key	Menu	Comments
Copy found set	Ctrl+Shift+C	Copies records to clipboard as text	
Copy record or Find request†	Ctrl+C	Nothing must be selected.	
Delete Record or Find Request†	Ctrl+E	Records ⇨ Delete Record, or Requests ⇨ Delete Request Command is mode-specific.	
Delete immediately	Ctrl+Shift+E		Bypass confirmation dialog box.
Duplicate Record or Find Request†	Ctrl+D	Records ⇨ Duplicate Record, or Requests ⇨ Duplicate Request	Command is mode-specific.
Modify Last Find	Ctrl+R	Records ⇨ Modify Last Find	
New record or Find request†	Ctrl+N	Records ⇨ New Record, or Requests ⇨ Add New Request	Command is mode-. specific

Continued

Table C-7 (*continued*)			
Command	*Key*	*Menu*	*Comments*
Next Record or Find Request	Ctrl+down arrow or Shift+ Page Down		
Omit a record	Ctrl+M	Records ⇨ Omit Record	
Omit multiple records	Ctrl+Shift+M	Records ⇨ Omit Multiple	
Open the layout pop-up menu	F2		
Previous record or Find request	Ctrl+up arrow or Shift+Page Up		
Replace a field's value	Ctrl+=	Records ⇨ Replace	
Select a record by number	Esc		
Show All Records	Ctrl+J	Records ⇨ Show All Records	
Sort[†]	Ctrl+S	Records ⇨ Sort	

[†]These commands can also be chosen from the pop-up menu that appears when you right-click a blank area of a layout in Browse or Find mode.

✦   ✦   ✦

Resources

I n addition to using this book and the material that came
with your copy of FileMaker Pro, you can turn to many
other resources for more information about the product.
These resources can help you accomplish the following:

+ Learn new database programming techniques and tricks

+ Work around or discover solutions to problems you have
encountered in using FileMaker Pro

+ Find out about upcoming versions of FileMaker Pro, as
well as utilities that enhance the program

+ Purchase ready-to-run FileMaker Pro templates that are
designed for your particular business

+ Hire a specialist to create a database template especially
for you

+ Try out free and inexpensive templates

Technical Support and General Help

If you need help with a problem that isn't explained in this
book or in the FileMaker Pro Help system, the best source of
information is the FileMaker Technical Support Department
(408-727-9004). Have your access code or product serial
number handy when you call.

If you have a fax machine or fax-modem, you can obtain a
wealth of technical information, troubleshooting notes, and
programming tips by calling the FileMaker Fax AnswerLine.
Dial 800-800-8954 from a touch-tone phone and request that a
catalog of document listings be faxed to you. After you receive
the catalog, you can call the same number to request that
additional documents be faxed to you. Although the Fax
AnswerLine is impersonal when compared to speaking with a
live technical support representative, it does provide answers

to many common (and not-so-common) FileMaker Pro questions. And, best of all, it's free!

If you have Internet access and a Web browser, you should visit FileMaker's Web site at `http://www.filemaker.com`. In addition to helpful tips and troubleshooting notes, you will find the site an invaluable source of FileMaker Pro templates.

If you have a FileMaker Pro programming problem or just want to pick up some great tips, you can subscribe to several free mailing lists sponsored by Blue World Communications, Inc. To obtain information on how to subscribe to the lists, go to Blue World's Web site at `http://www.blueworld.com/blueworld/lists/`.

Custom Programming and Vertical Applications

Because FileMaker Pro is such a popular database program, you probably won't be surprised to learn that some individuals and companies make their living by providing after-market materials, such as database templates, custom programming, and training materials.

FileMaker publishes a guide to third-party companies that provide FileMaker Pro solutions. A copy is included in the box with FileMaker. If you've lost your copy, you can view it on the Web at `http://www.co-media.com/FM2/`.

If your intent is to provide some FileMaker Pro solutions of your own, you can join the FileMaker Solutions Alliance (FSA) program for an annual fee of $249 by calling 800-325-2747.

Design Tips and Programming Tricks

In 1995, an enterprising FileMaker Pro developer named Matt Petrowsky decided the best way to spread the word about FileMaker Pro was to use it in a manner that FileMaker, Inc. never intended — to publish and distribute an electronic magazine called *FileMaker Magazine*. Dedicated to FileMaker Pro topics, this gorgeous monthly database contains scads of excellent design and programming tips. To download sample issues or to subscribe ($50/year), you can visit ISO Production's Web page at `http://www.iso-ezine.com` or contact them at the mailing address shown later in this section.

Tip Be sure to check out the enormous resource list compiled by ISO at `http://www.iso-ezine.com/resources.phtml`.

ISO maintains an Internet mailing list where users can exchange tips for publishing their FileMaker databases on the Web. To subscribe, send an e-mail message to `majordomo@filemakermagazine.com`. Type one of the following lines in the body of the message:

+ **subscribe fmweb-talk** (to receive a separate copy of each message as it is posted to the list)

+ **subscribe fmweb-talk-digest** (to receive a compilation of all messages posted to the list during each day)

ISO is also the publisher of several FileMaker-related CDs, including the *Everything CD for FileMaker Pro, Volume 3* ($49.99) and *Scriptology* ($79.99). The CDs can be purchased directly from the ISO Web site. To order by phone or mail, contact

ISO Productions, Inc.
4049 First Street, Suite 141
Livermore, CA 94550
Phone: 800-958-8999 or 250-752-1539
E-mail: iso@isoproductions.com

Magazines: An Additional Source for Tips

Several computer magazines occasionally provide FileMaker Pro tips and techniques. In addition to featuring in-depth reviews of new versions of programs (such as FileMaker Pro), they sometimes publish user tips and feature articles that explain how to get more out of FileMaker Pro.

Macworld magazine focuses primarily on the needs of business users. Following its merger with *MacUser* magazine, *Macworld* is now the primary source of Mac information for many users. *Mac Home Journal* caters more to novice users and the needs of individuals who have Macs at home. You should be able to pick up a copy of either of these magazines at a local newsstand, or you can contact the magazines directly for subscription information at the addresses below.

If you're not satisfied with scanning magazines for the occasional FileMaker article, give *FileMaker Pro Advisor* a try. This magazine is dedicated to FileMaker Pro and contains user success stories, technical articles, and tips and tricks. Subscriptions are $49 for six issues.

Macworld
Subscription Services

P.O. Box 54529
Boulder, CO 80328-4529
Phone: 800-288-6848 in U.S.; 303-604-1465 outside the U.S.
Web site: `http://www.macworld.com`

MacHome Journal
Subscripts @Mac Home Journal
703 Market Street, Suite 535
San Francisco, CA 94103
Web site: `http://www.machome.com`

FileMaker Pro Advisor
P.O. Box 469003
Escondido, CA 92046-9737
Phone: 800-336-6060
Web site: `http://www.advisor.com`

More Internet Resources

FileMaker developers are keenly aware of the need for an Internet presence; many have their own Web sites. To make it easy for you to find them, I've compiled a list of FileMaker-related sites that I think you'll find useful.

To make it easier for you to visit these sites, you'll find an HTML file named Resources.htm on the *FileMaker Pro 5 Bible* CD-ROM. Open this file in any Web browser (Internet Explorer or Netscape Navigator/Communicator, for example), and you can reach the sites by clicking links rather than typing the addresses.

✦   ✦   ✦

FileMaker Pro Function Reference

FileMaker Pro includes dozens of predefined functions that you can use to define formulas for Calculation fields (as explained in Chapter 14). The purpose of each of these functions is summarized in Table E-1.

Table E-1 FileMaker Pro's Built-In Functions	
Function Name	**Purpose**
Abs	Calculates the absolute value of an expression
Atan	Calculates the arc tangent of an expression, in radians, and returns a value between $-\pi$ and π
Average	Computes the average value (the arithmetic mean) of all values in one or more fields
Case	Performs a series of tests and selects one answer (or the default answer, if no test is found to be true)
Choose	Selects one answer from a series
Cos	Calculates the cosine of an argument expressed in radians, returning a value between -1 and 1
Count	Counts the number of valid, nonempty entries in one or more fields
DatabaseNames	Returns the filenames of all currently open FileMaker Pro databases
Date	Converts a numeric value into a valid date
DateToText	Converts a value in a Date field to text

Continued

Table E-1 *(continued)*

Function Name	Purpose
Day	Displays the day of the month, 1–31, for a given date
DayName	Displays the weekday name for a given date
DayofWeek	Displays the number of the day within a week, 1–7, for a given date
DayofYear	Displays the number of the day within a year, 1–365, for a given date
Degrees	Converts a value in radians into degrees
Exact	Returns "true" if two text expressions match exactly (including case)
Exp	Returns the antilog (base e) of an expression
Extend	Makes a nonrepeating field a repeating field (with the identical value in each place) for use in calculations with other repeating fields
External	When the FileMaker Pro Web Companion plug-in is installed, these functions return information about the individuals who access your database on the World Wide Web or an Intranet
FieldBounds	Returns the location and rotation angle of a given field in a particular layout of a database
FieldNames	Returns the names of all fields used in a particular layout (or in all layouts) of a specified database
FieldRepetitions	Returns the number of repetitions of a given repeating field as it is formatted on a particular layout of a database
FieldStyle	Returns information about how a field in a particular layout is formatted, as well as whether the field has a value list associated with it
FieldType	Returns the field definition for a specified field in a particular database
FV	Computes an investment's future value for a given payment amount, interest rate, and number of periods
GetRepetition	Presents the contents of a particular repetition in a repeating field
GetSummary	Calculates the value of a particular Summary field when the database has been sorted by the specified break field
Hour	Displays the number of hours in a time expression
If	Performs a logical test and completes one action if it is true, another if it is false
Int	Returns the integer portion of a numeric value
IsEmpty	Determines whether a value or field is blank
IsValid	Determines whether a related field can be found and contains valid data, and whether a related file can be found
Last	Shows the last valid, nonempty entry in a repeating field

Function Name	Purpose
LayoutNames	Returns the names of all layouts in a specified database
Left	Returns the specified number of characters of a text string, counting from the left
LeftWords	Returns the specified number of words from a text string, counting from the left
Length	Finds the number of characters in a given text string
Ln	Computes the natural (base e) logarithm of an expression
Log	Computes the common (base 10) logarithm of an expression
Lower	Converts a text string to all lowercase
Max	Displays the greatest value among those in specified fields
Middle	Returns a portion of a supplied text string, starting at a given position and extending a specified number of characters
MiddleWords	Returns the specified number of words from a text string, counting from the specified starting word
Min	Displays the smallest value among those in specified fields
Minute	Returns the minute portion of a time expression
Mod	Returns the remainder when an expression is divided by a given number
Month	Displays the number of the month in a date expression, within the range 1–12
MonthName	Displays the name of month in a date expression
NPV	Finds the net present value of an investment, using values in repeating fields as unequal payment values and the given interest rate
NumToText	Converts a numeric expression to text format
PatternCount	Returns the number of instances of a specified text string found within another text string or field
Pi	Returns the value of the mathematical constant pi
PMT	Calculates a loan payment, using the given principal, interest rate, and term
Position	Scans text for the specified string starting at the given position and returns the location of the first occurrence of the string
Proper	Converts the first letter of each word in the text string to uppercase (used to capitalize names, for example)
PV	Calculates the present value of an investment, using a given payment amount, interest rate, and periods

Continued

Table E-1 *(continued)*

Function Name	Purpose
Radians	Converts a degree value to radians (for use with trigonometric functions)
Random	Generates a random number
RelationInfo	Returns information about a particular relationship that has been defined for the current database
RelationNames	Displays the names of all relationships that have been defined for the specified database, separated by Returns
Replace	In a text string, starts at the given position, moves the specified number of places, and replaces the existing text with the specified new text string
Right	Counting from the right, returns a given number of characters in a text expression
RightWords	Returns the specified number of words from a text string, counting from the right
Round	Rounds off a numeric expression to the specified number of decimal places
ScriptNames	Returns the names of all scripts that have been created for a given database, separated by Returns
Seconds	Displays the seconds portion of a time expression
Sign	Examines a numeric expression and returns 1 for positive, - 1 for negative, or 0 for 0
Sin	Computes the sine of an angle expressed in radians
Sqrt	Computes the square root of a numeric expression (the same as expression ^ 0.5)
Status	Displays status information about the current time, operating system in use, version number of FileMaker Pro, name of the selected field, and so on (Note: There are currently 36 different status tests.)
StDev	Examines all values in any repeating or nonrepeating field and gives the sample standard deviation
StDevP	Examines all values in any repeating or nonrepeating field and gives the population standard deviation
Substitute	Substitutes one set of characters in a text string for another
Sum	Totals all values in specified fields
Tan	Computes the tangent for a given angle expressed in radians
TextToDate	Converts a text string into date format
TextToNum	Converts a text string to numeric format, ignoring alphabetic characters

Function Name	Purpose
TextToTime	Converts a text string to time format
Time	Converts three given numeric values into a time equivalent
TimeToText	Converts a time value into text format
Today	Returns the current date from the system clock
Trim	Strips the specified text expression of leading and trailing spaces
Truncate	Truncates a number to the specified number of decimal places
Upper	Converts a text expression to all uppercase
ValueListItems	Returns the items in a particular value list for a given database
ValueListNames	Returns the names of all value lists that have been defined for a given database
WeekofYear	Determines the number of the week in the year, 1–52, for the specified date expression
WeekofYearFiscal	Determines the number of the week in the year, 1–52, for the specified date expression (in accordance with the particular day that is considered the first day of the week)
WordCount	Returns the total number of words found in a text expression or field
Year	Returns the year part of the specified date expression

The functions are divided into 13 categories: text, number, date, time, aggregate, summary, repeating, financial, trigonometric, logical, status, design, and external. This appendix provides a detailed explanation for each of FileMaker Pro's built-in functions. The functions are listed alphabetically within the category to which they belong. In addition to an explanation of each function's purpose and an example of how the function is used, the sections include a statement that shows how to phrase the function and its arguments. (The order for arranging the function and its arguments is called the *syntax* of the function.) Special notes and cautions, as well as references to other, related functions, are included in the explanations of some of the functions.

To use a function in a Calculation field definition, double-click its name in the function list in the upper-right section of the Specify Calculation dialog box (see Figure E-1). Then replace the function's arguments with the appropriate field names or expressions.

Select related fields by first choosing the relationship from this pop-up menu

Field list

Operators

Specify the organization of the function list by
choosing an option from this pop-up menu

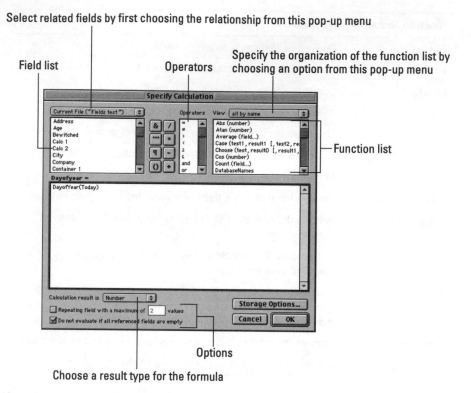

Function list

Options

Choose a result type for the formula

Figure E-1: The Specify Calculation dialog box

Aggregate (Statistical) Functions

These functions compute statistics on repeating and nonrepeating (normal) fields.
The result can be either repeating or nonrepeating. Although the arguments are
often Number fields, Date and Time fields can also be used.

The aggregate functions are as follows:

- ✦ Average
- ✦ Count
- ✦ Max
- ✦ Min
- ✦ StDev
- ✦ StDevP
- ✦ Sum

Using aggregate functions with repeating and nonrepeating fields

Although aggregate functions are commonly used with repeating fields, FileMaker Pro also enables these functions to be used with nonrepeating fields, as well as with a mixture of repeating and nonrepeating fields. Each aggregate function discussed in this section accepts a single repeating field or series of repeating and/or nonrepeating fields as arguments. Regardless of the result data type chosen (Number or Date, for example), you can optionally specify that the result be a repeating value and display a particular number of repetitions.

Average

Purpose: Computes the average value of all values in the specified field or fields. The fields may be repeating, nonrepeating (normal), or a combination of the two, and the result type can be repeating or nonrepeating. The average is calculated by adding all the appropriate values together and then dividing by the number of values added. The result is a numeric value or, in the case of a repeating result, a series of numeric values.

Syntax: Average (*field . . .*)

where *field . . .* is a list of one or more valid fields containing only numeric values.

Example: Suppose Prices is a repeating field containing the extended price of each item in an order. The following expression displays a message about the cost of these items:

```
"On average, the items you ordered cost $" &
NumToText(Average(Prices))
```

If Prices contains 5.00, 10.00, and 30.00, the expression produces the following message:

```
On average, the items you ordered cost $15.00
```

Example: If the nonrepeating fields F1, F2, and F3 contain 4, 6, and 8 in a given record, the formula Average(F1, F2, F3) returns **6**.

See also: Min, Max, Sum, StDev, StDevP.

Count

Purpose: Determines the number of nonblank entries in a repeating field, a series of nonrepeating fields, or a mixture of the two field types, returning the result or results as numeric values.

Syntax: Count (*field* . . .)

where *field* . . . is a list of one or more valid, nonempty repeating fields of any type, or a series of repeating and/or nonrepeating fields.

Example: If the repeating field Prices, formatted to contain up to ten values, actually contains 5.00, 10.00, and 30.00, then the following expression yields a message about the items ordered:

```
"You ordered " & Count(Prices) & " items. Thank you!"
```

In this case, the expression produces the following message:

```
You ordered 3 items. Thank you!
```

Max

Purpose: Finds the highest, latest, or greatest value among all values in a nonempty repeating field or in a series of nonrepeating and/or repeating fields. The result is returned in the appropriate format.

Syntax: Max (*field* . . .)

where *field* . . . is a list of one or more nonempty, valid fields of any type, or a series of repeating and/or nonrepeating fields.

Example: Suppose that Dates is a repeating field containing dates of orders in an invoice record. Suppose, further, that it contains three values: 03/17/99, 04/18/99, and 05/19/99. In that case, the following expression:

```
"Your last order was on " & Max(Dates)
```

produces this message:

```
Your last order was on 05/19/99
```

See also: Min.

Min

Purpose: Finds the lowest, oldest, or smallest value among all values in a nonempty repeating field or in a series of nonrepeating and/or repeating fields. The result is returned in the appropriate format.

Syntax: Min (*field . . .*)

where *field . . .* is a list of one or more nonempty, valid fields of any type.

Example: If Dates is a repeating field containing three values: 03/16/99, 04/17/99, and 05/18/99, then the following expression:

```
"Your first order was on " & Min(Dates)
```

produces the following message:

```
Your first order was on 03/16/1999
```

See also: Max.

StDev

Purpose: Computes the standard deviation for all values in a nonempty, numeric repeating field, a series of nonrepeating fields, or a mixture of the two field types. The standard deviation is a measure of how the values in a sample depart from the average value.

Note

The formula formerly used to calculate StDev in FileMaker Pro 2.1 is the one that is now used to calculate StDevP. If you have older FileMaker databases and want them to calculate a sample standard deviation, be sure you use StDev in the formula — rather than StdDevP.

Syntax: StDev (*field . . .*)

where *field . . .* is the name of a valid, nonempty repeating field containing numeric data only, or a series of repeating and/or nonrepeating fields.

Example: If the repeating field TestScores contains the values 98, 76, and 90, then the expression StDev (TestScores) yields **11.136**, the standard deviation of these test scores.

See also: StdDevP.

StDevP

Purpose: Computes the population standard deviation for all values in a nonempty, numeric repeating field, a series of nonrepeating fields, or a mixture of the two field types. The difference between StDev (described previously) and StDevP is that the former is assumed to be based on a sample, whereas the latter is a population statistic (that is, StDevP is not based on a sample).

Note   The formula formerly used to calculate StDev in FileMaker Pro 2.1 is the one that is now used to calculate StDevP. If you have older FileMaker databases and want them to calculate a sample standard deviation, be sure that StDev is used in the formula — rather than StdDevP.

Syntax: StDevP (*field . . .*)

where *field . . .* name is the name of a valid, nonempty repeating field containing numeric data only, or a series of repeating and/or nonrepeating fields.

Example: If the repeating field TestScores contains the values 98, 76, and 90, then the expression StDevP (TestScores) yields **9.09**, the population standard deviation of these test scores.

See also: StDev

Sum

Purpose: Adds the contents of each nonblank entry in a numeric repeating field or in a series of nonrepeating and/or repeating fields. The result returned is a numeric value.

Syntax: Sum (*field . . .*)

where *field . . .* is the name of a valid, nonempty repeating field containing numeric values only, or a series of nonrepeating and/or repeating fields.

Example: If the repeating field Prices contains the values 5.00, 10.00, and 30.00, then the following expression:

```
"Your item total is $" & Sum(Prices)
```

produces the following message:

```
Your item total is $45.00
```

See also: Average.

Date Functions

Date functions are used to find out various facts about dates entered by the user, to determine the current date from the system clock, and to convert date data into text format.

The date functions are as follows:

✦ Date

✦ DateToText

✦ Day

✦ DayName

✦ DayofWeek

✦ DayofYear

✦ Month

✦ MonthName

✦ Today

✦ WeekofYear

✦ WeekofYearFiscal

✦ Year

Date

Purpose: Determines the calendar date associated with three numbers, interpreted as days, months, and years, computed since January 1, 1 AD.

Syntax: Date (*month*, *day*, *year*)

where *month* is the number of the month, *day* is the number of the day, and *year* is the number of the year. (All are numeric expressions.)

Example: In a database, the fields DueMonth, DueDay, and DueYear are used to specify the due date of an invoice. If the fields contain 12, 19, and 1999, then the following expression:

```
"Your invoice was due on " & Date(DueMonth, DueDay, DueYear)
```

produces the following message:

```
Your invoice was due on December 19, 1999
```

Note   The result type for the formula must be set to Date. If it is set to Number, the displayed result is a serial number (730107) rather than the date previously shown.

See also: Day, Month, Year.

DateToText

Purpose: Changes the contents of a Date field into text format. The result can then be passed to another calculation that requires text input, or it can be printed directly. The text result appears in the form MM/DD/YYYY, so that September 2, 1996, appears as 09/02/1996.

Syntax: DateToText (*date*)

where *date* is a Date field or an expression yielding the Date data type.

Example: The following expression defines a Calculation field with text results, giving an invoice date after the text "This invoice was prepared on":

```
"This invoice was prepared on " & DateToText(Invoice Date)
```

If the invoice date were October 1, 1999, the field would contain the following message:

```
This invoice was prepared on 10/01/1999
```

See also: TextToDate.

Day

Purpose: Returns the number of the day in the month, from 1 to 31, for a specified date. The value returned is numeric.

Syntax: Day (*date*)

where *date* is a valid expression with a date format.

Example: If the field InvoiceDate contains the value 02/26/1999, then the expression Day (InvoiceDate) returns **26**.

See also: Month, Year.

DayName

Purpose: Returns a text string with the name of the day of the week for the specified date expression. The text returned is capitalized.

Syntax: DayName (*date*)

where *date* is a valid date.

Example: The following expression could be used as part of a message in a form letter:

```
"We missed you on " & DayName(Appointment Date)
```

If the Appointment Date field in the formula contains 10/23/1999, the following message is displayed:

```
We missed you on Saturday
```

See also: MonthName.

DayofWeek

Purpose: Returns a number representing the day of the week (from 1 to 7) on which the specified date falls. The number 1 is returned for Sunday, 2 for Monday, 3 for Tuesday, and so on.

Syntax: DayofWeek (*date*)

where *date* is a valid date expression.

Example: If a Birthday field contains 10/5/1999, the expression DayofWeek (Birthday) returns **3**, which represents Tuesday. To display the name of the day rather than a number, you could use the formula DayName (DayofWeek (Birthday)).

See also: DayofYear, WeekofYear.

DayofYear

Purpose: Returns the number of days elapsed in the appropriate year since the specified date. The result is a numeric value.

Syntax: DayofYear (*date*)

where *date* is a valid date expression.

Example: Assuming that today is February 9, 2000, the expression DayofYear (Today) returns **40** (since February 9th is the fortieth day of 2000).

Example: The following expression can be used to print a message about the Yuletide holiday:

```
"Only " & NumToText(358 - DayofYear(Today)) & " days until
Christmas!"
```

If today's date was 7/31/1999, then the expression would produce the following message:

```
Only 146 days until Christmas!
```

See also: DayofWeek, WeekofYear.

Month

Purpose: Returns a numeric value in the range 1 through 12, corresponding to the month in the specified date expression.

Syntax: Month (*date*)

where *date* is a valid expression in date format.

Example: If the Date field contains 03/16/2000, then the expression Month (Date) yields **3**.

See also: Day, Year.

MonthName

Purpose: Returns a text value with the proper name of the month in the given date expression. The text returned is capitalized.

Syntax: MonthName (*date*)

where *date* is a valid date expression.

Example: If the field Date contains the value 08/10/60, the following expression:

```
MonthName(Date) & " was a great month! You were born."
```

produces the following message:

```
August was a great month! You were born.
```

See also: DayName.

Today

Purpose: Obtains today's date, in proper date format, from the system clock. (To return the correct date, the computer's system clock must be set correctly.) Note that this function accepts no arguments.

Syntax: Today

Example: Use the Today function in a form letter layout to insert the current date (with the appropriate conversion) as follows:

```
DateToText(Today)
```

Tip   You can also obtain the current date with the Status(CurrentDate) function.

WeekofYear

Purpose: Calculates the number of weeks that have elapsed for a specified date in a given year. Fractional weeks at the start or end of a year are treated as full weeks, so possible values can range between 1 and 54. The value returned is in numeric format.

Syntax: WeekofYear (*date*)

where *date* is a valid date expression.

Example: If the Date field contains the value 2/9/2000, the expression WeekofYear (Date) returns the value **7**.

See also: DayofYear, WeekofYearFiscal.

WeekofYearFiscal

Purpose: Calculates the number of weeks that have elapsed for a supplied date in a given year, assuming that the week starts on a particular day. WeekofYearFiscal considers the first week of the year as the first one that contains four or more days—that is, when January 1 falls on a day between Monday and Thursday, that week is considered the first week of the year; otherwise, the next week is considered the first week. The returned numeric value is between 1 and 53.

Syntax: WeekofYearFiscal (*date*, *starting day*)

where *date* is a valid date expression and *starting day* is a number (1–7) that represents the day of the week that is to be treated as the first day of the week (1 is Sunday, 2 is Monday, and so on).

Example: January 1, 1996, fell on a Sunday. If the Date field contains the value 3/12/1996, the expression WeekofYearFiscal (Date, 1) returns the value **11**.

See also: DayofYear, WeekofYear.

Year

Purpose: Extracts the year portion of a date expression. The value returned is in numeric format and can be used in calculations.

Syntax: Year (*date*)

where *date* is a valid date expression.

Example: If the Date field contains the value 3/16/2000, then the expression Year (Date) yields the result **2000**.

The following expression yields the person's age after this year's birthday:

```
Year(Today) - Year(Birthday)
```

See also: Day, Month.

Design Functions

The design functions enable you to obtain information about the current database or any other database that is open, such as the names of all open databases, items in a value list, or the names of all fields used in a particular layout. The design functions are as follows:

- ✦ DatabaseNames
- ✦ FieldBounds
- ✦ FieldNames
- ✦ FieldRepetitions
- ✦ FieldStyle
- ✦ FieldType
- ✦ LayoutNames
- ✦ RelationInfo
- ✦ RelationNames
- ✦ ScriptNames
- ✦ ValueListItems
- ✦ ValueListNames

Caution

Database, layout, value list, field, and relationship names used in Design function expressions *must* be enclosed in quotation marks, such as LayoutNames ("Sales") or FieldNames ("Invoices.FP5", "Data Entry"). If you neglect to include quotation marks around these elements, the formula will *not* work!

Remember, too, that—when present—an extension is considered part of the filename. For a Windows FileMaker Pro 5 database called Artwork, the filename enclosed in quotation marks will normally be "Artwork.fp5," rather than "Artwork."

FileMaker Pro databases referenced in Design functions must currently be open.

DatabaseNames

Purpose: Returns the names of all currently open FileMaker Pro databases at the time the record is created. Filenames are listed alphabetically and are separated by Returns.

Syntax: DatabaseNames

Note that the DatabaseNames function takes no arguments.

Example: If the currently open FileMaker Pro databases are named Invoices and Sales.fp5, then the expression DatabaseNames returns the text strings **Invoices** and **Sales.fp5**, each on a separate line within the Calculation field.

FieldBounds

Purpose: Returns the location, size, and angle of rotation of a given field in a particular database layout. The result is type Text and in the form *a b c d e* (with each item separated from the others by a single space); where *a* is the distance from the field's left edge to the layout area's left edge, *b* is the distance from the field's top to the top of the layout area, *c* is the distance from the field's right edge to the layout area's left edge, *d* is the distance from the field's bottom edge to the top of the layout area, and *e* is the field's angle of rotation (clockwise). Items *a–d* are given in pixels. An unrotated field returns a rotation result of 0.

Syntax: FieldBounds (*database name*, *layout name*, *field name*)

Example: The expression FieldBounds ("Invoices", "Data Entry", "State") returns **42 267 85 283 0**. The first four items represent the distance of various edges of the State field from the top and left edges of the Invoices database's Data Entry layout. The final number (0) shows that the field is unrotated.

See also: FieldNames, FieldRepetitions, FieldStyle, FieldType.

FieldNames

Purpose: Returns the names of all fields used in a particular layout (or in all layouts) of a specified database. The result is of type Text. Successive field names are separated by Returns. To retrieve the names of all fields in all layouts, enter a pair of quotation marks as the layout name, as in FieldNames ("Sales", "").

Syntax: FieldNames (*database name*, *layout name*)

Example: The expression FieldNames ("Invoices", "Data Entry") returns the names of all fields used in the layout named Data Entry in the database named Invoices. Each field name is listed on a separate line within the field.

See also: FieldBounds, FieldRepetitions, FieldStyle, FieldType.

FieldRepetitions

Purpose: Returns the number of repetitions and the orientation of a given repeating field as it is formatted on a particular layout of a database. The result is of type Text, and the orientation returned is either "vertical" or "horizontal."

Syntax: FieldRepetitions (*database name*, *layout name*, *field name*)

Example: If a field named Rept is a repeating field that is formatted to display three repetitions in a vertical array, the expression FieldRepetitions ("Invoices", "Data Entry", "Rept") returns **3 vertical**.

See also: FieldBounds, FieldNames, FieldStyle, FieldType.

FieldStyle

Purpose: Returns a text string that describes the style of the specified field. Results can be Standard (a standard field), Scrolling (standard field with a vertical scroll bar), Popuplist, Popupmenu, Checkbox, or RadioButton. If the field has a value list associated with it, the name of the value list is also returned (separated from the returned style by a space).

Syntax: FieldStyle (*database name*, *layout name*, *field name*)

Example: The expression FieldStyle ("Invoices", "Data Entry", "State") returns **Standard**, if State is an ordinary text field. If State was formatted as a pop-up list and had a value list named State Names associated with it, the returned text would be **Popuplist State Names**.

See also: FieldBounds, FieldNames, FieldRepetitions, FieldType.

FieldType

Purpose: Returns information about the defined type of the specified field as a text string containing these four items, in order:

✦ Standard, StoredCalc, Summary, UnstoredCalc, or Global

✦ The field type (Text, Number, Date, Time, or Container)

✦ Indexed or Unindexed

✦ The maximum repetitions defined for the field (If the field is not a repeating field, 1 is returned.)

Syntax: FieldType (*database name*, *field name*)

Example: The expression FieldType ("Invoices", "State") returns **Standard Text Unindexed 1**, showing that the storage options have not been changed for the State field, it is of type Text, it is not indexed, and it is not a repeating field.

See also: FieldBounds, FieldNames, FieldRepetitions, FieldStyle.

LayoutNames

Purpose: Returns a list of the names of all layouts in a particular database, separated by Returns. Note that the specified database must be open for this function to return values.

Syntax: LayoutNames (*database name*)

Example: The expression LayoutNames ("Invoices") returns a list of the names of all layouts that are currently defined for the database named Invoices. (This assumes that Invoices is open when this Calculation field is evaluated. If Invoices is not open, the expression returns nothing.)

RelationInfo

Purpose: Returns information about a specified relationship. The four returned values are separated by Returns and consist of the name of the related database, the name of the match field in the master database, the name of the match field in the related database, and options that have been set for the relationship. Possible options include Delete ("When deleting a record in this file, also delete related records" has been set), Create ("Allow creation of related records" has been set), and Sorted ("Sort related records" has been set).

Syntax: RelationInfo (*database name*, *relationship name*)

Example: In the expression RelationInfo ("Invoices", "Cust ID"), Invoices is the current database for which the relationship Cust ID has been defined. The result might be **Call Log, ID, CustNum** (separated by Returns), indicating that "Call Log" is the related database, "ID" is the match field in the master database (Invoices), CustNum is the match field in the related database (Call Log), and no options have been specified for the relationship.

See also: RelationNames.

RelationNames

Purpose: Displays the names of all relationships that have been defined for the specified database, separated by Returns.

Syntax: RelationNames (*database name*)

Example: The expression RelationNames ("Customers") returns a list of all relationships that have been defined for the Customers database.

See also: RelationInfo.

ScriptNames

Purpose: Returns the names of all scripts that have been created for a given database, separated by Returns.

Syntax: ScriptNames (*database name*)

Example: In the expression ScriptNames ("Books 99"), a list of all scripts that have been defined for the Books 99 database is presented, separated by Returns.

ValueListItems

Purpose: Returns the items in a particular value list for a given database, separated by Returns.

Syntax: ValueListItems (*database name*, *value list name*)

Example: The expression ValueListItems ("Customers", "Sex") returns the list of items in a value list named Sex from the Customers database. The items returned, in this instance, might be **Male**, **Female**, and **Unknown**.

See also: ValueListNames.

ValueListNames

Purpose: Returns the names of all value lists that have been defined for a given database, separated by Returns.

Syntax: ValueListNames (*database name*)

Example: In the expression ValueListNames ("Sales"), the names of all currently defined value lists for the Sales database would be returned.

See also: ValueListItems.

Financial Functions

These functions perform investment-related calculations. They are used to determine loan specifications, how investments will grow over time, and the amount that investments are worth in constant money. They duplicate functions found on many financial pocket calculators.

The financial functions are as follows:

+ FV
+ NPV
+ PMT
+ PV

FV

Purpose: Computes the future value of an investment, based on the provided payment value, interest rate, and number of compounding periods. A numeric value is returned. The result is not the future value of an investment, starting with a certain balance; rather, it is the amount that accrues when equal payments are made over time to an account that bears a particular rate of interest.

Syntax: FV (*payment, rate, periods*) where *payment* is the amount of each payment, *rate* is the interest rate per period, and *periods* is the number of payment periods.

Example: The following expression:

```
FV(100, .05/12, 360)
```

returns **$83,225.86**, the value of an account if $100 payments are made each month for 30 years at an annual interest rate of 5 percent (.05/12).

Note   Payments are assumed to be made at the end of a period. Be sure to give the interest rate per period. Divide the annual rate by 12, as shown in the example, to obtain the monthly rate.

The following formula returns the future value of a continuously compounded investment, assuming a certain starting value:

```
Future Value = Present Value * Exp (Rate * Periods)
```

where Exp indicates the natural antilog of a number.

See also: NPV, PV.

NPV

Purpose: Calculates the net present value of a series of unequal payments made regularly to an account bearing fixed interest per period over the life of the payments.

Syntax: NPV (*payment, rate*)

where *payment* is a series of payment values or the name of a valid repeating field containing the numeric value of each payment, and *rate* is a numeric value indicating the interest rate per period.

Example: The following expression yields the profit on the transaction in today's dollars with an interest rate of 3 percent:

```
NPV(LoanAmt, .03)
```

When the repeating field LoanAmt contains the values -1000, 500, 600, 400, and 700, the result is **$1,008.73**. Note that the LoanAmt field contains five values that represent an initial loan of $1,000 (expressed as a negative value) and the values for the four annual payments.

See also: FV, PV.

PMT

Purpose: Calculates the payment needed to fully amortize a loan, given the loan amount, the interest rate per payment period, and the number of periods.

Syntax: PMT (*principal, rate, periods*)

where *principal* is a number representing the amount of the loan, *rate* is the interest rate per period, and *periods* is the number of payments.

Example: The following expression:

```
PMT(34100, 10.99/12, 60)
```

yields a payment of **$744.55**, which is the amount required to finance $34,100 at 10.99 percent annual interest over 60 months.

PV

Purpose: Calculates the present value of a series of equal payments, made at regular intervals, to an account bearing a fixed rate of interest.

Syntax: PV (*payment, rate, periods*)

where *payment* is the numeric amount of each payment, *rate* is the interest rate per period, and *periods* is the number of payments.

Example: The following expression:

```
PV (500, .03, 5)
```

yields the value of five annual $500 payments in today's dollars, assuming a 3 percent interest rate—in this case, **$2,289.85**.

See also: NPV, FV.

Logical Functions

In early versions of FileMaker Pro, If was the only logical function. In FileMaker Pro 3.0 and higher, the logical functions are as follows:

✦ Case

✦ Choose

✦ If

✦ IsEmpty

✦ IsValid

Case

Purpose: Evaluates a series of expressions and returns the result supplied for the first true expression that is found.

Syntax: Case (*test1, result1 [, test2, result2, default result] . . .*)

where *test* is any text or numeric expression and *result* is the result that corresponds to the expression.

Example: The Payment field is examined in the following expression:

```
Case (Payment="V", "VISA", Payment="M", "MasterCard", "Other")
```

If the Payment field contains a V, the result is **VISA**. If it contains an M, the result is **MasterCard**. If it contains anything else or is blank, the default result (**Other**) is returned.

See also: If, Choose.

Choose

Purpose: Selects one of a series of results based on an index value.

Syntax: Choose (*expression, result0 [, result1, result2] . . .*)

where the *result* of an expression yields a number (between 0 and the number of the last result specified) that indexes into the result list that follows, and *result* is one or more results. Choose can return text, a number, a date, a time, or a container.

> **Note**   As indicated in its syntax, Choose is a zero-based index. A result of 0 is needed to select the first result in the list.

Example: The following expression returns a random integer (whole number) between 0 and 3:

```
Choose(Int(Random*4), "0","1","2","3")
```

See also: If, Case.

If

Purpose: The If function is used when you want to perform one of a set of alternative actions based on the results of a logical test. Normally, the If function is used to choose between two actions; however, you can nest If functions within each other to add choices.

The If function works with the other logical operators, such as less than, equals, OR, AND, and NOT. You combine these operators to create a test that is evaluated for each record.

Syntax: If (*Test*, *Expression1*, *Expression2*)

where *Test* is a logical or numeric expression yielding a logical or numeric result, *Expression1* is an expression to be evaluated and whose value is assigned to the field if the test is true or is not equal to zero, and *Expression2* is an expression to be evaluated and whose value is assigned to the field if the test is false or is equal to zero.

Example: Consider this simple example:

```
If(Number > 0, "The number is positive.", "The number is less
than or equal to zero.")
```

If the Number field contains 35, then the expression produces the text: **The number is positive.**

If the Number field contains -11, the expression produces the text: **The number is less than or equal to zero.**

Remember, the function returns the value of the first expression if the test is true, and it returns the value of the second expression if the test is false.

You can put Ifs inside Ifs (called *nesting*) to add choices. The following example, derived from the first, can handle the additional case where the value in the Number field is equal to zero:

```
If(Number > 0, "The number is positive.", If(Number = 0, "The
number is zero.", "The number is negative."))
```

Note
The test does not have to be a logical expression. If you use a numeric expression, the first action will be performed if the test result is not zero, and the second action will be performed if the test result is zero.

The values of the two expressions should be the values that you want for the field as a whole, depending on which condition is met. For example, you can use the If function to define a Calculation field that gives the tax rate for mail order shipments. The following expression assigns a tax rate of 6 percent to shipments within the state if you're shipping from New Mexico; otherwise, the rate is zero:

```
If(State = "NM", .06, 0)
```

If the Calculation field has the name Rate, you can use it in calculations as follows:

```
Tax = Rate * Total
```

Sales tax is then automatically computed and added for in-state shipments and omitted (set to zero) for out-of-state shipments.

IsEmpty

Purpose: Determines whether a particular field or expression is empty. It returns **1** (true) if the field or expression is empty or **0** (false) if it is not empty.

Syntax: IsEmpty(*field*)

where *field* is a field name or a text or numeric expression.

Example: The following expression returns **1** if the Last Name field for the current record is blank; otherwise, it returns **0** (false), indicating that the field contains data:

```
IsEmpty(Last Name)
```

See also: IsValid.

IsValid

Purpose: Checks a related file for the presence of a given field. It returns **0** (false) if the field is missing or contains invalid data; otherwise, it returns **1** (true).

Syntax: IsValid (*related field*)

where *related field* is the name of a field in a related file.

Example: The following expression checks for a Customer Number field in the file specified by the relationship named ID:

```
IsValid(ID::Customer Number)
```

A result of **0** (false) is returned if any of the following conditions occur:

+ The related file cannot be found.
+ The field in the related file does not exist.
+ The value contained in the field in the matching record is invalid—that is, it is the wrong data type.

See also: IsEmpty.

Numeric Functions

These functions perform standard mathematical computations on numeric fields.

The numeric functions are as follows:

✦ Abs

✦ Exp

✦ Int

✦ Mod

✦ NumToText

✦ Random

✦ Round

✦ Sign

✦ Sqrt

✦ Truncate

Abs

Purpose: Returns the absolute value of a numeric expression. This function changes negative values to positive ones and leaves zero and positive values alone.

Syntax: Abs (*expression*)

where *expression* is a numeric expression or the name of a field that contains a numeric value.

Example: If the field Difference contains 125 or -125, then the following expression returns **125**:

```
Abs(Difference)
```

See also: Sign.

Exp

Purpose: Returns the natural antilog of the given numeric expression. This value is the result obtained when the constant e is raised to the power of the expression; e is approximately 2.7182818.

Syntax: Exp (*expression*)

where *expression* is a numeric expression or a field that contains a numeric value.

Example: The following expression calculates the number that has base e logarithm 2 (which is what is meant by the antilog 2):

```
Exp(2)
```

returns **7.389**, rounded to three decimal places.

See also: Ln, Log.

Int

Purpose: Returns the integer portion of a numeric expression. This portion is the part to the left of the decimal point. The portion to the right, if any, is simply dropped.

Syntax: Int (*expression*)

where *expression* is a numeric expression or a field containing a numeric value.

Example: The expression Int (Pi) is equal to **3**.

See also: Round, Truncate.

Mod

Purpose: Performs modulo arithmetic, which returns the remainder when a given number or expression is divided by another number.

Syntax: Mod (*expression*, *divisor*)

where *expression* is a numeric expression or numeric field, indicating the number to be divided, and *divisor* is a numeric expression or numeric field, indicating the number by which to divide. (Note that the expression determines the sign of the result. If the expression is positive, the result is positive; if the expression is negative, the result is negative.)

Example: The following expression is equal to **1**, which is the integer remainder when 10 is divided by 3:

```
Mod(10,3)
```

NumToText

Purpose: Changes the contents of a Number field into text format. The result can then be passed on to another calculation that requires text input, or it can be printed directly.

Syntax: NumToText (*number*)

where *number* is a Number field or a numeric expression.

Example: The following expression shows a field that tells the cost of an order:

```
"Your order came to $" & NumtoText(Grand Total)
```

If the Grand Total field contained 99.95, the expression's value would be: **Your order came to $99.95**

See also: TextToNum.

Random

Purpose: This function returns a random value in the range 0 to 1 inclusive. This function takes no arguments.

Syntax: Random

Example: The following expression yields a random integer between 1 and 52 inclusive:

```
Int(52 * Random) + 1
```

Such a number might represent a card drawn from a standard deck of playing cards.

Any of the following conditions causes the generation of a new random number:

> ✦ A new record is created.
> ✦ The Random function is newly assigned to a formula.
> ✦ Data is changed in any of the fields that are referenced by the formula containing the Random function.

Round

Purpose: Rounds off a numeric result to the specified number of decimal places.

Syntax: Round (*expression, places*)

where *expression* is a numeric expression or a field that contains a numeric value, and *places* is a numeric expression that indicates the number of decimal places to retain.

Example: The following expression returns the value of Pi to four decimals, or **3.1416**.

```
Round(Pi,4)
```

See also: Int, Truncate.

Sign

Purpose: Returns one of three values, depending on the value of the expression. If the expression is greater than zero (positive), Sign is equal to 1. If the expression is equal to zero, Sign is also equal to 0. If the expression is less than zero, Sign is equal to -1.

Syntax: Sign (*expression*)

where *expression* is a numeric expression or a field containing a numeric value.

Example: The expression Sign (163) has the value **1**.

See also: Abs.

Sqrt

Purpose: Returns the square root of the given expression. The square root is the number which, when squared, equals the original expression.

Syntax: Sqrt (*expression*)

where *expression* is a numeric expression or a field containing a numeric value.

Example: The expression Sqrt (9) is equal to **3**.

Tip

Other roots can be extracted by using the exponentiation operator (^). The nth root of a number is equal to that number raised to the reciprocal of n. Thus, the cube (or third) root of 27 can be calculated using the expression: 27 ^ (⅓).

Truncate

Purpose: Returns a number that is truncated to the specified number of decimal places. Numbers in additional decimal places (to the right) are dropped, not rounded off.

Syntax: Truncate (*number, precision*)

where *number* is a numeric expression or a field containing a numeric value, and *precision* is the number of decimal places.

Example: The expression Truncate (9.75621, 3) returns **9.756**. The expression Truncate (9.75621, 10) returns **9.75621**. (Because the additional decimal places do not exist, the original number is returned.)

See also: Int, Round.

Repeating Functions

Repeating functions enable you to convert a normal field so it can be treated as a repeating field in a calculation, reference a particular repetition in a repeating field, or find the last valid entry in a repeating field.

The repeating functions are as follows:

✦ Extend

✦ GetRepetition

✦ Last

Extend

Purpose: Extends a nonrepeating field for use in calculations with repeating fields. Every value in the extended field is identical — that is, the original value is simply duplicated.

Syntax: Extend (*nonrepeating field name*)

where *nonrepeating field name* is the name of a valid, single-entry field.

Example: The following expression enables you to calculate series of tax amounts, where Prices is a repeating field and TaxRate is a normal field that contains the state sales tax rate:

```
Prices * Extend(TaxRate)
```

GetRepetition

Purpose: Enables you to obtain the value of a specific repetition in a repeating field.

Syntax: GetRepetition (*repeating field name*, *repetition number*)

where *repeating field name* is the name of a valid, nonempty repeating field of any type, and *repetition number* is the number of the specific repetition within the field.

Example: If Prices is a numeric repeating field containing three values, 5.5, 10, and 30, then the expression GetRepetition (2) returns **10** (the value in the second repetition).

See also: Last.

Last

Purpose: Finds the last valid, nonempty entry in a repeating field. The entry is returned in the appropriate format.

Syntax: Last (*repeating field name*)

where *repeating field name* is the name of a valid, nonempty repeating field of any type.

Example: If Prices is a numeric repeating field containing three values, 5, 10, and 30, then the following expression:

```
"The last item you ordered cost $" & Last(Prices)
```

yields the following result:

```
The last item you ordered cost $30.00
```

See also: GetRepetition.

Status Function

The Status function can provide information about the current system on which FileMaker Pro is running, the number of records in the current file, the name of the current user, and more than 30 other useful tidbits. Unlike other function categories, the Status category consists of just one function—but it takes more than 30 preset arguments. The result of the Status function varies with the argument used.

Although you can type the argument to the Status function after choosing Status from the alphabetical function list presented in the Specify Calculation dialog box, you may find it difficult to remember the exact spelling and wording of the argument. The easy way to create an expression using the Status function is to choose "Status functions" from the View pop-up menu, and then select the correct argument, as shown in Figure E-2.

The following section provides a general description of the Status function and its arguments. For a more detailed explanation of the Status function arguments and the meaning of the data they return, choose "Status functions" from FileMaker Pro Help.

Choose "status functions" to see the supported arguments

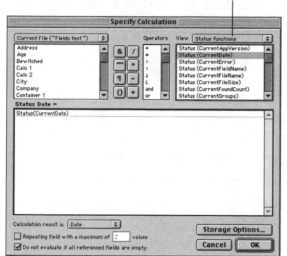

Figure E-2: Choosing an argument for the Status function

Tip

The variations of the Status function are extremely useful as script steps (several, in fact, are *only* useful as parts of scripts). For example, the expression Status (CurrentPlatform) is used to determine whether the database is running on a Macintosh or under Windows. Depending on the result of the Status (CurrentPlatform) check, you could have the script execute an AppleScript (if running on a Mac) or do something else (if running under Windows). Note that the Set Field step is often useful for adding status functions to a script.

When using the Status function, be sure to set the result type correctly, given the type of data that is returned. Status (CurrentTime), for example, returns **16:19:23** when the result type is Time, but returns a numeric string if the result type is set to Number.

Status

Purpose: Performs a check on the state of the database, hardware in use, and so on, and then returns this information in an appropriate form based on the result at the time of calculation.

Syntax: Status (*status flag*)

where *status flag* is one of the preset arguments supplied by FileMaker Pro 5. A given Status function can return a text string, a number, or a date, depending on its purpose. Status functions accept no parameters other than the preset arguments shown below:

✦ *Status (CurrentAppVersion):* Text string that shows the version number of the installed copy of FileMaker Pro, such as **Pro 4.0v2**

✦ *Status (CurrentDate):* Current date, according to the system clock

✦ *Status (CurrentError):* Number that represents a particular error condition (see Status (CurrentError) in the Help file)

✦ *Status (CurrentFieldName):* Name of the currently selected field

✦ *Status (CurrentFileName):* Filename of the current database

✦ *Status (CurrentFileSize):* Size (in bytes) of the current database file

✦ *Status (CurrentFoundCount):* Number of records in the current found set

✦ *Status (CurrentGroups):* Names of groups of which the current user is a member (according to his or her password)

✦ *Status (CurrentHostName):* Name of the host that is registered on the network

✦ *Status (CurrentLanguage):* Name of the language that is set for the current system

✦ *Status (CurrentLayoutCount):* Number of layouts that are defined for the database

✦ *Status (CurrentLayoutName):* Name of the current layout

✦ *Status (CurrentLayoutNumber):* Number of the current layout, according to the order reflected in the Set Layout Order dialog box

✦ *Status (CurrentMessageChoice):* Number representing the button the user clicked in response to a message created with the Show Message script step, as follows: **1** = OK, **2** = Cancel, **3** = third defined button.

✦ *Status (CurrentMode):* Number representing the current mode at the time of calculation, where **0** = Browse, **1** = Find, and **2** = Preview

✦ *Status (CurrentModifierKeys):* Number representing the current modifier key being pressed by the user, where **1** = Shift, **2** = Caps Lock, **4** = Control/Ctrl, **8** = Option/Alt, and **16** = Command (Mac)

✦ *Status (CurrentMultiUserStatus):* Number representing the current sharing status of the database, where **0** = single user; **1** = multi-user and the user is the host; and **2** = multi-user and the user is a guest.

✦ *Status (CurrentNetworkChoice):* Name of the current network protocol as set in the Application Preferences dialog box; blank if no network protocol has been selected

✦ *Status (CurrentPageNumber):* Number of the page currently being printed or previewed on-screen; **0** if not printing or previewing

✦ *Status (CurrentPlatform):* Number representing the type of computer system in use, where **1** = Macintosh and **2** = Windows

✦ *Status (CurrentPortalRow):* Number of the row that is selected in a portal. If a portal is not selected, **0** is returned

✦ *Status (CurrentPrinterName):* Name of the current printer

✦ *Status (CurrentRecordCount):* Total number of records in the current file

✦ *Status (CurrentRecordID):* The unique ID number of the current record

✦ *Status (CurrentRecordModificationCount):* Number of times that the current record has been modified. This number is incremented only when changes to the record have been committed — that is, when you switch to a different record, change to Find mode, or exit out of all fields in the record (pressing Enter on a Macintosh, for example). If the record has never been modified, **0** is returned.

✦ *Status (CurrentRecordNumber):* Number of the current record in the found set

✦ *Status (CurrentRepetitionNumber):* The number of the current repetition within a repeating field. The first repetition is **1**. If it is not a repeating field, **1** is also returned.

✦ *Status (CurrentRequestCount):* Number of find requests that are defined for the current database

✦ *Status (CurrentScreenDepth):* Given the display settings of the current computer, this is the number of data bits required to represent the color of a pixel. (When in 256-color mode, for example, the result is **8**; in thousands mode, the result is **16**.)

✦ *Status (CurrentScreenHeight):* Height (in pixels) of the current monitor on which the database is being run

✦ *Status (CurrentScreenWidth):* Width (in pixels) of the current monitor on which the database is being run.

✦ *Status (CurrentScriptName):* Name of the script that is currently running or paused

✦ *Status (CurrentSortStatus):* A number that indicates the sort status of the database: **0** = unsorted, **1** = sorted, or **2** = semi-sorted

✦ *Status (CurrentSystemVersion):* System software version number currently in use, such as **8.5.1**

✦ *Status (CurrentTime):* Current time of day

✦ *Status (CurrentUserCount):* Number of users currently accessing the file; **1** if in single-user mode, actual number plus one when the file is being shared on a network

✦ *Status (CurrentUserName):* Name of the current user, as specified in Preferences

Summary Functions

FileMaker Pro 5 contains only one summary function: GetSummary.
(The GetSummary function was called Summary in FileMaker Pro 2.1.)

GetSummary

Purpose: Returns the values for a particular Summary field when the database
is sorted by the break (grouping) field.

Syntax: GetSummary (*summary field, break field*)

where *summary field* is the name of the Summary field, and *break field* is the name
of the field that is used to group the records (the "when sorted by" field). The break
field can be a Text, Number, Date, Time, or Calculation field.

Example: Suppose you want to see year-to-date sales totals for the individual
members of your company's sales force. After the database has been sorted by
the Salesperson field, the following expression displays a different value for the
Sales Total field for each salesperson in the database:

```
GetSummary (Sales Total, Salesperson)
```

Note   To display a grand total for a Summary field rather than individual subtotals, use the
name of the Summary field as both arguments to the function:

```
GetSummary (Sales Total, Sales Total)
```

Text Functions

Text functions are used to compare text strings and to extract pieces of text strings.
They can also be used to insert text into a string.

The text functions are as follows:

- ✦ Exact
- ✦ Left
- ✦ LeftWords
- ✦ Length
- ✦ Lower
- ✦ Middle
- ✦ MiddleWords

- ✦ PatternCount
- ✦ Position
- ✦ Proper
- ✦ Replace
- ✦ Right
- ✦ RightWords
- ✦ Substitute
- ✦ TextToDate
- ✦ TextToNum
- ✦ TextToTime
- ✦ Trim
- ✦ Upper
- ✦ WordCount

Exact

Purpose: Compares two text expressions or fields and determines whether they are exactly the same. The comparison is case sensitive, so capitalization counts. The returned result is a logical value: **true** if the two strings are exactly the same, **false** if they are not.

Syntax: Exact (*first text, comparison text*)

where *first text* and *comparison text* are Text fields, expressions, or constants.

Note To create a text constant — such as Saturday, in the following example — you must surround it with quotation marks.

Example: The following expression is true if today's date is July 31, 1999:

```
Exact(DayName(Today), "Saturday")
```

Tip You can adapt the Exact function to perform a test that isn't case sensitive. Use either the Upper or Lower function to convert both text strings to all uppercase or lowercase, as in:

```
Exact(Upper(Field1), Upper(Field2))
```

See also: Position.

Left

Purpose: Returns a text result that equals the left-most part of a given Text field or expression, including only the specified number of characters.

Syntax: Left (*text*, *number*)

where *text* is a text expression or text from which the left-most part is to be taken, and *number* is a numeric expression or field specifying how many characters to use.

Example: The expression Left ("photocopy", 5) yields **photo**.

See also: LeftWords, Right, Middle.

LeftWords

Purpose: Returns a text result that equals the left-most part of a given Text field or expression, including only the specified number of words.

Syntax: LeftWords (*text*, *number*)

where *text* is a text expression or text from which the left-most part is to be taken, and *number* is a numeric expression or field specifying how many words to use.

Example: LeftWords ("The worst years of your life", 3) returns **The worst years**.

See also: RightWords, MiddleWords, Left.

Length

Purpose: Returns a numeric result that indicates the number of characters the specified text contains. When text length is calculated, alphanumeric characters, spaces, numbers, and special characters all contribute to the total.

Syntax: Length (*text*)

where *text* is a text expression, constant, or field that contains a text value.

Example: The expression Length ("photocopy") returns **9**.

See also: Trim.

Lower

Purpose: Converts the specified text string into all lowercase letters.

Syntax: Lower (*text*)

where *text* is a text expression, constant, or field containing a text value.

Example: The expression Lower ("PrintMonitor") yields **printmonitor**.

See also: Upper, Proper.

Middle

Purpose: Extracts a specified number of characters from a given text string, starting at a certain position.

Syntax: Middle (*text*, *start*, *number of characters*)

where *text* is a Text field, text constant, or text expression; *start* is a numeric value that indicates where to begin extracting characters; and *number of characters* is a numeric value that indicates the number of characters to extract.

Example: The following expression returns the letter **Q**:

```
Middle("John Q. Public", 6, 1)
```

Remember that spaces are characters, too.

See also: Left, Right, MiddleWords.

MiddleWords

Purpose: Enables you to extract a consecutive group of words from any text string, regardless of the starting position of the target word group.

Syntax: MiddleWords (*text*, *starting word*, *number*)

where *text* is the text expression or text from which the specified portion is to be extracted; *starting word* is a numeric expression or field that contains the number of the first word to be extracted; and *number* is a numeric expression or field specifying how many words to extract.

Example: The expression MiddleWords ("Baby animals must fend for themselves", 2, 3) returns **animals must fend**.

See also: RightWords, LeftWords, Middle.

PatternCount

Purpose: Returns the number of instances that a specified text string is found within another text string or field.

Syntax: PatternCount (*text*, *pattern*)

where *text* is the text expression or text to be searched, and *pattern* is the particular text string for which you are searching.

Example: The expression PatternCount ("You are the apple of my eye", "e") returns **5** because there are 5 e's in the text string.

Position

Purpose: Scans a specified text expression in an attempt to locate a particular instance of a search string, starting at a given position, and returns a numeric value equal to the position at which the search string starts within the larger string. If the search string is not found, the result is zero.

Syntax: Position (*text*, *search string*, *start*, *occurrence*)

where *text* is a text constant, field, or expression in which to search; *search string* is the text for which to search; *start* is a number that indicates at what character position to begin the search; and *occurrence* is a number, numeric expression, or field containing a number that indicates the particular occurrence of the string you want to find.

Examples: The expression Position ("bewitching beauty", "be", 1, 1) returns **1**; Position ("bewitching beauty", "be", 1, 2) returns **12**, as does Position ("bewitching beauty", "be", 10, 1).

See also: LeftWords, RightWords, MiddleWords

Proper

Purpose: Returns a text string in which the first letter of each word of the supplied text expression has been capitalized; all others are converted to lowercase. Some word processing programs refer to this as *title case*.

Syntax: Proper (*text*)

where *text* is a Text field, constant, or expression.

Example: The expression Proper ("SURF AND TURF") returns **Surf And Turf**.

See also: Upper, Lower.

Replace

Purpose: Inserts a specified text string into another text string, starting at a specified position and replacing a given number of characters. The number of characters replaced need not be equal to the number inserted.

Syntax: Replace (*text*, *start*, *size*, *replacement text*)

where *text* is a Text field, constant, or expression; *start* is a numeric value indicating the position at which to begin replacing; *size* is a numeric value that indicates the number of characters to replace; and *replacement text* is a Text field, constant, or expression to insert in the place of the specified characters.

Example: The expression Replace ("Clinton R. Hicks", 9, 2, "Robert") returns **Clinton Robert Hicks**.

See also: Substitute.

Right

Purpose: Starting at the right, extracts the specified number of characters from the specified text expression.

Syntax: Right (*text*, *number*)

where *text* is a Text field, expression, or constant from which to extract characters, and *number* is a numeric value that indicates how many characters to extract.

Example: The expression Right ("Rosanna", 4) returns **anna**.

See also: Left, Middle, RightWords.

RightWords

Purpose: Returns a text result that equals the right-most part of a specified Text field or expression, including only the specified number of words.

Syntax: RightWords (*text*, *number*)

where *text* is a text expression or text from which the right-most part is to be taken, and *number* is a numeric expression or field specifying how many words to extract.

Example: The expression RightWords ("These are the best days of our lives", 5) returns **best days of our lives**.

See also: LeftWords, MiddleWords.

Substitute

Purpose: Enables you to substitute one text string for another.

Syntax: Substitute (*text, search string, replacement string*)

where *text* is a text expression or Text field, *search string* is the text that is to be replaced, and *replacement string* is the text that is to be used as the replacement.

Example: The expression Substitute ("Paul was the walrus.", "Paul", "I") returns **I was the walrus.**

See also: Replace.

TextToDate

Purpose: Changes a text date value directly into date format. The supplied text must be in the format MM/DD/YYYY for this function to work correctly.

Syntax: TextToDate (*text*)

where *text* is a text constant or text expression in the form MM/DD/YYYY.

Example: The following expression converts a text constant into date format:

```
TextToDate ("03/23/1999")
```

This expression yields the following result in date format:

```
03/23/1999
```

See also: DateToText, Date.

Note TextToDate and the Date function are the only ways to enter a date constant into a formula that requires a date parameter, such as DayofYear and DayName.

TextToNum

Purpose: Converts the number part of a text expression into numeric format. The alphabetic portion is ignored.

Syntax: TextToNum (*text*)

where *text* is a text constant or a text expression.

Example: The following example defines a Calculation field in which nonnumeric data—such as a dollar sign and commas—are stripped from a price:

```
TextToNum(Price)
```

If the information in Price (a Text field) had been entered as $19,995.95, the Calculation field would contain **19995.95**.

See also: NumToText.

TextToTime

Purpose: Converts a text value or expression into time format. The results can then be passed on to a calculation that requires data in time format.

Syntax: TextToTime (*text*)

where *text* is a text constant or text expression. The data supplied must be in the form HH:MM:SS. Seconds are optional, and AM and PM may be used as suffixes.

Example: The following expression yields **14:15:00**:

```
TextToTime ("2:15 pm")
```

Tip The formatting of the converted text is initially determined by the result type that you select. If you select Time as the result type, the result returned is 2:15 PM—rather than the military time format used when Text is selected as the result type.

See also: TimeToText, TextToNum.

Note TextToTime and Time are the only ways to enter a time constant into a function or expression that requires data in time format.

Trim

Purpose: Removes leading and trailing spaces from a text expression or field.

Syntax: Trim (*text*)

where *text* is a Text field, constant, or expression.

Example: The expression Trim (" Johnny ") returns **Johnny** (with no surrounding spaces).

See also: Left, Right, Middle, Position.

Tip Some programs and computer systems require a set number of characters per field. Unused spaces in such fields may be padded with blanks. You can use the Trim function to remove these blanks when you import data from such programs and systems.

Upper

Purpose: Converts a given text string into all uppercase letters.

Syntax: Upper (*text*)

where *text* is a Text field, constant, or expression.

Example: The expression Upper ("Honorable") returns **HONORABLE**.

See also: Lower, Proper.

WordCount

Purpose: Returns the total number of words in a text string.

Syntax: WordCount (*text*)

where *text* is a Text field or expression.

Example: The expression WordCount (Comments) returns the number of words in the Comments field.

Time Functions

The Time functions are analogous to the Date functions described earlier in this appendix. You can use them to extract elements from a time expression or to convert number results into valid times — even if the numbers don't fall into the 0–60 and 0–24 ranges normally required for minutes and hours.

The time functions are as follows:

✦ Hour

✦ Minute

✦ Seconds

✦ Time

✦ TimeToText

Hour

Purpose: Extracts the hour part of a time expression or field, yielding a numeric result.

Syntax: Hour (*time*)

where *time* is a Time field or expression.

Example: If Current is a time field containing 12:30 PM, the expression Hour (Current) is equal to **12**. If the field contained 12:30 AM, on the other hand, the result would be **0**.

See also: Minute, Seconds.

Minute

Purpose: Extracts the minute part of a time expression or field, yielding a numeric result.

Syntax: Minute (*time*)

where *time* is a Time field or expression.

Example: If Current is a Time field containing 8:23:17, the expression Minute (Current) returns **23**.

See also: Hour, Seconds.

Seconds

Purpose: Extracts the seconds part of a time expression or field, yielding a numeric result.

Syntax: Seconds (*time*)

where *time* is a Time field or expression.

Example: If Current is a Time field containing 8:23:17 PM, the expression Seconds (Current) yields **17**.

See also: Hour, Minute.

Tip The Hour, Minute, and Seconds functions can be used together to obtain the decimal equivalent of a time value. You would need to divide the Minute result by 60 and the Seconds result by 3600, as shown in the following expression:

```
Hour(Current)+(Minute(Current)/60)+(Seconds(Current)/3600)
```

Time

Purpose: Returns a time value containing the specified number of hours, minutes, and seconds counted from midnight. The function compensates for fractional values, extracting seconds from fractional minutes and minutes from fractional hours.

Syntax: Time (*hours, minutes, seconds*)

where:

   ✦ *hours* is a numeric expression indicating the number of hours

   ✦ *minutes* is a numeric expression indicating the number of minutes

   ✦ *seconds* is a numeric expression indicating the number of seconds

Example: The expression Time (13, 70, 71) is equal to **2:11:11 PM**.

See also: Date.

TimeToText

Purpose: Converts a time into text format. The result may be printed directly or used in a text-based expression.

Syntax: TimeToText (*time*)

where *time* is a Time field or an expression yielding a time value.

Example: The following expression extracts the time from a field and prints it along with a message:

```
"Your order was prepared at " & TimeToText(Time Entered)
```

If the Time Entered field contained 02:15:00, the field would read as follows:

```
Your order was prepared at 2:15:00
```

See also: TextToTime.

Trigonometric Functions

This group of functions enables you to work with angles, degrees, and other geometric data. Note that the trigonometric functions are designed to work in radians. (There are 2π radians in 360 degrees.) You can use the Degrees function to convert radian results into degrees.

The trigonometric functions are as follows:

✦ Atan

✦ Cos

✦ Degrees

✦ Ln

✦ Log

✦ Pi

✦ Radians

✦ Sin

✦ Tan

Atan

Purpose: Returns the arc tangent (in radians) of the specified expression.

Syntax: Atan (*number*)

where *number* is a Number field, numeric expression, or constant. The returned value is between $-\pi$ and π.

Example: The expression Atan (Pi) is equal to **1.2626**, rounded to four decimal places.

See also: Tan, Degrees.

Cos

Purpose: Gives the cosine of the specified expression (assumed to be provided in radians).

Syntax: Cos (*number*)

where *number* is a Number field, numeric expression, or constant — in radians.

Example: The expression Cos (Pi) is equal to **-1**.

See also: Sin, Degrees.

Degrees

Purpose: Converts a value given in radians into degrees. There are 2π radians in 360 degrees.

Syntax: Degrees (*number*)

where *number* is a Number field, numeric expression, or constant — in radians.

Example: The expression Degrees (Pi) is equal to **180**.

See also: Radians.

Ln

Purpose: Returns the natural logarithm of the given numeric expression. The natural logarithm is the number which, when the constant e is raised to its power, gives the original number. In calculus, the natural logarithm of a number Ln (d) is the area under the curve 1/x evaluated from x = 1 to d.

Syntax: Ln (*number*)

where *number* is a numeric expression or a field containing a numeric value.

Example: The expression Ln (2) has the value **0.693**, rounded to three decimals.

See also: Log, Exp.

Log

Purpose: Computes the common (base 10) logarithm of the given numeric expression. Raising 10 to this power gives the original number. Thus, the log of 100 is 2, because 10 ^ 2 = 100.

Syntax: Log (*number*)

where *number* is a numeric expression or a field containing a numeric value.

Example: The expression Log (100 * 100) has the value **4**.

See also: Ln, Exp.

Pi

Purpose: Returns the value of the mathematical constant pi. Pi is defined as the ratio of a circle's circumference to its diameter. It is a transcendental number whose fractional part neither repeats nor terminates. This function takes no arguments.

Syntax: Pi

Example: If R is equal to 2, the following expression is approximately equal to **12.57**:

```
Pi * R ^ 2
```

This expression gives the area of a circle with a radius equal to R.

Radians

Purpose: Converts a value in degrees into radians, for use with calculations expecting a value in that form.

Syntax: Radians (*number*)

where *number* is a Number field, constant, or expression containing a value expressed in degrees.

Example: The expression Cos (Radians (45)) is equal to **0.707**, rounded to three decimal places.

See also: Degrees.

Sin

Purpose: Returns the sine of the given expression, interpreted as an angle expressed in radians.

Syntax: Sin (*number*)

where *number* is a Number field, constant, or expression given in radians.

Example: The expression Sin (Pi) is equal to **0**.

See also: Cos.

Tan

Purpose: Returns the tangent of the specified angle, assumed to be expressed in radians.

Syntax: Tan (*number*)

where *number* is a numeric field, constant, or expression given in radians.

Example: The expression Tan (Pi) is equal to **0**.

See also: Atan.

Web Companion External Functions

Purpose: When used in conjunction with FileMaker Pro 5's Web publishing features, the external functions enable you to get information about the users of your database, such as their domain name, current IP address, and the browser being used to view the database.

To use external functions, the Web Companion plug-in must be enabled. (This option is found in the Plug-Ins section of the Application Preferences dialog box.) The form of each external function is:

Syntax: External ("*function name*", *parameter*)

where *function name* is surrounded by quotation marks. Following are the variants of the External function:

+ *External ("Web-Version", 0):* Version number of Web Companion that is in use

+ *External ("Web-ClientAddress", 0):* If available, returns the domain name of the current user; otherwise, returns the user's current IP address.

+ *External ("Web-ClientIP", 0):* The user's current IP address

+ *External ("Web-ClientName", 0):* The name of the user, as entered in the database's password dialog box

+ *External ("Web-ClientType", 0):* Name and version of the Web browser being used by the current user

+ *External ("Web-ToHTML", field name)* or *External ("Web-ToHTML", text value):* The contents of a particular field or text string that is encoded in HTML (*HyperText Markup Language*)

+ *External ("Web-ToHTTP", field name)* or *External ("Web-ToHTTP", text value):* The contents of a particular field or text string that is encoded in HTTP (*HyperText Transfer Protocol*)

✦   ✦   ✦

Glossary

Although this book assumes you're familiar with the basics of operating a computer (using the mouse, choosing menu commands, selecting objects and text, and printing), everyone can use a little help now and then. This glossary includes definitions of some additional common terms that you may run into while using FileMaker Pro and reading this book.

access privileges Activities a user is allowed to perform when using a particular password.

alert box A program or system software dialog box that notifies you when something important has occurred or is about to happen. See also *dialog box*.

algorithm A series of steps for accomplishing a specific task.

alias A Macintosh stand-in icon for a program, file, folder, or disk. Double-clicking an alias results in the same action that occurs when you double-click the original icon. Under Windows 95 and 98, *shortcuts* serve similar functions to Macintosh aliases.

alphanumeric data Information consisting of letters of the alphabet, numbers, or a mixture of the two (for example, 1911 Oak Street).

AppleEvents Messages sent between Macintosh applications that enable the applications to interact. See also *AppleScript*.

Apple menu The menu at the far left side of the Macintosh's menu bar. You can place almost anything in the Apple menu, including frequently used programs, documents, folders, control panels, and aliases (stand-ins for programs, documents, folders, or disks).

AppleScript A programming language from Apple Computer (Macintosh only) that enables within- and between-program communications via AppleEvents. See also *AppleEvents*.

Application menu Found at the upper-right corner of the Macintosh's menu bar, this menu lists all programs that are currently running and enables you to switch from one program to another freely. The top half of the Application menu enables you to hide some or all of the programs temporarily, eliminating some of the desktop clutter. Under recent releases of the Mac OS, the Application menu can be "torn off" into a floating palette.

archive An archival copy of one or more files; frequently compressed. Archives can be created to save disk space, to reduce the time it takes to transmit (upload) and receive (download) the files by modem, or to serve simply as a backup copy (a personal safety net). See also *self-extracting archive*.

argument A value supplied to a function from which the function's value is calculated. See also *expression* and *function*.

arrow keys Keys on a standard keyboard that, when pressed, move the text insertion point within a FileMaker Pro database field or move a selected object when in Layout mode.

ascending sort A sorting order that starts with the smallest (or oldest) value and ends with the largest (or most recent) value. For numbers, values begin with the smallest value and proceed in numerical order. For text, values are arranged alphabetically (A–Z). Dates and times are sorted in chronological order. In fields that contain mixed data types (text, numbers, and characters), numbers appear first. See also *descending sort*.

ASCII Abbreviation for *American Standard Code for Information Interchange*; a code that associates a numerical value (0 through 255) with a character or control code. Control codes, letters, punctuation, and numbers are found in codes 0–127. Codes 128–255 (commonly referred to as *Extended ASCII*) consist of symbols and foreign language characters. See also *Extended ASCII*.

auto-entered value A value, text string, date, calculation, or other item that is automatically entered into a particular field when a new record is created. Auto-entry options are used to set a default entry for a field.

auto-entry field A database field that FileMaker Pro automatically fills in for each new or modified record.

auto-incrementing field A field that is automatically filled in when you create a new record. The entry in the field is based on an increment over the contents of that field in the previous record. This feature is useful for generating new invoice numbers, check numbers, record numbers, and so on.

Avery A manufacturer of specialized stock for printing a variety of labels, including disk labels and address labels.

backup *n:* An exact copy of a file.
  v: To create a duplicate of one or more files.

Balloon Help On a Macintosh, when the mouse pointer is passed over a program or system software object, menu item, or icon that has Help information attached to it, a cartoon-style Help balloon appears. To turn Balloon Help on or off, choose the appropriate command from the Balloon Help menu in the upper-right corner of the menu bar (System 7.*x*) or from the Help menu (OS 8.*x*).

bitmap A collection of individual picture elements (pixels or dots) that together constitute a graphic item.

body A layout part that contains the main record information.

book An icon in the status area of a FileMaker Pro database window. In Browse mode, you use the book to flip through database records. In Find mode, the book is used to view multiple find requests. In Layout mode, it is used to view different database layouts. In Preview mode, the book enables you to see additional pages of the current report.

Boolean A type of algebra in which expressions are evaluated for their truth value. Results are either true or false.

browsed records Those records in a FileMaker Pro database that are currently visible (not hidden).

button An object in a FileMaker Pro database layout that has a script attached to it. Clicking the button makes an associated script action or actions occur. In many dialog boxes, you also click buttons to select, confirm, or cancel an action.

cache An area in the computer's memory that is set aside for temporarily storing data that is on its way to and from a disk. Using a cache can greatly speed up operations because RAM is much faster to access than a disk.

Web browsers use hard disks to cache data downloaded from the Internet. By doing so, you can avoid having to waste time re-downloading Web page information on subsequent visits to the same site.

Calculation field A field type used to generate within-record computations. Formulas in Calculation fields can reference other fields, use FileMaker Pro's built-in functions, and contain constants.

CDML (Claris Dynamic Markup Language) An add-on to HTML (*Hypertext Markup Language*) that enables users to interact with FileMaker Pro databases that have been posted to the World Wide Web or a company Intranet. See also *HTML, XML,* and *Custom Web Publishing*.

check box A small box associated with an option in a dialog box or a type of field format in a FileMaker Pro layout. Clicking the box changes the state of the option from selected to deselected (and vice versa). Normally, you can choose multiple check boxes.

Chooser The Macintosh desk accessory you use to select a printer or other "printing" device (such as a fax modem) and, in some cases, to set options for that device.

click To press the mouse button once and then immediately release it. See also *double-click*.

Clipboard An area in memory that is used to store the most recently copied (⌘+C/Ctrl+C) or cut (⌘+X/Ctrl+X) object or text string. The contents of the Clipboard can be pasted (⌘+V/Ctrl+V) into other locations in the same document, another document, or even into another application.

clone An exact copy of a database — including all layouts, field definitions, and scripts — but without records. A clone is used as the basis for a new database. Other applications frequently refer to clones as *templates*.

close box The tiny box in the upper-left corner of some Macintosh windows or the tiny x in the upper-right corner of some Windows windows that, when clicked, closes or dismisses the window and any document it contains.

conditional test A logical test that — when executed — causes a script to take a particular action, depending on the result of the test.

constant A value that does not change. Pi, e, and 274 are all examples of constants.

Container field FileMaker Pro fields of this type can be used to store graphics, QuickTime movies and audio, OLE objects, or sound clips.

cosine The cosine of an angle is the ratio of the adjacent side in a right triangle to the hypotenuse, where the adjacent side and hypotenuse form the angle in question.

crash The cessation of functioning by a computer or a program. Signs that a computer has crashed include system crash dialog boxes on the Macintosh (which contain a bomb symbol), General Protection Fault error messages under Windows, and keyboard and mouse lock-ups.

current field The database field that is presently selected (by tabbing or clicking in the field). Only the current field can be modified.

current record The record that is presently selected. Only the current record can be modified.

cursor An on-screen indicator that moves in response to movements you make with the mouse or another pointing device. The mouse pointer changes its shape to reflect the activity you are performing.

Custom Web Publishing By using a combination of normal HTML and CDML, it is possible to publish FileMaker Pro databases on the Web that contain more advanced features than those made possible with Instant Web Publishing. See also *Instant Web Publishing* and *CDML*.

database An organized collection of information, normally with one central topic.

database program (or database management program) A program for entering, editing, and otherwise managing data records.

data-entry keys Keys on a standard keyboard that, when pressed, add data at the insertion point.

data validation User-specified criteria that instruct the database program to check a particular field's contents for allowable and unacceptable data. Validation criteria can include range checking and required fields, for example.

DDE Abbreviation for *Dynamic Data Exchange*; a Windows-based command sent to a program, instructing it to perform one or more specific commands. FileMaker Pro for Windows can send DDE commands (via the DDE Execute script step) but cannot receive them.

default The initial "factory setting" for a changeable value. This setting determines how an option or preference behaves if you never change the setting.

default value A common value that is automatically entered in a field when you create a new record. Using a default value saves typing time and ensures that information is entered consistently.

descending sort A sorting order that starts with the largest (or most recent) value and ends with the smallest (or oldest) value. An alphabetic sort in descending order begins with Z. See also *ascending sort*.

desktop The main work area on the computer screen.

dialog box A special type of window that applications and the system software use to present information that enables you to make choices. See also *alert box*.

dimmed command A menu command that cannot presently be selected — usually because it is irrelevant to the current operation. Dimmed items are also referred to as *grayed-out* and can appear in dialog boxes as well as in menus.

dogcow On a Macintosh, an icon in the LaserWriter Page Setup dialog box that demonstrates the combined effects of selected options. Sometimes referred to as Clarus (the fictional dogcow's name).

dot matrix A type of printer technology in which a print head that has many pins, each corresponding to one picture element (pixel or dot), is passed rapidly over a page, hammering out an impression through a ribbon.

double-click To press the mouse button twice in rapid succession. See also *click*.

download To elect to receive a file (usually via a modem and phone line) from the Internet, an information service, a bulletin board system, or another user's computer.

downloading The process of using a modem or network connection to retrieve a program or document file from the Internet, an online information service, a bulletin board system, or another user's computer.

drag To hold down the mouse button while moving the mouse pointer.

drag-and-drop Applications that support drag-and-drop technology enable you to drag text and graphics from one place in a document to another, from one document to another, as well as between different applications. In essence, drag-and-drop is simply a direct way of accomplishing a copy-and-paste operation without using the Clipboard as an intermediary.

emergency quit command A Macintosh keyboard command (⌘+Option-Esc) you can use to force a program to quit. You can sometimes use this command of last resort to quit a program that has locked up or crashed. The equivalent command under Windows 95/98/NT is Ctrl+Alt+Delete, which gives you an option of closing any current Windows task or program.

export To create a file in one program that can be read by other programs. To ensure compatibility with the program that will receive the data, most programs that export data can write it in a number of different file formats. See also *import*.

expression A mathematical statement consisting of one or more operators (such as + or *) that join two or more variables or constants. See also *argument* and *function*.

Extended ASCII Any ASCII character with a value higher than 127; the upper half of the ASCII character set. Special symbols and foreign language characters are found in Extended ASCII. See also *ASCII*.

external script A script in another FileMaker Pro database that is executed with the Perform Script step. When an external script is performed in this manner, the database that contains the script automatically opens. See also *internal script*.

Fat Binary A version of an application that can run on either a 68K-based Mac or a PowerMac because it contains sets of instructions for both processor types.

field Fields are the building blocks of which database records are composed. Each field is meant to store one particular type of information, such as a Social Security number or a birth date. See also *field type*.

field type Set in the Define Fields dialog box, a field type specifies the type of information that a particular field is intended to collect and display. Some common field types are Text, Number, Date, and Time. The main reason for declaring field types is to enable the database program to screen for invalid data so it can warn you if, for example, you have entered something other than a date in a Date field.

file Any named collection of information or instructions that is stored on disk. Programs, documents, and system software components are examples of files.

file dialog box Any dialog box that is designed to enable file-handling tasks, such as opening, saving, importing, and exporting files. Unlike most dialog boxes, file dialog boxes on the Macintosh frequently have no title. (Although this is *not* the case if you have a recent version of the Mac OS.) However, they are named under Windows 95 and 98 with titles — such as Save As — that indicate the operation about to be performed.

file format A standard specification for the way data is stored on disk and interpreted.

Find A command for locating a record or group of records based on criteria you establish. For example, you may want to find the address record for Ames Corporation or identify the records of all salespeople who earned more than $40,000 last year. Most database programs enable you to set multiple criteria when performing a find request.

flat-file database A flat-file database consists of a single file. Every field that is necessary must be in that file. See also *relational database program*.

folder A holder of documents, applications, and other folders on the desktop. Also called a *directory*.

footer A FileMaker Pro layout part that appears at the bottom of every record or report page. Page numbers and the current date are frequently placed in the footer. If you want to put special information on just the first or cover page of a report, use a Title Footer part. See also *header*.

found set The remaining visible (or browsed) records following a find procedure, such as a find request, Omit command, or Omit Multiple command. See also *Find*.

freeware Programs or templates that are offered to users free of charge. See also *shareware*.

function An operation performed on one or more values that yields a unique result for that value set. The function of two different value sets can be the same, but the function of a given value set can never differ from the original result. See also *argument* and *expression*.

Global field A Global field is used to hold the same value for all records in the database. Any value which, by its nature, must be constant throughout the database is a candidate for a Global field. Examples might include a fixed shipping charge, a user's name, and various preference settings. A Global field can also be used to temporarily store script results.

grayscale Objects and text are displayed in shades of gray rather than in color. As with color, most grayscale displays can support multiple gray shades (4, 16, and 256, for example).

group A set of objects in a layout to which you have applied the Group command so you can treat them as a single entity rather than as a collection of objects. To work again with the individual components of a group, use the Ungroup command.

guest Any user who opens a shared database after the host has opened it. See also *host*.

handle A black dot that appears at the corners of an object when it is selected in Layout mode. You can drag the handles to change the size of the object.

header A FileMaker Pro layout part that appears at the top of every record or report page. The report title is often placed in the header. If you want to put special information on just the first or cover page of a report, use a Title Header part. See also *footer*.

header record A special first record that is frequently included as part of an export file. The header identifies (by name) all fields that are present in the file and indicates the order in which they can be found. The header record can also specify the separator (such as tab- or comma-delimited text) and field types and sizes (as found in a dBASE file, for example). See also *export*.

hierarchical menu A menu in which one or more menu items contain a submenu.

host The user who first opens a FileMaker Pro database and sets its status to multiuser, enabling other users on the network to share that database. In subsequent sessions, other users may become the host. See also *guest*.

HTML Abbreviation for *Hypertext Markup Language*; the simple programming language used to create pages for the World Wide Web. See also *CDML*.

import To bring data from another program into the current program. Importing saves you the effort of needlessly retyping data. FileMaker Pro, for example, can read any tab-delimited text file — regardless of what program actually created the file. See also *export*.

index FileMaker Pro maintains an internal list of data that includes the contents of selected Text, Number, Date, Time, and Calculation fields. Indexes are responsible for the speed with which FileMaker Pro executes find requests. In versions of the program prior to 3.0, indexing was automatically performed for every appropriate field type. In FileMaker Pro 3.0 and higher, indexing is an option that must be turned on individually for desired fields. See also *sort*.

inkjet A type of printer technology in which ink is forced at high pressure onto the page. Inkjet printers are frequently inexpensive, while being capable of matching or surpassing the resolution and quality of many laser printers.

insertion point A blinking vertical line that indicates the point at which the next typed, pasted, or imported data will appear.

installer A special program provided to enable users to copy a program, templates, and supporting files to their hard disks. Also called a *set-up program*.

Instant Web Publishing Using the Web Companion plug-in, you can publish a FileMaker Pro database to the Internet or a company Intranet by merely specifying a few options in the Web Companion Configuration dialog box. Individuals who view the published database can interact with it by creating new records, sorting, and performing other basic database operations. See also *Custom Web Publishing*.

internal script A script that is contained in and executed from the current FileMaker Pro database. See also *external script*.

invalid data Information that does not adhere to the specific format for a given field or that falls outside the acceptable range of values for that field. This term also refers to data of the wrong type, such as character data in a Number field.

keyboard shortcut Keys you press as an alternative to using the mouse to select a command from a menu or a dialog box option. Also called a *keyboard equivalent*.

laser printing A printing technology in which laser light creates an image of a page on a rotating drum, magnetizing the drum. Toner particles adhere to the magnetized drum and are then transferred onto paper, where they are fused at high heat. This technology works like a conventional photocopier.

layout In FileMaker Pro, a particular arrangement of fields, graphics, and static text. Unlimited layouts can be designed for each database, each with a different purpose. For example, some layouts may be used for data entry and others for generating printed or on-screen reports.

layout parts The major sections in a database layout. Depending on the purpose of the layout, it may contain a body, header, footer, and summary parts, for example.

List View Using the View as List command, you can display records in a continuous scrolling list rather than one record per screen. See also *Table View*.

lookup A field option that instructs FileMaker Pro to search an external database for a record that contains a match to the data entered in the current database. If a match is found, data from another field in the external database is automatically copied into a field in the current database. For example, entering an inventory part number in one database can trigger a lookup in another database of a price and description for that part.

lookup field A field in the current database into which data will be copied when a lookup is triggered. See also *match fields*.

lookup file The database in which data is looked up (in response to data being entered or edited in the trigger field in the current file).

mail merge Combining address and other personal or business information (usually from a database) with a form letter to generate a series of "personalized" letters. You can generate a merge directly within a FileMaker Pro 3.0 or higher layout.

master password A special password that provides complete access to a FileMaker Pro database, including permission to change the design of the database, set or change passwords and access privileges, and establish or change groups. See also *password*.

match fields When performing a lookup, the fields in the two database files that are compared. These fields define the relationship between the files. To identify associated records, a Social Security or customer identification number might serve as match fields in the two files. See also *lookup field*.

menu A list of choices, presented by a program or the operating system, from which you can select an action. Menus appear when you click menu titles in the menu bar.

menu bar In a Macintosh program or in the Finder, the horizontal strip at the top of the screen that contains the menu titles; in a Windows program, the horizontal strip at the top of the current window that contains the menu titles.

merge The process of combining information from a database with a text document, such as for a form letter (also known as a mail merge). See also *mail merge*.

modal dialog box Any dialog box that you must respond to before you can continue working. See also *modeless dialog box*.

mode A state of a FileMaker Pro database in which you can perform only one global type of activity. The four modes are Browse, Find, Layout, and Preview.

modeless dialog box A dialog box that you can leave open while you attend to other work; it does not require an immediate response or dismissal. See also *modal dialog box*.

modifier key A key or keys that, when pressed in combination with a letter, number, or punctuation key, change the meaning of the second key. When you are typing text, for example, the Shift and Option keys frequently act as modifier keys. Similarly, pressing the ⌘ (Macintosh) or Ctrl key (PC) in combination with a second key issues a program command. On a Macintosh keyboard, modifier keys include Shift, Option, ⌘, and Control. On a PC, modifier keys include Shift, Alt, and Ctrl.

monochrome Refers to a two-color display (typically black-and-white).

ODBC Abbreviation for *Open Database Connectivity*; a protocol used to interact with and request data from other databases. FileMaker Pro 5 can act as an ODBC client program and request data from other sources, such as Oracle or Sybase databases. The reverse is also true; that is, FileMaker can respond to ODBC queries from other applications. Some non-database applications, such as Microsoft Word and Excel, can also import data via ODBC.

OLE Abbreviation for *Object Linking and Embedding*; a Microsoft technology that enables objects to be inserted into OLE-compliant programs, such as FileMaker Pro. Using Windows, OLE objects can be inserted and edited. When using a Macintosh, however, OLE objects can only be viewed, cut, copied, or pasted; they cannot be inserted nor edited in any manner.

omit To remove a record from a found set temporarily, hiding it from view. If you select the Omit option when performing a find request, FileMaker Pro shows only the records that do *not* match the search criteria. For example, if the search criterion was State = CA, clicking the Omit option would result in a found set of records from all states *except* California.

open To load a copy of a document from disk into a program. You can also open folders and desktop windows for disks by double-clicking the icons that represent them.

operator A symbol indicating that a certain mathematical process should be performed on the entities surrounding the operator symbol. Both + and / are examples of operators.

operator precedence See *order of operations*.

options See *preferences*.

order of operations (or precedence) Refers to the way in which algebraic expressions in formulas are evaluated. Exponents are evaluated first, then multiplication and division, then addition and subtraction. When operators are of equal precedence, they are evaluated from left to right. You can include parentheses in an expression to alter the order of operations. Expressions in the innermost set of parentheses are evaluated first. See also *expression*.

password A string of characters a user must type when opening a protected FileMaker Pro database. Different passwords are often associated with different privileges, specifying what a user can or cannot do with the database. See also *master password*.

platform A particular computer/operating system combination. The Macintosh, Windows 95, and Windows 98 are common platforms.

plug-in A software add-on that enhances FileMaker Pro by giving it new capabilities. For example, Web Companion is a FileMaker Pro plug-in. Other programs, such as Adobe Photoshop and PageMaker, may also support plug-ins.

portal A rectangular area on a layout created with the Portal tool; used to display multiple records from a related file. Think of a portal as a window into a related database.

precedence See *order of operations*.

preferences Program-specific or document-specific options you set to govern how certain aspects of a program behave. Preferences are often referred to as *options*.

Preview A FileMaker Pro mode that enables the user to see what a printed report or other document will look like on-screen prior to committing it to paper.

print driver A software program used to control a specific printer. Macintosh print drivers are accessed in the Chooser. Windows print drivers can be selected in either the Print or Print Setup/Page Setup dialog boxes.

PrintMonitor (or desktop printer) Apple programs that watch over and control background printing jobs.

questionable spelling The term that FileMaker Pro's spelling checker uses to identify a word that is not contained in the current main or user dictionaries.

QuicKeys A Macintosh macro utility from CE Software that enables users to automate functions in most programs. When you use the Send Apple Event script step, QuicKeys macros that access other programs can be executed from within FileMaker Pro.

QuickTime An Apple-created system extension that enables you to play or display video, picture, and sound data on any Macintosh. QuickTime support is also available on Windows-based PCs. QuickTime movies and audio clips can be inserted into Container fields.

radio button In dialog boxes, buttons that present a series of mutually exclusive options or settings (for example, enabling or disabling background printing). Fields can be formatted as radio buttons in FileMaker Pro in order to present a set of choices.

RAM Abbreviation for *Random Access Memory*; the memory the computer uses to run programs, temporarily store data, and so on.

range checking A database program feature that prevents input errors by making certain each entry in a particular field is within acceptable ranges. For example, numeric entries for student grades might have to be between 0 and 4.

Read Me file A text file that provides information about a program or template. Manufacturers of commercial programs often include a Read Me file on disk to inform users about important topics that are not covered in the program's manual. Although these files do not have to be named "Read Me," such a name encourages users to open the file and examine its contents.

reader (or viewer) A utility program that enables the contents of a document to be read, regardless of whether or not the user has his or her own copy of the program in which the document was created. A reader typically provides the user only with "read" privileges; that is, the user can read documents created with a particular program, but cannot "write" (create new documents of that type). Adobe Acrobat Reader is a common reader application for both Macs and PCs.

record The basic unit of every database. All databases are composed of records, each storing information for a single entity, such as a person, catalog item, video-tape, or recipe.

relational database program A program in which key fields link information in multiple database files, enabling you to generate reports and display information based on data from more than one database. See also *flat-file database*.

relationship A relationship between two FileMaker Pro databases is defined by a pair of matching fields in the files, such as a customer ID number or Social Security number. When a relationship has been defined, either database can draw/display data from the other for viewing on-screen or use in reports. For example, using Customer Email Address as the matching field between two databases (Tech Support and Customers), a case record in the Tech Support database could display contact information for each customer by pulling it from the related record in the Customers database.

Relookup A Records menu command that causes all lookups for a database to be executed again (for every record currently being browsed). Choosing this command ensures that all lookup fields contain current data.

repeating field A field option that enables a single field to store and display multiple values, such as the names of purchased items in an invoice database.

report A copy of selected information from a database, consisting of specified records in a certain layout, often presented in a particular sort order.

required field (not empty) A field that must be filled in before finalizing the information for the record. The record is checked for completeness only when you press Enter; attempt to switch to a different record, layout, or mode; close the database; or try to quit FileMaker Pro while the database is still open.

reset switch A hardware switch or button that causes the computer to go through its start-up sequence. Refer to your owner's manual for the availability and location of the switch or button. Normally, the reset switch should only be pressed to recover from a system crash.

resources In a FileMaker Pro database, these are the layouts and the fields. When defining access privileges associated with a particular group, the database designer or administrator can prevent users from modifying or even seeing particular resources.

root The top or highest level of any disk. When a disk icon is first opened, the root is the part of the disk you first see.

save To store a current copy of a document on disk.

script A user-defined sequence of commands and actions that automates FileMaker Pro tasks. A script consists of one or more commands associated with a specific database that FileMaker will execute automatically or when instructed to do so by the user. External (non-FileMaker) scripts can be created in other applications and programming environments, such as Visual Basic for Applications (Windows) and AppleScript (Mac).

ScriptMaker The FileMaker Pro component you use to design scripts.

scroll arrow The arrow icon at either end of a scroll bar. When you click the arrow, the window's contents move in the opposite direction of the arrow.

scroll bar A rectangular bar along the right side or bottom edge of a window. Clicking or dragging in a scroll bar changes your view of the window's contents. Document windows and large text fields often have scroll bars.

scroll box The box in a scroll bar. The position of the scroll box indicates the position of what is displayed in the window relative to the entire document.

SCSI (pronounced "scuzzy") Abbreviation for *Small Computer Systems Interface*. Enables devices, such as hard disks, CD-ROM drives, tape drives, and scanners, to be connected in series to a computer. Until recently, SCSI was the standard hardware interface on all Macintoshes, and it could be found on some PCs. In current hardware, SCSI is being supplanted by FireWire and USB.

search criteria Information used as a reference in search or find operations.

self-extracting archive One or more compressed files that contain a built-in file extraction program. When a user double-clicks the icon of a self-extracting archive, a file dialog box appears that enables the user to select a destination disk and folder for the expanded (normal) files. See also *archive*.

set-up program See *installer*.

shareware Programs or templates that are distributed to users on the honor system. If you decide to keep the program or template, you send the author the requested fee. See also *freeware*.

Shut Down A command in the Mac's Special menu and Windows 95/98's Start menu that you use to shut down the computer and devices that are connected to it.

sine For a right (90-degree) triangle, the ratio of the opposite side to the hypotenuse for one of the other two angles.

size box Refers to the box in the lower-right corner of some Macintosh windows. Dragging the size box changes the size of the window. (In recent versions of the Mac OS, three diagonal lines in the lower-right corner of the window have replaced the size box. In Windows 95/98, you can change the size of windows by clicking and dragging any window corner or edge.)

sort To rearrange database records in a different order than the one in which they were originally entered. Most database programs — including FileMaker Pro — can simultaneously sort on multiple fields. The more powerful database programs enable you to specify key or index fields (special sort fields that are automatically maintained by the program). Indexes are particularly useful for very large databases, where a normal sort would be extremely time consuming. Indexing can be specified for most types of FileMaker Pro fields. See also *index*.

sort order The order in which a field is sorted. Every FileMaker Pro database field can be sorted in one of three sort orders: ascending, descending, or according to the entries in a value list.

source code In a computer program, source code is the set of instructions that makes a program do what it was intended to do. The instructions are in a human-readable form (usually in a programming language such as Pascal, C, BASIC, FORTRAN, or assembly language). In a FileMaker Pro template, script definitions, DDE instructions, and AppleScript instructions may be considered the equivalent of source code.

standalone document A document that contains its own reader and, hence, does not require the user to own a specific program to open and read the document. The document is a program. For example, on the Macintosh, all documents created in the shareware program DOCMaker are standalone documents.

standalone program After FileMaker Pro Developer's Edition is used to compile a template, the template becomes a standalone program. It can be run on any Mac or PC, and the program does not require that a copy of FileMaker Pro be installed.

status area The area on the immediate left of a FileMaker Pro database window. In Browse mode, the status area contains controls that enable you to select a different layout, navigate among records, change the magnification (zoom), and show or hide the status area. Information on the current state of the database (such as whether it is sorted, the number of records being browsed, and the current record number) is also displayed in the status area.

step (or script step) A single action set for a FileMaker Pro script.

sub-script Any FileMaker Pro script that is performed by another script.

Summary field A type of field used to summarize the information in the same field across all currently browsed (visible) records.

System file A critical component of the Macintosh system software, located in the System Folder on the startup disk.

system software Software that supports application programs by managing system resources, such as memory and input/output devices.

Table View In Table View (a new feature of FileMaker Pro 5), data is displayed in spreadsheet format. Each row corresponds to a record and each column is a field. See also *List View*.

tangent In a right (90-degree) triangle, the ratio of the opposite side to the adjacent side for one of the two other angles.

TCP/IP A network protocol (supported by FileMaker Pro 4.0 and higher) that is used to connect to the Internet.

template (or stationery document) A partially completed document that serves as a starting point for other documents. In a word processing program, for example, you might create a memo template that contains appropriate headers and text formatting, making it simple for you to create each new memo without unnecessarily having to retype basic text. The equivalent document in FileMaker Pro is known as a clone and is created using the File ⇨ Save a Copy As command. See also *clone*.

text box (or text-edit box) A rectangular area in a dialog box or program that is used to enter or edit information. A common example is the space provided for a filename in Open and Save dialog boxes.

text file (also called text-only file) A file saved without formatting (a single font and no style or size options). Most text editors, such as BBEdit on the Macintosh and Notepad under Windows, automatically save documents in this format. You can usually create such files by using a word processing program's Save As command and choosing Text-Only or Text as the format. In general, you create pure-text files so other programs or other types of computers can read them.

title bar The horizontal bar at the top of a window that shows the name of the window's contents. You can move a window by dragging its title bar.

trigger field A field in the current database that, when data is entered or modified, initiates a lookup in another database.

uncompressing (or extracting) To shorten the length of time required to download files from an information service, a utility program is often used to compress the files into an archive (making the files smaller). Uncompressing or extracting the contents of an archive restores the files to their original size and format. See also *archive*.

unique field A field that can contain only data that is not duplicated in any other record.

user name A unique name assigned to a computer or its primary user; normally used to distinguish that computer from others on a network.

value list A list of choices or values that are associated with one or more fields. Using value lists can help speed data entry and ensure the consistency of information. Value lists can be displayed as pop-up lists, pop-up menus, radio buttons, or check boxes.

variable A value in an expression that may change, usually indicated by a letter or name. A field can be considered a variable because its contents may change from record to record.

windoid A tiny, special-purpose window that is typically provided as a user-control tool. FileMaker Pro's Size tool and the various tear-off palettes, such as the ones used to apply colors or textures to objects, are examples of windoids.

Web page A page on the World Wide Web, frequently consisting of a mixture of text, graphics, and multimedia elements (such as sound and movie clips).

World Wide Web A graphically rich portion of the Internet, consisting of millions of pages programmed in HTML (*Hypertext Markup Language*). Users can move from page to page by clicking text or graphic links.

XML This is *eXtensible Markup Language*, an emerging standard for next-generation documents delivered via the Internet. As the standard is evolving, you can track it on the Internet at `http://www.xml.com`.

zoom Changing the magnification level or view of the database by enlarging or reducing all elements on a layout.

zoom box On a Macintosh, this is a tiny box in the upper-right corner of all resizable windows (System 7.*x*) or second from the right (OS 8). Under Windows, this box is beside the close box (the tiny x) and is referred to as "Maximize/Restore." Click the box to expand the window to its maximum size. A second click returns the window to its original size.

Index

F

Family Medical Expenses template, 607
Field Borders command, 230
Field Borders dialog box, 229
field definitions, 70
    changing, 171–172
    modifying, 125
    printing, 373, 390–397
    setting, 123–144
Field Format command, 84
Field Format dialog box, 85, 95, 160–161
    Include vertical scroll bar check box,
       231
    Repetitions section, 232
field labels
    editing, 103
    formatting, 80–83, 221
field options
    Auto-Enter options, 147–154
    data validation options, 154–158
    indexing and storage options, 165–167
    repeating fields, 158–164
    setting, 72, 73–77, 144–167
    setting, after data entry, 146
field tool, 45
    adding fields with, 210–211
field types, 6, 126–144
    Calculation, 133–134. *See also*
       Calculation fields
    Container, 130–132. *See also* Container
       fields
    Date, 128–129. *See also* Date fields
    Global, 134. *See also* Global fields
    Number, 128. *See also* Number fields
    Summary, 135–144. *See also* Summary
       fields
    Text, 127–128. *See also* Text fields
    Time, 130. *See also* Time fields
fields
    adding to layout, 209–211, 246
    auto-incrementing, 6
    baselines for, 229–230
    borders for, 83–84, 223, 229

complex, breaking up, 126
copying, 291–293
Ctrl+clicking/right-clicking on, 225
current, 272
default values for, 6
defined, 4
deleting, 168–169
display formatting for, 224–232
duplicating, 170, 211
empty, searching for, 310–311
fill colors and patterns for, 94, 230
formatting, 221–236
Go to scripts for, 440–441
grouping, in columnar reports,
    188–189
indexing, 126–127
inserting data, scripts for, 450–457
moving, 211, 224
naming, 124–125, 167–168
options, changing or deleting, 172–173
order of, 143–144, 182
options for, 170–171
placement of, 85–92
redefining, 171, 211
removing from layout, 169
repeating, 137. *See also* repeating fields
replacing contents, 317–319
required, 6, 74
resizing, 85–92, 102, 224
scripts for, 431–432, 449–457, 467–470
scroll bars for, 230–231
serial numbers for, 318–319
Set Field script, 449–450
tab order, 235–236
text attributes of, 80–83
text formatting options, 226
3D effects for, 230
validation options for, 74
file dialog box, 26–27
file-extraction utilities, 525
file formats, 56, 497–501
    for exporting, 512
    for importing, 501

Continued

Continued

U

Notes

Notes

_____
_____
_____
_____
_____
_____
_____
_____
_____
_____
_____
_____
_____
_____
_____
_____
_____

Notes

Notes

Notes

Notes

Notes

Notes

Notes

Notes

_____

_____

_____

_____

_____

_____

_____

_____

_____

_____

_____

_____

_____

_____

_____

_____

IDG Books Worldwide, Inc. End-User License Agreement

READ THIS. You should carefully read these terms and conditions before opening the software packet(s) included with this book ("Book"). This is a license agreement ("Agreement") between you and IDG Books Worldwide, Inc. ("IDGB"). By opening the accompanying software packet(s), you acknowledge that you have read and accept the following terms and conditions. If you do not agree and do not want to be bound by such terms and conditions, promptly return the Book and the unopened software packet(s) to the place you obtained them for a full refund.

1. **License Grant.** IDGB grants to you (either an individual or entity) a nonexclusive license to use one copy of the enclosed software program(s) (collectively, the "Software") solely for your own personal or business purposes on a single computer (whether a standard computer or a workstation component of a multiuser network). The Software is in use on a computer when it is loaded into temporary memory (RAM) or installed into permanent memory (hard disk, CD-ROM, or other storage device). IDGB reserves all rights not expressly granted herein.

2. **Ownership.** IDGB is the owner of all right, title, and interest, including copyright, in and to the compilation of the Software recorded on the disk(s) or CD-ROM ("Software Media"). Copyright to the individual programs recorded on the Software Media is owned by the author or other authorized copyright owner of each program. Ownership of the Software and all proprietary rights relating thereto remain with IDGB and its licensers.

3. **Restrictions On Use and Transfer.**

   (a) You may only (i) make one copy of the Software for backup or archival purposes, or (ii) transfer the Software to a single hard disk, provided that you keep the original for backup or archival purposes. You may not (i) rent or lease the Software, (ii) copy or reproduce the Software through a LAN or other network system or through any computer subscriber system or bulletin-board system, or (iii) modify, adapt, or create derivative works based on the Software.

   (b) You may not reverse engineer, decompile, or disassemble the Software. You may transfer the Software and user documentation on a permanent basis, provided that the transferee agrees to accept the terms and conditions of this Agreement and you retain no copies. If the Software is an update or has been updated, any transfer must include the most recent update and all prior versions.

4. **Restrictions on Use of Individual Programs.** You must follow the individual requirements and restrictions detailed for each individual program in the "About the CD-ROM" appendix of this Book. These limitations are also contained in the individual license agreements recorded on the Software Media. These limitations may include a requirement that after using the program for a specified period of time, the user must pay a registration fee or discontinue use. By opening the Software packet(s), you will be agreeing to abide by the licenses and restrictions for these individual programs that are detailed in the "About the CD-ROM" appendix and on the Software Media. None of the material on this Software Media or listed in this Book may ever be redistributed, in original or modified form, for commercial purposes.

5. **Limited Warranty.**

   (a) IDGB warrants that the Software and Software Media are free from defects in materials and workmanship under normal use for a period of sixty (60) days from the date of purchase of this Book. If IDGB receives notification within the warranty period of defects in materials or workmanship, IDGB will replace the defective Software Media.

   (b) **IDGB AND THE AUTHOR OF THE BOOK DISCLAIM ALL OTHER WARRANTIES, EXPRESS OR IMPLIED, INCLUDING WITHOUT LIMITATION IMPLIED WARRANTIES OF MERCHANTABILITY AND FITNESS FOR A PARTICULAR PURPOSE, WITH RESPECT TO THE SOFTWARE, THE PROGRAMS, THE SOURCE CODE CONTAINED THEREIN, AND/OR THE TECHNIQUES DESCRIBED IN THIS BOOK. IDGB DOES NOT WARRANT THAT THE FUNCTIONS CONTAINED IN THE SOFTWARE WILL MEET YOUR REQUIREMENTS OR THAT THE OPERATION OF THE SOFTWARE WILL BE ERROR-FREE.**

   (c) This limited warranty gives you specific legal rights, and you may have other rights that vary from jurisdiction to jurisdiction.

6. **Remedies.**

   (a) IDGB's entire liability and your exclusive remedy for defects in materials and workmanship shall be limited to replacement of the Software Media, which may be returned to IDGB with a copy of your receipt at the following address: Software Media Fulfillment Department, Attn.: *FileMaker Pro 5 Bible*, IDG Books Worldwide, Inc., 7260 Shadeland Station, Ste. 100, Indianapolis, IN 46256, or call 1-800-762-2974. Please allow three to four weeks for delivery. This Limited Warranty is void if failure of the Software Media has resulted from accident, abuse, or misapplication. Any replacement Software Media will be warranted for the remainder of the original warranty period or thirty (30) days, whichever is longer.

(b) In no event shall IDGB or the author be liable for any damages whatsoever (including without limitation damages for loss of business profits, business interruption, loss of business information, or any other pecuniary loss) arising from the use of or inability to use the Book or the Software, even if IDGB has been advised of the possibility of such damages.

(c) Because some jurisdictions do not allow the exclusion or limitation of liability for consequential or incidental damages, the above limitation or exclusion may not apply to you.

7. U.S. Government Restricted Rights. Use, duplication, or disclosure of the Software by the U.S. Government is subject to restrictions stated in paragraph (c)(1)(ii) of the Rights in Technical Data and Computer Software clause of DFARS 252.227-7013, and in subparagraphs (a) through (d) of the Commercial Computer—Restricted Rights clause at FAR 52.227-19, and in similar clauses in the NASA FAR supplement, when applicable.

8. General. This Agreement constitutes the entire understanding of the parties and revokes and supersedes all prior agreements, oral or written, between them and may not be modified or amended except in a writing signed by both parties hereto that specifically refers to this Agreement. This Agreement shall take precedence over any other documents that may be in conflict herewith. If any one or more provisions contained in this Agreement are held by any court or tribunal to be invalid, illegal, or otherwise unenforceable, each and every other provision shall remain in full force and effect.